Supercomputing Systems

Supercomputing Systems

Architectures, Design, and Performance

Svetlana P. Kartashev and Steven I. Kartashev
International Supercomputing Institute, Inc.

VAN NOSTRAND REINHOLD
_____New York

Copyright © 1990 by Van Nostrand Reinhold

Library of Congress Catalog Card Number 89-5267
ISBN 0-442-25615-9

Printed in the United States of America

Designed by Universities Press

Van Nostrand Reinhold
115 Fifth Avenue
New York, New York 10003

Van Nostrand Reinhold International Company Limited
11 New Fetter Lane
London EC4P 4EE, England

Van Nostrand Reinhold
480 La Trobe Street
Melbourne, Victoria 3000, Australia

Nelson Canada
1120 Birchmount Road
Scarborough, Ontario M1K 5GH, Canada

16 15 14 13 12 11 10 9 8 7 6 5 4 3 2 1

Library of Congress Cataloging in Publication Data

Supercomputing systems: architecture, design, computations,
    applications, and performance evaluation/[compiled by] Svetlana P.
    Kartashev & Steven I. Kartashev.
        p. cm.
    Includes bibliographies and index.
    ISBN 0-442-25615-9
    1. Supercomputers. I. Kartashev, Svetlana. II. Kartashev,
Steven I.
QA76.5.S8984   1989
004.1'1—dc19   89-5267
                                                                    CIP

CONTENTS

Introduction   xi

List of Contributors   xxxi

PART 1 SUPERCOMPUTER ARCHITECTURES   1

1 Supercomputer Architectures: Evolution and Implementations   3

Svetlana P. Kartashev and Steven I. Kartashev

   Industrial and Prototype Architectures 3
   Major Factors that Affect Evolution of Industrial and Prototype
      Architectures 4
   Survey of Existing Techniques of Performance Improvement 7
   Evolution of Industrial Architectures 70
   Industrial Pipelined Multiprocessors 70
   Industrial Array Systems 81
   Prototype Architectures 91
   Survey of Projects in Adaptable and Data-Flow
      Architectures 95
   Conclusions 99
   References 102

2 Designing and Programming the CHoPP Supercomputer   106

*Theodore E. Mankovich, Leonard Allen Cohn, Val Popescu,
Herbert Sullivan, Bruce D. Lightner, Thomas McWilliams, and
Theodore R. Bashkow*

   Introduction 106
   CHoPP Principles of Operation 108
   Performance of CHoPP on the Livermore Loops 123
   Design and Simulation of the CHoPP Supercomputer Using
      SCALD 138
   References 153

3 The Unisys Integrated Scientific Processor System   154

*Jane R. Kessler, James A. Hodek, David S. Dunn, Francis A.
Stephens, and Keith Besaw*

The Unisys 110/90 ISP System Integrated Supercomputing   154
Introduction   156
Integration   157
Technology   157
ISP Characteristics   158
Software   167
Performance   172
Conclusion   175

Performance Results on an Integrated, Interactive
   Supercomputer   176

Introduction   176
System Integration   176
Interactive Supercomputing   178
System Performance   179

Processor Scheduling Algorithms for a Heterogeneous Vector
   and Scalar Computer System   186

Introduction   186
Overall System Design Considerations   187
Hardware Considerations   189
Software Considerations   190
Memory Bandpass Considerations   191
Heterogeneous Multiprocessor Scheduling
   Algorithm   192
Conclusion   193

Advanced Techniques for Vectorizing Dusty Decks   193

Introduction   193
Background   194
Basic Theory   195
The REVERSE Dependency for Expanded
   Scalars   200
The REVERSE Dependency in IF-to-MASK
   Conversions   207
Mask Construction   209
An Algorithm to Compute Control
   Expressions   212
Conclusions   217

References   219

4 A Scaleable Architecture for Exploiting Demand-Driven and Data-Driven Parallel Communication   **221**

A. A. Faustini, E. A. Ashcroft, and R. Jagannathan

Introduction   221
Operator Nets   228
Mathematical Semantics   230
Abstract Operational Models   233
A Programming Language for Operator Nets   239
Equivalent Semantics   251
An Eazyflow Architecture   252
Conclusions   264
References   265

PART 2 SOFTWARE AND HARDWARE DESIGN OF
        SUPERCOMPUTERS   269

5 Software Development for Parallel Processing in a Distributed Computer Architecture   **271**

Noah S. Prywes and Boleslaw K. Szymanski

Introduction   271
The MODEL Approach   273
International Econometric Modeling Example   276
The Operation of the MODEL Compiler   283
Configuration Processing   286
Run-time Environment   288
Conclusions   290
References   290

6 Cache Coherence in Mind Systems: A Petri Net Model for a Minimal State Solution   **292**

Jean-Loup Baer and Claude Girault

Introduction   292
Cache Memories   294
Informal Description of the Architecture and Protocols   296
Modeling with Petri Nets   302
Detailed Model   309
Extensions and Improvements   321
Conclusions   326
References   326

7   **The Optimization of a Hierarchical Memory System for High-Speed Scientific Computers**   **329**

J. A. Davis and A. V. Pohm

Introduction   329
Hierarchical Memory Structure   332
Optimizing the Memory Hierarchy   341
An Illustrative Example   345
Conclusions   346
References   346

8   **Testing Techniques for Complex VLSI/WSI Processing Arrays**   **348**

F. Distante, M. G. Sami, and R. Stefanelli

Introduction   348
Behavioral Testing: The Multiple-level Approach   350
Some Approaches to Testing of Processing Arrays   355
A Behavioral Testing Technique for a Class of Fault-tolerant
   Arrays   357
Concluding Remarks and Further Developments   365
References   365

**PART 3 SUPERCOMPUTER COMPUTATIONS,
              APPLICATIONS, AND PERFORMANCE
              EVALUATIONS**   **367**

9   **Supercomputers and Multiparameter Systems Theory**   **369**

John Jones, Jr.

Introduction   369
Computation of Various Generalized Inverses of Multiparameter
   Matrices   370
Similarity and Equivalence of Matrices   380
Conclusions   387
References   387

10   **Supercomputer Applications in Modeling and Image
       Processing for Space and Earth Sciences**   **389**

*Milton Halem, Barbara H. Putney, Judith E. Devaney, P. J. Camillo,
R. J. Gurney, Hudong Chen, William H. Matthaeus, Don J. Lindler,
Sara R. Heap, James P. Strong, H. K. Ramapriyan, James J. Little,
and Michael J. McAnulty*

MODELING OF PHYSICAL PROCESSES

Producing an Accurate Gravity Model on a CYBER 205 Vector Supercomputer   391

A SIMD Implementation of a Hillslope Water Flow Model   399

Magnetohydrodynamic Cellular Automata: Theory and Potential for Applications to Massive Parallelism   412

IMAGE PROCESSING FOR REMOTE SENSOR OBSERVATIONS

Restoring Blurred Astronomical Images with the MPP   421

Massively Parallel Correlation Techniques for Determining Local Differences in Pairs of Images   437

Vision Modules on the Connection Machine   448

Limitations of Inherently Parallel Graphics Algorithms   465
References   477

11   Supercomputer Applications of the Hypercube   **480**

John Apostolakis, Clive Baillie, Robert W. Clayton, Hong Ding, Jon Flower, Geoffrey C. Fox, Thomas D. Gottschalk, Bradford H. Hager, Herbert B. Keller, Adam K. Kolawa, Steve W. Otto, Toshiro Tanimoto, Eric F. Van de Velde, J. Barhen, J. R. Einstein, and C. C. Jorgensen
Introduction   480
The Caltech Concurrent Computation Program   481
The Hypercube as a Supercomputer   485
The Design of a Portable Parallel Multigrid Algorithm for the Hypercube   503
Lattice Gauge Theories on Hypercubes   520
Applications of the Hypercube in Geophysics   530
Multiple-target Track Initiation on a Hypercube   538
Advances in Concurrent Computation for Machine Intelligence and Robotics   550
References   570

12   Stochastic Petri Nets as a Tool for the Analysis of High-Performance Distributed Architectures   **578**

M. Ajmone Marsan, G. Chiola, and G. Conte
Introduction   578
Overview of PN Definitions and Notation   582
Timed Petri Nets   585

Stochastic Petri Nets   585
Models of Multiprocessors with Cache Memories   598
Numerical Results   606
Conclusions   610
References   611

Index   **614**

INTRODUCTION MODERN TRENDS IN SUPERCOMPUTING

Svetlana P. Kartashev and Steven I. Kartashev

Supercomputing can be conceived as an assortment of scientific and industrial disciplines that attempt to compute high-performance processes with due regard to their current performance requirements. Its place is within the computer sciences, since its major objective is to take advantage of all the available performance potential that can be offered at different levels of computational processes. However, it is strongly impacted by other contributing sciences associated with high-performance scientific and industrial applications, since their practitioners view supercomputing as the way to achieving their own performance objectives.

Thus, supercomputing has become a true mixture of various scientific and industrial components aimed at achieving a sustained and superior performance of high-performance application processes.

REQUIREMENTS – CAPABILITY CORRESPONDENCE

Further evolutionary developments in supercomputing are aimed at dynamically sustaining the correspondence between supercomputer *requirements* generated by the users and the supercomputer *capabilities* of modern and future supercomputers in satisfying these requirements.[1]

The roles of *producer* and *consumers* in relation to the pair, *requirements–capabilities,* are fulfilled by users and computer designers, but their roles interchange depending on which element of this pair is considered. Thus, the *producers* of supercomputer *requirements* are users of high-performance applications who generate specific demands on timing, tolerated errors, and cost of computation for their processes. The *consumers* of the *requirements* are computer designers of supercomputers at hardware and software levels whose task is to conceptualize, design, and manufacture cost-efficient supercomputing structures that meet the users' requirements.

On the other hand, the *producers* of *capabilities* are supercomputer designers who design supercomputers with certain performance ranges dependent on their cost. The *consumers* of these machines' *capabilities* are *users* whose criteria for supercomputer selection becomes • *efficiency* with which each particular machine meets specific performance demands, and • the *cost* of this machine for the user.

Supercomputer efficiency is a broad term which includes not only timing characteristics of the machine but also the ease and simplicity of its programming is measured as • *degree of users' effort* required to implement a complex high-performance application process, and • *availability of automatic software environment* within the supercomputer, which allows smooth and automatic running and servicing of the process together with other application processes that are run concurrently.

TECHNOLOGICAL DEVELOPMENTS

The advent of supercomputing was largely the result of technological developments that allowed creation of faster and more affordable hardware.[2] The technology has offered the following sources of performance improvements.

- higher rates of computer operations achieved by dramatic reduction of clock periods, and
- very high computational concurrency extended to operations and processes and achieved through microminiaturization of components.

As a result of these technological shifts, the objective of all the computing disciplines that participate at various stages of the computational process has become that of mastering this greatly expanded and easily affordable parallelism by improving existing and creating new cost-effective computing structures at different levels of computation.

Supercomputer Architectures

Supercomputer architectures are influenced by the following developments.
1. Bold exploration of extended concurrency/complexity trade-offs
2. Investigation of two different orders of execution triggered by
   (a) completion of instructions, and
   (b) arrival of operands.

CONCURRENCY/COMPLEXITY TRADE-OFFS

Trade-off of concurrency with complexity is associated with proliferation of the following outlooks in designing current and future architectures.

1. The use of fewer structural units, each of which is supposed to be quite complex.[3,4] This approach has been implemented in the majority of industrial supercomputers and multiprocessors.

2. The use of a great number of structural units each of which is supposed to be sufficiently simple. This approach was implemented in massively parallel architectures.[5-8]

The interconnections between structural units can be *direct* as in message-passing architectures[7,8] or *reconfigurable*[9,10] The degree of implemented reconfiguration is also varied, from very modest by reconfiguring devices and registers, to very dramatic as is done in dynamic architectures that perform a total restructuring of hardware resources under software control.[9-12]

Industrial (CRAY-type) Supercomputers and Multiprocessors

More detailed description of their evolutionary trends as well as current statuses of implementation of supercomputer architectures can be found in Chapters 1–3 of this book. Here, we will deal only with major highlights and their economic outline justification.

The evolutionary development of industrial architectures is influenced by the following factors.

F1. Gradual and mostly quantitative changes in basic architectural characteristics of a current industrial architecture are caused by economic demands on the reuse of the entire software development for its predecessor.

F2. To be economically feasible and to satisfy user performance needs, an industrial architecture of the current generation must take maximum cost and speed advantage of the component technology that is used.

We can now trace the following evolution in Control Data/ETA architectures in terms of F1.

First generation		Second generation		Third generation
STAR-100 (1974)	$\rightarrow$	CYBER 205 (1981)	$\rightarrow$	ETA-10 (1986)

Similar evolution is true for the CRAY supercomputer family starting with the CRAY-1 and ending with CRAY X-MP/4 and CRAY-2:

First generation		Second generation		Third generation
CRAY-1 (1976)	$\rightarrow$	CRAY X-MP/2, X-MP/4 (1982)	$\rightarrow$	CRAY-2, CRAY-3 (1984)(1988–?)

As for the numerous minisupercomputers, their architectural evolution cannot be traced yet, since we are witnessing proliferation of their first generations manufactured mostly since 1984.

We can identify further evolutionary influences in terms of F2.

Cost optimization. The major source of the cost optimization is associated with minimization in the number of module types used for supercomputer design.

For instance, the STAR-100, built from SSI parts, required 300 different module types each of which was mapped onto a separate board. For the CYBER 205, this approach became infeasible economically because of a peculiarity of LSI cost considerations. To realize cost factors of LSI technology, the total number of different chip types for CYBER-205 was reduced to 14 for scalar unit and 11 for vector and I/O modules.[4]

Speed optimization is achieved by:

- reducing the clock period;
- expanding device parallelism inside each structural unit;
- expanding the process concurrency by gradual increase (not very dramatic) in the number of structural units for each new generation of supercomputers.

Massively Parallel Architectures (MPA)

Massively parallel architectures enjoy popularity in both industrial and academic communities. The most representative architectures are implemented in the following machines.

- *Massively Parallel Processor* (*MPP*), developed jointly by Goodyear Aerospace Corporation and NASA-Goddard Space Flight Center, was delivered in 1982.[13,14] The MPP processor has 16 896 one-bit PEs arranged in a 128 row × 132 column rectangular array.[5]
- *Connection Machine,* developed at Thinking Machines Corporation is a parallel computing machine having between 16K and 64K 1-bit processors operating under the control of a single instruction stream broadcast to all processors.
- *Hypercube Supercomputer,* developed at Caltech with the first hardware version, Cosmic Cube, having 64 nodes.[7] Subsequent versions were Mark II and Mark III. The final 128-node version Mark III fp is to be completed in the Summer of 1988.[17]

Note. Strictly speaking, Hypercube lies between the CRAY-type and MPA, since it has a much smaller number of nodes than a classical MPA and each node is a quite complex computer, although not as complex as a typical node (CRAY-1 or CYBER-205) in the latest generations of industrial supercomputers made from 8 to 16 such nodes. However, architecturally, the Hypercube provides the advantages and faces the problems of an MPA in view of the total privacy of each node memory and limited communication capabilities among nodes achieved only with the use of *message-passing*.

CONTROL FLOW VERSUS DATA FLOW

As indicated above, a second factor that has influenced the evolution in supercomputer architectures was the use of two alternative models of computation. The first one, called *control flow,* represents program as a sequence of instructions in which sequentiality is maintained with the use of step operations and conditional and unconditional branches.

The second model, called *data flow,* also assumes that the program is a sequence of operations. However, the order of execution is maintained by the availability of operands, that is, by data flow. For this model, two operations are sequential only if they are data-dependent, that is, the second one *consumes* the data *produced* by the first one.

Otherwise, they can be executed in parallel. Thus, ideally, as many operations can be executed in parallel as there are available operand pairs.

Control-flow supercomputers implement both *operation* (fine-grain) and *task* (coarse-grain) parallelism. Fine-grain parallelism is implemented in:

- *array systems* in which the same operation is performed over a set of different data pairs;
- *pipelined systems,* in which different phases of the same operation (process) are performed in parallel over a set of different data pairs; and
- *long instruction word architectures,* which implement operation parallelism with the use of very long instruction.[19]

Coarse-grain or task parallelism is implemented in multicomputers/ multiprocessors that run independent and asynchronous tasks.

By definition, *data-flow supercomputers implement mostly fine-grain parallelism.* As for task parallelism, it is restricted to data-dependent tasks only within a single data-flow program so that each task producer knows of all task consumers that need its data. If two data-dependent tasks belong respectively to two independent programs, the task-producer may not know in advance of all independent task-consumers that may need the produced data. Therefore, any such task-consumer must access the needed data array itself rather than wait until it become available on its node's arcs. Handling all such cases requires introduction of control flow of operation when the task-consumer initiates the task-rendezvous process with an independent task-producer. Apparently, to implement unrestricted task parallelism requires a hybrid supercomputer that implements both data and control flow orders of execution.

Presently, no consensus exists as to which computational mode gives better performance.

Proponents of control flow argue that it allows improved performance in comparison to data-flow computation because of better utilization of resources.[21] Also, for realistic programs, actual resources involved in data-flow computations are much smaller than the entire complexity of a data-flow supercomputer leading to a considerable resource waste.[20]

The time-overhead created with data-flow supercomputing is associated with (a) the necessity to control the movement of highly distributed data items rather than program instructions; (b) the complexity of allocation algorithms because of the requirement to take into account the locality of both instructions and data; (c) the excessive manipulation with tags during each data entry into a program loop, and so on.

On the other hand, in spite of these drawbacks, data-flow concept remains an attractive architectural idea because of its promise to maximize the potential instruction parallelism, which by definition is beyond the reach of control-flow architecture.

Apparently, a future high-performance supercomputer should be a hybrid that can take advantage of both data-flow and control-flow modes of operation in order to achieve maximal operation parallelism and process concurrency uninhibited by the problems encountered in both types of computation.

State-of-the-art research using prototypes of sufficient power will provide excellent opportunities to alleviate all these problems and build such a supercomputer.

Software Developments

The advent of supercomputing has triggered the following developments in software structures.

• Massive efforts to parallelize execution and simplify development of complex *application programs* through parallel algorithm design and component reuse
• Developing *high-level languages* suitable for parallel computation
• Developing *parallel programming environments* for supercomputers that allow parallel monitoring and servicing of concurrent application programs.

APPLICATION PROGRAMS

In the area of application programs, two major research explorations are taking place aimed respectively at:

1. improving the performance of complex application program, and
2. reducing the amount of time and effort spent on program development processes.

Program Performance

Program performance is optimized provided the following conditions apply.

• It is implemented with fast parallel processing algorithm.
• It is optimally coded and efficiently mapped onto supercomputer architecture.
• Supercomputer architecture and its servicing software introduce minimal delays in program computation and serving data needed by the program.

The major objective of parallel algorithm design is obtaining fast parallel-processing algorithms for application processes. This is achieved by performing equivalent transformations wthin the algorithm in order to make it suitable for computation by synchronous and asynchronous parallel architectures used in supercomputers. *Synchronous* parallel architectures are *arrays* and *pipelines*. *Asynchronous* parallel architectures are *multicomputers/multiprocessors*.

Extraction of maximal performance from the array or pipeline requires efficient parallelization for arrays and vectorization for pipelines of the respective data structures used in computations since, essentially, each array and pipeline execute one instruction stream at a time.

Computation of an application algorithm efficiently by multicomputer/ multiprocessor requires its parallel decomposition into various segments that can run in parallel and asynchronously. Therefore, current work in parallel algorithm design is directed at:

- parallelization and vectorization of data structures to make algorithms suitable for array and pipeline computations;
- parallel decomposition of the application algorithms to make them suitable for computation by multicomputers/multiprocessors.

Also, parallel algorithm design remains the area of interest for two scientific disciplines dependent on the form of algorithm presentation.

If an algorithm is abstracted from specific software implementation, its parallel design methodology was and continues to be the domain of *computational sciences*. On the other hand, when it is presented as a high-level program, its parallel design becomes an object of interest for *software design* directed at developing program and data decompositions that not only perform program and data parallelization and data vectorization, but efficiently map the program and data onto supercomputer architectures. These software design techniques are sometimes attributed to compiler methodologies.

Parallelization and Vectorization of Data Structures

Parallelization and vectorization of data structures is understood as follows. Given an n-element data array:

1. Assign one data element per each PE for array (parallel) data structure or k data elements per PE for pipeline (vectorized) data structure.
2. Perform such equivalent transformations within an application algorithm that it can concurrently control the array of n PEs for array processing or pipeline of p PEs for pipeline processing, where $p = n/k$.

The difference between array and pipeline processing is as follows. Each engaged PE in an array made of n PEs at any moment of time executes the same operation over a different pair of operands; in a pipeline of p PEs, organized into p stages, each PE conceived as the ith stage of the pipeline ($i = 1, \ldots, p$) and, assigned a separate pair of operands, executes the ith phase of the process (operation) assigned to the entire pipeline.

Consequently, both modes of operation imply data parallelism, which is applied at each step of the same operation for arrays or different phases of the same operation (process) for pipelines. Thus, array and pipeline modes of operation require development of data-parallel algorithms that at each step deal with an array of different operand pairs. To become efficient, a data-parallel algorithm must be capable of processing an n-element array in less than n steps, otherwise there is no justification for introducing n PEs for array processing or p PEs for pipeline processing. The typical speed improvement for array processing is $\log_2 n$; that is, instead of n steps required by serial processing of n data elements, the same algorithm is executed in $\log_2 n$ steps. For a fully engaged pipeline, an n-element array is processed in $p + k$ steps, where p is the number of pipeline stages, and k is the number of operands (or operand pairs) assigned to each stage.

The major and most obvious drawbacks of data-parallel computations as a class are as follows.

D1. By nature, they are not universal but *dedicated*. Thus, for all non-data-parallel applications, array and pipeline supercomputers show inferior performance, although a significant body of research work is now aimed at broadening the class of data-parallel applications, that is, finding the parallel method of execution for algorithms that used to be regarded as entirely serial.[16,23]

D2. *Limited communication capabilities* among different PEs. For arrays, the most typical connection among PEs is a grid, which may prove to be insufficient for nongrid type data exchanges. In all such cases, data words need to be routed among PEs in order to reach their destination. This introduces significant communication overhead and diminishes the benefits of speed-up due to array processing as a concept. For pipelines, the communication capabilities among PEs are even more limited, totally precluding data exchanges among arbitrarily selected PEs while the pipeline is working.

Parallel Decomposition of Application Algorithms

Here we will deal with this problem in the context of software design, assuming that the algorithm has already been brought to a suitable parallel computational form by available numerical methods.

In a supercomputer organized as multiprocessor/multicomputer if two concurrent tasks are data-independent, their parallel computation presents no problem. The problem arises if tasks are data-dependent, that is, if the first one uses the computational data produced by the second one. Organization of parallel computation among such tasks requires proper organization of such tasks, rendezvous process, which features minimal synchronization delays caused by interrupting the task-consumer if the requested data have not yet been produced by the task-producer.

The major thrust of the literature on software design in parallelization/vectorization of data-dependent tasks, however, is directed at concurrentization and vectorization of program loops which feature various types of data dependencies during successive loop iterations (true dependence, anti-dependence and output-dependence[22]).

Loop concurrentization means correct parallel computation of consecutive loop iterations with minimal delays introduced by synchronization processes aimed at passing data-dependent variables from one loop iteration to the next.

Loop vectorization means correct pipeline computation of consecutive loop iterations with the use of vector instructions. Since many supercomputers have vector instruction sets, and a limited number of processors,[3,4] loop vectorization becomes an important factor of their speed-up.

Reducing Program Development Costs

A supercomputing program is usually very complex, requiring many man-hours of program development efforts. Therefore, considerable effort is now expended to reduce the amount of time needed by a program development process. Major approaches here are (a) component reuse, and (b) software design.

Component Reuse

This concerns construction of programs from reusable components (modules) with or without the use of composition principles. The composition approach provides for some abstract initial representation of reused program modules, then the use of a composition technique such as parameterized programming,[25] the Unix pipe mechanism,[38] or special specification techniques,[26] to construct a complex program from reusable modules with the interfaces specified by the composition technique.

The second approach involves the creation of libraries of reused components that do not need preliminary specifications to be connected to each other.[27]

Software Design

This concerns the development of synthesis techniques for automatic generation of an application program. To be most efficient, these generation techniques should apply to all of the software of the supercomputer. Accordingly, any target program is first represented in an abstract and very high-level notation related to the problem domain.[28,29] The executable program is then generated from the initial simplified representation using automatic synthesis techniques.

PARALLEL PROGRAMMING LANGUAGES

The effect of supercomputing on high-level languages is via two approaches.

- *Theoretical approach* aimed at developing an ideal high-level language concept for future supercomputers
- *Practical approach* aimed at improving existing programming languages and creation of new programming languages for existing industrial supercomputers

Theoretical Approach

Theoretical work in high-level languages is focused on the following.

1. Raising the level of abstraction by developing *very high-level languages* that allow:
(a) programming an application with fewer and more powerful language constructs;
(b) efficient translation of the resulting program into a variety of supercomputer architectures.
2. Higher utilization of concurrency present in application with the use of the *declarative* versus the *imperative* style of programming.[30]

Very High-Level Languages

The basic ideas behind *very high-level languages* is to use declarative and concurrent semantics based upon equational logic.[30] This implies that the programs written in such languages are presented as sets of logical axioms and computation is conceived as a set of rules derived from the equations by a compilation process.[32] The current state of computation is defined by substitution of the "pattern" (usually left-hand side of the expression) in place of a replacement template that is a portion of the right-hand side of the expression and which satisfies the logical conditions attached for such a replacement. When the pattern replaces the matching replacement template, the new result is obtained by instantiating (activating) specific values of variable(s).

These substitutions can be applied concurrently to all the available replacement spots, requiring no specific concurrency constructs at the language level.

Another feature of such languages is that by definition they are *declarative* and not imperative. In the beginning, before the compilation process begins, available sets of equations declare the problem that has to be solved. The task of the compiler is to detect all the available parallelism by concurrent application of substitution rules for all available replacement templates that instantiate computations to specific values. Therefore, the only sequentiality that is introduced by such languages is through data dependence, defined by the rules of precedence present in equations. By contrast, the practical supercomputer languages of today are *imperative* in the sense that they explicitly specify the sequence of commands; that is, not only do they say what to do but also when and where to do it.[30] This is the restriction that reduces the concurrency that can be extracted from high-level application programs.

Practical Approach

The practical approach (a) improves existing high-level languages by adding parallel constructs that implement typical supercomputer operations, (b) develops specific machine-parallelism languages that are well suited for available and popular supercomputers,[31] and (c) attempts to express problem-parallelism directly without reference to the hardware of the underlying machine.[33]

Improving Existing High-Level Languages

Most high-level languages currently used to program supercomputers are conventional scientific languages with added concurrent programming constructs.[34,35] Of these, FORTRAN is highly popular because FORTRAN computations are numeric in nature and supercomputers are now mostly used for numeric computations. Current work on FORTRAN modification is aimed at making FORTRAN programs more suitable for array and pipeline computations.[34,37]

Machine Parallelism Languages

A basic characteristic of such languages is their ability for direct expression of *machine parallelism*.[36,37] This allows generation of efficient code during the compilation stage. These languages provide suitable data representation as well as algorithm construction features that encourage explicit expression of parallelism within the algorithms.

Their major drawback is that the high-level programs generated with their use are overly architecture dependent and are not portable from one architecture to another.

Direct Expression of Problem Parallelsim

The major objective of the third approach in supercomputer languages is to provide for the direct and natural expression of process parallelism (a) unhindered by improving or fixing an existing sequential language, and (b) avoiding dependence of the language on the hardware with all its negative consequences.[31]

The independence of such languages of the architecture is achieved via their ability to give the user the right to define the maximal size of parallelism at compile stage and to adjust the program to a smaller than maximal size at execution time. Also, these languages are portable and equally suitable for vector and array types of computation.[33]

However, their wide adoption by the user community is hindered by the fact that existing industrial supercomputers, for economic reasons, tend to preserve the software developed for earlier generations and thus mostly rely on the languages (say, FORTRAN), in which this software has been written in the past, rather than use new languages that overcome the bottlenecks of sequentiality and dependence on the hardware for improving program performance.[3,4]

PARALLEL PROGRAMMING ENVIRONMENT

The creation of parallel programming environments is aimed at achieving the following goals:

- parallel monitoring of computations,
- parallel servicing of computations.

These functions are performed by distributing operating systems, parallel compilers, and debuggers.

Operating Systems

Current research in operating systems is going in the following directions.

1. Standardization of the OS functions for improving the user's access to supercomputers with the use of industry standard user interface and file systems networked with standard workstations.[38,39]
2. Equipping the OS with the techniques aimed at automatic scheduling and synchronization of multiple processes run on multiple and distributed resources.
3. Concurrent implementation of the OS functions with those of computations in order to exclude or minimize the OS overhead introduced into computations.[40,41]

Standardization of the OS Functions

Currently, the most widely used standard OS in supercomputers is the UNIX OS, which provides facilities for running programs and a file system for managing information.[42] A *file system* is organized as a tree in which each leaf is a *file* or a *directory*. When a user turns on UNIX, a command interpreter accepts commands from the terminal as requests to run program. Any such request includes the program name, which accesses the required file in a file system. If this file exists and is executable, it is loaded as a program.

One of the most productive aspects of UNIX environment is a rich set of software tools for serving programs. The UNIX software is written in the C language. Since C is available on a variety of machines, C programs are portable from one machine to another. Also, the UNIX system contains a variety of facilities that encourage software reuse ranging from the library of standard functions to basic architectural mechanisms called *UNIX pipe* which, acting as a standard buffer interface, allows one user program-producer to generate data for another user program-consumer.

Applied iteratively, the UNIX pipe allows practical and effortless organization of very complex *hierarchical* software systems that would be very difficult if not impossible to organize otherwise.

Distributed Hardware Operating System

The major drawback of standard OS software of the Unix type is that it introduces a considerable time overhead into program computation because almost all program requests for service are accompanied by program interrupts caused by interference of the OS. In a supercomputing environment, to reduce or minimize the OS overhead into computations requires hardware implementation on distributed resources of scheduling and synchronization algorithms. This leads to hardware implementation of basic OS functions, since this is an efficient way of achieving concurrentization of the OS functions with those of computations.[40,41,43] The intention of the hardware-implemented OS is in absolute minimization of program interrupts.

In a typical computational situation, most program interrupts originate from the necessity for the OS to interfere in the *task rendezvous* process between two programs. To perform process synchronization, the OS stops both the program-consumer when it issues a request for rendezvous and the program-producer when it accepts the rendezvous request.

Only following this synchronization stage, does the OS allow the rendezvous to proceed, that is, to send data array to task-consumer memory domain. However, interrupt of both task-producer and task-consumer can be avoided if the task-rendezvous algorithm is implemented via hardware and can be activated locally inside each PE. It allows avoidance of the following interrupt cases.

Case 1. Neither task-producer (TP) and task-consumer (TC) is interrupted if the data are produced before they are requested; that is, if the *accept* statement issued by the TP precedes the *request* for rendezvous issued by the TC. The hardware OS organizes storage of the requested data in a particular destination and informs TC through the mailbox system about the storage location, requiring no interrupt for either task.

Case 2. TP is not interrupted; TC is interrupted if the data are produced after they are requested, that is, if the *accept* statement issued by the TP follows in time the *request* for rendezvous issued by TC. The hardware OS again uses the same mailbox system with storage location to allow the interrupted TC to resume computations when the data produced by TP are ready.

Hence, for task-rendezvous, implementation of a hardware OS abolishes all interrupts of the task-producer and minimizes interrupts of task-consumer.

Parallel Servicing Software
On-going research in the area of parallel servicing software pursues the following objectives.

- Automatic generation of compilation and debugging systems, given a description of supercomputer architecture
- Implementation of a comprehensive software portability concept that allows creation of retargetable software systems and greatly improves software productivity.

Both objectives will lead towards creation of comprehensive software environments for supercomputers through the use of:

- automatic synthesis applied to software generation, and
- reuse of basic software tools, which becomes possible through implementation of the portable software concept.

However, in the supercomputer environment, both concepts are applicable only for *stored* application programs, since the time overhead they introduce becomes that of program preprocessing aimed at its compilation and debugging, which is not additive to program computation time. Thus, they may become ingredients of standard OS, greatly enriching its repertoire. On the other hand, *dynamic* or *arriving* programs require hardware implementation of compilation systems as a part of its OS hardware aimed at automatic scheduling and resource allocation in real-time.

Applications

Users are the major beneficiaries of these new developments in supercomputing. There is a broadly formed consensus that supercomputing has already established itself as the third mode of scientific research, that is, that it has significantly broadened the traditional base of scientific pursuits formerly restricted to (1) experimentation and (2) theoretical analysis.[44]

The advent of supercomputing in the area of applications was marked by the following milestones.

Milestone 1 Improved match between more precise modeling techniques and high-performance scientific and industrial applications.

Milestone 2 Cost-efficient computerization of new applications with very demanding performance requirements that were unthinkable targets for attempted computerization in the past owing to their complexity and timing demands. (For instance, many mission-critical computations in aerospace are characterized by continuing and dramatic reduction in the time of computer responses to real-time input data acquired from sensors because of the rapid progress in the systems aimed at detecting, intercepting, and homing each real-time target. Similar timing limits are imposed by advanced nuclear and chemical processes controlled by supercomputers; and so on.)

Milestone 3 Comprehensive automation applied to complex application processes which allows a much greater degree of exclusion of human intervention than it was possible to achieve in the past through the use of:

- *intelligent expert systems* with automatic decision making process, and
- *automatic software systems* made of complex application programs and the parallel-programming environment in which they are run.

Milestone 4 Creation of comprehensive numerical laboratories for complex supercomputer applications with all the supporting mechanisms that facilitate understanding of computational results via the use of:

- *visual presentation* of time-dependent multidimensional computational results and their effect on the behavior of modeled application processes;
- *time-dependent multidimensional simulations* of complex application processes; and
- ability to perform *automatic comparison of numerical data with those obtained through the use of laboratory experiments* with far-reaching consequences for improving the human understanding of complex scientific application processes and aiding scientific discovery.[45]

The following categories of users become principal beneficiaries of these advances.

- Users of important industrial applications such as high-speed aerodynamic design, robotics, biotechnology, structural materials, electronic and optical technologies, and so on

- Users of scientific applications in astronomy, virology, biochemistry, nuclear and chemical sciences, earth and space sciences, and so on
- Key manufacturing industries, which will be able to improve their productivity via more comprehensive and efficient automation applied at the level of engineering design, product fabrication and product testing
- Predictive activities in weather forecasting, global financial stability, and monetary policies, and economic modeling[46]

Thus, the advent of supercomputing can be seen to have become synonymous with rapid acceleration of the entire technological progress in a modern society.

- Supercomputing as a discipline expedites making and improves the quality of fundamental scientific discoveries that affect modern technological society.
- Supercomputing allows faster and more comprehensive technology transfer aimed at moving the results of state-of-the-art activity pursued in sciences to the world of technology.
- Supercomputing greatly expands the productivity of manufacturing industries through the use of comprehensive automation and/or computerization of industrial processes.

ABOUT THIS BOOK

While the preceding sections of this Introduction have attempted to capture major technical developments that are taking place in a broad field of disciplines united under the banner of supercomputing, this book gives an opportunity to become familiar with specific technical developments mentioned above. Its chapters cover the following fields:

Part one. Supercomputer Architectures
Part two. Software and Hardware Design of Supercomputers
Part three. Supercomputer Computations, Applications, and Performance Evaluations

Supercomputer Architectures

The area of supercomputer architecture is represented by four chapters.

Chapter 1 performs an overall analysis, investigates all the existing techniques of performance improvement, studies the evolution of major industrial architectures and explores the performance potential offered by major research approaches: adaptable and data flow architectures.

Chapter 2 is dedicated to the CHoPP supercomputer, which is the product of CHoPP Corporation. It describes its basic feature aimed at minimization or total elimination of memory conflicts by the use of hardware operating system. It analyzes CHoPP's performance in executing the Livermore benchmarks and gives details on automatic computer-aided design and simulation of CHoPP circuits through the use of SCALD technology.

Chapter 3 is dedicated to another supercomputer manufactured by the Unisys Corporation. The major feature of the Unisys approach is that it allows addition of a fast array/vector add-on system integrated with the Unisys mainframe. The chapter gives a comprehensive technical description of this integrated supercomputer along with its performance results, allocation, and scheduling techniques, as well as advanced software design aimed at loop vectorization.

Chapter 4 deals with the data-flow approach to supercomputing. It classifies available data-flow approaches (data-driven and demand-driven) and proposes a hybrid model of computation—the Eazyflow model—that provides one with the benefits of both models. It then introduces basic programming concepts for data-flow computations and outlines major characteristics of easy-flow architecture.

Software and Hardware Design of Supercomputers

The second part of the book practices the top-down approach, starting with high-level languages and ending with hardware design.

Chapter 5 explores the benefits of equational languages and declarative style of programming for programming large-scale computations. It introduces the MODEL equational language and shows that its use allows creation of powerful software environment. These tools can make the programming, debugging, and modifying of parallel computations similar in complexity and difficulty to preparing software for sequential processing.

Chapter 6 considers the design of the cache–primary memory interface in systems composed of several processors. Each processor is provided with a local cache interconnected via a switching scheme to the main memory. The major problem in such systems is cache coherence, which is aimed at preventing individual processors from modification of their local cache without the use of a centralized notification mechanism that allows broadcast of every individual modification to all caches. The proposed solutions are divided into: (a) software-based solutions; (b) solutions for shared-bus systems; and (c) directory-based solution. Chapter 6 contributes to a directory-based solution by presenting a formal model based on Petri nets that allows creation of correct protocols for local cache modifications in complex multiprocessing environments.

Chapter 7 outlines the techniques for optimization of the entire hierarchical memory system for supercomputers. It presents a methodology aimed at organization of a high-speed memory system with the use of linear hierarchical organization employed in buffered (cache) memories and shows how this organization can optimize both the time of access and the overall memory size. Iterative application of the cache principle to successive memory levels allows organization of a powerful memory pyramid in which each next level has a smaller size and can be accessed faster than preceding level and will act as its cache.

Chapter 8 deals with automatic hardware design aimed at development of behavioral testing techniques for complex systolic arrays. The authors introduce an augmented fault-tolerant interconnection structure between all the available PEs, which allows them to reconfigure-out faulty PEs from computations. This interconnection structure allows independent access to all single PEs and thus it is not hindered by the global nature of the architecture. The authors define a testing strategy that allows minimization of the overall testing time while preserving the behavior nature of the device being tested.

Supercomputer Computations, Applications, and Performance Evaluation

As follows from its title, this section deals with supercomputer applications at the level of algorithms (Chapter 9), description of applications (Chapters 10 and 11) and their performance evaluation (Chapter 12).

Chapter 9 explores basic mathematical theory and algorithms for handling multidimensional multiparameter systems on supercomputers. It considers matrices belonging to a vector space over two rings. Such problems require large amounts of storage and many arithmetic operations, and hence necessitate supercomputers and parallel processing.

Chapter 10 deals with supercomputer applications in modeling and image processing for earth and space sciences. Part A describes modeling applications of remotely sensed data and explores the ways in which these modeling techniques can be implemented. In Part B, the authors address the use of supercomputing for image processing, covering (a) the use of parallel programming techniques for restoration of astronomical images that have been blurred by imperfections of sensors; (b) the use of image matching techniques for tracking the motion of objects by detecting differences between successive images of the same object; (c) the use of supercomputers for vision applications (including problems involving edge detection, vision levels, and an analysis of a current project to implement vision modules on the Connection Machine; (d) limitations of parallel graphics algorithms on a massively parallel processor.

Together all the topics discussed in Chapter 10 help explain why new supercomputer architectures and algorithms are necessary and what performance benefits for these applications are expected.

Chapter 11 surveys early applications of the hypercube to computationally intense probelms in science and engineering. The presentation is based on actual experience of the authors at Caltech. It also includes the experience accumulated with the use of commercial hypercubes at Ametek, Floating Point Systems, Intel, and NCUBE.

The chapter also summarizes the current status of the Caltech Concurrent Computation Program, describes the hypercube and its position in the taxonomy of parallel machines, and provides an in depth discussion of several Caltech hypercube applications concerning the multigrid approach to partial differential equations, quantum chronodynamics theory in high-energy physics, geophysics, and the Kalman filtering used in multitarget tracking. Finally, the chapter covers the pioneering work at Oak Ridge Laboratory on the use of the commercial NCUBE as a controller for a robot: a real-time application.

Chapter 12 surveys the use of stochastic Petri nets for evaluating supercomputer performance. Classical methodologies of performance evaluation have the goal of assessing and comparing different supercomputers in order to remove their bottlenecks and predict the effectiveness of upgraded configurations. In the case of supercomputing, another objective is quantitative assessment of design alternatives during the definition stages. Modeling techniques become compulsory and allow a computer designer to alleviate many problems during functional hardware and software design of the system. This chapter describes several classes of Petri net models suitable for analysis of complex computing systems. The models presented do not incorporate all the details of the multiprocessor behavior, but they are examples of modeling a specific function.

CONCLUSIONS

We believe that the reader will be happy with this collection of papers. The authors attempt to present the topic of supercomputing from the viewpoint of disciplines which they are pursuing as professionals. The advantage of such an approach is to become acquainted with insights and knowledge accumulated in a variety of scientific and industrial areas that have a strong association with supercomputing.

REFERENCES

1. Hanson, Harold P. (1988). "Supercomputing as a multidisciplinary approach to technological progress," *Proceedings of the Third International Conference on Supercomputing,* Vol. I, pp. ix–xii. International Supercomputing Institute, Inc., St. Petersburg, Fla.

2. Bashkow, T. R. (1987). "Supercomputers: Always in the fast lane," *Computer Technol. Rev.,* Vol. VII, No. 12.

3. Steiner, K. (1988). "Supercomputer design challenges," *Proceedings of the First International Conference on Supercomputing Systems,* pp. 3–7. International Supercomputing Institute, Inc., St. Petersburg, Fla.

4. Lincoln, N. R. (1982). "Technology and design trade-offs in the creation of a modern supercomputer," *IEEE Trans. Computers,* Vol. C-31, No. 5, pp. 349–363.

5. Batcher, K. E. (1982). "Bit-serial parallel processing systems," *IEEE Trans. Computers,* Vol. C-31, No. 5, pp. 377–385.

6. Fiebrich, R. D. (1987). "Data parallel algorithms for engineering applications," *Proceedings of the Second International Conference on Supercomputing,* Vol. II, *Industrial Supercomputer Applications and Computations,* pp. 17–23. International Supercomputing Institute, Inc., St. Petersburg, Fla.

7. Seitz, C. L. (1985). "The Cosmic Cube," *Commun. ACM,* Vol. 28, No. 1, pp. 22–34.

8. Fox, G. C., M. A. Johnson, G. A. Lyzenga, S. W. Otto, S. K. Salmon and D. Walker. (1988). Prentice Hall, Englewood Cliffs, N.J. *Solving Problems on Concurrent Processors.* The software supplement to the book is edited by I. Angus, G. Fox, J. Kim and D. Walker.

9. Kartashev, S. P. and S. I. Kartashev. (1978). "Dynamic architectures: Problems and solutions," *Computer*, Vol. II, July, pp. 26–40.

10. Kartashev, S. P. and S. I. Kartashev. (1978). "LSI modular computers, systems, and networks," *Computer*, Vol. II, July, pp. 7–15.

11. Kartashev, S. P., and S. I. Kartashev. (1979)."A multicon. er system with dynamic architecture," *IEEE Trans. Computers*, Vol. C-28, No. 10, pp. 704–721.

12. Kartashev, S. P. and S. I. Kartashev. (1980). "Supersystems for the 80s," *Computer*, Vol. 13, Nov. pp. 11–14.

13. Batcher, K. E. (1980). "Design of a massively parallel processor," *IEEE Trans. Computers*, Vol. C-29, pp. 836–840.

14. Fung, L. W. (1977). "A massively parallel processing computer," in *High-Speed Computer and Algorithm Organization*, (ed. D. J. Kuck et al.), pp. 203–204. Academic Press, New York.

15. Hillis, D. (1985). "The Connection Machine," MIT Press, Cambridge, Mass.

16. Hillis, D. and G. L. Steele. (1986). "Data parallel algorithms," *Commun. ACM*, Vol. 29, No. 12, pp. 1170–1183.

17. Apostolakis et al., Ch. 11, this volume.

18. Dennis, J. B. (1980). "Data flow supercomputers," *Computer*, Vol. 13, No. 11, pp. 48–57.

19. Fisher, Joseph A. (1987). "Very long instruction word architectures: Supercomputing via overlapped execution," *Proc. of the Second International Conference on Supercomputing*, Vol. 1, pp. 353–362. International Supercomputing Institute, Inc., St. Petersburg, Fla.

20. Veen, Arthur H. (1986). "Data flow machine architecture," *ACM Computing Surveys*, Vol. 18, No. 4, pp. 365–398.

21. Gaiski, D. D., D. A. Padua, D. J. Kuck and R. H. Kuhn. (1982). "Second opinion on data flow machines and languages," *Computer*, Vol. 15, No. 2, pp. 58–69.

22. Kuck, D. J. (1978). *The Structure of Computers and Computations*, Vol. 1. Wiley, New York.

23. Padua, D. A. and M. J. Wolfe. (1986). Advanced compiler optimizations for supercomputers," *Commun. ACM*, Vol. 29, No. 12, pp. 1184–1202.

24. Biggerstaff, T. J. and A. J. Perlis. (1984). "Forward," *IEEE Trans. Software Eng.*, Vol. SE-10, No. 5, pp. 474–477.

25. Goguen, J. A. (1984). "Parameterized programming," *IEEE Trans. Software Eng.* Vol. SE-10, No. 5, pp. 528–544.

26. Litvintchouk, S. D. and A. S. Matsumoto. (1984). "Design of Ada systems yielding reusable components: An approach using structured algebraic specification," *IEEE Trans. Software Eng.*, Vol. SE-10, No. 5, pp. 544–552.

27. Lanergan, R. G. and C. A. Grasso. (1984). "Software engineering with reusable design and code," *IEEE Trans. Software Eng.*," Vol. SE-10, No. 5, pp. 498–502.

28. Cheng, T. T., E. D. Lock and N. S. Prywes. (1984). "Use of very high level languages and program generation by management professionals," *IEEE Trans. Software Eng.* Vol. SE-10, No. 5, pp. 552–564.

29. Neighbors, J. M. (1984). "The Draco approach to constructing software from reusable components," *IEEE Trans. Software Eng.*, Vol. SE-10, No. 5, pp. 564–574.

30. Goguen, J., C. Kirchner, J. Meseguer and T. Winkler. (1987). "OBJ as a language for concurrent programming," "Proceedings of the Second International Conference on Supercomputing", Vol. I, pp. 196–198. International Supercomputing Institute, Inc. St. Petersburg, Fla.

31. Perrott, R. H. and A. Zarea-Aliabadi. (1986). "Supercomputer languages," *ACM Computing Surveys*, Vol. 18, No. 1, pp. 5–23.

32. Winkler, T. C., S. Leinwand and J. Goguen. (1987). "Simulation of concurrent term rewriting, in

Proceedings of the Second International Conference on Supercomputing, Vol. 1, pp. 199–208. International Supercomputing Institute, Inc., St. Petersburg, Fla.

33. Perrott, R. H. (1979) "A Language for array and vector processors," *ACM Trans. Program. Lang. Syst.* Vol. 1, No. 2, pp. 177–195.

34. Control Data Corporation. (1982). *Cyber 200 Fortran, Version 1, Reference Manual.* Pub. 60480200, CDC, St. Paul, Minn.

35. CRAY Research. (1982). *Fortran (CFT) Reference Manual.* Pub. SR-0009.

36. Stevens, K. G. "CFD—A Fortran-like language for the Illiac-IV," SIGPLAN Notices, Vol. 10, No. 3, pp. 72–80.

37. International Computers Ltd. (1978). "DAP: Introduction to Fortran programming." ICL Tech. Pub. 6755, ICL, London, UK.

38. Kernighan, B. W. (1984). "The UNIX system and software reusability," *IEEE Trans. Software Eng.* Vol. SE-10, No. 5, pp. 513–519.

39. Curry, G. A. and R. M. Ayers (1984). "Experience with Traits in the Xerox Star Workstation," *IEEE Trans. Software Eng.* Vol. SE-10, No. 5, pp. 519–528.

40. Kartashev, S. I. and S. P. Kartashev. (1982). "A distributed operating system for a powerful system with dynamic architecture," *The 1982 National Computer Conference, AFIPS Proc.,* pp. 105–116.

41. Mankovich, T. E., V. Popescu and H. Sullivan. (1987). "CHoPP principles of operation," *Proceedings of the Second International Conference on Supercomputing,* Vol. 1, pp. 2–11. International Supercomputing Institute, Inc., St. Petersburg, Fla.

42. Kernighan, B. W. and R. Pike (1984). *The Unix Programming Environment.* Prentice-Hall, Englewood Cliffs, N.J.

43. Kartashev, S. P. and S. I. Kartashev (1989). "Supercomputer architectures: Evolution and implementations," *Supercomputing Systems,* Ch. 1. Van Nostrand, New York.

44. Raveche, H. J. (1987). "Report of the Sub-Panel on Applications of High-Performance Computing in Engineering and Science," *SIAM Workshop,* Leesburg, Va., Feb. 2–3, 1987, pp. 11–46.

45. Winkler, K.-H. A., J. W. Chalmers, S. W. Hodson, P. R. Woodward and I. N. J. Zabusky. (1988). "A numerical laboratory," *Physics Today,* pp. 28–37.

46. "A national computing initiative: The agenda for leadership," *Executive Summary, SIAM Workshop,* Leesburg, Va., Feb. 2–3, 1987, pp. 3–11.

CONTRIBUTORS

M. Ajmone Marsan
Università di Milano, Dipartimento di Scienze dell'Informazione, Milan, Italy

John Apostolakis
California Institute of Technology, Caltech Concurrent Computation Program, Pasadena, California

E. A. Ashcroft
Arizona State University, Department of Computer Science, Tempe, Arizona

Jean-Loup Baer
University of Washington, Department of Computer Science, Seattle, Washington

Clive Baillie
California Institute of Technology, Caltech Concurrent Computation Program, Pasadena, California

J. Barhen
Oak Ridge National Laboratory, Engineering Physics and Mathematics Division, Center for Engineering Systems Advanced Research, Oak Ridge, Tennessee

Theodore R. Bashkow
Columbia University, Department of Computer Science, New York, New York

Keith Besaw
ETA Systems, Inc., St. Paul, Minnesota

P. J. Camillo
NASA-Goddard Space Flight Center, Laboratory for Terrestrial Physics, Greenbelt, Maryland

Hudong Chen
Bartol Research Institute, University of Delaware, Newark, Delaware

G. Chiola
Università di Torino, Dipartimento di Informatica, Torino, Italy

Robert W. Clayton
California Institute of Technology, Caltech Concurrent Computation Program, Pasadena, California

Leonard Allen Cohn
CHoPP Computer Corporation, La Jolla, California

G. Conte
Università di Parma, Istituto per le Scienze d'Ingegneria, Parma, Italy

J. A. Davis
Iowa State University, Department of Electrical Engineering and Computer Engineering, Ames, Iowa

Judith E. Devaney
ST Systems Corporation, Lanham, Maryland

Hong Ding
California Institute of Technology, Caltech Concurrent Computation Program, Pasadena, California

F. Distante
Politecnico di Milano, Milan, Italy

David S. Dunn
Unisys Corporation, Roseville, Minnesota

J. R. Einstein
Oak Ridge National Laboratory, Engineering Physics and Mathematics Division, Center for Engineering Systems Advanced Research, Oak Ridge, Tennessee

A. A. Faustini
Arizona State University, Department of Computer Science, Tempe, Arizona

Jon Flower
California Institute of Technology, Caltech Concurrent Computation Program, Pasadena, California

Geoffrey C. Fox
California Institute of Technology, Caltech Concurrent Computation Program, Pasadena, California

Claude Girault
Université Paris VI, Paris, France

Thomas D. Gottschalk
California Institute of Technology, Caltech Concurrent Computation Program, Pasadena, California

R. J. Gurney
NASA-Goddard Space Flight Center, Laboratory for Terrestrial Physics, Greenbelt, Maryland

Bradford H. Hager
California Institute of Technology, Caltech Concurrent Computation Program, Pasadena, California

Milton Halem
NASA-Goddard Space Flight Center, Space Data & Computing Division, Greenbelt, Maryland

Sara R. Heap
NASA-Goddard Space Flight Center, Laboratory for Astronomy and Solar Physics, Greenbelt, Maryland

James A. Hodek
Unisys Corporation, Roseville, Minnesota

R. Jagannathan
Computer Science Laboratory, SRI International, Menlo Park, California

John Jones Jr.
Air Force Institute of Technology, Department of Mathematics and Computer Science, Dayton, Ohio

C. C. Jorgensen
Oak Ridge National Laboratory, Engineering Physics and Mathematics Division, Center for Engineering Systems Advanced Research, Oak Ridge, Tennessee

Steven I. Kartashev
International Supercomputing Institute, Inc., St. Petersburg, Florida

Svetlana P. Kartashev
International Supercomputing Institute, Inc., St. Petersburg, Florida

Herbert B. Keller
California Institute of Technology, Caltech Concurrent Computation Program, Pasadena, California

Jane R. Kessler
Unisys Corporation, PO Box 500, Blue Bell, Pennsylvania

Adam K. Kolawa
California Institute of Technology, Caltech Concurrent Computation Program, Pasadena, California

Bruce D. Lightner
Science Applications International Corporation, La Jolla, California

Don J. Lindler
Advanced Computer Concepts, Inc., Potomac, Maryland

James J. Little
Massachusetts Institute of Technology, Cambridge, Massachusetts

Michael J. McAnulty
University of Alabama, Birmingham, Alabama

Thomas M. McWilliams
Valid Logic Systems, San Jose, California

Theodore E. Mankovich
CHoPP Computer Corporation, La Jolla, California

William H. Matthaeus
Bartol Research Institute, University of Delaware, Newark, Delaware

Steve W. Otto
California Institute of Technology, Caltech Concurrent Computation Program, Pasadena, California

A. V. Pohm
Iowa State University, Department of Electrical Engineering and Computer Engineering, Ames, Iowa

Val Popescu
CHoPP Computer Corporation, La Jolla, California

Noah S. Prywes
University of Pennsylvania, Department of Computer and Information Sciences, Philadelphia, Pennsylvania

Barbara H. Putney
NASA-Goddard Space Flight Center, Laboratory for Terrestrial Physics, Greenbelt, Maryland

H. K. Ramapriyan
NASA-Goddard Space Flight Center, Space Data & Computing Division, Greenbelt, Maryland

M. G. Sami
Politecnico di Milano, Milan, Italy

R. Stefanelli
Politecnico di Milano, Milan, Italy

Francis A. Stephens
Unisys Corporation, Roseville, Minnesota

James P. Strong
NASA-Goddard Space Flight Center, Space Data & Computing Division, Greenbelt, Maryland

Herbert Sullivan
CHoPP Computer Corporation, La Jolla, California

Boleslaw K. Szymanski
Rensselaer Polytechnic Institute, Department of Computer Science, Troy, New York

Toshiro Tanimoto
California Institute of Technology, Caltech Concurrent Computation Program, Pasadena, California

Eric F. Van de Velde
California Institute of Technology, Caltech Concurrent Computation Program, Pasadena, California

PART ONE

Supercomputer Architectures

1

SUPERCOMPUTER ARCHITECTURES: EVOLUTION AND IMPLEMENTATIONS

Svetlana P. Kartashev and Steven I. Kartashev

At every stage of their development, large computer architectures have manifested the efforts of their designers to achieve the maximum speed attainable. In their quest, computer architects have traveled a long but illustrious path marked by such milestones as von Neumann computers, microprogrammed computers, and parallel systems, including multiprocessors, multicomputers, arrays and pipelines.

INDUSTRIAL AND PROTOTYPE ARCHITECTURES

From the very beginning, the evolutionary development in supercomputer architectures has formed two clearly established and independent paths aimed at

- *development of industrial architectures* produced by major industrial manufacturers in a significant number of copies;
- *development of prototype (research) architectures* produced by research groups associated with industry and/or academia in a single or limited number of copies.

3

MAJOR FACTORS THAT AFFECT EVOLUTION OF INDUSTRIAL AND PROTOTYPE ARCHITECTURES

Basic evolutionary trends for both types of architectures are governed by the factors discussed in pp. 4–5 for industrial architectures and in pp. 6–7 for prototype architectures.

Basic Factors of Industrial Architecture Evolution

The evolutionary development of industrial architectures has been influenced by the following factors.

> IF1. Gradual and mostly quantitative changes in basic architectural characteristics of a current industrial architecture are necessitated by economic demands on the reuse of the entire software development for its predecessor.
>
> IF2. To be economically feasible and to satisfy user performance needs, an industrial architecture of the current generation must take maximum cost and speed advantage of the component technology used.

Let us give more details on each of factors IF1 and IF2.

GRADUAL AND QUANTITATIVE CHANGES IN BASIC ARCHITECTURAL SOLUTIONS

Each new-generation supercomputer is aimed at satisfying growing user needs that cannot be met by the supercomputers of the preceding generation.[1] For instance, the main economic reason behind the appearance of the CYBER-205 was the vast user need for fast solution of algorithms associated with three-dimensional modeling. (Previously, the user had been satisfied with two-dimensional solutions.) However, a transition from a two-dimensional to three-dimensional modeling requires a 100-fold increase in memory volumes and arithmetic speed. This necessitates the construction of a new supercomputer of the next generation.[2]

To satisfy the new user needs in a cost-effective manner requires extensive reuse of the software developed for the architecture of the preceding generation. This leads to architectural compatibility between the current and past architectures.

As was indicated by Neil Lincoln:[2]

> The motivation for a user to procure a supercomputer is ... rather the need to fit an increased model size or computing speed requirement. The motivation for a manufacturer to produce a supercomputer is to realize sufficient sales and profit to justify launching expensive and risky development efforts.

Realization of these economic causes leads to factor IF1 for industrial architectural evolution. For instance, we can now trace the following evolution in Control Data/ETA architectures:

First generation STAR-100 (1974)	$\rightarrow$	Second generation CYBER-205 (1981)	$\rightarrow$	Third generation ETA-10 (1986)

Similar evolution applies for the CRAY supercomputer family, starting with the CRAY-1 and ending with CRAY X-MP/4 and CRAY-2:

First generation CRAY-1 (1976)	$\rightarrow$	Second generation CRAY X-MP/2, X-MP/4 (1982)	$\rightarrow$	Third generation CRAY-2, CRAY-3 (1984)

MAXIMUM COST AND SPEED ADVANTAGE OF THE USED COMPONENT TECHNOLOGY

A second factor of industrial architectural evolution is associated with the full utilization of available technological advances for component technologies.

Cost Optimization via Reduced Module Type Count

The major source of the cost optimization is associated with minimization in the number of module types used for supercomputer design. Let us illustrate this phenomenon by considering transition STAR-100 $\rightarrow$ CYBER-205.[2]

Since STAR-100 was built from SSI parts, the engineers of its design team were free to develop as many module types as were needed to improve the performance of this machine. This resulted in over 300 different module types, each of which was mapped onto a separate board.

For CYBER-205, this approach became economically infeasible because of a peculiarity of LSI cost considerations. To realize cost factors of the LSI technology employed, the total number of different chip types for CYBER-205 was reduced to 14 for scalar unit and 11 for vector and I/O modules.

Speed Optimization

In existing industrial supercomputers, the speed is usually improved via:

- reducing the clock rate by taking advantage of smaller propagation delays affordable with LSI technology;
- introduction of functional-device parallelism into supercomputer design;
- reduction in memory-management overhead;
- reduction in I/O overhead and other factors.

Let us consider how all these factors can be illustrated for the STAR-100 $\rightarrow$ CYBER-205 transition.

Reducing the clock rate by taking advantage of smaller propagation delays affordable with LSI technology. A 40 nsec clock rate for STAR-100 was reduced to 13.3 nsec in CYBER-205.[2] A major stumbling block in achieving a 13.3 nsec rate was the old Register File of STAR-100, which was required in order to allow each new instruction to fetch all its operands and write the computational results obtained. Since the instruction rate for CYBER-205 was set at one instruction per clock, all operand/result accesses had to be made during a 13.3 nsec period. This objective was achieved with the use of innovative file organization made with 4×16-bit memory chips, each of which could perform a concurrent read and write of two operands at a time with the speed of 8–10 nsec.

Introduction of functional parallelism for scalar and vector operations. For STAR-100 the economy of SSI dictated that scalar and vector functions be performed sequentially by the same arithmetic unit. In CYBER-205 the economy of LSI has allowed a cost-efficient creation of parallel arithmetic functions for scalar and vector operations, respectively.

Reduction in memory management overhead created by huge virtual memory was achieved via increase in the number of possible page sizes, with each page size conceived as a unit of a physical memory allocation.

The I/O overhead was significantly reduced via

- the use of much faster I/O channels, and
- increase in the number of terminals that could be connected with the CYBER-205, via network connection of terminals with this supercomputer versus dedicated interconnection of terminals in STAR-100.

Factors of Prototype Architecture Evolution

The factors that have governed the development of prototype architectures are just the opposite of those for the industrial ones. These factors are:

PF1. More innovative and daring use of the available and new architectural approaches.

PF2. No prototype architecture, as a rule, fully utilizes the available advances of component technologies associated with the use of the newest high-speed components, development of dense packaging, and organization of efficient cooling and heat-dissipation systems.

INNOVATIVE USE OF NEW ARCHITECTURAL APPROACHES

In contrast to industrial architectures, the prototype architectures are more innovative in introducing nonorthodox computing structures that possess potential for improving performance. The origin of this phenomenon is again economic. While the objective of a successful industrial supercomputer is to achieve absolute minimization of its hardware and software costs while meeting new user throughput demands, the actual cost of a prototype architecture becomes a factor of smaller importance.

Indeed, the objective of a feasible prototype architecture is to evaluate the performance/cost potential for a new or modified principle of computing not used before in other prototypes. Since the designers of an architectural prototype are not restricted by the software compatibility demands, their architectural thinking is more unrestrained concerning the types of architectural solutions that can be accomplished.

INCOMPLETE UTILIZATION OF THE AVAILABLE TECHNOLOGICAL ADVANCES

The reasons for this factor are again economic. As a rule, a typical prototype architecture is implemented by a small group of computer scientists and engineers who are incapable, owing to financial constraints, of organizing the large-scale component technology research that is customarily performed by their industrial counterparts. For instance, an LSI module used for designing the CYBER-205 is a newly developed high-powered LSI circuit that was the result of a research effort started in Control Data Advanced Design Laboratory as far back as 1972 in conjunction with several key semiconductor vendors.[2] Parts counts, interchassis wiring, and power and cooling considerations dominate the production of real usable industrial supercomputers, with architecture becoming a necessary but secondary consideration.[2] On the other hand, for a prototype architecture, the component technology factors become of secondary importance, since the major task of its research team is to check the feasibility of innovative software and architectural solutions before embarking into huge component technology costs aimed at optimal technological implementation of these solutions.

SURVEY OF EXISTING TECHNIQUES OF PERFORMANCE IMPROVEMENT

The economic factors of architectural evolution for industrial and prototype architectures that we have noted have clearly shaped the way these architectures have been developed by various manufacturers (industrial and research). Before describing specific evolutionary trends demonstrated by architectures analyzed under the influence of factors IF1 and IF2 for industrial architectures and PF1 and PF2 for prototype architectures, we consider the existing techniques of performance improvement. Thereafter, we will describe how these techniques have been used in the long path of architectural evolution under the economic restraints of factors IF1 and IF2, and PF1 and PF2.

Two Levels of Performance Improvement in a Computer System

The performance of a computer system can be improved at two levels:

• design level,
• architectural level.

The border between design level and architectural level is blurred (Fig. 1-1). For simplicity, under *design level* we mean all performance optimizations associated with execution of a single or multiple operations in a single or different functional

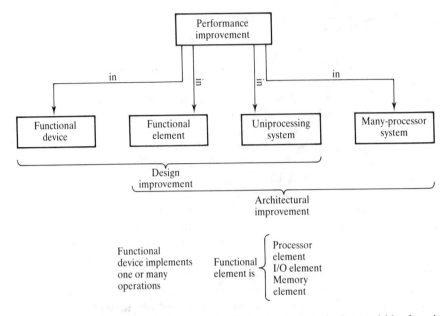

Figure 1-1. Performance improvement within functional devices; within functional elements; within uniprocessing systems; and within many-processor systems. A functional device implements one or many operations; a functional element is a processor element, an I/O element or a memory element.

units (processor, memory, I/O). Under *architectural level* we mean all performance optimizations achieved at the level of *machine instructions for a single machine level program or multiple machine-level programs.*

Therefore, roughly, a *design improvement* can be achieved by speeding up operation(s) execution times within:

- functional devices;
- functional elements (which is understood as either a processor element, PE, memory element, ME, or I/O element); and
- a uniprocessing system assembled from one PE and other functional elements.

Likewise, an *architectural improvement* is achieved by speeding up execution of one instruction at a time in a uniprocessing system or many instructions at a time in a many-processor system.

Therefore, the architectural level implicitly takes into account the interactive work under program control of several functional units (processor, memory, and I/O), whereas the design level takes into account the work of one or several functional devices or elements. Although, under this classification, for some architectures multiple operations in different functional units may be attributed to architectural improvement, for simplicity we will consider them design optimizations (Fig. 1-1).

Design Optimization

For a supercomputer, there are two types of operations:

- non-memory-access operation, performed in PE or I/O; and
- memory-access operation, performed in ME (Fig. 1-2).

OPTIMIZATION OF NON-MEMORY-ACCESS OPERATIONS

For any *non-memory-access operation*, the design improvement can be made inside a single functional device (adder, multiplier, division unit, etc.) via its parallelization for fast scalar and vector computations and/or pipelining for vector computations (Fig. 1-2). For complex iterative operations, device parallelization and pipelining can be combined. For instance, floating-point division can be represented by a parallel division algorithm implemented as a parallel division fragmented into a sequence of simple additions and/or subtractions. Thus, the functional device becomes pipelined.

> **Example 1.** Figure 1-3 shows a 32-bit multiplication pipeline for STAR-100, which implements parallel carry–save multiplication algorithm. *Parallelization* of the algorithm is achieved by having parallel Partial Adders, PA, at the first and successive levels of the multiplication diagram. *Pipelining* of the algorithm is achieved via its segmentation into a sequence of parallel additions in which parallel adders of each pipeline level generate partial sums that are fed as addends to the next level until only two addends remain. These are then added (or merged and added) outside the multiplier.

OPTIMIZATION OF MEMORY-ACCESS OPERATIONS

For a *memory-access operation*, design improvement in memory access is achieved via

- memory interleaving;
- memory overlap with processor or I/O operation; and
- use of buffer (cache) memories (Fig. 1-2).

Memory Interleaving

Memory interleaving allows a PE to access a data word stored in ME at the clock rate t_0 of this PE, which is a divisor of the clock period, T_0, of ME. If a memory is p-interleaved, then $T_0 = p \cdot t_0$ and each PE is connected in parallel with p ME$\{ME_1, ME_2, \ldots, ME_p\}$.

This requires that each ME_i $(i = 1, \ldots, p)$ stores every $(m \cdot p + i)$th word, where $m = 0, 1, 2, \ldots$.

> **Example 2.** Figure 1-4(a) shows the 4-interleaved memory consisting of ME_1, ME_2, ME_3, and ME_4, connected with one PE. Therefore, $p = 4$. Here t_0 is the clock period of PE, and T_0 is the clock period of each ME (Fig. 1-4(b)). As seen, $T_0 = 4 \cdot t_0$, and during each t_0, one word is accessed by PE, in spite of the fact that each internal memory cycle, $T_0 = 4t_0$. For ME_1, $i = 1$, and the words stored in it are w1, w5, w9, etc. Similarly, one can define the words stored in other memory modules.
>
> As can be seen, the processor clock period, t_0, is shifted with respect to the

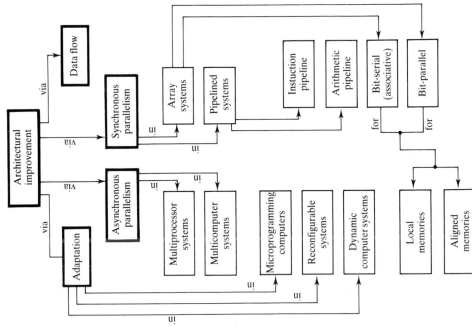

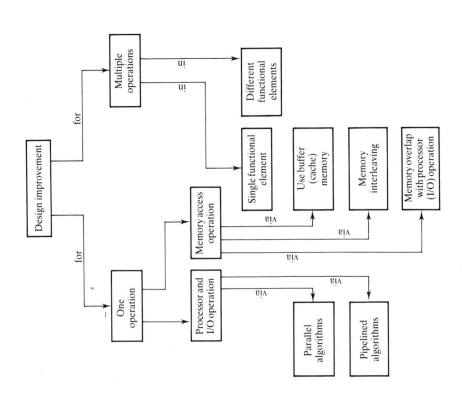

Figure 1-2. Performance improvement at design and architectural levels.

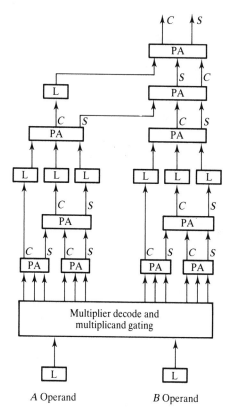

Figure 1-3. Parallel carry-save multiplication algorithm for the STAR-100. PA, partial adder; L, latch; S, Partial sum; C, partial carry.

memory clock period, T_0, for the following reason. During the writing pulse μ of T_0, the word w is written from the memory to the Memory Data Register, MDR, ($M \rightarrow MDR$). The same word can be thus written to PE only during the writing pulse τ of t_0, which must immediately follow the writing pulse of μ of T_0.

Memory Overlap

Memory overlap with the processor or I/O operation allows a total elimination of the memory access operation—which is sequential to operation execution—from the time of instruction execution. It is mostly used in uniprocessor pipelines.

Example 3. Consider a pipelined execution of the addition $A_i + B_i \rightarrow C_i$ over the data array of 100 operand pairs, A_i and B_i. For simplicity, consider this execution with a 3-addressed instruction format I_1 (Fig. 1-5(a)), where three address fields, A_1, A_2 and A_3 store base addresses for **A**, **B** and **C** vectors and vector components are contiguous. Therefore the I_1 instruction should be preceded by the I_0 instruction which stores the size k of **A**, **B** and **C** vectors and indexing increment II. For our example, $k = 100$, $II = 1$. The I_1 instruction consists of seven phases (Fig. 1-5(b)), of which FM1 is the instruction fetch phase; F1 is the A1 address modification phase; F2 is the A_i-operand fetch and A2 address modification phase; F3 is the B_i operand fetch phase; F4 is a register-to-register transfer phase; F5 is the operation phase; F6

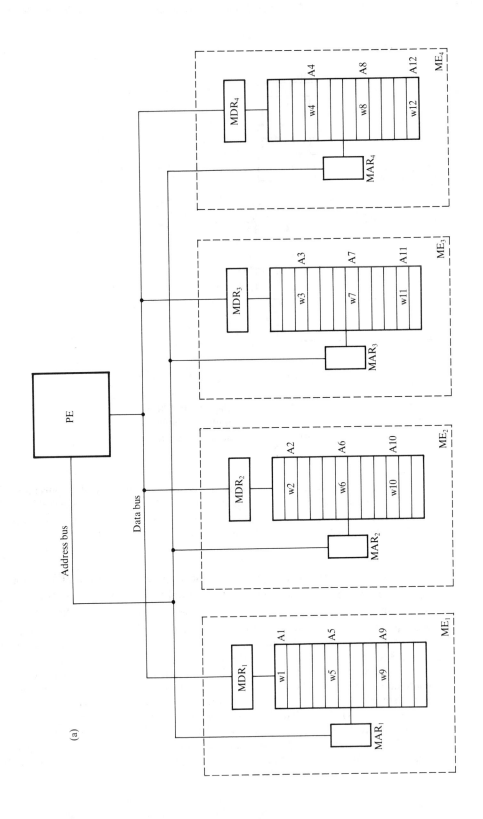

(a)

12

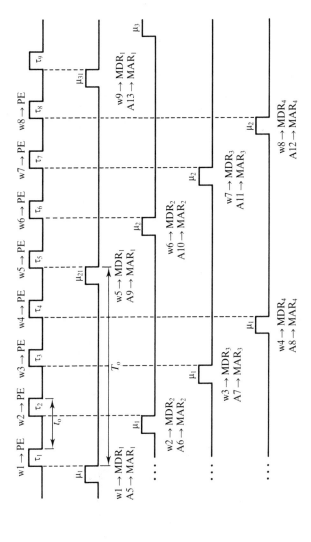

Figure 1-4. (a) The four-interleaved memory made of ME_1, ME_2, ME_3, and ME_4. (b) Four-interleaved memory synchronization. T_0 is memory clock period; t_0 is processor clock period.

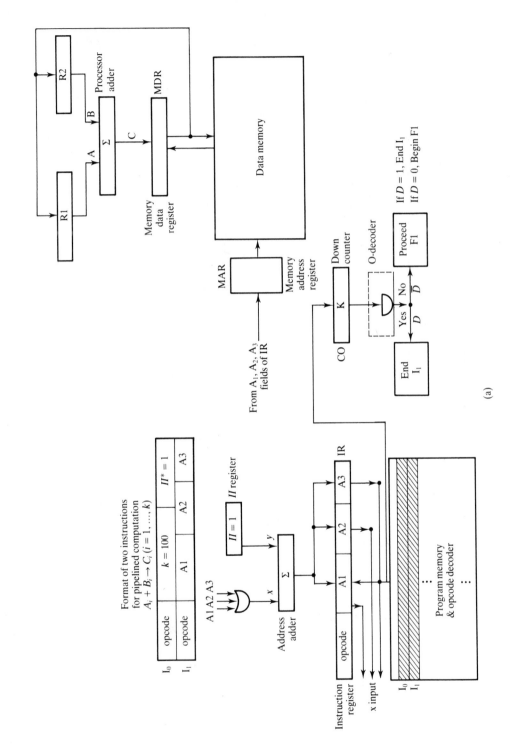

14

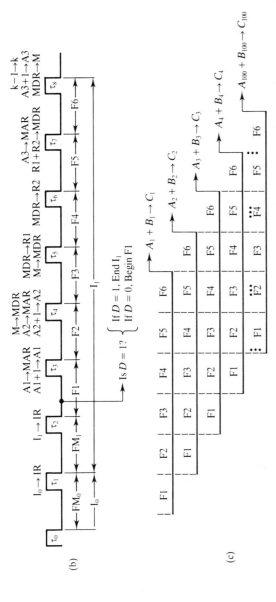

Figure 1-5. (a) Pipelined execution of the addition $A_i + B_i \rightarrow C_i$ with a three-address instruction. (b, c) Timing diagram of pipelined addition, $A_i + B_i \rightarrow C_i$; (b) assigning pipeline phases to synchronization sequence; (c) phase overlap.

15

is the write result phase. As can be seen, the operation $A_i + B_i$ is performed by a single computational phase (F5). All the remaining phases are noncomputational in the sense that they are aimed at (a) memory access of instruction, its operands and computational result; (b) address modification; (c) moving operands inside the processor. However, by overlapping consecutive microprograms that execute $A_i + B_i \rightarrow C_i$, one can obtain a total elimination of all overhead phases from the time of computation and the time of one clock period for obtaining each result $C_i = A_i + B_i$ (Fig. 1-5(c)). The entire array of 100 C_i is obtained during 107 clock periods, where 7 clock periods are spent filling this pipeline with the initial information.

Cache Memories

A major function of cache memories is to reduce the memory access time via

- including a relatively small and fast memory (cache) into the processor, PE, and
- performing regular data transfers between cache and the main memory to fill the cache with missing memory pages.

Usually, the speed of cache memory is identical to that of the processor PE. Also, since cache by definition is much smaller in size than the main memory, the PE-processor is provided with a special mapping table, the "directory system," aimed at transforming a larger effective page address of the main memory, MEA, into a much smaller current effective address, CEA, of the needed page in the cache (Fig. 1-6). If a needed page is missing from the cache, then a special page-replacement algorithm is activated that finds an already used page in the cache and replaces it with a needed page fetched from the main memory.

Example 4. A typical algorithm for the cache access is as follows.[3]

Given: a *m*ain (memory) *e*ffective *a*ddress, MEA, of the wanted page generated inside PE.

Find: the *c*ache *e*ffective *a*ddress, CEA, where this page is or will be stored.

Current storage implies that the wanted page is available in the cache; *future storage* implies that the wanted page is missing and must be transferred to the cache from the main memory.

To simplify the address translation of MEA into CEA, (MEA $\rightarrow$ CEA), MEA must be partitioned into separate address fields that perform the following functions:

F1. A separate field of MEA must be used as the effective address, DA, of the directory system (Fig. 1-6).

F2. A relative address, RA, within the wanted page specified by its MEA, must be directly transferrable to CEA (Fig. 1-7).

F3. Since MEA size is larger than that of CEA, there are unique Δ bits, where $\Delta = $ MEA $-$ CEA, which specify the location of this page in the main memory (Fig. 1-7). This field can be used as a unique tag stored in the directory system that identifies the mapping page function MEA $\rightarrow$ CEA (Fig. 1-8).

F4. To minimize the number of page misses, a single directory word specified by the DA address must store not a single page base address, BA, but k page

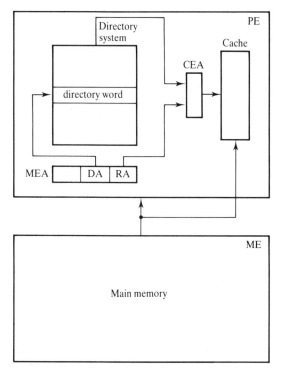

Figure 1-6. Interactions between cache and main memories within one computer element made of one PE and one ME.

base addresses in s bits, with the size $|s| = \log_2 k$ (Fig. 1-8).

F5. Since $CEA = BA + RA$, where $+$ is the concatenation operation, BA must properly contain the DA-address to access the directory system and its specific directory slot, DIS, using s bits, where a given mapping $MEA \rightarrow CEA$ is stored. This specifies $BA = DA + S$ (Fig. 1-7).

F6. To perform a parallel comparison of each page tag Δ stored in the MEA register with K tags included into K DIS-fields of a single directory word fetched from the directory system, there must be a separate tag field

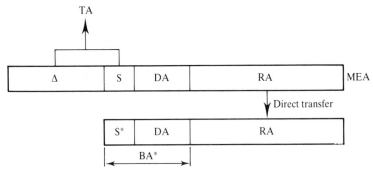

Figure 1-7. Designation of fields in **m**ain memory and **c**ache **e**ffective **a**ddresses (MEA and CEA).

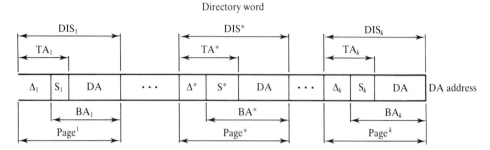

Figure 1-8. Formatting a directory word.

(Fig. 1-8):

$$\mathbf{TA} = \Delta + \mathbf{S}$$

This organization allows a wanted available page to be identified by equality, $TA = TA^*$; where TA is stored in MEA; TA^* is stored in one of k DIS-fields. Its effective cache address is: $CEA^* = BA^* + RA$, where BA^* is taken from the accessed directory word; RA is directly transferred from MEA register to CEA register.

F7. If the needed page is not available, then a special page-replacement algorithm is activated which performs the following actions.

    a. It finds a most recently used and unneeded page residing in the same directory word. (This page becomes released from the cache.)

    b. It writes the updated page address information to the directory slot, DIS, formerly occupied by the released page, RP.

    c. It organizes a data transfer of wanted page information from the main memory to the cache.

OPTIMIZATION OF MULTIPLE OPERATIONS

For *multiple operations*, the most obvious improvement is in parallel execution of several operations, each of which handles a different pair of operands. This parallelism can be achieved inside a single functional unit (processor) or at the level of several functional units. For instance, multiple operation parallelism at the level of a single functional unit is illustrated by parallel implementation of scalar and vector operations in two separate arithmetic units for CYBER-205.

The example below elaborates on the evolution of the multiple-operation concept in the same functional unit for STAR-100 → CYBER-205 evolutionary family.

    Example 5. As was shown in ref. 2, in STAR-100, scalar and vector operations were sequential; in CYBER-205 they became parallel. Indeed, in STAR-100, because of the unique register file that contained initial operands and computational results for both scalar and vector operations, these two operations became interlocked, in the sense that in any time interval the performance of only one operation (scalar or vector) has been allowed. However, even during STAR-100 development, the decision to run these two operations in parallel has become highly evident. However, the full impact of this decision was realized only in CYBER-205 because of LSI technological advances.

Indeed, the small-scale integration technology (SSI) used for STAR-100 fabrication made it an economic necessity that the same hardware perform both scalar and vector operations. For CYBER-205, manufactured from LSI components, such an economic constraint was no longer viable and separate implementation of scalar and vector operations became economically justifiable. As a result, a unique register file of STAR-100 was removed from its virtual memory and was duplicated in the processor of CYBER-205 to serve vector and scalar operations in parallel.

Architectural Optimization

The following are the existing sources of architectural performance improvement:[6]*

- architectural adaptation;
- use of data-flow principles;
- use of synchronous parallel computing structures; and
- use of asynchronous parallel computing structures (Fig. 1-2).

ARCHITECTURAL ADAPTATION

An *architectural adaptation* means software-controlled adaptation of the architecture to executing program. It can be achieved at the following levels of reconfiguration (Fig. 1-9).

a. *Microprogramming level* extended to reconfiguration of separate devices within a single processor in microprogrammable computers;

b. *Reconfigurable system level* extended to reconfiguration of separate functional units in parallel systems (arrays, multicomputers, multiprocessors, pipelines); and

c. *Dynamically partitionable system level* extended to module level reconfigurations aimed at forming various computing structures with variable architectural parameters (variable number of dynamic computers with changeable word sizes; variable dynamic arrays, pipelines, etc.).[4]

---

* We do not discuss here the architectural performance improvement offered by message-passing architectures, of which the most famous is the *Cosmic Cube* (Hypercube) described in the January 1985 CASM by C. L. Seitz. Since these machines support cube-type connections among nodes and have no interconnection network, they are not suitable for typical multiprocessing applications whereby one processor PE_i can access nonlocal data computed by another processor PE_j and stored in local ME_j through direct PE_j–ME_j interconnection activated dynamically. For more details of the applications of the *Cosmic Cube* (Hypercube), see Chapter 11.

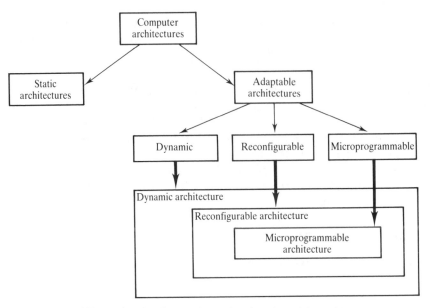

Figure 1-9. Different levels of reconfiguration in adaptable architectures.

The examples below illustrate the essence of architectural adaptations to an executing program achieved at microprogramming level (Example 6); reconfigurable system level (Example 7); and dynamically partitionable system level (Example 8).

Example 6: Microprogramming Level of Adaptation. Figure 1-10(a) contains the processor portion of a microprogrammed computer with 18 reconfiguration

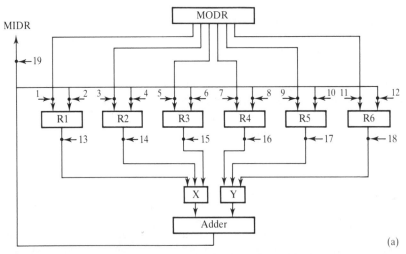

(a)

Figure 1-10. Microprogramming level of adaptation. (a) Processor portion of a microprogrammed computer. (b) Logarithmic encoding of microoperations. (c) Linear encoding of microoperations. (d) Encoding example of the microinstruction R1 ⊕ R6→ R2, MIDR.

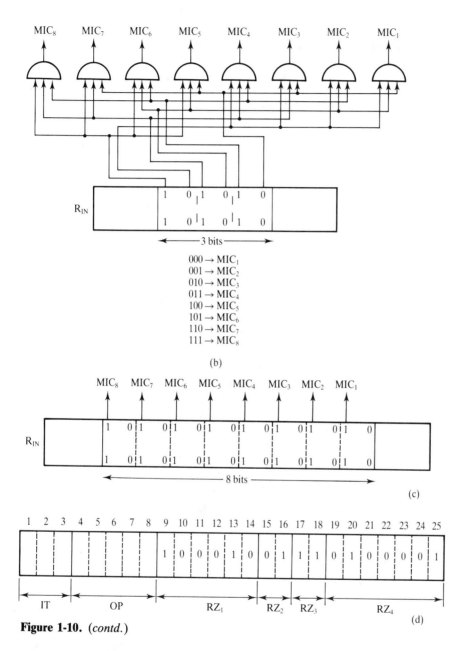

$$000 \to MIC_1$$
$$001 \to MIC_2$$
$$010 \to MIC_3$$
$$011 \to MIC_4$$
$$100 \to MIC_5$$
$$101 \to MIC_6$$
$$110 \to MIC_7$$
$$111 \to MIC_8$$

(b)

(c)

(d)

Figure 1-10. (*contd.*)

microoperations.[4] These microoperations may be assembled into four groups, GR_1 through GR_4. Each GR_i is assigned with one zone RZ_i ($i = 1, \ldots, 4$) of the reconfiguration field in a microinstruction format shown in Figure 1-10(d). The microoperations of every group GR_i are encoded either *logarithmically*, whereby the size $|RZ_i| = \log_2 |GR_i|$, or *linearly*, whereby $|RZ_i| = |GR_i|$ (Fig. 1-10(b, c)). Logarithmic encoding is used for minimization of the zone size. However, it allows execution of only one microoperation at a time. Linear encoding is used to increase microoperation parallelism by allowing parallel execution of any combination of microoperations contained in one group. However, it increases the bit size of the encoding zone. Group GR_1 contains microoperations that connect a common memory output data register, MODR, with registers R1–R6: $GR_1 = \{1, 3, 5, 7, 9, 11\}$. It must be encoded linearly, since a word stored in MODR can be sent to any combination of R1–R6 in parallel. This gives six bits for RZ_1. In Figure 1-10(d), $RZ_1 = 100010$ means MODR → R1, R5.

Group $GR_2 = \{13, 14, 15\}$ includes microoperations that connect R1, R2, and R3 with the X-terminal of the adder. This zone is encoded logarithmically, since an adder may receive only one word at a time through each of its terminals. Thus $|RZ_2| = \log_2 3 = 2$, and $RZ_2 = 01$ means that R1 stores the X-operand (Fig. 1-10(d)). Similarly, Group $GR_3 = \{16, 17, 18\}$ includes microoperations that connect R4, R5, and R6 with the Y-terminal of the adder. It is also encoded logarithmically and $RZ_3 = 11$ means that R_6 stores the Y-operand. Finally, Group $GR_4 = \{19, 2, 4, 6, 8, 10, 12\}$ comprises microoperations that connect the adder output with the MIDR and R1–R6. It is encoded by the field RZ_4. The encoding is linear, since a result can be sent to any of the registers in parallel. In Figure 1-10(d), $RZ_4 = 0100001$ means that $X + Y$ is sent to R2 and MIDR.

Improving performance by virtue of microprogramming is achieved as follows. By writing various codes into different zones of the reconfiguration field of a microinstruction format, a programmer is capable of performing the architectural reconfiguration at microprogramming level by selecting the registers that store operands and computational results. The net result is a better tuning of the instruction microprogram to an executing algorithm, and eliminating the overhead time caused by register-to-register transfers that are to be performed in the absence of microprogrammable reconfiguration.

Example 7: Reconfigurable Level of Adaptation. This type of reconfiguration is exemplified by Figure 1-11, showing reconfiguration of eight computer elements identified with nodes N_0 through N_7 into a particular binary tree configuration.[5]

This is accomplished with the use of n-bit code, *bias*, and a special n-bit shift-register, SRVB, residing in each tree node (Fig. 1-12(a)). (Here, n is the number of levels in a tree.) The shift-register residing in node N finds the code N^* of its successor in the tree via the following operation. $N^* = 1[N]_0 + B$, where $1[N]_0$ is a one-bit noncircular shift of N to the left and B is the control code, bias, brought to every node by the reconfiguration instruction. For instance, in Figure 1-11, bias $B = 101$ allows obtaining the following $N \to N^*$ connections of node N with its successor N^* in a given tree configuration:

$$\text{For } N_2 = 010, \ N^* = 1[010]_0 + 101 = 100 + 101 = 001;$$
$$\text{For } N_1 = 001, \ N^* = 1[001]_0 + 101 = 010 + 101 = 111; \text{ etc.}$$

As seen from Figure 1-12, this reconfiguration technique allows each tree configuration to be established during the time of one mod-2 addition operation. Since there are 2^n different n-bit biases, it is possible to generate 2^n different trees using this reconfiguration technique (Fig. 1-12(b)).

Improving performance is achieved as follows. By writing a new control code into each functional and/or computer element of a reconfigurable computer

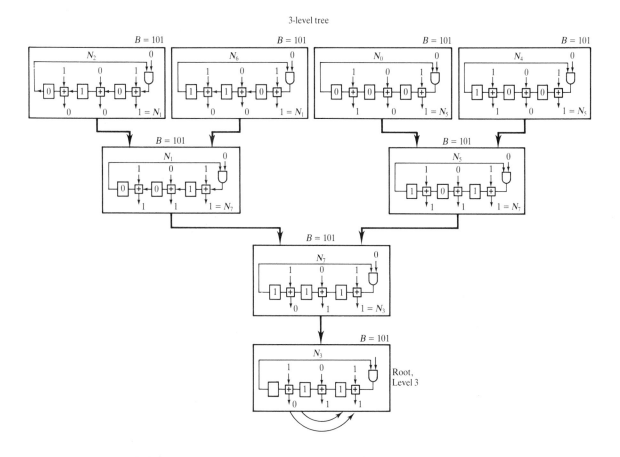

Figure 1-11. Example of a reconfigurable level of adaptation. Using this technique, each binary tree configuration is established during the time of MOD 2 addition and with the use of single n-bit code, B, where n is the number of tree levels.

system, a programmer may allow activation of different interconnections among these elements. The net result is an improved time for data exchanges because of

- direct connections among processors and memories (for multiprocessor systems);
- direct connections among separate computers (for multicomputer systems);
- application determined topological structures among separate computer nodes (trees, stars, rings, hypercubes, etc.).

Example 8: Dynamically Partitionable System Level. This is exemplified by Figure 1-13, in which a system of four 16-bit computer elements, CE, is partitioned into various combinations of concurrent computers with selectable word sizes.[6,7] This system contains n computer elements, CE, $(n-1)$ connecting elements, MS, and

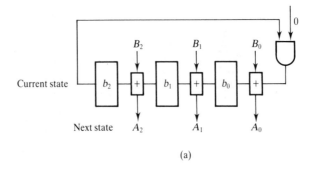

Current state

Next state A_2 A_1 A_0

(a)

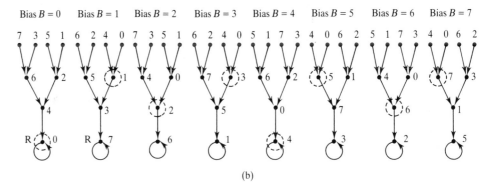

(b)

Figure 1-12. The SRVB-technique.

one monitor, V (not shown). One CE processes h-bit words in parallel and it includes one PE, one ME, and one I/O element, GE. Assume $h = 16$. A pair of adjacent CEs is separated by one connecting unit, MS, which may assume the following modes: right transfer, left transfer, or no transfer. For a right transfer, a 16-bit word is transferred by MS to the next right-adjacent CE. For a left transfer, a 16-bit word is transferred by MS to the next left-adjacent CE. For no transfer, a 16-bit word is not transferred between CEs. A dynamically partitionable system may form concurrent computers of variable sizes, labeled $C_i(k)$. Each $C_i(k)$ computer $(k = 1, \ldots, n)$ integrates k computer elements and $(k - 1)$ connecting elements. The subscript i indicates the position of the computer's most significant CE. This computer handles $16 \cdot k$-bit words in parallel which are stored in $16 \cdot k$-bit wide memory. By changing the number of computer elements in $C_i(k)$, one obtains 16, 32, 48, or $16 \cdot n$-bit computers.

This system may assume 2^{n-1} different architectural states. The difference between states is in the sizes, positions, and numbers of computers operating concurrently.

In Figure 1-13, $n = 4$. Thus, this architecture may assume $2^{n-1} = 2^3 = 8$ different states, $N_0, \ldots, N_7$. State N_0 is characterized by formation of a single 64-bit computer that integrates all CEs and all connecting elements, MS. State N_1

means coresidence of two concurrent computers:

- a 48-bit computer, $C_1(3)$, formed from CE_1, CE_2, and CE_3; and
- a 16-bit computer, $C_4(1)$, formed from CE_4.

$CE_1(3)$ integrates two connecting elements MS_1 and MS_2, assuming a transfer mode (left and/or right) for instruction fetch and no transfer mode for parallel data fetch; $C_4(1)$ integrates no connecting elements; $C_1(3)$ and $C_4(1)$ are separated by MS_3, assuming a no-transfer mode during the existence of state N_1. Transition of this dynamically partitionable architecture from one state to another is performed by a special architectural switch instruction $N \rightarrow N^*$, where N is the current state; N^* is the next state. This architecture may perform any transition $N \rightarrow N^*$; i.e., no transition constraints exist. Since, for each transition, at least one computer in the present state must give up its resources to form another computer in the next state, any architectural transition may occur at the moment of time when all computers that sacrifice their resources finish their tasks. This moment is identified by the monitor.

Improving performance is achieved as follows. By writing new control codes to separate CEs of the resources, a programmer may affect a dynamic partitioning or redistribution of the resources into concurrent computing structures with variable characteristics. This variability is broadly applied to the following parameters:

- the number of concurrent computing structures being formed;
- the word size of each component of the respective structure.

Therefore, a programmer may affect each program computation in a minimal computing structure. This maximizes the number of programs computed concurrently by available resources redistributed dynamically.

Difference Between the Three Different Levels of Reconfiguration
The differences between the three different levels of reconfiguration are as follows.

- For *microprogramming level*, reconfiguration affects each component module internally, in the sense that all its external connections remain the same.
- For *reconfigurable system level*, reconfiguration affects each component module only externally, in the sense that this module continues to hold the same computing structure that it held before. However, the interconnections of this structure with other concurrent structures may be changed.
- For *dynamically partitionable system level*, reconfiguration allows redistribution or dynamic partitioning of the resources into different computing structures. Therefore, component modules are allowed to be integrated into changeable computing structures in a way that they have never been allowed for the other two levels of reconfiguration.

Hence, reconfiguration in dynamically partitionable systems (otherwise

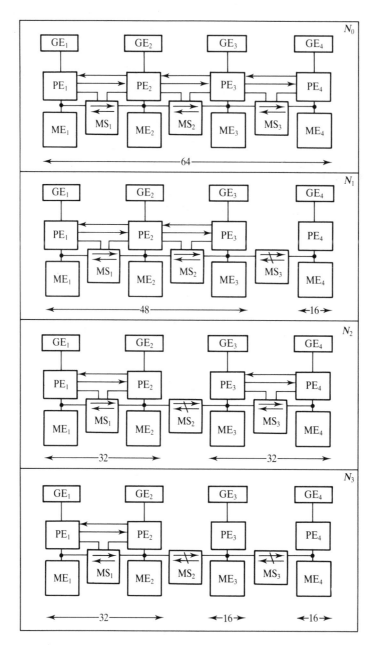

Figure 1-13. Dynamic architecture made of four computer elements.

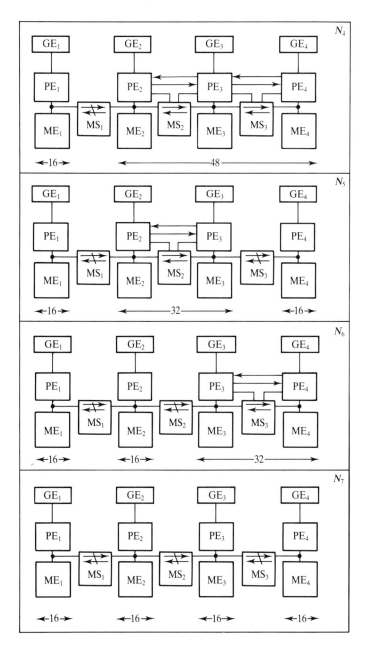

Figure 1-13. (*contd.*)

called dynamic architecture) is more complete, in the sense that it may include

a. microprogramming level inside each module;
b. reconfigurable system level between modules; and
c. dynamically partitionable level among modules by allowing their assembly into various computing structures under program control during computations.

USE OF THE DATA-FLOW PRINCIPLE

The use of the data-flow principle means exploiting the maximal parallelism present in programs unimpeded by bottlenecks emanating from a need to control the execution of multiple programs on multiple resources.[8] Therefore, data-flow architectures take advantage of the data-flow principle inherent in a modern program structure by allowing execution of each instruction as soon as its operands arrive. The architecture is thus capable of fully exploiting computational concurrencies present in the program, since each time it may execute as many instructions in parallel as are ready for execution, that is, these instructions receive both operands needed for computation.

Data-Flow Graph

To apply the data-flow principle in a most efficient way, for any program one must construct a data-flow graph that specifies the computational precedence present in the program and not the one caused by specific program and data allocations, and/or used programming laguages.

As a matter of fact, all data-flow programming languages are graph-based, that is, they begin with constructed data-flow graphs as the input.

In a data-flow graph, each node is assigned one operation and its operands (Fig. 1-14). The node finds the computational result of this operation and sends it to one or several destination node(s) that use this result as an operand. Therefore, nodes N and N^* are connected in a data-flow graph if node N generates an operand (or fires a token) for node N^*.

Example 9. Consider the following expression:

$$(x + y - k) \cdot w = z$$

The data flow graph for this expression is shown in Fig. 1-15(a). As seen, the two operands (tokens) x and y are used for the Add node. The result is sent as an operand to the SUBnode together with another operand k waiting at the input line.

(a)   (b)

Figure 1-14. Operation node in a data-flow graph.

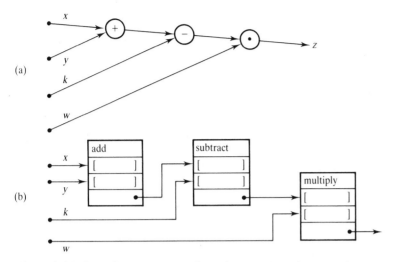

Figure 1-15. Data-flow representation of expression: $(x + y - k) \cdot w = z$: (a) graph form; (b) memory-storage form.

The SUBnode fires to generate an operand for the MUL node. This produces result z, which is sent to further destinations (Fig. 1-15(b)).

In general, the following are the basic principles present in all data flow schemes.

P1. Data-flow graphs are constructed using primitive node operations by connecting appropriate inputs and outputs.

P2. Arcs in data-flow graphs may represent primitive as well as structured values.

P3. Each operational node acts as a dedicated function and it cannot modify its inputs. It only produces the output(s) appropriate to its inputs (operands).

P4. The basic model works by keeping track of the results produced by each operation as tokens residing on graph arcs; when an operation executes, it consumes input tokens and produces the output token(s) (Fig. 1-16).

Merge and Switch Nodes

The node type discussed so far describes computations requiring operands. Program structures for conditional transitions and looping require different types of nodes. The following new types of nodes appear:

merge(MG) and switch(SW).

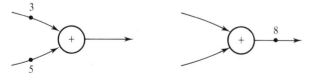

Figure 1-16. Firing a node in a data-flow graph.

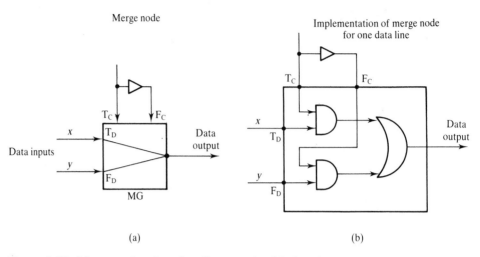

Figure 1-17. Merge node of a data-flow graph: (a) functional description; (b) logical diagram.

A *merge node, MG,* (Fig. 1-17(a)) has two data inputs sent to true and false data channels, T_D, F_D, and two control lines that receive control signals, T_C and F_C used to control the data transfer from T_D or F_D to the only output data terminal of MG. If $T_C = 1$, a data word received through the T_D channel is passed through the MG node. If $F_C = 1$, a data word received through the F_D channel is passed through the node.

A *switch node, SW*, (Fig. 1-18(a)) performs just the opposite function. It passes the word received through its only data input either to the true data output, T_D, or the false data output, F_D, depending on the values of the control

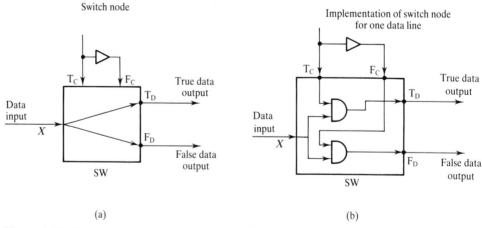

Figure 1-18. Switch node of a data-flow graph: (a) functional description; (b) logical diagram.

signals received via true control line T_C or false control line F_C. If $T_C = 1$, data word is transferred to T_D; if $F_C = 1$, data word is transferred to F_D. Therefore, these two nodes can be implemented as follows: the merge node can be implemented via two-level logic AND–OR (Fig. 1-17(b)). The switch node requires only one level of AND gates for its implementation (Fig. 1-18(b)).

These two types of nodes can perform a simple implementation of DO-loops and other control structures with the two outcomes T and F. If a control structure has more than two outcomes, it is implemented as a consecutive connection of several SW nodes.

Example 10. Consider data-flow implementation of the following program construct:

$$\text{While } x > 0, \text{ DO} = x - 5.$$

A data-flow program scheme for this DO loop is shown in Figure 1-19. Figure 1-20 shows its hardware implementation. As seen, to implement this scheme requires:

1. four registers, R1–R4, for variable x, constant 5, variable $x - 5$ and the final result $y \leq 0$;
2. logical circuits for implementing one MG node and one SW node;
3. one decoder, which decodes > 0.

The decoder generates F_C or T_C control signals for both nodes MG and SW. Control signal F_C indicates the end of the iterative process $x - 5$ over variable x stored in R1 and beginning of the new process over a new value x which is then transferred to R1.

Therefore, to store F_C requires flip-flop TT, since it will affect the next iterative process specified by a new x.

Consider the timing of this DO-loop execution by the hardware diagram of Figure 1-20. For simplicity, assume $x = 7$, that is, for $x = 7$ the DO loop $x - 5$ takes

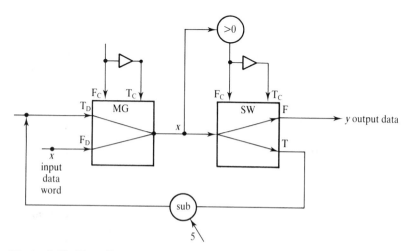

Figure 1-19. Data-flow program scheme for the DO loop, *while $x > 0$, $DO = x - 5$.*

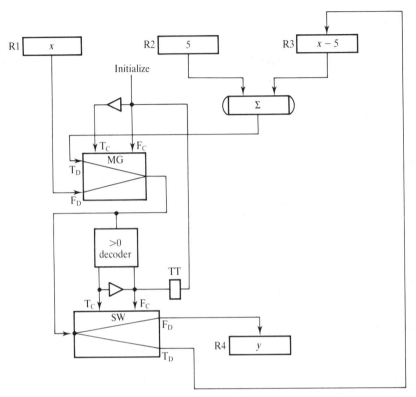

Figure 1-20. Hardware implementation of the DO loop, *while $x > 0$, DO $= x - 5$.*

only one iteration with the true outcome. At the second iteration, the DO ends. We assume that by the time period T_1, all the required data words are available in registers R1 and R2, that is, R1 stores $x = 7$, R2 stores 5 (Fig. 1-21).

In the beginning, control signal F_C is generated by the control unit. Thereafter, it is generated by the schema automatically. However, regardless of the source of F_C generation, F_C always lasts one clock period. As for T_C, it can last longer than one clock, since it is the negation of F_C.

Since variable $x = 7$ is sent to the F_D input of the MG node and $x > 0$ is true, it is passed by the SW node and written to register R3 during clock pulse t_2.

During clock period T_2, $F_C = 0$ activates $T_C = 1$. Therefore, the difference $\Delta = R3 - R2$ is allowed to pass through the MG node. Since $\Delta = 7 - 5 = 2$, the decoder generates $T_C = 1$, which allows Δ to be written to R3 during pulse t_3. During clock period T_3, adder executes $\Delta - 5 = 2 - 5 = -3$. $T_C = 1$, so that -3 is passed by the MG scheme. The >0 decoder generates $F_C = 1$, which writes -3 to R4. Thus, we obtain $y = -3$. Concurrently, $F_C = 1$ is written to flip-flop TT. This occurs during pulse t_4. Since TT is connected with the F_C input of the MG scheme, it signals the end of the preceding DO loop and beginning of the new DO loop caused by new value of variable x stored in register R1. As can be seen, the schema begins to work automatically.

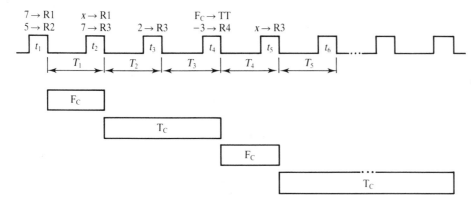

Figure 1-21. Synchronization of the DO loop, *while* $x > 0$, $DO = x - 5$.

THE USE OF SYNCHRONOUS PARALLEL COMPUTING STRUCTURES

Implementation of synchronous parallel computing structures is achieved in array systems and pipeline systems (Fig. 1-22).

In an array system, an operation attributed to one instruction is executed in parallel or synchronously over the array (vector) of data operands. The performance improvement in array systems is therefore due to synchronous data parallelism whereby, at the time of one operation, a single instruction handles a vector of N operand pairs (A_i, B_i), where N is the number of PEs in the system (Fig. 1-22). In pipeline systems, the performance improvement is due to phased operation parallelism whereby a pipelined system made of n stages executes n different operations at a time, each of which is performed over a separate pair of operands and each of which is in the ith phase of execution, where i is the number of pipeline stage (Fig. 1-23). The speed of data movement in a pipeline is that of the longest operation assigned to a pipeline stage. Both systems implement a *synchronous operation parallelism*, where synchronization is

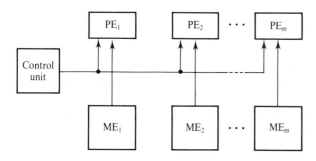

Figure 1-22. Array system.

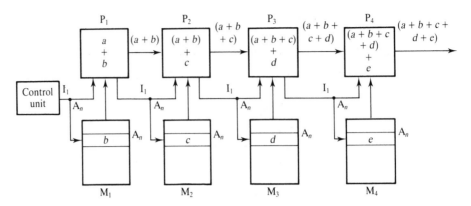

Figure 1-23. Pipeline system.

achieved via

- *synchronous movement of operands* to the processing elements of both types of systems, and
- *synchronous execution of the operation* assigned to each processing element of a system.

The major distinction between arrays and pipelines is that each PE in an array executes all phases of one instruction microprogram locally, whereas, in a pipeline, each PE (one operation unit) executes only one phase of the instruction microprogram; the next phase is executed by the next PE (operation unit) consecutively connected with the given PE (operation unit). Two other differences are of a smaller scale, since they are direct consequences of the major distinction:

- For arrays, the operation assigned to each PE_i ($i = 1, \ldots, N$) is always the same, since each PE_i executes the same microprogram in concert with other P_j; for pipelines, PE_i and PE_{i+1} may execute different operations if these are different and consecutive phases of the instruction microprogram.
- For arrays, each PE fetches both operands; for pipelines, only one operand is ever fetched by the local PE; the other operand may be supplied by the preceding stage.

Array Systems: Classification

Bit-Serial and Bit-Parallel Arrays
The existing arrays systems are divided into the categories bit serial, and bit parallel.

In a *bit-serial array system*, each processing element, PE, handles one bit of a data word at a time, so that an array of N PEs handles N 1-bit slices of N data words at a time. Therefore, a bit-serial array processes $N h$-bit words during h clock periods.

Since each PE handles only one bit of data at a time, it can be made very simple. As a consequence, N can be made very large.

In a *bit-parallel array system*, each PE handles the entire data word at a time, so that an array of m PEs handles m full data words at a time.

Let us evaluate which array system, bit-serial or bit-parallel, is more efficient in the sense that it can handle a larger number of h-bit data words per time interval T.

For such an evaluation, we must assume that the total bit size K that identifies the complexity of the system must be the same for bit-serial and bit-parallel arrays. For any bit-serial array, $K = N$; for any bit-parallel array, $K = h \cdot m$—that is, $N = h \cdot m$.

Any objective throughput measure of the system, $\text{TM}(h)$ must measure the number of h-bit data words handled during $l \cdot h$ clock periods, T_0, since $h \cdot T_0$ is the time for the bit-serial array to complete processing of a single h-bit data word. Thus, assume that $T = (h \cdot T_0) \cdot l$.

For bit-serial arrays, $\text{TM}_s(h) = N \cdot h \cdot l$.
For bit-parallel arrays, $\text{TM}_p(h) = m \cdot h \cdot l$.
Find the ratio,

$$r = \frac{\text{TM}_s(h)}{\text{TM}_p(h)} = \frac{N \cdot h \cdot l}{m \cdot h \cdot l} = \frac{h^2 \cdot m \cdot l}{h \cdot m \cdot l} = h$$

Therefore, the bit-serial system is h times more efficient than the respective bit-parallel system having the same bit or hardware complexity of the resources.

Memory Organization

Another major division of the existing array systems is related to organization of primary memory for their PE elements. Accordingly, the existing array systems are divided into local-memory array systems, and aligned-memory array systems.

For *local-memory array systems* (Illiac-IV, ICL DAP) each processor PE_i can fetch only those operands that are stored in local ME_i. If PE_i need to access a nonlocal ME_j, it can do so only by communicating with the PE_j local to ME_j, using available routing or direct interconnections among PEs.

For *aligned-memory array systems,* the processor and memory resources made of m PEs and m MEs are connected together via an interconnection network that allows each PE_i to access nonlocal ME_j (Fig. 1-24).

An obvious advantage of aligned-memory array systems is in a greatly reduced data exchange time in comparison with the local memory arrays. Indeed, since each PE_i can be connected directly with any nonlocal ME_j, there is no need to perform a data transfer from ME_i to ME_j (via a routing network that introduces an associated data-transfer overhead) in order that PE_i can access this data array.

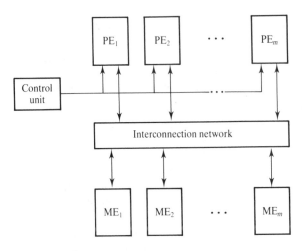

Figure 1-24. Aligned memory array system.

The major problem for aligned-memory arrays, however, is in organization of concurrent nonconflicting memory accesses of m MEs by m PEs under the conditions that data arrays accessed by m PEs may be stored locally or nonlocally.

The existing efforts in organization of nonconflicting concurrent memory accesses[10-12] have been centered on development and refining of so-called *skewed storage schemes* that allowed conflict-free accesses to major substructures of arrays, such as

- rows and columns;
- rows, columns, and major diagonals;
- all linear subarrays, and so on.

Example 11. Consider organization of the memory storage for the classical rows and columns skewage. Figure 1-25 shows a trivial memory storage scheme that provides concurrent conflict-free access of rows. However, column data words cannot be accessed concurrently, since each column is stored in the same ME. To overcome this restriction, the following memory skewage is used: each PE_i ($i = 1, 2, 3, 4$) accesses the consecutive addresses of data words stored in the following circular shifting sequence of MEs: $1 \to 4 \to 3 \to 2$ (Fig. 1-26(a)), where i is the initial member of this sequence.

For PE_1, this sequence is: $1 \to 4 \to 3 \to 2$ (Fig. 1-27(a)). Thus, the first element of the array is stored in ME_1; second element is in ME_4, third element is in ME_3; and fourth element is in ME_2. For PE_2, this sequence is: $2 \to 1 \to 4 \to 3$ (Fig. 1-27(b)). This determines ME_2 as storing the first element, ME_1 as storing the second element, ME_4 as storing the third element, and ME_3 as storing the fourth element. Figures 1-27(c) and 1-27(d) illustrate storage schemes for PE_3 and PE_4.

The original array skewed among different ME_i and PE_l is shown in Figure 1-26(b). As is seen, conflict-free memory access is extended to all its rows, columns, and backward diagonals, since all these subarrays are stored in distinct ME_i. The only exception is a set of all forward (sub)diagonals (such as $\{A_{11}, A_{21}, A_{31}, A_{41}\}$ or $\{A_{12}, A_{22}, A_{32}\}$ or $\{A_{13}, A_{23}\}$, etc.), each of which is stored in the same ME_i ($i = 1, 2, 3, 4$) and thus must be accessed sequentially.

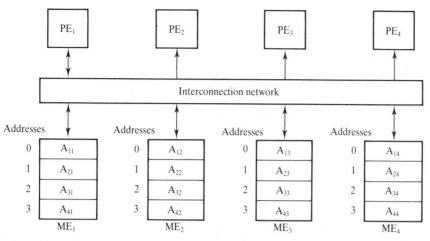

Figure 1-25. A memory storage scheme with conflict-free row and nonconflict-free column memory accesses.

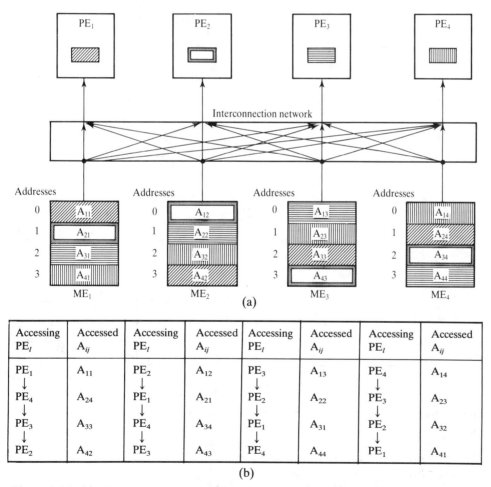

(a)

Accessing PE$_l$	Accessed A$_{ij}$	Accessing PE$_l$	Accessed A$_{ij}$	Accessing PE$_l$	Accessed A$_{ij}$	Accessing PE$_l$	Accessed A$_{ij}$
PE$_1$ ↓	A$_{11}$	PE$_2$ ↓	A$_{12}$	PE$_3$ ↓	A$_{13}$	PE$_4$ ↓	A$_{14}$
PE$_4$ ↓	A$_{24}$	PE$_1$ ↓	A$_{21}$	PE$_2$ ↓	A$_{22}$	PE$_3$ ↓	A$_{23}$
PE$_3$ ↓	A$_{33}$	PE$_4$ ↓	A$_{34}$	PE$_1$ ↓	A$_{31}$	PE$_2$ ↓	A$_{32}$
PE$_2$	A$_{42}$	PE$_3$	A$_{43}$	PE$_4$	A$_{44}$	PE$_1$	A$_{41}$

(b)

Figure 1-26. (a) Memory skewage described by the sequence $(1 \rightarrow 4 \rightarrow 3 \rightarrow 2)$. (b) Skewing of the original array of 16 elements among four PEs and four MEs.

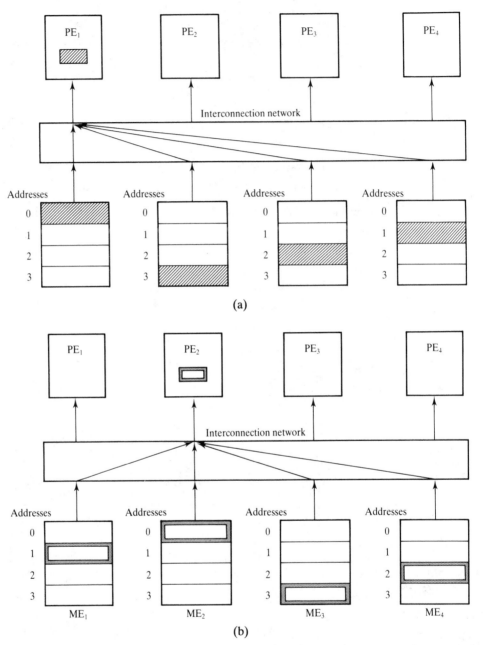

Figure 1-27. ME sequences of consecutive addresses in one array accessed by one PE$_i$, where:

(a) PE$_i$ = PE$_1$, giving access sequence $1 \rightarrow 4 \rightarrow 3 \rightarrow 2$;
(b) PE$_i$ = PE$_2$, giving access sequence $2 \rightarrow 1 \rightarrow 4 \rightarrow 3$;
(c) PE$_i$ = PE$_3$; giving access sequence $3 \rightarrow 2 \rightarrow 1 \rightarrow 4$;
(d) PE$_i$ = PE$_4$, giving access sequence $4 \rightarrow 3 \rightarrow 2 \rightarrow 1$.

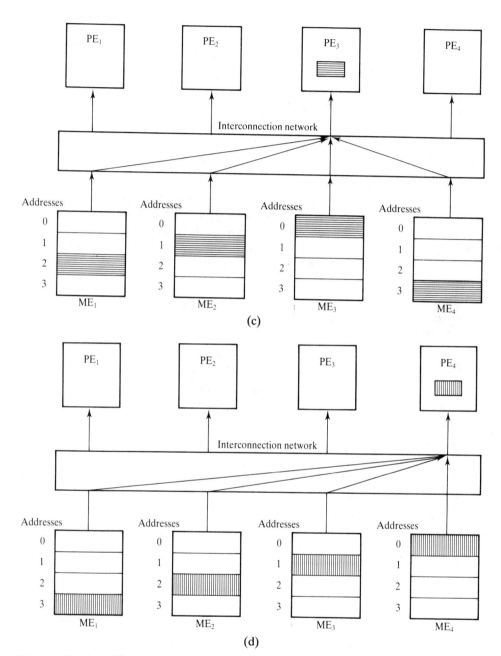

Figure 1-27. (*contd.*)

Pipeline Systems: Classification

Existing pipeline systems are divided into arithmetic pipelines, and instruction pipelines.

Arithmetic pipelines fragment the arithmetic operation assigned to an instruction into phases. The operation can represent

- an arithmetic expression made of the sequence of several simple arithmetic operations, or
- a single operation represented by a multistep computational algorithm (multiplication, division and floating-point operations).

Instruction pipelines fragment into phases the memory access process aimed at fetching the instruction and its operands from the memory and moving them in the processor before they reach an executional unit. For many instruction pipelines, the entire processor operation assigned to the instruction is treated as a single phase. However, if an arithmetic operation(s) is also pipelined, then the two pipelines merge together.

Arithmetic Pipelines

There are two types of arithmetic pipelines:

- *pipelined uniprocessor* aimed at pipeline execution of one or several operations in a single processor;
- *pipelined multiprocessor* aimed at pipelined execution of an arithmetic expression made of several operations in a sequence of processors connected together so that the ith processor, P_i becomes the ith stage of the pipeline.

A classical pipelined uniprocessor is exemplified by the CRAY-1, which features arithmetic pipelining of all functional units.[13] Also, for the CRAY-1, several pipelined operations can be executed as a sequence with the use of *chaining*. The result is a significant speed-up that is a function of m, the number of chained operations, and n, the size of data vector(s).

Indeed, as was shown in ref. 14, if m operations are *unchained*, that is, if they are assigned to m vector instructions, each of which handles a data vector(s) made of n words or operand pairs, then the time t_u of unchained pipeline execution of m operations in the CRAY-1 is

$$t_u = m(n-1) \cdot T_0 + \sum_{i=1}^{m} (s_i + l_i) \cdot T_0$$

where s_i is the start-up time of the ith operation ($i = 1, \ldots, m$); l_i is the number of pipeline phases in the ith operation; T_0 is the time of the clock period. On the other hand, if m operations are *chained*, they are assigned to a single vector instruction, which handles a sequence of m operations over a data array made of n operand pairs for each operation; then the time t_c of the chained pipeline execution in CRAY-1 is:

$$t_c = (n - 1) \cdot T_0 + \sum_{i=1}^{m} (s_i + l_i) \cdot T_0$$

The speed-up $\Delta = t_u - t_c$ obtained via chaining is

$$\Delta = m(n - 1)T_0 - (n - 1)T_0 = (m - 1) \cdot (n - 1) \cdot T_0$$

Therefore, the larger m and n, the larger the speed-up Δ accomplished via chaining.

Note: In the expression for t_u, the size n of the data vector was taken to be the same for all unchained operations. Although on first examination this sounds like an unnecessary restriction, constant n was adopted to obtain fair conditions of comparison, in as much as, for the chained sequence of m operations, n *must be the same for all operations*.

Otherwise, the chained pipeline stops after processing the last word of the vector with the minimal size n_{min}, where

$$n_{min} = \min(n_1, n_2, \ldots, n_m)$$

and n_i is the size of the vector for the ith operation.

For $m = 4$, $n = 50$, $\Delta = (4 - 1) \cdot (50 - 1) \cdot T_0 = 3 \cdot 49 \cdot T_0 = 147T_0$.

As is seen, chaining is an efficient concept for arithmetic pipelines in uniprocessors. The expected speed-up is significant even for small data arrays.

Pipelined Multiprocessors

As an example of pipelined multiprocessor, consider a *dynamic pipeline system* that can perform several useful adaptations to an algorithm.[15]

Example 12. This dynamic pipeline system organized as a multiprocessor may adapt on operation sequence, on pipeline length, on the time of operations in a stage, and so on, achieving a considerable speed-up as a result and eliminating the major problem of conventional arithmetic pipelines, which consists in introducing a significant time overhead because of disparity between the pipeline and algorithm being executed.

Before explaining how these adaptations can be accomplished, let us consider the hardware implementation of the dynamic pipeline described in refs. 6 and 15. Its hardware resources may be formed into one computer supervisor, C_0, and several $k \cdot h$-bit computers, $C_1, C_2, \ldots, C_F$, forming consecutive pipeline stages (Fig. 1-28). Each computer C_i $(i = 0, \ldots, F)$ is conceived as a single dynamic computer that may change its word size.[15,17] Computer C_0 stores instructions in memory M_0 and fetches them to processor P_0. Its size matches that of one instruction. Each pipeline computer C_i has memory M_i for storing data for processor P_i and a general register set RM_i that stores the temporary results required by P_i. This data is produced by P_i or by other processors. Two consecutive pipeline stages, C_i and C_{i+1}, are separated by the connecting element MSE_i, which may assume two modes of operation as follows.

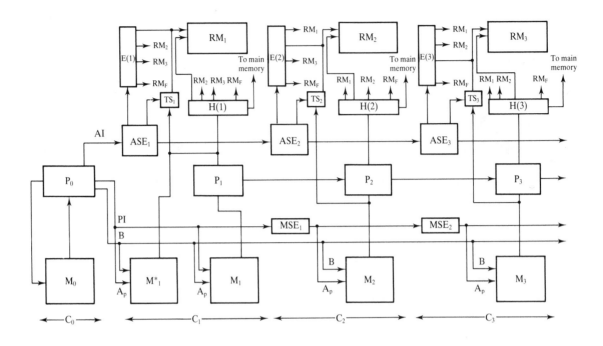

Figure 1-28. Block diagram of dynamic pipeline.

1. *Right transfer.* MSE_i receives the pipelined instruction and sends it to stage C_{i+1} with a delay of one time interval.
2. *No transfer.* The instruction received is not transferred to C_{i+1}.

The connecting elements, $ASE_1, \ldots, ASE_F$ are connected into a shifting sequence and transfer several addresses. Each time that pipeline stage C_i receives an operand and executes the operation assigned to it by the program instruction, the connecting element ASE_i receives a word shifted from ASE_{i-1}; that is, ASE_i is synchronized by stage C_i and holds data from ASE_{i-1} while C_i is executing. If the result of this operation is to be written to a general register set, RM_j, ASE_i sends the address of that set to stage C_j, and the result obtained in C_i is sent to RM_j. Thus, the number of MSE and ASE connecting elements is the same and matches F, the number of pipeline stages. Both an MSE and an ASE may be implemented by a universal LSI module equipped with modular control organization.[17]

Each instruction fetched from M_0 to P_0 includes two portions—a pipeline portion, PI, and an address portion, AI. By passing through the bus made of MSE connecting elements, the pipeline portion propagates through consecutive pipeline stages with a delay of one interval for each stage and causes execution of an operation assigned to each stage. At the same time, the address portion of the instruction propagates through the bus made of ASE connecting elements. It specifies both the pipeline stage, C_i, that should output the result and the general register set, RM_j, that should receive this result.

The pipeline instruction, PI, stores several control codes that perform adaptations eliminating the following causes of delays common in conventional pipelines.

1. *Operation sequence.* On currently implemented pipelines, if a sequence of operations in the program does not correspond to the sequence of operational units connected into the pipeline, the pipeline must be switched into a new configuration matching the one in the program.[19,20] This process introduces the additional delay associated with such a reconfiguration.

   In a dynamic pipeline, no such delay occurs because each pipeline stage is a processor P_i, capable of executing any operation.

2. *Pipeline length.* In conventional pipelines, a disparity between the number of consecutive operations in the instruction and the number of stages in the pipeline that processes this instruction creates additional delays. These dummy time intervals are associated either with instruction propagation through unneeded stages or with conflict resolution when the instruction bypasses the unneeded stages and encounters operands prepared for some of its predecessors.[19,20]

   In a dynamic pipeline, no such delays occur. The number of stages through which the instruction propagates is defined by the code, w, contained in the instruction itself. After passing through w stages, the instruction completes its execution.

3. *Time of operation in a stage.* In existing pipelines, the time for noniterative processor-dependent operations—such as addition, subtraction, and comparison—is constant and does not depend on data word sizes. However, selection of a standard operation time in each stage requires that it be the time of the longest operation (addition handling maximal word sizes). All faster operations—processor-dependent operations handling smaller word sizes, Boolean operations, and so on—are slowed down because they are executed during the time of the longest processor-dependent operation.

   No such slowdown occurs in a dynamic pipeline. The processor at each stage can reconfigure into the minimal size required by the data word fetched by the instruction, and the modular control organization—implemented at that and every stage[15]—generates minimal operation times for all computer operations. A dynamic pipeline, therefore, is capable of working at a variable rate. If it is filled with short operations, it fans out results at the rate of the short operation.

4. *On-line feeding of temporary results to the pipeline stages needing them.* Additional waiting times occur in existing pipelines when the computational result obtained from one instruction in one stage is required as an operand for another instruction in another stage. For instance, if the pipeline executes $(A - B)^2 + D \cdot K$, the temporary result $(A - B)^2$ cannot be used on-line as an operand for some other pipeline stage.

For a dynamic pipeline, however, the addressing procedure used allows each stage C_j to receive on-line a temporary result produced by another stage C_i by way of its general register set RM_j (Fig. 1-28). In this way, the waiting time associated with grouping and feeding temporary results to the pipeline stages needing them may be eliminated.

5. *Redistribution of the pipeline resource.* Existing pipeline systems cannot partition their available resources into a variable number of parallel pipelines, each of which is provided with a changeable number of stages. As a result, the number of instruction streams cannot be changed. Likewise, selection of pipelines with a fixed number of stages delays the execution of instructions requiring a smaller number of stages.

On the other hand, a dynamic pipeline architecture may perform multiple on-line switching of the resources into different states, maximizing the number of instruction streams computed by the same equipment. The ability of a dynamic pipeline to form different states is convenient for handling conditional branching, since no time is lost by selection of the instruction sequence not currently filling the main pipeline. Switching a dynamic pipeline into stages with multiple pipelines also allows one to organize multiport branching.

Instruction Pipelines

In existing supercomputers, the major function of instruction pipelines is continuously to bring vectors of data to arithmetic units in order to enable their continuous performance as arithmetic pipelines with the rate T_0 of processor clock period.

This idealistic expectation is greatly hindered by the discrepancy in clock periods T_0 and T_{0M} of processor and memory operations, respectively. Indeed, usually T_0 is a divisor of T_{0M} so that the main memory is p-interleaved to provide access of each data word at the rate of one T_0, where $p = [T_{0M}/T_0]$. For instance, for CRAY-1, $T_0 = 12$ nsec; $T_{0M} = 50$ nsec; and $p = 4 = [50/12]$. Thus, consecutive data words of the data array are stored in four successive locations of memory units that are connected with the same data port (Fig. 1-4).

The requirement to interleave the main memory in order to achieve processor rates for accessing data leads to the following major causes of pipeline disruptions in instruction pipelines of industrial supercomputers.

C1. *Limited bandwidth* of memory units that may store data vectors needed for pipeline access.

C2. *The problem of conditional branches* becomes far more severe than for conventional instruction pipelines.

C3. *Nonconsecutive locations* of data words in successive memory units may cause pipeline disruptions for as many as $(p-1)$ clock periods, which is the time of two consecutive accesses to the same memory unit.

Let us consider each of these problems in more detail.

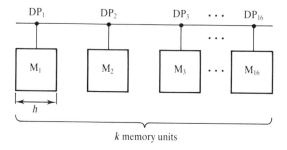

Figure 1-29. The maximal bandwidth MB $= k/T_{0M}$, where k is the number of data ports and T_{0M} is the time to access one data word.

Problem 1: Limited memory bandwidth is a direct consequence of the p-interleaved memory, since for such memories p memory units are connected to the same data port. Conventionally, the memory bandwidth, MB, defines how many data words can be accessed per second by a computer system,

$$MB = \frac{k}{T_{0M}}$$

where k is the number of memory units that can be accessed concurrently; T_{0M} is the time to access one word (Fig. 1-29).

For instance, for the CRAY-1, $k = 16$, $T_{0M} = 50$ nsec, giving MB $=$ 320 Mwords/sec. However, for the p-interleaved memories,

$$MB_I = \frac{k}{T_0 \cdot p}$$

since p memory units are connected to the same data port DP_i (Fig. 1-30(a)).

Here T_0 is the time of the processor clock. The effective MR_I is further reduced if data operands needed for the pipeline expression are stored in such interleaved locations connected to the same data port.

For instance, in Figure 1-30(a), the instruction pipeline achieves the maximal rate of MB_I, since data operands for the vector expression $\mathbf{a} + \mathbf{b} \rightarrow \mathbf{c}$ are accessed via separate data ports DP_1, for the $\mathbf{a}$ vector, DP_2 for the $\mathbf{b}$ vector and DP_3 for the $\mathbf{c}$ vector, where $\mathbf{a} = (a_1, a_2, a_3, a_4)$, $\mathbf{b} = (b_1, b_2, b_3, b_4)$, and $\mathbf{c} = (c_1, c_2, c_3, c_4)$. However, if the $\mathbf{c}$ vector is accessed through the same data port used to access $\mathbf{a}$ or $\mathbf{b}$ (Fig. 1-30(b)), the instruction pipeline is disrupted, since each pair c_i and a_i cannot be accessed concurrently.

Problem 2: Conditional branching is a conventional problem of all instruction pipelines, whereby an actual successor (I_{2F} or I_{2T}) of the conditional branch instruction (I_1) may be fetched only *following the completion of I_1*, leading to a disruption in phase overlap (Fig. 1-31). Therefore, for conventional instruction pipelines, conditional branch may lead to a replacement of phase overlap with sequential execution of phases.

However, since modern supercomputers use memory interleaving, the

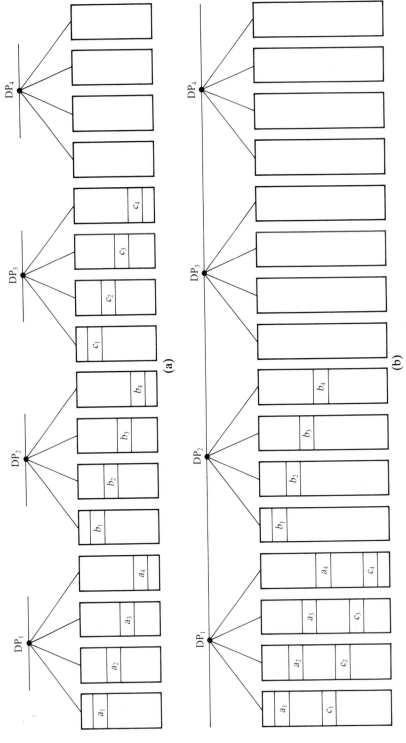

Figure 1-30. Reduction in memory bandwith caused by the four-interleaved memory.
(a) Nondisrupted pipelined execution of $\mathbf{a} + \mathbf{b} \rightarrow \mathbf{c}$ for interleaved memory locations;
(b) Disrupted pipelined execution of $\mathbf{a} + \mathbf{b} \rightarrow \mathbf{c}$ for the memory locations connected to the same data port.

46

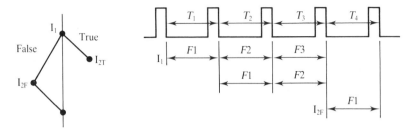

Figure 1-31. Disruption of phase overlap during conventional conditional branches.

problem of conditional branches in their instruction pipelines becomes far more acute, inasmuch as it may result in pipeline idleness for as many as $PDT_{max} = (p-1) \cdot T_0$ clock periods if an actual successor and the conditional branch instruction that finds this successor are stored in the same memory unit.

Example 13. Suppose that the instruction memory is 4-interleaved and I_4 fetched from M_4 is the conditional branch instruction that has true successor I_{T1} stored in M_1 and false successor T_{F1} stored in M_4 (Fig. 1-32). Suppose that in actual execution the I_4 will be followed by I_{F1}. Since memory M_4 may be accessed again only at the fourth clock period T_0 following the fetch of I_4, the instruction pipeline becomes idle for the time $(p-1) \cdot T_0$.

Problem 3: Non-consecutive locations of consecutive data words in the same data vector also may cause severe pipeline disruption,[2] since it becomes impossible to perform a perfect p-interleaving of the offending data vector in p memory units. This leads to a situation in which two consecutive data words w_j and w_{j+1} of this vector are not stored in two successive memory units M_i and M_{i+1} and the instruction pipeline loses valuable clock periods to access w_{j+1} following the access of w_j. The worst case of this type of disruption occurs when the indexing increment d is a multiple of p, as $d = p \cdot l$, where $l \geq 1$, and p is the index of p-interleaving. For this case, two consecutive words $w_j = w_i$ and $w_{j+1} = w_{i+d}$ of the used data array $v' \subset v$ to be accessed by the instruction pipeline (Fig. 1-33(a)) are stored in the same memory unit and the pipeline waits again for as many clock periods as the time $PDT_{max} = (p-1) \cdot T_0$ to access w_{j+1} following the access of w_j (Fig. 1-33(b)). Therefore, elimination of this cause of pipeline disruption requires the use of such d_s that allow perfect p-interleaving.

This may require a separate storage of some subvectors v' of the original vector v if each such v' is to be used in independent pipelining. A requirement that some (if not all!) subvectors v' of v be stored separately is severe and fundamentally cannot be implemented in many computational situations. The most typical of them is the one in which a subvector v' is found dynamically. For this case, it becomes impossible to predict a priori what subvector v' of v needs additional storage, since its size is determined by a current (dynamic) number of loop iterations. In all such cases, the pipeline disruptions due to Problem 3 are

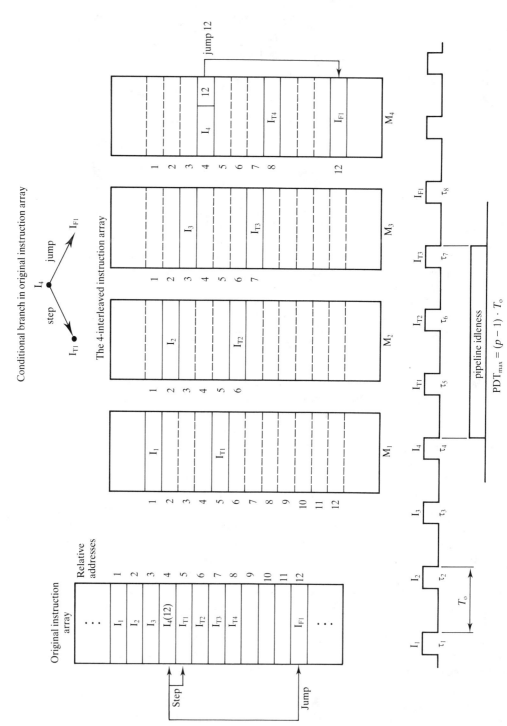

Figure 1-32. Problem of conditional branch in an instruction pipeline that features memory interleaving.

inevitable, although the number of clock periods lost may not be as large as the maximal case of $d = p \cdot l$, where $l \geq 1$, and p is the index of interleaving.

Note. In industrial supercomputers, independent storage of pipelined data vectors is usually organized with the use of such popular operations as *Gather* and *Scatter,*[14,39] where *Gather* organizes a new storage of each vector $\mathbf{v}'$ that must be used in pipelining by collecting consecutive vector elements from their original and irregular storage locations. On the other hand, the *Scatter* operation restores the elements of the $\mathbf{v}'$ vector to their original locations. Specifically, *Gather* and *Scatter* implement the following DO loops, respectively:

```
        Gather                Scatter
     DO J=1,N              DO J=1,N
     B(J)=A(IL(J))         A(IL(K))=B(J)
     Continue              Continue
```

ASYNCHRONOUS PARALLEL COMPUTING STRUCTURES

The asynchronous parallelism is implemented in the two types of computing structures: multicomputer systems, and multiprocessor systems.

Multicomputer Systems

A multicomputer system is a parallel system assembled from N computers in such a way that any two computers may communicate with each other via the interconnection bus connected with their I/O devices[22,29] (Fig. 1-34). The I/O device that performs this communication in each computer is, as a rule, a buffer memory (BM), that is connected to the local processor and the primary memory (Fig. 1-35).

If computer A has to write to its primary memory, M_A, a block of data words stored in the primary memory M_B of computer B, then the interconnection bus of the multicomputer system activates the following path between computers A and B (Fig. 1-35):

1. The block requested in computer B is transferred from memory M_B to its buffer memory, BM_B.
2. From BM_B it is transferred to BM_A, the buffer memory of computer A.
3. From BM_A it is sent to its destination, memory M_A. A block of data must therefore be written to two buffer memories, first to BM_B and then to BM_A, before going to its destination memory M_A. This slows down the information sent between computers significantly.

Another kind of bottleneck between computers is associated with the restricted bandwidth of the interconnection bus. If a system is assembled from a number of large computers, then parallel word exchange among these computers leads to an interconnection bus of significant complexity. To reduce this complexity, the bandwidth of the bus is often restricted. This may be done by replacing parallel word transmission by a sequential byte transmission. For instance, in a 16-bit interconnection bus, a 64-bit word is transferred via 16-bit

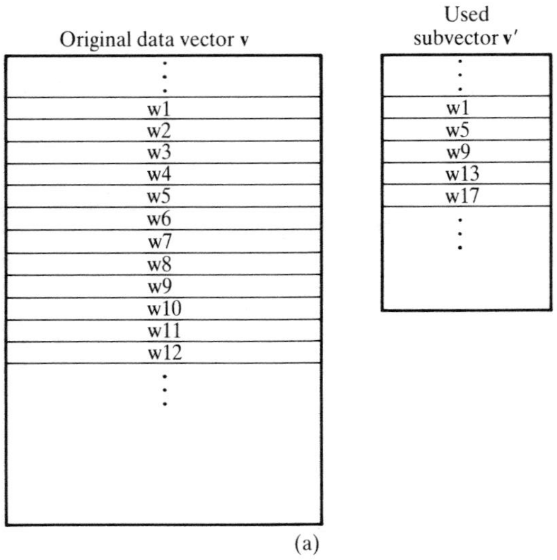

Figure 1-33. Pipeline disruption due to nonconsecutive locations of consecutive data words—worst case: (a) memory storage; (b) synchronization diagram for memory accesses.

50

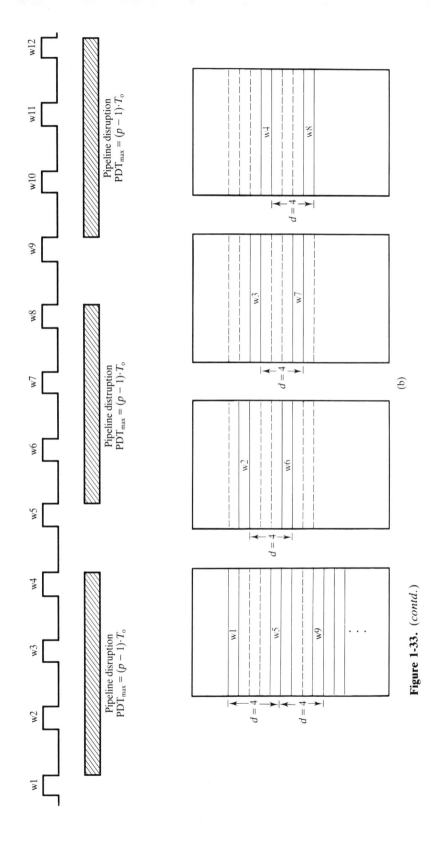

Figure 1-33. (*contd.*)

(b)

51

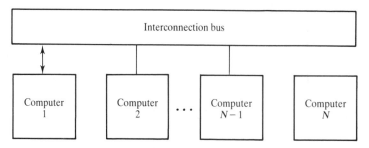

Figure 1-34. Multicomputer system.

bytes, thus requiring four time intervals to transmit one word. Byte transfer therefore leads to another source of increasing the time of between computer communication.

It follows from the above that a multicomputer system assembled from N computers may compute N instruction sequences concurrently, where each instruction may handle a pair of operands at a time. The relatively slow data transmission between computers makes a multicomputer system effective in computing those algorithms that have infrequent data exchanges between instruction sequences computed in different computers since each such exchange will require a significant amount of time to perform.

Therefore as a rule, industrial and prototype supercomputer architectures avoid using this classical multicomputer scheme in view of its obvious proclivity for slowing down all nonlocal processor–memory and memory–memory communications that can be effectively remedied by alternative multiprocessor systems, since the latter have direct nonlocal processor–memory interconnections.

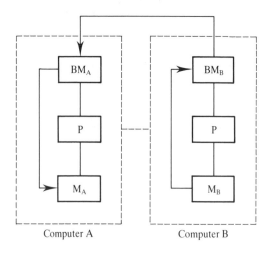

Figure 1-35. A communication path between two computers A and B in a multicomputer system.

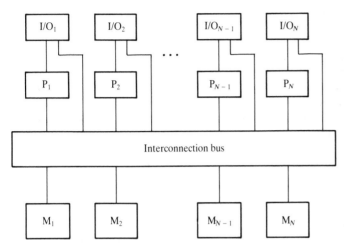

Figure 1-36. Multiprocessor system.

Multiprocessor Systems

A multiprocessor system is assembled from the same functional units (processors, memories, I/Os) that are used in a multicomputer system. However, the interconnection bus of the multiprocessor system allows activation of a direct communication path between any two functional units contained in the system (Fig. 1-36).[22-35]

A multiprocessor system can therefore provide direct data exchanges between any processor and any memory, or any two processors, or any two memories, and so on. For instance, if processor P_2 needs a block of data words stored in the memory M_N, then the interconnection bus reconfigures into a direct path between P_2 and M_N, allowing such an exchange directly rather than by using two buffer memories, as is done in multicomputer systems (Fig. 1-37).

Such an organization of data exchanges will require the complexity of the interconnection bus to be even greater than for a multicomputer system. To make this complexity problem manageable, some systems have restrictions on direct communications among functional units. Their interconnection bus will, as a rule,

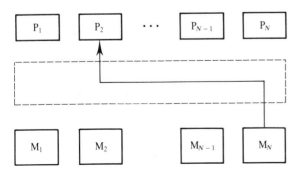

Figure 1-37. PE_2–ME_N data exchange in a multiprocessor system.

support only direct processor–memory exchanges. Other exchanges, such as processor–processor or I/O-memory, may be prohibited. As with multicomputers, multiprocessors may reduce the bus complexity by restricting its bandwidth. This again introduces word transmission by bytes and leads to a slowing down of communications. In general, multiprocessor systems are effective for executing complex algorithms having a high interaction between the concurrent instruction sequences computed in different processors; that is, one sequence needs blocks of data words computed by another sequence.

Multiprocessor systems make efficient use of the above-mentioned techniques of cache memories and memory interleaving for reducing the time of local and nonlocal memory accesses. The major problems of multiprocessor systems are associated with the time and space memory overheads.

The *time overhead* is introduced because of the following.

- *Memory conflicts*, whereby memory ME_i serving processor PE_j is accessed by another processor PE_k. (Here i may coincide with j or k.) This causes a conflict between PE_j and PE_k for accessing ME_i.
- *Missing free memory clocks*, whereby ME_i becomes idle because of imperfect interleaving. However, ME_i (although free) cannot be accessed by processor PE_j because this ME_i is engaged in an interleaving access that involves another group of processors. Thus PE_j must wait before this interleaving access will end.
- *Cache misses*, when a wanted page is not stored in the cache and thus must be relocated from the main memory to the cache. The program run on processor PE_i that needs this page must wait until this relocation is completed.

The *space overhead* is associated with the unused memory space because of strict restrictions on data locations imposed by the interleaving process. Especially severe are these restrictions for the memory interleaving during multiprocessing.

Below we describe existing techniques that minimize the impact of the time overhead during memory conflicts and time and space overheads during interleaving.

Minimizing the Impact of Memory Conflicts

This will be exemplified for a dynamic architecture assembled from building blocks called DC groups.[55] Each DC group features the multiprocessing type of interconnections between its ME and PE resources, each of which is made of n units (PE or ME).

Since resolution of memory conflicts requires the interference of the operating system, let us briefly introduce relevant features of the architecture of one DC group and its operating systems. Basic principles of dynamic architecture were given in Example 8.

A dynamic architecture is assembled from building blocks called dynamic computer (DC) groups. Each DC group is capable of partitioning its resources into a selectable number of dynamic computers with changeable word sizes.

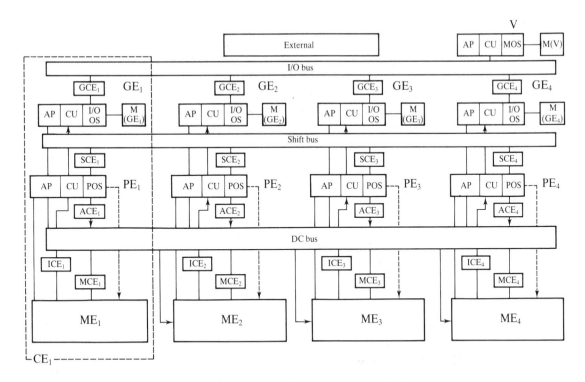

Figure 1-38. Block diagram of one DC group containing four computer elements.

Each DC group contains n h-bit computer elements, PE; n h-bit memory elements, ME; and n h-bit I/O elements, GE (Fig. 1-38). In Figure 1-38, the DC group includes 4CE (i.e., $n = 4$); DC-group may form dynamic computers $C_i(k)$. Each dynamic computer handles $h \cdot k$-bit words; it is assembled from k consecutive CE (CE_i, $CE_{i+1}, \ldots, CE_{i+k-1}$), and the i subscript indicates the position code of its most significant CE. The word sizes formed are multiples of 16 (16, 32, 48, 64, etc.), whereas the number n of CEs may be 4, 8, or 16. Thus, the DC-group may be conceived as a subsystem of a supercomputer system.

If computer B needs a data array stored in a memory page of computer A, then this page is connected with computer B. For this architecture, by loaning its page(s), computer A does not interrupt its program, whereas computer B begins to work with a loaned page as if it belonged to its own memory.

Loaning the memory resource for temporary use by another computer requires interference of the local processor operating system, POS, which resolves conflicts arising each time two or more computers request the same memory page of the local ME_i.

PROCESSOR OPERATING SYSTEM

If the same page of computer A is requested by two or more other computers, the POS_A residing in PE_A has to decide which computer request for

$ME_A \rightarrow PE_B$ or $ME_A \rightarrow ME_B$ exchanges should be granted. To solve these conflicts, each program is assigned a priority code, PC, that shows the relative importance of this program among all others that are being computed by the system. Also, each request for a page is provided with another important characteristic—the tentative duration of a data exchange, TDE.

These two codes will provide the user with a much better quality of service, since the programs with low PCs and small TDE may be granted requests because the requested exchange will take a short time. Should a page request be characterized by the PC code alone, it would be impossible for a program of low priority to request data exchanges of short durations.

Thus, if a page of computer A is requested, the POS_A receives two characteristics of each page request: the priority code, PC, of the requesting program and the tentative duration, TDE, of the exchange.

GENERATION OF PAGE ADDRESSES

In each CE a local computing program may use two busses: the local data bus, which receives data words from the local ME; and the instruction bus, which broadcasts instructions fetched from the local ME to all CEs of the dynamic computer, provided a current program segment is stored in this ME (Fig. 1-38).

For convenience of programming, it is arranged that the data words needed by a current program may be stored not in one but in four pages. The respective four-page addresses are stored in four 8-bit registers, R1–R4 (Fig. 1-39). Each data-fetch instruction that organizes an operand fetch from the local ME stores a 2-bit code m that specifies which of the registers R1–R4 stores a current page address. This register is then connected with the 8-bit local page address for the local data bus. In Figure 1-39, the following ms are used: If $m = 00$, R1 stores a current page address; if $m = 01$, it is stored in R2; and so on.

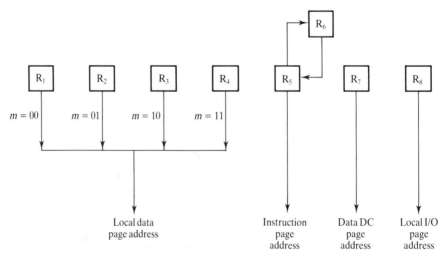

Figure 1-39. Page address registers.

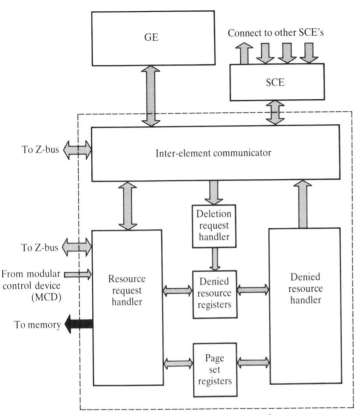

Figure 1-40. Block diagram of the processor operating system.

Similarly, it is arranged that the instructions for a currently executed program segment be stored in two pages whose addresses are stored in R5 and R6, where R5 stores the page address that is connected to the instruction bus and R6 stores the next page address. If a program needs to jump to a page address stored in R6, the following transfers are performed: R5→R6 and R6→R5; that is, a current address is saved in R6 and a new address is transferred to R5. This is done with a special instruction that transfers control to a new program segment whose page address was in R6.

For the DC bus and the local I/O bus, the respective page addresses are stored in R7 and R8; that is, a programmer may work with one page for each of these busses. All these registers (R1–R8) are included in the page set registers of the POS (Fig. 1-40).

HANDLING PAGE REQUESTS

All POSs of the DC-group may exchange with 16-bit messages. Each message may belong to one of the following categories:

1. it may be a *page request*, or
2. it may be a *Yes* or *No response* on a page request.

There are other types of messages that are not discussed here.

A page request to a given POS_A from all of the POS_B is broadcast via connecting element SCE_A local with CE_A. The DC group has n SCEs that are forming the P-bus considered above. In Figure 1-40, $n = 4$; therefore the SCE has four 16-bit channels, of which three are input channels for receiving page requests from other CEs and one is the output channel for sending its own page request to other CEs. Further, as was indicated above, every POS_A may receive a 16-bit request from the local I/O POS_A via a 16-bit data bus that connects PE_A and the local GE_A.

Since each POS_A may receive up to $n - 1$ concurrent page requests from other POSs, these requests form a queue in the *inter-element communicator* that allows only one request to be handled at a time. After this request is finished, the next request in a queue is processed, and so on. Having received a page request, each POS_A initiates a *resource request handler* that initiates the actions discussed in the next sections.

RESOURCE REQUEST HANDLER

The received page address is compared concurrently with all those stored in R1–R8 to find out whether a requested page, RP, is busy. If it is free, the POS_A performs the following functions.

- Generates a "Yes" response to the external requester, POS_B.
- Writes this page address to the R7 register that connects it to the DC bus (Fig. 1-39).
- Activates the data channel in the connecting element, SCE_A, that connects the local memory element, ME_A, with its destination processor element, PE_B, that requested this page. This establishes the $ME_A \rightarrow PE_B$ data path whereby a local page in ME_A was loaned to Computer B (Fig. 1-38).

If a requested page, RP, is busy, its address is stored in one of the registers, R1–R8. This means that this RP-page is used by one of the following programs (Fig. 1-39).

1. If it is stored in the R1–R6 registers, it is used by the local program, AP, computed by Computer A.
2. If it is stored in the R7 register, it is used by another computer, C, which borrowed this page via the DC bus. Thus this page is used by the CP program.
3. If it is stored in the R8 register, it is used by the local program, GEP, computed in the local I/O element, GE_A.

To generate a Yes or No response to a page request, the operating system, POS_A, must compare the received PC_B and TDE_B parameters (where PC_B is the priority code and TDE_B is the tentative duration of the data exchange of the requester B) with those of the program that is currently using the requested page, RP. It is one of AP, CP, or GEP. The priority code and tentative duration of each of these programs is stored in the resource request handler.

ESTIMATE TABLE

To find out which of the programs must use the requested memory page, RP, the POS_A performs a priority analysis that consists of the following. It analyzes a special *estimate table* (Table 1–1) whose rows are marked by priority codes, PC, and columns by TDE times. In the system under consideration, there are seven levels of priorities; thus, PC is a three-bit code and $PC_7 > PC_6 > \cdots > PC_1$.

Assume that the TDE code ranges from 10^2 clock periods to 10^6 clock periods. Thus, the estimate table will have seven rows and five columns.

The intersection (PC, TDE) of the given PC row and the TDE column gives an integer called *program weight* (PW) that shows what actions should be taken by the POS_A. For instance, in Table 1-1, if $TDE = 10^2$ and $PC = 1$, then $PW = 20$. If $TDE = 10^4$ and $PC = IV$, then $PW = 25$, and so on.

It should be noted that the estimate table is made up on the basis of statistical analysis of algorithms that are computed by the DC group. Each estimate table can be augmented with new columns and new rows to reflect given computational requirements. Further, since the estimate table is stored in the memory, its expansion requires no hardware changes. Row and column entries may also be changed to reflect a change in a set of programs that are under execution.

DECISIONS MADE BY THE POS_A

To make a decision concerning a requested page, RP, the POS_A must find two program weights, PW_U and PW_B, where PW_U is the program weight of the program that is currently using a requested page and PW_B is the program weight of the program that is requesting this page. If $PW_U \geq PW_B$, a requester, POS_B, receives a No response. If $PW_U < PE_B$, a requester, POS_B, receives a Yes response.

Handling the No response is considered in the next section. As for the Yes response, the type of actions undertaken by the POS_A—following comparison of PW_U and PW_B—depends on what type of programs have been using a requested page, RP. There are four cases, considered below.

Case (a). Local AP program using a local data bus. If a requested page, RP,

Table 1-1. Estimate table

Program priority	Tentative duration (TDE)				
	10^2	10^3	10^4	10^5	10^6
I	20	15	10	5	1
II	25	20	15	10	5
III	30	25	20	15	10
IV	35	30	25	20	15
V	40	35	30	25	20
VI	45	40	35	30	25
VII	50	45	40	35	30

is used by the AP program, for data fetches, its address is stored in one of the registers R1–R4 (Fig. 1-39). If this page is granted to computer B, its address should be written to the R7 register connected with the DC bus, whereas the register that stored it before should be reset. However, the local AP program may continue its execution until it starts data fetches from the requested page. In this case the AP program will be interrupted only when it fetches a data-fetch instruction with 2-bit code, m, that connects a requested page granted to computer B with the data page address. Such an organization allows elimination of unnecessary interrupts. Thus the AP becomes interrupted only when such interrupt is absolutely necessary.

Case (b). Local AP program using an instruction bus. If a requested page is used by the AP program for instruction fetches, its address is stored either in R5 or R6 registers. If the request on this page to POS_B is granted and a requested page is stored in the R5 register, R5 is reset, and the AP program is interrupted. If a requested page is stored in the R6 register, R6 is reset and the execution of program AP proceeds until it fetches the instruction that transfers control from R6 to R5.

Case (c). External CP program using a DC bus. If a requested page is used by the external CP program, its address is stored in register R7. If the POS_A decides to give the requested page to the POS_B, then the following actions are performed.

1. The resource request handler of the POS_A sends a message to POS_C that a page in ME_A will be denied for further use by CP program.
2. Having received this message, POS_C acknowledges its reception.
3. POS_A establishes a new path in the DC bus by connecting ME_A with PE_B.
4. POS_A sends a Yes response message to POS_B, indicating that its page request is granted.

Case (d). Local GEP program using a local I/O bus. Actions similar to those in case (c) are performed if a requested page has been used by the local GEP program.

DENIED RESOURCE HANDLER

If the POS_A denies a page request made by the POS_B, this request is remembered in the denied resource table (Table 1-2) that is stored in the Denied Resource Handler unit (Fig. 1-40).

The table that stores denied requests has $n + 1$ rows, where n rows are assigned for n CEs of the system and the last row is assigned for the local I/O element, GE_A.

Table 1-2. Denied resource table

CE_1	5, VI, 3	6, III, 5	7, V, 10	22, II, 10
CE_2	6, III, 5	5, IV, 2	—	—
CE_3	—	—	—	—
CE_4	16, VI, 5	—	—	—
GE_3	5, IV, 4	—	—	—

The table contains d columns, where d specifies the number of denied requests from one POS_B that can be stored. Each row marked by CE_B stores denied page requests made by the POS_B residing in CE_B to POS_A. Since local POS_A does not make page requests to itself, its row CE_A is empty. This is accomplished to preserve the circuit identity of all POSs. This last row, GE_A, stores denied page requests made by local I/O OS_A. For instance, if the DC group has four CE ($n = 4$) and $d = 4$ is selected, then Table 1-2 has five rows and four columns. The entry (i, j) of the ith row and the jth column stores the following *page request parameters*: the address RPA of requested page, RP; the priority code PC of the program that requests RP; and the tentative duration of an exchange, TDE.

Example 14. For the DC group with four CEs ($n = 4$), consider Table 1-2 stored in POS_3 local with CE_3. This means that row CE_3 is empty; in the first four rows this table will store all page requests on the pages of ME_3 made by POS_1, POS_2, and POS_4. In the last (fifth) row, the requests made by local I/O OS_3 will be stored. The row CE_1 stores all page requests made by POS_1. There are four such requests. Request 1 is on Page 5, for the program with PC = VI. The page is needed during 10^3 clock periods. Request 2 is on Page 6 for the program with PC = III during 10^5 clock periods; and so on. The local GE_3 row stores only one page request on Page 5 for the program with PC = IV during 10^4 clock periods.

HANDLING DENIED REQUESTS

For each POS_A, Table 1-2 stores two types of denied requests: external and internal. External denied requests are from all other POSs. Internal requests are from the local I/O OS_A.

To satisfy an external request requires that the DC bus be free and the requested page, RP, be free. To satisfy an internal page request requires that only the requested page be free. Consider handling external denied requests only, since handling internal denied requests is a simple extension of this more general procedure. Each time the DC bus is free and one page of ME_A is released—that is, its address called *released page address* (RPA) is taken away from one of the registers, R1–R8—the RPA address is sent to the denied resource handler.

Thereafter, RPA is compared with all page addresses stored in Table 1-2. If it is not stored in Table 1-2, the next released page is analyzed. If it is stored in Table 1-2, assume that it is stored in row B and column 1—that is, it is requested by POS_B for the first time. Upon fetching this request, the POS_A informs the POS_B that the requested page can be connected to the computer element CE_B. If the POS_B agrees to accept this page, the POS_A writes this RPA address to register R8—which is connected with the DC bus—and deletes this request from Table 1-2. If POS_B does not agree to accept this page, then again this page request is deleted from Table 1-2. If the same released page address, RPA, is stored in several entries of Table 1-2, this means that the same page is requested by several programs. All such requests having the same RPA are fetched; and, using Table 1-1, their program weights, PW, are found. Thereafter the request with the highest PW is satisfied and deleted from Table 1-2. The remaining requests continue to be stored in Table 1-2.

Example 15. Suppose that the DC bus is free and ME_3 releases Page 5 (i.e. RPA = 5). In Table 1-2, the same RPA = 5 is stored in three requests: request 1, made by POS_1; request 2, made by POS_2; and request 1, made by the local I/O OS_3. Using Table 1-1, we find that the program weights of these requests are as follows:

Request #1 (POS_1) $PW_1 = 40$ (row VI, col. 10^3)
Request #1 (POS_2) $PW_2 = 35$ (row IV, col. 10^2)
Request #1 (I/O OS_3) $PW_3 = 25$ (row IV, col. 10^4)

Since PW_1 is the highest program weight, Request 1 (POS_1) is granted. This means that POS_3 informs POS_1 that Page 5 can be connected with CE_1.

If POS_1 agrees to accept this page, POS_3 writes RPA = 5 to register R8 and deletes this request from Table 1-2 (Fig. 1-9).

If POS_1 informs POS_3 that it does not currently need Page 5, request 1 (POS_1) is deleted from Table 1-2.

Perfect Interleaving for a Multiprocessor

The effect of time and space overhead during interleaving can be significantly reduced or even eliminated if the conditions of perfect interleaving are satisfied.

PERFECT INTERLEAVING FOR A UNIPROCESSOR

For the p-interleaved memory, which serves a single processor, PE, the value of p must be selected so that $p = T_0/t_0$, where T_0 is the clock period of the memory and t_0 is the clock period of the processor (Fig. 1-4). This completely excludes any time overhead in accessing consecutive words in the data array allocated among p interleaved memories, ME_i. However such an allocation creates a considerable space overhead, since in each ME_i every interleaved data word w_j is separated from the next word of the local data array stored in the same ME_i by p empty locations. Elimination of the space overhead can be accomplished if, in each local data array A_i of ME_i, consecutive data words are stored in contiguous memory locations (Fig. 1-41(a)). However, this necessitates that the processor PE be provided with p address counters CO_i $(i = 1, \ldots, p)$, each CO_i storing relative address ACO_i of the respective ME_i. The effective memory address, E, for accessing ME_i is defined as the concatenation $E = M_i ACO_i$, where M_i is the position code of ME_i stored in mod p counter M, and ACO_i portion of the address is activated from the respective CO_i (Fig. 1-41(b)).

Mod p counter M contains p states: $M_1, M_2, \ldots, M_p$. Each state, M_i is identified with the position code of the respective ME_i (Fig. 1-41(a)). Every transition $M_i \rightarrow M_{i+1}$ (mod p) is performed during each processor clock period t_0 under the respective clock pulse t. Every state M_i generates a signal O_i $(i = 1, \ldots, p)$ that is sent to the relative address counter CO_i to enable the following actions.

Action 1   Transfer of the current relative address ACO_i to the address bus ACO of the processor PE (Fig. 1-41(b)).

Action 2   Increment of current relative address ACO_i to obtain $ACO_{i+1} = ACO_i + 1$, so that CO_i will store the next relative address ACO_{i+1}.

The next ACO_{i+1} will be sent to the ACO bus as soon as the next O_i signal is generated. (Instead of the relative address counter one can use the relative address adder, $\text{ACA}_{i+1} = \text{ACA}_i + d$ where $d \geq 1$ is an indexing increment.)

Example 16. Consider the timing diagram of the perfect interleaving for a uniprocessor that eliminates both the time and space overheads. Assume that $p = 4$, that is, $T_0 = 4t_0$, and the original array A consists of 24 data words partitioned into four local arrrays, A_I, A_{II}, A_{III}, and A_{IV}. Each local array A_i ($i = \text{I, II, III, IV}$) is given with the two relative addresses, left-hand side ACO_i and right-hand side AA_i, where ACO_i shows the local relative address within ME_i and AA_i shows the absolute relative address within the original A array (Fig. 1-41(a)). Since the memory is 4-interleaved, giving $p = 4$, the M-counter includes four states: $\text{M}_1 = 00$, $\text{M}_2 = 01$, $\text{M}_3 = 10$, and M_4. For the 4-interleaved memory, there are four relative address counters CO_1–CO_4. The timing diagram for all the register-to-register transfer actions involved in this perfect 4-interleaving process is shown in Fig. 1-41(c).

As seen, during each clock pulse μ_i of the memory ME_i (Fig. 1-41(c)) one data word a_i is accessed as $a_i \rightarrow \text{MDR}$ from the respective local array A_i ($i = \text{I, II, III, IV}$) (Fig. 1-41(a)). Thus no time overhead is created since there are no lost memory and processor pulses. The processor clock sequence τ is shifted with respect to the memory clock sequence μ_i ($i = 1, 2, 3, 4$). This allows each word accessed from the memory ME_i to its data register MDR to be transferred to PE ($\text{MDR} \rightarrow \text{DR}$) with the next arriving pulse τ (Fig. 1-41(c)). The lower portion of Fig. 1-41(c) shows the timing in generating ACO addresses. Those are changed in PE with the rate of the processor clock τ under signal O_i, so that each ACO_i is changed to ACO_{i+1} when counter M holds state M_i. The effective address $E = \text{M}_i \text{ACO}_i$ is sent to ME_i, when it issues its clock pulse μ_i ($i = 1, 2, 3, 4$). The next pulse τ of the processor increments this ACO_i, since it coincides with the O_i signal. As seen, no memory space overhead is created, since in each local array A_i ($i = \text{I, II, III, IV}$) consecutive data words are contiguous.

CONDITIONS OF PERFECT INTERLEAVING FOR UNIPROCESSOR

As follows from the Example 16, the following are the conditions of perfect p-interleaving for a uniprocessor.

C1. The original data array A must be made of data words spaced from each other with the same distance $d \geq 1$ to allow its partitioning into p local arrays A_i ($i = 1, \ldots, p$).

The number of words, k, in the original array A must be a multiple of p, so that each local array will have k/p words.

C2. The index p of interleaving must be defined as $p = T_0/t_0$, where T_0 is the memory clock period and t_0 is the processor clock period.

C3. To minimize space overhead, each local array A_i must be stored in the relative locations of ME_i separated with the same distance $f \geq 1$ so that the next relative addresses $\text{ACO} = \text{ACO}' + f$ is generated by the local relative address adder for $f > 1$ or counter for $f = 1$.

C4. The effective memory address is defined as $E = \text{M}_i \text{ACO}_i$ where the M_i portion of the address is stored in the mod p counter M which specifies a current ME_i address and the ACO_i portion of the address is stored in the relative address adder CO_i ($i = 1, \ldots, p$).

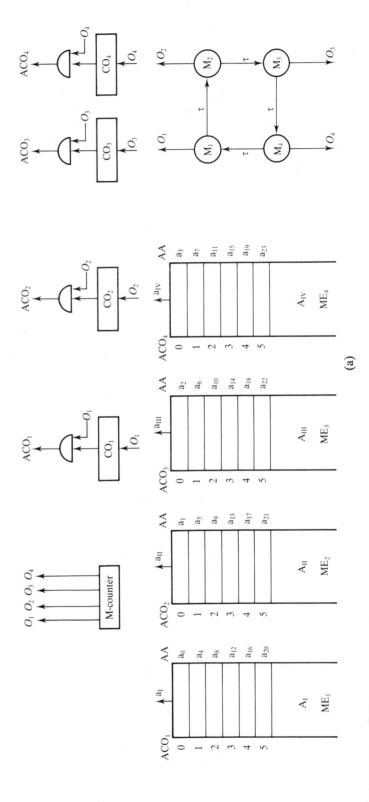

(a)

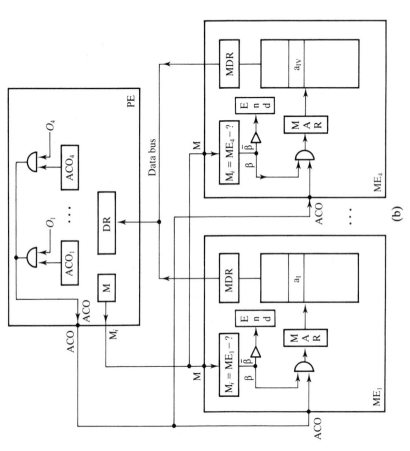

Figure 1-41. (a) Elimination of the space overhead in each ME during perfect memory interleaving in a uniprocessor. (b) Hardware diagram of perfect 4-interleaving in a uniprocessor. (c) Timing diagram of perfect 4-interleaving in a uniprocessor.

65

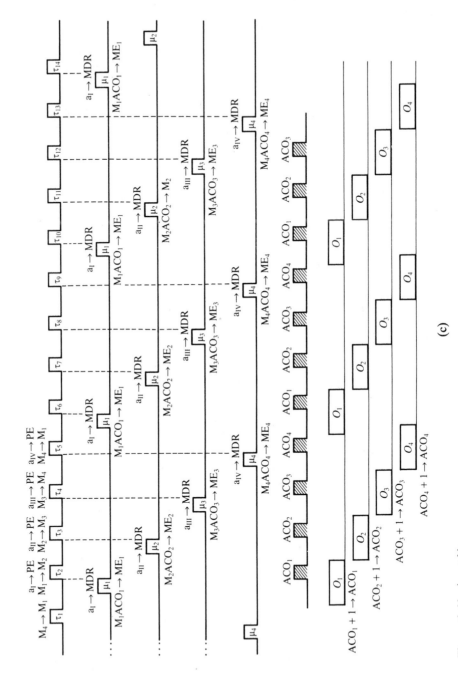

Figure 1-41. (contd.)

66

PERFECT INTERLEAVING FOR A MULTIPROCESSOR

As follows from the preceding sections, perfect interleaving for a uniprocessor prevents any other processor from being connected to the same interleaving memory, since there are no idle memory cycles when this memory can be accessed by a new processor. To allow several processors to be interleaved with the same memory requires adding additional memory units so that the total number k of interleaved memories becomes larger than $p = T_0/t_0$.

Therefore if $p = T_0/t_0$, the p-interleaving becomes *minimal* and applicable only for the uniprocessor. To connect m processors into the same interleaving memory requires selection of m such that $m = k/p$. Indeed, each interleaving cycle IC consists of k memory accesses from consecutive memories ME_1, $ME_2, \ldots, ME_k$, that is, $IC = k \cdot t_0$. Each memory ME_i becomes free for the next access by a new processor(s) during the time $(k/p) \cdot t_0$, giving the total number of processors m that can be interconnected into the same interleaving scheme as $m = k/p$.

Example 17. Figure 1-42(a) shows the two processors interconnected into the same interleaving memory consisting of six ME—that is, having $k = 6$. Assume that $T_0 = 3t_0$, that is, each ME_i is 3-interleaved (Fig. 1-42(b)). Since one interleaving cycle IC is made of six accesses to ME_1 through ME_6, and each memory ME_i is 3-interleaved, during each interleaving cycle IC, it can be accessed by $m = 2$ processors PE_1 and PE_2, where $m = 6/3$. In Figure 1-42(b) consecutive memory pulses are identified with the processors that send E-addresses to the respective memories. As is seen, if $m = k/p$ and $p = T_0/t_0$, no time overhead is created during accesses, since each module ME_i is engaged during every memory cycle T_0.

Note. Since, during each memory pulse μ, there exists m memory modules ME_i that are accessed concurrently by m processors PE_i, each ME_i must be provided with m data buses and m address buses.

In Figure 1-42(a), $m = 2$, requiring two dedicated data and address buses for each ME_i $(i = 1, 2, \ldots, 6)$ of which one pair of this bus is used by PE_1 and another pair is used by PE_2. Each PE_i is sending the entire E address information to all ME_j concurrently through the dedicated address bus. The ME_j with the position code identical to that of the effective address, E, is activated into the memory access (Fig. 1-42(a)): that is, it is allowed to receive the relative portion of the E-address.

In Figure 1-42(b), what is eliminated through correct selection of k, p, and m is only the time overhead. The space overhead remains, since only one relative address counter is used in each PE_i $(i = 1, 2)$ for generating consecutive relative addresses of the original array A. These addresses become noncontiguous and thus create space overhead. Elimination of the space overhead requires the use of $k = 6$ relative address counters in each PE_i.

CONDITIONS OF PERFECT INTERLEAVING FOR MULTIPROCESSORS

These conditions for multiprocessors basically repeat those for the uniprocessor. The only change is in $m = k/p$.

For uniprocessors, $m = 1$ and $k = p$.

For multiprocessors, m and p are divisors of k, and k is necessarily greater than m and p.

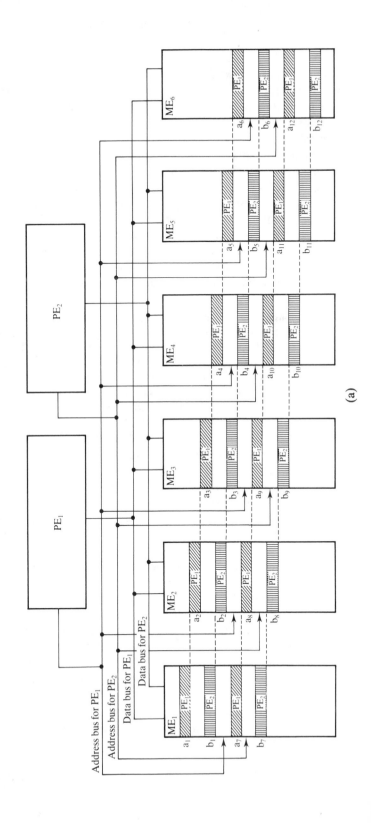

(a)

68

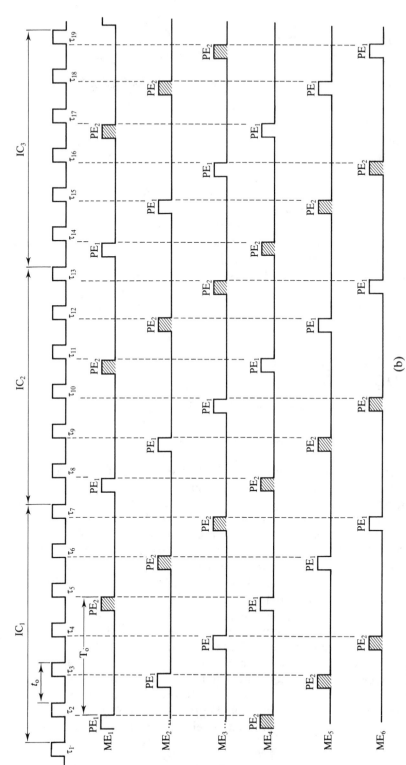

Figure 1-42. (a) Perfect 2-processor 3-interleaving. Interleaving parameters; $p = 3$, $m = 2$, $k = p \cdot 2 = 6$. $IC = k \cdot t_0$. (b) Timing diagram of the perfect 2-processor 3-interleaving.

(b)

EVOLUTION OF INDUSTRIAL ARCHITECTURES

Further evolution in the industrial architectures proceeded along the following lines:

- pipelined systems;
- array systems;
- multiprocessor systems;
- multicomputer systems.

All these systems implemented limited adaptation capabilities achieved via system and microprogrammable reconfiguration.

No data-flow project has yet been implemented industrially in the sense of the definition we have made. The data-flow concept still remains a daring architectural idea that is waiting its turn to be implemented in a form of a viable industrial and commercially available supercomputer. Dynamically partitionable supercomputers, too, still represent prototype architectures, in view of the obvious industrial conservatism in implementation of unorthodox architectural principles.

INDUSTRIAL PIPELINED MULTIPROCESSORS

Development of industrial pipelines began with the appearance of IBM's STRETCH, which was the first computer that implemented the instruction pipeline aimed at prefetching of instructions and its operands.[36]

After this historic event, pipeline systems began to be very popular in the industry. In fact, since the appearance of the STRETCH computer, instruction and arithmetic pipelines have become the major choice of industrial manufacturers in view of obvious speed advantages of pipelined computations.

As industrial pipelines were refined in the 1970s with technological advances it became possible to have pipelined multiprocessors instead of the former pipelined uniprocessors. Therefore, we will consider first evolutionary architectural refinement of industrial pipelined uniprocessors and then show what architectural features have been added to them in order to make them multiprocessors. We will discuss two industrial families: CDC-ETA and CRAY, and show how they progressed along the general evolutionary lines outlined above.

Only two industrial families are selected because only these two families contain at least three generations of supercomputers, so that the industrial evolutionary trends we have outlined can be clearly followed and identified. The market is now replete with supercomputers and minisupercomputers produced by other manufacturers. However, in each such case the respective family has just begun and includes the newest supercomputers of the first generation. As a matter of fact, all these systems are completely specified by the classification given above.

Control Data-ETA Evolutionary Family

The Control Data-ETA evolutionary family includes three generations of machines:

$$STAR-100 \ (1974) \rightarrow CYBER-205 \ (1981) \rightarrow ETA-10 \ (1986)$$

THE STAR-100 ARCHITECTURE

The basic organization of Figure 1-43 shows the STAR-100 processor.[2] There are four main units: memory and storage access control (SAC), two floating-point pipelines, a string unit, and a stream-control unit.

The stream-control unit controls the whole system and performs simple logical operations over arithmetic and scalar operands. All processing in STAR-100 is performed in one of two pipes and string unit.

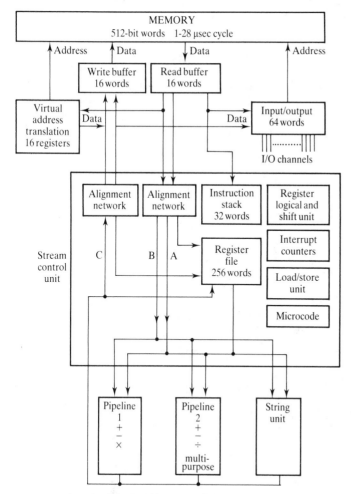

Figure 1-43. The STAR-100 processor.

Both pipeline units perform floating-point addition, subtraction, and multiplication. The memory is 512 bits wide and assembled into 64k words. Its cycle time is 1.28 μsec and it is paged. Control functions for this machine are performed by stream control unit, which performs the following functions.

- Streams and aligns A, B, and C operands ($A * B = C$) for the two vector pipelines for memory-to-memory operations under the control of the microcode stored in a special high-speed memory.
- Executes simple logical operations over scalar operands.
- Organizes pipelined execution in vector pipelines of arithmetic expressions containing more than one arithmetic operation with the use of a register file containing 256 words. This file chains vector pipelines together by storing initial operands and intermediate results for vector pipelines.
- Organizes an instruction prefetch for up to 16 instructions with the use of the instruction stack containing up to 64 instructions packaged into 32 words (two instructions per word).

All vector processing is performed in three pipelines that can operate concurrently. Of these three, two (pipeline 1 or pipeline 2) are equipped with floating-point capability. A basic component of both floating-point pipelines is the five-phased floating-point addition pipeline with an option of postnormalization (Fig. 1-44). This pipeline is reconfigurable in the sense that it can operate over two streams of 64-bit operands A and B as $A_1 * B_1$ and $A_2 * B_2$, where * stands for

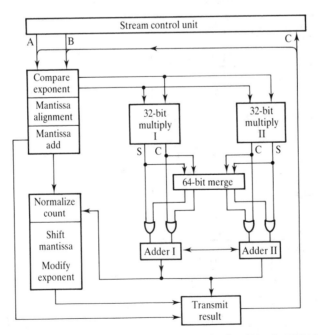

Figure 1-44. Floating-point-addition pipeline-I in the STAR-100 processor.

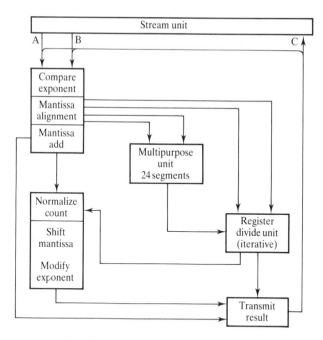

Figure 1-45. Floating-point-addition pipeline-II in the STAR-100 processor.

$(+)$ or $(-)$ or four streams of 32-bit operands $A_1 * B_1$, $A_2 * B_2$, $A_3 * B_3$ and $A_4 * B_4$. This reconfiguration doubles the rate of processing. The maximal potential speed of STAR-100 is 10^8 floating-point operations per second over 32-bit operands. Hence the name STAR-100. The difference between the two pipelines is that the first one can perform pipelined multiplication over 32-bit operands (Fig. 1-44), whereas the second can perform scalar division and multipurpose functions (square-root, vector division, and vector multiplication (Fig. 1-45)).

To improve the memory bandwidth, the main memory has the following properties.

- It is provided with a very wide parallel access of 512 bits partitioned among 32 memory modules. The memory clock period is $T_0 = 1.28\,\mu$sec. A superword of 512 bits can be accessed from or to 32 memory banks concurrently with a speed of 1.28 μsec, achieving a rate of 1600 megabytes per sec.[39]
- The memory is 32-interleaved, where $32 = 1.28\,\mu$sec $\div$ 40 nsec, so that each 16-bit byte of the 512-bit superword is fetched during 40 nsec to provide the required 40 nsec rate for the two floating-point pipelines. This constitutes 4×64-bit operands, 2×64-bit results, and the remaining 128 bits are assigned for the control vectors and other general input/output for the memory.

The storage access control unit maps 512 superwords accessed during 32 accesses with the speed of 40 nsec per access into narrower operands that can be 64-bit words, 32-bit words, 16-bit bytes, or even bits.

CYBER-205 ARCHITECTURE

The next supercomputer, CYBER-205, essentially repeats the structure of STAR-100. The modifications introduced were as follows.[2]

1. Regularization and aggregation of design to allow a feasible LSI implementation.
2. Parallelization of scalar and vector operation.
3. Providing several different page sizes to reduce the memory overhead of virtual memory management.
4. Elimination of direct connections of terminals with the central processor. Instead, the loosely coupled network was designed to increase the number of terminals.

Both STAR-100 and CYBER-205 are uniprocessors in the sense that they operate over a single process at a time.[2]

In accordance with this general modification strategy, specific quantitative changes in CYBER-205 are as follows (Fig. 1-46). One superword of 512 bits is accessed from the memory during 20 nsec for CYBER-205 rather than 1.28 μsec for STAR-100.[14] All 512-bit superwords are assembled into four M words. Each M word is organized into 16 memory modules each having a 32-bit data path.

Thus, each M word is 16-interleaved, giving $k = 16$; since the memory clock period $T_0 = 80$ nsec, and the processor clock period $t_0 = 20$ nsec, the minimal interleaving index is $p = T_0/t_0 = 4$. Therefore, for each M word there are $k/p = 4$ concurrent accesses of 32-bit half-words, giving the total size of 128 bits ($32 \times 4 = 128$) fetched from each M word concurrently. Since there are four M words, in all 512-bits (or one superword) are accessed during each t_0.

Also, each memory module of 32-bit data width is provided with an additional 7-bit width for single-error correction and double-error detection (SECDED bits) giving the total number of 112 SECDED bits for one 512-bit word, where $112 = 7 \times 16$. In general, the memory is accessed by s-words (512 bits) for vectors and by words (64 bits) and half-words (32 bits) for scalars. The memory interface unit assembles this data into 128-bit wide data paths each connecting the memory interface unit with scalar and vector processing units via three read (R1, R2, and R3) and two write (W1 and W2) paths (Fig. 1-46). In all, the memory interface unit is connected via ten 128-bit data paths with the processing units and I/O units of the computer, each of which has a maximum transfer rate of 128-bits per each 20 nsec clock period of the processor.

All data paths to the vector section pass through the scalar section. The scalar section contains the instruction pipeline that issues one 32-bit instruction with the processor rate of 20 nsec. The size of instruction stack is 128 32-bit instructions or 64 64-bit instructions, or a combination of both, so that one 64-bit

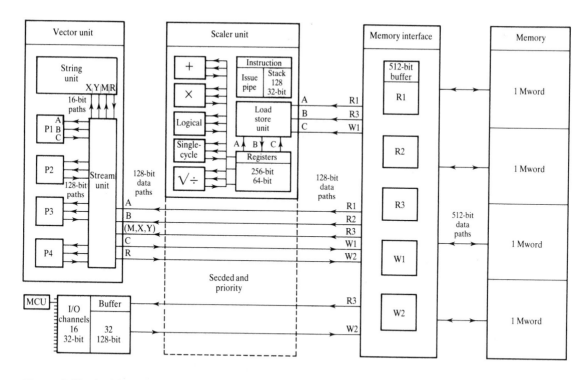

Figure 1-46. Architectural diagram of the CDC CYBER-205.

instruction is stored in the two consecutive locations of the instruction stack. The instruction pipeline generates instructions for scalar and vector units.

Operations over vectors or strings of characters are performed in the vector section, which consists of up to four floating-point pipelines and a string unit. These are fed with data streams by the use of the stream unit. All vector operations are memory-to-memory.

Each of the floating-point pipelines (P1, P2, P3, and P4) consists of five pipelined functional units for addition, multiplication, shifting, logic operations, and delay connected via the data interchange. Division and square-root are performed in the multiplication unit (Fig. 1-47).

The string unit performs all bit-logical and character-string operations on strings of bits and bytes. It also processes the control vectors associated with the masking of floating-point operations.

All data paths to the string unit are 16 bits wide. There are three input paths X, Y, M: X and Y for character strings and M for masking.

ETA-10 SUPERCOMPUTER

The next supercomputer of this family is the ETA-100 supercomputer announced by ETA in 1986.[37] This is a pipelined multiprocessor made of eight uniprocessors

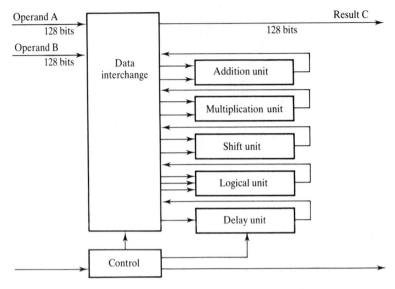

Figure 1-47. Floating-point pipeline for the CDC CYBER 205.

of CYBER-205 type (Fig. 1-49). Each of the eight uniprocessors is shown in Figure 1-48. As seen it has parallel scalar and vector operation, local memory (central processor memory) and access to the shared memory of the multiprocessing system.

Figure 1-49 shows possible multiprocessor configurations. In spite of only an 8-fold increase in complexity caused by connecting eight uniprocessors of the

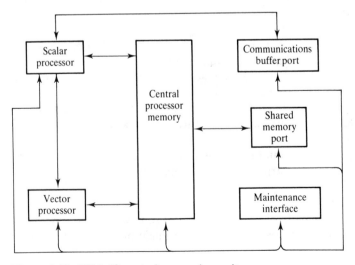

Figure 1-48. ETA-10 central processing unit.

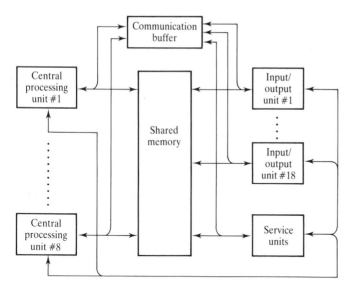

Figure 1-49. ETA-10 Functional Diagram.

CYBER-205 type, the maximal range of performance increase is up to 30 times in comparison with CYBER-205.[37]

CRAY Research Evolutionary Family

We describe the CRAY-1 supercomputer in more detail and then give the evolutionary changes that are also quantitative in nature. The CRAY Research evolutionary family is shown below:

$$\text{CRAY-1 (1976)} \rightarrow \text{CRAY-X-MP/2, X-MP/4 (1982)} \rightarrow \begin{cases} \text{CRAY 2} \\ \text{CRAY 3} \end{cases} \text{(1984)}$$

CRAY-1 ARCHITECTURE

The CRAY-1 architecture is shown in Figure 1-50. It centers around the main memory feeding data to and from a set of scalar and vector registers. Logical and arithmetic operations are performed in 12 functional units interconnected with the registers. The memory width is 64 bits. Its access time is 50 nsec.

The memory is divided into 16 or 8 memory banks that can operate concurrently at the rate of one 64-bit word per 50 nsec, giving the maximal memory bandwidth as

$$\text{MB} = \frac{16}{50 \text{ nsec}} = 320\text{M word/sec}$$

The entire memory is also 16-interleaved, giving the following parameters for concurrent interleaved memory access: minimal interleaving index, $p = 50 \text{ nsec}/12 \text{ nsec} = 4$, $k = 16$, $m = k/p = 4$—that is, four 64-bit data words can be fetched with the rate of $t_0 = 12.5$ nsec.

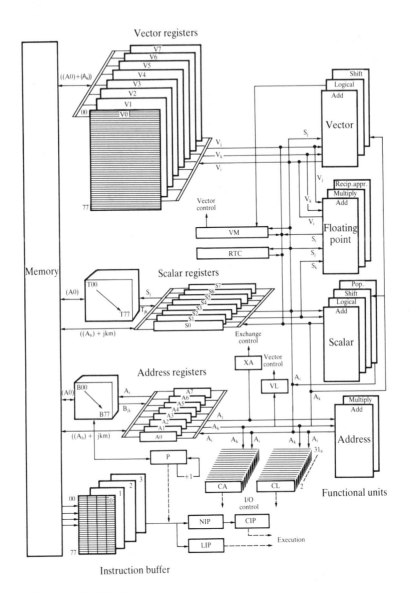

Figure 1-50. CRAY-1 supercomputer.

The maximal memory capacity of 320M word/sec is maintained only between the memory and the instruction buffer consisting of four buffers each containing 64 16-bit instructions. Each buffer is connected with a 64-bit bus with the memory. Therefore for the perfect interleaving, the entire buffer can be filled during $16 \cdot t_0 = 2 \, \mu\text{sec}$.

For data transfer, only a quarter of this rate is used, giving $MB_D = 80M$ word/sec and only one 64-bit data channel, which transfers one 64-bit word every 12.5 nsec (80M word/sec $= 1/(12.5 \cdot 10^{-9}) = 10^9/12.5$).

The minimal memory bandwidth MB_{min} is 20M word/sec. It is applied when consecutive words are drawn from the same memory bank, which is accessed with the speed of 50 nsec ($MB_{min} = 1/(50 \cdot 10^{-9}) = 20M$ word/sec).

The data path between the main memory and the registers can be conceived as a single 64-bit pipeline involved in either reading or writing data from and to the memory. Since there is only one data port for data transfer, concurrent read and write are precluded. The length of this pipeline is 11 clock periods.

As was noted in ref. 14 the major deficiency of CRAY-1 is an insufficient data rate of only 80M word/sec which is used for maintaining a considerable arithmetic capability of 160M flop/sec (80 million floating-point multiplications and 80 million floating-point additions). To maintain this arithmetic speed requires the availability of three operands for each operation, giving the required $MB_R = 480M$ word/sec. Since $MB_D = 80M$ word/sec at best, CRAY-1 utilizes only 1/6 of the required bandwidth that supports its arithmetic power.

The CRAY-1 registers are divided into the following categories.

- Eight 24-bit address registers (A0–A7), otherwise called A-registers
- Eight 64-bit floating-point registers (S0–S7) for scalar operations (S-registers)
- Eight 64-bit floating-point registers (V0–V7) for vector operations (V-registers). Each vector register contains 64 data words.

Address registers A0–A7 are separated from the main memory by 64 buffer registers (B-registers: B00–B77), each of which is 24 bits long. The same type of buffering is performed for the scalar registers, which are connected with the memory with the use of 64 T-registers (T0–T77) each of which is 64 bits long.

The memory operates at the rate of one word per clock period t_0 with B, T, and V registers. A and S registers may have direct communication with the memory at the rate of one word per two clock periods or via buffer B or T registers that may communicate with A and S sets every clock period.

Vector processing is accomplished with the use of three floating-point arithmetic units (add, multiply, and reciprocal approximation) and three additional vector units for addition, logical operations, and shifting. All six units are segmented and can function concurrently. To overcome the limitation on the memory bandwidth in providing adequate operand rates, results from one vector operation stored in V registers can be used as input operands to another operation. This process is called *chaining*. It allows formation of arithmetic pipelines with more than one operation. The speed improvement achieved with chaining has been discussed earlier.

The next important feature of the CRAY-1 is pipelining of all vector operational units.

The three attributes of the CRAY-1 that account for its fast arithmetic performance are

- fast vector registers;
- pipelined functional units with parallel operation; and
- chaining.

These features allow CRAY-1 to achieve a very high processing rate in vector processing over data arrays. Another factor that contributes to fast performance is a short start-up time for pipelined units. Thus, for a series of similar operations, vector performance becomes more beneficial than a series of scalar operations for vectors containing five or more elements.[39]

The major restriction of CRAY-1 is a restricted memory bandwidth that cannot support the maximal arithmetic rate for memory–memory operations. However, memory interleaving can proceed over noncontiguous memory locations that can be separated by the permanent distance d (called stride): that is, interleaving in the CRAY-1 is more flexible than in the STAR-100, which allows only $d = 1$ (see ref. 2).

CRAY X-MP SERIES

The second generation of the CRAY architecture is CRAY X-MP, containing up to four processors of CRAY-1 type[40] (Fig. 1-51).

As can be seen, the following modifications are introduced: (a) central shared memory for data exchanges among separated uniprocessors; (b) inter-CPU for control in data exchanges; and (c) SSD for storing large data sets that are used repetitively, and the like.

The operating system of the CRAY X-MP can support independent processes at each of the CPU; multiprocessing of a single job performed by up to four processors; and multitasking of one or two programs that feature data dependencies.

The X-MP supercomputer offers as much as a 5-fold increase in speed

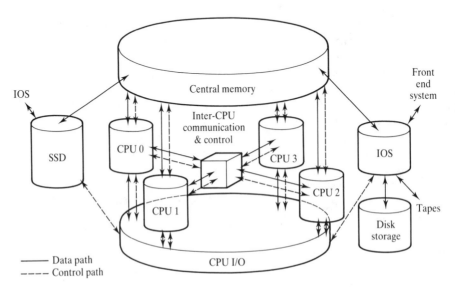

Figure 1-51. CRAY-X-MP supercomputer.

because of shorter clock period, higher memory bandwidth, and guaranteed chaining.

The third-generation CRAY-2 and CRAY-3 are provided with 4 and 16 processors, respectively.

Let us give more details of the CRAY X-MP/2 computer. It is a two-processor supercomputer with a 4M word memory that features 32-interleaving. The arithmetic portion of the machine repeats that of the CRAY-1.

A significant improvement of the CRAY X-MP/2 is an increased memory bandwidth in comparison with the CRAY-1, due to

- increase in the number of M words that can be accessed concurrently, and
- increasing index k of nonminimal interleaving; since $k = 32$, which allows partitioning of the memory into 32 memory modules, and $p = 4$ as in CRAY-1, then $m = 32/4 = 8$.

Thus, eight 64-bit words can be accessed in parallel with the rate of $t_0 = 9.5$ nsec, the processor clock period. This accounts for the maximal memory bandwidth, $MB_M = 880M$ word/sec.

INDUSTRIAL ARRAY SYSTEMS

As has been indicated, an array system is made of one control unit and multiple PEs under central program control. One array executes one instruction at a time over the vector of operands (Fig. 1-22). The idea of array computations is due to Unger.[41] The Unger paper is remarkable for its time because it not only suggests the architecture of future machines like Solomon,[42] Illiac-IV,[43] and DAP,[44] but also foresees the essential role of monolithic integrated circuitry in implementing any machine with so many components.

The industrial array processors fully comply with the division into the two categories (see p. 34):

- *Bit-parallel*, whereby each processor of the array processes a full word of each operand at a time. Most notable representatives of bit parallel arrays are the Illiac-IV and BSP
- *Bit-serial*, whereby each processor of the array processes one bit of a word at a time (STARAN, DAP, and MPP)

Industrial Bit-Parallel Array Systems

The most famous arrays of this group have been made by Burroughs. The first bit-parallel array designed (not produced) was the one named Solomon and proposed by Slotnick in 1962.[42] It was a 32×32 array of intercoupled processors with 4096 words of local storage.

A much more powerful machine based on the Solomon idea was the Illiac-IV, produced in 1972 by Burroughs.[43] The next array machine in this evolution was BSP produced by Burroughs in 1980, which overcame many

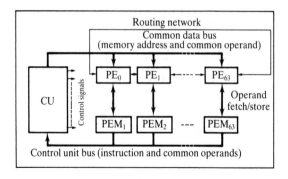

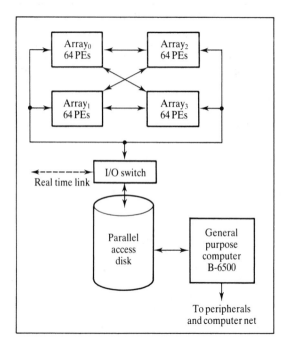

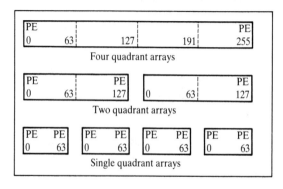

Figure 1-52. The Illiac-IV supercomputer.

drawbacks of Illiac-IV. The evolution is shown below:

Solomon (1962) → Illiac-IV (1972) → BSP (1980)

The Illiac-IV, although sharing the architectural idea of Solomon, was too advanced for the available technology and suffered from many difficulties arising from being the first in using bipolar monolithic technology on a massive scale (Fig. 1-52). Actually, only one configuration of 64 processors has ever been built.

Despite the difficulties, Illiac-IV was very effective in solving a large number of application problems. The principal difficulty of Illiac-IV was not the aggregate processor power available but the difficulty of maintaining a fast accessing rate for each PE that would have matched the fast rate of array processing. Each PE had direct access only to a 4096 word memory. To solve this problem, Burroughs undertook another machine, the BSP.

The BSP was an outcome of the Illiac-IV experience but was free from many of the difficulties. BSP took advantage of the VLSI circuitry. Also, the principal difference was that all parallel PEs were coupled to main memory not via a set of local banks but through the alignment network (Fig. 1-53).

Although the maximum throughput of BSP is only 50M flop/sec in comparison with 80–100M flop/sec possible for the Illiac-IV, the BSP can maintain a large percentage of its maximal throughput whereas the Illiac-IV as a rule worked with less than a quarter of its maximal power.[14] The major technical accomplishment of BSP was in its ability to maintain a continuous flow of operands for all its 16 processors. This was achieved by a relatively large random-access memory with up to 8M words backed by fast electronic file memory.

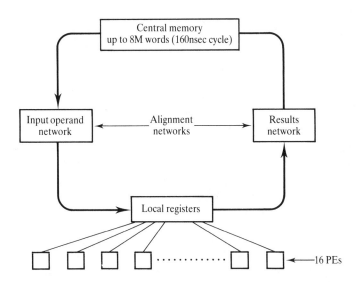

Figure 1-53. The BSP supercomputer.

Figure 1-53 shows how 16 PEs can access any part of central memory for input operands and results. The number of PEs was restricted to 16. The memory cycle is 160 nsec and most PE operations take 2 cycles.

The total executional loop is pipelined. This pipeline contains the following stages.

1. Read parallel memory for operands
2. Align operands with 16 arithmetic processors
3. Perform operation
4. Align results with destination memory units
5. Store results in parallel memory

Each stage requires a different number of clock periods, depending on the number of operands fetched and operations to be performed. Thus, the pipeline becomes asynchronous. Although the entire executional cycle is pipelined, the array PEs are concurrent—they work over operands in parallel and not as a pipeline.

The BSP uses 48-bit PEs of which 36 bits are assigned for the mantissa and 11 bits are assigned for exponents. The most interesting feature of BSP is its parallel memory consisting of 17 memory banks. Such a number of memories allows concurrent conflict-free access to all linear subarrays provided that the indexing increment between consecutive elements of a data vector is not a multiple of 17.

This memory organization was described in ref. 10. It is a particular case of a skewed storage scheme described on p. 37, when $m \neq N$, where m is the number of PEs and N is the number of MEs.

Example 18. Consider how the BSP memory organization works for the 4×4 array of 16 elements. Figure 1-54(a) gives the 4×4 matrix which elements a_{ij} are given with two addresses:

a. the a-address which shows the element position within this matrix when it is stored as a one-dimensional array;
b. the ij-address which gives its i and j locations in column i and row j.

According to this scheme, to provide a conflict-free access for rows, columns and backward diagonals of this matrix requires $N = 5$ memory modules, one module more than the number m of processors PE; that is $N = m + 1$ and N must be prime. The following addressing scheme is used for mapping this array onto the memory made of N MEs:

• the address μ of ME is defined as $\mu = a(\mathrm{mod}\, N)$, where a is its a-address
• the relative address r within each ME is defined as $r = \lfloor a/m \rfloor$, where m is the number of PEs and $\lfloor \; \rfloor$ is the integer smaller than or equal to a/N.

Using these formulae, we can map the 4×4 matrix of Figure 1-54(a) as shown in Figure 1-54(b). Consider, as an example, a conflict-free access of the row $(a_{21}, a_{22}, a_{23}, a_{24})$ of the matrix. Its a-addresses form the following **a** vector: $\mathbf{a} = (1, 5, 9, 13)$. Its μ addresses form the $\boldsymbol{\mu}$ vector: $\boldsymbol{\mu} = (1, 0, 4, 3)$, since $N = 5$

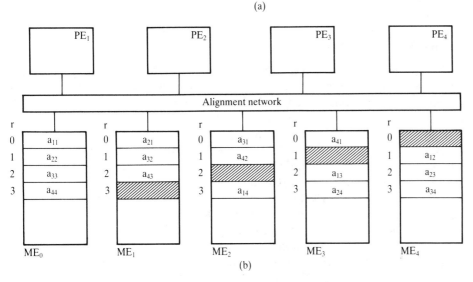

a-address	ij address	a address	ij address	a address	ij address	a address	ij address
0	a_{11}	4	a_{12}	8	a_{13}	12	a_{14}
1	a_{21}	5	a_{22}	9	a_{23}	13	a_{24}
2	a_{31}	6	a_{32}	10	a_{33}	14	a_{34}
3	a_{41}	7	a_{42}	11	a_{43}	15	a_{44}

(a)

(b)

Figure 1-54. The skewed storage technique used in the BSP. The table in (a) The 4-4 matrix array represented with the *a*- and *ij*-addresses.

and $1 \equiv 1 \pmod 5$, $5 \equiv 0 \pmod 5$, $9 = 5 + 4 \equiv 4 \pmod 5$ and $13 = 2 \cdot 5 + 3 \equiv 3 \pmod 5$. Its relative addresses form the **r** vector: $\mathbf{r} = (\lfloor 1/4 \rfloor, \lfloor 5/4 \rfloor, \lfloor 9/4 \rfloor, \lfloor 13/4 \rfloor) = (0, 1, 2, 3)$. The **μ** and **r** vectors are generated in the control processor and then sent component-wise to each PE_i. Each PE_i fetches an operand defined by μ_i and r_i addresses.

As follows from Figure 1-54(b), for the 4×4 matrix this memory scheme achieves conflict-free access of rows, columns, and backward diagonals, since all their elements are stored in different MEs. The forward diagonals are stored in a single ME, and their concurrent accessing therefore causes memory conflicts.

Industrial Bit-Serial Array Processors

In this section we discuss three such processors: STARAN, MPP, and DAP. Of these three, STARAN and MPP form an evolutionary family.

STARAN

The most famous bit-serial array processor is STARAN produced by Goodyear in 1972.[47] Figure 1-55 shows one module of STARAN, of which there are 32. All modules are attached to an external host computer. A basic module is 256 processors, each of which is of one bit long coupled to a 256×256 bit memory. The processor and memory modules are connected by the alignment network, called Flip-network. The function of the flip-network is to access 256 bits using the following types of accessing:

- bit slice;
- word slice mode; or
- a number of mixed modes (words and bits).

STARAN was a pioneering architecture that implemented the idea of associative search whereby at each clock period one word w stored in an associative memory (content-addressable memory) is fetched and compared with the key-word, k. If $k \neq w$, the next word is fetched. If $k = w$, search ends and the next step of an algorithm is performed (Fig. 1-56).

A peculiar feature of the STARAN architecture is its flip-network, which allows various types of permutations and shifts to be performed over bit slices or word slices during their accessing by 256 1-bit processors.

The memory of STARAN consists of 256 words, each of which is of 256 bits. It is connected with three 256-bit registers X, Y, and M via the flip-network (Fig. 1-57). The X and Y are the registers equipped with the Boolean logic, which implements 16 Boolean functions of two variables. These functions can be performed over the following operand pairs: $A * B$, where $A, B \in \{X, Y, W\}$, and X and Y are stored in X and Y registers and W is an outside word from one of the

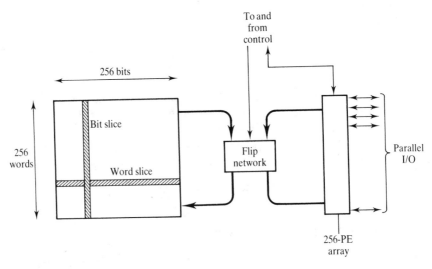

Figure 1-55. One STARAN module.

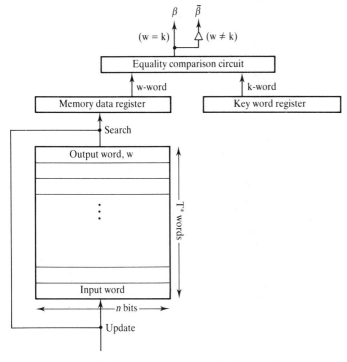

Figure 1-56. Basic algorithm of an associative search.

following destinations:

- memory;
- flip-network,
- processors, and so on.

M is the mask register, which allows selective activation of the $A_i * B_i$

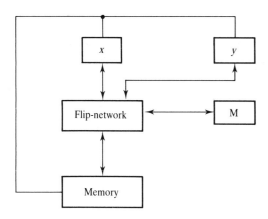

Figure 1-57. Interconnection of the STARAN memory with the flip-network.

operation depending on the content of its bit M_i. If $M_i = 1$, $A_i * B_i$ is activated. Otherwise, it is deactivated.

Similarly, X and Y registers can act as a mask for operations performed over other operand pairs. The flip-network allows a wide range of permutations over any of the words X, Y, W, and M or the results of their operations. The permutations performed are divided into the two categories: *flip permutations* and *shift permutations*.

Flip Permutations

Flip permutations are performed over 256 data lines with the use of eight control lines ($8 = \log_2 256$). Since through eight control lines it is possible to transfer 256 different control codes, the flip-network may perform 256 flip permutations PM_i, each identified with the control code CC_i ($i = 1, \ldots, 255$). The mapping for PM_i is defined as follows: Let $X_s(i)$, $Y_d(i)$ be, respectively, the source input and destination output data lines of the flip-network ($s, d = 0, \ldots, 255$). For permutation PM_i:

$$Y_d(i) = X_s(i) \oplus CC_i, \qquad \text{where } \oplus \text{ is mod-2 addition}$$

Example 19. Figure 1-58 shows the fiip-permutation defined by $CC_i = 5$ in the flip-network with eight data lines. The mapping is defined as follows: for $X_s = 0$, $Y_d = 0 + 5 = 5$; for $X_s = 1$, $Y_d = 1 + 5 = 4$, and so on.

Shift Permutations

Each flip permutation can be followed by a shift permutation. The flip-network implements $(n^2 + n + 2)/2$ shift permutations where $n = 8$. This includes the identity permutation (with no shift) and $n^2 + n/2$ different m-bit shifts to a set of 2^p data lines, where $0 \leq p \leq n$, and n is the number of control lines. All possible shifts of mod 2^p are thus implemented.

MASSIVELY PARALLEL PROCESSOR

The next bit-serial array processor in this evolution was the Goodyear Massive Parallel Processor announced in 1982. It consists of 128×128 single-bit PEs designed to operate in parallel on concurrent data streams.

PEs are coupled only to the nearest neighbors, since interconnection among PEs was difficult to implement. MPP is intended mostly for image processing.

The PEs are in the array unit (Fig. 1-59). Other major blocks of the

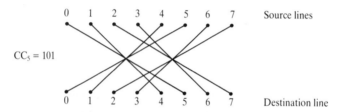

Figure 1-58. Flip permutation defined by $CC_i = 5$.

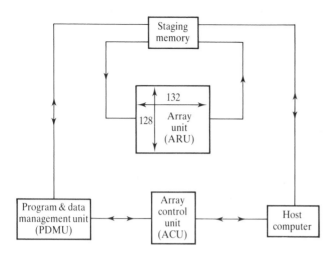

Figure 1-59. Block-diagram of the Goodyear MPP.

MPP are

- the array control unit;
- staging memory;
- program and data management units; and
- interface to a host computer.

The array control unit controls execution of the application program, the PEs array unit, and I/O operation. This allows concurrent array processing, scalar processing, and I/O operation.

The staging memory is used for two functions:

- reformatting data before they become suitable for array processing in 1-bit PEs; and
- buffering information between array and I/O.

Program and data management units can control the overall flow of programs and data in and out of the MPP. The program development software package for the MPP is also executed in the program and data management unit.

Much of the software development is written in FORTRAN. The host interface is based on selecting DEC VAX-11/780 as a host computer.

DISTRIBUTED ARRAY PROCESSOR OF THE ICL

DAP exemplifies the ICL approach to array processing, which balances computational power with the technology. The result is an inexpensive product that achieves a high performance/cost ratio. Essentially, DAP is 64 × 64 array of 1-bit PEs. The design of DAP began in 1974; its basic ideas are described in two major publications.[50,51]

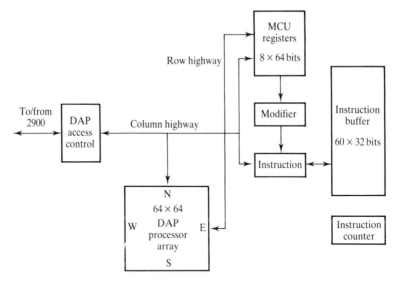

Figure 1-60. The, architecture of the DAP array processor.

The two major contributions of the DAP approach to the serial array processing are:

- Each 1-bit PE_{ij} of the DAP array located in row i and column j can be accessed from the master control registers (MCU) via two orthogonal 1-bit data paths: row highway and column highway (Fig. 1-60).
- The highly distributed and autonomous nature of processing realized in DAP is designed to emulate a memory module for an ICL mainframe computer.

DAP instructions are stored two per one memory word. For repeated execution they can be stored in the instruction buffer. Each PE is 1-bit; its diagram is shown in Figure 1-61. Each PE is connected with its four adjacent neighbors at N, S, W, and E directions. The instructions can operate over planar or cyclic PEs connected in the edges of rows and columns.

Instructions are executed in two phases: fetch and execute. Each of the phases takes the duration of one clock period, $T_0 = 200$ nsec. Since two instructions are fetched concurrently (inasmuch as they are packaged in one memory word), they are defined by one fetch cycle and two execute cycles ($3T_0$), giving the time per instruction as $1.5T_0$. However, this rate per instruction can be significantly improved if an instruction is not loose but appears in the scope of a special DO-loop implement. For this case, the first phase of each instruction will only be performed once during the first iteration of the DO.

During successive DO iterations, no instruction fetches are necessary, since all instructions are available in the control unit. The maximal length of the DO is

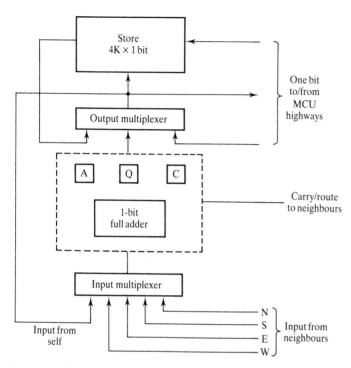

Figure 1-61. DAP 1-bit processor element.

60 instructions and DO can have up to 254 iterations. In the DO scope, the rate of instruction execution thus becomes higher and asymptotically approaches one instruction per T_0. Although the normal mode of processing is bit-serial over 4096 words, DAP can feature other parallel modes over fewer data words with larger bit sizes. These are shown below. They are described in ref. 14. Accordingly, DAP implements the following concurrent variable-word-size processing capabilities:

- 4096 1-bit words, or
- up to 1344 2-bit words, or
- up to 768 4-bit words, or
- up to 256 8-bit words, or
- up to 128 16-bit words, or
- 64 32-bit words.

PROTOTYPE ARCHITECTURES

The evolution of prototype architectures led to application of the innovative architectural techniques of adaptation and data flow to synchronous and asynchronous parallel systems,[52] resulting in

a. *Adaptable architectures,* conceived as
   • *reconfigurable systems* (reconfigurable arrays, pipelines, multicomputers/multiprocessors)
      • *Dynamic computer systems,* which perform a complete dynamic partitioning of the resources under program control into variable subsystems of different dedication (dynamic arrays, pipelines, multicomputers/multiprocessors)[6]
b. *Data-flow architectures* organized mostly as multiprocessors, since each instruction must have direct access to other nonlocal memories to deposit computational results it computes.[8] So far, no project has been announced whereby the data flow concept is implemented in pipeline and array systems, although some research efforts have been made in this direction.

Adaptable Architectures

In general, as was noted on p. 19 adaptable architectures attempt to obtain higher throughputs through dynamic adaptations to executing algorithms that are performed with the use of reconfiguration.[6] Therefore, their major rationale for performance improvement is to achieve a much better utilization of hardware resources than can be achieved in any nonreconfigurable (static) system that does not feature such extensive reconfiguration.

The consequence of such a match between architecture and algorithm is an additional speed-up achieved on the same resource. Also, adaptable architectures are amenable to LSI technology for the following reasons. LSI technology has introduced modularity as basic to the organization of a computer's architecture. All the latest industrial architectures are LSI modular in their designs: they cannot otherwise compete in the cost realities of modern LSI implementations. Each LSI module from which a supercomputer is assembled may be equipped with simple control circuits for software-controlled activation and deactivation of interconnections with other modules.

For instance, processor modules may be switched among several main memory modules, which may reduce the time required for processor–memory communication. Alternatively, one processor may reconfigure into several smaller-sized processors in an array-parallel system, increasing the size of the data vector processable by a single instruction. Finally, a modular architecture supports a complete dynamic redistribution of the available hardware by reconfiguring hardware resources into different numbers of variably sized computers, arrays, or pipelines, or mixed architectures that feature co-residence of several subsystems of various dedications formed dynamically under software control.[4,17] This allows the computer to adjust to the changeable number of information streams encountered in complex algorithms. Thus, a computer architecture assembled from LSI modules may adapt much more closely to the needs of the algorithm than was ever achieved in industrial supercomputing systems.

It is safe to predict that LSI technology will lead to a proliferation of adaptable architectures for supercomputers that can perform many new and cost-effective adaptations to algorithms that have never been attempted on traditional systems.[4] Furthermore, since LSI technology significantly reduces the cost and enhances the reliability of computer components, it makes feasible the design of reliable modular computer systems containing many more hardware resources than ever before. This should sharply increase the number of instruction and data streams that can be computed. Consequently, LSI technology has greatly influenced the emergence of *architectural adaptation*, and *enhanced computational prallelism* as powerful methods for increasing throughput. This encourages the creation of prototype supercomputers with throughputs greatly exceeding those of systems from previous generations. As a result, LSI technology is shifting the upper bound of computerization upwards.

Current Research Trends in Adaptable Architectures

Research in adaptable architectures is heading in the direction of furnishing them with new adaptations that improve the performance of the available resources. The objective of these adaptations is to increase throughput of supercomputing systems without increasing their complexity, since this is already extremely high.

The computational specifics of some complex real-time algorithms provide computer designers with some ways to increase throughput through architectural adaptations. These algorithms sometimes have portions (tasks) requiring different types of computation: multicomputer, array, or pipeline. For instance, a task may be characterized by a large number of parallel instruction streams with little interaction. This task could be computed by a multicomputer system with as many computers as instruction streams. Suppose that the next task of the algorithm employs a great deal of data parallelism—that is, each program instruction has to handle a data vector of large dimension. This task requires an array system. The next task may require increased speed, which can be accomplished through pipelining.

To process this algorithm in minimum time, it must be computed by three separate systems employing different types of architecture: multicomputer, array, and pipeline. Such a resource would be exceptionally complex, with each of its systems engaged in computation of one task only, and idle during the execution of the remaining tasks. To reduce this complexity, the supercomputing system should be provided with the ability to reconfigure its resources, via software, into different types of architecture: array, multicomputer, pipeline, or multiprocessor.

The performance of supersystems, however, depends not only on the types of adaptations that are implemented but also on the quality of each adaptation; namely, on how precise the match between the dynamically created architecture and the algorithm is sustained. For pipeline architectures, this means a minimization of dummy intervals created in the pipeline because of the disparity between the structure of the pipeline and of the algorithm. For arrays, the architecture must be capable of partitioning its resources into a variable number of concurrent arrays. Within each array it must be able to change the dimension of each data vector as well as the word size of each processor that computes one component of this vector.

For multiprocessors, optimization means reducing the time spent by any pair of resource units involved in communication; that is, one must construct fast, reconfigurable paths that transmit data words in parallel between any pair of resource units. For multicomputers, the architecture must provide fast parallel exchanges both between a pair of computers and between any pair of functional units from two different computers. Thus, the objectives for optimizing multiprocessors and multicomputers are similar and consist of creating fast reconfigurable busses that support parallel word exchanges between any pair of functional units, either from the same or from different computers.[4]

Data-Flow Architectures

Whereas the objective of adaptable architectures is to improve performance via a better utilization of resources achieved by various dynamic adaptations to algorithms, a data-flow architecture tries to achieve the same objective via dynamic formation of the data-flow graph of an executing program from the available hardware resources.

Data-flow graphs can be *static* or *dynamic*.[8] Static graphs cannot change during execution, so if one portion of a graph is called by several callers, all multiple copies of this portion are provided by the compiler for each caller. For dynamic graphs, connections with each node can change. If a called portion is used by several callers, it is stored in a separate location. Each caller fetches this location and creates a dedicated flow-graph that specifies connections of the called portion with all its destinations.

From this viewpoint, both architectures owe their improvement in performance to adaptation to algorithms. The differences between these adaptations are as follows.

A-D1. Task-level adaptations. For *adaptable architectures*, the hardware resources reconfigure at the level of tasks. Thus they conform to task needs.

A-D2. Release of redundant resources into additional computations. The redundant hardware resources are released into additional computations; that is, additional parallelism is obtained because of better utilization of resources.

D-D1. Instruction-level adaptations. For *data-flow architectures*, dynamic adaptation to an algorithm is extended to a much lower hardware level—the level of machine instructions. As many instructions are executed in parallel as are ready for computation, that is, whose operands are available.

D-D2. Non-release of redundant resources. For *data-flow architectures*, redundant resources not engaged in computations are idle and are not released into additional computations as is the case for adaptable architectures.

It remains to be seen which approach is better when viable prototype architectures are constructed and objective scientific experiments can be performed.

SURVEY OF PROJECTS IN ADAPTABLE AND DATA-FLOW ARCHITECTURES

This section will concern itself with a brief survey of the most representative projects in adaptable and data-flow architectures and succinct presentation of one adaptable and one data-flow prototype.

Projects in Adaptable Architectures

Adaptable-architecture projects are shown in Table 1-3, which illustrates their basic features. By no means is this table exhaustive; it merely illustrates some representatives that are either operable or sufficiently mature to suggest successful completion.

Basic features of these projects can be found in the major publications referenced in column 7, of Table 1-3.

Kartashev Dynamic Computer
The block of diagram of the Kartashev dynamic computer is shown in Fig. 1-38, described earlier on pp. 54–62. This architecture can form

- dynamic computers with selectable sizes (Fig. 1-13);
- dynamic arrays with variable number of processors and word sizes of each processor (Fig. 1-62);
- dynamic pipelines with variable number of stages and variable word sizes of each stage (Fig. 1-28);
- dynamic network configurations—trees, stars, and mixed—with variable characteristics.

Figure 1-11 shows one binary tree configuration that can be established instantaneously during the time of one logical operation. Each new computing structure can be formed with the use of one program instruction during the time not exceeding addition operation. This project is now operable.

Table 1-3. Survey of projects in adaptable architectures

Principal investigator(s)	Institution	Project name	Basic feature	Interconnection scheme	Major publication
1. Lax, Kalos, Gottlieb	NY Univ.	NYU Ultra-Computer Project	Reconfigurable multiprocessor with up to 512 PE	Shuffle (multistaged) interconnection	Gottlieb et al., "The NYU Ultracomputer—Designing an MIMD Shared Memory Parallel Computer," *IEEE Transactions on Computers*, Feb. 1983, Vol. C-32, No. 2, pp. 175–189.
2. Kuck, Lawrie, Davidson, Sameh	Univ. of Illinois	CEDAR	Collection of PEs and local MEs grouped into clusters connected to global memory through a shuffle network	Shuffle (multistaged) interconnection	D. Gajski et al., "CEDAR: A Large Multi-processor," *Computer Architecture News*, Vol. 11, No. 1, March 1983, pp. 7–11.
3. Kartashev, Kartashev	DCA, Inc.	DC Group	Dynamic architecture forming dynamic computers of various sizes and variable arrays, pipelines, multiprocessors, and mixed architectures	Cross-bar system and subsystem interconnection (single-staged)	S. P. Kartashev and S. I. Kartashev, "A Multicomputer System with Dynamic Architecture," *IEEE Transactions on Computers*, Oct. 1979, pp. 704–721.
4. Browne	Univ. of Texas–Austin	TRAC	Array computer with static reconfiguration	Banyan (multistaged) interconnection	Sejnowski et al., "An Overview of the Texas Reconfigurable Array Computer," 1980 Natl.

					Comp. Conf., *AFIPS Conf. Proc.*, Vol. 49, pp. 631–641.
5. Siegel	Purdue Univ.	PASM	Reconfigurable array and multiprocessor with 30 PE	Cube (multistaged) interconnection	Kuehn et al., "Design of a 1024-Processor PASM System," *Int. Conf. Parallel Processing*, Aug. 1985, pp. 232–235.
6. Bolt, Beranek, Newman	BBN Advanced Computers	Butterfly Multi-processor	A machine of 128 nodes interconnected via shuffle (butterfly) network. PEs are implemented via Motorola 68000 microprocessors; memory is managed by AMD-2901 bit slice processors. BBN is currently developing the next-generation prototype	Shuffle (multistaged) interconnection	G. E. Schmidt, "The Butterfly Parallel Processor," *Proc. 2nd Intl. Conf. on Supercomputing,* Vol. I, pp. 362–365, May 1987. International Supercomputing Institute, 1987.
7. Nosenchuck, Littman	Princeton Univ.	Navier–Stokes Computer (NSC)	Prototype NSC will consist of 128 nodes. It features nearest-neighbor interconnection. Each node is provided with dynamically reconfigurable pipeline connected with the interleaved memory	Nearest-neighbor interconnection	(Not known)

Code of state	Architectural configuration	Symbolic notation of the architecture
N_0	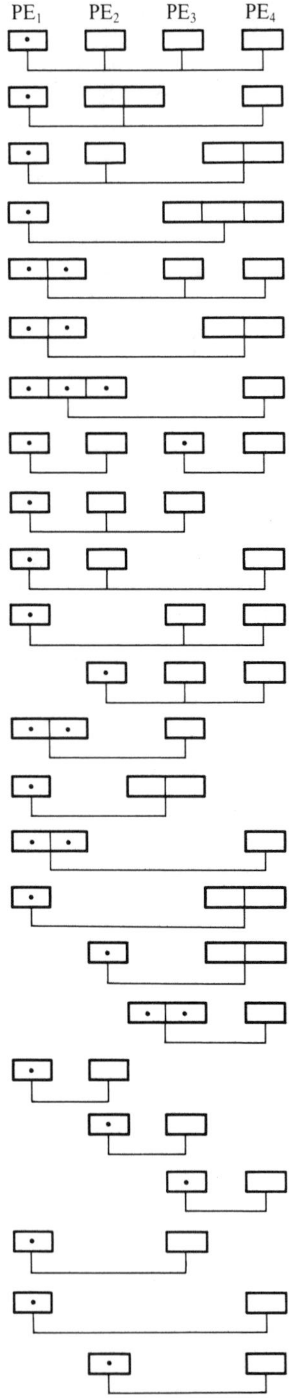	$PE_1 \rightarrow PE_2 \,.\, PE_3 \,.\, PE_4$
N_1		$PE_1 \rightarrow (PE_2, PE_3), PE_4$
N_2		$PE_1 \rightarrow PE_2, (PE_3 \,.\, PE_4)$
N_3		$PE_1 \rightarrow (PE_2 \,.\, PE_3 \,.\, PE_4)$
N_4		$(PE_1 \,.\, PE_2) \rightarrow PE_3 \,.\, PE_4$
N_5		$(PE_1 \,.\, PE_2) \rightarrow (PE_3 \,.\, PE_4)$
N_6		$(PE_1 \,.\, PE_2 \,.\, PE_3) \rightarrow PE_4$
N_7		$PE_1 \rightarrow PE_2 : PE_3 \rightarrow PE_4$
N_8		$PE_1 \rightarrow PE_2 \,.\, PE_3$
N_9		$PE_1 \rightarrow PE_2 \,.\, PE_4$
N_{10}		$PE_1 \rightarrow PE_3 \,.\, PE_4$
N_{11}		$PE_2 \rightarrow PE_3 \,.\, PE_4$
N_{12}		$(PE_1 \,.\, PE_2) \rightarrow PE_3$
N_{13}		$PE_1 \rightarrow (PE_2 \,.\, PE_3)$
N_{14}		$(PE_1 \,.\, PE_2) \rightarrow PE_4$
N_{15}		$PE_1 \rightarrow (PE_3 \,.\, PE_4)$
N_{16}		$PE_2 \rightarrow (PE_3 \,.\, PE_4)$
N_{17}		$(PE_2 \,.\, PE_3) \rightarrow PE_4$
N_{18}		$PE_1 \rightarrow PE_2$
N_{19}		$PE_2 \rightarrow PE_3$
N_{20}		$PE_3 \rightarrow PE_4$
N_{21}		$PE_1 \rightarrow PE_3$
N_{22}		$PE_1 \rightarrow PE_4$
		$PE_2 \rightarrow PE_4$

Figure 1-62. Array architectural states of dynamic architecture made of four PEs.

Survey of Data-Flow Projects

Data-flow projects are listed in Table 1-4. As can be seen, the difference between them is in (a) the use of static or dynamic program graphs; (b) data-flow language; and (c) interconnection networks.

Dennis Machine

Dennis and his coworkers proposed a data flow interconnection scheme whereby each instruction is equally accessible to result packets generated by any other instruction, regardless of where they reside in the machine.[53,54] Accordingly, their data-flow principle is implemented with the use of a multiprocessor architecture in which separate processors are interconnected with memories using interconnection networks. Dennis and Misunas use a multistaged network because it is less complex.

The conceptual diagram of this machine is shown in Figure 1-63. It consists of a large set of instruction cells, IC, each of which holds one activity template of a data-flow program graph.

Instruction cells are grouped into cell blocks, CB, shown in Figure 1-63. Each cell block is connected via an interconnection network with one of the processors $P_1, \ldots, P_k$. When an instruction is ready for computation, it is sent to one of the processors. The result of this operation is sent via the distribution network to CB again.

CONCLUSIONS

We have analyzed evolutionary trends in industrial and prototype architectures. We have seen that over the years, industrial supercomputer architectures took a conservative course in adopting new architectural ideas because of the economic realities faced by their designers.[1,2] These realities dictate that the architectures from different generations be architecturally compatible in order to preserve and enlarge the supercomputer software created and being created over decades. Thus, implementation of radical architectural ideas in successive generations becomes cost-prohibitive and the architectural design of a new supercomputer is much overshadowed by technological considerations.[2]

As has been demonstrated in this chapter, all major industrial supercomputer architectures rely on technology and accompanied concurrency and microminiaturization as the major factor of improving their speed, innovative architectural solutions remaining beyond their grasp.

The latter become the matter of concern for prototype architectures—a field now regarded as the true battleground for testing and implementing new architectural concepts for future supercomputers.

Prototype supercomputer architectures have clearly established two classes—adaptable (reconfigurable) and data-flow—which represent state-of-the-art activity.

Table 1-4. Survey of data-flow projects

Principal investigator(s)	Institution	Project name, system name	Basic feature	Language used	Interconnection scheme	Major and easily accessible publications
1. Compte, Syre, Hifdi	Center for Studies & Research, Toulouse, France (CERT)	Lau (completed in 1979)	Static flow graph	Original data flow language	Ring interconnection scheme	Syre, Compte, and Hifdi, "Pipelining, Parallelism and Asynchronism in LAU System," *Proceedings of the 1977 International Conference on Parallel Processing*, pp. 87–92.
2. Dennis	MIT, USA	MIT-Dennis	Static flow graph	VAL	Multistaged interconnection network	Dennis, "Data-Flow Supercomputers," *Computer*, Nov. 1980, pp. 48–56.
3. Arvind, Thomas	MIT, USA	MIT-Arvind	Static flow graph	ID	Packet-switching	Arvind and Gostelow, "The U-Interpreter," *Computer*, Feb. 1982, pp. 42–49.
4. Guard, Watson	Univ. of Manchester, UK	Manchester-Guard (operational since 1982)	Static flow graph	Graph-based assembler	Ring structure	Watson and Guard, "A Practical Data-Flow Computer," *Computer*, Feb. 1982, pp. 51–57.
5. Davis	Univ. of Utah	Utah-Davis	Dynamic flow graph	High-level graphical language	Tree interconnecton	Davis and Keller, "Data-Flow Program Graphs," *Computer*, Feb. 1982, pp. 26–41.
6. Keller, Lindstrom	Univ. of Utah	Utah-Keller	Demand-driven execution, model, dynamic data-flow graph	Graphic and textual language	Not known	Keller, Lindstrom, and Patil, "A Loosely-Coupled Applicative Multi-Processing System," Proceedings of the 1979 National Computer Conference, *AFIPS Conference Proceedings*, June 1979, pp. 613–622.

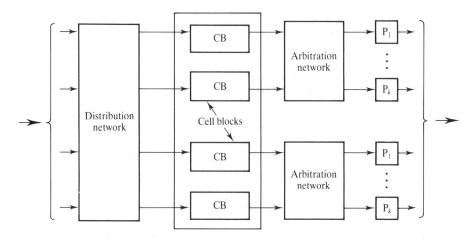

Figure 1-63. Dennis cell block architecture.

Adaptable Architectures

The feasibility of adaptable architectures is due to the LSI technology which gave birth to new modular architectures with complexity ranging from one or several LSI modules used to assemble a microcomputer to the thousands of LSI modules that are to be included into a powerful parallel system (supercomputing system).

Thus, technological advances in the 1970s have given a new momentum to research into and development of new architectures for supercomputing systems. These architectures are capable of reconfiguring the available resources into variably sized computers (processors); different types of architectures (array, pipeline, multicomputer, or multiprocessor); processors with selectable instruction sets; etc. They allow the creation of supercomputing systems with enormous throughput that maintain a high level of reliability.

New adaptation properties exhibited by these architectures will lengthen the life cycles of supercomputing systems, since they allow the attainment of higher throughputs from the available resources. This is an extremely important goal in supercomputing system design inasmuch as the cost of these systems is exceedingly high.

The appearance of supercomputing systems with adaptable architectures requires the creation of adaptation systems conceived as the software that performs preprocessing of algorithms and determines the best architectures for their execution. Research on adaptation systems may become a milestone in the computer sciences, as happened in the past with operating systems, whose appearance in the 1960s was caused by creation of parallel systems.

Data-Flow Architectures

What are the prospects for data-flow supercomputers? Machines based on the concepts we have presented are being built today. A machine having up to 512 processing elements or cell blocks seems feasible. For example, a 4×4 router for packets, each sent as a series of 8-bit bytes, could be fabricated as a 100-pin LSI device, and fewer than one thousand of these devices could interconnect 512 processing elements or cell blocks. If each processing unit could operate at two million instructions per second, the goal of a billion instructions per second would be achieved.[8]

Yet there are problems to be solved and issues to be addressed. It is difficult to see how data-flow computers could support programs written in FORTRAN without restrictions on and careful tailoring of the code. Study is just beginning on applicative languages like Val and ID. These promise solutions to the problems of mapping high-level programs into machine-level programs that effectively utilize machine resources, but much remains to be done. Creative research is needed to handle data structures in a manner consistent with the principles of data-flow computation. These are among the problems under study in the most advanced data-flow projects.[8,57]

Another major problem of data-flow computing that received prominent attention is gross underutilization of resources, otherwise referred to as the resource waste.[56,57] As was shown in ref. 56, for realistic programs, the actual resources used in data-flow computations become much smaller than the entire resources complexity of a data-flow supercomputer, leading to a considerable resource waste. Also, fundamentally, data-flow computing as an architectural concept creates a significant time overhead caused by

1. the necessity to control movement of highly distributed data items rather than that of program instructions used conventionally;
2. complexity of allocation algorithms for large data structures because of the requirement created dynamically to take into account the locality of both instruction and data items that must be accessed;
3. excessive tag manipulation during each data re-entry and exit to and from a program loop;
4. fine granularity of instruction parallelism.

Prototypes of sufficient power that are likely to be available will provide excellent research opportunities for alleviating all of these problems.

REFERENCES

1. Steiner, K. (1985). "Supercomputer design challenges," *Proceedings First International Conference on Supercomputing Systems*, pp. 3–7. International Supercomputing Institute, St. Petersburg, Fla.

2. Lincoln, N. R. (1982). "Technology and design trade-offs in the creation of a modern supercomputer," *IEEE Trans. Computers*, Vol. C-31, No. 5, pp. 349–363.

3. Matick, R. E. (1975). "Memory and storage," In *Introduction to Computer Architecture*, pp. 175–247. SRA Publishing House, Chicago.

4. Kartashev, S. P., S. I. Kartashev, and C. R. Vick (1982). "Historic progress in architectures for computers and systems," In *LSI Modular Computer Systems, Vol. 1*, (ed. S. P. Kartashev and S. I. Kartashev), pp. 3–94. Designing and Programming Modern Computer Systems Series. Prentice-Hall, Englewood Cliffs, N.J.

5. Kartashev, S. P. and S. I. Kartashev (1986). "Data exchange optimization in reconfigurable binary trees," *IEEE Trans. Computers,* Vol. C-35, No. 3, pp. 257–274.

6. Kartashev, S. P., S. I. Kartashev, and C. R. Vick (1980). "Adaptable architectures for supercomputers," *Computer,* Vol. 13, No. 11, pp. 17–37.

7. Kartashev, S. I. and S. P. Kartashev (1979). "A multicomputer system with dynamic architecture," *IEEE Trans. Computers,* Vol. C-28, No. 10, pp. 704–721.

8. Dennis, J. B. (1980). "Data flow supercomputers," *Computer,* Vol. 13, No. 11, pp. 48–57.

9. Barnes, G., R. M. Brown, M. Kato, D. J. Kuck, D. L. Slotnick, and R. A. Stokes (1968). "The Illiac-IV computer," *IEEE Trans. Computers,* Vol. C-17, No. 8, pp. 746–757.

10. Budnik, P. and D. J. Kuck (1971). "The organization and use of parallel memories," *IEEE Trans. Computers,* Vol. C-20, pp. 1566–1569.

11. Shapiro, H. D. (1978). "Theoretical limitation on the efficient use of parallel memories," *IEEE Trans. Computers,* Vol. C-27, pp. 421–428.

12. Lawrie, D. (1975). "Access and alignment of data in array processor," *IEEE Trans. Computers,* Vol. C-24, pp. 1145–1155.

13. "CRAY-1 computer system," *1976 Reference Manual,* CRAY Research, Inc., Publication 2240004.

14. Hockney, R. W. and C. R. Jesshope (1981). *Parallel Computers: Architecture, Programming and Algorithms,* Adam Hilger, Bristol, U.K.

15. Kartashev, S. P. and S. I. Kartashev (1981). "Adaptable pipeline system with dynamic architecture," *Proceedings of the National Computer Conference,* pp. 111–123. AFIPS Press, Montvale, N.J.

16. Kartashev, S. P. and S. I. Kartashev (1984). Memory allocations for multiprocessor systems that incorporate content addressable memories," *IEEE Trans. Computers,* Vol. C-33, No. 1, pp. 28–45.

17. Kartashev, S. I. and S. P. Kartashev (1978). "Dynamic architectures: Problems and solutions," *Computer,* Vol. 11, No. 7, pp. 26–40.

18. Kartashev, S. P. and S. I. Kartashev (1987). "Analysis and synthesis of dynamic multicomputer networks that reconfigure into rings, trees, and stars," *IEEE Trans. Computers,* Vol. C-36, No. 7, pp. 823–845.

19. Watson, W. J. (1972). "The TI ASC—a highly modular and flexible supercomputer architecture," *AFIPS 1972 Fall Joint Computer Conf.,* Vol. 41, pp. 221–228. AFIPS Press, Montvale, N.J.

20. Ibbett, R. N. and P. C. Capon (1978). "The development of the MU5 computer system," *Commun. ACM,* Vol. 21, No. 1, pp. 13–24.

21. Thomasian, A. and A. Avizienis (1976). "A design study of shared-resource computer system," *Proceedings Third Annual International Symp. Computer Architecture,* pp. 105–111.

22. Bell, C. Gordon (1971). *Computer Structures: Readings and Examples.* McGraw-Hill, New York.

23. Davies, D. W., K. A. Bartlett, R. A. Scantlebury, and P. T. Wilkinson (1967). "A digital communication network for computers giving rapid response at remote terminals," *ACM Symposium on Operating System Principles,* Gatlinburg, Tenn.

24. Robertson, J. E. (1958). "A new class of digital division methods," *IRE Trans.,* Vol. EC-7, No. 3, pp. 218–222.

25. Segal, R. J. and H. P. Guerber (1961). "Four advanced computers—key to Air Force digital data communication system," *Proc. AFIPS Eastern Joint Computer Conf.,* Vol. 20, pp. 264–278. AFIPS Press, Montvale, N.J.

26. Davis, R. G. and S. Zucker (1971). "Structure of a multiprocessor using microprogrammable building blocks," *Proceedings National Aerospace Electronics Conference,* pp. 186–200. IEEE Press, Dayton, Ohio.

27. Davis, R. L., S. Zucker, and C. M. Campbell (1972). "The building block approach to multiprocessing," *AFIPS 1972 Spring Joint Computer Conf.*, pp. 685–703. AFIPS Press, Montvale, N.J.

28. Reigel, E. W., D. A. Fisher, and V. Faber (1972). "The interpreter—A microprogrammable processor," *AFIPS Conf. Proc.*, Vol. 40, pp. 705–723. AFIPS Press, Montvale, N.J.

29. Enslow, Jr., P. H. (1977). "Multiprocessor organization—A survey," *ACM Comput. Surveys*, Vol. 9, No. 1, pp. 103–129.

30. Enslow, Jr., P. H. (Ed) (1974). *Multiprocessors and Parallel Processing*, Wiley, New York.

31. Swan, R. J., S. H. Fuller, and D. P. Siewiorek (1977). "CM—A modular, multimicroprocessor," *AFIPS Conf. Proc.*, Vol. 46, pp. 637–643. AFIPS Press, Montvale, N.J.

32. Swan, R. J., A. Bechtolsheim, K. Lai, and J. Ousterhout (1977). "The implementation of the CM multimicroprocessor," *AFIPS Conf. Proc.*, Vol. 46, pp. 645–655. AFIPS Press, Montvale, N.J.

33. Pariser, J. J. and H. E. Maurer (1969). "Implementation of the NASA modular computer with LSI functional characters," *AFIPS Conf. Proc.*, Vol. 35, pp. 231–245. AFIPS Press, Montvale, N.J.

34. Anderson, G. A. and E. D. Jensen (1975). "Computer interconnection structures, taxonomy, characteristics and examples," *ACM Comput. Surveys*, Vol. 7, No. 4, pp. 197–213.

35. Baer, J. L. (1976). "Multiprocessing systems," *IEEE Trans. Computers*, Vol. C-25, pp. 1271–1277.

36. Bloch, E. (1959). "The engineering design of the STRETCH computer," *Proc. Eastern Joint Computer Conference, 1959*, pp. 48–59.

37. *ETA Systems* (1986). Vol. 2, No 2. ETA Systems, St. Paul, Minn.

38. *CRAY-1 Hardware Reference Manual*, No. 2240004, Rev. E., 1980.

39. Zakharov, V. (1984). "Parallelism and array processing," *IEEE Trans. Computers*, Vol. C-33, No. 1, pp. 45–79.

40. CRAY Research, Inc. (1984). *The CRAY X-MP Series of Computer Systems*. Technical Brochure. Aug.

41. Unger, S. H. (1958). "A computer oriented towards spatial problems," *Proc. IRE*, Vol. 46, pp. 1744–1750.

42. Slotnick, D. L., W. C. Borck, and R. C. McReynolds (1962). "The Solomon computer," *Proc. AFIPS FJCC*, Vol. 22, pp. 97–107.

43. Barnes, G. H., R. M. Brown, M. Kato, D. J. Kuck, D. L. Slotnick, and R. A. Stokes (1968). "The Illiac-IV computer," *IEEE Trans. Computers*, Vol. C-17, pp. 746–757.

44. Reddaway, S. F. (1973). "DAP—A distributed array processor," *Proceedings First Annual Symposium on Computer Architecture*, Fla, pp. 61–65.

45. Kuck, D. J. and R. A. Stokes (1982). "The Burroughs scientific processor," *IEEE Trans. Computers*, Vol. C-31, No. 5, pp. 363–377.

46. Budni, K. P. and D. J. Kuck (1971). "The organization and the use of parallel memories," *IEEE Trans. Computers*, Vol. C-20, pp. 1566–1569.

47. Batcher, K. E. (1972). "Flexible parallel processing and STARAN," *Proc. WESCON Technical Papers*, Vol. 16, pp. 1–3.

48. Batcher, K. E. (1982). "Bit-serial parallel processing systems," *IEEE Trans. Computers*, Vol. C-31, No. 5, pp. 377–385.

49. Batcher, K. E. (1976). "The flip network in STARAN," *Proceedings 1976 International Conference on Parallel Processing*. IEEE Computer Society, Long Beach, Calif.

50. Reddaway, S. F. (1973). "DAP—A distributed array processor," *First Annual Symposium on Computer Architecture*, Fla.

51. Reddaway, S. F. (1979). "The DAP approach," *Infotech State of the Art Report*: *Supercomputers,* Vol. 2, (ed. C. R. Jesshope and R. W. Hockney), pp. 311–329.

52. Kartashev, S. P. and S. I. Kartashev (1980). "Supersystems for the 80's: Guest Editors' Introduction," *Computer,* Vol. 13, No. 11, pp. 11–17.

53. Dennis, J. B. and D. P. Misunas (1975). "A preliminary architecture for a basic data-flow processor," *Proceedings Second Annual Symposium Computer Architecture,* Houston, Tex., pp. 126–132.

54. Dennis, J. B., C. K. C. Leung, and D. P. Misunas (1979). "A High Parallel Processor Using a Data Flow Machine Language." Laboratory for Computer Science, MIT, CSG, 134-1, June 1979, p. 33.

55. Kartashev, S. I. and S. P. Kartashev (1982). "A distributed operating system for a powerful system with dynamic architecture," *The 1982 National Computer Conference, AFIPS Proceedings,* pp. 105–116. AFIPS Press, Montvale, N.J.

56. Gaiski, D. D., D. A. Padua, D. J. Kuck, and R. H. Kuhn (1982). "A second opinion on data flow machines and languages, *Computer,* Vol. 15, No. 2, pp. 58–69.

57. Veen, A. H. (1986). "Dataflow machine architecture," *ACM Comput. Surveys,* Vol. 18, No. 4, pp. 365–398.

2

DESIGNING AND PROGRAMMING THE CHoPP SUPERCOMPUTER

Theodore E. Mankovich, Leonard Allen Cohn, Val Popescu, Herbert Sullivan, Bruce D. Lightner, Thomas M. McWilliams, and Theodore R. Bashkow

INTRODUCTION

Until quite recently, the commercially available general-purpose digital computer had sufficient speed to satisfy most users' needs. However, the requirements of certain scientific users, especially the large government laboratories such as Los Alamos, Lawrence Livermore, and so on, were not met by these machines. This led to the development of specialized pipelined computers (vector processors) that were capable of meeting some of these demands. However, these specialized designs only performed well when the problems led to certain types of computations. Thus, if a computation contains large numbers of long data vectors upon which matrix or vector operations were performed, the vector machines have dazzling speeds—approaching their peak performance potential. However, a relatively minor dilution of these special data types causes a severe degradation in performance. In 1975 Herb Sullivan and Ted Bashkow at Columbia University began a research study on the possibility of designing a general-purpose super high-speed computer, whose performance would not degrade in this manner. Their aim was to develop a computer that would achieve high performance if there was sufficient parallelism in the problem to be solved, regardless of the specific form that it took. This effort, known as the CHoPP project, culminated in the CHoPP 1 computer. (CHoPP is an acronym for Columbia Homogeneous Parallel Processor.) This is a machine comprising a multiplicity of nodes that are connected together. Each node has a number of functional units (processing units), which operate in parallel. The nodes share a common memory space.

In order to use such a machine, the problem to be solved must be broken down into component parts (tasks) that can be solved simultaneously.

It is well known that there are difficulties in using such a machine.

1. Since all data and programs are in a common memory, when more than one node attempts to access the same data or the same instruction, there is memory contention to be resolved.

2. Any demand by a processor for memory information suffers a delay, since the request must traverse the interconnection network to get to memory and again traverse it to return the information. This memory latency can degrade performance if not overcome.

3. Given one node may require information supplied by a different node (and in fact must do so if they are cooperating), how can these requesters and suppliers be synchronized so that, for example, data is not read before it is written?

4. How are the various tasks to be assigned to the various nodes? How are they scheduled?

5. If the problem has a large number of tasks, then clearly it can be run effectively and speedily on a number of nodes (large-scale granularity). What if the problem has only few tasks, or only one? Then the few or single task must be run very fast itself: one must exploit small-scale granularity.

The next section explains how the CHoPP 1 attacks these problems.

In the design and development of a machine there is a natural desire to predict its performance. This is a difficult problem. In principle, for a general-purpose computer, one would need to predict its performance over every possible program. The compromise that was used by the CHoPP Computer Corporation was to focus the efforts on the Livermore Loops bench marks, which, though limited, give some insight into the structure of at least some types of scientific computation. The Loops were analyzed in order to exhibit their data dependency structure and then were hand-coded in CHoPP machine language. Because a single superinstruction is executed in one clock time, an analysis of the hand-coded loops gives fairly good estimates of machine performance. The details are given in a later section.

Since the CHoPP 1 is a very innovative design, not only in its internal logical structure, but in its packaging, there was considerable initial discussion as to the design tools to be used. Not only was the machine to be designed, it needed to be simulated to insure the validity of the design. To reduce some of the complexity, it was decided initially to design and build a "demonstration unit," which is basically a CHoPP node without all of the circuitry needed to interface to the interconnection network. The Valid Logic Systems SCALD system was chosen as the computer-aided design system. The utilization of this system in designing the demonstration unit will be described.

CHoPP PRINCIPLES OF OPERATION

The CHoPP computer is a general-purpose high-performance computer, suitable for any computationally intensive application. Two innovative architectural mechanisms are employed to enable the highest performance in a general-purpose environment. Within a processing node, nine functional units can issue and can complete nine instructions every clock period to provide high sequential speed. In addition, multiple processing nodes are configured sharing a common conflict-free memory and employing fast task-switching hardware to provide high parallel task speed. (In this discussion, a single instruction thread controlled by a single program counter with its own register sets is known as a task. A more detailed definition is given later.) With these two complementary mechanisms, both the sequential and parallel code within a program achieve high performance.

In previous high-performance computers, the architecture increased computational speed by arranging multiple functional units in one or more pipelines controled by scoreboard-type mechanisms or by vector instructions. The goal of such architectures has been to enable the issuing of one instruction for every clock cycle. During vector operations and with certain code sequences, this goal is achieved. However, at the start and end of vector operations and generally at branch instructions, the sequence of instructions flowing through the pipe is broken. During these breaks, fewer than one instruction per clock cycle is issued. Only when the pipeline again is full is one instruction per clock cycle achieved. With these breaks, a performance somewhat less than one instruction per clock is achieved. For these computers, software can push the performance toward the goal by increasing the length and proportion of vector operations, and by suitable arrangement of sequential instructions to minimize breaks. However, even with this software tuning, the performance falls short of the goal of one instruction per clock cycle. As a further architectural aid, the manufacturers of these computers are adding multiple computing units with some shared storage to permit more than one processor to work on the same problem.

It is generally agreed that higher performance can be achieved only through the exploitation of parallelism. One currently popular approach to accomplishing this is by interconnecting a great number of microprocessors in an interesting scheme like an n-cube. Unfortunately, when the problem presents little or no properly structured opportunity for concurrent execution, the performance of these multi-micro architectures falls drastically. The overall performance then becomes dominated by this "sequential" portion of the problem that is executed relatively slowly.

The CHoPP philosophy is to provide high performance on all aspects of general-purpose problems. Architectural balance is the key to delivering high performance. In the environment of general-purpose computationally intensive programs, both parallel and sequential execution must be fast. And within the parallel execution, both large-granularity parallelism and small-granularity parallelism must be supported. The CHoPP architecture achieves this balance. It delivers high sequential performance by issuing multiple instructions on each clock cycle, by having zero-delay branch instructions, and by having very fast execution of individual computational instructions. It gives high parallel performance by having multiple processors sharing a conflict-free memory and by having very fast task context switching hardware. The conflict-free memory eliminates memory contention problems and the fast task switching permits execution of even small-granularity tasks without system overhead becoming significant. The following architectural mechanisms contribute to the architectural balance of the CHoPP machine.

- Issuing of up to nine instructions per computing node every clock.
- RISC-type instructions controlling each of the nine functional units.
- Each functional unit takes only a single clock to complete any of its operations.
- Special instruction-fetch hardware prevents branch instructions from causing any break in the pipeline. The instruction following the branch is ready for execution regardless of which way the branch goes.
- A very short pipeline minimizes the pipeline breaks caused by the computing node switching between parallel tasks. When another task is ready for execution (up to 63 per processing node may be ready), only three clocks are needed both to save the state of the present task and to begin the execution of the other task.
- Prioritized queuing and scheduling of parallel tasks and the distribution of tasks among the nodes are handled by specialized fast task-management hardware without software intervention.
- Synchronization is performed using shared conflict-free memory. Suspension and readying of parallel tasks, owing to the unavailability of synchronization data or the presence of a waiting task when synchronization data becomes available, is handled by fast task-management hardware without software intervention.
- The computational synchronization operations such as Fetch and Add are executed within the conflict-free memory network to prevent a sequential bottleneck from many parallel tasks simultaneously executing these operations.

The remainder of the section presents a detailed overview of the unique features of the CHoPP architecture as seen by the user. Illustrating the features from the users' viewpoint gives the reader an appreciation of how the CHoPP architecture can be used to give both high sequential performance and high parallel performance. The explanation of the operation and control of the multiple functional units demonstrates how high sequential speed is achieved. The paragraph on the task defines the CHoPP concept of the task and shows how special task-handling and synchronization hardware enables high parallel performance on both small- and large-granularity tasks. Though space does not permit the detailed examination of the memory protection and job control features, they are mentioned to emphasize the fact that the CHoPP architecture provides all the mechanisms necessary to fit the CHoPP into the general-purpose high-performance computer environment.

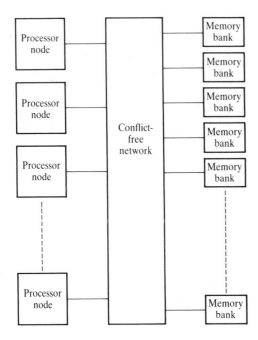

Figure 2-1. CHoPP is a shared-memory MIMD machine.

Functional Block Diagram

CHoPP is configured as 4, 8, or 16 computing nodes (hereafter referred to as nodes) sharing a common conflict-free memory as shown in Figure 2-1. It is an MIMD (**m**ultiple **i**nstruction stream, **m**ultiple **d**ata) machine executing code and using data entirely from the shared memory. I/O paths are associated with each node and have a direct path to the shared memory.

The Computing Node

Figure 2-2 illustrates the basic structure of a computing node. All of the major functional units are illustrated with their data paths. The functional units operate on the contents of registers to produce a result to be stored in a register and/or sent to memory. They also compute addresses in order to send a memory request to the memory request unit. Both load and store type instructions result in a response from memory that is routed by the memory response unit. Instructions are fetched from the instruction cache. If the cache does not contain the requested instruction, a request is sent to the memory request unit and instruction execution is temporarily suspended. When the request is filled, the instruction is routed by the memory response unit to the instruction cache and execution resumes.

The task manager monitors the progress of the functional units. If an instruction fault (divide by zero, illegal opcode, etc.), hardware fault (memory

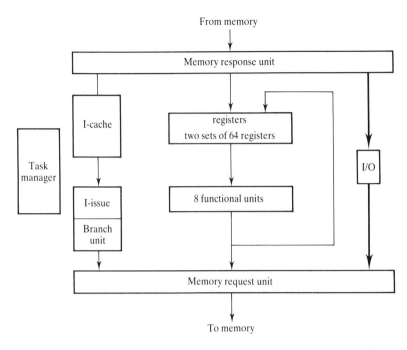

Figure 2-2. CHoPP processing node.

parity), or synchronization fault (data unavailable) occurs, the task manager causes the executing task to be suspended and starts up the highest priority task that is ready to run. In addition, the task manager supports preemptive scheduling. If a task with a higher priority than the running task becomes ready, the task manager causes the executing task to be suspended and starts the higher-priority task running.

External I/O devices generate requests directly to the memory request unit. Input data from external devices flows through the memory request unit. Output data is routed through the memory response unit.

Interaction of Functional Units and Registers

Figure 2-3 shows a more detailed view of the interaction of the nine functional units with the registers. The figure is the view of the registers and functional units as seen by a single instruction thread. Instructions are fetched and executed according to the program counter, which is normally incremented by 1 unless there is a branch taken. The registers are divided into two sets of 64 (64-bit) registers; each set is served by four functional units. The address register set is used in address calculation and the computational register set is used to hold computational results. Calculations performed in the functional units can cause

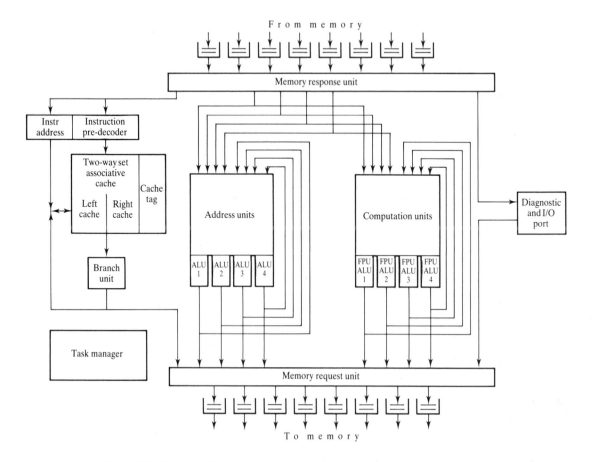

Figure 2-3. Functional units and registers.

the setting of the condition code registers, which are then available fo. testing by the branch functional unit.

The operations performed by the nine functional units are controlled by a 256-bit wide superinstruction. (In the remainder of this chapter "superinstruction" refers to the 256 bits that are executed by the nine functional units on each clock; "instruction parcel" refers to the bits that are used to control one of the nine functional units. Wherever it is unambiguous, the word "instruction" can be used to refer to either of these.) It is this superinstruction that is fetched and executed on each clock cycle. The 256 bits of the superinstruction are divided into nine instruction parcels, one for each functional unit. Figure 2-4 shows the layout of the superinstruction. The leftmost parcel controls the single branch functional unit. The next four parcels are instructions for the four address functional units

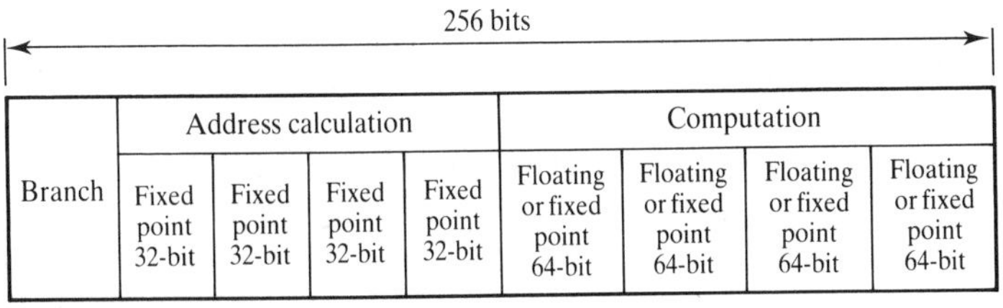

| | 256 bits | | | | | | | |

	Address calculation				Computation			
Branch	Fixed point 32-bit	Fixed point 32-bit	Fixed point 32-bit	Fixed point 32-bit	Floating or fixed point 64-bit	Floating or fixed point 64-bit	Floating or fixed point 64-bit	Floating or fixed point 64-bit

Superinstruction format

Figure 2-4. Layout of superinstruction.

(address units). The final four parcels are instructions for the four computational functional units (computational units).

At each clock, one superinstruction is executed; that is, four address calculations are made, four computational calculations are made, and a branch may be taken. Thus, nine operations (conventional instructions) are executed on each clock.

The instruction parcels for the nine functional units are very much like the instructions for a standard RISC architecture. The branch unit executes branch instructions. The address units are restricted to integer and logical address arithmetic. The computational units can perform floating-point operations as well as integer and logical operations. The total instruction set for these parcels can be subdivided into five types of instructions.

- *Register-to-register computational instructions.* One or two operands are fetched from registers and the result is stored in a third register.
- *Load and store memory reference instructions.* A load instruction uses an address computed by an address unit to send a request to the memory request unit to load a datum into either an address register or a computational register. A store instruction sends an address computed by an address unit and a datum from either an address unit or a computational unit to the memory request unit for storage in memory.
- *Branch instructions.* The branch unit tests the contents of one or both of the two condition-code registers and updates the program counter accordingly.
- *Task manager control instructions.* The task manager contains a local store of state and control information related to the tasks in a node. These instructions manipulate the data in the local store. Most of these instructions are privileged.
- *Intertask synchronization instructions.* To the functional units, synchronization instructions operate like load and store instructions. Addresses are calculated in the address units and a datum or request for datum is sent to the memory request unit. The actual synchronizing operations are accomplished mostly in memory and the task manager.

Each of the register sets contains 64 registers, each register being 64 bits wide. Each register set is available to four functional units. The register set is shared totally by the four functional units. All registers are available to them for operands or results on every superinstruction. This means that, in the same cycle, four functional units can use the same register for operands. They may also use identical registers for results. Multiple use of the same results register in the same superinstruction causes the contents of that register to be the logical OR of the data from the multiple functional units.

Some of the instructions for the address and computational units may optionally set one of the two condition-code registers as a result of their operation. The condition codes may then be tested by the branch unit to determine whether a branch should be taken. Once a condition code is set, it remains set until it is again set by another instruction. The condition code is available for testing by a branch instruction in the superinstruction following the superinstruction containing the setting parcel.

The single branch unit controls the altering of the program counter for the superinstructions. Branch instructions test one or both of the two condition-code registers and branch accordingly. The branch address is either given by a program counter relative immediate operand in the branch parcel of the superinstruction or is given by the contents of a register. When it is a program counter relative branch, the processor anticipates the branch and always has the target super-instruction available for execution. This branching is always zero-delay. Regard-less of whether the branch is taken, the next superinstruction is available for execution on the clock following the branch instruction. If a register is to be used, a "prepare-to-branch" instruction can be used to guarantee that the target instruction is ready for execution on the next clock cycle. If the prepare-to-branch instruction precedes the related branch by two instructions, there is again zero-delay branching.

Conflict-free Memory

The memory for the CHoPP is addressed by memory reference instructions using addresses computed in the address functional units. Each address is the unique storage location for a 64-bit datum. In addition to the data bits, there are two control bits used for synchronization operations. Since every memory location is available for synchronization operations, every memory location has these control bits. Figure 2-5 shows the organization of a memory location.

The two control bits are used in the Send/Receive and Get/Put synchroni-zation operations that are explained in detail below. The empty/full bit indicates whether the synchronization datum has yet been stored in the location. The

Empty	Wait	
		64-bit data
Full	No wait	

Figure 2-5. Memory location structure.

wait/no-wait bit indicates whether a recipient task has arrived prior to the storing of the datum and is presently waiting.

Even though Figure 2-2 shows the conflict-free memory as separate from the memory request/response units at the computing nodes, logically they are all part of the memory system. The memory request/response units contain the first and last stage of routing and conflict-resolution hardware that creates the conflict-free property of the memory. The conflict-free property means that regardless of the access pattern, memory requests do not interfere with each other to create a sequential bottleneck. All of the processors can access the same or any pattern of different locations, and they are all serviced equally without having to wait in line for access to a particular memory bank or particular memory location.

As was shown in a previous section, each processing node is capable of generating up to four address calculations and therefore up to four memory requests on each clock. The memory request unit, the conflict-free memory, and the memory response unit have sufficient bandwidth to handle four requests and four responses from every node on every clock.

The conflict-free property and the sufficient bandwidth make it possible for the programmer largely to ignore the properties of the memory, even in writing complex, multitasked software. At all times the memory can be considered as a conventional uniprocessor memory with a certain latency. No special consideration need be made when multiple tasks are going to access memory in a particular pattern.

In order to permit the programmer to compensate easily for memory latency, the load and store instructions are accomplished asynchronously. That is, the node does not wait for the completion of the load or store in order to go on to the next instruction. The load instruction is routed to memory, filled, and routed to the requesting register simultaneously with the node continuing to execute further instructions. If the node attempts to make use of a register that has not yet received its datum from the outstanding load, the node temporarily suspends the execution of instructions and waits for the completion of the load. The wait is accomplished by special hardware and need not be of concern to the programmer. To achieve the highest performance, however, the programmer should allow sufficient time between the load instruction and the use of the register to cover the memory latency. The store instruction also proceeds asynchronously but, since data are being sent to memory, no wait is necessary.

A load instruction uses one of the address functional units to compute the address. The computation can be either the adding of two registers or the adding of an immediate value to the contents of a register. The result is used as the effective address. The result can also be stored in a register. Using this feature, the address can be incremented or decremented in the same instruction parcel as is used for the memory reference.

When a store operation is performed, the datum to be stored is derived from the results of either an address unit or a computational unit. Any operation normally performed by the functional unit creating the datum can be used to create the value to be stored. As in any calculation, the result may be sent to a register in addition to being sent to memory. Also, the address calculation can be stored back in a register. Note that, since the store operation is sending a value to memory, it requires two functional units, one to compute the address and one to compute the value.

The Task

The current great interest in configurations of multiple processors has given rise to a plethora of words to describe the programming units that exploit parallelism. There are processes, monitors, partitions, tasks, microtasks, contexts, instruction threads, and so on. These can have a meaning in hardware and/or software, operating system, and microcoded control. In the present document, where the goal is the technical explanation of the hardware of the CHoPP machine, the term "task" has specific relevance only to the hardware. A *task* is the object that is created by a Task Spawn instruction. A task is the object whose state is saved when a program interrupt occurs. A task is the contents of the hardware registers stored in the register files and local store and associated with a particular task number. As defined previously using slightly more abstract terminology (abstract, that is, with respect to actual physical hardware), it is the single thread of instructions and related data associated with a particular program counter and its progress. The relation of this hardware-delimited task to any of the more abstract programming concepts connected with the exploitation of parallelism is not purely coincidental, but here we leave to the reader to make these relational associations. We have undertaken only to explain the organization of the hardware that manipulates and controls the CHoPP task.

Figure 2-6 elaborates the depiction of the CHoPP hardware presented in earlier figures to illustrate the special hardware structure that creates, schedules, and synchronizes tasks.

Whereas Figure 2-3 showed each register file as just 64 registers, the actual register file has storage for 64 of these sets of 64 registers. Each of these sets of 64 registers is associated with a single task. In one processing node there can be 64 tasks resident, each with 64 address registers and 64 computational registers. Each of these 64 locations for register sets is referred to as a *task slot*, or simply a *slot*. A task is assigned to one of these slots at creation. A task is then uniquely identified by the node on which it lives and the task slot it occupies within the node. Only one task in each node is currently running at any one time and thus only its registers are accessible to the functional units for computation. The currently running task is known as the *active task*.

The task manager contains a local store where the remainder of the state information for a task is kept. There are 64 slots in the local store of a node corresponding to the 64 possible tasks in a node. Task slots can be in one of four states. Figure 2-7 illustrates the possible state transitions:

Empty   There is presently no task assigned to the slot.
Active   The task in the slot is currently executing instructions.

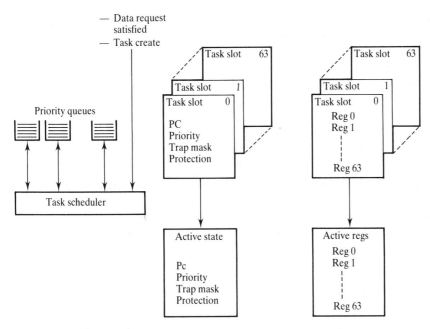

Figure 2-6. Task-manipulation hardware.

Ready   The task in the slot is ready to run. That is, all of the registers
            contain valid data for the next instruction to execute.
Waiting   The task is not ready to run. That is, one or more of the registers
            needed by the current instruction have not yet received the data
            requested from memory by a synchronizing instruction.

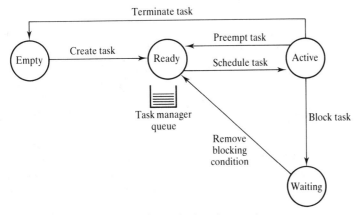

Figure 2-7. State diagram for task slots in a node.

The ready tasks are kept in queues in the task manager according to their priorities. The task manager uses a preemptive scheduling algorithm. If a task with priority higher than the currently active task becomes ready to run, the current task is preempted and the higher priority task is made active. There is no set order to the execution of tasks of equal priority. Any one of the ready tasks of the highest priority can be selected by the task manager to become the active task.

The exchange of the current active task for another of the tasks in a node is called a *task swap*. A task normally remains active until there occurs one of the four events that cause the swap of the active task:

- *Task termination.* The active task executes a task termination instruction or the task manager receives an external request to terminate the task.
- *Unavailable register.* The next instruction to be executed needs to use a register that has not yet received its requested synchronization datum. Note that a task swap does not occur when a register is unavailable owing to the memory latency on an ordinary load-from-memory instruction. In that case, the node simply waits for the datum to become available and no swap occurs.
- *Task preemption.* A task with a priority higher than the active task becomes ready. The active task is preemptively swapped for the higher-priority task.
- *Program interrupt.* The current instruction causes an interruption to occur. The interruption may be a trap instruction, supervisor call instruction, divide by zero, loss of precision, and so on.

It is important to note that the entire control and management of the tasks is handled by the hardware task manager. The functional units and the program do not get involved except to directly or indirectly generate the event that triggers the task manager. Having these actions performed in hardware enables a very fast context switching between tasks, and in many cases the task manager is able to perform its activities in parallel with ongoing computations.

Once an event occurs that instigates a task swap, the following actions occur.

1. The active program counter and task status words are placed back in their task slot in local store. The program counter and task status words for the new active task are made active.
2. the active register sets are placed in their background slot and the register sets for the new task are brought from their slot into the active position.
3. The first instruction to be executed comes through the pipeline to reach the functional units.

All of these actions proceed in parallel, so that only three clocks are needed to swap tasks. By keeping this swap time very low, the CHoPP machine can efficiently execute code that has very few instructions between task-swapping events (i.e., small-granularity tasks).

Under program control there are instructions that can manipulate tasks by performing actions that may cause swapping events. In addition, there are a number of maintenance instructions whereby supervisory tasks can direct and control the actions of the task manager. All of these instructions can be classified under the three fundamental mechanisms in the CHoPP architecture for dealing with tasks.

- *Task creation and termination.* There are specific instructions that can be placed in a superinstruction to create or terminate a task.
- *Task synchronization.* There are specific instructions that permit the synchronized transfer of data between tasks.
- *Task management.* There are specific instructions that manipulate the tasks within a node. These instructions can examine and alter certain state information concerning any task within a node. Some of these instructions are privileged. In addition, the task manager hardware maintains the queues of tasks and determines the order of execution of tasks without any software or functional unit intervention.

Task creation is done totally under program control. The instruction set includes two instructions for creating tasks. One instruction creates a single task, and the other instruction creates multiple tasks. An important and necessary characteristic of the CHoPP architecture is that the hardware is in control of the assignment of tasks to nodes. When a single task is created, the hardware assigns it to a processing node. When multiple tasks are created in a single instruction, the created tasks are distributed equally among the processors. The hardware task manager is in control of all task assignments to nodes and therefore it can maintain an efficient distribution of tasks.

At creation, each task is given a program counter, a priority, a unique number, and a single parameter. The number and parameter can be used to transfer information to enable the task to establish its own working space in memory. Once a task is created, it is available to be executed whenever it is not blocked waiting for synchronizing information and it has the highest priority of ready tasks in the processing node where it currently resides. The termination instruction simply removes the task state information from the node slot it is currently occupying, making the slot available for another task.

INTERTASK COMMUNICATIONS

The shared conflict-free memory is the only communication path between the nodes. Therefore, all transfer of information among tasks is accomplished through the memory. Three types of communication are possible. Shared memory can simply be read and written by multiple tasks. Tasks can be directly synchronized using special instructions that implement the synchronized transfer of data. Finally, a number of memory reference instructions that alter memory in an indivisible way are available to efficiently implement some common uses of shared memory.

TASK SYNCHRONIZATION

Task synchronization is accomplished by two sets of instructions for the synchronous transfer of a datum between tasks. The Get/Put pair of instructions is used for the transfer of a 64-bit word between two tasks. The Send/Receive pair of instructions is used to have one task distribute copies of a 64-bit word to multiple tasks. These are synchronous transfers in that a task attempting to use a synchronous datum is held in the Wait state until the datum is created and Sent by a task.

Figure 2-8 shows the changes in memory location state as the synchronous exchange between single tasks, using the Get/Put interactions, proceeds. The memory location has two control bits, empty/full and wait/no wait, as was described earlier. There are two cases shown: the Putter arrives before the Getter, and the Getter arrives before the Putter.

If the Putter arrives first (Fig. 2-8(a)), the datum is deposited in the location and the empty/full bit is set to full. The wait/no wait bit remains at no wait since there are not any waiting tasks. When the Getter arrives, it finds the location set to full and takes the datum resetting the bit to empty.

If the Getter arrives first (Fig. 2-8(b)), it discovers that the location is set to empty. It then deposits identification information in the location (node, task slot, receiving register) and sets the wait/no wait bit to wait to indicate that a task is waiting for the datum. When the Putter arrives, it finds the location set to wait. It takes the datum and sends it to the register in the task slot specified by the identification information found in the location. It resets the word to no wait and empty. Note that a Get/Put pair is the passing of a datum between tasks: the datum need not ever be in memory.

The Send/Receive instruction pair permits the synchronous transmission of a single 64-bit word from one task to many tasks. The transmission is fundamentally different from that achieved by the Get/Put pair. In Send/Receive, copies of the datum are delivered to each Receiver, whereas with Get/Put a single 64-bit object is transferred and no copies are made. Figure 2-9

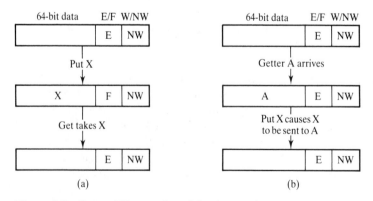

Figure 2-8. Get and Put synchronizing instructions.

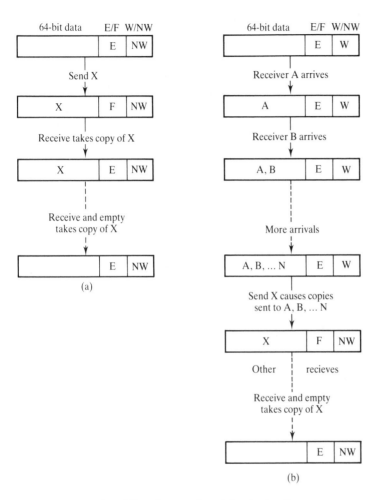

Figure 2-9. Send and Receive synchronizing instructions.

shows the changes in the memory location state as the Send/Receive instructions proceed. Two cases are shown: Sender arriving before any Receivers, and several Receivers arriving before the Sender.

If the Sender arrives first (Fig. 2-9(a)), the datum is deposited in the location and the empty/full bit is set to full. As each Receiver arrives, it takes a copy of the datum back to the requesting register. Since the Receiver in this case normally takes no action with regards to the control bits, additional instructions are needed to permit the resetting of these bits. Instructions are provided to permit the empty/full bit to be cleared either in combination with a Receive or as a separate instruction.

If one or more Receivers arrive first (Fig. 2-9(b)) they are kept waiting for the datum. For illustrational purposes, the multiple waiting Receivers are shown as being stuffed into the single 64-bit location. In reality, a special hardware mechanism effectively permits the queueing of waiters. The wait/no wait bit is set to wait on the arrival of the first Receiver. When the Sender arrives with the datum, the empty/full bit is set to full and a copy of the datum is sent to each of the receivers. The datum is then stored in the location for any following receivers. These later Receivers simply take a copy of the datum. Since the list of waiting Receivers can be quite long, special hardware mechanisms are provided to permit the distribution of the datum to the Receivers without sequentially transmitting it to each receiver on the list. In fact, the datum is transmitted to all of the Receivers in a time similar to that which would be taken for all of the Receivers to Load a datum from one location in the conflict-free memory.

At the node, the synchronization instructions receive somewhat special treatment. The Send and the Put instruction look very much like a Store to memory instruction. A request is sent to the memory request unit and passed along to memory. Likewise, the Get and the Receive instructions look very much like the Load from memory instruction. As far as the task is concerned it is loading a 64-bit value into a register. The difference from the task's point of view is that with this synchronizing load the determination of the latency is more complex. Since the receipt of the datum is dependent on when the creating task Puts or Sends it, the latency can only be determined by a detailed analysis of the program. Even then it is not certain, because the scheduling of tasks by the task manager influences the timing. If the task attempts to use the register to which it has done a Get or Receive and the datum has not yet arrived, the task manager changes the status of that task slot to waiting and swaps in another ready task. When the datum finally arrives, the task manager changes the status to Ready. If the task has a higher priority than the active task, it is immediately swapped into the active position. Otherwise it remains Ready and the task manager can swap it in according to its priority.

INDIVISIBLE INSTRUCTIONS FOR SHARED DATA
When multiple tasks share memory locations, it is often desirable to have data in memory altered without having to invoke the overhead of exchanged signals using synchronization instructions. On the CHoPP machine, two instructions are provided to permit indivisible operations on memory locations. A Match and Replace instruction performs a comparison with the contents of a memory location and if successful replaces the contents with a new value. This instruction permits the efficient implementation of so-called blackboard algorithms.

A Fetch and Add instruction allows the addition of a value to a memory location and the returning of its original contents. The CHoPP architecture implements this operation in special hardware to allow combining of simultaneous Fetch and Add instructions to the same location without having to perform the additions sequentially. Thus, this instruction is considerably more efficient than using synchronizing instructions to make the standard three-instruction sequence load, add, and store indivisible.

Job Control

The CHoPP machine contains specific hardware and instructions to permit the grouping of tasks into units called *jobs*. Like the task information, the task manager maintains job information in its local store. Information for up to 2048 jobs can be resident on the machine. During normal task creation, execution, and swapping, the job identification is simply part of the task's state information in the node. As a consequence, the task manager incurs no extra overhead when switching from a task in one job to a task in another job. This makes the CHoPP machine particularly efficient in a multiprogramming environment. Such a multiprogramming environment becomes very important for efficient machine utilization when jobs have a dynamic number of active tasks. When one job has very few active tasks and therefore can use only a few processing nodes, the CHoPP task manager hardware immediately permits other jobs access to the processing power. Grouping tasks by jobs permits the accessing of jobs by groups for accounting, control, and termination.

Memory Protection

A memory protection scheme is implemented on the CHoPP machine to restrict a task's access to code and data. There are separate mechanisms for code and data memory.

PERFORMANCE OF CHoPP ON THE LIVERMORE LOOPS

The Livermore Loops benchmark is a set of FORTRAN code fragments, called kernels. Each kernel is short (median length is eight lines of executable code) and contains at least one DO loop. These loops are designed to be representative to the inner loops of some of the codes used at the Lawrence Livermore National Laboratory (LLNL). They are one benchmark LLNL uses in evaluating computer performance. We, at CHoPP Computer Corporation, have also found them useful. Before making a computer with a new architecture, one would like to have some ballpark idea of how well the new architecture will perform. The fact that the Livermore Loops are short enables one to hand-compile them for the new architecture and estimate the performance. It should be noted that a good estimate of performance does not guarantee that all aspects of the machine perform well on all codes. For example, I/O performance is not measured by the loops. However, if some of the loops do not produce good performance estimates, then areas of weakness can be found and something can be done about them.

The remainder of this section discusses four aspects of instruction execution, gives an example of the structure of CHoPP code, analyzes the data dependency structures we found in the Livermore Loops, and gives the estimated megaflop rates for each of the 24 Livermore Loops on the CHoPP 1 computers. Table 2-1 contains a one-phrase description of each kernel. The original Livermore Loops code may be obtained from: Frank McMahon, L-35 University of California, Lawrence Livermore National Laboratory, P.O. Box 808 Livermore, Calif. 94550.

Some Aspects of Instruction Execution

There are several aspects of instruction execution that seem to arise in the execution of many programs. Since these aspects seem to arise often, we believe that any high-performance computer must handle them all well. Some, but not all of these, exist in executing the Livermore Loops and thus, we feel that the Livermore Loops serve as a useful probe in trying to discover the eventual CPU performance of the computer.

MEMORY LATENCY

In large computers it is often the case that many clock periods elapse between the time that a processor makes a request for data from memory and the time that the data is delivered to it. In CHoPP 1, this time interval will probably be between six and ten clock periods. If the processor cannot be doing useful work during this time period, performance is seriously eroded. As an example of this, consider Loop 12.

$$DO\ 12\ K=1,N$$
$$12 \quad X(K)=Y(K+1)-Y(K)$$

For each new item of data obtained from the Y array, a single floating point operation can be performed. Having to wait for the next value from memory could easily slow the processor down by more than a factor of 2. Other high-performance machines have the ability to do useful work during a pending memory request. The 360/91 has reservation stations,[7] the 6600 has the scoreboard,[6] and vector computers can access memory in pipeline fashion.[5]

The CHoPP computer has a valid bit associated with each register. Whenever the processor requests data from memory, the register that is to receive the data has its valid bit set to the invalid state. When the data arrives from memory and is stored in the register, the bit is set valid. As long as the registers used by the processor have their valid bits set valid, the processor keeps on executing instructions, even if there are many outstanding memory requests. Notice that many outstanding memory requests means that there need to be many registers.

When a short loop is encountered, such as Loop 12 above, one needs to make memory fetch requests by more than one loop iteration in advance, say J iterations, in order to compensate for the memory latency. For example, when computing $X(K)$, it may be desirable to initiate a memory fetch request for $Y(K+J)$. This leads to unrolling the loop by J iterations. Note that, with this arrangement, we effectively have the advantages of vector overlap without a vector unit and its restrictions. A vector pipe can only perform one operation at a time from its vector instruction set and, in some machines, two or more pipes can be chained together. However, in CHoPP, any set of ordinary instructions can be combined into a single vector-type operation.

INSTRUCTION ISSUE RATE

In each clock period, most computers issue either one new instruction or no new instructions. Because some instructions may take more than one clock to finish, several instructions may be in progress at the same time. Nonetheless, the issue rate is never better than one per clock, and often lower than that. However, it is often the case that more than one instruction could be issued at the same time if the hardware would only allow it. As an example of this, consider Loop 7.

```
DO 7 K=1,N
X(K)=    U(K  )+R*(Z(K  )+R*Y(K    ))+
      T*(U(K+3)+R*(U(K+2)+R*U(K+1))+
      T*(U(K+6)+R*(U(K+5)+R*U(K+4))))
   7   CONTINUE
```

First, three multiplies could be done at the same time, $R*Y(K)$, $R*U(K+1)$ and $R*U(K+4)$. Then, three additions could be done at the same time, then another three multiplies, then three more adds. After that, a single multiply, then a single add, then another single multiply and, finally, a single add to finish the computation. If up to three instructions could be executed each clock, these 16 operations could be done in a total of eight clocks, giving an average instruction issue rate of two per clock. One can do even better. If up to four instructions could be issued each clock, one could start the next iteration of the loop halfway through the current iteration. Then, the one-instruction-per-clock issue rate during the last half of one iteration occurs at the same time as the three instructions per clock issue rate of the next iteration, thus providing a steady four-instructions-per-clock issue rate all the way through the loop. Since there also needs to be data fetching, result storing, and loop control going on at the same time, the average number of instructions issued per clock could be even higher than four.

Instruction execution in CHoPP is organized by superinstructions. Each superinstruction consists of nine parcels and these parcels contain the instructions executed. Up to four computational instructions (floating-point, fixed-point, logical), plus up to four address instructions (memory reference, fixed point, logical), plus one branch instruction may be contained in each superinstruction. On each clock, the next superinstruction containing its nine parcels is issued, provided all the registers needed by the superinstruction are valid. No-operation instructions are placed in leftover parcel positions if not all nine positions are used. The four computational parcels have equal access to 64 computational registers and the four address parcels have equal access to 64 address registers.

Notice that with more than one parcel in a superinstruction one can perform some computation in one parcel and, in a second parcel, instruct that the result of the first parcel operation be stored in memory at the location computed in the second parcel. Thus, a "compute a value and store it in memory" can be accomplished in only one superinstruction. A consequence of being able to issue up to four memory requests per superinstruction is that a large bandwidth between the processor and memory must be provided.

SEQUENTIAL CODE

It would not do much good to have a million processors during a section of code that keeps all but one of them idle. We think that most practical programs have such sections. This can occur in a loop, as shown here:

```
      DO 61 K=1, N
      IF (X satisfies some property) GO TO 60
      X=function 1 (X)
      GO TO 61
                .
                .
                .
   60    X=function 2 (X)
   61    CONTINUE
```

Livermore Loop 17 is of this form, where function 1 is the STEP MODEL and function 2 is the LINEAR MODEL. We cannot compute any value of X until the previous value is known, since, until the previous value is available, we do not even know which function to apply. For this reason, we believe that a small number of very powerful processors is better than a large number of weak ones. Thus, CHoPP1 will be available with 4–16 extremely powerful processors instead of thousands of micros.

FREQUENT BRANCHING

Performance of any computer on code that contains a lot of branch instructions suffers if the branch instruction takes many clock periods. An examination of machine code for most any program shows a high percentage of branch instructions, often between 10 and 20%.[1] Because CHoPP executes up to nine instructions in each superinstruction, one may think that there might be a branch instruction in nearly every superinstruction. In practice, this is not so. For example, loop unrolling may reduce the number of branch instructions needed. However, the percentage of superinstructions containing a branch instruction (instead of a no-op in the branch parcel) is expected to be high. Indeed, in programming applications, we have encountered nontrivial examples where an entire loop fits in one superinstruction and so it branches to itself while in the loop.

Livermore Loop 16 is an example of a high-frequency of branch instructions.

```
410     J2=(N+N)*(M-1)+1
        DO 470 K=1, N
        KE=K2+1
        J4=J2+K+K
        J5=ZONE (J4)
        IF (J5-N        )       420, 480, 450
415     IF (J5-N+II    )        430, 425, 425
420     IF (J5-N+LB    )        435, 415, 415
425     IF (PLAN(J5)-R)         445, 480, 440
430     IF (PLAN(J5)-S)         445, 480, 440
435     IF (PLAN(J5)-T)         445, 480, 440
440     IF (ZONE(J4-1))         455, 480, 470
445     IF (ZONE(J4-1))         470, 480, 455
450     K3=K3+1
        IF (big expression)     445, 480, 440
455     M =M+1
        IF (M-ZONE(1) )         465, 465, 460
460     M =1
465     IF (I1-M       )        410, 480, 410
470     CONTINUE
480     CONTINUE
```

The branching is controlled by condition codes in CHoPP. In normal execution, a new superinstruction is issued each clock. In one clock, the superinstruction could set the condition code. The superinstruction executed on the next clock could branch, depending on that condition code setting. On the very next clock, the correct superinstruction (fall-through if branch is not taken, target if branch is taken) is executed. No idle clocks exist (assuming only that all needed instructions are in the instruction cache and that all needed registers are valid). Because the other eight parcels of the superinstruction can be doing useful work, the branch execution is completely overlapped with other instruction execution. Hence, we call this a "zero-time" branch. Every superinstruction may contain a branch instruction with no loss of efficiency because, during a branch, the condition code may be reset for the branch in the next superinstruction. That is, a superinstruction can be executed every clock period, even when every one contains a branch.

An Example of the Structure of CHoPP Code

Livermore Loop 12 serves as the basis for this example.

```
DO 12 K=1, N
12    X(K)=Y(K+1)-Y(K)
```

There is not much to do on each iteration of this loop. Only one value, $Y(K + 1)$, needs to be fetched from memory since the other value was obtained on the previous iteration. A subtraction is then performed and the result of the subtraction is stored in memory. It would seem that there is not enough to do in this loop to make efficient use of the superinstruction. However, since the iterations of this loop are independent, we can do two of them at the same time: we can load two values, then perform two subtractions and store two results. This can all be accomplished in one superinstruction if the values being loaded are for future use. The first superinstruction of the loop contains the following parcels:

Computation
    2 subtractions

$$Y(K + 1) - Y(K) \text{ and } Y(K + 2) - Y(K + 1)$$

    2 unused, contain NO−OP, indicated by dashes
Address
    2 stores (the result of the subtractions)

into $X(K)$ and $X(K + 1)$

    2 fetches for future use

$$Y(K + 16) \text{ and } Y(K + 17)$$

Branch
NO−OP as the loop is unrolled for memory latency, indicated by dashes

$Y(K + 16)$ and $Y(K + 17)$ are fetched because the loop is unrolled to contain eight superinstructions and so once around the loop of superinstructions computes 16 values of the X array. Figure 2-10 shows the structure of the unrolled loop. The store parcel adds the contents of an address register and a small constant to obtain the memory reference location. The result of this addition is not only used in the memory reference, but is also stored into a register. The way the loop uses this is to add the value of 2 to the previous memory reference location to obtain the new memory reference location, and the register that contains the new memory reference location is the same register that contained the previous memory reference location. Thus, two registers contain pointers into the X array. The two pointers into the X array are updated each superinstruction. The fetch parcels do not store the memory reference location back into a register, so the fetch parcel cannot update a pointer in order for the next superinstruction to use it. Instead, a third register contains the origin of the Y array, plus 18 minus the origin of the X array. The value of this register when

Label	Branch parcel	Address parcels	Computation parcels
LOOP12	---	Store into X(K) Store into X(K + 1) Fetch Y(K + 16) Fetch Y(K + 17)	Y(K + 1) − Y(K) Y(K + 2) − Y(K + 1) --- ---
	---	Store into X(K + 2) Store into X(K + 3) Fetch Y(K + 18) Fetch Y(K + 19)	Y(K + 3) − Y(K + 2) Y(K + 4) − Y(K + 3) --- ---
	---	Store into X(K + 4) Store into X(K + 5) Fetch Y(K + 20) Fetch Y(K + 21)	Y(K + 5) − Y(K + 4) Y(K + 6) − Y(K + 5) --- ---
	---	Store into X(K + 6) Store into X(K + 7) Fetch Y(K + 22) Fetch Y(K + 23)	Y(K + 7) − Y(K + 6) Y(K + 8) − Y(K + 7) --- ---
	---	Store into X(K + 8) Store into X(K + 9) Fetch Y(K + 24) Fetch Y(K + 25)	Y(K + 9) − Y(K + 8) Y(K + 10) − Y(K + 9) --- ---
	---	Store into X(K + 10) Store into X(K + 11) Fetch Y(K + 26) Fetch Y(K + 27)	Y(K + 11) − Y(K + 10) Y(K + 12) − Y(K + 11) KK = KK + 16 ---
	---	Store into X(K + 12) Store into X(K + 13) Fetch Y(K + 28) Fetch Y(K + 29)	Y(K + 13) − Y(K + 12) Y(K + 14) − Y(K + 13) Compare KK to KLIMIT ---
	JUMP < LOOP12	Store into X(K + 14) Store into X(K + 15) Fetch Y(K + 30) Fetch Y(K + 31)	Y(K + 15) − Y(K + 14) Y(K + 16) − Y(K + 15) --- ---

Figure 2-10. Example of CHoPP code structure.

added to each of the two *X* array pointer registers provides the fetch location. Notice that each of these three registers is read by two different parcels at the same time. Not only is this permitted, but, in fact, the hardware would permit all four parcels to read the same register at the same time.

Since pointers into the arrays are used and these pointers are updated by the store instruction itself (instead of using origin of an array and an index into the array), there is no value of K actually in the address parcels and, hence, no updating of K, the subscript of the arrays, need be done. The only thing left in this loop is control for getting out of the loop. Since all address parcels are already used in this example, this control function is done using the computation parcels. The value of K is placed in one of the computational registers. This is referred to as KK instead of K to indicate that this value is not used elsewhere in the loop. This register is incremented by 16 each time around the loop and then compared to a limit. Based on this compare, the branch parcel in the last superinstruction of the loop controls the exit from the loop. Finally, notice that there is nothing very complicated in this example. In fact, preliminary work on a FORTRAN compiler indicates that it will not be difficult to develop a compiler that creates code that is just about as efficient as this. Loop unrolling, while well understood, does not seem to be discussed in the literature from the point of view of compensating for memory latency. Rather, it is discussed from the point of view of reducing branch overhead.

Data-Dependency Structures

A data dependency occurs when one computation needs a result that another computation produces. The first computation may not proceed until the needed data has been computed by the other computation. Programming a parallel computer causes one to become more aware of the data-dependency structures. In programming a sequential computer, not much attention need be paid to the form of the data-dependency structures. Some parallelism is introduced with pipelined processors, with or without a vector unit, and, for efficient use of pipelined processors, one needs to be concerned with some data dependencies. This is most apparent in determining when a loop can be vectorized.[4] Likewise, one needs to be concerned somewhat with data dependencies in making good use of the parcels in the superinstructions. This seems to be about as difficult as it is for a pipelined, nonvectorized processor and is less constrained (and, hence, easier) than a vector processor. When a computer has multiple processors, the data-dependency structures become very important indeed. Careful consideration of the data-dependency structures is necessary in order to make good use of multiple processors.

The Livermore Loops were studied to determine their data-dependency structures at an iteration level. That is, the major concern was dependencies from one iteration of the loop to some other iteration, rather than the dependencies within an iteration. At this level, only five structures were needed to be able to classify all 24 loops:

1. Independent
2. Tree
3. Linear recursion
4. Equivalence set
5. Sequential

The likely success of a loop being able to use a vector unit has a strong correlation with the data-dependency structure it has.

STRUCTURES THAT ARE LIKELY TO VECTORIZE

Two of the data-dependency structures are likely to be able to take advantage of a vector unit. Although CHoPP does not have a vector unit, these structures are important because they also allow the utilization of multiple processors.

In the independent structure, each iteration is independent of all the others. That is, no iteration needs any information from any of the other iterations. This structure is shown in Figure 2-11. Each dot represents some computation and each line segment represents a data dependency. The dependency direction is from the top of the figure to the bottom, hence, the computation represented by the dot at the upper end of a line segment must be finished before the computation represented by the dot at the lower end of the same line segment may start.

An example of this is forming the sum of two vectors. That is, computing

$$A(K) = B(K) + C(K)$$

for each value of K. Clearly, all of these sums could be done at the same time. Another example is Livermore Loop 12 discussed above. Indeed, one-third of the Livermore Loops (kernels 1, 7, 8, 9, 10, 12, 15, 22) have this independent structure. In addition, kernel 18 has this structure repeated sequentially three times; kernel 2 has it repeated sequentially $\log(n)$ times; and kernel 6 has it repeated sequentially n times, where n is the size of the largest loop. The independent structure performs well on CHoPP because the iterations can be spread across the processors with no communication needed among them other than notification of the completion of work.

The tree data-dependency structure, shown in Figure 2-12, does not occur in the Livermore Loops as originally coded. However, an appropriate transformation can be applied to some of the kernels to arrive at this structure. As an

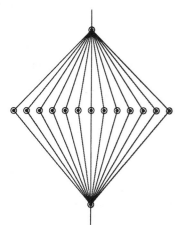

Figure   2-11. Independent data-dependency structure.

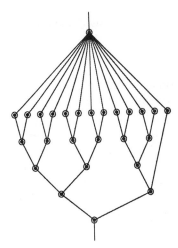

Figure 2-12. Tree data-dependency structure.

example, consider finding the sum of the first 8 numbers in an array X:

```
        Q=0
        DO 10 K=1,8
10      Q=Q+X(K)
```

The output of each iteration is used as the input to the next iteration and, as it stands, this is an example of the sequential data-dependency structure. The general case of the sequential structure is considered below, but here we can take advantage of the fact that the operation (addition) is associative. This DO loop is functionally equivalent to

$$Q=((((((A+B)+C)+D)+E)+F)+G)+H$$

Here the values $X(1)$, $X(2)$, $X(3)$, ... are now called A, B, C, ... Applying associativity, one can put this into the tree structure,[2] obtaining

$$Q=((A+B)+(C+D))+((E+F)+G+H))$$

When the operation performed is associative, one can transform all or only part of the problem from either structure to the other. Thus, a problem may be divided into pieces. Each processor uses the sequential data structure on its piece, and then these results can be combined using the tree structure.

Kernels 3 and 24 can be transformed into the tree structure. Further, kernels 4 and 21 can be transformed into a combination of the tree structure and the independent structure. That is, both of these kernels break up into several independent groups, but each group has the tree structure.

Although CHoPP can always efficiently execute any problem when the data dependencies are in either form given so far (independent or tree), the same is not true for a vector processor, owing to the limited set of operations a vector processor can perform. Livermore Loop 15 has the independent structure discussed above, yet, owing to the conditional tests within each iteration, the

CIVIC compiler was unable to use the vector processor of the Cray X-MP and so the Cray achieved only about 4.2 megaflops. As another example, consider a program to do payroll. Each person's earnings, deductions, and so on can be computed independently of each other person's. Various totals may need to be obtained, such as the total federal income tax withheld from all checks, and these can be obtained using the tree structure. But owing to the way the Tax Tables are constructed, with different rules for different ranges of income, the procedure to compute tax withheld actually changes, depending upon income, and so does not lend itself to vector operation. Yet none of this is any problem for CHoPP. Each node can proceed with various individual computations. There is no requirement that any two of them carry out the same function.

STRUCTURES THAT USUALLY DO NOT VECTORIZE

The third structure is called linear recurrence. Whereas the previous structure was illustrated by the summing of a set of numbers, here all the partial sums of a vector of numbers, from the start of the vector to position K for each k, is desired. That is

$$A(1)=B(1) \text{ and}$$
$$A(K)=B(K)+A(K-1) \text{ for } K>1$$

Another example is given by

$$A(1)=B(1) \text{ and}$$
$$A(K)=B(K)+C(K)*A(K-1) \text{ for } K>1$$

Although these examples have sequential data-dependency structures, they can be transformed into the linear recurrence structure shown in Figure 2-13. Kernels

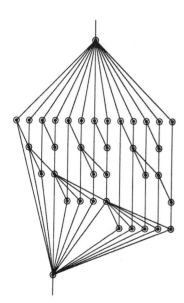

Figure 2-13. Linear recursion data-dependency structure.

5 and 11 both have this structure. This structure occurs sequentially twice in kernel 19 and five times in kernel 23.

The next structure we call the equivalence set data-dependency structure. The previous structures are static. That is, they do not depend upon the numerical value of the data. Without knowing the value of the data, we know which pieces of data are combined with which other pieces and in what order. In this case, however, each iteration of the loop uses the value of the data to determine membership of an equivalence class. The data for that iteration is then combined with the rest of the data of the same equivalence class. This structure is shown in Figure 2-14, where the combining in each equivalence class has the tree data structure. CHoPP has the FETCH & ADD instruction to permit parallel execution of the processors in the presence of this data dependency structure. Kernels 13 and 14 both have this structure.

The last data dependency structure in the Livermore Loops is the sequential data dependency structure. Although some pre- and postprocessings of kernels 16, 17, and 20 have the independent data structure, the essence of these kernels is of the form

$$\text{IF } X(K-1) < 0$$
$$\text{THEN } X(K) = f(X(K-1))$$
$$\text{ELSE } X(K) = g(X(K-1))$$

The function performed to determine $X(K)$ is dependent upon the value computed for $X(K-1)$; thus $X(K-1)$ needs to be determined before $X(K)$. This data structure is illustrated in Figure 2-15. The top horizontal row of dots

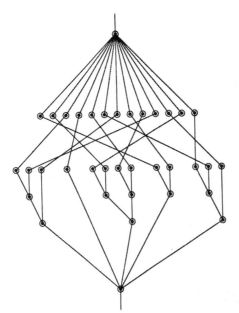

Figure 2-14. Equivalence set-dependency structure.

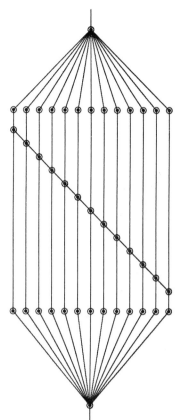

Figure 2-15. Sequential
data-dependency structure.

represents some preprocessing and the bottom row of dots represents some postprocessing. The dots in between are the sequential portion. It is commonly believed that such nonlinear recursion cannot be parallelized in general.[2]

CHoPP Performance Estimates

Each of the 24 Livermore Loop kernels was coded for the CHoPP architecture. Since no high-level language compiler was available when they were coded, they were hand-coded in assembly language. Since no hardware was available then, running time had to be estimated. Estimating the running time of a code can be very tricky in some computers, especially those with pipelines, because of data dependencies. However, in the CHoPP supercomputer, data dependencies do not disturb the pipeline flow. The main uncertainties in estimating performance are delays due to memory access.

There are two sources of memory delay: instruction fetch and data fetch. Instruction-fetch delay only occurs when there is a cache miss. Since the

Livermore Loops are very short, only a few cache misses in the first iteration of a loop brings the code for the entire loop into the cache. All subsequent iterations have no cache misses and, hence, no delay due to instruction fetch. Thus, there is negligible performance degradation due to instruction-fetch delay. Data-fetch delays are neglibible also, because one can almost always code fetch instructions sufficiently early enough that when the data is needed it is already in a register. This was illustrated in the code for the main loop of Livermore Loop 12 given

Table 2-1. Performance of CRAY-X-MP (measured) and CHoPP1 (estimated) on the 24 Livermore Loops.

				Megaflop rates			
Livermore loop kernel descriptions					Code for CHoPP1 processors		
Kernel	Description	Kernel #	X-MP CIVIC	1	4	16
1	Hydro Fragment	1	136.0	53	200	643
2	Incomplete Cholesky-Conjugate Gradient Excerpt	2	22.0	25	88	242
3	Inner Product	3	84.9	56	181	405
4	Banded Linear Equations	4	47.8	41	152	460
5	Tri-diagonal Elimination, Below Diagonal	5	5.4	21	40	124
6	General Linear Recurrence Equations	6	4.3	55	137	412
7	Equation of State Fragment	7	162.2	65	249	823
8	ADI Integration	8	119.0	52	205	751
9	Integrate Predictors	9	153.9	60	212	569
10	Difference Predictors	10	45.5	25	87	223
11	First Sum	11	3.3	29	55	201
12	First Difference	12	68.0	26	66	108
13	2-D Particle In Cell	13	4.1	11	35	74
14	1-D Particle In Cell	14	18.1	11	35	74
15	Casual FORTRAN, Development Version	15	4.2	10	39	156
16	Monte Carlo Search Loop	16	3.6	5	5	5
17	Implicit Conditional Computation	17	9.2	37	55	62
18	2-D Explicit Hydrodynamics Fragment	18	115.9	40	152	522
19	General Linear Recurrence Equations	19	7.1	25	40	99
20	Discrete Ordinates Transport, Conditional Recurrence	20	12.2	27	54	54
21	Matrix * Matrix Product	21	46.7	36	136	432
22	Planckian Distribution	22	62.9	25	96	350
23	2-D Implicit Hydrodynamics Fragment	23	13.6	55	204	250
24	Find Location of First Minimum Array	24	2.6	30	41	46
		harmonic mean	9.3	22.6	46.4	67.5

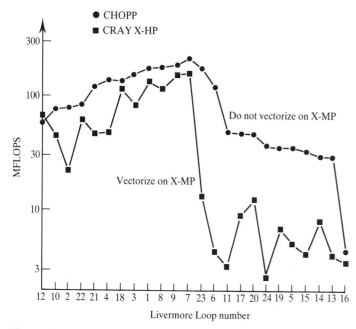

Figure 2-16. Comparison of CHoPP1 and CRAY X-MP magaflop rates. ● 1/4 CHoPP 1/16; ■ 1/4 CRAY X-MP/48.

above. Because of loop unrolling, data dependencies do not interrupt the pipeline flow and so all superinstructions take one clock period. One can estimate the execution time by simply counting the number of superinstructions executed and multiplying this count by the time for each clock period. This is the way the estimates given below were obtained. The clock period on the CHoPP1 is anticipated to be 60 nsec. Each kernel was first programmed to use just one processor. In most cases, we would expect a reasonably good FORTRAN compiler to achieve performance close to the hand coded results using the original FORTRAN code as input (no reprogramming). Half of the kernels, those that were vectorized well for the Cray X–MP, ran faster on the Cray. The other half ran faster on a one-node CHoPP. The harmonic mean (a measure of throughput) on all 24 loops shows CHoPP1 running faster by more than a factor of 2. Each kernel was then reprogrammed for multiple processors. Execution time estimates were obtained for a 4-processor and for a 16-processor CHoPP1 system. All of these results are given in Table 2-1. It is particularly interesting to compare the 1-processor Cray X-MP results with those for the four-node CHoPP1, because these machines contain about the same number of components. Also, both are one-fourth of the maximum configuration. This comparison is given in Figure 2-16.

DESIGN AND SIMULATION OF THE CHoPP SUPERCOMPUTER USING SCALD

CHoPP Computer Corporation purchased its first SCALD design station from Valid Logic Systems in March 1986. The SCALD system was selected after an extended survey of the computer-aided design market. CHoPP Computer felt that the SCALD system stood a good chance of standing up to the unusual demands the CHoPP supercomputer design and engineering project would place on a computer-aided design and simulation system. One of the reasons we were convinced that the SCALD system might satisfy our need to handle very large and complex logic designs was that SCALD was originally born of a need to create an equally large and complex supercomputer, namely the S-1.[3]

This section provides some background on the SCALD system, a discussion of the CHoPP design philosophy, and a brief description of the CHoPP demonstration unit's physical packaging. The section concludes with a discussion of CHoPP Computer Corporation's experiences in applying the SCALD system's design tools to the problem of designing the CHoPP supercomputer demonstration unit.

SCALD Design Methodology

Structured computer-aided logic design (SCALD) was developed by Dr. Thomas M. McWilliams and Dr. L. Curtis Widdoes at Lawrence Livermore National Laboratory and Stanford University in the late 1970s. It is a graphics-based design system that allows large digital systems to be designed in a structured, hierarchical manner similarly to the structured design of large, complex computer programs. SCALD automates time-consuming and error-prone processes, thus allowing engineers to concentrate their efforts on the creative aspects of electronic design and development. SCALD came into existence when McWilliams and Widdoes, as directors of the Navy-funded S-1 supercomputer project, were charged with developing supercomputer performance systems with limited time and limited resources. Development of such an advanced computer demanded advanced design tools that did not then exist. Their first task, therefore, was to develop the design tools.

They set two primary goals for their design tools. The first was to create a design methodology that would allow engineers to express their designs on the level at which they think about them. They reasoned that engineers do not think about their designs in terms of component types and netlists, but rather in terms of functional modules and data paths, and the design tools should allow them to express their designs in those terms.

Designs created using SCALD offer a number of advantages over conventional logic design techniques. In general, SCALD designs are easier to understand. They are uncluttered and easy to read because SCALD allows a single block to represent a large amount of logic; it allows a single line to represent a multi-bit bus; it allows a single component symbol to represent multiple chips.

McWilliams' and Widdoes' second goal was to allow designs to be re-compiled rapidly as new circuit technologies become available, thus allowing engineers to take advantage of advancing technology without starting over from scratch.

SCALD eliminates the need to draw out all of the logic of a design. Because a design in SCALD is done in a hierarchical manner, repetitive circuits need only be drawn once, then repeated as often as necessary. Since individual segments of logic are defined in terms of a macro language, they can be expanded in a number of ways. Initially, they may be expanded as a relatively large number of small-scale (SSI) or medium-scale (MSI) integrated circuits. As more advanced technology becomes available, the macros can be redefined to take advantage of a smaller number of large-scale (LSI) or very large-scale (VLSI) devices. Re-defining macros to take advantage of new technology still requires work, but it is much easier than with "flat" designs (i.e., designs defined in terms of their lowest-level components).

The Original SCALD Implementation

Originally, SCALD was designed to allow engineers to input a high-level graphic description of a digital system, and to get as output a wire list to drive manufacturing systems. It was a system specifically geared to the design and implementation of wire-wrap circuit boards. Three modules made up the original SCALD system: the Stanford University Drawing System (SUDS) graphics editor, the macro expander, and the wire lister.

The SUDS graphics editor was used to enter drawings directly on a graphics terminal and to create macro definitions of logic segments. The macro expander would read the output of SUDS, along with a hand-generated layout specification, and expand hierarchical drawings into a connection list (netlist) and other lists to document the design. The wire lister read the connection list and an integrated-circuit definition file, and created the necessary documentation to drive a wire-wrap machine. The SCALD system was sophisticated in that it could not only generate new boards but could automatically read the state of an old board and generate the needed instructions to change the board into a new state. For example, changes could be made by editing a source drawing and running the SCALD system again. The wire lister would read the old board state, and output a new board state complete with a wrap/unwrap list to update finished boards to the newest level.

SCALD proved to be successful. The first SCALD project was the S-1 computer itself: a 10 MIPS, 5500-IC, ECL-10K system with power comparable to an IBM 370/168. With SCALD, it was designed and implemented with only 2 man-years of effort.

In recognition of their achievement, the Institute of Electrical and Electronics Engineers (IEEE) presented McWilliams and Widdoes with the W. Wallace McDowell award in 1984.

SCALD Commercial Implementation

While the original SCALD implementation is in the public domain, McWilliams and Widdoes reasoned that it had commercial possibilities. In 1981 they founded Valid Logic Systems in order to make the SCALD methodology available commercially. The other founders of Valid Logic Systems were Dr. Jared Anderson, the founder and former president of Two Pi Corporation; Mr. Ray King, a manufacturing executive at Hewlett-Packard; and Mr. Jeffrey Rubin, a member of the S-1 project team and a senior programmer in the artificial intelligence group at Stanford University.

Valid Logic recognized that the SCALD methodology alone was not enough. To be commercially viable, SCALD had to be implemented in an open system, based on recognized industry standards, which would allow the SCALD tools to work with other design tools in an engineering environment. Valid's choice to implement an open system allows third-party hardware and software to be integrated into Valid's SCALD environment, and allows Valid's software to communicate with other systems, thus providing more complete engineering solutions.

Valid chose to implement the SCALD tools under the UNIX operating system because that is a de facto standard operating system for scientific and engineering applications. Ethernet was chosen for local area networking so that the SCALD tools could communicate with other systems. Since IBM Corporation and Digital Equipment Corporation (DEC) mainframe computers are dominant in the engineering environment, Valid chose to be compatible with these systems by porting Valid's design verification software to them. Providing a link between IBM and DEC computers and Valid-supported workstations allowed Valid's workstations to be integrated into existing engineering environments. Valid's SCALD software is also available on engineering workstations produced by IBM and DEC.

Today, the SCALD methodology, although based on the original concepts, incorporates a set of tools that span a much broader range of engineering efforts. No longer simply geared to the design and implementation of wire-wrap boards, today's SCALD helps engineers produce ASICs, full-custom chips, boards, and complete systems.

We list below the tools in the SCALD methodology as implemented by Valid Logic Systems today.

- The original SUDS graphics editor was replaced by ValidGED, a powerful and easy to use schematic capture system. With it, engineers can enter and edit designs quickly and accurately.
- The original SCALD system has no design verification capability. Engineers still had to build breadboards to see whether their designs worked. That is no

longer necessary. ValidSIM, a sophisticated logic simulator, and ValidTIME, a powerful timing analysis program, allows engineers to exercise their schematics as if they were breadboards.

- The old SCALD macro expander and wire lister has been replaced with ValidPACKAGER, which now provides the link between logical and physical designs. The package automatically assigns parts, generates netlists, and checks for electrical problems such as signal loading errors. The package's open and expandable architecture can support all modern packaging technologies. Valid's "flattener" can be used to automatically generate conventional "low-level" schematics diagrams from a packaged physical design.
- Valid added hardware modeling to its SCALD tools in early 1984. The Realchip hardware modeling system, invented by Widdoes, was the industry's first hardware-modeling system. It allows the SCALD tools to create and verify designs containing complex VLSI devices such as microprocessors and their peripheral chips. In 1986, Widdoes was awarded a patent for his Realchip hardware modeling invention.
- Valid also introduced the Realfast simulation accelerator in 1984. Developed by McWilliams, its speed and simulation capacity extend workstation-based interactive simulation into the realm of very large, very complex designs.

CHoPP Design Philosophy

The design of the CHoPP demonstration unit was carried out under a strict set of guidelines. One overriding concern was to insure that software simulations of the CHoPP machine would be true tests of the validity of the logic of the machine. After all, simulations are only effective if the test vectors exercise the logic of the design in a way that actually tests the intended function of the logic. Therefore, the ability to execute basic machine instructions on large blocks of logic, representing the major parts of the CHoPP machine, was one of the basic goals that drove our design philosophy. The basic design philosophy that has guided the development of the CHoPP demonstration unit includes the following points.

1. Provide the capability to execute CHoPP assembly code on the simulator.
2. Maintain an automated, closed loop from schematic entry and simulation through PCB layout and testing.
3. Fully automate DC testing with test jigs and an automated link to simulator.
4. Use computer simulation to take the place of wire wrap prototypes, oscilloscopes and logic analyzers.
5. Design, debug, and maintain all logic at a "high level."
6. Design the CHoPP demonstration unit from "off-the-shelf" parts.

ASSEMBLY LANGUAGE ON THE SIMULATED MACHINE

We felt from the beginning that the ability to execute CHoPP assembly code on the simulator was important for proper debugging of the machine design. Coding in assembly language is a convenient way to generate a large number of meaningful test patterns for the simulated design. Therefore, we have provided the capability to down-load simulated CHoPP memory with instruction sequences that are created using a simple assembler and linker. This has proved to be very effective in debugging the logic of the machine.

CLOSED-LOOP DESIGN SYSTEM

We felt that it was essential to maintain an automated, closed loop linking the design, simulation, construction, and testing phases. No human interfaces were allowed between any of the phases. Valid Logic's SCALD system matched well with this philosophy, providing the needed automated, bidirectional interfaces between the design and simulation system and the PCB layout system. Because the SCALD system architecture is an "open" one, we were able to provide the missing automated links to our in-house DC board-test system.

AUTOMATED DC TESTING

We decided to include an automated DC testing capability in the normal design/simulation/PCB layout loop. Because all of the CHoPP demonstration unit's printed circuit boards have an identical form factor, we were able to design a single test jig that can be used to perform DC tests on all the machine's circuit boards. By linking the test jig to the SCALD simulator, test vectors for actual boards can be derived as a normal byproduct of the design-simulation phase. The same test patterns that were used to debug the simulated design can be used to drive the DC tester against the physical design. Test results can then be compared to those predicted by the SCALD simulator.

SIMULATION TO REPLACE HARDWARE PROTOTYPES

After careful consideration of a number of factors, including the current state of industry-standard computer-aided design and engineering hardware and software, the perceived complexity of the CHoPP demonstration unit, and the scheduling constraints of the project, a decision was made to use a logic simulation software to replace one of the classic design stages of a new computer, namely the wire-wrap prototype, with its attendant horde of technicians and engineers, tangled in a maze of oscilloscope probes and logic analyzer clip leads, wreaking havoc with wire-wrap guns. The decision to use software to debug logic designs has not eliminated long nights spent peering at schematics, trying to figure out what the heck is going on, but no one has burned their knuckles on bus buffer ICs driving a bus at the wrong time. Certainly, once found, design errors are much easier to fix using a software simulator in place of a wire-wrap prototype.

If simulation is used properly, what is left to debug after a PC board is constructed? The answer is timing. Although the SCALD system does have a timing-analysis facility, it does not have perfect information (e.g., individual wire delays) and therefore it cannot do a perfect job. What remains to be done after the printed circuit boards have been constructed are AC tests. These are performed in the usual way, by plugging together boards to construct a running machine. If the logic of the machine is created using the proper synchronous design rules based on a single master clock, the majority of initial timing problems can be eliminated by simply slowing down the master clock. The machine is first brought up using a slower than normal master clock. Systematic testing is used to identify areas of logic that are limiting the clock speed. The slower logic is "tuned up," and eventually the entire machine can be brought up to the clock rate set as part of the original design goals.

"HIGH-LEVEL" LOGIC DESIGN

The logic of the CHoPP demonstration unit is maintained at a "high level" using the hierarchical design capability of the SCALD system. In fact, with SCALD the engineer can design, debug and maintain all his or her logic at a "high level," never having to deal with mundane tasks such as allocating integrated circuits packages to perform specific logic functions. One really begins to appreciate the importance of this capability when one has to deal with a logic system as complex as a supercomputer.

For example, SCALD's package automatically assigns high-level logic functions to individual IC packages, assigning pins and component numbers. A 256-bit bus can be buffered by placing a single symbol on a "high-level" drawing. The final circuit board will get the necessary 32 bus-buffer ICs, with all 640 pins assigned automatically. The designer does not have to deal with the low-level logic unless he wants to. If requested though, the SCALD system's flattener will automatically draw "conventional" schematics from the packaged "high-level" design, showing each individual IC with each pin labeled and a signal wire attached.

We have found that the logic of the original "high-level" schematic is completely lost in the clutter of the detailed "flat" schematic. In the past, with large logic designs, in order to preserve the "high-level" design, people were forced to maintain two sets of schematics, one at the "high level" and one at the "detailed level." The two sets of schematics never agreed perfectly because a human being was responsible for maintaining consistency. SCALD has changed this.

In fact, we have found surprisingly little use for the more than one thousand pages of detailed schematics that can be derived from the CHoPP demonstration unit "high-level" schematics. This is partly due to the fact that automated DC testing has eliminated much of the need to deal with indivdual ICs and pins. When the engineer needs to deal with the circuit board at the lowest level, cross-references relating signal names, boards, component IDs, and pin numbers are available on-line using a computer terminal.

"OFF-THE-SHELF" PARTS

The intent of the CHoPP demonstration unit is to establish the power of the CHoPP architecture using conventional integrated-circuit technologies and a conservative clock period. The CHoPP architecture allows one the flexibility to design a supercomputer-class machine without using exotic and risky packaging and integrated-circuit technologies.

For the CHoPP demonstration unit we chose to design with standard parts that could be ordered out of manufacturer's catalogues and purchased "off-the-shelf," wherever practical. As a result, the bulk of the demonstration unit is constructed from standard Advanced Schottky and FAST transistor–transistor logic (TTL) integrated circuits, with heavy use of high-speed programmable logic devices (i.e., "D" type PALs) for the "glue" logic. Several "off-the-shelf" very-large-scale integrated circuits perform a number of complex functions (e.g., ALU, multiplication, barrel-shift, etc.). A minimal amount of emitter-coupled logic (ECL) is used for clock distribution. We did need to design one large compacted gate-array integrated circuit to provide a 16-port register file for the CHoPP demonstration unit. The machine's basic clock period is 60 nanoseconds.

CHoPP Demonstration Unit Packaging Scheme

The logic of the CHoPP demonstration unit consists of over 6000 LSI and VLSI integrated circuits packed into a 4-cubic-foot volume. All the integrated circuits are housed in either conventional dual-inline packages (DIP) or pin grid array (PGA) packages, mounted on multilayer printed circuit boards (PCBs). There are a total of 19 circuit boards measuring about 2 feet on a side, each with the same form factor. Each printed circuit board has either two or three power planes and two ground planes. The number of signal layers varies from six to eight.

Instead of using a backplane to conduct signals between the many boards in the system, a novel high-density interconnect scheme was devised. This scheme greatly increases the number of available interboard connection points, thereby adding another degree of freedom to the printed wiring network.

The CHoPP demonstration unit is an interconnecting "sandwich" of 19 circuit boards, stacked one on top of another. Each board in the sandwich is capable of conducting 2096 signals to its upper neighbor via its top surface and another 2096 signals to its lower neighbor via its bottom surface. These board-to-board interface signals are conducted by 24 custom high-density connector assemblies, which are "sandwiched" between the printed circuit boards. The connector assemblies conduct signals between aligned gold-plated pads on the top and bottom surfaces of each board. Because each signal is paired with a separate ground return, the actual number of electrical connections is double the number of signals quoted above, a total of 8384 connection points per board.

The interface between any two boards in the CHoPP "sandwich" can be probed with the machine running by installing a special "extender" board designed for that purpose. The "extender" board is installed between any two boards of interest. The "extender" taps each of the 2096 interboard signals, buffers each signal, and then makes the buffered signal available at an edge connector for convenient probing with a logic analyzer or an oscilloscope. DC tests of a single board may be performed using a special test jig. The test jig consists of two boards that are used to make up a three-board "sandwich," with the board under test in the middle. The outer boards mate with and make electrical contact with all the pins of all connectors on the board under test. Under control of a DEC MicroVAX II minicomputer, the test jig can apply a TTL level to and/or read the TTL level of any pin of any connector on the board under test. The test jig also has control over the ECL master clocks to the board under test. Software in the MicroVAX computer allows a person to create and run test patterns against the board under test. Test vectors created by the SCALD simulator can also be run against the board under test.

Interboard Wiring in the CHoPP Demonstration Unit

By distributing many high-density connectors over the top and bottom surfaces of each circuit board, the designer is free to route signals in three dimensions. By using through-plated via holes to conduct signals through intervening circuit boards in the PCB "sandwich," the designer can distribute a signal between any two boards in the CHoPP unit using no more than 11 inches of interboard wiring (the height of the PCB sandwich). With careful planning and correct logic partitioning and parts placement, the added trace length from interboard wiring can be kept very small indeed (less than a few inches).

The flexibility offered by the added wiring dimension allows important signal busses to be allocated where they are most needed, for example, in the middle of the circuit board, instead of always at the edge of the board. Bus buffers and line drivers and receivers that would normally be needed to drive long busses can often be eliminated because the circuit runs can be much shorter. With capacity to conduct 4192 signals to/from a circuit card, interboard wiring paths are plentiful. Bus multiplexors can often be eliminated from a design by using two or more wires where only one wire might be used in the conventional edge-connector/backplane interconnection scheme.

With an added wiring dimension, it is now possible to partition logic in a different way. A given section of logic can be allocated a vertical "slice" through the PCB "sandwich," and distributed among a number of boards with only a small penalty for interboard wiring delay.

Unfortunately, the added flexibility of the CHoPP interconnection scheme brings added complexity. The large number of available interconnections in the CHoPP demonstration unit must be managed carefully and in an intelligent way.

The order in which boards are stacked in the "sandwich" is very important. Certain board orderings will tend to minimize the number of interboard wiring paths required; other orderings will result in a shortage of interboard wiring paths. For example, if two boards in the "sandwich" need to share 100 signals and the two boards are stacked in adjacent positions, then only 100 signal contacts need be allocated on a single side of each circuit board. No via holes would be required for the interboard signal distribution. However, if the two boards are stacked in positions 1 and 12 in the "sandwich," then ten additional boards would be affected. Each of the ten intervening boards would need to reserve 100 top-to-bottom signal vias and 200 signal contacts, thereby consuming over 2000 extra interboard wiring contacts and requiring over 1000 extra signal vias.

Although we felt that a computer program could do a more optimal job, the interboard wiring in the CHoPP demonstration unit is managed by hand and simply checked by computer. One person has responsibility for the master list, which details exactly which signals appear on each of the 150 912 interboard contacts in the CHoPP "sandwich." Each signal that flows over the interboard wiring system has a responsible engineer (usually the engineer who designed the board on which the signal originates). Moving, adding, deleting, or changing signals requires the consent of the person in charge of the master list. This is because most changes impact other engineer's signals, which must be moved to make room for any changes. The keeper of the master list is often simply an arbitrator who arranges swaps of precious interboard wiring space.

Recognizing that placement and trace length are critical for certain components and signals in the design, we have kept the responsibility for component placement and interboard wiring with the design engineer. All components (ICs) are placed on a template of the CHoPP circuit boards by the board's logic designer before the board is released for PCB layout. An inhouse computer program takes component placement information from the SCALD system and translates it into a form suitable for the PCB layout system. Both the component placement and the allocation of interboard wiring remain manual functions.

Experiences with SCALD

CHoPP Computer Corporation purchased its first SCALD workstation in March 1986. Since that time the original SCALD system hardware has been upgraded extensively by adding a second SCALD processor unit, exchanging the MC68010 processors for MC68020s, adding more graphics stations, installing 10 Mbytes of semiconductor memory in both processors, adding four high-performance Fujitsu Eagle disk drives (total of 1688 Mbytes of disk storage), adding an electrostatic printer/plotter, attaching a simulation accelerator (Realfast), and installing an Ethernet local area network.

The SCALD system has been attached to a local DEC MicroVAX II minicomputer in order to provide a convenient link (via DECnet) to a remote DEC VAX 8650 computer. The remote VAX 8650 computer is used to run SCALD logic simulations that are too large to run on the local Valid Logic processors. The SCALD hardware is in continuous use 24 hours per day, seven days per week in a batch-processing mode. The graphics design stations are in use about 14 hours per day, by two overlapping enginering shifts.

One feature of SCALD that CHoPP Computer Corporation has found very attractive is that its architecture is "open." This means that the internal structure of the SCALD system is documented and this documentation is made available to the average user of the system. Most design data stored in the SCALD system is in the form of simple ASCII text files. The various programs that make up the SCALD system communicate through these text files. The user is free to do his own special processing on these text files, or he can even replace a SCALD program's processing function with a program of his own design.

The SCALD user is free to add new parts to the SCALD device libraries or create his own separate device libraries. The user can correct errors or oversights detected in the SCALD device libraries supplied by Valid Logic Systems. The user can create new device models for simulation and timing analysis purposes. Complex devices that cannot be constructed simply from the devices in the SCALD primitive library can be simulated using the "user-coded primitive" feature of the SCALD system.

Because the SCALD workstations are based on the UNIX operating system, a flexible and powerful (though sometimes cryptic) interface is available for adapting the SCALD system to a user's particular needs. A full Berkeley UNIX version 4.3 program-development and text-processing system is delivered with each SCALD workstation system.

If there is any drawback to the "open" and flexible architecture of the SCALD system, it might be that the average engineer must learn a fair amount about the UNIX operating system in order to take full advantage of the system. As many will testify, learning UNIX from the documentation supplied with a typical UNIX system is sometimes painful. Valid Logic Systems' UNIX documentation is "typical" in that respect. However, once mastered, the UNIX standard "tool box" becomes a very useful part of the design and documentation processes. It also helps to have at least one UNIX expert available to answer "hard" questions and to keep the casual UNIX user out of trouble.

Adapting SCALD to Meet our Needs

CHoPP Computer Corporation has taken full advantage of the flexibility of the SCALD system. Without the latent power delivered with the basic SCALD system, we could not have met the challenge of designing a supercomputer with the resources available.

FACTORY SUPPORT

The excellent factory support from Valid Logic Systems and timely access to the latest Valid "beta-release" software have been the key to our success with the SCALD system. The CHoPP supercomputer design pushed Valid's standard-release SCALD software past its design limits on a number of occasions. Valid Logic Systems "hot-line" support has proved to be both useful and responsive. Valid has always been quick to respond with fixed and/or work-arounds where the problems have been theirs and not ours.

USER-CODED PRIMITIVES

CHoPP Computer Corporation has made extensive use of SCALD's "user-coded primitive" feature. "User-coded primitives," also called UCPs, are specially coded Pascal subprograms that are designed to emulate a particular logic device, such as an integrated circuit. UCPs give the SCALD user the option of creating a "behavioral model" of a device, instead of a hardware "gate-level model" of the device. A very complex device can often be modeled as a Pascal UCP program with much less work than the equivalent hardware model. In the case of extremely complex devices (e.g., microprocessors), the UCP might only model a small subset of the device's full functions. We have created UCPs for a number of the more complex integrated circuits in the CHoPP demonstration unit.

One technique we have found useful is to model a complex device as a hybrid combination of software UCPs and hardware primitives. For example, a complex 32-bit arithmetic logic unit (ALU) might be modeled as follows. The core section of the ALU, which performs the logic functions would be coded as a Pascal UCP. All the data paths, multiplexor, parity generation/checking logic, and tristate buffers would be modeled with hardware primitives from the SCALD library. This hybrid modeling scheme makes sense because certain logic functions are easy to do with software (e.g., complex arithmetic operations), but other logic functions are more efficiently done with simple hardware primitives (e.g., multiplexing, parity checking).

One drawback to using "user-coded primitives" in our situation is that the Pascal compilers on the SCALD workstations and VAX 8650 processor are not compatible. The UNIX Pascal code must be modified slightly if it is to be compiled on the VAX for simulations there. We manage this problem by using a "preprocessor" program and coding UCPs in a special Pascal preprocessor language. The preprocessor program takes in the Pascal preprocessor source code and emits either Valid Logic Systems or DEC VAX Pascal source code. In this way, we can maintain one source code file which serves both processors.

CUSTOM DESIGN TOOLS

CHoPP Computer Corporation has created a number of special design tools in order to support the design of the CHoPP supercomputer. Most of these tools were written in the C language and execute under UNIX on the SCALD workstations. The following is a selected list of the tools we have developed.

Makedesign. A utility that combines any number of drawings (logic designs) into a single integrated design. Makedesign also automatically processes any programmable devices (e.g., PALs) that are moved as part of the design integration.

Makeconn. A utility that processes the master interboard wiring list for the CHoPP computer and automatically creates connector drawings and assigns connector via holes for each printed circuit board.

Checkconn. A utility that checks the master interboard wiring list against the "top-level" drawings for each printed circuit board in the CHoPP computer. This utility insures that each printed circuit board has the correct interboard signals connected to it.

Listconn. A utility that checks the master interboard wiring list for consistency and produces a three-dimensional mapping of all interboard signals in the CHoPP demonstration unit "sandwich."

Listboard. A utility that shows the allocation of interboard signals for each printed circuit board by connector. As an option, a drawing of the circuit board can be produced, with the location (connector and pin) of each signal shown.

Simasm. A CHoPP machine code assembler that produces SCALD simulator control files that can be used to load CHoPP programs into the simulator for testing purposes.

Compileprom. A utility that reads an ASCII text document describing the format of each of the CHoPP superinstructions and produces PROM programming files for the CHoPP superinstruction decode logic.

Stripexp. A utility that removes unneeded information from SCALD compiler expansion files in order to speed up the simulator "loading" phase.

Stripsyn. A utility that removes unneeded information from SCALD compiler signal name synonym files in order to speed up the simulator "loading" phase.

Squashexp. A utility that compresses SCALD compiler expansion files in order to speed file transfer to the VAX computer.

Telplace. A utility program that converts component-placement information derived from placement drawings on the SCALD system to a form usable by the Telesis PCB layout system.

Batch. A utility program that manages batch queues used to schedule lengthy SCALD processes. Large SCALD compilations, batch simulations, and other processing operations execute more efficiently when executed one at a time, instead of concurrently via the UNIX timesharing system.

DCtest. A utility subsystem that drives the DC test fixtures on the MicroVAX II to perform DC tests. Physical packaging information and test vector are derived from the SCALD system. Tests are performed either interactively or as batch processes using a CRT terminal on the MicroVax system.

Findsig. A utility that allows an engineer to access a cross-reference data base that is used to locate signals on a circuit board. The cross-reference relates signals names to boards, component locations, and component pins.

Besides the above-mentioned utility programs, we have developed a large number of UNIX shell scripts that provide a number of special functions related to the engineering of the CHoPP demonstration unit.

One interesting use of the SCALD system was to verify the logic of the compacted gate array IC that CHoPP Computer designed in order to provide a 16-port register file for the arithmetic section of the processor. Test vectors were taken from the VAX 8650 where the IC was designed and simulated (using LSI Logic's logic design and simulation system). The vectors were converted into a form compatible with the SCALD simulator. A simple test design was generated that included one of the gate array ICs. The test vectors were run against the simple design using the SCALD simulator.

The tests verified a number of things. They verified that the Pascal "user-coded primitive" model matched the actual IC design. They also verified that the same "high-level" conception of the IC was shared by three different people: the engineer who was designing with the IC, the programmer who produced the Pascal "behavioral" model (i.e., the UCP) and the engineer who designed the IC itself. There was now some assurance that the gate array IC, as designed, matched its intended purpose.

Design Management Structure

The design of the CHoPP demonstration unit with the SCALD system is managed in such a way that many engineers can work cooperatively and efficiently on the single large design that is the CHoPP computer. Three separate UNIX file systems were set up to manage the design of the machine; the file systems are called *int, master,* and *pcb.* The file systems contain the drawings and SCALD files which represent the logic of the CHoPP computer.

The *int* file system is used for design integration, and is where engineers' individual designs are collected for integration with other parts of the CHoPP computer. All simulation testing is done in the *int* file system. In general, simulation testing is done in *int* by "plugging together" large pieces of the machine and then running test vectors interactively.

The *master* file system is where fully tested, and hopefully correct, designs are stored. Special permission from a responsible librarian is required to make changes to the *master* file system. Designs can be "checked out" of *master* for testing purposes. However, if changes are made to these designs, the librarian must be consulted before *master* can be updated. The librarian is responsible for insuring that *master* always contains a collection of designs that correctly describe a working CHoPP computer.

The *pcb* file system is used to prepare designs for transmission to the Telesis printed circuit board (PCB) layout system. The "high-level" designs are "packaged" and "flattened" in the *pcb* file system. This process reduces the original "high-level" design to a "flat" design, with the logic of the design expressed as actual integrated circuit packages and with package pin numbers assigned to individual signals. Once released for printed circuit board layout, designs in *pcb* cannot be changed until "back annotation" information from the Telesis layout process has been transmitted back into the SCALD system. The *pcb* file system holds the physical design information for the CHoPP computer's printed circuit boards. It therefore is used by the automated DC test system and is consulted when probing circuit boards in the assembled machine.

If errors are detected and/or design improvements are needed, then changes are made to a copy of the affected design taken from the *master* file system. Tests are performed using the *int* file system. Once the design changes have been verified, the improved design replaced the older design in master. When approval is given for a new printed circuit board, the improved design is moved to *pcb* and new circuit boards are produced.

This separation of designs into three file systems allows new design and simulation to be carried out in a simple way without affecting the validated master design, and without interacting with the previously constructed and in-process printed circuit boards. Printed circuit board engineering is effectively decoupled from the "high-level" design of the machine.

Experiences with the SCALD Simulator

Our biggest problem with relying on simulation is that the simulation run times tend to get very long as the various pieces of the CHoPP computer design are integrated into a single design simulation. Simulation turn around times have gone from minutes, to hours, and even to days as more and more of the machine's logic is "plugged" together.

In general, we have found that the limiting factor is not the speed at which the simulation actually "runs," but the time spent leading up to the actual circuit simulation. This "lead" time is spent in the SCALD compiler and in the "loading" of the compiled design into the SCALD simulation program. Improvements in the original SCALD compiler software by Valid Logic Systems, especially the incremental compilation feature ("page compiler"), have improved the compilation times greatly. However, the simulation "load" times remain quite long.

LARGE SIMULATIONS
Our designs tend to be large, with compiler "expansion" files in the range of 20 to 50 Mbytes. Under ideal conditions, such large designs can take over five hours to re-compile and a similar number of hours to "load" into the simulator. What determines these times is the speed at which the processor can "page" virtual memory blocks to and from the backing store (i.e., the disks). With only ten million bytes of main store in our virtual memory MC68020 processor unit, the 20 to 50 Mbyte virtual data structures being manipulated by the SCALD compiler and simulator simply do not fit in the physical memory of the processor.

Clearly, the "working set" of the compiler and simulator programs do not fit well with the available physical memory in the processor. More physical memory is not an option because we are already near the maximum offered with our SCALD system units. As might be expected, when we upgraded our UNIX system to use the high-performance disk drives for backing store, we found our compiling and simulation times improved by over a factor of 2, a direct result of the faster "paging" offered by the high-performance drives.

Moving larger designs to the VAX 8650 superminicomputer for simulation has reduced simulation times radically, in the cases where the design fits within the physical memory of the VAX. We must still compile the designs on the Valid Logic processors. For example, a large simulation (20 Mbyte expansion file) that took over 15 hours using the MC68020 Valid Logic SCALD station completes in less than 1 hour on the VAX. This simulation required about 60 Mbytes of {\it virtual} memory space on the VAX. We observed that the "working set" of that simulation was about 40 Mbytes. (Before the VAX 8650 was upgraded from 32 to 64 Mbytes of physical memory, the same simulation took about 5 hours to complete on the VAX, although the elapsed "CPU time" was only 45 minutes.)

With sufficient memory installed in the VAX 8650, this design required about 45 minutes of wall clock time to "load" into the simulator and about 10 minutes of wall clock time to execute the simulation test vectors. A single machine cycle (one 60 nanosecond clock period) requires about 10 seconds of "CPU time" (about 10 seconds of wall clock time when the "working set" of the simulation fits into the physical memory of the VAX processor).

MEMORY LIMITS ON THE VAX

At the present time we are facing a frustrating problem with simulation on the VAX 8650. Although we can upgrade the VAX 8650 processor to support over 128 Mbytes of physical memory, a single program running under the VMS operating system cannot have more then 32 Mbytes of physical memory assigned to it. Memory beyond this limit is "paged out."

Under VAX's virtual memory operating system, virtual memory pages that have been marked for "page out" to the disk are actually cached in a "pool" that resides in unused physical memory in the machine. Therefore, "page faults" need not generate backing store disk accesses, given sufficient unused memory. This offers a way to increase the physical memory assigned to a single program, as the operating system's "page cache" increases the apparent size of the program's "working set" by substituting quick "virtual" page faults for much slower "real" page faults.

However, the VAX operating system places an arbitrary upper limit on the number of modified pages that can be held at any time in the "page cache." This limit restricts the amount of modified memory in the "page cache" to no more than 8 Mbytes. The net result is that, when running on a VAX, the SCALD simulator program will begin to "page out" to disk after it has created about 40 Mbytes of internal data structure (32 Mbytes in the program plus 8 Mbytes in the "pool"). After this limit is passed, the program's efficency drops radically, and the execution speed becomes paced by the speed at which the operating system can "page out" memory to the disk. This is in spite of the fact that plenty of unused memory is available in the processor. At this time we are exploring a number of possibilities aimed at correcting this problem.

REALFAST HARDWARE ACCELERATOR

The Realfast hardware accelerator has proved effective in speeding up the execution of simulation test vectors. We have seen execution improvements of the order of a factor of 10. This has proved most useful for "batch" (noninteractive) simulations which execute a large number of test vectors.

The Realfast accelerator does not change the simulation "load" time substantially. It therefore is of marginal use for the more common short interactive simulation sessions. The Realfast accelerator also suffers from the problem that its memory is limited. Unlike its software counterpart, the Realfast has no automatic virtual memory paging scheme. If a design is too large for the Realfast unit's memory, the design cannot be run using the Realfast. There are, however, tricks that can be used to conserve the Realfast's simulation memory. For example, one trick is to substitute custom "user-coded primitives" for the standard library memory parts in designs that have a large number of memory integrated circuits. Because "user-coded primitives" are not executed in the Realfast accelerator, the demand for Realfast memory is reduced, at the price of a reduced execution speed.

Result

The Valid Logic Systems SCALD system has allowed the CHoPP development team to effectively design and debug the logic of the CHoPP demonstration unit by running test vectors created from CHoPP assembly language source programs. Complex interactions of machine instructions, including conditional branches, exception handling, and hardware task switching, have been tested and debugged with an efficiency that is unattainable using conventional hand-generated board-level test vectors. This level of design verification has allowed us to skip the traditional breadboard prototype stage of a computer design.

REFERENCES

1. Gibson, J. C. (1970). *The Gibson Mix*, Report TR.00.2043, IBM System Development Division.

2. Kuck, D. J. (1972). *The Structure of Computers and Computations*, Vol. 1, Wiley, New York.

3. McWilliams, T. M. and L. C. Widdoes Jr. (1978). "SCALD: structured computer-aided logic design," *Proceedings 15th Design Automation Conference*, pp. 271–276.

4. Padua, D. A. and M. J. Wolfe (1986). "Advanced compiler optimizations for supercomputers," *Commun. ACM*, Vol. 29, No. 12, pp. 1184–1201.

5. Russell R. M., (1979). "The CRAY-1 computer system," *Commun. ACM*, Vol. 21, No. 1, pp. 63–72.

6. Thornton, J. E. (1970). *Design of a Computer—The Control Data 660.* Scott Foresman, Glenview, Ill.

7. Tomasulo, R. M. (1967). "An efficient algorithm for exploiting multiple arithmetic units," *IBM Journal*, pp. 25–33, January.

3

THE UNISYS INTEGRATED SCIENTIFIC PROCESSOR SYSTEM

Jane R. Kessler, James A. Hodek, David S. Dunn,
Francis A. Stephens, and Keith Besaw

In June 1986, Unisys Corporation delivered its first 1100/90 ISP system; in May 1987, Unisys introduced the system at The Second Annual International Conference on Supercomputing, in a series of papers describing the system.

The introduction of this system represented the first time a tightly coupled system operating under one operating system including one or more general-purpose mainframe processors and one or more Class VI supercomputer processors had been brought to the computer marketplace as a commercially available product. This set of heterogeneous processors, instruction processors (IPs), input/output processors (IOPs), and supercomputing processors (ISPs) is tightly integrated into a mainframe environment by means of a shared memory with high bandpass.

The significant attributes of this system are:

- Supercomputer performance transparently accessible to the user. A high-performance processing system that achieves through its many degrees of parallelism a greater percentage of peak power than any machine in the industry and through its integration a high throughput capability.
- A supercomputing system with all the capabilities of a mainframe product, including interactive supercomputing, database processing accessible from

FORTRAN, multitasking, and multiprocessing, as well as a full spectrum of development tools to maximize productivity and performance.

- Fault-tolerant supercomputing with 100% through checking satisfying all the normal mainframe requirements of reliability, maintainability, installability, and manufacturability.
- Tight integration, through a memory with high bandpass, into a mainframe environment that permits in excess of 96 percent of the ISP cycles to be dedicated to user's production work. Additionally, the ISP operation has little impact (less than 4 percent) on the operating system running on the IP.
- No data motion in this system, which enhances throughput and maintains data integrity for the user as well as providing the user with productivity benefits due to more rapid algorithm development.
- "State of the art" vectorizing compiler that vectorizes more of the user's FORTRAN (old or new) than any other compiler in the industry.
- A supercomputer system that is readily field-upgradable from one to two ISP processors. Instantly site-reconfigurable to one or two complete systems, depending on security and production demands.

The four major sections included in this chapter are (1) "The Unisys 1100/90 System—Integrated Supercomputing," which is an overview of the 1100/90 ISP System including the components of system integration, the ISP organization, and hardware. In addition, the software support system for software development and performance enhancement is presented. The performance of the machine is briefly covered for major metrics. (2) "Performance Results on an Integrated, Interactive Supercomputer," which covers the objectives and performance results of the design concept of an integrated mainframe supercomputing environment. Topics include performance in the area of system integration, interactive supercomputing, and overall system performance. (3) "Processor Scheduling Algorithms for a Heterogeneous Vector and Scalar Computer System," which discusses task scheduling for the 6-by heterogeneous multiprocessor 1100/94 + 2 ISPs system. The key hardware design element for performance is having the memory bandpass to adequately support these six processors and the four input/output processors. Next comes the processor scheduling algorithms. Ninety-six percent user utilization of the vector processors can be demonstrated. (4) "Advanced Techniques for Vectorizing Dusty Decks," which is one of a series of papers that have been published describing the Universal Compiling System. The focus of this paper is the techniques developed within the compiler to make the migration of older FORTRAN programs—"dusty decks"—easy for the user. This paper explores two techniques designed into the UCS FORTRAN compiler for converting existing programs to parallel execution—scalar expansion and IF-to-MASK conversion—and explores a new dependency that simplifies the two techniques, called *REVERSE dependency*. In order to explain the generation of REVERSE dependencies for IF-to-MASK conversion, another topic, *control expressions*, is also explored.

The Unisys 1100/90 ISP System Integrated Supercomputing*

In late June 1986, Unisys made the first customer delivery of a unique supercomputing system—the 1100/90 ISP (Integrated Scientific Processor). This is the first system that integrates a complete supercomputing system directly into a mainframe computer. The following is an overview of the ISP, covering its architecture, hardware, special software, and performance.

INTRODUCTION

The Unisys 1100/90 ISP system integrates a supercomputer class processor into the normal multiprocessor environment of the 1100/90 system. Prior to the integration of the ISP, the 1100/90 system had already provided up to four 1100/90 instruction processors (IPs) and four input/output processors (IOPs) sharing access to a large central memory. The ISP (of which there may be two added to an 1100/90 ISP System) now adds another processor type that is especially designed for and dedicated to handling scientific processing. The overall structure of the 1100/90 ISP system is seen in Figure 3-1. The basic 1100/90 ISP system consists of one IP, one ISP, one IOP, and one Scientific Processor Storage Unit (SPSU). Additional IPs, an ISP, IOPs or SPSUs may be added to the system as a field upgrade.

The ISP is a general-purpose scientific processor having both scalar and vector capabilities. Through use of simple compile time directives, user programs may be written to run either on the 1100/90 IP or the ISP (or both). The operating system automatically allocates the processors (IPs and ISPs) in the

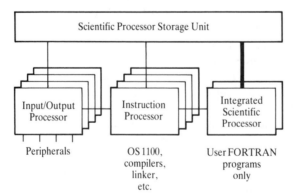

Figure 3-1. ISP integrated structure.

---

* This section was contributed by James A. Hodek.

system between those jobs requiring the ISP and those requiring the IP. The 1100/90 ISP system is therefore a heterogeneous multiprocessing system consisting of different types of processors with specific characteristics that are optimized for unique tasks.

The ISP is a special-purpose processor in that it is dedicated exclusively to running user programs. No portions of the operating system or system software such as compilers or linkers execute on the ISP and, therefore, do not steal ISP time from user FORTRAN programs. Ideally, the ISP should be used for those programs that can utilize its vector processing capabilites. Pure scalar programs (those that contain no vectors) can be run on either the 1100/90 IP or the ISP but do not take particular advantage of the ISP.

INTEGRATION

The ISP is fully integrated into the 1100/90 system. Since the Series 1100 is an established hardware/software system, this provides the ISP user with access to a large collection of proven software systems. Constructing an application for the ISP is precisely the same as for the 1100/90. An ISP application can be built using all the tools the mature mainframe 1100 system provides.

An ISP user therefore has access to the following kinds of software which represent thousands of man-years of development effort:

- Various modes of processing: timesharing; batch; realtime; transaction
- Interactive development aids (OS 1100 and UNIX based): editors; compilers; assembler; linker; debuggers; performance-measurement tools
- File-management system
- Database management
- Communications networking
- Extensive application packages

The 1100/90 IP should not be regarded as a "front end" for the ISP because the 1100/90 IP and ISP share the same memory and have identical data formats, and therefore, there is no data movement or data conversion required when the operating system gives the ISP a task to perform. This is an important advantage of the total integration of the ISP into a general-purpose system—the 1100/90. Furthermore, the absence of data movement between processing environments permits the use of the ISP supercomputer in interactive applications.

The use of identical floating-point formats on the IP and ISP ensures that there are no problems of differences in precision or convergence when moving an algorithm developed on the IP to the ISP. These problems may often arise when using a front-end processor with a different floating-point format.

TECHNOLOGY

The ISP shares the same component and fabrication technology as the 1100/90 IP. This generation of packaging is called "high-performance packaging" or HPP. The circuits used are large-scale integration (LSI) and medium-scale integration (MSI). The circuit type used in the ISP is emitter-coupled logic (ECL) with a switch time of less than 500 picoseconds. The ISP makes extensive use of custom gate arrays. In total, the ISP contains over 1 300 000 gates.

The ISP circuits are packaged on multilayer cards. Two cards are connected to form a card pair. Between the cards of the card pair is a "cold plate." Distilled water is circulated through the cold plate to remove heat generated by the ECL logic. The ISP contains 50 such card pairs.

Because of the high logic density, each circuit card has connectors on three sides. The card pairs are inserted into a card deck. The card deck interconnects the circuit cards via a multilayer backpanel (containing 31 layers).

The hardware technology of the ISP was selected to satisfy mainframe manufacturability and reliability criteria and hence exotic technology was consciously not employed.

ISP CHARACTERISTICS

The ISP consists of two components: the scalar module (SM) and the vector processing module (VM). The SM provides general instruction control, address translation, and a complement of scalar arithmetic units. The VM is a pipelined vector processor containing several arithmetic and move units that may operate in parallel.

The functional units of the VM can automatically "chain" operations together; for example, the first result from the vector multiply pipe may be used immediately by the vector add pipe. ISP chaining is general in that any pipe will chain from the results of another without special considerations. This feature has assisted the special software developed with the ISP to utilize efficiently a high percentage of the machine's peak processing power.

The SM and VM portions of the ISP are also overlapped so that, where possible, scalar computations may be done in parallel with vector computations.

ISP Organization

The major architectural components of the ISP are shown in Figure 3-2.

Registers

The ISP is a register-based vector processor. Vector operations are performed between vector registers or, possibly, between vector registers and scalar registers.

SCALAR REGISTERS
The ISP contains 16 general-purpose (G) scalar registers. These registers may hold single- (36-bit) or double- (72-bit) precision floating-point numbers,

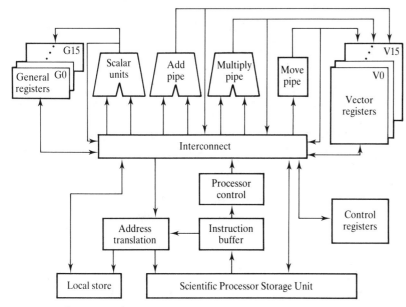

Figure 3-2. ISP organization.

integers, addresses, and vector address strides (distance between vector elements). The G registers may be used in operations with other G registers, with
storage, and also in combination with the vector registers. When used in vector
operation, a G register is treated as a vector of identical elements.

VECTOR REGISTERS
There are 16 vector registers in the ISP. Each vector register contains 64 36-bit
elements. A vector register may hold 64 single-precision (36-bit) floating-point or
integer operands or it may hold 32 double-precision (72-bit) floating-point or
integer operands.

LOOP-CONTROL REGISTERS
The ISP contains eight vector and eight element loop-control registers that
together with loop-control instructions manage the execution of and bookkeeping
for vector and element loops.

A vector loop is a loop in which vector operations process a 64- (or 32-)
element vector strip during each iteration. The active vector loop-control register
controls the length of vector operations within the loop.

An element loop is a loop that processes a single element from within a
vector strip on each iteration. The active-element loop-control register specifies
which element is accessed from within a vector register during each iteration.

The ISP loop-control structures were especially designed to match the types
of loops used in FORTRAN programs.

STATE REGISTERS

The ISP contains 16 (36-bit) state (S) registers. These registers are used for various purposes in association with ISP instructions or for machine execution control. The following are of particular interest.

S4, S5   *The vector mask register pair.* Each register contains 32 bits of the 64-bit mask generated by vector comparisons. The vector mask register is used by the ISP FORTRAN compiler to vectorize conditional (IF statements) operations in vector loops. A vector operation may use the mask register to select a subset of the elements in the vector register to be used in the operation.

S6   Scalar condition code. Set by scalar compare instructions.

S7   *Local storage stack-control word.* A special feature of the ISP hardware is the provision for a high-speed stack that resides in local store. Instructions are provided to push and pop the local store stack. The ISP FORTRAN compiler takes advantage of this facility for temporary storage in subroutines. Items in the local store stack may be accessed in one cycle.

S14   Breakpoint address. The breakpoint address may be used to set instruction or data breakpoints in a program. This facility in combination with a software debugging system (PADS: Programmer Advanced Debugging System) provides an efficient and interactive means for debugging FORTRAN programs on the ISP.

S15   Internal interval timer. The internal interval timer is a count-down 36-bit register that is decremented by one at each machine cycle. On expiration, an interval timer interrupt is generated. The interval timer is utilized by software in two ways:

- To obtain an accurate measure of actual execution time utilized by a program from one point to another. This time is available to user FORTRAN programs from a library subroutine.
- When combined with a special software package, the Program Execution Evaluation Routine (PEER), the S15 interval timer interrupt provides a means for statistical evaluation of where an ISP program spends its execution time. Since very little overhead is incurred, this evaluation may be performed on long-running programs to determine where there is potential for optimization. The PEER software can produce a report that shows the percentage of time spent in each part of a program.

ISP Processor Control

OS 1100 is responsible for assigning tasks for the ISP to perform and thus keeping the ISP busy. Typically, the 1100/90 ISP system will have a mixture of jobs to run. The ISP is treated as a special resource by the operating system to be shared among the executing job mix. Each job will receive a portion of the ISP processing power. Switching the ISP between jobs is an OS task that represents a necessary overhead in a multiprocessing environment. The operating system has been optimized in this area to minimize this overhead. Since switching overhead has been minimized, it is possible to keep the ISP over 98 percent busy in a multiprocessing environment while incurring only a small IP overhead of 1.5 percent.

In order to direct and control the ISP, the hardware contains four control structures. These are the mailbox, the quantum timer, hardware status registers, and the scientific processor control block.

MAILBOX

Control of the ISP by OS 1100 is accomplished via a "mailbox." The mailbox contains various pieces of control information used by both the operating system software and the ISP hardware. Among these are:

- a control code (determines the ISP function to be performed);
- a pointer to the scientific processor control block;
- the current status of the ISP;
- the current execution address for the ISP;
- a copy of the hardware status registers.

By means of the mailbox and interprocessor interrupts, the operating system controls execution of each ISP program on the ISP. Each ISP job receives a quantum of time to execute. It may use all of its time quantum or give up control voluntarily. Typical reasons for relinquishing control would be to perform I/O, reference a package available only on the IP or to obtain service from the operating system.

QUANTUM TIMER

The actual duration of execution time on the ISP for each activity is controlled by the quantum timer. The quantum timer is loaded and controlled by the operating system. Each ISP instruction executed causes the quantum timer value to be decreased by a specific amount. This amount is the approximate execution time of the instruction. This approximate time is not dependent on job mix and will be reproducible between runs of the same program. When the quantum timer value crosses zero, an external interrupt occurs.

HARDWARE STATUS REGISTERS

The hardware status registers (HSR 0, 1, 2, 3) consist of four 36-bit registers that indicate the state of the ISP. These are used by OS 1100 to determine the state of the ISP upon completion of an ISP activity (normal or otherwise). If an activity terminates abnormally owing to a hardware problem, the HSRs may be used to determine the nature of the ISP-detected hardware problem. This information may be used by the operating system to automatically initiate diagnostics to determine required maintenance action.

The HSRs may also contain information on software problems detected by the hardware, for example, addressing errors.

SCIENTIFIC PROCESSOR CONTROL BLOCK

The scientific processor control block contains (or contains pointers to) all the information necessary to begin (or suspend) the execution of an activity on the ISP. This information is managed by the hardware and software to control the execution of programs using the ISP.

The ISP uses the information in the SPCB to control the acceleration (startup) or deceleration (stop) of a program's quantum of time on the ISP.

Local Storage

The ISP contains a special directly addressed internal storage called *local store*. The size of local store is 4096 36-bit words. Its principal use is to provide fast access to scalar operands. Data may be moved to/from local store in one cycle.

Local store is actually part of a specially addressed storage segment which may be up to 64K words in size. Data in the accelerated 4096-word portion of this segment is local to each activity executing on the ISP and is loaded/stored on each activation/deactivation of an activity.

Special care has been taken in the design of the system software for the ISP (compilers, libraries, and linker) to optimize the use of local store. Uses for local store include a pool of commonly used constants, common scratch areas, scalar user variables, array descriptors, parameter descriptors, and expression temporary storage.

A special feature of the ISP hardware is the provision for a stack that resides in local store. Instructions are provided to push and pop this local store stack. A stack frame is 32 words. The ISP FORTRAN compiler takes particular advantage of this facility for temporary storage in subroutines.

Instruction Set

All ISP instructions (both scalar and vector) are 36 bits in length. The general format of scalar and vector computational instructions is shown below:

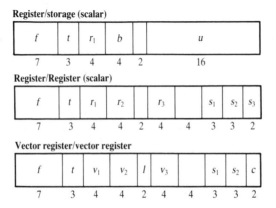

Register/storage (scalar)

f	t	r_1	b		u
7	3	4	4	2	16

Register/Register (scalar)

f	t	r_1	r_2		r_3		s_1	s_2	s_3
7	3	4	4	2	4	4	3	3	2

Vector register/vector register

f	t	v_1	v_2	l	v_3		s_1	s_2	c
7	3	4	4	2	4	4	3	3	2

f   Is the 7 bit function code

t   Indicates the type of the operation:

    0   Single precision integer

    1   Double precision integer

    2   Single precision floating point

    3   Double precision floating point

b   Indicates the index G register or special addressing

    0   Reference to local storage segment

    1–14   Reference to an index G register

    15   Reference to the current local store stack frame

r   Specifies a G register number or a vector register element (determined by *s*). In general $r3 \leftarrow r1$ op $r2$ (RR) $r1 \leftarrow$ storage (or $r1 \leftarrow r1$ op storage) (RS).

s   Indicates whether the associated operand is a G register, S register or a V register. For vector operations, *s* indicates that the register is either a replicated G register or a V register.

v   Specifies either a V register or a replicated G register for use in a vector operation. In general, $V_3 \leftarrow V_1$ op V_2.

l   Selects the vector length from four possibilities (from the loop-control register).

    0   Element count

    1   Next element count

    2   Alternate 1

    3   Alternate 2

c   Indicates what mask control is to be used with the vector operation:

    0, 2   Process all elements

    1   Process elements that correspond to 0s in the mask

    3   Process elements which correspond to 1s in the mask

The following instructions are implemented on the ISP:

Scalar instructions

Add	Convert (Integer/Float,
Add negative	Single/Double)
Multiply	Shifts (Right Logical, Right
Divide	Algebraic,
Absolute value	Left Logical, Left Circular)
Count Signs	Load
Logicals (And, Or, Xor)	Store
Compare	Move Register
	Move Negative

Vector instructions

Add	Divide
Add Negative	Absolute Value
Multiply	Negate

Shifts (Right Logical, Right Algebraic, Left Logical, Left Circular)
Count Signs
Logical (And, Or, Xor)
Compare
Convert (Integer/Float, Single/Double)
Sum Reduction
Product Reduction
Max Reduction
Min Reduction
Load

Store
Generate Index Vector
Indexed Load
Indexed Store
Move
Compress
Distribute
Load Alternating (used for complex arithmetic)
Store Alternating (used for complex arithmetic)
Extract Population Count
Extract Population Parity

Control instructions
Build Element Loop
Build Vector Loop
Jump Vector Loop
Jump Element Loop
Conditional Jump
Increment and Jump Less
Decrement and Jump Greater
Load Address and Jump
Jump to External Segment
Load Multiple

Store Multiple
Store L Registers
Load L Registers
Advance and Retract Local Storage
Stack Pointer
Adjust Loop Register Pointers
Generate Interrupt
Test and Set/Test and Clear
Diagnose Read
Diagnose Write

Pipelines

To achieve high performance, a large amount of parallelism is designed into the ISP. As discussed previously, the vector and scalar portions of the ISP may execute in parallel. In addition to this, the vector unit contains several parallel functional units called *pipes* or *pipelines*. These are:

Add pipe	adds
	subtracts
	converts
	shifts
	logicals
Multiply pipe	multiplies
	divides
	population count
Move pipe	register to register
	compression/distribution
	population parity
	precision conversion

Load/store pipe	load vector register from storage
	storage vector register to storage
Scalar access pipe	access scalar register for vector operation

Each of these pipes may be in execution at the same time. For example, the ISP may be simultaneously performing a vector addition $(A + B)$, a vector multiplication $(C * D)$ and a vector load or store. The ISP, therefore, may produce four single-precision floating-point results or two double-precision floating-point results per machine cycle.

Storage

A special high-performance scientific processor storage unit (SPSU) is provided for the ISP. The SPSU may be configured in 4 194 304-word cabinet increments up to a maximum of four cabinets of SPSU. Each SPSU cabinet can support up to four IPs, four IOPs, and two ISPs.

The SPSU supports a very high load/store bandwidth, which is balanced with the processing capability of the ISPs, IPs, and IOPs. This balance has been selected to assure that there is no storage access bottleneck on the ISP even at peak processing speeds.

The characteristics of the ISP processor and the SPSU storage are summarized as follows.

- Overlapped scalar and vector processing modules
- Three parallel vector processing pipes (multiply, add, and move)
- Parallel load/store access to storage
- 30-nanosecond clock period
- Four single-precision floating point results per cycle (or two double-precision)
- Single- and double-precision integer arithmetic
- Single- and double-precision floating-point arithmetic
- 16 72-bit general (G) registers
- 16 36-bit state (S) registers (with vector mask registers)
- 16 64-element vector (V) registers
- 4096-word local storage
- 8 vector loop control registers
- 8 element loop control registers
- 16 256-word instruction buffers
- 255 basic instructions

Scientific processor storage

- One to four 4 194 304-word memory cabinets
- 4 194 304 to 16 777 216 36-bit words (plus six check, one check parity and one data parity)
- 8 interleaved banks per cabinet (524 288 words per bank)
- 90-nanosecond cycle time

- 1420 million words/sec throughput (355 million word/sec per cabinet)
- Two ISP Ports (scientific processor—receives four words per clock period; 133 million word/sec per port)
- Four ports (1100/90) (15 million word/sec per port)
- Four IOP ports (input/output processor) (8 million word/sec per port)

Addressing

The ISP uses the same 36-bit virtual addresses that are used by the 1100/90 extended architecture. For performance reasons, however, the conversion mechanism from a virtual address to a real memory address is different. The ISP uses an activity segment table (AST) to convert addresses. There may be up to 32 entries in the AST and thus, 32 segments in the ISP program. (A segment is a contiguous region of real memory.) A typical program, however, might use only five or six segments. ISP segments may be created by the static linking feature of the OS 1100 linking system.

Loading and Storing Vectors

Vector registers are loaded and stored by Load Vector (LV) and Store Vector (SV) instructions. These instructions reference a G register that holds the vector virtual address. In addition to the virtual address, the G register may also hold a stride, which is the distance between vector elements and will be used to determine the storage address of each vector element loaded or stored. Alternatively, an implicit stride of +1 (single precision) or +2 (double precision) may be selected by the instruction.

Where the elements of a vector are not being referenced in such an orderly fashion (e.g., in FORTRAN, where the array subscript is itself an array reference) the ISP provides vector-indexed Load and Store instructions (LVX, SVX). In these instructions a vector register is referenced in the Load or Store. That vector register will be used to obtain the offsets to the vector elements to Load or Store. These instructions provide a "scatter/gather" capability and are quite useful in many vector processing applications including sparse-matrix handling.

Error Detection

Fully 30 percent of the ISP logic is dedicated to assuring the reliability and maintainability of the system. All of the ISP data paths, address paths, and external interfaces carry parity checks to assure that data passed through is not corrupted. All data registers and storages are also parity-checked. ISP microcode storage is similarly protected. Both the scalar and vector arithmetic units employ parity-prediction logic to ensure data integrity.

The ISP design also incorporates fault-isolation logic to assist in readily locating failing components. This capability, together with diagnostic software, is intended to minimize repair time if a hardware problem arises. The intention is to minimize down-time. Both the fault-detection and fault-isolation capabilities of the ISP meet the requirements of a normal mainframe environment.

In a multi-ISP configuration, the operating system allocates ISP processing equally between the available ISPs in an exactly similar fashion as in handling multiprocessing with IPs. If a problem occurs on one ISP, only the program actually using that ISP at the time of the failure is lost, and this is the case only if no checkpoint has been applied. The rest of the workload continues on the remaining ISP.

The failing ISP is automatically taken offline. Diagnostic information is taken for fault isolation and repair. After repair, the ISP may be dynamically added back into the application.

For long-running programs, the operating system provides the capability to periodically take checkpoints of the program. If a failure occurs affecting the program, it may be restarted from its most recent checkpoint.

SOFTWARE

The key to the performance of a supercomputer is the ability easily to access the full power of the machine from a high-level language. There are two principal vehicles for accessing this power: an efficient vectorizing compiler and high-performance library routines implementing common mathematical algorithms.

Since the bulk of scientific code is written in FORTRAN, the presence of a vectorizing FORTRAN compiler is essential. Users depend upon the compiler to do a good job of utilizing the machine.

Vectorizing FORTRAN Compiler

A new FORTRAN compiler was developed specifically for the ISP. This compiler contains an extensive vector optimization capability and has demonstrated in independent tests that it vectorizes "more difficult" loops than any other compiler in the industry.

COMPILER ARCHITECTURE

The new FORTRAN compiler is part of a "family" of compilers sharing a unique architecture. This family is called the "Universal Compiling System" or UCS. The UCS system has defined a common, language-independent, intermediate form into which programs written in various languages may be translated. A "front-end" translator exists for each language handled by UCS (currently FORTRAN, COBOL, and PASCAL). The front end translates the source program to the common intermediate form. A single, common, code generation and run-time support system called the Language Support System (LSS) is used to translate and optimize the intermediate form of the source program into object code. The structure of UCS is shown in Figure 3-3.

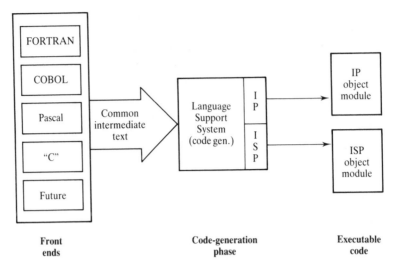

Figure 3-3. Universal compiling system.

This design allows new languages to be added easily to the UCS compiling system and provides for easy use of multiple languages in writing a program. It is expected that additional languages will be offered for the ISP in the future.

FORTRAN VECTORIZATION

The FORTRAN compiler performs a complete analysis of a FORTRAN program's branching structure to determine those regions where vector operations are possible. This analysis in combination with a sequence of vectorization algorithms eventually produces a transformation of the original FORTRAN program into ISP object code, which performs vector operations.

The vectorizing process of the ISP FORTRAN compiler is broken into the following steps.

1. *Flow analysis, blocking and information gathering.* This step is fundamental to the vectorization process. At this step the loop areas of the program are located and information is gathered about the interaction between the variables and arrays in the program.

2. *Loop normalization.* Loops are transformed into a common form for common treatment by the remaining steps. For example, DO Loops are transformed to begin at 1 with a step size of 1.

3. *DO variable substitution.* Scalars that are functions of the DO variable are eliminated from the loop. Where used, they are replaced by equivalent expressions involving the DO variable.

4. *Dependency analysis.* The use and definition of array elements and scalar variables within loops is examined. The dependency between definition and

use must be determined to learn whether array operations can be vectorized safely.

5. *Scalar renaming.* Scalars are often used in vectorizable loops as a convenience to the expression of the algorithm. Scalar definitions and uses are examined to determine which are independent of each other and which may be eliminated.

6. *Scalar expansion.* In certain vectorizable loops scalars may be defined as the result of array-element expressions. These may be vector intermediate results and are recognized as such by the compiler.

7. *Loop distribution.* A DO loop containing several independent functions may be broken up into several loops for more efficient vector code generation. This also splits vectorizable statements from nonvectorizable portions of loops when possible.

8. *Loop interchange.* Loops that are nested may be interchanged (the inner loop becomes the outer loop and the outer loop becomes inner loop) where such interchange is feasible and results in more efficient vector code.

9. *Special casing.* The ISP FORTRAN compiler contains checks for certain special-case FORTRAN loops for which the ISP contains special hardware instructions. In addition, certain special FORTRAN loops that might not be considered vectorizable on the basis of a simple analysis of their array element dependencies are vectorized by the compiler. These special cases include:
   - Reductions (SUM, PRODUCT, MIN, and MAX)
   - Linear recurrences, for example, $A(I) = B(I) \times A(I-1) + C(I)$
   - Loop re-rolling. Loops that have been unrolled by the FORTRAN programmer to expose additional scalar operations for optimizing scalar compilers and hardware are re-rolled and vectorized. For example:

```
DO 2 K=1, 996, 5
S=S+Z(K)*X(K)+Z(K+1)*X(K+1)
 ·    +Z(K+2)*X(K+2)+Z(K+3)*X(K+3)         (3-1)
 ·    +Z(K+4)*X(K+4)
2 CONTINUE
```

is recognized as equivalent to:

```
DO 2 K=1, 1000
S=S+Z(K)*X(K)                              (3-2)
2 CONTINUE
```

and is vectorized as a dot product

10. *Special hardware optimization.* The ISP FORTRAN compiler is designed to utilize efficiently the special nature of the ISP hardware at the detailed instruction level. Instructions may be reordered to take advantage of the multiple pipelines of the ISP as well as the overlap between vector and scalar

operations. In vector loops, operands for the next iteration of the loop are preloaded at the end of loops so that the loading may overlap processing during the loop.

A unique feature of the ISP FORTRAN compiler is that it will generate code for both the 1100/90 IP as well as the ISP. This assures that there are not subtle source-language incapabilities that could arise if two different compilers were present. A compiler option indicates on which machine (IP or ISP) the program is intended to be run.

Since the 1100/90 ISP system may be configured with two ISP processors, it is possible to put both ISPs to work on a single problem. ISP FORTRAN provides a multitasking facility that can be used for this purpose. By means of a "fork and join" capability, a problem can be broken into two parallel parts that may execute on two ISPs in one-half of the time using only one ISP.

ISP FORTRAN conforms to American National Standard FORTRAN, ANSI X3.9-1978 (FORTRAN 77), but it also implements many of the array-programming extensions planned for the emerging 8X standard:

- Array-valued expression and assignment statements.
- Identified arrays
- Array sections
- Conditional array statements
- PACK and UNPACK statements
- Array-valued intrinsics

It is therefore possible to code FORTRAN programs for the ISP that use vector syntax directly, rather than DO Loops, to perform vector processing. In either case, the ISP FORTRAN compiler will generate vector code for the program.

Vectorizer

Since the ISP FORTRAN compiler accepts the vector syntax of the proposed FORTRAN standard, a special FORTRAN source vectorization processor (UVEC) is supplied as a part of the ISP software for migrating FORTRAN source to vector syntax.

UVEC accepts a FORTRAN source program, recognizes vectorizable constructs in a similar manner to the ISP FORTRAN compiler, and produces a new FORTRAN source program that replaces those FORTRAN statements that were vectorizable with explicit vector syntax. UVEC also generates a report indicating which FORTRAN loops were vectorized and which were not. When vectorization is not possible, a reason is given as to why not.

UVEC may be used to produce a new version of FORTRAN source that uses vector syntax rather than DO loops. This is a way to start "thinking in vector terms." Alternatively, the reporting feature of UVEC may be used to restructure FORTRAN programs to be more vectorizable by the ISP FORTRAN compiler.

PEER—Program Execution Evaluation Routine

As mentioned previously, the ISP hardware provides an interval timer that may be used to interrupt a program at specified intervals. A performance-evaluation software package (PEER) is also provided to complement and take advantage of this capability. PEER may be invoked by the ISP programmer to determine where within a program the execution time is spent.

PEER uses the interval timer to interrupt the execution of a program at uniformly distributed random intervals. At each interrupt, PEER records the program address at which the interrupt occurred. This information is subsequently sorted and may be analyzed to generate a report showing the frequency of execution of each part of the program being studied. This information is quite useful in understanding the operation of the program and in determining where effort might best be spent in optimizing the execution of the program.

Since PEER introduces a reasonably small amount of overhead into the execution of a program, it is practicable to use it on large production executions. Programs may, therefore, be analyzed in their actual execution environment.

Program Debugging

A large scientific application, like any complex software package, requires a good development environment for fast, easy, and reliable construction. A keystone of the 1100/90 ISP development environment is its excellent high-level language debugger—PADS (Programmer's Advanced Debugging System).

The PADS system provides three principal functions useful in developing, debugging, and maintaining a program.

- A means for interactively displaying data during the execution and debugging of a program by using the actual variable names used in the program—memory dumps and machine expertise are not required.
- A means to interrupt the execution of a program and gain interactive control at specified source line numbers, labels, or subroutines. Interactive control may also be obtained upon all or specific program error conditions or upon explicit debugging calls.
- A complete debugging language that may be used to write debugging procedures specific to the algorithms and data structures of an application. These procedures may be retained in a library associated with the application and may be used to maintain the application as well as to debug it initially.

The debugging language of PADS is independent of the source language program being debugged and may be used with multiple source languages. PADS supports all the languages compiled by the UCS compilers (currently FORTRAN, COBOL, and PASCAL) but uses the same debugging language for each.

Mathematical Libraries

The ISP FORTRAN system is supported by two sets of mathematical libraries. Basic mathematical functions defined in the FORTRAN language are provided in the Common Math Library. These functions include square-root, sine, cosine, and so on. The Common Math Library provides assembly-language implementations for both scalar and vector versions of these routines.

The ISP is also supported by a library extended beyond FORTRAN requirements. These routines may be used as building blocks by writers of scientific applications. Currently, the Extended Math Library provides:

Fast fourier transforms
Convolution routines
Correlation routines
LINPACK
EISPACK
Basic linear algebra subroutines (BLAS)

Interpolation routines
Normal moveout
Wiener filter
Arithmetic precision inquiry
Date and time
Access to ISP interval timer

PERFORMANCE

The ISP peak performance rates are in the "medium" range as supercomputers are measured (see Table 3-1). Peak rates, however, are only one measure of a supercomputer. More important are sustained rates. A *sustained* rate is dependent on how well the raw power of a machine can be applied to a real algorithm expressed in a programming language (such as FORTRAN) and translated to machine code by a compiler.

The 14 Lawrence Livermore National Laboratory kernels have been frequently used to measure supercomputer performance. Indeed, they provide one definition of what kind of performance constitutes a supercomputer. (A "supercomputer" produces an average performance, in double precision, of greater than 20 MFLOPS—millions of floating point operations/second—on FORTRAN versions of the 14 Livermore kernels.)

The ISP performance using FORTRAN and a single ISP processor on the 14 Livermore kernels is shown in Table 3-2.

Another measurement of performance used in comparisons of various

Table 3-1. ISP peak MFLOP rates

	Number of ISPs	
	1	2
Single precision	133	266
Double precision	66	133

Table 3-2. ISP Livermore Loop performance

| Kernel number | MFLOPs | |
	Double	Single
1. Hydro exerpt	43.2	80.2
2. MLR, inner product	46.0	96.9
3. Inner product	46.0	96.9
4. Banded linear equation	22.1	25.0
5. Tri-diagonal elim. (below)	2.1	2.4
6. Tri-diagonal elim. (above)	3.9	7.0
7. Equation of state excerpt	52.9	100.6
8. PDE integration	31.9	35.8
9. Integer predictors	39.8	49.8
10. Difference predictors	12.8	14.4
11. First sum	3.2	6.0
12. First difference	19.4	37.7
13. 2-D particle pusher	2.5	2.9
14. 1-D particle pusher	2.7	3.4
Average	23.4	40.0

scientific computers is performance on the LINPACK Standard Linear Equations Software from Argonne National Laboratories. The ISP performance on LINPACK using FORTRAN is shown in Table 3-3.

In both of these benchmarks, the performance of the ISP is a high percentage of its peak processing power. This suggests two things. First, the ISP's design is well balanced and its power is applicable to these benchmarks. Second, the ISP FORTRAN compiler is sophisticated enough to be able to apply the ISP's power to FORTRAN codes.

Synergy

How the capability of the ISP hardware and the ISP FORTRAN compiler come together to maximize system performance is best seen in an example.

FORTRAN (Livermore Loop #1)

```
     DO 1 K=1, 400
     U1(K)=T+V1(K)*(R*W1(K+10)+S*W1(K+11))          (3-3)
1    CONTINUE
```

Table 3-3. ISP MFLOPs on LINPACK

Test	Order	Precison	MFLOPs
LINPACK	100	Double	12
LINPACK	100	Single	15
DLU	300	Double	35
SLU	300	Single	49

This FORTRAN loop contains five floating-point operations per iteration and, in total, executes 2000 floating-point operations. It is vectorizable with a vector length of 400.

For this kernel, the ISP FORTRAN compiler generates the following code.

```
 1.  BSVL   0,(400)                 Build vector loop
 2.  L      G4,(ADCON W1)           Virtual address of W1
 3.  L      G5,E_CONSTANTS$+20
 4.  AR     G4,G5,G6                G6=Virtual Address of
                                       W1(11)
 5.  DLV    V4,G6 ELCT              Preload strip of W1(11)
                                    thru W1(42)
 6.  L      G7, E_CONSTANTS$+2
 7.  AR     G4,G7,G8
 8.  L      G9,(1998)
 9.  AR     G8,G9,G10               G10=Address of V1(1)
10.  L      G11, E_CONSTANTS$+20
11.  AR     G8,G11,G5               G5=Virtual Address of
                                       W1(12)
12.  L      G6,(+84)
13.  AR     G6,G4,G7                G7=Virtual Address of
                                       W1(11+64)
14.  A      G8,(+3998)              G8=Address of U1(1)
15.  DL     G4,T                    Preload the scalar T
16.  DL     G11,S                   Preload the scalar S
17.  DL     G9,R                    Preload the scalar R
18.  DFMV   G9,V4,V5 ELCT           Form R*W1(K+10)
19.  DLV    V6,G5 ELCT              Load W1(K+11)
20.  DFMV   G11,V6,V6,ELCT          Form S*W1(K+11)
21.  DFAV   V5,V6,V5 ELCT           Form R*W1(J+10)+S*W1(K+11)
22.  DLV    V7,G10 ELCT             Load V1(K)
23.  DFMV   V7,V5,V5 ELCT           Form
                                    V1(K)R*W1(K+10)+S*W1(K+11)
24.  DFAV   G4,V5,V5 ELCT           Add T to form complete
                                    expression
25.  JLRZ   $+2 NELC                Skip next instruction if
                                    ''next element count''=0
26.  DLV    V4,G7 NELC              Preload next strip of W1
27.  DSV    V5,G8 ELCT              Store result to U1
28.  A      G10, E_CONSTANTS$+64    Increment addresses by 64
                                    words
29.  A      G5, E_CONSTANTS$+64
30.  A      G7, E_CONSTANTS$+64     (32 elements)
31.  A      G8, E_CONSTANTS$+64
32.  JVL    0,Line #18
```

The short FORTRAN program generates 32 instructions of which 15 are in the vector loop. This loop demonstrates several of the hardware and software features described above.

1. Instruction 3, 6, 10, 28, 29, 30, 31 access a system constant pool that is maintained in local store.
2. A vector strip and all scalars in the loop are preloaded outside the loop.
3. Most instructions in the loop use the "element count" (ELCT) of the current vector strip, however a preload near the end of the loop references the "next element count" (NELC).
4. All vector instructions in the loop operate on 32 double precision floating point numbers except the last (13th) iteration which processes a strip of 16 elements.
5. All scalar operations in the loop are overlapped by the vector operations and do not add to execution time.

Pipeline Activity

Figure 3-4 shows the parallel activity of the ISP Load/Store, Multiply and Add vector pipes as well as the ISP scalar unit during the execution of the loop body of Livermore Loop #1. Note how vector operations chain from (overlap) the computation of their operands.

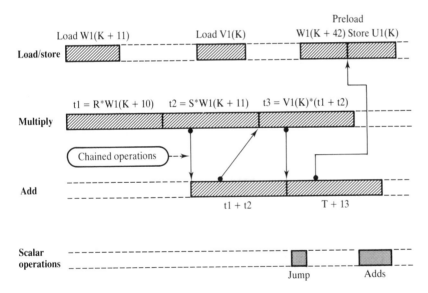

Figure 3-4. Pipeline activity.

CONCLUSION

The Unisys 1100/90 ISP system has for the first time integrated a complete supercomputer into an established mainframe system. The ISP supercomputer is exclusively dedicated to processing user applications. A sophisticated optimizing FORTRAN system is provided to develop applications for the ISP. The ISP offers excellent performance over a broad class of scientific applications.

Performance Results on an Integrated, Interactive Supercomputer*

INTRODUCTION

The Unisys Integrated Scientific Processor System is a set of processors tightly coupled and integrated through a central shared memory with a high bandpass. The processor components, as shown in Figure 3-5, are the 1100/90 IP (the instruction processor), the IOP (the input/output processor) and the ISP, a Class VI supercomputer instruction processor, with vector and scalar capabilities (Hodek 1987). To the user, this system can exist in a complete range of configurations from an 1100/91 plus one ISP to an 1100/94 plus two ISPs with the requirement that at least one of each type of processor is configured. The central shared memory is available in 4 Mword increments each with a bandpass of 355 Mwords/sec to a maximum bandpass of 1.4 Gwords/sec.

SYSTEM INTEGRATION

Objectives

The fundamental concept in the ISP system design was that it should be a "supercomputer system" and that the user of the 1980s and 1990s required a total supercomputer facility with all the "ease of use" capabilities of a typical

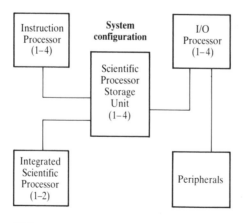

Figure 3-5. System configuration.

---

* This section was contributed by Jane R. Kessler.

mainframe system. The bottom line was that the age of "bit twiddling" for performance was over. The supercomputer system should be transparent to the user. The user needed the full range of capabilities—for example Data Base Management access and tools to achieve high user productivity and performance in a supercomputer environment.

The premise was that the user, whether in a research or a production environment, cared only about three fundamental tasks:

- developing new applications and algorithms;
- executing production runs on a high-performance machine;
- manipulating and displaying the results.

All other activities, such as moving data around, reformatting data, interacting with multiple operating systems and waiting on I/O, were counterproductive to the tasks outlined above. They were not "useful" work.

It was, therefore, a requirement of the system design team to permit the three tasks to occur simultaneously and concurrently with as little interference among them as possible. As a result, the following design decisions were made.

- No operating system on the ISP processor
- Compilation and linking on the IP processor
- A central shared memory with sufficient bandpass capable of servicing all processors in the system. No data motion and no data reformatting
- Code execution on the IP or ISP by user direction
- A complete set of tools for development and performance
- System balance with regard to ISP, IP, and IOP processing

Results

In describing the results of these design decisions as they impact integration, only the most important will be highlighted, because all of them contribute to the overall system performance discussed in the last section.

1. Since no operating system executes on the ISP, 98.6 percent of the cycles of the ISP are available for production work (Dunn and Stephens 1987). This has been demonstrated as achievable for sustained periods of time (625 hours) on a test suite of 78 user-application codes in an environment in which 96 percent of the IP was loaded with batch and demand processing.
2. The decision to permit processing on the IP and ISP by user direction has led to significant capability for rapid code migration of large programs (500 000 lines of source code) and for good performance results. Codes originally designed for serial processors may have many small utility subroutines of perhaps only a few lines of code each. These utilities may be called by many different subroutines.

    For example assume both A and Q call B and C, which are both small utility routines. If A is a subroutine with no vectorizable content, an I/O routine for example, and Q is a subroutine with a large amount of vectorizable code, then it makes sense to perform the ABC envelope on the IP and QBC on the ISP. Processor switching is avoided and the most useful work is performed on the appropriate processor. Tools such as PEER, the Program Execution Evaluation Routine, assist the user in making these determinations.

3. Because there is no data motion—no file transferring among processors—the data is available for the process that requires it whether it be I/O processing by the IOP, database preprocessing by the IP, or supercomputer processing by the ISP. The data is there, available for use by whichever processor requests it at a bandpass of sufficient width to sustain the processor.

4. That there is no data reformatting among processors means that a user can switch processors during algorithm development and achieve "correct" results and algorithm convergence and closure without having to be concerned about a variety of floating-point representations and word sizes. The user's only concern need be perhaps in the area of differences between optimization levels and multiply/add precedence methodologies that occur in all optimizing and vectorizing compilers. However, it should be noted that compiler options and debugging tools provide rapid detection methods for isolating these artifacts. This is an important "ease of use" and productivity factor.

INTERACTIVE SUPERCOMPUTING

Objectives

The objectives in the area of interactive supercomputing were that the system be transparent to the user at the terminal level and the system be balanced so that all activities required by many users wishing to do interactive processing could be satisfied. In meeting this requirement, all of the design decisions discussed previously contribute; however, the third and sixth are key.

Results

"Ease of use" or transparency is not demonstrable on paper. However, most users with any experience of compilation, linking, and execution in the normal mainframe environment will find only a one- or two-word modification of the job-control language required. This is all that is necessary for the user to do interactive supercomputing from his/her terminal. Everything else is handled by the system.

> **Example 1. Ray Trace Simulation.** The user wished to continuously modify the input data to develop the best solution. It is an issue of performing many runs sequentially after examining the previous results. In the normal environment, the time elapsed between runs was 40 minutes, which meant the user would perform other tasks in the interval and disrupt his/her concentration on the problem. Now the end-to-end time has been speeded up by a factor of 8, reducing the elapsed time to 5 minutes.

This speed-up on the program execution time was with modest grooming of less than 2 percent of the code.

Example 2. Weather Model. The Unisys 1100/91 + ISP system has been bench-marked against an 1100/91 plus CRAY X-MP system. The model is currently running at a government site and the user was interested in throughput or the total elapsed time from process initiation to process completion. The data obtained were

1100/91 + ISP	27 min 44 sec
1100/91 + CRAY X-MP 1/4	30 min 00 sec

on code optimized for the CRAY system. This excellent throughput is due to the system integration in the areas of data collection and verification for consistency in conjunction with high-performance processing and the fact that there is no data motion.

SYSTEM PERFORMANCE

Objectives

The objectives in the design were:

- Performance of at least 6–9 times the performance of the 1100/90 IP processor for suitable applications
- Performance on the Livermore Loops and Linpack sufficient to achieve Class VI supercomputer designation
- Hardware capable of sustained high performance on two-, three-, and four-dimensional physical problems
- Vector length necessary to achieve 1/2 the performance at infinite vector length must be short
- "State of the art" vectorizing compiler capable of making the burst rate of the machine accessible to the user without effort and permitting "dusty decks" to achieve performance easily
- System throughput environment in which all system users achieve performance improvements

These objectives were in addition to those outlined in previous sections.

Results on Kernels

The performance of the ISP relative to the 1100/90 instruction processor for kernels is given in Table 3-4.

Livermore Loop performance	Double Precision 23 MFLOPs
	Single Precision 40 MFLOPs
Linpack performance	Linpack (100 * 100)
	Double Precision 16 MFLOPs
	Single Precision 19 MFLOPs
	Linpack (300 * 300)
	Double Precision 35 MFLOPs
	Single Precision 49 MFLOPs

Table 3-4. Performance on kernels. Relative performance ISP vs. 1100/91 (6–9 times for suitable applications)

	Performance ratio ISP vs. 1100/91	Groomed?[a]
Livermore Loops DP 1–14	12.4	No
LINPACK DP 100 * 100	5.5	No
LINPACK DP 300 * 300	18.9	No
SP 300 * 300	17.1	No
Sandia SP 1–5	5.3	Yes
Livermore Loops DP 1–24	6.8	No
Whetstones	7.9	No
French benchmarks	10.0–20.0	No
Spanish benchmarks	6.0–10.0	No
ACCU	4.7 Average	No
(30 programs)	0.8–18.9	

[a] Groomed means modest changes have been applied to take advantage of ISP architecture as an integrated vector processing system.

These results are slightly higher than those reported (Dongarra 1986) due to later compiler releases.

Two aspects of this performance data should be pointed out:

1. The significant increase in performance achieved in going from the Linpack (100 * 100) to the Linpack (300 * 300) is primarily due to the memory bandpass of the system and the fact the hardware is optimized for nested DO loops—for example, a multidimensional problem space.

2. While these are only small kernel results for a system whose major goal is system performance and throughput, one can see how well the system performs on the Linpack (100 * 100) equations relative to the competition in terms of accessible power and useful work as shown in Figure 3-6. Operating system overhead has been factored out to obtain useful work. No attempt has been made to factor out code development overhead as that is not quantifiable as it varies site to site. Obviously, however, code development as well as operating system overhead reduce the number of cycles available to the user attempting to perform production work.

Results on Benchmarks

The performance of the ISP relative to the 1100/90 on benchmarks is shown in Table 3-5. Some of these benchmarks will be discussed relative to other supercomputers. Additionally, other aspects of the system will be discussed.

The floating-point word size on the IP and ISP is 36 bits single-precision and 72 bits double-precision, as shown in Table 3-6. Because the floating-point representation is optimized with a 27-bit mantissa for the 36-bit single-precision and a 60-bit mantissa for the 72-bit double-precision, often problems do not require a double-precision calculation. An example of this is the Cholesky

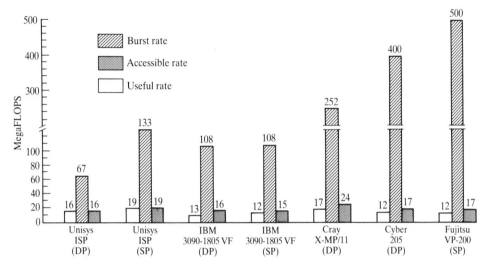

Figure 3-6. Relative performance of various supercomputers results on benchmarks.

Decomposition problem, which consists of 200 000 20×20 matrix inversions as shown in Table 3-7. In this example, the performance relative to the CRAY X-MP is shown in double precision. However, the user is satisfied with the single precision result at a significant performance improvement and with reduced memory requirements.

In a similar benchmark run on a Plasma Code (Genztsch 1987a, b), a precision of 36 bits was adequate. In Figure 3-7 it should be noted that on the IBM 3090 VF single and double precision arithmetic have approximately the same performance.

Table 3-5. Performance on benchmarks. Relative performance ISP vs. 1100/91 (6–9 times for suitable applications)

	Performance ratio ISP vs. 1100/91	Groomed?[a]
FIDISOL	9.8–13.2	Yes
Ray trace	8.4	Yes
Bracknell model	5.1	Yes
Danish benchmark	12–14.3	Yes
Scatter model	11.1	Yes
HIRAS model	4.2	Yes
Sptral	7.5	No
BMRK	6.6	Yes
Cholesky	16.8	Yes
Weather application	24.0	No
Thermal diffusion	6.0	Yes

[a] Groomed means modest changes have been applied to take advantage of ISP architecture as an integrated vector processing system.

Table 3-6. Small machine constants

	Single precision	Bits	Double precision	Bits
Unisys	0.149E − 07	27	0.173E − 17	60
Cray			0.711E − 14	48
CDC	0.218E − 07	26	0.711E − 14	48
IBM	0.954E − 06	21	0.222E − 15	53

Table 3-7. Cholesky decomposition. 200 000 20 × 20 matrix inversions

Unisys	Single precision (min:sec)	Double precision (min:sec)
1100/81	19:21	32:33
1100/91	05:19	08:25
ISP	02:48	05:36
	$00:10\frac{1}{2}$	$00:21\frac{1}{2}$ (Hand-compiled)
	00:14	00:30 (Optimized FORTRAN)
Cray X-MP/1	—	05:05 00:25 (Optimized FORTRAN)

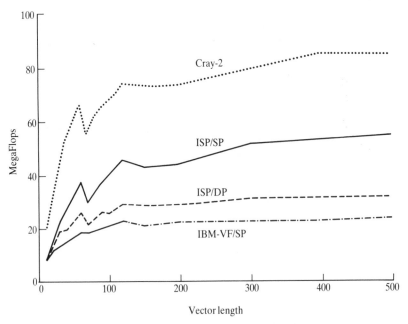

Figure 3-7. Plasma code.

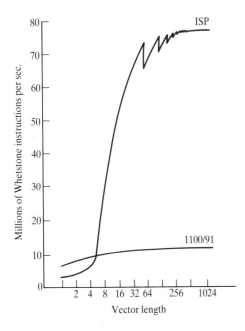

Figure 3-8. Vectorized Whetstones.

The next result is the vector length necessary to achieve 1/2 of the performance obtained at infinite vector length. This is shown in Figure 3-8. At a vector length of approximately 20, the ISP achieves 1/2 the infinite vector length performance. Therefore, the ISP has achieved its goal of being a good short-vector machine. If one has a physical problem that inherently has a vector length of 5 or less, then one should execute on the 1100/90 instruction processor. This is due to the overhead of starting up the vector pipes. However, one also finds in older code that there may be sections of the program that are written for short vectors and other sections for long vectors. There is no inherent limitation due to the physics of the problem; however, it would require major restructuring to change the code to all long vectors. The user can compile the sections for each processor and execute the best task on the best processor without having to restructure the entire program before achieving good results. In a multiuser environment, the best task is then being performed on the best processor and overall throughput is enhanced.

Another aspect of the system that has a significant impact on overall performance is the capability of accessing data from memory for code that has strides or increments differing from unity. This means the user does not have to rethink his problem in order to achieve a good level of performance. The following program was executed (van Kats, and van der Steen 1987) with different values of INCR:

```
        DO 10 I=1,INCR*1000,INCR
        S=S+A(I)*B(I)                           (3-4)
    10  CONTINUE
```

Table 3-8. Performance of the inner-product kernel for different values of increment

INCR	Cyber 990 vector (SDOT)	DPS-90 vector	IBM 3090 vector	Unisys ISP vector
1	32.3	3.9	20.8	32.7
2	13.9	3.9	18.9	26.0
3	14.5	3.8	13.4	26.0
4	13.6	2.4	8.1	24.4
5	14.1	1.6	4.6	26.0
6	13.0	1.5	3.8	26.0
7	14.3	1.3	3.3	23.7
8	13.1	1.1	3.0	18.5
9	15.0	1.2	2.9	26.0
10	14.7	1.2	2.8	26.0
11	14.3	1.2	2.8	26.0
12	14.3	1.2	2.7	24.4
13	14.4	1.2	2.7	26.0
14	14.2	1.2	2.5	26.0
15	15.5	1.2	2.5	15.0
16	10.6	1.1	2.5	10.4

and the results are shown in Table 3-8 for various systems.

As shown in Figure 3-6, the optimizing compiler makes the power of the ISP accessible to the user. Averaged over a range of applications, the user should see between 30 and 50 percent of peak performance on "dusty-deck" code. Occasionally, results as shown in Table 3-9 occur. On a seismic benchmark on groomed FORTRAN code, the ISP achieves sustained performance of 98 percent. A comparison of the ISP's vectorization capabilities is shown in Figure 3-9 and further information is available in the literature (McKie 1987; Coleman 1987; Besaw 1987).

The last result to be discussed is the impact on the entire computing environment of adding an ISP into a typical 1100/92 environment. This is shown

Table 3-9. Seismic benchmark

System	Single-precision results per unit of time	Comments[a]
Sperry ISP	80K	UFTN compiler (no modification)
	330K (128 MFLOPS[b])	UFTN compiler (groomed FORTRAN)
IBM 3090-200 VF	56K	Degree of optimization unknown;
	255K (102 MFLOPS[b])	assembled coded FFTs
Cray X-MP/1	137K	CFTN compiler (no modification)
	450K (180 MFLOPS[b])	CFTN compiler (groomed FORTRAN)

[a] UFTN = Sperry Universal Compiler (FORTRAN), CFTN = Cray Compiler (FORTRAN).
[b] Peak speed: ISP = 133 MFLOPS; IBM = 108 MFLOPS; X-MP/1 = 250 MFLOPS.

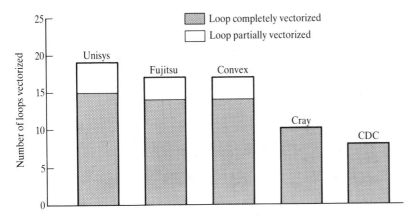

Figure 3-9. Comparison of vectorization capabilities. Source for other vendors: Lawrence Livermore National Laboratories Report UCRL-53745 (June 1986).

in Figure 3-10. If one has a computational load of 10 jobs, each of which takes 10 minutes each, then on average, in the 1100/92 environment, all jobs whether scientific or nonscientific will be completed in 50 minutes. If one has an environment of five scientific jobs (each taking 10 minutes) and five nonscientific jobs (each taking 10 minutes) and one adds an ISP, then the users see the following performance improvements:

Nonscientific   all jobs complete in 25 minutes
Scientific jobs   all jobs complete in 6–9 minutes

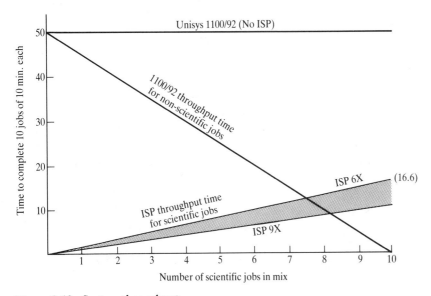

Figure 3-10. System throughput.

Both set of users obtain benefits. This is a result of a system design that envisioned a truly heterogeneous multiprocessing mainframe and supercomputer environment for the user of the 1980s and 1990s.

The Unisys 100/90 ISP system has introduced the concept of integration of supercomputing into a mainframe environment that permits interactive supercomputing while maintaining a high level of performance.

Processor Scheduling Algorithms for a Heterogeneous Vector and Scalar Computer System*

The UNISYS 1100/90 ISP (Integrated Scientific Processor) computer system, makes available a vector processor capable of supercomputer performance on suitable scientific work within the framework of a general-purpose computer environment. This section does not describe the system in detail but rather concentrates on the overall system, hardware, and software design objectives of providing a heterogeneous multiprocessor system. However, it must be stressed that the ISP has its own scalar and vector capabilities.

INTRODUCTION

The UNISYS 1100/90 ISP computer system is the first system to integrate a vector processor directly into a mainframe computer environment in order to offer supercomputer performance for scientific work. The system can have up to four regular instruction processors (IPs) and four input/output processors (IOPs) in addition to the two ISPs, as shown in Figure 3-11. The ISPs, IPs and IOPs all share access to the same physical memory and provide the unified computing system required by many of today's users. The direct result of this design is that the data to be used on the ISP need not be moved from IP/IOP visible memory to ISP visible memory in order to be addressed. Another benefit of this design is that the format of data as seen by the IP and the ISP is the same. No data conversion is necessary when going from a data-preparation task phase on the IP to the ISP. Similarly for any form of postprocessing on the IPs, like graphics output, data is immediately available. The key hardware design element for high vector-processing performance is having adequate memory bandpass to support these six processors, particularly the vector pipe rate of the two ISPs, and the four IOPs. In other words, the ISP(s) are truly functionally integrated into the 1100/90 computer system.

The following sections will describe the various design considerations that

---

* This section was contributed by David S. Dunn and Francis A. Stephens.

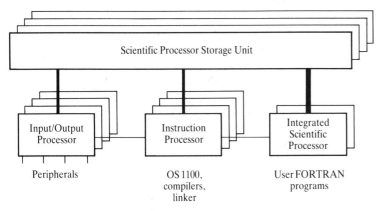

Figure 3-11. ISP integrated structure.

went into the final make-up of the overall system. We devote some discussion to the memory bandpass of the scientific processor storage unit (SPSU) to underline the importance and value of the scheduling of the six processors. This designed memory bandpass of 355 million words per second per SPSU cabinet (maximum four for total of 16 million words) is sufficient to keep all of the processors running at close to rated speed in parallel with one another. In the concluding sections, results extracted during system operation of differing work profiles are presented as a measure of the scheduling efficiency of this heterogeneous multiprocessor system.

OVERALL SYSTEM DESIGN CONSIDERATIONS

No operating system software executes on the ISP. This means that 100 percent of the ISP machine cycles after task switch are theoretically available for the execution of user code. This feature greatly streamlines the software design, since the only operating system (OS) code written was in adapting the 1100 Exec Operating System. No mini-operating system needs to run on the ISP because all ISP and memory scheduling is performed on the IP(s). This also means that only one task is issued to an ISP at a time. The task once dispatched to the ISP will execute until one of the following occurs:

1. the user task voluntarily gives up control of the ISP;
2. the user task generates an internal program error that requires processing by the operating system rather than in user code (i.e. arithmetic exception processing to be performed on the IP);
3. the user task's ISP quantum (time-slice) expires;

4. the ISP hardware detects an error requiring operating system notification;
5. the operating system signals the ISP task to come to an orderly halt.

Item 4 is a hardware exception condition of a fatal nature requiring operator intervention and item 5 is an Exec assist feature currently used in memory management. SIP (System Instrumentation Package) results measured in live operation show this function to be very infrequent.

A direct result of this IP-controlled scheduling of the ISP and the lack of operating system code on the ISP means that the concept of dual register sets found on the 1100 IP for the Exec was not necessary, thus allowing hardware register complexity to be channeled for user performance.

The ISP hardware is set up to process exception conditions—for example, arithmetic underflow and overflow conditions—by taking an interrupt/jump to ISP code (user-written or system-supplied run-time library routine). The user can, if desired, direct this exception processing to the IP. Handling of these conditions proceeds without forcing a processor switch if handled internally. Another hardware design decision that led to less complexity within the ISP was to distinguish between overlapped (high-speed) and nonoverlapped running for the purposes of error recovery. The terms *overlapped* and *nonoverlapped* refer to overlapping instruction execution. For an exception in nonoverlapped mode the hardware returns the failing instruction, so all that is necessary is the correction and reissue of that one instruction. For an exception detected in overlapped mode, several instructions may have to be reissued or the code backed up to a checkpoint.

In any multi-processor system with cached processors, mechanisms must exist to decide which is the latest valid copy of any data item and provide interprocessor signalling. The ISP has a one-cycle (30-nsec) access local store for the high-speed reference of scalar variables rather than its own cache. Each ISP has a totally separate local store. It was decided not to have the ISP issue cache invalidates to the IP caches memories, as the IPs do to each others' caches, when SPSU memory is modified. This was deemed to be too much of an IP performance hit to handle cache invalidates at ISP vector load/store speeds. Instead, Exec code in the IPs issues DIA (diagnose/cache handling) instructions to invalidate their own operand buffers. Special hardware was introduced into the 1100/90 to allow an IP cache complete invalidate to be issued in 640 nsec. Test and Set/Clear type instructions exist on both the IP and ISP to allow data exchange without running into cache multiply-copy problems. These instructions force reference to real memory rather than using a cache copy if available.

Since only one task is to be issued to an ISP at one time, the system was designed to keep the ISP busy executing user tasks whenever requests for ISP service exist in the system. The mechanism (both H/W and S/W) employed to accomplish this task switch was conceived to allow for 96 percent user availability of the ISP.

A software design goal was set of 400 μsec from the time the ISP interrupts the IP until the ISP is again executing this or another task is established. This is discussed further under Software Considerations.

HARDWARE CONSIDERATIONS

For vector processors, the state (register) save/restore time is a key determining factor in the choice of time-slice. This hardware time is a fixed factor in the scheduling algorithm and its effect is discussed in greater detail below.

The ISP hardware was designed for the IP to be able to dispatch a new task to the ISP (accelerate) and remove a task from the ISP (decelerate) quickly as compared to the execution time on the ISP. This process is called a task switch. The hardware times achieved are typically 30–50 μsec for an acceleration and 25–35 μsec for a deceleration. The hardware times we quote in this section of this chapter were measured with an external hardware monitor—a TESDATA 88 monitor.

The value chosen for the time-slice (quantum) on the ISP should lead to the ISP being capable of achieving a 96 percent user task utilization. The time-slice chosen was approximately 25 msec and is controlled by software using a hardware quantum timer register. The measured ISP task-switch time was 305 μsec for a one-ISP system and slightly longer on average for a two-ISP system. Benchmark results have shown a 98.5 percent user utilization on one-ISP and 96 percent on a two-ISP system.

The ISP cannot issue Exec requests (ERs) or CALL requests directly to the 1100 OS for Exec service. This forces a task switch to the IP to issue the service request, for example, an I/O request. In order to keep the ISP busy, the ISP task should not perform excessively frequent I/O operations, for example, greater than 100 I/O operations per second with four disk controllers. For greatest efficiency, tasks should request as much data as possible in each request. The I/O issue is discussed further under Software Considerations below.

The bandwidth to and from memory must be great enough to handle requests from the four IP/IOPs and two ISPs possible in the maximum configuration for the 110/94 plus two ISPs. Most tasks show that even when there is memory contention there is little or no performance degradation. Even with the ten multiprocessors, memory contention results in a maximum of only 25 percent performance degradation of the ISP with one SPSU memory cabinet for the worst case. See the discussion on memory bandpass below.

Hardware features of the ISP that add to its performance include the following.

- Ability to overlap vector and scalar operations
- Multiple vector pipelines
- Ability to perform vector operations with chaining and overlap
- High speed local store for scalar access

To reduce the ISP task switches, the ISP will not necessarily generate an external interrupt for all arithmetic and addressing fault conditions. Some errors may be captured and handled internally by user-supplied code. The choice of whether to handle a certain error condition internally or externally is up to the individual user.

The IP and ISP principal design directions were clearly controlled by the suitability for the general-purpose and scientific work profiles, respectively, but given these hardware characteristics, scheduling algorithms have been developed to obtain the most user work out of each of the processors.

SOFTWARE CONSIDERATIONS

The software (i.e., Exec code) pathlengths for the ISP scheduling code have been optimized to provide as short a task-switch time as possible on the 1100/90. Having established the basic overall system and hardware parameters for ISP scheduling, the Exec software modifications to optimize ISP task switching are as discussed below.

Executive Software Modifications

There is one ISP work list that contains activities requiring ISP service. The general principles of processor scheduling in an 1100 apply in many instances to the following discussion. The ISP work list is ordered by Type and Level (TAL) such that the highest-priority job is the first on the list. This allows the dispatching algorithm to find the next activity simply by picking up the first job on the work list. There are 150 priority levels available.

The Exec software data structures necessary for controlling the activity on the ISP are permanently allocated. This means that no buffer acquisition is necessary as part of the dispatching process. In addition, there is no buffer release as part of interrupt postprocessing.

The ISP dispatcher is designed so that in multiple ISP configurations dispatching for one ISP does not block dispatching for another ISP except for a very small amount of time. There is only one work list for the two ISPs.

The 1100/90 has two modes for instruction execution. Extended mode allows for greater addressability of individual user data banks. Therefore, the ISP adapt code for the Exec was written, where possible, in extended mode. This allows multiple data banks to be simultaneously accessed, thus reducing the bank switching overhead previously incurred in basic mode.

When an ISP activity gives up control of the ISP and returns to the IP, the activity's TAL priority is increased. This gives the activity a slightly higher IP switching priority and greatly improves the ISP system throughput for tasks with moderate I/O request rates.

There is no preemption of tasks executing on the ISP; that is, tasks are not interrupted as soon as a higher-priority one becomes available on the ISP queue. Higher-priority tasks become candidates for ISP execution only at task-switch time, as defined in the section Overall System Design Considerations.

I/O Handling

For the greatest efficiency in I/O handling, the general principle is that I/O should be blocked up as much as possible. This means that I/O requests should be grouped into fewer occurrences of larger amounts. The FORTRAN language constructs of the BUFFERIN and BUFFEROUT form are available to the user programs as is common with larger systems. It is possible with these constructs to overlap I/O and computation on the ISP. In addition, the I/O complete tests are set up with ISP TEST/SET instructions thus avoiding an ISP task switch. ISP code runs in the extended mode environment of the 1100/90, making easily available large data areas for I/O buffers.

The 1100 operating system provides IP multitasking as a standard feature and this has been expanded to allow an IP task to create ISP tasks. The benefits of the quick activation of the ISP make IP/ISP multitasking efficient for the FORTRAN user program.

When there is only one task on the ISP work list, the time quantum is doubled.

MEMORY BANDPASS CONSIDERATIONS

The key item for discussion in this section is the *memory bandpass* and the *interprocessor interaction*. This is measured as effective performance under different conditions. Each SPSU cabinet (maximum of four per system) has a maximum memory bandpass of 355 Mwords (36-bit) per sec. This is an eight-bank access of four words per access cycling in 90 nsec. This peak performance exceeds the sum of the peak transfer rates of the 10 separate processors, assuming no bank conflicts. Each ISP has a peak of 133 Mwords/sec SPSU memory transfer rate to support the vector arithmetic section.

Requester access priority for each processor component is IOP/IP/ISP, with the IOPs having the highest priority and the ISPs the lowest. The IOPs each have 6.67 Mwords/sec (30 Mbytes/sec) transfer rate to each SPSU cabinet. The IPs corresponding transfer rates are 15 Mwords/sec.

The IOPs having the highest priority into the SPSU's memory interface, allow the time-critical I/O transfers to occur, but also have the performance effect of theoretically being able to reduce the ISP transfer rate by 25 percent under peak I/O transfer rate conditions.

It is possible to configure an 1100/90 with a lower total bandpass memory utilizing another memory type (MSU) for use without the ISP. There can be mixed configurations, but still a maximum of four memory cabinets in total. Whereas the IPs and IOPs can access both memory types, the ISPs can only access the SPSU memory. IP multiprocessor performance out of one SPSU should be a little better than out of the other memory type (MSU) because of the additional banks (eight in an SPSU as opposed to four in MSU). The IP performance executing out of SPSU should be affected only marginally by ISP transfers to/from SPSU. IOP transfer into MSU is 8.33 Mwords/sec.

HETEROGENEOUS MULTIPROCESSOR SCHEDULING ALGORITHM

The previous sections have laid out the characteristics of the 1100/90 plus ISP computer system. The final form of the scheduling algorithm is to have frequent task switching on the IPs and less frequent on the ISPs. In a heavy workload batch and interactive environment, the IPs will typically run between 2000 and 3000 instructions between interrupts and have a task-switch time of about 290 μsec. At approximately 6 million instructions per second, this is 333 to 550 μsec task slice time on the 1100/90 IP. This time is determined by interrupt rate. In the scientific/batch examples presented below, the interrupt rate (typically lower than in commercial applications) is up to 1662 total interrupts per second or 415 per IP second (2.4 msec slice). The ISP tasks run up to 25 msec between interrupts and have a switch time of about 305 μsec.

As examples, two weather-industry codes were run in various combinations. The first job was capable of being executed on the IP or ISP, that is, the same FORTRAN source compiled for the IP or ISP as required, and was CPU-bound in both cases. The second job was compiled to target it for running on the ISP and in addition to taking 50 ISP seconds, required 230 Mbytes of I/O in 150 elapsed seconds. The tasks are labeled A, B, and C, respectively for the IP, ISP CPU-bound tasks, and the ISP task with I/O task (see Table 3-10). The Exec busy time for each case is given in milliseconds per IP second. The IP(s) interrupt rate and the ISP slice time are given in total number of interrupts per second and milliseconds per ISP slice time respectively. The IP task executes about 5.8 billion instructions and the same task vectorized for the ISP runs about nine times faster.

In Table 3-10 the numbers of processors and jobs gives the work capacity for job test mix. The IP and ISP processor utilization is given as percentage per IP or ISP. The design goal is to maximize the ISP processor utilization, and this is

Table 3-10. 1100/94 plus two ISPs: processor utilization, interrupt rates, and IP Exec time for various job mixes

IP(s)	Utilization (percent)	ISP(s)	Utilization (percent)	Task A	B	C	Exec busy MS/IP Sec	IP interrupt rate	ISP slice time (average)
1		0		0	0	0	1.290	5.607	0.
4		0		0	0	0	0.464	3.352	0.
1	95.4	0		1	0	0	3.352	12.793	0.
4	91.0	0		4	0	0	4.555	101.966	0.
1		1	95.5	0	1	0	20.736	22.072	45.306
1		1	26.6	0	0	1	29.922	80.340	12.447
4		2	96.9	0	16	0	35.451	81.414	24.556
4	89.5	1	97.9	4	8	0	25.023	423.168	22.229
4	88.1	2	95.9	4	16	0	46.061	756.800	22.616
4	86.5	2	94.4	4	16	10	79.875	1662.192	17.893

seen to approach 98 percent in the one-ISP case. The IP processor utilization remains high despite work required to schedule the tasks and processors. The peak processor utilization required to drive the system in this series of tests was 79.875 msec of IP time per second, or 8 percent.

One other major point to make about the progression of ISP jobs with I/O versus ISP jobs with little I/O is shown in the first example. To a first approximation, the 16 CPU-bound ISP jobs consume ISP processor time at a uniform rate of 0.09 ISP processor-busy seconds per elapsed second. The ISP jobs with I/O were run in two groups of five and used 0.23 ISP processor-busy seconds per elapsed second. Without the ISP task priority promotion on voluntary give-up for I/O, these I/O jobs finish after the CPU-bound jobs, thereby missing the chance to overlap I/O with computation. The IP scheduler also works this way. This technique can be looked on as getting the I/O started as quickly as possible to maximize overlap of I/O and computation.

The first two lines of Table 3-10 show background utilization of the idle system. Under increasing load on the system, the user processor utilization remains high and the IP Exec processor time to drive the system rises only modestly to 8 percent of the IP time.

CONCLUSION

With the scheduling algorithms discussed and coding efficiencies used, the processor utilization for the ISPs can be kept in the 95 percent and better region. The Exec processor time to drive the system in these examples only goes up to 8 percent and the IP utilization of user work is in the 80–90 percent range.

The work capacity potential of the system has been maximized by the choice of these scheduling algorithms for this 1100/90 ISP 6-by heterogeneous multi-processor system.

Advanced Techniques for Vectorizing Dusty Decks*

INTRODUCTION

Unisys has developed a processor for computation-intensive applications—the ISP (Integrated Scientific Processor)—that has a vector architecture similar to that of the CRAY machines. The process of translating a user's program into a form that can take advantage of the power of a vector machine is known as vectorization. Unisys has a vectorizer within its UFTN FORTRAN compiler. Because the majority of the programs expected to be run on the ISP would be

---

* This section was contributed by Keith Besaw.

"dusty deck" FORTRAN programs, prime considerations in the design of the Unisys vectorizer were to do very well in the transformations known as scalar expansion and IF-to-MASK conversion. Additionally, neither of these transformations should result in the use of large temporary arrays, as is commonly done by other vectorizers.

A primary tool in meeting these requirements is a new dependency called a *REVERSE dependency*. This chapter shows how the REVERSE dependency is used to improve scalar expansion and covers its part in IF-to-MASK conversion. Another important part of the IF-to-MASK conversion within the Unisys vectorizer is the generation and use of "control expressions"; the generation algorithm is covered in some detail within this paper. Many examples are included to show how the REVERSE dependency and control expressions are used within the vectorizer to transform FORTRAN source into vectorized object code.

BACKGROUND

A vector machine such as the Unisys ISP has instructions that perform the same operation on many (usually 32 or 64) elements of a program's array operands. On the ISP, for example, a code segment that picks up 64 elements of an array B, does an element-by-element add to 64 elements of an array C, and stores the 64 results into 64 elements of an array A might look as follows:

```
L  G1,addr-of-first-elt-of-B
L  G2,addr-of-first-elt-of-C
LV V1,G1       Load 64 elements of B
LV V2,G2       Load 64 elements of C
AV V1,V2,V3 Element-by-element add
L  G3,addr-of-first-elt-of-A
SV V3,G3       Store 64 results into A
```

G1, G2, and G3 are the usual general-purpose registers. V1, V2, and V3 are called vector files. On the ISP, a vector file can contain up to 64 single-precision items or 32 double-precision items. They are used in the same way as registers except, for example, when a single-precision vector add instruction is performed on two entire vector files, the add is performed on 64 pairs of operands and produces 64 results. The problem is knowing when it is possible to convert a FORTRAN DO loop, written to be executed serially, into a form that performs 64 iterations of the original loop in parallel using vector instructions. This is the task of a vectorizer.

The new Unisys UFTN vectorizing compiler is a portion of the Unisys Universal Compiling System (UCS) (Gyllstrom et al. 1979; McKie 1985). This compiling system has several machine-independent front ends (e.g., FORTRAN, C, COBOL, and Pascal). These front ends feed machine-dependent code generators through a machine- and language-independent intermediate form. UFTN is actually the name of the machine-independent FORTRAN front end. The programmer uses the VECTOR compiler option to invoke the ISP code generator. The vectorizer is part of the language-independent ISP code generator; although the ISP code generator currently is not very language-independent in that few constructs are handled other than those required for FORTRAN.

With this compiling system, it is possible for a programmer to compile a FORTRAN program for the Unisys 1100/90 (serial) architecture or the ISP (vector) architecture without source modifications. The only difference to the programmer is the code generator compiler option. It is also possible for a subroutine compiled for the 1100/90 to call one compiled for the ISP without special FORTRAN source. The operating system does all the work necessary to make the machine switch; no help is needed from the programmer. This makes the ISP an exceedingly easy-to-use vector machine.

But an easy-to-use machine is not good enough. The compiler also must be easy to use so that the overall system is attractive to the large market of users who are experts in their field but do not have the time to be experts on vector architectures. Many parallel machines currently suffer from the deficiency that users must be knowledgeable of the machine architecture in order to get reasonable benefit from its capabilities.

The goal of the UFTN vectorizer was to vectorize existing (dusty deck) FORTRAN programs well enough to make the ISP attractive to those who do not want to modify their programs or will only make modifications that conform to the current FORTRAN standard. To do this, UFTN had to have very good scalar expansion and very good IF-to-MASK conversion (including arithmetic IFs and IFs with GOTOs), and it had to assume little or no help from the programmer via special parallel FORTRAN syntax or compiler directives. They cover up a weak compiler and are used incorrectly even by experts.

BASIC THEORY

Before describing the REVERSE dependency and control expressions and their use in scalar expansion and IF-to-MASK conversion, it is necessary to understand the basic theory upon which UFTN vectorization is based.

Dependency Analysis

Kuck and his research group at the University of Illinois at Urbana-Champaign developed a dependency analysis theory that formed the basis for UFTN's initial design (Banerjee 1976; Kuck 1976, 1977, 1978, 1980, 1981; Leasure 1976; Muraoka 1971; Padua et al. 1980; Padua and Wolfe 1986; Towle 1976; Wolfe 1976). Four basic dependency types from this theory are used with the UFTN compiler, three of which have two distinct flavors.

FLOW dependency

```
        DO 10 I=1,N
S1         S=A(I)+B(I)        FLOW
S2         C(I)=D(I)-S        on S
    10     CONTINUE
```

(3-5)

This is also called a TRUE dependency by Kennedy and Allen in their work at Rice University (Allen 1983, 1984; Kennedy 1980). There is a data flow from the definition of S in statement S1 to the use of S in statement S2. The dependency arc places an ordering on the statements in that the tail of the arc (statement S1) must be executed before the head of the arc (statement S2).

ANTI dependency

```
        DO 20 I=1,N
S1         A(I)=S+B(I)        ANTI
S2         S=C(I)-D(I)        on S
    20     CONTINUE
```

(3-6)

The variable S must be used in statement S1 before it is defined in statement S2.

OUTPUT dependency

```
        DO 30 1=1,N
S1         S=A(I)+B(I)        OUTPUT
S2         S=C(I)-D(I)        on S
    30     CONTINUE
```

(3-7)

The variable S must be defined in statement S1 before it is redefined by statement S2.

CONTROL dependency

```
        DO 40 I=1,N
S1         IF(A(I).LE.B(I))GOTO 40    CONTROL
S2         C(I)=D(I)
    40     CONTINUE
```

(3-8)

Statement S2, which defines $C(I)$, is executed under control of the IF statement S1. Unlike the three previous dependencies, which are called data dependencies, a CONTROL dependency represents both an execution ordering and an execution control; that is, the tail of the dependency arc (S1 above) can prevent execution of the head of the arc (S2 above).

In the definitions of the FLOW, ANTI, OUTPUT, and CONTROL dependencies, the dependencies occur completely within a given iteration of the loop. Take the example used to show a FLOW dependency and an arbitrary iteration, say the "fifth": statement S1 on the "fifth" iteration of the loop defines the variable S whose value is used by statement S2 only on the "fifth" iteration. They are called *EQUAL* dependencies because for the dependency to occur the values of the loop-control variables must all be equal in the statements making up the head and tail of the dependency arc. Elsewhere in the literature they are also referred to as *LOOP-INDEPENDENT* dependencies.

The three data dependency types come in two flavors, the EQUAL form just described and another form called CARRY dependencies:

```
      DO 50 I=2,N
S1        B(I)=A(I-1)     ⟵  CARRY
S2        A(I)=C(I)+D(I)  ⟋  FLOW on A                (3-9)
   50     CONTINUE
```

The above shows a *CARRY-FLOW* dependency; the FLOW dependency "carries" from a given iteration of the loop to a later one. For example, the first iteration of the loop defines $A(2)$ while the second iteration uses the value of $A(2)$ defined by the first iteration. CARRY dependencies are referred to elsewhere in the literature as *LOOP-CARRIED* dependencies.

For the remainder of this chapter, if the term CARRY is not explicitly stated, the dependency is assumed to be an EQUAL dependency.

Like an EQUAL-FLOW dependency, a CARRY-FLOW dependency also places an ordering on the execution of the statements. It is easy to see that the ordering exists for EQUAL dependencies, since the statement at the head of the dependency arc must be executed before the statement at the tail of the dependency arc in the same iteration of the loop. For a CARRY dependency, some iteration of one of the loops containing the two statements making up the dependency arc must be executed before another iteration of the same loop. Later examples show CARRY dependencies for multiply-nested loops.

The {pi}-graph

Once the UFTN vectorizer constructs a dependency graph for a loop and all of its nested loops, the loop is separated into strongly connected regions at each loop level using the directed dependency arcs. A strongly connect region is a group of statements S1, S2, S3, . . . , Sm such that a dependency arc exists with tail S1 and head S2, and another arc exists with tail S2 and head S3, and so on until the last with tail Sm and head S1. A single statement can be a strongly connected region if there exists a dependency arc whose head and tail is the given statement.

One of the important aspects of a strongly connected region is that the statements in a strongly connected region at a given loop level cannot have all iterations performed in parallel (which in most cases means the statements cannot be vectorized). The cycle of directed dependency arcs that place a group of statements in a strongly connected region can only be caused by later iterations of statements in the group being dependent upon earlier iterations of statements in the group. The first example in the later section on Introduction to Scalar Expansion shows a two-statement, strongly-connected region, the cycle of directed dependency arcs that place the two statements in the region, and why the two statements cannot have multiple iterations performed in parallel.

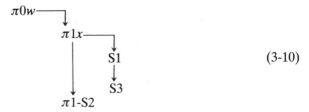

```
        DO 10 I=1,N
S1        A(I)=B(I-1)+C(I)   ⟩ FLOW   ⟩ FLOW  ⟵⟩ CARRY
S2        D(I)=A(I)*E(I)     ⟵  on A  ⟩ on A   ⟩ FLOW
S3        B(I)=A(I)+F(I)                ⟵      ⟩ on B
   10     CONTINUE
```

Figure 3-12. Singly nested loop with strongly connected region.

The result of separating a loop into strongly connected regions is represented by a {pi}-graph similar to that used by Kuck (Allen 1983; Kuck 1976;
Kuck, 1977; Kuck 1978; Towle 1976). An algorithm developed by Tarjan (Tarjan
1972; Shimon 1979) is used to construct this {pi}-graph. Two contrived examples
will give a feel for what a {pi}-graph looks like. The first (see Fig. 3-12) shows a
singly nested loop having a strongly connected region containing two statements
and a third statement not contained in a strongly connected region. The
{pi}-graph for this loop is:

$$\pi 0w \longrightarrow$$
$$\pi 1x \longrightarrow$$
$$S1$$
$$S3$$
$$\pi 1\text{-}S2$$

(3-10)

Each node in the {pi}-graph is called a {pi}-block. For {pi}-block {pi}1x, the 1
signifies that the {pi}-block is at loop level 1 and the x is a unique identifier for
the {pi}-block. {pi}0w is used as a dummy outer {pi}-block to which the level 1
{pi}-blocks can be linked. S1 and S3 are in the strongly connected region
represented by {pi}1x because of the FLOW dependency from S1 to S3 and the
CARRY-FLOW dependency from S3 to S1. S2 is not part of a strongly connected
region at loop level 1; there is no list of directed dependency arcs beginning at
statement S2 that returns to S2. This is represented by making a {pi}-block at
loop level 1 whose unique identifier is $-S2$, that is the statement's identifier is
attached to {pi}1 to form the {pi}-block's full name.

Notice that {pi}1x appears before {pi}1-S2 in the list attached to {pi}0w and
S1 appears before S3 in the list attached to {pi}1x. The {pi}-blocks and
statements are ordered using the appropriate dependency arcs, which happen to
be the two EQUAL-FLOW dependencies in the above {pi}-graph.

The second example (see Fig. 3-13) shows how multiple loop levels are
handled. This is important since UFTN vectorizes more than just the innermost
loop level. The CARRY-FLOW dependency from the $A(I)$ that is defined by
statement S2 to the $A(I)$ that is used in S2 is a CARRY from one iteration of the
J loop to the next. The 2 in FLOW-2 is used to specify that the CARRY-FLOW

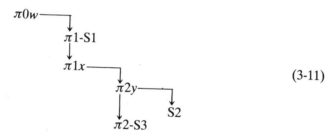

```
       DO 10 I=2,N
S1        A(I)=0                              FLOW-1
          DO 20 J=1,M                         on A
S2            A(I)=A(I)+B(I-1,J)              CARRY    CARRY    CARRY
S3            B(I,J)=B(I,J)+A(I-1)           FLOW-1   FLOW-1   FLOW-2
       20     CONTINUE                        on A     on B     on A
       10  CONTINUE
```

Figure 3-13. Treatment of multiple loop levels.

dependency carries on the "DO J" (or second) loop level. The other two CARRY-FLOW dependencies are from one iteration of the I loop to the next, that is, they CARRY on loop level 1.

The {pi}-graph looks like:

$$
\begin{array}{l}
\pi 0w \longrightarrow \\
\quad \pi 1\text{-}S1 \\
\quad \pi 1x \longrightarrow \\
\qquad \pi 2y \longrightarrow \\
\qquad \qquad S2 \\
\qquad \pi 2\text{-}S3
\end{array}
\qquad (3\text{-}11)
$$

Statement S1 is not in a strongly connected region but is at loop level 1; this is represented by {pi}1-S1. Statements S2 and S3 are in a strongly connected region at loop level 1, which is represented by {pi}1x. At loop level 2, S2 is in a strongly connected region containing only itself (caused by the CARRY-FLOW dependency from S2 to itself), which is represented by {pi}2y. Statement S3 is not in a strongly connected region at loop level 2 and is represented by {pi}2-S3.

The process of constructing the {pi}-graph is called *loop distribution* because it essentially distributes a separate loop around each strongly connected region of statements within the original loop. Each {pi}-block actually represents a loop. For example, there are two {pi}-blocks at loop level 1: {pi}1-S1 and {pi}1x. A "DO I" loop can be placed around S1 and another around the two statements S2 and S3, producing a program that gives the same answers as the original loop.

Our implementation of loop distribution proceeds from outer loop to inner loop. When determining a strongly connected region at a given loop level, all dependencies at that loop level and below are used. Those dependencies at outer loop levels are ignored. Therefore, loop distribution first breaks the statements into {pi}-blocks at level 1 using all of the dependencies. Then, taking each {pi}-block constructed at level 1, level 2 {pi}-blocks are formed and attached to the level 1 {pi}-block. In forming level 2 {pi}-blocks, all of the dependencies at level 2 and below whose head and tail are within the same level 1 {pi}-block are used.

After any transformations have been performed on the {pi}-graph (e.g., special reduction cases, loop fusion, or loop interchange), *loop reconstruction* uses the {pi}-graph to re-form the program for use by the rest of the code generator. Loop reconstruction generates the appropriate loop structures according to the {pi}-graph, places statements in the loop associated with the {pi}-block in which they are contained, orders the statements and nested loops according to the dependency arcs, marks vectorizable statements (those in {pi}-blocks that do not represent strongly connected regions), and generates masks or control transfers as appropriate (discussed later).

Loop reconstruction takes the {pi}-graph from the above example and generates the following FORTRAN approximation:

```
         DO 11 II=2,N,64    Vector Loop
S1         A(II:II+63)=0
    11     CONTINUE
         DO 12 I=2,N
         DO 21 J=1,M
S2         A(I)=A(I)+B(I-1,J)
    21     CONTINUE
         DO 22 JJ=1,M,64  Vector Loop
S3         B(I,JJ:JJ+63)=
     !          B(I,JJ:JJ+63)+A(I-1)
    22     CONTINUE
    12     CONTINUE
```
(3-12)

The "DO *I*" loop has been distributed around S1 and around the two statements S2 and S3. The "DO *J*" loop has been distributed around S2 and S3. FORTRAN array syntax such as

$$A(II:II+63)=0 \qquad (3\text{-}13)$$

is used to represent vector instructions on a machine whose vector length is 64. Since S1 and S3 ended up in {pi}-blocks that did not represent strongly connected regions at loop levels 1 and 2, respectively, S1 was vectorized at level 1 and S3 at level 2.

The "DO 11" and "DO 22" loops are called vector loops because the increment of loop control variable is 64, the machine's vector length.

THE REVERSE DEPENDENCY FOR EXPANDED SCALARS

Introduction to Scalar Expansion

Scalar expansion is done to allow multiple iterations of a loop to be performed in parallel. The loop in the example used to show a FLOW dependency can have

```
      DO 10 I=1,N
         S=A(I)+B(I)    ⟩FLOW  ↖ CARRY ↴ CARRY OUTPUT
         C(I)=D(I)-S    ↙ on S ⟩ ANTI    S to itself
10       CONTINUE               on S
```

Figure 3-14. Loop with full complement of dependencies.

multiple iterations performed in parallel if the scalar S is expanded. In addition to the FLOW dependency, there is a CARRY-ANTI dependency from the use of S back to the definition and a CARRY-OUTPUT dependency from the definition to itself. Figure 3-14 shows the loop with its full complement of dependencies. Figure 3-15 shows an unrolled version of the first couple of iterations of the loop, clearly showing the CARRY dependencies.

Notice that each iteration of the loop must wait for the previous one to complete. Each statement, in the fully unrolled loop, must wait for the previous statement to complete (which is what the dependencies represent). The loop could have been written as:

```
      DO 10 I=1,N
         SA(I)=A(I)+B(I)   ⟩FLOW
         C(I)=D(I)-SA(I)   ↙ on SA
10       CONTINUE
```
(3-14)

which eliminates the CARRY-ANTI and CARRY-OUTPUT dependencies and allows all iterations of the loop to be performed in parallel. The scalar S has been expanded into the array SA. One negative aspect of scalar expansion is that a potentially large temporary array is required, $SA(N)$.

On a vector machine, the object code (using a FORTRAN approximation) should look like:

```
      DO 10 II=1,N,64          Vector Loop
         VS(0:63)=A(II:II+63)+B(II:II+63)
         C(II:II+63)=D(II:II+63)-VS(0:63)
10    CONTINUE
```
(3-15)

In this case, each iteration of the "DO 10" vector loop picks up 64 elements of A beginning at $A(II)$ and adds them to 64 elements of B beginning at $B(II)$ and places the 64 results in one of the machine's vector files (represented by the

```
S=A(1)+B(1)   ⟩FLOW              ↘ CARRY      Iteration 1
C(1)=D(1)-S   ↙ on S ....⟩CARRY...⟩OUTPUT.....................
S=A(2)+B(2)   ⟩FLOW  ↙ANTI  ↙ on S          Iteration 2
C(2)=D(2)-S   ↙ on S    on S
```

Figure 3-15. Loop showing CARRY dependencies.

64-element array $VS(0:63)$). Those 64 results are subtracted from the 64 elements of D beginning at $D(II)$ and stored into the 64 elements of C beginning at $C(II)$.

Generating the REVERSE Dependency

Several things are done by the compiler to expand scalars and to expand them only to the size of a vector file. The following are the most important.

1. *Assume* each loop is split into two loops, a vector loop and element loop pair. Elsewhere in the literature a *vector* loop may be referred to as a *block* loop and an *element* loop as a *strip* loop. Because this chapter is directed towards vector architectures, and not the more general cases, the terms vector and element are used. The following example and discussion should make the vector/element loop pair concept more clear.
2. Do not generate CARRY-ANTI or CARRY-OUTPUT dependencies for scalars that are going to be expanded (there are some exceptions mentioned later).
3. Generate all other normal dependencies at the element (even) loop levels.
4. Generate a REVERSE dependency in the opposite direction of each EQUAL-FLOW dependency but at the immediately containing vector (odd) loop level.

Using the above example, the loops are assumed to have the vector/element loop pair and the dependencies as shown in Figure 3-16. The {pi}-graph produced by loop distribution is then:

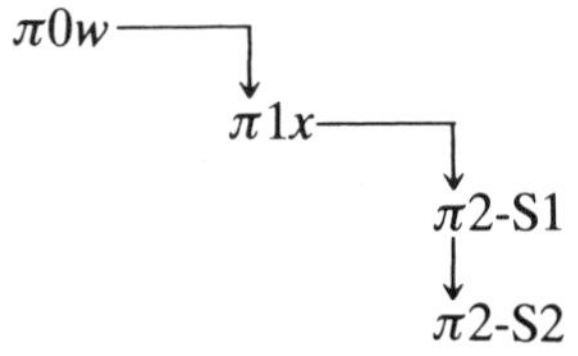

$$
\begin{array}{l}
\pi 0w \longrightarrow \Big\downarrow \\
\qquad \pi 1x \longrightarrow \Big\downarrow \\
\qquad\qquad \pi 2\text{-}S1 \\
\qquad\qquad \Big\downarrow \\
\qquad\qquad \pi 2\text{-}S2
\end{array}
\qquad (3\text{-}16)
$$

The FLOW-2 dependency along with the REVERSE-1 cause statements S1 and S2 to form a strongly connected region at loop level 1, the vector loop level. This is represented by the {pi}-block {pi}1x. Neither statement is in a strongly connected region at loop level 2 (the only dependency at the element-loop level

```
            DO 10 II=1,N,64          Vector loop
              DO 11 I=0,63           Element loop
S1              S=A(II+1)+B(II+1)      ⤶ FLOW-2   ↩ REVERSE-1
S2              C(II+1)=D(II+I)-S      ⤶ on S     ↩ on S
        11      CONTINUE
        10    CONTINUE
```

Figure 3-16. Vector/element loop pair with dependencies.

or below is the FLOW-2 dependency). This is represented by {pi}2-S1 and {pi}2-S2. Since neither statement is in a strongly connected region at their inner element-loop level, both are vectorizable. Both statements are held in the same vector loop because they are in the same strongly connected region at that loop level. This ensures that the scalar S only needs to be expanded to the size of a vector file (64 elements on the Unisys ISP).

There is a direct relationship between the element loop and vector instructions. If loop distribution places a statement in a {pi}-block at the element-loop level that does not represent a strongly connected region, loop reconstruction changes the element loop into vector instructions.

If not all element loops immediately contained in a vector loop vectorize, then it is possible to recombine the element and vector loops and eliminate the double loop level. In fact, recombination is not done for the Unisys ISP; advantage is taken of the architecture's well designed vector/element loop structure to partially vectorize statements. Vector loads are performed immediately preceding and vector stores immediately following element loops containing unvectorizable statements; within the element loops, the vector files are referenced element by element. Vectorizable subexpressions are also moved out of element loops, and the vector files containing their results are referenced element by element.

Scalar Expansion Examples

The following, more complicated, example shows more of the advantages of the REVERSE dependency, as used in scalar expansion, and how easily the resulting loops can be generated from the {pi}-graph.

```
           DO 10 I=1,N
S1            S=A(I)+B(I)
S2            T=S-C(I-1)
S3            C(I)=T+D(I)                  (3-17)
S4            E(I)=C(I)*2
        10    CONTINUE
```

With vector/element loops, the dependencies are as shown in Figure 3-17.

```
      DO 10 II=1,N,64              Vector Loop
         DO 11 I=0,63              Element Loop
S1          S=A(II+1)+B(II+1)      FLOW-2    REVERSE-1 on S
S2          T=S-C(II+I+1)          on S        FLOW-2     REV-1     CARRY
S3          C(II+1)=T+D(II+1)      FLOW-2      on T       on T      FLOW-2
S4          E(II+1)=C(II+1)*2      on C                             on C
   11       CONTINUE
   10    CONTINUE
```

Figure 3-17. Scalar expansion with vector/element loops.

REVERSE dependencies have been created to reverse each EQUAL-FLOW dependency of the potentially expandable scalars S and T. The level of the REVERSE dependency is 1 less than its related FLOW dependency.

The {pi}-graph produced by loop distribution is:

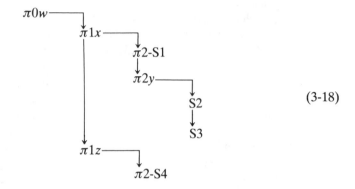

$$(3\text{-}18)$$

Statements S1, S2, and S3 are in the same {pi}-block at level 1 (the vector-loop level) because the FLOW and REVERSE dependencies generated for the scalars S and T make the three statements a strongly connected region at loop level 1. Since the three statements are in the same {pi}-block at the vector-loop level, loop reconstruction places them in the same vector loop. Now all statements using S and T are in the same vector loop. Now all statements using S and T are in the same vector loop and therefore S and T need only be expanded to the size of the contained element loops, which is 64, the size of the vector files.

Statement S1 is not in a strongly connected region at level 2 (represented by {pi}2-S1) and so is vectorizable. Statements S2 and S3 are in a strongly connected region at level 2 and so are not vectorizable. Notice that all uses of T are in the same strongly connected region at loop level 2. UFTN recognizes this and does not expand T even though it originally set up the REVERSE dependencies in an attempt to expand T. Statement S4 need not even be in the same vector loop as the other 3 statements and is vectorizable (represented by {pi}2-S4).

The output of loop reconstruction (using a FORTRAN approximation) is:

```
        DO 10 II:1,N,64        Vector Loop
S1        VS(0:63)=A(II:II+63)+B(II:II+63)
        DO 11 I=0,63           Element Loop
S2        T=VS(I)-C(II+I-1)
S3        C(II+I)=T+D(II+1)
    11    CONTINUE
    10  CONTINUE
        DO 12 II=1,N,64        Vector Loop
S4        E(II:II+63)=C(II:II+63)*2
    12  CONTINUE
```

$$(3\text{-}19)$$

```
DO 10 II=1,N,64          Vector Loop
    DO 11 I=0,63          Element Loop
        IF(rel-exp)THEN
        S=A(II+1)
        ELSE
S2      S=B(II+1)
        ENDIF
S3      C(II+1)=S+D(II+1)
    11  CONTINUE
    10  CONTINUE
```

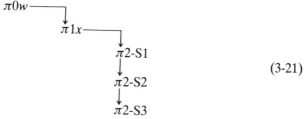

Figure 3-18. Loops and data dependencies after loop reconstruction.

Statements S1 and S4 can be executed with vector instructions rather than an element loop; that is, multiple iterations of the loop can be performed in parallel for statements S1 and S4.

A scalar defined on two or more paths and used after the paths have rejoined is a common occurrence. Generating the REVERSE dependencies to oppose the EQUAL-FLOW dependencies, as described above, makes vectorization of this case a simple task. For example:

$$
\begin{array}{ll}
& \text{DO 10 I=1,N} \\
& \quad \text{IF(rel-exp)THEN} \\
\text{S1} & \qquad \text{S=A(I)} \\
& \quad \text{ELSE} \\
\text{S2} & \qquad \text{S=B(I)} \\
& \quad \text{ENDIF} \\
\text{S3} & \quad \text{C(I)=S+D(I)} \\
\text{10} & \quad \text{CONTINUE}
\end{array}
\tag{3-20}
$$

The assumed loops and their data dependencies (ignore for now the CONTROL dependencies caused by the IF statement) are shown in Figure 3-18.

The {pi}-graph produced by loop distribution (again ignore the IF statement) is:

$$
\begin{array}{l}
\pi 0w \longrightarrow \\
\quad \pi 1x \longrightarrow \\
\qquad \pi 2\text{-S1} \\
\qquad \downarrow \\
\qquad \pi 2\text{-S2} \\
\qquad \downarrow \\
\qquad \pi 2\text{-S3}
\end{array}
\tag{3-21}
$$

The three statements are in a strongly connected region ({pi}1x) at the vector-loop level, but none is in a strongly connected region at the element-loop level, and so all are vectorized.

The resulting object code looks similar to:

```
      DO 10 II=1,N,64            Vector Loop
         M(0:63)=rel-exp(II:II+63)
S1       VS(0:63)=A(II:II+63)?M(0:63)
S2       VS(0:63)=B(II:II+63)?.NOT.M(0:63)              (3-22)
S3       C(II:II+63)=VS(0:63)+D(II:II+63)
   10 CONTINUE
```

Statements S1 and S2 are performed under control of a mask expression (represented by the MASK operator ? (question mark), which is defined more fully later along with a more complete discussion of masks). A masked operation is performed for an element of a vector file if the associated element of the mask is TRUE. For example, taking the 25th assign performed by vector instructions generated for statement S2 on a given iteration of the "DO II" vector loop, $B(II+24)$ is assigned to $VS(24)$ if-and-only-if the value of the 25th mask expression, .NOT.M(24), is TRUE. Vector architectures normally have the capability of performing vector instructions under the control of a mask.

The world is always more complex than the common examples, so less amiable cases had to be considered in the implementation of UFTN. For example:

```
      DO 10 I=1,N
S1       IF(A(I).NE.0)S=A(I)                (3-23)
S2       B(I)=C(I)/S
   10    CONTINUE
```

The S used in statement S2 has a CARRY-FLOW dependency from statement S1 as well as the simple EQUAL-FLOW dependency. It is better to leave this loop unvectorized. More generally stated, when a CARRY-FLOW exists for a scalar and there may be an iteration of the loop on which the scalar is not defined, then the normal CARRY-ANTI and CARRY-OUTPUT dependencies are generated. (This is not as difficult to recognize as might be expected; in UFTN it falls out of the information in the "definition-reaches" bit vector computed in the CARRY dependency analysis pass.)

In the above example, a CARRY-ANTI dependency is generated at the element-loop level rather than a REVERSE dependency at the vector-loop level. This places S1 and S2 in a strongly connected region at the element-loop level, so neither statement is vectorized.

The {pi}-graph, resulting from the use of the REVERSE dependency, separates, at the element-loop level, the vectorizable definitions and uses of a scalar from its unvectorizable definitions and uses while keeping all references to the scalar in the same vector loop. This makes partial vectorization of a loop a simple process. For example:

```
      DO 10 I=1,N
S1       S=S+A(I)
S2       B(I)=S                             (3-24)
   10    CONTINUE
```

```
      DO 10 II=1,N,64      Vector Loop
         DO 11 I=0,63      Element Loop
S1          S=S+A(II+I)  ⌐ FLOW-2  ⌐ REV-1  CARRY FLOW-2
S2          B(II+I)=S    ← on S    ← on S   and CARRY
      11    CONTINUE                        OUTPUT-2
      10    CONTINUE                        on S
```

Figure 3-19. Loop dependencies for the example of (3-23).

The assumed loops and their dependencies are shown in Figure 3-19.
   The {pi}-graph produced by loop distribution is:

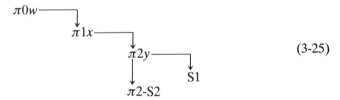

$$\text{(3-25)}$$

S1 is in a strongly connected region by itself ({pi}2y) at the element-loop level
and so is not vectorized. S2 is not in a strongly connected region at the
element-loop level and is therefore vectorized. Loop reconstruction takes the
{pi}-graph and produces:

```
         G1=S
         DO 10 II=1,N,64      Vector Loop
            DO 11 I=0,63      Element Loop
   S1          G1=G1+A(II+I)
               VS(I)=G1
      11       CONTINUE
   S2          B(II:II+63)=VS(0:63)
      10       CONTINUE
```

$$\text{(3-26)}$$

G1 is one of the general-purpose registers. *VS* (the expanded version of the scalar
S) is placed in one of the machine's vector files. The vector file is defined one
element at a time using the result of statement S1 in the "DO 11" element loop
(the ISP's architecture makes this a very simple task). Statement S2 is vectorized as
represented by the FORTRAN array syntax. If *S* has uses following the loop then
the final value computed in *VS* (the expanded version of *S*) must be assigned to *S*
at the loop's exit.

THE REVERSE DEPENDENCY IN
IF-TO-MASK CONVERSIONS

Converting the normal test-and-branch execution of IF statements into statements
executed under mask control can be made to look like scalar expansion with the

addition of a MASK operator ? (question mark). The left operand of a ? is a FORTRAN statement; the right operand is a logical expression. For example,

$$A(I)=B(I)+C(I)?MASK \qquad (3\text{-}27)$$

means that $B(I)$ is added to $C(I)$ and stored to $A(I)$ if-and-only-if the logical (or boolean) value of MASK is .TRUE..

This operator was introduced with little explanation in an earlier scalar-expansion example. The proposed 8X FORTRAN WHERE statement could have been used to represent a vectorized statement executed under a mask. The ? operator was chosen instead, because it makes statements look more like the vectorized object code they are being used to repesent.

A loop such as:

```
        DO 10 I=1,N
S1        IF(D(I).EQ.0)GOTO 20
S2        A(I)=B(I)/D(I)                        (3-28)
     20   CONTINUE
     10   CONTINUE
```

can be thought of as:

```
        DO 10 II=1,N,64      Vector Loop
          DO 11 I=0,63       Element Loop
S1          MASK=D(II+1).EQ.0
S2          A(II+I)=                            (3-29)
  !             B(II+I)/D(II+I)?.NOT.MASK
     11   CONTINUE
     10   CONTINUE
```

MASK is just a scalar that is defined by statement S1 and used by statement S2. MASK can be expanded and its definitions and uses can be vectorized like any other scalar. A CONTROL dependency becomes another name for an EQUAL-FLOW dependency. The dependency graph for the above is given in Figure 3-20.

Once the CONTROL and associated REVERSE dependencies are inserted into the dependency graph, the {pi}-graph is constructed in the same way as presented in the scalar-expansion discussion. The statement S1, which defines MASK, and statement S2, which uses MASK to control its own execution, are placed in the same {pi}-block at the vector-loop level owing to the strongly connected region formed from the CONTROL and associated REVERSE

```
        DO 10 II=1,N,64                                      Vector Loop
          DO 11 I=0,63                                       Element Loop
S1          MASK=D(II+1).EQ.0                                CONTROL-2  R.
S2          A(II+1)=B(II+1)/D(II+1)?.NOT.MASK
     11   CONTINUE
     10 CONTINUE
```

Figure 3-20. Loop dependencies including MASK statements, once the CONTROL and associated REVERSE dependencies are inserted.

dependencies. The resulting object code is similar to:

```
          DO 10 II=1,N,64        Vector Loop
S1          MASK(0:63)=D(II:II+63).EQ.0
S2          A(II:II+63)=B(II:II+63)                     (3-30)
          !    /D(II:II+63)?.NOT.MASK(0:63)
          10  CONTINUE
```

On this Unisys ISP, the expanded scalar MASK(0:63) requires only 64 bits. Statement S1 is performed with vector instructions that load the next 64 elements of D and compare them to 0. The vector compare instruction sets the 64 bits of the ISP's mask register. The jth bit of the mask register is set to 1 (.TRUE.) if-and-only-if $D(II + j)$ is equal to 0. Statement S2 is then performed with vector instructions that load 64 elements of B and D beginning at $B(II)$ and $D(II)$, performs the 64 divides, and stores the results in 64 elements of A beginning at $A(II)$ all under control of the 64-bit mask register. So, $B(II + j)$ is divided by $D(II + j)$ and stored to $A(II + j)$ if-and-only-if the jth bit of the mask register is 0.

MASK CONSTRUCTION

The literature seems to make the construction of the masks (or GUARDS as they are often called) a complex task (at least, the GUARD expressions quickly become complex) (Towle 1976; Allen 1983). The method used in UFTN, while fairly simple, handles arbitrary "logically" forward branching. The mask expressions remain no more complex than the IF expressions in the original source, and the vectorization of a mask is independent of the vectorization of its uses. An example of the last statement is:

```
          DO 10 I=1,N
S1            IF(A(I-1).EQ.3)THEN
S2                A(!)=B(I)
S3                B(I)=C(I)+3                          (3-31)
              ENDIF
          10    CONTINUE
```

While the mask $A(I - 1).EQ.3$ and the assignment to $A(I)$ are strongly connected at the element-loop level (and so unvectorizable) the assignment to $B(I)$ is vectorizable. The resulting object code (with statement S3 vectorized) looks as follows:

```
          DO 10 II=1,N,64        Vector Loop
          DO 11 I=0,63           Element Loop
S1          MASK(I)=A(II+I-1).EQ.3
S2          A(II+I)=B(II+I)?MASK(I)
          11  CONTINUE                              (3-32)
S3          B(II:II+63)=
          !          C(II:II+63)+3?MASK(0:63)
          10  CONTINUE
```

The Flow Graph

The algorithm first assumes that the program has been divided into basic blocks. A basic block is a group of consecutive statements that have a single entrance (e.g., a labeled statement) and a single exit (e.g., an IF statement). The "flow graph" is constructed for the basic blocks containing such information as the predecessors and successors of each block, the loop structure, and the dominance ordering of the blocks. Loosely, a block precedes another in the dominance ordering if it is executed first on a nonlooping path from procedure entrance to exit.

The blocking is done by the routines that perform the task for UFTN's standard optimizer (i.e., the optimizer that performs constant folding, strength reduction, common expression elimination, etc.). The blocking algorithms are based on the theory in Aho et al. (1977). Given the flow graph of the program, a logical "control expression" is constructed for each block, which reflects the program flow to that block. For simplicity, the discussion of control expressions deals only with blocks with one or two successors (IF–THEN–ELSE-like branching). The following algorithms are extended only slightly within UFTN to handle multiple-successor (CASE) blocks or multiple-exit loops. Except for some simple early-exit loops, it is generally not useful to vectorize CASE-like structures of multiple-exit loops.

Some compiler developers may actually implement the following algorithms and need a start as to how to handle CASE-like structures and multiple-exit loops. In the following algorithms, a THEN/ELSE flag is used in the control expressions for blocks with two successors so that the actual control flow path is known at each point. In UFTN, a count of the number of rejoined forks is kept for CASE branching or multiple-exit loops (replacing the THEN/ELSE flag). While the actual path is not known, it is known at what point all forks from a CASE branch or all exit paths from a loop have rejoined and attempts can again be made to vectorize statements.

The three-branch arithmetic IF

$$IF(exp)10,20,3 \qquad\qquad (3\text{-}33)$$

looks like two statements, each with two successors, to the UFTN vectorizer (barring special casing when two labels are equal); that is,

```
IF(exp=0)GOTO 20
IF(exp<0)THEN GOTO 10          (3-34)
ELSE GOTO 30
```

The following loop will be used in discussing the algorithm used to computer control expressions. The upper-case letters at the left denote the basic blocks.

```
        DO 10 I=1,N
A         IF(AA(I).NE.0)GOTO 2
          GOTO 4
B 2       IF(AB(I).NE.0)GOTO 5
E 3       AE(I)=EXPE
          GOTO 6
```

```
C 4       IF(AC(I).NE.0)GOTO 3
F         AF(I)=EXPF
          GOTO 7                              (3-35)
D 5           IF(AD(I).NE.0)THEN
G                 AG(I)=EXPG
          ELSE
H                 AH(I)=EXPH
          ENDIF
I 6       AI(I)=EXPI
J 7       AJ(I)=EXPJ
   10     CONTINUE
```

This should be sufficiently complex, with many GOTOs (including a physically backward, though logically forward, branch) and a block-IF. The flow graph of the program (ignoring the loop latch branch from block J to block A) looks like:

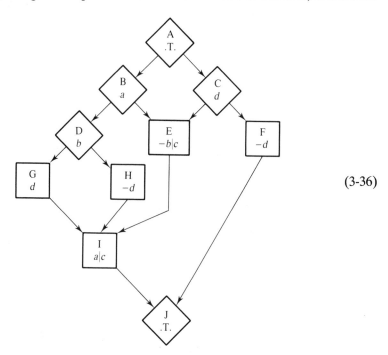

(3-36)

The upper case letter in the diamond or box is the block's identifier. Below the block's identifier is the control expression that the UFTN vectorizer generates for the block. A lower case letter in a control expression represents the control flow from the last statement of the associated upper case lettered block. If the lower case letter is prefixed with a — then it represents the ELSE branch from that block, otherwise the THEN branch is being represented. The symbol | represents a logical OR, and .T. means the block is always executed.

Notice that the GOTO 4 statement (the second statement in the loop body) has been drawn into the preceding IF statement when blocking. The GOTO 4 statement could have been placed in a separate block having one predecessor (the IF statement) and one successor (statement 4) without affecting the control expressions generated by the algorithm given later. Either way, loop reconstruction eliminates GOTOs when reconstructing vectorized loops. Even for loops analyzed by the UFTN vectorizer but only partially vectorized, the unvectorized portions are regenerated by loop reconstruction using the {pi}-graph with the existing GOTOs eliminated.

Take block I and examine its control expression $a \mid c$. This control expression reflects the fact that block I is executed if either the THEN branch of the fork out of block A is taken or the THEN branch of the fork out of the block C is taken.

Once the branches of a fork have rejoined, the information about that fork is useless but the path to that fork block is still important. In the case of block I, the two paths caused by the fork at the end of block B have rejoined at block I, but rather than keep $b \mid -b$ in the control expression for block I, the path to block B—that is block B's control expression—a becomes the first subexpression of the control expression for block I.

It is unneccessary to keep the full subexpression representing the other possible path to block I, which is from A to C to E to I. The full subexpression representing the forks is

$$(-a \; \& \; c)$$

but since executing the THEN branch of C implies that the ELSE branch of A has been executed, the $-a$ can be dropped. It is only necessary to keep the fork type (THEN or ELSE) of each of the nearest forks that cause a block to be reached.

AN ALGORITHM TO COMPUTE CONTROL EXPRESSIONS

Formally, the algorithm to compute the logical control expressions for all blocks of a loop is:

```
procedure compute_control_expressions
Define the control expression for the block which is
the head of the loop to be .TRUE. (it is always
executed).
   for each remaining block, in dominance order, do
      Call curnt_blk the block being processed.
      Set blk_exp to .FALSE..
      for each predecessor of curnt_blk do
         Call pred_blk the curnt predecessor block.
         if curnt_block is the only successor of pred_blk
         then begin
            Set pred_exp to the control expression
```

```
                    computed for pred_blk.
                    blk_exp=OR(blk_exp, pred_exp)
end
              else begin
                    Let pred_blk_ace be an atomic control
                    expression (i.e., just a block-name/fork-type)
                    whose block-name is pred_blk.
                    if curnt_blk is the THEN branch of pred_blk
                    then Set the fork-type of pred_blk_ace to THEN
                    else Set the fork-type of pred_blk_ace to ELSE
blk_exp=
  OR(blk_exp, pred_blk_ace)
              end
            end for each predecessor
          Set the control expression for curnt_blk to blk_
          exp.
          end for each block
        end compute_control_expressions

     procedure OR(old_exp, new_exp) RESULT log_exp
RECURSIVE
     for each atomic OR'ed subexpression in new_exp do
        Call new_or_atom the subexpression being
        processed.
        Call new_or_blk the block that new_or_atom
        represents.
        for each atomic OR'ed subexpression in old_exp do
           Call old_or_atom the subexpression of old_exp
           being processed.
           if the block of old_or_atom is the same as the
           block of new_or_atom (i.e., new_or_blk in both
           cases)

           then delete old_or_atom from old_exp and make
           an early exit from the current for each loop.
           The early exit is performed when the paths from
           the THEN and ELSE forks out of block new_or_blk
           (one path is represented by old_or_atom and the
           other by new_or_atom) have come back together.
        end for each
           if no early exit from the just closed loop
           then add a copy of new_or_atom to the list of
           OR'ed
           atomic subexpressions in old_exp. Note, if old_exp
           was simply .FALSE. then adding a copy of new_or_
```

atom results in old_exp just containing the copy.
```
else begin
```
    Since the two forks of new_or_blk have come back
    together, the block for which old_exp is being
    computed is no longer under control of new_or_
    blk's branching. However, it is still under
    control of the branching that caused new_or_blk to
    be reached.

    Call pred_exp the control expression that has
    already been computed for block new_or_blk.
    old_exp=OR(old_exp, pred_exp)
```
    end
  end for each
  return old_exp
end OR
```
Assume that the control expression blk_exp is
going to be computed for block I in our earlier
example using the above procedures. All blocks except
J and F dominate block I and so their control
expressions have already been computed.
```
blk_exp=.FALSE.
```
    Initialize.

```
blk_exp=blk_exp|−b|c
```
    The third predecessor of I is block E which has
    only one successor so OR in E's control
    expression (which is −b|e).
```
blk_exp=blk_exp|−d
```
    Second predecessor of I is H which has only one
    successor so attempt to OR in H's control
    expression (which is −d).
```
blk_exp=d|−d=b
```
    Since both forks from block D have come back
    together at block I, instead of OR'ing in −d, d
    is removed and the control expression computed
    for block D (which is b) is OR'ed into blk_exp.
```
blk_exp=blk_exp|−b|c
```
    The third predecessor of I is block E which has
    only one successor so OR in E's control
    expression (which is −b|e).
```
blk_exp=b|−b|c=a|c
```
    Since both forks from block B have come back
    together at block I, eliminate the information
    on b from blk_exp and OR in the control
    expression computed for block B (which is a).

Constructing the CONTROL and REVERSE Dependencies

The construction of the CONTROL and REVERSE dependencies for a statement in a block under control of a conditional branch is straightforward from the resulting control expression.

For a statement S in an arbitrary block X whose control expression is y perform the following loop:

For each atomic subexpression ae of y perform the following steps.

1. Let Z be the block of ae.
2. Let LS be the last statement in block Z. LS is the statement causing the conditional branching at the end of block Z.
3. Construct a CONTROL dependency at the element-loop level from statement LS to statement S.
4. Construct a REVERSE dependency at the vector-loop level from statement S to statement LS.

Using the assign to $AI(I)$ in block I from the earlier example, the control expression $a \mid c$ means that a CONTROL dependency is required from the last statement in block A {IF(AA(I).NE.0)} to the assign to $AI(I)$, along with a REVERSE dependency back, and a CONTROL dependency is required from the last statement in block C {IF(AC(I).NE.0)} to the assign to $AI(I)$, and again, a REVERSE dependency back. The dependency graph (assuming no data dependencies) for the whole loop is shown in Figure 3-21.

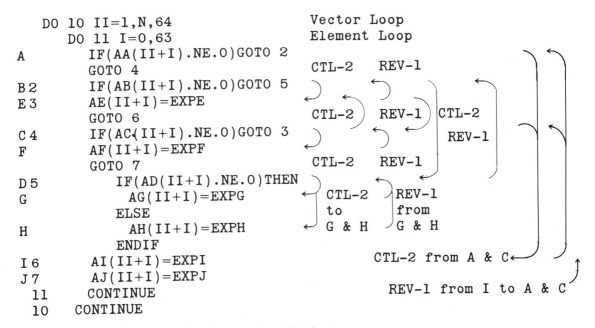

Figure 3-21. Dependency graph for the example of (3-35).

Notice that no complicated logical expression simplifier is required to compute the control expressions and, as we will see, no logical expression simplifier is required for constructing the actual execution-time masks. The control expressions are easy and fast to generate and they translate directly into the CONTROL and REVERSE dependencies required.

Generating the mask expressions from this information is not too difficult, although it can get a bit tricky for things such as constructing the ELSE mask computed in a block executed under another ELSE mask where the definition is unvectorizable and the use is vectorizable. A few comments on object-code generation for mask expressions and a FORTRAN approximation of the object code for the example loop follow to give a feel of what loop reconstruction must do.

Comments on Code Generation for Loops with Mask Expressions

For each of the blocks whose last statement is a conditional branch (blocks A, B, C, and D) a THEN mask and an ELSE mask must be created if needed for use in executing later statements. Call A_THEN_MASK(0:63) block A's THEN mask for the current iteration of the vector loop. A_THEN_MASK(j) is .TRUE. if-and-only-if the THEN branch is taken by the last statement in block A in the $II + j$th iteration of the original loop, given that II is the equivalent vector loop's loop control variable. A_THEN_MASK is used, for example, in executing statements in block B. In a given iteration of the vector loop to be constructed, A_THEN_MASK is computed with the statement:

$$A\_THEN\_MASK(0:63)=AA(II:II+63).NE.0 \qquad (3\text{-}37)$$

A_ELSE_MASK is simply the .NOT. of A_THEN_MASK. However, since a vector instruction on the Unisys ISP can be performed under the mask or the .NOT. of the mask, A_ELSE_MASK need not be computed. The statements of block C can simply be executed using the .NOT. of the mask A_THEN_MASK.

The statements in block D must be executed under the mask computed for the THEN branch out of block B. Since block B is only executed when the THEN branch of block A is taken, an element of B_THEN_MASK(0:63) must be .FALSE. if the same element of A_THEN_MASK(0:63) is .FALSE.. The Unisys ISP hardware sets the elements of a mask to .FALSE. where the control mask is .FALSE. for a mask computed under mask control. So the vector instructions used to perform

$$\begin{aligned}&B\_THEN\_MASK(0:63)=\\&\quad AB(II:II+63).NE.0 \ ? \ A\_THEN\_MASK(0:63)\end{aligned} \qquad (3\text{-}38)$$

set an arbitrary element B_THEN_MASK(j) to .FALSE. if the element of the control mask A_THEN_MASK(j) is .FALSE. or if AB($II + j$).EQ.0.

The statement

$$AH(I)=EXPG \tag{3-39}$$

in block H is under control of the ELSE branch of the fork in block D (since the mask expression for block H is $-d$). One cannot simply do an element-by-element (bit-by-bit) logical .NOT. of D_THEN_MASK(0:63) to come up with D_ELSE_MASK(0:63), since both must be .FALSE. for those elements associated with iterations of the loop in which block D is not executed. However, the computation is still trivial. Since the mask for executing statements in block D is the THEN mask from block B, the mask for the ELSE branch out of block D is:

$$D\_ELSE\_MASK(0:63)=$$
$$D\_THEN\_MASK(0:63) \quad XOR \tag{3-40}$$
$$B\_THEN\_MASK(0:63)$$

Since our expanded scalar masks are only 64 bits large, the XOR is done with scalar (not vector) instructions.

For mask definitions that cannot be vectorized (or defined by XORing or NOTing known masks), the big difficulty is getting all elements (bits) of the expanded scalar mask initialized to .FALSE. at a convenient point. As for XOR and NOT, a scalar instruction is used to initialize all 64 bits to 0 (FALSE). The element loops defining these masks need only set the .TRUE. elements of the masks.

The only other real problem is knowing when not to generate a mask because it is not needed (e.g., when there are no statements in an ELSE block). This task is, for the most part, a bookkeeping problem.

Given the above comments and assuming everything vectorized, you can get an idea of the actual mask construction from a FORTRAN approximation (including the earlier-defined mask operator ?) of the object code generated for the example loop in Figure 3-22. Those statements marked "sca" are performed with scalar, rather than vector, instructions.

It is assumed that the expressions EXPE, EXPG, EXPH, EXPI, and EXPJ are vectorized, that is, that the values of the expressions for 64 consecutive iterations of the original loop can be computed using vector instructions.

CONCLUSIONS

The REVERSE dependency provides a simple way to keep the definitions and uses of expanded scalars or the definitions and uses of masks in the same vector loop. One big advantage is that expanded scalars (or masks) need only be expanded to the vector size of the machine (which is 64 for single-precision vector operations on the Unisys ISP). No large temporaries are ever required. A second big advantage is that an expanded scalar is almost always kept loaded in one of the ISP's 64-element vector files from definition to last use. Equivalently, a 64-bit mask is usually kept either in the ISP's mask register or one of its general-purpose registers from definition to last use.

```
        DO 10 II=1,N,64                                    Vector Loop
A       A_THEN_MASK(0:63)=AA(II:II+63).NE.0
B       B_THEN_MASK(0:63)=AB(II:II+63).NE.0  ?A_THEN_
        MASK(0:63)
sca     B_ELSE_MASK(0:63)=B_THEN_MASK(0:63).XOR.A_THEN_
        MASK(0:63)
D       D_THEN_MASK(0:63)=AD(II:II+63).NE.0  ?B_THEN_
        MASK(0:63)
G       AG(II:II+63)=EXPG(next 64 iterations)    ?D_
        THEN_MASK(0:63)
H       AH(II:II+63)=EXPH(next 64 iterations)    ?D_
        MASK(0:63)
C       C_THEN_MASK(0:63)=AC(II:II+63).NE.0  ?.NOT.A_
        THEN_MASK(0:63)
sca     C_ELSE_MASK(0:63)=C_THEN_MASK(0:63).XOR.
  !                        .NOT.A_THEN_MASK(0:63)
F       AF(II:II+63)=EXPF(next 64 iterations)  ?C_ELSE_
        MASK(0:63)
sca     E_MASK(0:63)=B_ELSE_MASK(0:63).OR.C_THEN_
        MASK(0:63)
E       AE(II:II+63)=EXPE(next 64 iterations)    ?E_
        MASK(0:63)
sca     I_MASK(0:63)=A_THEN_MASK(0:63).OR.C_THEN_
        MASK(0:63)
I       AI(II:II+63)=EXPI(next 64 iterations)    ?I_
        MASK(0:63)
J       AJ(II:II+63)=EXPJ(next 64 iterations)
   10   CONTINUE
```

Figure 3-22. MASK construction for the example of (3-35).

Little additional code was required in UFTNs vectorizer to get this payoff. Loop distribution, which was in place in UFTN to separate vectorizable from unvectorizable statements, was modified slightly to speed the processing of vector-loop levels with no REVERSE dependencies. The existing dependencies were placed on the even (element) loop levels, and REVERSE dependencies were added to oppose the existing CONTROL and FLOW dependencies on the odd (vector) loop levels. Lastly, a few changes were made to loop reconstruction to handle a {pi}-graph with vector/element loop levels. These minor changes eliminated the problem of scalar expansion resulting in large temporary arrays and, as an added benefit, resulted in better object code.

Also shown in this chapter is the algorithm UFTN uses in generating control expressions to represent the program flow. Control expressions are used to generate the REVERSE dependencies needed for IF-to-MASK conversion.

Control expressions and REVERSE dependencies are two important parts of UFTN's method of vectorizing loops with conditional branches. Overall, this method has shown itself to be simple, thorough, and fast, and to result in better code than any other method investigated.

Not explored in this chapter, because it is has yet to be implemented in the UFTN compiler, is the potential use of the REVERSE dependency to reverse an INPUT dependency. An INPUT dependency is like an OUTPUT dependency, except that rather than definitions at the head and tail of the dependency arc, there are uses, both of which use exactly the same definition(s) of the variable. The REVERSE dependency could reverse an INPUT dependency when it was desired to keep the two uses of the variable in the same vector loop. This would be valuable, for example, if the variable being used was a vector strip of an array, since a vector file could be loaded once and used twice within the vector loop.

REFERENCES

Aho, Alfred V. and Jeffrey D. Ullman (1977). *Principles of compiler design.* Addison Wesley, Reading, Mass.

Allen, John Randal, Ken Kennedy, Carrie Porterfield, and Joe Warren (1983a). "Conversion of control dependence to data dependence." *Conference Record of the 10th Annual ACM Symposium on Principles of Programming Languages,* Austin, Tex.

Allen, John Randal (1983b). "Dependence analysis for subscripted variables and its application to program transformations." PhD Thesis, Rice University, Houston, Tex.

Allen, John Randal (1984). "Automatic loop interchange," Symposium on Compiler Construction, *SIGPLAN Notices,* Vol. 19, No. 6, pp. 233–246.

Banerjee, Utpal (1976). "Data dependence in ordinary programs." Department of Computer Science Rep. UIUCDCS-R-76–837, University of Illinois, Urbana-Champaign, Ill.

Besaw, Keith V. (1987). "Advanced techniques for vectorizing dusty decks." *Proceedings Second International Conference on Supercomputing,* Vol. I, Part 1, pp. 111–132. International Supercomputing Institute, St. Petersburg, Fla.

Coleman, Howard B. (1987). "The vectorizing compiler for the unisys ISP," *1987 International Conference on Parallel Processing Proceedings,* St. Charles, Ill., pp. 567–576.

Dongarra, Jack J. (1986). *Performance of Various Computers Using Standard Linear Equations Software in a FORTRAN Environment.* Argonne National Laboratory, Technical Memorandum No. 23, August 5, 1986.

Dunn, D. S. and F. A. Stephens (1987). "Processor scheduling algorithms for a heterogeneous vector and scalar computer system." *Proceedings Second International Conference on Supercomputing,* Vol. I, Part 1. pp. 133–137. International Supercomputing Institute, St. Petersburg, Fla.

Gentzch, W. (1987a). Benchmark results from the UNISYS 1100/90 " Private communication to Unisys Corporation.

Gentzch, W. (1987b). "The efficient use of the UNISYS 1100/90 " Private communication to Unisys Corporation.

Gyllstrom, Hans C., Ross C. Knippel, Larry C. Ragland, and Karen E. Spackman (1979). "The Universal Compiling System." *SIGPLAN Notices,* December 1979, pp. 64–70.

Hodek, James A. (1987). "The Unisys 1100/90 ISP System, integrated supercomputing," *Proceedings Second International Conference on Supercomputing,* Vol. I, Part 1, pp. 38–150. International Supercomputing Institute, St. Petersburg, Fla.

Kennedy, Ken (1980). *Automatic Translation of FORTRAN Programs to Vector Form.* Rice Technical Report 476-029-4, Rice University, Houston, Tex.

Kuck, David J. (1976). "Parallel processing of ordinary programs." In *Advances in Computers,* Vol. 115 (ed. Morris Rubinoff and Marshal C. Yovits), pp. 119–179. Academic Press, New York.

Kuck, David J. (1977). "A survey of parallel machine organization and programming." *Comput. Surveys,* Vol. 9, No. 1, pp. 29–59.

Kuck, David J. (1978). *The Structure of Computers and Computations,* Vol. 1. John Wiley, New York.

Kuck, David J., R. H. Kuhn, Bruce R. Leasure, and Michael J. Wolfe (1980). "The structure of an advanced vectorizer for pipelined processors," *Proceedings IEEE Computer Society Fourth International Computer Software and Applications Conference,* Chicago, Ill., pp. 709–715.

Kuck, David J., R. H. Kuhn, David A. Padua, Bruce R. Leasure, and Michael J. Wolfe (1981). "Dependence graphs and compiler optimizations," *Conference Record of the Eighth ACM Symposium on Principles of Programming Languages,* Williamsburg, Va., pp. 207–218.

Leasure, Bruce Robert (1976). "Compiling Serial Languages for Parallel Machines," Masters Thesis, UIUCDCS-R-76-805, University of Illinois, Urbana-Champaign, Ill.

McKie, Sarah R. (1985). "A Unified Code Generator for Multiple Architectures," *Proceedings of the 1985 ACM Annual Conference,* Denver, Colorado, October 1985, pp. 412–426.

McKie, Sarah R. (1987). *A Multiple Architecture Code Generator.* Internal Unisys Corp. Document.

McMahon, Frank (1986). *The Livermore Fortran Kernels, A Computer Test of the Numerical Performance Range.* Report UCRL-53745, Lawrence Livermore National Laboratories, Livermore, Calif.

Muraoka, Y. (1971). "Parallelism Exposure and Exploitation in Programs, " PhD Thesis, Report 71-424, University of Illinois, Urbana-Champaign, Ill.

Padua, David A., David J. Kuck, and Duncan H. Lawrie (1980). "High-speed multiprocessors and compilation techniques," *IEEE Trans. Computers,* Vol. C-29, No. 9, pp. 763d–776.

Padua, David A. and Michael J. Wolfe (1986). "Advanced Compiler Optimizations for Supercomputers," *Commun. ACM,* Vol. 29, No. 12, pp. 1184–1201.

Shimon, Even (1979). *Graph Algorithms,* pp. 64–66. Computer Science Press, Rockville, Md.

Tarjan, Robert (1972). "Depth First Search and Linear Graph Algorithms," *SIAM Journal of Computing,* Vol. 1, No. 2, June 1972 pp. 146–160.

Towle, Ross (1976). "Control and Data Dependence for Program Transformations," PhD Thesis, Rep. 76-788, University of Illinois, Urbana-Champaign, Ill.

Van Kats, J. M. and A. J. van der Steen (1987). "Mainframes with supercomputer speed," ACCU Reeks 51, Academic Computer Utrecht, State University of Utrecht, Utrecht, The Netherlands.

Wolfe, Michael J. (1976). "Techniques for Improving the Inherent Parallelism in Programs," Masters Thesis, Department of Computer Science Rep. UIUCDCS-R-78-929, University of Illinois, Urbana-Champaign, Ill.

4

A SCALEABLE ARCHITECTURE FOR EXPLOITING DEMAND-DRIVEN AND DATA-DRIVEN PARALLEL COMPUTATION

A. A. Faustini, E. A. Ashcroft, and R. Jagannathan

INTRODUCTION

The term *supercomputer* is not well defined and as a consequence is used in widely divergent contexts. Despite this diversity of usage, the term usually carries with it a "high-performance" connotation. A *supercomputing system* can be thought of as a computer system that significantly outperforms, usually with respect to a particular domain of application, the standard "mainframes" of its time. Supercomputers of this era ($\sim$1987) are still predominantly Cray class machines that excel in scientific computations involving vector or matrix computations. This success has led to a much narrower view of supercomputer systems. In this narrower view, a supercomputing system is thought of as a fourth-generation architecture with vector-processing capabilities. In our opinion, supercomputing systems need not be tied to a particular generation of architecture because they change as our requirements for computation evolve. For example, over the next decade we will no doubt see the emergence of supercomputing systems for the symbolic processing requirements of artificial-intelligence applications. In addition, we predict that in the same time frame we

This work was supported mainly by NSF Grants DCR-84 15618 and DCR-84 13727, and in part by funds from the DARPA Strategic Computing Program, monitored by the Office of Naval Research under ONR Contract N000014-85-C-0775.

221

shall see the conventional sequential supercomputer architectures yielding some of their ground to scaleable parallel architectures. In this chapter we present a candidate scaleable parallel architecture that exploits the advantages of both demand-driven and data-driven computation.

We regard demand-driven dataflow and Reduction [p. 97 of ref. 1] as different evaluation strategies. In Reduction both program and data are indistinguishable and both are transformed during evaluation, whereas only data is transformed in demand-driven computation. This has important implications for fault-tolerance.[2] On the other hand, reduction and demand-driven dataflow treat function evaluation in the same way (i.e., call-by-need).

Computational Physics

Traditionally, supercomputers have been developed in an attempt to satisfy the extraordinary computational needs of physicists. Bill Buzbee of the Los Alamos National Laboratory has stated that the driving force behind the early development of supercomputing systems was, and to a large extent is still, the Navier-Stokes equation. The numerical solution to this equation requires millions of floating point operations to be performed per second (FLOPS). In fact the speed at which a floating point operation can be performed is so important that it has become a standard by which supercomputers are currently measured. Cray Research, one of the leading manufacturers of supercomputers, has machines with peak performance ratings ranging from 80 MFLOPS (10^6 FLOPS) for the CRAY1-S to over one GFLOP (10^9 FLOPS) for the CRAY2 (4 CPUs). These peak performance figures are misleading. A more meaningful measure is the sustained performance with respect to an application or set of benchmark programs.[3] J. J. Dongarra at the Argonne National Laboratory has compared the performance of about 100 computers, ranging from a Motorola 68000 to a CRAY X-MP. The benchmarks he used are for solving dense systems of linear equations of order 100. More specifically, they are based on the LINPACK software in a FORTRAN environment.[4] His results show that the CRAY1-S runs his benchmarks at 23 MFLOPS.* Jim McGraw, a researcher at the Lawrence Livermore National Laboratory (LLNL), has stated that the goal of researchers at LLNL is to have applications running on Cray class machines at sustained rates that are 75% of the peak performance. In practice, applications running on the CRAY1-S perform at between 15 and 55 MFLOPS depending on the application (i.e., 20% to 70% of peak performance).

The success of Cray class supercomputers can be traced to ingenuity in the architecture, use of state-of-the-art components, excellent assembly-language programming for critical code sections and, more recently, effective vectorizing FORTRAN compilers. Moreover, this success has been achieved within the

---

* We include this to illustrate the difference between *peak* performance and *benchmark* performance. The reader should refer to Jack Dongarra's report before drawing any further conclusions.

framework of the conventional sequential von Neumann model of computation. Although machines such as the CRAY-X MP or the CRAY2 have up to four CPUs, each of these is a single von Neumann machine enhanced to permit operations in vector mode. In this mode a machine is able to perform a floating-point operation in one machine cycle. The CRAY-X MP has a cycle time of 8.2 nanoseconds (nsec), giving it a peak performance rating of about 120 MFLOPS per processor. The success of corporations like Cray Research leaves no doubt that there are domain-specific applications that require super-computer performance. Unfortunately, not all problems fall into this category and for those that do not the Cray solution is inappropriate and expensive.

Japan's Fifth-Generation Computing Systems (FGCSs) Project

Japan's FGCSs project has recently emerged as a new driving force behind a new class of supercomputer architectures for symbolic processing. The FGCSs project attempts to "extend the frontiers of computer science and engineering to the point where intelligent, superpowerful computers might be capable of serving as expert consultants to government . . . applications would . . . increase produc-tivity, conserve energy, provide medical, educational, and other social support.† This new driving force seems to encompass a wider range of applications than those of computational physics. Some of these applications are as computationally demanding as those of the physicists. For example, one of the goals of FGCSs is to enable a machine to interact with humans through spoken natural language. To achieve continuous (speaker-independent) speech recognition with a vocabulary of 20 000 words requires a machine capable of 100 000 MIPS.† Moreover, the algorithms involved may not be amenable to evaluation in a vector mode. Other requirements of the FGCSs include computer vision, robotics, and the codifying of human knowledge in machine form for utilization by intelligent systems.

Central to the FGCSs goals is the development of a symbolic programming language based on first-order predicate calculus, called KL1 (for Kernel Lan-guage 1). This language is a derivative of the logic programming language Prolog. It is interesting to note that to meet many of the goals set for FGCSs requires "super" implementations of KL1. Consequently, the designers of architectures for symbolic computation, following their counterparts in the world of numeric computation, have devised a means of measuring the performance of their implementations. In the case of Prolog, the measure used is called a *logical inference*. Implementations are measured in terms of logical inferences per second (LIPS). This measure is not as well defined as a FLOP. The reason for this is that a LIP is the amount of time that it takes to invoke and successfully complete a Prolog clause. A clause might be as simple as $p :- q$ or it might be a more

---

† See the Special Issue of the *IEEE Spectrum* on fifth generation computing systems, November, 1983.

complex clause involving complex subgoals such as $d(X, Y):-a(X, Z)$, $b(Z, X, W)$, $c(W, Y)$, where the predicates a, b, c are themselves defined in terms of further subgoals. Thus, a logical inference can be simple or extremely complex depending on the complexity of the clause. To overcome this problem the logic programming community has informally agreed (at least for sequential implementations of Prolog) upon performance measures based upon a number of standard benchmarks. The most popular of these benchmarks is the determinate concatenation of two lists. For more details, see ref. 5. On the basis of this benchmark, the best commercially available implementations of Prolog run at 100 000 LIPS on SUN 3 Workstations, VAX class machines, and microcoded Symbolics 3600s. The more recent implementations of Prolog are native code compilers that, whenever possible, translate Prolog into the native code of the target machine.

A number of experimental "super" implementations of Prolog are being developed that run on either large main frames such as an IBM 3080 (500 000 LIPS) or special-purpose VLSI implementations such as the Berkeley PLM[6,7] (270 000 LIPS). One notable symbolic architecture that is similar in spirit to the early CRAY machines is the LOW RISC machine.[8] This design built with moderate technology (an instruction cycle time of 100 nsec) is reported to run Prolog at bursts of up to 3 000 000 LIPS. If CRAY class technology were used on the LOW RISC (5 nsec cycle time), it might be possible for it to run at bursts of up to 60 MLIPS. (The simplicity of the LOW RISC machine (40 000 transistors) means that it could be built with emerging GaAs technology.) Thus, we begin to see the emergence of supercomputer systems for symbolic processing. We note that the requirements of FGCSs applications will require machines capable of performing in the range of 100 MLIPS to 1 GLIPS.

THE SEQUENTIAL NATURE OF THE CONVENTIONAL APPROACH

The supercomputing systems described above share one common property, that is, they are all, even the previously cited Prolog implementations,[9] machines based primarily on the von Neumann model of computation. Conventional supercomputing systems derive their performance from ingenious ways of organizing the architecture to suit a particular application domain. Techniques used include internal pipelining of instructions, the exploitation of subinstruction parallelism, vector-mode processing, and other clever optimization techniques. Supercomputing systems based on the von Neumann model of computation have been and will continue to be amongst the most successful computational tools for problem solving for both numeric and symbolic applications.

Our Approach to Supercomputing Systems

Note that for the remainder of this chapter we will use the term supercomputer and multiprocessor architecture interchangeably.

Architectures based on the von Neumann model of computation are not the only way of attaining supercomputer performance. We feel that the successful harnessing of parallelism, available at different levels of granularity, will result in significant performance improvements. Our approach to computation is based on a parallel model of computation that is mathematically oriented in contrast to the von Neumann approach, which is machine-oriented. Figure 4-1 gives an overview

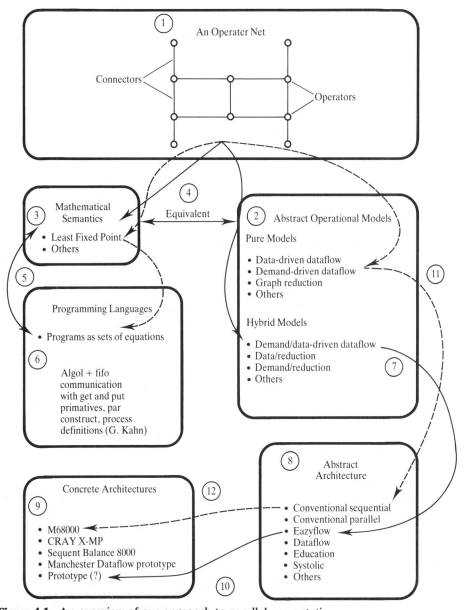

Figure 4-1. An overview of our approach to parallel computation.

of our approach to parallel computation. The keystone to our approach is a structured uninterpreted net called an *operator net*. An example net is shown in box 1 of Figure 4-1. The nodes of an operator net are called *operators* and the arcs *connectors*. We will show how both an operational and a mathematical interpretation can be given to these nets.

Operational interpretations (or semantics) are dynamic interpretations in which an operator net is to be thought of as an abstract computing device. Under one interpretation operators might be continuously operating determinate computing devices, and in another they might be nondeterminate devices. The connectors in one interpretation might be FIFO queues of length 2, in another they might be LIFO queues, and so on. Thus, the concept of an operator net together with an operational interpretation can be used to define many different abstract models of parallel computation. However, in this chapter we are restricting outselves to operational models in which the nodes are continuously operating determinate computing devices and the arcs are communications channels along which travel data or requests for data. In particular, we are interested in date-driven dataflow (traditional *dataflow*), demand-driven dataflow (called *eduction*[10]) and a hybrid of these two models called *eazyflow*.

Operator nets can also be given a mathematical interpretation (or semantics) that is to be thought of in a "static" or "absolute" sense. Although there are no restrictions on the mathematical semantics, other than computability constraints, in this chapter we consider only a mathematical semantics that is based on fixpoint theory.[11] The mathematical semantics is defined by a set of equations that is associated with an operator net. The meaning of the net is given by the least fixed-point solution to these net equations.

Although the operational and the mathematical semantics are different ways of interpreting operator nets, it turns out that under certain conditions the two are equivalent. If this is the case, as it is with the interpretations we will use, then the power of mathematics can be brought to bear on the design of programming languages, compilation techniques, and computer architectures. Roughly speaking, equivalence means that the data values that flow along the connector of an operator net are precisely those values that the least fixed point generates for the mathematical object corresponding to the connector.[12]

Since we have selected a mathematical semantics to work with, namely the fixpoint semantics of Kahn, it can be used as a standard for determining the *correctness* of different operational models.

In his original paper, Gilles Kahn[11] defines a simple language for parallel processing based on an extension to ALGOL 60. The extension involves the introduction of communication channels, process declarations and *put* and *get* primitives for writing to and reading from named channels. Although it is possible to coerce a conventional language into "a simple language for parallel processing," it turns out not to be necessary. The reason for this is that the net equations are themselves an elegant equational programming language that we get for free. We shall see later that different data algebras can be associated with operator nets, resulting in a family of equational languages. Each member of the family is determined by a different data algebra.

Eazyflow engines are a new family of computer architectures based upon a model of computation that combines the advantages of both data-driven and demand-driven computation.[1,13] Most of the members of this family are used for special-purpose applications such as signal processing, image processing, and real-time process control.[14] What is significant is that all eazyflow architectures are variants of one standard architecture. In this chapter we present the standard architecture, that is, an architecture that is to be found at the heart of any eazyflow engine. The main features of all the eazyflow engines are the following.

- The machines are all operational realizations of a mathematical algorithm specification model called operator nets.[15]
- The computational model employed is a hybrid of demand-driven and data-driven computation, called eazyflow.[13,16]
- The different engines will be programmed using different members of the Lucid[17,18] family, and these will be the assembly languages of the machines. (We will see that the choice of Lucid is very natural, because Lucid programs are essentially the textural forms of operator nets.)
- Lucid is a very high-level language, but, since it is the assembly language of the machines, it is very close to the basic architecture of the machines. Other languages can be run on the machines in the normal way, by using compilers that compile into the assembly languages of the machine in question, that is, into the appropriate member of the Lucid family.
- The architecture presented in this chapter is based on the successful architecture of the Manchester Dataflow Machine. It uses unidirectional pipelined rings that carry tagged data packets.
- The machine is composed of several submachines that are joined together by having their rings intersect through a switch. Because the rings are heavily pipelined, the delay through the switch will not significantly reduce the performance of the machine.

The ideas presented all stem from a reexamination of the basic concepts in the area of asynchronous, highly parallel computation in the light of usability and, in particular, programmability. At the same time, mathematical elegance and simplicity have been goals, particularly for models and languages. One result of this is that the conventional ideas of dataflow have been found wanting, and the operational concept of dataflow network has been replaced. The approach taken now, which is simpler and yet is an extension, is to take, instead, the mathematical concept of operator net as the most basic idea. The problem of giving operational interpretations to operator nets is a separate problem from that of giving a mathematical meaning to nets. Thus, different modes of operational behavior can be studied (including traditional dataflow). This allows different operational interpretations to be compared and it has permitted the design of a novel operational interpretation. This interpretation, which is a hybrid of two of the basic interpretations (data-driven and demand-driven dataflow), takes advantage of the strengths of both while largely avoiding their drawbacks. The hybrid operational interpretation, called eazyflow, is the basis for the architecture. The architecture is based on several submachines joined together through an interconnection switch. The architecture should be scaleable in the sense that the number of submachines can be increased without the performance of the individual submachines being degraded.

Alternative Paths in Our Approach

In Figure 4-1 the black arrows indicate a path through the boxes that is the basis of the work described in this chapter. This is not the only path that can be taken. The dotted arrows indicate an alterntive path, one in which Lucid (or operator nets) are run on a sequential machine such as a 68000. This involves the development of Lucid Abstract Sequential Machine.

Alternatively, different paths can be combined to form a hybrid path. For example, it would be very interesting to take the work on compiling Lucid for sequential machines[19,20] and use it together with the work described in this chapter to produce an effective implementation of operator nets (Lucid) on machines such as a CRAY-X MP, a Sequent Balance 8000 or a Mark 3 Hypercube. The reader is encouraged to pursue these alternative paths of investigation.

OPERATOR NETS

Operator nets can be thought of as a generalization of the "simple language for parallel processing" originally defined by Gilles Kahn.[11] The syntax or form of operator nets is briefly described below. The reader interested in more details should read ref. 15.

An *operator net* is a main directed graph together with subsidiary named operator nets that are called *function definitions*. All of the directed graphs, the main one and those contained within the subsidiary operator nets, use only the following six types of nodes.

- *Operator nodes,* which are associated with operator symbols
- *Function nodes,* which are associated with the names of function definitions
- *Subcomputation nodes,* which correspond one-to-one with particular subsidiary operator nets
- *Fork nodes,* which are used for replicating data
- *Input nodes* and *output nodes,* which are used to form semantic interfaces with enclosing operator nets or the "outside world"

The operator net shown in Figure 4-2 illustrates almost all of the features of operator nets. The input and output ports are small shaded squares, the fork nodes are small black circles, operators nodes are ovals, and function nodes are rectangles. Note that the subcomputation node "sqroot" contains a subsidiary operator net. Numbers have been placed next to the input arcs of nodes that will subsequently be given an interpretation in which the relative order of the input arcs is important. Examples are the arithmetic operators "minus" and "division."

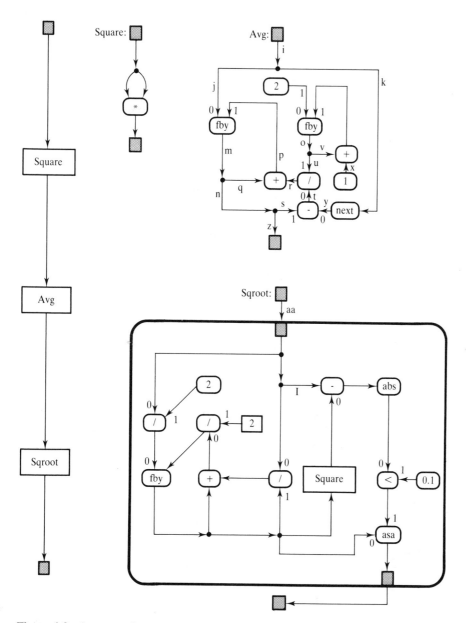

Figure 4-2. An example operator net.

MATHEMATICAL SEMANTICS

We assign a meaning to our operator nets in a mathematical way, using fixpoint theory. Each connector in the net is associated with a mathematical equation (one equation for each connector in the main directed graph and one for the output connector of each function definition). Each of the function-definition equations contains the equations for the subsidiary operator net associated with the function definition. Also, the equations for subcomputation nodes will contain the equations for the operator nets associated with its connectors. This means that the equation sets will be structured in the same manner as the operator nets.

Gilles Kahn[11] was the first to show how it is possible to give operator nets a mathematical meaning. Kahn discovered a way of associating a set of equations with a network of parallel computing agents. Moreover, he noted that it was possible to take as the mathematical meaning of the net the least fixed point of these equations. We now illustrate this by showing how to associate a set of equations with the net called *counter* shown in Figure 4-3.

Following Kahn we associate with each arc of the net a name. For example v0 is associated with the input arc and v3 with the output arc. Given the labelling in Figure 4-3, we can build up the following set of equations:

```
v0=input;
v1=+(v4, v5);
v2=fby(v0, v1);
v3=v2;
v4=v2;
v5=1;
```

Abstracting from this, we can see that in general each connector in an operator net has associated with it an equation of the form:

```
vi=fi(v0, v1, . . . ,vn).
```

Counter:

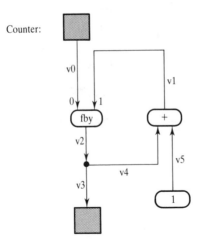

Figure 4-3. The labeling of a simple operator net.

Consequently the set of equations for an entire net can be expressed in the form:

$$V \quad = \quad F(V).$$

where $V = (v0, v1, \ldots, vn)$ and $F = (f0, f1, \ldots, fn)$.

Equations like the above are used to specify the mathematical semantics of the net. This can only be done once the operator symbols are associated (interpreted) over an appropriate algebra (see next section). The semantics or meaning of the net is then specified in a relatively straightforward way using conventional fixpoint theory.[21]

As a consequence of the fixpoint semantics, the "=" symbol in the above equations really does define an equality. This means that we can substitute the use of a name $v5$ for its value 1. If we repeatedly apply this substitution rule, then the above equations reduce to the following single equation:

```
v2=fby(input, +(v2, 1))
```

As an exercise the reader is asked to verify that the operator net in Figure 4-4, which is simply a labeling of the operator net in Figure 4-2, corresponds to the following set of equations:

```
d            =sqroot(avg(square(a)));
square(e)  =*(e,e);
avg(i)     =m
             [     m=fby(i,+(m,r));
                   r=/(-(next(i),m),o);
                   o=fby(2,+(o,1));
             ]
sqroot(aa)=asa(V,<(K,0.1))
             [     A≈aa;
                   V=fby(/(A,2),/(+(V,/(A,V)),2));
                   K=abs(-(square(V),A))
             ]
```

The net-description equations are structured in the same manner as the original operator net. (Note that $A \approx aa$ is not an equation; it simply indicates that the edge labeled by A is the input edge of a subsidiary operator net of the subcomputation node, the one corresponding to incoming edge labeled aa. A precise definition of "≈" is given in Ashcroft's paper on "The syntax and semantics of Lucid".[22]

Algebras

The uninterpreted graphical language of operator nets is given a meaning by associating with the graph different continuous sequence algebras.* The elemen-

---

* Intuitively the data objects in the universe of the algebra will, in our operational interpretations, correspond to the data objects that travel along the arcs connecting the nodes or computing devices. The operators of the algebra will correspond to the computing devices at each node.

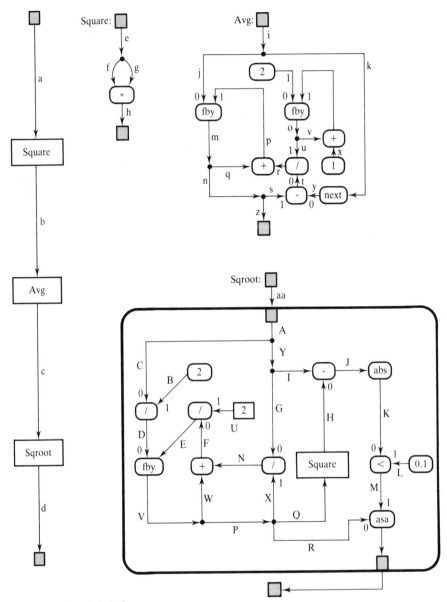

Figure 4-4. A labeled operator net.

tary data objects in the universe of an algebra A will often be such things as integers, reals, and Booleans, but they may be lists, arrays, and character strings. Since A has to be a continuous algebra, the universe must be a cpo (complete partial order) and the operators on the elementary data objects must be continuous. Thus there must be a least element, which we will denote by $\perp$ and sometimes refer to as *bottom*. The operators of A do not need to be strict. A strict operator or function requires all of its arguments to be defined (that is, they cannot be $\perp$) if the result of applying the operator or function is to be defined. A typical nonstrict operator is the ternary operator *if-then-else*.

For simplicity, we will assume for the rest of this chapter that the universe of A is a flat cpo (that is, the only ordering is that *bottom* is less than everything else) and that it contains integers, reals, and Booleans. Also, we will assume that A has the usual arithmetic and logical operators and *if-then-else*.

The infinite sequences algebra $I(A)$ has, as its universe, the set of all infinite sequences of elements of the universe of A and the ordering on it is the pointwise extension of the ordering on A. (The least element is the infinite sequence of $\perp$ elements.) All the operators of A are the pointwise extensions of the corresponding operators in A. (This means, for example, that the nullary operator symbols, like "3" and "true," will denote infinite sequences, in this case, of 3s and trues.) It is easy to see that $I(A)$ is a cpo. Notice that the sequences in the universe of $I(A)$ can be intermittent; that is, they can have $\perp$ elements preceding non $\perp$ elements. Also, all the operators are pointwise; that is, the ith element in the sequence produced depends only on the ith elements of the arguments to which the operator is applied. For pointwise operators or functions, we can define the concept of *pointwise strictness*. A pointwise strict operator or function is one that, for all i, requires all of its arguments to be defined at point i (that is it cannot be the least element of the data algebra A) for the result of applying the operator or function to be defined at point i.

The algebra $E(A)$ is an enlargement of $I(A)$ in which there are several special nonpointwise operators with names like *first, next, followed-by* (or *fby*), *as-soon-as* (or *asa*) and *whenever* (or *wvr*). The unary operator *next*, for example, returns a sequence that is identical to its argument except that the first element of the argument is missing: the ith element of the result is the $(i + 1)$th element of the argument. The binary operator *fby*, for example, adds the first element of its first argument to the front of the sequence that is its second argument: thus, the ith element of the result is the $(i - 1)$th element of the second argument for i not equal to 0, otherwise it is the first element of its first argument.

An example of an algebra that is a specialization of $E(A)$ is the algebra $P(A)$ whose universe is the set of nonintermittent sequences. This algebra is induced by the continuous surjection $\phi_{P(A)}$ that maps an intermittent sequence to a nonintermittent sequence by simply making the elements of the sequence $\perp$ forever as soon as the first $\perp$ is encountered. The algebra $P(A)$ is essentially the same as the algebra whose universe is the set of all finite and infinite sequences of elements of the universe of A, as originally studied by Kahn in 1974.

Using either $E(A)$ or $P(A)$, the operator net in Figure 4-4 computes the running root-mean-square of its input.

ABSTRACT OPERATIONAL MODELS

Although there are many interesting operational interpretations that can be given to operator nets, we will concentrate on the "dataflow" interpretations. There are two basic interpretations that are of interest; the first and the most widespread is data-driven dataflow[23] and the second is demand-driven dataflow or eduction[10] (a less-known form of dataflow). It turns out that both these operational models have strengths and weaknesses and these have been well documented.[15] This section concludes with a description of a hybrid operational model that combines the benefits of demand-driven dataflow with the benefits of data-driven dataflow.[13] The two pure models complement each other, resulting in the removal of the disadvantages of both models but at the same time including the benefits of both.

Data-Driven Computation—Dataflow

We assume that the reader is familiar with the classic data-driven model of dataflow.[1,23] In data-driven dataflow, an operator or user-defined function will fire as soon as there are sufficient datons (units of data or tokens) on the incoming edges of the node.

Demand-Driven Computation—Eduction

In contrast to the data-driven model, in the demand-driven method, an operation associated with an operator of a node will be executed only if there is a demand for the result of the operation and if, as before, there are sufficient datons on the incoming edges. If there is a demand but there are not sufficient datons on the incoming edges, then demands for appropriately tagged datons are made, so as to remedy the insufficiency. These demands are made to the nodes at the source of each edge for which there is a missing daton. When, as a result of such demands, there is a daton on each necessary incoming edge, the operator fires. This firing could produce a daton to satisfy an earlier demand from the edge's destination. Eventually, when no more demands need to be sent, data will begin to flow back through the net to produce the desired output. The result is sent out along the node's outgoing edge.

The demands can be visualized as traveling through the dataflow net in the reverse direction to that of the data. We call these demands *questons* (from the word "request").

Although the careful propagation of questons can avoid unnecessary computation, queston propagation does not come without cost.

Operator Attributes

Operators or node functions can be classified in a variety of ways. These classifications can be extremely useful in providing different types of operations that can be used to test the strength or weakness of different operational interpretations.

We note that the standard approach to dataflow computation is to take a select set of primitive dataflow operations such as select, distribute, merge, ... together with the usual arithmetic and logical operations. These primitives then become the machine language of a dataflow architecture. Programming languages such as Lisp or single assignment languages such as VAL or ID[23] are then compiled into this dataflow assembly language. This totally removes the user from the underlying architecture, which is good—unfortunately it also removes them from the dataflow model of computation. They do not program in a dataflow language but use a "clean" von Neumann language that is translated by a compiler to run on a dataflow engine. This is not the case in our approach and we will see later that the Lucid programmer actually thinks in terms of the dataflow model when solving problems.

An operator is said to be *pointwise* if the production of the ith output is solely dependent on the ith inputs. A node is said to be *strict* if the ith output requires all the ith inputs to be present before it can fire. The definitions of *nonpointwise* and *nonstrict* are merely the complements of the above. Figure 4-5 names examples of each of these types of operator. The "plus" node is pointwise in that it requires a daton on each of its inputs in order to produce the next output. Thus, the ith output is indeed determined by the ith inputs. The *if-then-else-fi* node requires three arguments in order to fire. It always needs the first argument, which is always a predicate. The next argument required will depend on the value of the predicate. If it is true then the second argument is needed and the last argument is ignored. Conversely, if the predicate is false then the third (or last) argument is required and the second is ignored. Thus, in a data-driven mode, one of the branches will have been computed only to be thrown away. Note that this node cannot be implemented in a strict manner, because to do so would mean that a value would have to arrive on all inputs and it is often the case that *if-then-else-fi* is being used to avoid a nonterminating or undefined computation associated with the branch that was not needed. Note that there are dataflow architectures that permit only strict dataflow nodes.

The operator labeled Avg is an example of a nonpointwise strict function. This node computes the running average of its inputs. Thus it always requires its

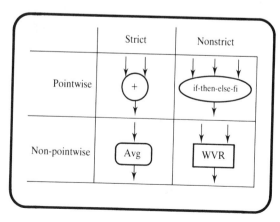

Figure 4-5. Different types of operators.

input (i.e., it is strict) and yet the output depends on more than just the current value of the input (it is dependent on the entire history of the input). The node labeled WVR (pronounced "whenever") is an example of a nonpointwise, nonstrict node. It passes on the ith value of its left argument but only if the ith value of its right argument is true. Thus, even if some of the values associated with the false arguments are undefined, it can still compute. Moreover, the ith output is almost never associated with the ith input.

Another classification is to divide the operators into two disjoint classes either predictably heedless or unpredictably heedless. An operator is *predictably heedless* if the datons it requires to compute are syntactically determinable. An *unpredictably heedless* operator is one whose input can only be determined at runtime (i.e., semantically). The reader is asked to explain the relationship between our two classifications. How do they relate? Are nonstrict operators the same as unpredictably heedless or can nonpointwise strict nodes be unpredictably heedless?

These various classifications permit us to look at different interpretations to see what type of operators can be handled. For example, nets that are made up only of predictably heedless operators are best suited to data-driven computation. In contrast, if an operator net contains unpredictably heedless nodes, it is better evaluated in a demand-driven manner.

Tagged Versus Piped Dataflow

There are two different ways in which an operator net is usually interpreted operationally. One is to consider the edges in the operator net to be piped along which datons flow, in a FIFO manner. In other words, the edges are considered to be queues acting as buffers between the nodes. (Often these queues are required to have a bounded length.[24]) We call this the *piped* method of evaluation.

The other is to interpret the edges in operator nets as simple routes that datons must take when flowing from one operator to the next. The buffers between the operators are not queues, they are multisets. These are generally considered to be unbounded. Some discipline must be imposed on the order in which a node takes datons from the incoming edges; this is achieved by associating the datons with appropriate tags. This method of interpreting operator nets is called the *tagged* method of evaluation.

It turns out that piped evaluation is unable to correctly implement operators that are pointwise nonstrict like the *if-then-else* above. The reason for this is that piped demand-driven or data-driven computation cannot skip over a value in a pipe; it must be evaluated. As we stated previously, it is often the case that the *if-then-else* has been used to avoid a non-terminating computation. Thus before piped evaluation can proceed it must evaluate an unending computation. Only then can it get the next daton in the queue or pipe. Arvind and Gostelow[25] formally proved that the operational model corresponding to tagged evaluation is stronger than that corresponding to piped evaluation. This simply means that the tagged method can produce more results than the piped method. For the rest of the chapter we will generally assume that we are only considering tagged evaluation.

Disadvantages of the Data-driven Approach

Dataflow (data-driven computation) exploits parallelism in a natural way, and gets completely away from such von Neumann machine concepts as flow control, memory, addresses, and imperative programming in general. These are the positive steps; but data-driven dataflow itself has some problems. The following summarizes some of them.

- A major problem with dataflow networks is that the operators in nodes must be strict. This makes it difficult to translate some languages into dataflow networks.
- Even with languages that do not need nonstrict operators other than *if-then-else-fi,* dataflow networks are not easy to write programs for. That is, it is difficult to translate programs automatically into dataflow networks, even programs in languages that are designed for exactly that. This is partly because it is not simple for an automatic translator to discover appropriate triggers for constants. Also, it can be difficult for an automatic translator to express complicated interrelationships between conditional expressions, for example, in terms of select and distribute nodes, the nodes that are available for expressing the desired conditional-evaluation behavior.
- It is a drawback to dataflow networks that not all networks constructed from the different types of nodes are meaningful or represent an expressible computation. The different types of nodes must be put together in certain ways in order to make sense. For example, one combination of select and distribute nodes will give the effect of *if-then-else-fi,* and another will give the effect of looping, but others may make no sense at all.
- Another problem with dataflow networks is that it is difficult to handle data structures. Consider a program that uses a one-dimensional array A. If there are places in the program where elements of the array are referred to, say by expressions A[I] and A[J], the normal dataflow behavior would send copies of A (all of it) to the parts of the network corresponding to these expressions. This is clearly inappropriate. What is really needed is that the values of I and J be used to produce demands for particular elements of A, and that no copies of A be made. The array A must be stored somewhere and referred to, which goes against the normal idea of dataflow. We have seen that, in dataflow, user-defined functions must be strict; the parameter-passing mechanism must be call-by-value. There are definite reasons why, in some languages, the parameter-passing mechanism must be call-by-need. These languages cannot easily be implemented using dataflow, and this is another reason why dataflow can be inadequate.

Disadvantages of the Demand-driven Approach

Although the demand-driven approach computes only what is absolutely necessary to produce all the required output, it suffers from the following disadvantages.

- There is additional overhead required to propagate demands through the net.
- Copy or duplicate nodes cause a memory management problem. The reason for this is that, when a demand travelling in the reverse direction to the data enters a copy node, there is no way for it to know whether the other branches leading out of the copy node (in the data flow direction) also require that value or even whether they have already demanded that value. When the value associated with the original demand arrives at the copy node it is only sent along those arcs that have requested it. Otherwise the node would compute something that was not necessary to compute because the daton flowing down an arc will trigger further computations. Thus, a record must be kept of who has requested a value. Each copy node needs to have memory associated with it, which in turn needs to be managed (they are not self-cleaning, as they are in the data-driven case).

Despite these disadvantages tagged demand-drive dataflow is the strongest of the interpretations.

Eazyflow—A Hybrid Model of Computation

It is in fact possible to combine the pure data-driven model with the pure demand-driven model in order to reap their benefits while largely avoiding their drawbacks.[13] The eazyflow model is such a hybrid. The term *eazyflow* is derived from two words: *ea*gerflow, referring to eager-evaluation or data-driven computation, and the term la*zyflow*, referring to lazy-evaluation or demand-driven computation.

The basic idea is that we want to avoid unnecessary computations whenever possible, but if we know we have no choice then we might as well do that part eagerly. To achieve this, the operator net needs to be partitioned into lazy and eager subnets. This is accomplished by partitioning the connectors into two disjoint sets by coloring the arc either green or red. Initially, all arcs in the net are colored green. An edge is colored red if at least one of the following conditions holds.

- The source node is unpredictable. (Eager-evaluation of such an operator would result in wasteful computation.)
- The destination operator is partial. (Eager-evaluation of a partial operator could result in nonterminating computation.)
- At least one of the incoming edges of the source operator is red. (Unless the incoming edges are green, the operator cannot be eager-evaluated.)

Thus, the set of red edges of an operator net is the smallest set of edges having the above properties. Data-driven and demand-driven models interact where green edges lead into operators with red outgoing edges. In this model, demand-driven computation has priority, triggering data-driven computation in certain cases, for a certain time, or for a certain number of datons. Consequently, datons produced in a data-driven manner are controlled.

Demands propagate in the reverse direction along red edges. Demand for a daton causes the operator producing the daton to be applied to appropriate datons from the incoming edges. This can be done immediately if the required datons are already available. Otherwise, if a daton is expected on a red incoming edge, a further demand is made for it by propagating a demand. If a daton is expected on a green incoming edge, no demand is made for it, since the daton should be produced using eager-evaluation. Instead, a trigger is sent that initiates a bounded amount of data-driven computation of precursor datons. These will eventually cause the desired daton to arrive on the green incoming edge. That is, by permitting data-driven computation to produce a certain number of datons on certain green edges, the desired daton is eventually produced automatically. For each edge e, the desired daton is eventually produced automatically. This is because there is a set of green edges such that, if values are produced on those edges, the datons will automatically be produced on edge e when eager-evaluating.

If a data-driven computation proceeds with no heed as to whether the datons it generates are needed or not, then an unbounded build-up of datons could result on green edges leading into nodes with red edges. Hence, data-driven computation has to be controlled sufficiently so that unbounded build-up does not occur. At the same time, data-driven computation should be allowed to produce a bounded number of extra datons in anticipation of their use. In the eazyflow model, the demand-driven model has priority, triggering data-driven computation only when possible, and when useful. This way, it can be guaranteed that the amount of extra datons is always bounded.

A PROGRAMMING LANGUAGE FOR OPERATOR NETS

If we are abandoning dataflow networks, we should be sure that the replacement—operator nets—is usable as dataflow networks for the specification of algorithms. We want to know that operator nets can be programmed relatively easily. Nets are two-dimensional objects, at best, and it is difficult to display them on terminals, write them into files, and so on. What is needed is some textural representation, a language, that can express useful computations.

As it happens, there is a programming language that corresponds exactly to operator nets. This language is called Lucid. Lucid programs can be thought of as linearized forms of operator nets (and, conversely, operator nets as graphical forms of Lucid programs). The translation from one to the other is trivial (in marked contrast with the difficult translation of other programming languages, or even Lucid, into dataflow networks). Lucid is actually a family of languages; a particular member of this family is determined by the data-objects that programs use and the basic data-operations over these objects. In operator-net terms, this corresponds to choosing which datons are going to pass along the arcs of the operator nets and which operators are available for association with nodes.

Lucid is a family of *declarative* programming languages. The term declarative programming language is usually applied to a language that is based on a formal system such as the lambda calculus or the predicate calculus. Existing declarative languages can be broken down into two further subdivisions: those languages that are *purely declarative* and those that have been extended to include *extralogical features*. Included in the former are SASL[26] and Lucid[17,27] and in the latter are Lisp and Prolog. Languages like SASL and Lucid are completely free of side-effects, which makes them more suited to parallel execution. The following sections are devoted mainly to programming in Lucid. Those interested in a more rigorous treatment of the semantics of the language should refer to ref. 27.

Data Algebras and Simple Expressions

Lucid is a family of programming languages in which each member of the language is determined by a data algebra. A data algebra consists of a universe and a set of operations over subsets of the universe. Thus the data algebra determines the types of objects that can be manipulated in the language. An example of a simple algebra would be one with a universe of numbers (including rationals) and the usual operations over these numbers. In terms of operator nets this means that the objects flowing along arcs would be numbers and that operators themselves would have interpretations such as addition, multiplication, and so on.

A more significant algebra would be one based on the data types and operations provided by the language POP-2.[28] The universe of this algebra consists of numbers, strings, atoms, lists, and two special objects: error and eod (end of data). The operations would be head, tail and cons for lists, substring and string append for strings, and so on. This member of the Lucid family is called pLucid. The following three expressions are pLucid programs:

```
x+8
`abc' ^substring(1,2, `efg')
hd tl [1 2 3]
```

The Form and Structure of Programs

Programs for all members of the Lucid family take on the same syntactic form. This form is derived from P. J. Landin's language called ISWIM.[29] A program is an expression in which operators and operands appear. The operators are those associated with the algebra defining a particular member of the family and a set of core Lucid operators (explained below). The operands are either constants, again from the underlying algebra, or variables defined in the program. Following Landin's notation an expression is defined in terms of a *where-clause*. The where-clause has a *head* and a *body*. The head of the where-clause is an expression involving operators and operands that could conceivably contain other where-clauses. The body consists of a set* of *definitions* that define the variables used in the head or in other definitions of the same body. Thus, the scope of a variable is the head and body of the where-clause in which it is defined. A definition is a simple equation in which a variable is defined to be equal to an expression. The variable may be a simple name (a *nullary variable*) or it may be a parameterized name (a *nonnullary variable,* often referred to as a function). The expression part of a definition contains operands and operators and, conceivably, additional where-clauses. Variables that appear in either the body or the head of a clause and have no defining equation are assumed to be inputs from the external environment (usually the user keyboard or a file).

The following are some examples of simple Lucid programs, which are included to familiarize the reader with the syntax of the language. It should be immediately obvious, without explaining the semantics of the language, what the value of each of the following expressions or programs is.

```
x+y   where                // Program 1
        x=1;
        y=27 div 8;
      end;


f(z)  where
          f(x)=x+1;        // Program 2
          z   =a+b;
          a   =7;
          b   =9;
      end;


f(x)*g(v)-1/y
        where              // Program 3
          f(x)=x*x/PI
                  where  PI=3;  end;
          g(x)=x*4;
      end;
```

Expressions of this form correspond to modules that have one output (the head of the clause) and multiple inputs (the undefined or free variables of the

---

* The order of the equations is not relevant because they are simply specifications of data dependencies. There is no syntactically implied order of execution.

clause). For applications requiring modules with multiple outputs and multiple inputs, the definition of a program can be extended from being a simple expression into being a set of equations. In this scheme, a subset of the defined variables would have to be distinguished as the output variables associated with named output ports.

Nonstrict Conditional Expressions

Most members of the Lucid family permit conditional computation by including the conditional expression* *if-then-else-fi*. This operator is nonstrict, since it can compute on the basis of only a subset of its arguments. If the predicate part of the conditional expression is true, then the result of the expression will be the value of the true branch regardless of the value of the false branch (even if it is ⊥). A similar interpretation is given if the predicate part is false, except that this time the false branch is taken. After having read the next section on sequence algebras, the reader should take the time to understand why the following program produces as output ⟨1, 4, 5, 8, 9, 12, 13, . . .⟩ and *not* ⟨1, 2, 3, 4, 5, 6, 7, 8, . . .⟩

```
output where
        output    =if alternate then odd else even fi;
        odd       =1 fby odd+2;
        even      = odd+1;
        alternate =true fby not alternate;
    end;
```

Simple Iteration and Sequence Algebras

The reader who took the time to evaluate the above programs will have concluded that Program 1 produced 4 and that Program 2 produced 17. Although these answers are correct there is an extended interpretation to the above programs that is related to their correspondence to operator nets. In our interpretation of operator nets we assumed that the operators were continuously operating and consequently the value of a variable or a constant is the entire sequence or stream of activity associated with its corresponding edge in the operator net. In this light the above programs do not simply produce a simple constant (4 or 17) as output, but rather a stream or sequence of such constants. The programmer is encouraged to think of these streams temporally or iteratively. In Program 1 the value produced at the first point in time (on the first iteration) is 4, at the second point in time (or the second iteration) the value is 4, and so on. To enable the specification of programs that produce outputs that are

---

* We assume that these members of the Lucid family include a simple Boolean algebra whose data objects are *true* and *false* and whose operators are *and, or, not*.

not endless constants but change with time, we introduce the temporal Lucid operators.

Temporal Operators

Lucid can often be viewed as a language that deals with objects that change in a temporal sense, even though it is a functional language in the purest sense. The (unchanging) values of variables in Lucid are actually infinite sequences, but the variables should be thought of as objects that change with time. For example, the Lucid definition*

$$x=1.05 \text{ fby } x+0.05;$$

defines the value of x to be the sequence $\langle 1.05, 1.1, 1.15, \ldots \rangle$, but it is natural and useful to think of the value of x as an object, which is initially 1.05 and subsequently changes to $1.1, 1.15, \ldots$. This simple idea has many consequences. It means that the language enjoys all the advantages of a functional language, such as referential transparency, provability, and so on, while retaining an operational iterative flavor. The following definition of the operator fby may help explain why the above program behaves as stated:

$$(A \text{ fby } B)_t = \begin{cases} A_t & \text{if } t = 0 \\ B_{t-1} & \text{if } t > 0 \end{cases}$$

where t belongs to $\{0, 1, 2, 3, \ldots\}$, the set of natural numbers, and A and B are arbitrary expressions in the language. Consequently, x in the above program is 1.05 at time $t = 0$ and at time $t > 0$, x is defined to be the value x at the previous point in time $(t - 1)$ plus 0.5. Thus at time $t = 2$, x is $1.05 + 0.05 = 1.1$, and so on.

It is not always the case that we want to produce a time-varying stream based solely on the value at the previous point in time. We may want to compute using a future point in time. Consequently there is a unary operator that enables access to the value of a variable at the next time point. This operator is called next and is used to define the Fibonacci numbers in increasing order:

fibonacci=1 fby 1 fby fibonacci+next fibonacci;

Readers should take time to verify that this is correct. They may find the following definition of next useful when doing so. Note that A is an arbitrary expression in the language.

Let t belong to $\{0, 1, 2, 3, \ldots\}$ the set of natural numbers then

$$(\text{next } A)_t = A_{t+1}.$$

To further help the reader we note that the usual precedence of operators defined for Lucid[30] means that the equation defining fibonacci is parsed as:

fibonacci=(1 fby(1 fby (fibonacci+(next fibonacci))))

---

* The operator fby is to be read as *followed by*.

We include the parentheses here purely as an aid to understanding. The original equation would run correctly on current Lucid implementations.*

Nested Iteration

Nested iteration is analogous to nested for-loops in an imperative programming language. The operator net in Figure 4-4 contains a nested iteration. In operator net terms, nested iteration corresponds to subcomputation nodes. The Lucid program corresponding to the net in Figure 4-4 is as follows:

```
sqroot (avg(square(a)))
    where
        square(e)=e*e;
        avg(i)=m    where
                        m=i fby m+r;
                        r=(next i-m)/o;
                        o=2 fby o+1;
                    end;
        sqroot(aa)=v asa K<0.1
                    where
                        A is current aa;
                        V=A/2 fby (V+A/V)/2;
                        K=abs(square(V)-A);
                    end;
    end;
```

The similarity to the simplified equation for the net in Figure 4-4 should be apparent. To compute a value for `sqroot(X)` at time i requires an entire Lucid subcomputation to take place inside of `sqroot`. This means that the variables A, V and K go through an entire simple iteration process in order to produce a result for the outer variable at a single point in time. See ref. 30 for more details on nested iteration and the `is current` declaration.

User-defined Functions

User-defined functions in Lucid are functions from infinite sequences to infinite sequences, which, in operational terms, means that they are filters that produce outputs as inputs are fed in. The simplest user-defined functions are similar to those used in Program 2 and Program 3 in functions such as:

```
f(x)=x+1;
```

---

* A Lucid (pLucid) interpreter written in C running under either System V or Berkeley 4.2BSD is available from A. Faustini, Department of Computer Science, Arizona State University, Tempe, AZ 85287.

These simple functions are called *pointwise functions* because their output at time *t* depends simply on their inputs at time *t*. The inputs in this case are the actual parameters of the functions. The function f also is *strict*. Each output requires all the inputs to be present (in this case simply x). The following is an example of a pointwise function that is *nonstrict*:

```
ns(x)=if alt then x+1 else 2 fi
             where
                  alt=true fby false fby alt;
          end;
```

The reason that it is nonstrict is that x at time *t* is not always needed to produce ns(x) at time *t*. Why is the following function pointwise strict or nonstrict?

```
ps(x)=if alt then x+1 else x+2 fi
             where
                  alt=true fby false fby alt;
          end;
```

Nonpointwise Functions

User-defined functions need not act "pointwise"—the output can depend on all or some of the previous inputs. For example, we can write a function that produces a running average of its inputs, as follows

```
Avg(x)=s/next index
        where
             s          =first(x) fby s+next x;
             index      =0 fby index+1;
             first(x)   =x fby first (x);
          end;
```

Note that `index` and `first` are so commonly used that they are usually built into an implementation hence the user need not define them as we have done. More precisely, there is an index variable associated with each clause and `first` is a prefix operator like `next`; thus, it need not have parentheses associated with it. Taking all of this into account, the above program can be rewritten as

```
Avg(x)=s/next index where s=first x fby s+next x; end;
```

From this point on we will no longer define `first` or `index`, we will simply use them. Operationally, the filter `Avg` keeps around a local variable s (for each invocation of `Avg`, that is, for each distinct lexical occurrence of `Avg(e)` in the program) that "remembers" the running sum (of e). It also means that all Lucid programs are essentially continually operating programs or coroutines, which are given infinite sequences of inputs and produce infinite sequences of outputs.

Recursive nonpointwise functions

There are a number of very useful filters that can be defined in Lucid itself with the following recursive definitions. The following are so useful that they are usually included as primitive binary operators having an infix notation. These are wvr (pronounded whenever), upon, and asa (pronounced as soon as). The first argument (or the left argument) is the data argument and the second is a predicate or control argument. The recursive definitions for these filters are

```
wvr(x,p)=if first x then x fby z else z fi
              where
                  z=wvr(next x, next p);
              end;
```

This filter outputs the members of the stream x for which there is a corresponding true predicate. Thus if p were never true this node would never produce an output. If p is an alternating stream of trues and falses then the output is every other member of x. Note, in general, that we cannot tell by analyzing a program in which wvr is used whether this operator will ever produce any output or if it does how far along x it will need to go before producing an output. Because of this uncertainty characteristic, we call nodes like the wvr node (or function), *unpredictable.*

```
upon (x,p)=x fby if first p then upon (next x, next p)
                          else upon (x, next p) fi;
```

The upon filter acts very much like a valve and an internal buffer. The first value of flow into the node (x at time 0) is stored in the internal buffer and is also output. Thereafter, output is determined by the predicate p. If p is false, the value in the internal buffer is output again and the x input is held by a valve. If p is true then the valve opens and the next x input is stored in the internal buffer (overwriting the previous contents) and is also output. It should be obvious from this description that this node is nonpointwise. Thus, if p is always true then the node acts as an identity filter for x. Otherwise x is stretched out in some manner, which in the worst case would be an endless stream of the first value of x.

It is possible to think of upon as the functional description of a single element in a RAM where the x is a data path and the p the read/write path. The reader should return to this potential use of upon after having read the section on spatial Lucid and ask the question "Why does the definition of upon given here as the description of a single element in a RAM also work for arbitrary size RAMs?"

```
asa(x,p)=first wvr(x,p);
```

The asa node is simply the first value produced by a whenever repeated forever. The asa node is useful in subcomputation evaluation when a stream of values associated with a subcomputation node needs to be collapsed to provide a value for a single point in time for a variable immediately outside the subcomputation (see the program corresponding to the operator net in Figure 4-4).

Finite and Infinite Sequences

Although an equation in Lucid corresponds to an unending stream of datons (infinite) it is possible in practice to have definitions that define what appears to be a finite stream of datons. To achieve this, we augment the universe of an algebra with the special object "eod" (the end of data object). If the term `eod` appears in a program, it defines an infinite sequence consisting of the special object "eod." In practice, when an implementation of Lucid attempts to output the "eod" object the program is forced to terminate output on that stream. In the case of modules with one output this means that the module terminates. The program

```
x where x=1 fby 2 fby eod; end;
```

outputs 1 followed by 2, then it terminates. The effect on input variables is also the same; if an "eod" object is input, then the corresponding input stream is closed. If input is from a file, an "eod" object will be generated when the end of file marker is encountered. If input is from a user, an "eod" is generated when a special control sequence is typed, usually "control-D" in a UNIX environment. This completes the description of the object "eod" as it applies to a module's input or output.

Internally the "eod" object combines with other objects in the algebra's universe in a manner defined by the operators. Since "eod" is a means of making an infinite stream appear finite, we are in a sense forcing finiteness into the computation. Given this assumption, we extend the definitions of the operators to include the "eod" object. In general, when "eod" is an argument to an operator, the result is almost always "eod." Thus 1 + "eod" is "eod," true *and* "eod" is "eod," and so on. Two operators that do not propagate "eod" are a unary predicate for testing for "eod" called `iseod` and the `if-then-else-fi` expresion. The latter only propagates "eod" when it appears as the predicate or as the result of the selected branch. Thus

```
if eod    then 4 else 6    fi is equivalent to eod
if true   then 4 else eod fi is equivalent to 4
if false then 4 else eod fi is equivalent to eod
```

A precise description of how `eod` combines with other objects in an algebra is described in ref. 30. Note that as far as the mathematical semantics are concerned all streams are infinite.

Spatial Lucid Operators

A natural extension to Lucid is to allow values to vary in space as well as in time. By adding such values to Lucid, the language becomes much more expressive and, in particular, can express a massive amount of implicit parallelism. In the mathematical semantics of Lucid, the values of variables are infinite sequences of data items. Nevertheless, the developers of the language strongly recommended that Lucid not be thought of as a language for manipulating infinite sequences. Rather, the variables should be thought of as having values that change with time. This gives the language an operational, iterative flavor, and it is felt that it is much easier to program in this way. There are programs, however, for which it is appropriate to think in terms of infinite sequences and it is these that are expressible in space extended Lucid. The idea is to change the semantics of Lucid by having the values of variables be (time) sequences of elements that themselves vary in space. New operators are added that work in space in the same way that the Lucid operators work in time. (These operators work pointwise in time.) The following are the definitions of the space analogs of fby, first and next. Note that with space we have arbitrary numbers of space dimensions (the k subscript) and associated with each dimension are the cby k (pronounced "continued by" in dimension k), initial k and rest k operators. Let t and s belong to $\{0, 1, 2, 3, \ldots\}$, the set of natural numbers, and A and B be arbitrary expressions in the language:

$$(A \text{ cby } k \, B)_t^{s0, s1, \cdots} = \begin{cases} A_t^{s0, s1, \ldots, s^{(k-1)}, s^{(k+1)}, \ldots} & \text{if } s_k = 0 \\ B_t^{s0, s1, \ldots, s^{(k-1)}, s^k-1, s^{(k+1)}, \ldots} & \text{otherwise} \end{cases}$$

$$(\text{rest } k \, A)_t^{s0, s1, s2, \cdots} = A_t^{s0, s1, \ldots, s^{(k-1)}, s^k+1, s^{(k+1)}, \ldots}$$

$$(\text{initial } k \, A)_t^{s0, s1, s2, \cdots} = A_t^{s0, s1, \ldots, s^{(k-1)}, 0, s^k, s^{(k+1)}, \ldots}$$

All operations that were pointwise extensions of data operations are now pointwise extensions in space as well as in time, and the Lucid operators (which are not pointwise in time) are pointwise in space. There are also operations that convert from time to space, and from space to time. The resulting language is called Flucid. For a more complete discussion see refs. 27, 31, 32. A particularly nice property of Flucid is that basic operations and user-defined functions are serendipitous. This term comes from an early paper by Ashcroft,[33] which introduced the term "the serendipity principle," in connection with APL. In APL, a function that is written to work on scalars, say, often also works when applied to vectors or arrays of higher rank, forming higher-rank objects from the results of applying the function to the individual elements of the arguments. This extension to higher ranks seems, in the APL case, to be "a good thing that happens by chance" (i.e., the function appears to have serendipity), but, in fact, there are logical reasons why it works in some cases but not in others. In Flucid, this extension works in all cases. We will see examples of this when we look at particular applications. (For historical reasons we will still use the terms "serendipitous" and "the serendipity principle" even though no chance is involved.) There are many examples of Flucid programs that use Flucid's "serendipity principle" to good effect and that allow implementations to use massive parallelism. These are often found in scientific calculations. The following example is one of these. It is the outline of a program to solve Laplace's equation in a two-dimensional space of size N by M, using the usual relaxation method where the next value at each point in space is the average of its four neighbors.

```
s asa settled
    where
        s        =ORIG fby cond
                            OUTSIDE   : 0:
                            ELECTRODE : POTENTIAL;
                            default   : f(s);
                        end;
        f(A)     =(up A+down A+left A+right A)/4;
        ORIG     =if ELECTRODE then POTENTIAL else 0 fi;
        OUTSIDE=sindex0>=N or sindex0<=0 or
                sindex1>=M or sindex1<=0;
    end
```

Note that sindex$i$=0 cby$i$ sindex$i$+1, like index, is usually a built-in feature of the language. In addition to operators like next and rest$k$ that enable the programmer to access the next time or space point, there are also special operators that enable the programmer to access the previous time or space point. The reader should be able to construct their definitions from the above definitions of next and rest$k$. What happens when we apply a "previous" operator at the origin of time or space? We go into negative time or negative space. To facilitate this we extend the time and space indices to permit negative indices. In the above program, operators like up and right are really rest0 and rest1, respectively. The down and left operators are the "previous" space point operators for space dimension 0 and 1, respectively.

The best way of understanding the above program is to think of each value of s as being a two-dimensional plane of potentials, with nonnegative coordinates. Initially, s is everywhere zero, except at electrodes. At each step in the subsequent computation the potentials of the electrodes stay the same, as does the part of the plane outside the N by M region we are considering. Each of the other points changes to the average of the potentials of the four surrounding points, except for the points along the edges of the plane (i.e., with one of the coordinates being zero) that stay at zero potential. The program is only an outline because the constant arrays ELECTRODE and POTENTIAL, the initial conditions, and the termination condition, settled, are not specified.

The following extended example of the Laplace program for three dimensions is a good example of how easy it is to extend programs to higher dimensions:

```
s asa settled
   where
      s        =ORIG fby cond
                       OUTSIDE   : 0;
                       ELECTRODE : POTENTIAL;
                       default   : f(s);
                       end;
      f(A)     =(up A+down A+left A+right A
                +front A+rear A)/6;
      ORIG     =if ELECTRODE then POTENTIAL else 0 fi;
      OUTSIDE          =sindex0 > = N or sindex0 < = 0
                       or sindex1 > = M or sindex1 < = 0
                       or 0 > = sindex2 or sindex2 < = 0;
   end
```

As a final example, we present two versions of the sieve of Eratosthenes, one written with time and function calling and the other written in time and space. In the first program, a new recursive call is made of sieve each time a new prime is to be output. Thus, the number of primes output is directly proportional to the depth of the function calling. Each call of sieve can be thought of as spawning a new coroutine. The first call is a coroutine that removes multiples of the first element of nats (i.e., 2) from the stream nats. The 2 is output as a prime and nats stream with multiples of 2 removed is sent to a new call of sieve which does exactly the same as the first in that it removes all multiples of the first element 3 of the new input stream and so on. The reader should spend some time to try to understand what is going on in this program, as it is very instructive. Note that the activations of sieve never die off; they simply provide additional filtered numbers to deeper calls.

```
sieve (nats)
   where
      nats     =2 fby nats+1;
      sieve(n)=n fby sieve (n wvr n mod first n ne 0);
   end;
```

The following is the time/space version of the same program. The primes in this program also appear in time; that is, the ith prime is the time i (space 0) output of the program. An infinite vector of natural numbers beginning with $2, 3, 4, 5, \ldots$ is the starting point for an iterative process that removes all multiples of the first entry in the vector to produce the next vector in time:

```
initial sieve
        where
           sieve=nats fby sieve whvr sieve mod
                initial sieve ne 0;
           nats =2 cby nats+1;
        end;
```

Note that whvr is the space analog of wvr; in fact, the definition of whvr is the same as wvr except that fby and next are replaced with cby0 and rest0. We usually drop the subscripting when we are dealing with the first space dimension.

As a final challenge, we ask the reader to explain why the following program produces as output a "running histogram" (in the first space dimension) of the distribution of natural numbers occurring in the time sequence data, which is only partially defined in the program below. Any sequence of integers could be used and so we could substitute the right-hand side of the definition of data used below with index mod 256. In practice, it would be an input to the module and so no definition would be required:

```
next histogram
        where
             histogram=index upon data eq sindex;
             data       =2 fby 5 fby 67 fby 999 fby ....;
        end;
```

Lucid is a high-level language with several interesting characteristics. There are no concepts of "flow of control" and sequencing, and computations are naturally "distributed," since there is nothing to stop computations from proceeding in different places at the same time. With the emphasis on iteration rather than recursion, the language can be programmed in very conventional ways; yet it can also be programmed in ways that take advantage of some of its more unusual features, such as coroutines. Semantically, the language is based on the idea of infinite sequences, and continuous, unending operation. It is not surprising that it turns out to be the linearized form of operator nets.

EQUIVALENT SEMANTICS

The equivalence between the operational and the mathematical semantics of operator nets is significant. The reason for this is that the "static" and relatively simple mathematical semantics can be brought to bear on the complex operational interpretations. An excellent example of this in practice is the cycle-sum test for dataflow deadlock. When developing complex operator nets (or Lucid programs) it is possible to define networks with extremely complex feedback behavior. If great care is not taken, the program (or operator net) could easily deadlock* because variables associated with feedback loops could be defined in such a way that they are dependent either directly or indirectly on their current or future value. We illustrate this test with a number of simple examples and refer the interested reader to Wadge.[34] Following Wadge we assign integers to the input arcs of the primitive operators of a Lucid program as seen in Figure 4-6.

---

* Deadlock can also occur in a concrete architecture owing to lack of resources. This is not what we are discussing at this point. Here we are interested in the program or operator net as a specification and the test is aimed at ensuring that there is no deadlock in the specification.

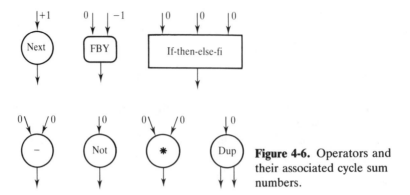

Figure 4-6. Operators and their associated cycle sum numbers.

Note that the pointwise data operations like −, ∗ and `if-then-else-fi` have a 0 associated with their input arcs because they are pointwise. On the other hand, the Temporal Lucid operator `next` has +1 associated with its input arc because the output is 1 ahead of the input. In other words, the output at time t is the input at time $t + 1$. In a similar manner, the `fby` node has associated with it a 0 for the first argument and −1 with the second argument, which is delayed by one.

A deadlock can occur in a program specification if the program contains at least 1 feedback loop. Examples of nets with feedback loops, some of which cause deadlock, are shown in Figure 4-7. Assuming that a module is never starved of its inputs, the cycle sum test can be stated as follows:

> For all loops in the net (program), sum the numbers assigned to each arc making up the loop. If all loops independently have loop sums that are negative, then the net is guaranteed not to deadlock. If this is not the case, then nothing can be said about deadlock.

The equivalence between the operational and the mathematical semantics means that the cycle sum test can be validated by using the mathematical rather than the operational semantics. In fact, Wadge[34] has already used this approach.

AN EAZYFLOW ARCHITECTURE

In this section we will describe a multiprocessor architecture called an *eazyflow engine*. We do not intend this section to be a detailed account of the architecture, rather a relatively complete description of an interpreter for Lucid (or operator nets) expressed as a multiprocessor architecture. The reader interested in the fine details of the architecture (actual size of the tags, etc.) should consult Lee[35] and DeForest.[36] The latter reference is a companion to an eazyflow simulator that is written in portable C.*

---

* A copy of the Eazyflow simulator (including source code and user manuals) is available from Tony Faustini, Department of Computer Science, Arizona State University.

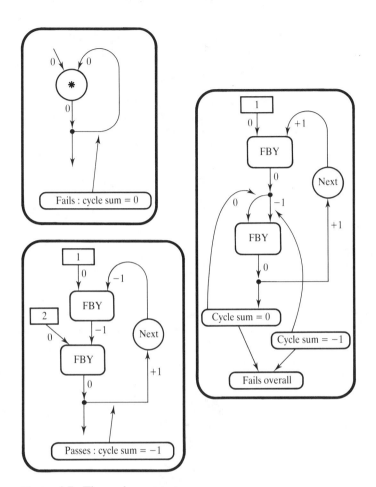

Figure 4-7. The cycle sum test.

The eazyflow engine is programmed directly using textural representations of operator nets (by which, of course, we mean Lucid programs). When given an operator net (i.e., a Lucid program), the eazyflow engine acts like the network, in the sense that the appropriate operations are performed on the appropriate data, with appropriate degrees of parallelism.

The basic idea in eazyflow is that the edges of a net can be distinguished so that those parts of the net that can be executed in a data-driven manner are separated from those parts that must be demand-driven.[13] When this is expressed in terms of Lucid programs, it corresponds to a partitioning of the Lucid variables into two sets. Certain variables in the Lucid program, the eager variables, can be eager-evaluated (that is, they can be computed in a data-driven manner) and the rest, the lazy variables, must be lazy-evaluated (that is, they must be computed in a demand-driven manner). This partitioning is *done automatically* on the basis of the definitions of the variables; *it is not decided by the programmer.* The data-driven computation is controled by demands for other variables that must be lazy-evaluated. When a demand is made for a lazy variable that needs eager variables, demands will be produced for some or all of the eager variables. This is the only way in which eager variables are demanded. When an eager variable X is demanded at time i, and that time is *close* to the limit of the values of X that have been, or will be, produced, the limit for X is increased by a fixed number N, and eager-evaluation is triggered for the most basic variables on which the eager variable depends. (These variables are necessarily eager.) Only N values of these variables will be produced. (To get more produced, there must be another demand for X, for a time that is *close* to the new limit for X.) The values of N and *close* are parameters of the system, and good values for them will be found by experiment.

Mapping a Program Onto the Architecture

An eazyflow engine is typically composed of one or more submachines. Each submachine is a parallel machine in its own right and will be described shortly. A single submachine on its own is capable of evaluating an entire Lucid program. However, when there are many submachines it is preferable that the workload be distributed in an equitable manner amongst the available submachines. There are several approaches that could be taken. One might be to exploit locality properties in Lucid programs. In this case a compiler would decide, based on locality properties, where the different parts of the net would be evaluated.

In our engines we will distribute computations based on a hash function applied to the tag part of either a daton or a demand for a daton. In this manner we will generate a uniformly random distribution of requests across the submachines.

A Single Submachine

Each submachine essentially consists of three intersecting rings, one for handling demands (*the demand ring*), one for applying operators to the results of demands (*the application ring*, also referred to as the eduction rings), and one for computing values in a data-driven manner (*the dataflow ring*). The dataflow ring is essentially the same as the single ring of the dataflow machine at Manchester, and the second eduction ring (application) also is somewhat similar to the ring of the Manchester machine, since once an operator has been demanded it works in a data-driven way. The whole design is a generalization of the proven architecture of the Manchester machine. In fact, Ian Watson, one of the two designers of the Manchester machine, made contributions to the design when he was working with Ashcroft at SRI. The rings constituting a submachine are unidirectional pipelines, around which tagged tokens flow in a quasisynchronized manner. Each ring contains a queue to balance the flow of packets. The three rings are interconnected because the demand ring can produce results for the application ring, and the application ring can produce demands (when nonstrict operators are tentatively applied, as when the `if-then-else-fi` operator produces a demand for one of the branches after it receives the result of the test). The demand ring can affect the dataflow ring (when data-driven computation is initiated or resumed as a result of a demand), and the dataflow ring can produce results for the demand ring (when a value is produced, in a data-driven manner, for an eager variable that occurs in a lazy definition). Each ring will be described separately. Each ring picks up processors from a pool of processors, and we propose to use one pool for all the rings. The structure of the submachine is shown in Figure 4-8.

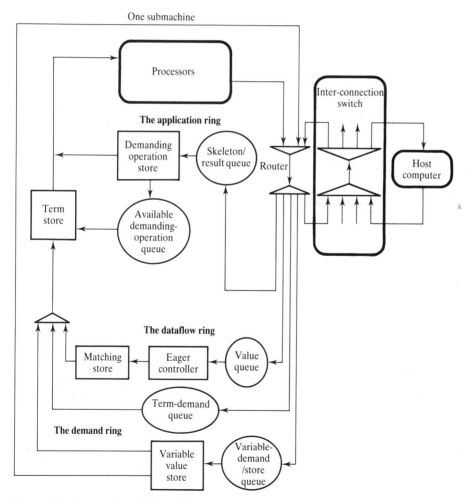

Figure 4-8. An eazyflow submachine.

THE DEMAND RING

Demands are handled by two rings, one for demanding terms that are simply variables and the other for handling demands for general terms. It often turns out that the demand for a simple variable can be satisfied immediately, since it may already have been demanded previously and its associated value will have been stored in the variable-value store. A demand for a general term usually generates more demands.

Three of the main components in the rings are the previously mentioned pool of processors, the term-demand queue, and the variable-demand queue. In addition, there is a variable-value store, and a term store, in which programs are stored in the form of intermediate code. This intermediate code is very simple. It is basically a linearized form of the parse tree of the program in question. One feature of the intermediate code is that the address of the term defining a variable or function, or the term occurring in the declaration of a variable, will be used to identify the variable or function in the intermediate code, and in the variable-value store.

The whole operation of the rings can be simply explained by describing what happens to the demand packets that come off the term-demand queue and the variable-demand queue. A *demand packet* represents a demand for the tagged value of a term that is not a basic constant.

A demand packet is of the form (a, t, r); a is the address in the term store of the term being demanded (together with two bits to indicate whether the term is a variable, or a basic operation applied to operands, or a function applied to actual parameters, or a Lucid or system operation applied to operands); t is the tag; and r is the return address. The last, $r,$ is the address of the demanding-operation that has been promised the result of the demand, and an indication of the position, in the demanding-operation, in which the result is to be put. (Demanding operations also contain return addresses.)

The demand packets are routed to the appropriate queue as a result of inspecting the two bits in the address of the term. Each demand that comes off the variable-demand queue goes to the value store, where the tagged value of the variable is located, if it has such a tagged value. This value is sent to the result queue, which we will consider later. If there is no value, but there is an indication that the value is "being computed," the return address of the demand is put on a list of return addresses associated with the variable value, in the value store. If there is no value at all for the tagged variable, an indication that the variable is "being computed" is left in the value store, and, after the demand is modified by incorporating the variable-value store address of the variable, the demand travels on to the term store.

Each demand that comes off the term-demand queue goes directly to the term store. When a demand arrives at the term store, the following things happen. First of all, a packet is constructed, consisting of the contents c of address $a,$ together with the demand itself. Next, if the term is a basic operation applied to operands, or is simply a variable, an address s of an available demanding-operation is taken from the queue of addresses of available demanding-operations, and put in the new packet. Finally, this packet is sent to the processor pool.

At the processor pool, a processor is chosen, and this processor then performs various actions, depending on the sort of term being demanded. If the term is a defined function applied to actual parameters, so that c denotes the address in the term store of the defining term of the function, the tag is modified by adding the address a to the "calling sequence" embodied in the original tag t. A demand is then sent off to the demand queue for the value of c with this new tag, and with the original return address r.

If the term is a basic (pointwise) operation applied to arguments (which means that c denotes the operation), then demands are made for the values of the operands of the operation and space is set up to hold these values until they have all been produced and the operation can be applied. This will be explained in more detail.

The first thing that happens is that a skeleton is created for a demanding-operation. The skeleton will consist of the address s of the demanding-operation, the operation c that will wait there for operand values, and the return address r to which the result of the operation will eventually be sent. The skeleton is sent around the inner ring (the queue that holds results also will hold skeletons) and, when it gets to the demanding-operation store, it causes the appropriate demanding-operation to be set up at address s.

A demanding-operation contains the op-code for the operation that is the event to be performed (in this case c), the return address of the demand that generated the demanding-operation (in this case r), and space in which to put the values of the arguments when they are eventually produced.

For nonstrict basic operations, like `if-then-else-fi`, essentially the same thing happens, only the space for operand values in demanding-operations will also be used to hold pointers to the arguments that are to be evaluated later, as well as the tag for which they are to be evaluated. (Actually, this will be a pointer to a separate block of storage in which the original demand is put, since this demand will give all the relevant information.)

The other thing that happens when c is a basic operation is that demand packets are created for the necessary arguments of the basic operation and are sent to the demand packet queue. The addresses of these operands will be obtained from the address a by simply adding an offset corresponding to the operand number, and the return addresses of these demands will be s together with the positions, in the demanding-operation at s, in which the results of these demands are to be put. The tags of the demands will be t.

If any of the arguments are basic constants, like "3" or "[A B C]," the demand is not sent off to the demand queue. (Remember that demands in the demand queue should not be demands for constants.) In fact, the demand packet will not be constructed. Instead, a result packet is constructed using c (which will be the value of the constant, or, as in the second example, a pointer to the value) and the return address. This is sent around the inner ring to the demanding-operation store.

If the operation c is a Lucid (nonpointwise) operation, or a system operation, the processing of the demand is completely different. No demanding-operation is created. Instead, a new demand packet is set up for an argument of the Lucid operation or system operation, with the same return address but with a different tag. For example, if the term is next E, the new demand will be for E, with the tag increased by 1. If it is E fby F, and the tag corresponds to Lucid-time 0, the new demand is for E, with tag corresponding to Lucid-time 0; if the tag corresponds to a Lucid-time greater than 0, the new demand is for F, with the Lucid-time (tag) decreased by 1. Since all other temporal Lucid operations can be defined in terms of next and fby, using recursion, we do not need to consider them here. However, we could add special actions into the machine to handle them directly. The previous argument can also be applied to the spatial Lucid operators using cby and rest. We will not describe such actions here.

If the term is just a variable, a tagged value of that variable must have been absent in the variable-value store, and now a demand has to be sent off for the term defining the variable (namely that addressed by c), with tag t and return address s. Before doing this, a skeleton must be sent off to the demanding-operation store, for the special operation, *store*. The demanding-operation is put in location s. The demanding-operation will contain the address in the variable-value store of the variable that is being demanded. (This was picked up, by the demand, at the time the "being computed" flag was set.)

No other cases need be considered here for the actions of the processor dealing with a demand. We have glossed over the system operations, which occur in the intermediate code, for manipulating tags. These deal with subcomputations (the effects of is current), with references to global variables of functions, and with references to formal parameters, which must give access to the actual paramters via tag modification and reference to the intermediate code. These features, though crucial and distinctive to this implementation of Lucid, are too complicated to be explained simply here, see Faustini and Wadge.[37]

THE APPLICATION RING

We saw that the values of already-calculated variables, when demanded, are sent to the result queue. The result packets on the result queue consist of data together with return addresses. (The demand for the already-calculated variable, mentioned in the last paragraph, came with a return address, and this return address was combined with the variable value to give the result packet that was sent to the result queue.) As these result packets come off the result queue, they go to the demanding-operation store, where the data value is put into the correct demanding-operation, at the correct place, as indicated by the return address.

If this data value completes the set of operands for the demanding-operation, the information in the demanding-operation is made into a packet that is sent to the processor pool. The address of the demanding-operation is added to the list of addresses of available demanding-operations.

When a completed demanding-operation packet reaches the processor pool, it takes a processor, which then applies the appropriate operator to the data values in the packet. The result is made into a result packet by adding the return address of the demanding-operation, and this is added to the result queue. The only exception to this is when the operator is a store. In this case, the operator performed is the identity function, but there is another effect in addition to the production of a result packet. The value, which is the argument of the store operator, together with the address in the variable-value store of the tagged variable (that address being found in the demanding-operation), is made into a store packet. This store packet is sent off to the variable-value store. (The variable-demand queue can also hold store packets.) When this packet reaches the variable-value store, the value is put into the appropriate address and the value is used to make result packets for all of the suspended demands for the variable that have been kept in the variable-value store. These result packets are sent to the result queue. This completes the description of the eduction rings. We will now consider the dataflow ring.

THE DATAFLOW RING

The dataflow ring contains a matching store, exactly like the matching store of the Manchester machine. It also contains a value queue and a stage called the *eager controller,* which will be explained shortly. It is to the eager controller that triggers are sent from the term store. Also arriving at the eager controller are values produced by processing completed packets from the matching store. These packets contain operators to be performed, together with their operand values, the tag that the result is to have, and the destinations to which the results are to be sent. Each value produced will be an ordinary data value, like those stored in the variable-value store, together with a tag and the destination to which it is to be sent. A destination consists of the operator to be performed and the address in the term store of the variable whose definition contains the occurrence of the operator in question and an indication of whether this is the value of one of the basic eager variables on which the values of other eager variables depend.

When a value packet arrives at the eager controller, if the destination indicates that the value is not one for a basic eager variable, the packet is passed on to the matching store. If the value is for one of the basic eager variables, the relevant part of the tag is compared with the limit for this variable. (The limit is stored in the eager controller.) If the relevant part of the tag is less than the limit, the packet is passed on to the matching store. If the relevant part of the tag is greater than the limit, the packet is stored in the eager controller.

When a value packet reaches the matching store, a search is made for a packet in the matching store that has the same operator and variable address as given by the destination field in the value packet, and has the same tag. If one is found, the value is put into this packet at the appropriate point. (Which is the appropriate point is part of the destination also.) If one is not found, such a packet is created, and the value is inserted at the appropriate point. If doing either of these things results in a packet in the matching store that has a full complement of operands (the operand is bound to be predictably heedless, so "fullness" is easily determined), the full packet travels to the term store. There the packet is changed to several packets, one for each of the places in which the result of applying the operator is to be used in an eager definition. (This information is contained in the term store, as mentioned earlier, and is found by using the address of the variable in question.) These packets then travel to the processor pool, where a processor is used to apply the operator to the operands, yielding a result packet that travels to the eager controller.

If the variable in question is used in lazy definitions (possibly in addition to being used in eager definitions), a packet is created, at the term store, that contains the operator, the operands, the variable, and the tag. When this packet gets to the processor pool, the operator is applied to the operands and the result is combined with the variable name and the tag to produce what we call an *insert packet*. This insert packet is sent to the variable-value store, where the value is given to the appropriate variable with the appropriate tag. This is done using an associative match, unlike the other way of giving values to variables via store packets using actual addresses in the variable-value store. If there is nothing in the variable-value store for that variable and tag, a place is created. If there is something there it will be an indication that it is "being computed," and there will be at least one demand for the variable and value being held there. As happens with store packets, these values are sent to the application ring, and put in the demanding-operation store.

When a trigger for a variable arrives at the eager controller, the limit number for that variable and tag (ignoring the time in the tag) is increased to be N plus the time in the tag in the trigger, if this is greater than the current limit. Also, the values for that variable held by the eager controller that are below the new limit are sent off to the matching store.

This completes the description of the dataflow ring, and thus completes the description of the whole submachine. The description is quite complicated, but it is basically a relatively complete description of an interpreter for the high-level language Lucid, expressed as an architecture. Language interpreters are generally complicated things, and usually no attempt is made to describe them relatively precisely in English, as we have done here. The fact that we could do it indicates that there is a good match between the language's syntax and semantics and also that the language is simple and elegant.

Storage Management

The overall architecture of submachines is inadequate in one respect: values are never removed from the pool of variable values, even though the value may never be demanded again. In practice, the architecture will be somewhat different from that described above, because it will have storage management built in. It will embody a management scheme employing a "future usage count" that is able to throw away a (tagged) value when its future usage count gets down to zero.

The current Lucid interpreter handles this problem with a heuristic called the "retirement plan."[37] If a tagged variable value passes retirement age, that is, has not been demanded for some time (measured in terms of the number of garbage collections it has survived), it is retired at the next garbage collection. The retirement age is adjusted dynamically if tagged values have to be recomputed because they are demanded after they have been retired.

A heuristic method of handling a similar problem has been proposed by Keller and Sleep.[38] They want to avoid recomputing terms like $f(e)$, in applicative languages, and propose that the programmer supply an *initial count function* which, depending on the value of e, gives an initial usage count for $f(e)$. If, after the count reaches zero and the value of $f(e)$ has been thrown away, $f(e)$ is subsequently demanded, it can be re-evaluated from the definitions, so no real harm results from choosing an incorrect initial count function. In contrast to the above two schemes, the usage count scheme is not heuristic.

In Lucid it is possible to devise an algorithm using future-usage counts that ensures that, when a value is thrown away, it will never be demanded again. We will demonstrate the basic principle by going through an example program:

```
x where x=1 fby x+1; end;
```

In this example x is used twice, once in the head of the where-clause and once in the recursive definition of x. The fact that x is used twice in the programs means it has a usage count of 2. Thus, x at time i will only be used twice at that point in time. Consequently, when x at time i is used for the second time we know that its entry in the variable-value store can be purged. In fact, for simple programs like the one above the usage count scheme gives a perfect usage to the variable-value store. Unfortunately, not all programs are as simple-minded as the above and those that are not cause problems. Again we will illustrate this through an example program:

```
x+a where x=if p then a else 1 fi; end;
```

If we assign usage counts in the usual way, then we see that x and p have usage counts of 1 each and a has a usage count of 2. We know by looking at the program that in this case, because the program involves an unpredictable operator, the usage count of a is 2 only if p is true at all time contexts. If p is never true, then we will have an extra copy of a around for all time contexts. This is because not evaluating the true branch of if-then-else-fi means that we are not using a and so its usage count never gets to zero. The solution we have adopted in current implementations of the usage count scheme is to "unevaluate" the redundant branch of the if-then-else-fi. We do this by sending "fake" demands to the redundant branch so that usage counts can be appropriately decremented. Note we need not perform any of the associated data operations, since they will have no use. Thus, the usage count is a completely general scheme for memory management.

Another solution to this problem is to make a hybrid memory management scheme that uses a heuristic scheme for memory management for variables that are unpredictable and a usage count scheme for those that are predictable. In fact, we can use exactly the same partitioning of variables as we did when we divided variables into lazy and eager. The hybrid scheme could be implemented by a single variable-value store or it could be that a variable-value store is needed for each part of the hybrid. A hybrid scheme will probably be implemented in our final machine design.

The Interconnection Topology

An eazyflow engine consists of several submachines connected together using the same switch, as indicated in Figures 4-8 and 4-9. Packets are routed to particular submachines by the switch, depending on the tags or the return addresses in the packets. For some packets, such as result packets, skeleton packets, store packets and insert packets, the submachine to go to is specified directly in the packet. For demand packets and value packets, the submachine is determined by the tag, using a fixed random hashing function. (All submachines use the same hashing function.) The hashing distributes the computational activity among the submachines in a random way and balances the load on the various processors.

Although each eazyflow subengine is a parallel machine in its own right, parallel evaluation of a program will come mainly from the cooperative efforts of multiple submachines. These cooperative efforts take place when submachines interact in evaluating a program. This is done through the routing of packets from one submachine to another. It is therefore obvious that the switch will determine

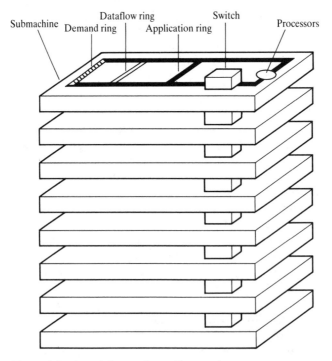

Figure 4-9. A multilayered eazyflow engine.

the extent to which the architecture is scaleable. Consequently, the switch must perform so that it does not become the bottleneck of the system.

There are many ways in which a number of submachines might be connected. These range from a full crossbar switch to some form of fast bus. Since our architecture relies heavily on the pipelining of packets from one component in the architecture to another, our switch is a buffered multistage delta network.

BUFFERED MULTISTAGE DELTA NETWORKS

In our current design, the switch will be a binary buffered delta network, with buffering between each of the stages. The transit time across the switch will depend logarithmically on the number of submachines. This will not limit the number of submachines that can be used, because the number of stages in the pipelines is increased accordingly, and the pipelines should be full. A major concern with an interconnection network of this type is that contention could result in gaps in the pipelines and consequently degrade the performance of the entire machine.

Figure 4-10 is taken from a study on the simulated performance of a multistage switch.[39] We recommend that interested readers obtain a copy of this excellent report. The report includes results from various experiments that are designed to observe the effects of load, buffer size, switch size, and "hot spots" on throughput.

With uniform distribution of packets through the switch, the results are quite positive. They indicate that the throughput percentage decreases gradually as the size of the switch is increased. This indicates that the switch is indeed scaleable. In addition, the results show that performance can be significantly

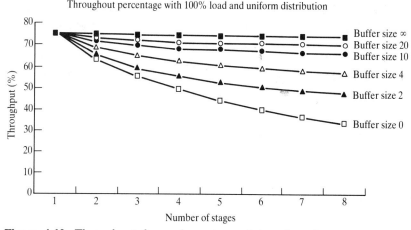

Figure 4-10. Throughput for various size switches (based on pregenerated addresses, 10 000 cycles).

improved either by increasing the buffer size (see Fig. 4-10) or by reducing the load into the switch.

Results published by Pfister and Norton,[40] regarding hot spots in multistage switches, show that the degradation in performance due to hot spots are quite dramatic. Lee's report confirms those findings. In addition, it asserts that when the source of the hot spot is localized there is a marked improvement in throughput. Hot spot contention would, at first sight, seem to negate the claims made about the scaleability of the machine. This appears not to be the case, since we have been unable to find a Lucid program that, when evaluated on the eazyflow simulator, generated hot spots even though we have tried to write programs that we thought might generate such behavior.

We feel that determining the best hashing function, which will uniformly distribute computation based on the tags, will probably be a major factor in the fine-tuning of the machine for optimum performance.

OTHER POSSIBLE INTERCONNECTION STRATEGIES

The multistage delta networks described above are a simple and elegant solution to the interconnection problem, but this is by no means the only solution. It may turn out that locality properties inherent in Lucid programs will allow an even simpler type of interconnection, which would still give the machine the property of scaleability, the ability to be expanded in terms of the number of processors used, and so on, without requiring changes in existing hardware other than simple additions. One possibility is a hybrid topology in which small clusters of submachines are connected through a crossbar switch and each cluster is connected with a multistage delta network. Each cluster would contain computations that are in some sense closely related, such as the variables of a particular function call. This exact topology is the interconnection network of a Japanese dataflow machine called the Sigma-1.[41]

A completely different approach is to try to directly implement operator nets on some form of reconfigurable array of nodes. The Lucid operators such as `next` and `fby` and a very simple data algebra can easily be implemented by simple finite automata. If in addition we take the piped evaluation approach, then a reconfigurable array of automata could be configured to act literally as the net. This approach would probably not lead to a general-purpose machine for the execution of operator nets, but it might provide a workable subset for limited domains of applications such as signal processing or image processing. If supercomputer performance is the goal, then this avenue is probably worthy of investigation. Lucid (because of its simple mathematical semantics) is well suited to the sophisticated compile-time analysis that would be required in this alternative approach.

CONCLUSIONS

The architectures we propose solve a number of important problems facing supercomputer systems. The most important of these are *programmability* and *scaleability*. Each eazyflow engine is programmed in a member of the Lucid family of programming languages.[27]

Members of the Lucid family are really a textural form for operator nets. Our architectures are based on the successful multilayered architecture of the Manchester dataflow machine and are thus scaleable.[42] This means that an n-fold increase in the computing "resources" of an engine will produce close to an n-fold increase in performance if there is enough parallelism in the problem.

To a large extent, the Manchester machine can be considered to be a precursor of the eazyflow engine proposed here, and lessons can be learned from the experience with that machine. Evidence from use of the Manchester machine[42,43] indicates, by extrapolation, that the eazyflow engine should be able to utilize its processors efficiently and thus be a very fast machine. The actual performance of the machine cannot be predicted before more details of the hardware, such as the processors to be used and the hardware hashing technique to be employed, have been settled.

Nevertheless, it can confidently be predicted that the unidirectional pipeline structure of submachines will work, and the main unknown is how effective the connection of submachines is. This can really be determined only by actually building a machine, but analysis of the simulations we have carried out on the performance of the switch indicate that the machine will be scaleable. Experience with the Manchester machine leads us to believe that there is no difficulty finding problems with enough parallelism to exercise the computing power of the machine. Moreover, the problems do not have to be regularly structured (as they must for vector machines) or even numerically oriented. Apart from its effectiveness, another reason for building this machine is that it will be the first eazyflow engine, and we confidently expect that analysis of our simulations will show that eazyflow is better than straight (data-driven) dataflow, in most cases, both for programmability and speed of computation.

ACKNOWLEDGMENTS

Special thanks go to Darin DeForest, Jon Mills and Skip Lewis who helped in various ways in the preparation of this document.

REFERENCES

1. Treleaven, P. C., D. R. Brownbridge, and R. P. Hopkins (1982). "Data-driven and demand-driven computer architecture," *ACM Comput. Surveys,* Vol. 14, No. 1, pp. 93–143.

2. Jagannathan, R. and E. A. Ashcroft (1986). "Fault-tolerant aspects of the education model and architecture," In *Proceedings of the 7th Digital Avionics Systems Conference.* IEEE.

3. Hack, James, J. (1986). "Peak vs. sustained performance in highly concurrent vector machines," *IEEE Computer,* Sept. pp. 11–19.

4. Dongarra, J. J. (1984). *Performance of Various Computers Using Standard Linear Equations Software in a Fortran Environment.* Technical Memorandum No. 23, August 1984, Revision 2. Argonne National Laboratory, 9700 S. Cass Ave., Argonne, IL 60439.

5. Mills, J. W. (1986). *A RISC Architecture for Prolog.* TR-86-008. Department of Computer Science, Arizona State University, Tempe, AZ.

6. Dobry, T. et al. (1985). "Performance studies of a Prolog machine architecture," *12th International Symposium on Computer Architecture, June 1985.*

7. Kogge, P. M. (1988). *The Architecture of Logic-based Computing Systems.* Addison-Wesley, Reading, Mass.

8. Mills, J. W. (1989). "A high-performance LOW RISC machine for logic programming," *J. Logic Programming* (in press).

9. Warren, D. H. D. (1983). *An Abstract Prolog Instruction Set.* Technical Report, Note 309. SRI International, 333 Ravenswood Avenue, Menlo Park, CA 94025.

10. Ashcroft, E. A., A. A. Faustini, and B. Huey (1985). "Eduction—A model of parallel computation and the programming language Lucid," In *Proceedings of the IEEE Fourth Annual Conference on Computers and Communications,* March 1985, pp. 9–15.

11. Kahn, Gilles (1974). "The semantics of a simple language for parallel programming," In *Proceedings of the 1974 IFIP Congress* (ed. J. L. Rosenfeld), pp. 471–475.

12. Faustini, A. A. (1982). "The equivalence between an operational and a denotational semantics for pure dataflow," PhD dissertation, University of Warwick, UK.

13. Jagannathan, R. and E. A. Ashcroft (1984). "Eazyflow: a hybrid model for parallel processing," In *Proceedings of August 1984 International Conference on Parallel Processing,* pp. 514–523. IEEE.

14. Faustini, A. A. and E. B. Lewis (1986). "Towards a real-time dataflow language," *IEEE Software,* Vol. 3, No. 1, pp. 29–35.

15. Ashcroft, E. A. and R. Jagannathan (1986). "Operator nets," *Fifth Generation Computer Architectures: Proceedings of the IFIP TC 10 Working Conference on Fifth Generation Computer Architectures. UMIST Manchester, July 1985* (ed. J. V. Woods). North-Holland, Amsterdam, 1986.

16. Jagannathan, R. and E. A. Ashcroft (1985). "Eazyflow engine architecture," *Proceedings of the Phoenix Conference on Computers and Communications. March 1985,* pp. 161–165. IEEE.

17. Ashcroft, E. A. and W. W. Wadge (1976). "Lucid—A formal system for writing and proving programs," *SIAM J. Computing,* Vol. 5, No. 3, pp. 336–354.

18. Ashcroft, E. A. and W. W. Wadge (1977). "Lucid, a nonprocedural language with iteration," *Commun. ACM,* Vol. 20, No. 7, pp. 519–526.

19. Flamig, B. (1985). "The sequential compilation of Lucid," MSc, Department of Computer Science, Arizona State University, Tempe, AZ.

20. Bagai, R. (1986). "Compilation of the dataflow language Lucid," MSc thesis, Department of Computer Science, University of Victoria, B.C., Canada.

21. Manna, Z. (1974). *Mathematical Theory of Computation.* McGraw-Hill, New York.

22. Ashcroft, E. A. (1984). "The syntax and semantics of Lucid," *Technical Report SRI International, Computer Science Laboratory,* April 1984.

23. Arvind and T. Agerwala (1982). "Data flow systems," *IEEE Computer Magazine,* Vol. 15, No. 2 [Special issue on Dataflow.]

24. Dennis, J. B. and D. P. Misunas (1975). "A preliminary architecture for a basic data-flow processor," In *Proceedings of the Second Annual Symposium on Computer Architecture.* ACM, Jan. 1975.

25. Arvind and K. P. Gostelow (1977). "Some relationships between asynchronous interpreters of a dataflow language," In *Formal Descriptions of Programming Languages.* IFIP working group 2.2, 1977.

26. Turner, D. A. (1979). "A new implementation technique for applicative languages," *Software Practice and Experience,* Vol. 9, Sept. pp. 31–49.

27. Wadge, W. W. and E. A. Ashcroft (1985). *Lucid, the Dataflow Programming Language.* Academic Press, London, UK.

28. Burstall, R. M., J. S. Collins, and R. J. Popplestone (1971). *Programming in POP-2.* Edinburgh University Press, Edinburgh, UK.

29. Landin, P. J. (1966). "The next 700 programming languages," *Commun. ACM,* Vol. 9, pp. 157–166.

30. Faustini, A. A., S. G. Matthews, and A. G. A. Yaghi (1984). *The pLucid Programmer's Manual.* Technical Report TR84-004, Computer Science Department, Arizona State University, Tempe, AZ.

31. Faustini, A. A. and Darin DeForest (1986). *The Array Lucid (Flucid) Programmer's Manual.* Technical Report TR86-016, Computer Science Department, Arizona State University, Tempe, AZ.

32. Ashcroft, E. A. (1985). "Ferds—massive parallelism in Lucid," In *Proceedings of the IEEE Fourth Annual Conference on Computers and Communications,* March 1985, pp. 16–21.

33. Ashcroft, E. A. (1974). "Towards an APL compiler," *Proceedings of APL6,* Anaheim, ACM, May 1974.

34. Wadge, W. W. (1981). "An extensional treatment of dataflow deadlock," *Theor. Comput. Sci.,* Vol. 13, pp. 3–15.

35. Lee, Rosanna (1985a). *Emulating Eazyflow.* Technical Report CSL-#148. Computer Science Laboratory, SRI International, 333 Ravenswood Avenue, Menlo Park, CA 94025.

36. DeForest, D. and A. A. Faustini (1986). *The Design and Implementation of a Simulator for a Multiprocessor Architecture.* Technical Report TR86-015. Department of Computer Science, Arizona State University, Tempe, AZ.

37. Faustini, A. A. and W. W. Wadge (1987). "An inductive interpreter for the language pLucid," In *Proceedings 1987 ACM SIGPLAN Conference on Interpreters and Interpretive Techniques.* St. Paul, Minn., pp. 91–94.

38. Keller, R. M., and M. R. Sleep (1981). "Applicative caching: Programmer control of object sharing and lifetime," In *Proceedings of the 1981 Conference on Functional Programming Languages and Computer Architecture,* pp. 131–140. ACM.

39. Lee, Rosanna (1985b). *Simulated Performance of a Multi-stage Switch.* Technical Report. Computer Science Laboratory, SRI International, 333 Ravenswood Avenue, Menlo Park, CA 94025.

40. Pfister, G. F. and V. A. Norton (1985). "'Hot spot' contention and combining in multistage interconnection networks," *IEEE Transactions on Computers,* Vol. C-34, No. 10, pp. 934–948.

41. Hiraki, K., T. Shimada, and K. Nishida (1984). "A hardware design of the SIGMA-1—A dataflow computer for scientific computations," In *Proceedings of August 1984 International Conference on Parallel Processing.* IEEE.

42. Gurd, J. R., C. C. Kirkham, and I. Watson (1985). "The Manchester Prototype Dataflow Computer," *Commun. ACM,* Vol. 28, No. 1, pp. 34–52.

43. Watson, I. and J. Gurd (1982). "A practical dataflow computer," *Computer,* Vol. 15, No. 2, pp. 51–57.

PART TWO

Software and Hardware Design of Supercomputers

5

SOFTWARE DEVELOPMENT FOR PARALLEL PROCESSING IN A DISTRIBUTED COMPUTER ARCHITECTURE

Noah S. Prywes and Boleslaw K. Szymanski

INTRODUCTION

Procedural programming for parallel computers is intrinsically more difficult than for sequential machines. In addition to the usual challenges, one must consider communication overhead and synchronization problems. It is also necessary to balance the computational load assigned to individual processors. The balancing can be done reliably only after the software has been developed and, therefore, it leads to costly postdevelopment tuning.

Specialized parallel computing hardware often requires software to be developed in dialects of standard languages. Varying communication primitives of different parallel computers have led to major software incompatibilities. A focus on software efficiency additionally increases complexity of software development.

In the assertive programming paradigm, a computational problem is expressed as a set of assertions about its properties and not as a sequence of steps leading to the solution. Solution procedures are automatically generated from the assertive description. The programmer is not involved in the implementation, whose efficiency and correctness are assured by the underlying language translator.

This work was supported in part by the Office of Naval Research under Contracts N00014-83-K and N00014-86-K-0442, and in part by the Army Research Office under Contract DAAL03-86-K-0112.

Depending on the type of assertions used as a basis for a notation, different languages for assertive programming have been proposed. In equational languages, assertions are expressed as algebraic equations (Ashcroft and Wadge 1977; Hoffman and O'Donnell 1982; Chen 1986; Szymanski and Prywes 1988). Such languages are naturally suited to mathematical modeling. They have also been proved to be an effective tool for describing general computational tasks (Baron et al. 1985).

In equational programming, the envisaged role of the computer is not to execute, step by step, prescribed operations, as in procedural programming, but to find those values of unknown variables that make all stated assertions become true. As the programmer specifies rather than prescribes the computation, we shall refer to assertive programs as *specifications*. Clearly, a specification translator has to be much more sophislated than ordinary compilers or interpreters. In addition to typical functions of a compiler, it has to transform a specification into efficient programs for the individual parallel processors.

A truly large-scale computation must be partitioned into smaller computational tasks, here called *modules,* that are candidates for parallel execution.

There are two tasks in defining the complete parallel computation. First, it is necessary to define semantically correct computation, independently of the way the computation will be executed. Second, it is also necessary to define efficient ways of its execution. In parallel programming, the first task roughly corresponds to programming-in-the-small, and the second one to programming-in-the-large.

In traditional programming, those two tasks are interdependent and it is difficult to do them separately. In our approach, the first task corresponds to defining equations describing the computation. The important feature of equational specification is independence of its meaning from equation distribution among program modules. The equations yield the same results no matter whether they are consolidated into one large specification and executed on a sequential, single-processor machine or partitioned into several modules and run on a multinode distributed architecture. The equational specification can be developed and tested without considering the efficiency and parallelism at all. In our approach, such specification defines data transformations done by the module.

In the second task, defining the mapping of computation onto the processors and specifying data flow are of concern. The programmer has to be able to define routes and identities of data exchanged between communicating processes and to map the program modules onto the processors, but not to describe the computation itself. Such description of communication and mapping is called a configuration. The simple, path definition-oriented language, called CSL (Configuration Specification Language), has been designed for that purpose.

The paper describes use of the MODEL and CSL languages for parallel software development. It is organized as follows. In the next section we give the general description of our approach based on the integrated use of software tools built for the MODEL equational language. An example of international econometric modeling developed with the assistance of those tools is given in the following section. We then describe the MODEL language compiler. The

Configurator is presented next and then the run-time environment is discussed. The final section offers conclusions regarding the use of equational languages for parallel processing.

THE MODEL APPROACH

In the following we assume that the hardware consist of a number of interconnected processors, each with its own memory. The processors can cooperate in performing an integrated parallel computation. The software consists of operating systems and compilers that will largely hide from the programmer the parallel computation aspects.

The programmer is envisaged as performing the following steps:

1. The programmer will partition the entire computation into independent *modules* that are candidates for execution in parallel. Such partitioning is frequently natural to the application being programmed.
2. Each module will be programmed independently of the other modules. The programmer will regard the communications with other modules in the same way as ordinary input/output. Namely, the intermodule communications are viewed in the same way as if the communication was conducted with a passive input/output device, such as a terminal or a disk, without requiring from the programmer special knowledge of concurrency. The modules can be then compiled and individually tested, if the data to be communicated are provided as external files.
3. A collection of modules will be synthesized into an integrated computation by merely specifying the interconnections between modules. This will be done in a very high-level language, called CSL (the Configuration Specification Language), specially designed for programming in-the-large. Within each module, the delays between inputs and outputs will be estimated during compilation on the basis of the maximum sizes of data structures and the operations performed. Those delays and the network connections specified in the configuration enable the programmer to evaluate the performance of the global computation.
4. Modularity features ease splitting or fusing of modules and substituting, modifying or adding modules. By fusing or splitting modules, the programmer can revise the configuration to remove bottlenecks that limit throughput or cause uneven load distribution.

Thus the parallel programming effort will require only the composing of program fragments (the modules in steps 1 and 2) and the synthesizing of them (in step 3). These steps will be no more difficult, and sometimes easier, than the corresponding steps in conventional sequential programming.

Jobs consisting of parallel modules and their synthesis will be submitted into a queue for parallel execution, similarly to the submission of conventional sequential jobs. They will then be scheduled in parallel and executed with several-fold greater speed.

The MODEL system, discussed below, simplifies these steps by the following means.

1. Providing the users with an equational language for specifying the program modules in step 2. The MODEL compiler will generate respective parallel-executable programs from these equational specifications.
2. Eliminating the need for programming input and output (including inter-process communications). The input/output events are implied from the equations and data declarations (step 2). They are invisible to the programmer and are generated entirely by the compiler.
3. Providing the users with a programming in-the-large language and its translator, called *MODEL Configurator,* for easily synthesizing or altering a computation composed of a large number of modules (step 3).
4. Eliminating the need to sequence statements or to use any control or input/output constructs. Equational specifications can be fused or split at will, to create modified modules without requiring internal reordering. Further, the interconnecting network can easily be modified to include, delete, or substitute modules.
5. Simplifying proofs of correctness of the equational specifications, and there-fore improving program reliability and user confidence in the software. There are checks and facilities for preventing deadlocks of consumable resources and for synchronizing termination of concurrent processes (Szymanski et al. 1985).

The hardware and operating system environment that is considered here consists of a VAX front-end-processor (FP) operating under the VMS operating system, and a cluster of Micro VAX II associated-processors (APs), each operating under the VAXELN operating system. Each processor has its own memory (M). There is no memory sharing. All communications and synchroniza-tion use messages. All input/output (I/O) is connected to the front-end-processor (FP). The processors are connected by a communication network. This is illustrated in Figure 5-1. In the experimental system, the communications are via Ethernet. Considerably faster communications can be provided in the ultimate system.

Three software tools have been developed to support the software develop-ment process.

1. A configurator for the Configuration Specification Language, CSL, used to define modules' communication and to map the modules onto a network of associated processors for execution.
2. A compiler for the equational language used to define modules' operation. This compiler produces programs for the respective processors.
3. A timer for estimating the delays inherent in the modules.

The Configuration Specification Language, CSL, is used for the description of the configuration. The objects of this language are modules (and their aggregates) and sets of data (files or collections of communicated messages). Statements of CSL represent relations between modules and data sets. Those relations include production, consumption, or update done on different levels of

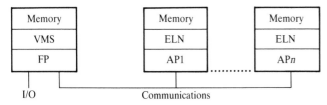

Figure 5-1. Distributed parallel architecture.

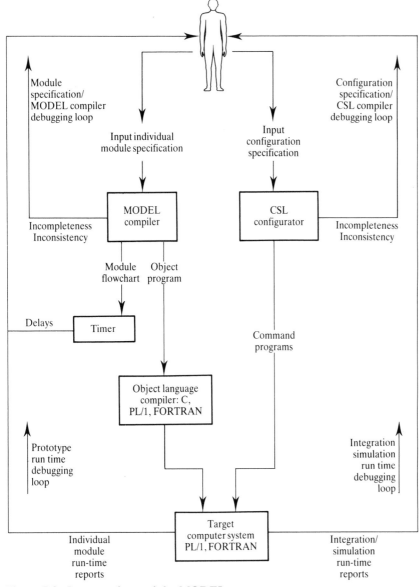

Figure 5-2. Integrated use of the MODEL system components.

data structures. More detailed description of CSL is presented later. CSL has been implemented in the VAX/VMS and VAXELN environment. The configurator produces data for setting up communications channels and invoking, scheduling, and synchronizing modules (processes) to maximize interprocess concurrency.

Modules are specified in the MODEL equational language. Currently, the compiler of the MODEL language produces optimized object code in FORTRAN, C, and PL/1. The integrated use of the MODEL compiler, configurator, and timer is further illustrated in Figure 5-2.

The programmer familiar with representing problems through equations is shown at the top. The programmer can input partial or complete configuration specifications to the configurator, and individual module specifications to the MODEL compiler. Debugging is illustrated in Figure 5-2 through the feedback to the programmer. The static debugging is performed by the configurator and the MODEL compiler, which conduct analysis of specifications' completeness and consistency. A program is generated once the MODEL compiler determines that a specification is acceptable. In dynamic debugging of the individual module, a generated program can be executed with test data (simulating interactions with other modules) and the results can be displayed to the programmer to verify that it performs as intended. Similarly, a multiprocess test, in which several modules are executed and interact with each other, may be performed using the command-language program produced by the configurator. This testing constitutes a system-wide debugging loop. All required changes and corrections are made in the MODEL and CSL languages and not in the generated procedural-object programs. Finally, module delays are reported by the timer during module compilation. The programmer associates them with modules in the configuration and evaluates total delays along critical paths in the configuration graph. Repartitioning of modules may be necessary, if estimated performance is not satisfactory.

INTERNATIONAL ECONOMETRIC MODELING EXAMPLE

Introduction

Our approach is illustrated by a computation of a worldwide econometric model in the LINK project (Klein 1975). This is a computation-intensive large-scale system requiring substantial computational resources. It is typical of problems encountered in scientific modeling, in which the inflexibility of large-scale computation limits the benefits of use of computers for research.

The LINK project integrates many econometric models of countries or regions. Those models were first developed independently, and only later did the need arise for integrating them together. This mode of activity is called *cooperative computation* (Prywes 1984). In this mode, a local model is defined historically through the interest and expertise of local developers. The developers are typically initially uncoordinated and dispersed organizationally and geographically. The motivation for synthesizing models into an integrated system comes later. The advantage in synthesizing a global system may be viewed as follows. In an isolated model, the variables that are imposed by the external environment are considered as parameters and their values are assumed by the user. In contrast, in a global system the variables external to one model are derived from others and can be evaluated, which makes the modeling more reliable. The main difficulty in synthesizing models is caused by the difference in definitions given to common variables in independently developed interacting models. An agreement must be made between authors of such models on transformations of these variables to obtain a common meaning and structure. Such an agreement is called a *contract* (Gana 1978) and is sometimes defined by adding an interfacing model.

Project LINK is a classic example of cooperative computation. It consists of institutions that have been developing stand-alone econometric models, typically for their own country or region. The large databases and hundreds to thousands of econometric equations in each model are in constant flux, following political and economic changes. Since the respective economies are highly interdependent, it is important to synthesize the models. Also, results must be obtained quickly to alert the economists to changes that may be needed in economic policies and plans.

The parallel computation of the example below represents a simulation of economic interactions in the Pacific Basin. The economies simulated and their corresponding models are those of the USA, Japan, Taiwan, Korea, the Philippines, and Thailand. They also interact with a reduced model of the rest of the world. Each model forms a process (module). In the following sections we first describe local process specification and then describe interprocess configuration of the global system.

Local Process Specification

Each process (module) is developed independently as if it were standing alone (left path of the diagram in Figure 5-2). The steps in a process development consist of repeatedly (1) preparing a specification, (2) generating a program, (3) testing through running the program with data, and (4) evaluating results and reformulating the specification, if necessary. All changes are made by modifying the specification in the MODEL equational language. The underlying implementation, including the generated program, are of no concern to the programmer.

An equational specification of a country econometric model is presented through a simplified example. For brevity, a small econometric model with nine variables is illustrated diagrammatically in Figure 5-3 and its specifications are shown in Figure 5-4.

For each econometric model, there are interior variables, which are defined by the given model, and exterior variables, which are determined outside the

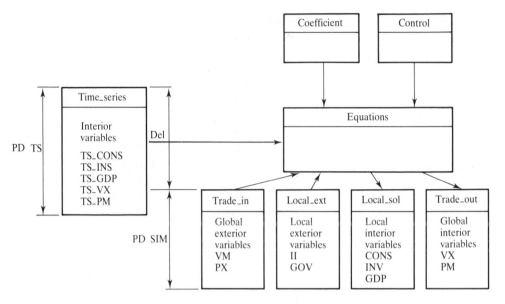

Simplified schematic diagram

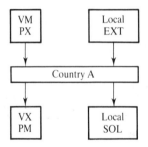

Figure 5-3. Diagram of the country econometric model. CONS, consumption; INV, investments; GDP, gross domestic product; II, government investments; GOV, government expenditures; VM, volume of imports; VX, volume of exports; PM, price index of imports; PX, price index of exports.

model. In addition, we will distinguish variables local to the single-country model from those that are global—that is, those that are used by more than one model. All variables are viewed generally as arrays. Arrays are members of respective files. In each model, there are five interior variables defined by respective equations. Local and global variables are kept in separate files. The local exterior variables are kept in the files: Coefficients, Control and Time_series. The Coefficients file contains the values of the coefficients in the equations, assumed to have been previously computed using estimation methods. The Control file contains three parameters: PD_TS, the number of periods in the Time_series file; PD_SIM, the number of periods in the simulation (forecast); and DEL, the number of periods from the beginning of the time series to the beginning of the simulation. The Time_series file contains historical values for the interior variables. These historical values are used as the initial values for the simulation. In a stand-alone model, there are two files for exterior variables (Local_ext and Trade_in) and two files for interior variables (Local_solution and Trade_out). The four global variables in Trade_in and Trade_out files consist of volumes and prices of exports and imports. This type of a model can be represented by a simplified diagram, shown at the bottom-left corner of Figure 5-3.

Figure 5-4 shows the MODEL language specification of the example. The header at the top of the figure identifies the name of the program to be generated (A), and the names of the five source (input) and two target (output) files. The

```
/* * * * * * * * * * * * * HEADER * * * * * * * * * * * * */
MODULE: COUNTRY_MODEL;
SOURCE FILES: TIME_SERIES, CONTROL, COEFFICIENTS,
TRADE_IN, LOCAL_EXOG;
TARGET FILES: LOCAL_SOL, TRADE_OUT;
/* * * * * * * * * * * * DATA DESCRIPTIONS * * * * * * * * * * * * */
1 CONTROL IS FILE,
 2 C_RECORD IS RECORD,
  3 (PD_TS,PD_SIM,DEL) IS FIELD (PIC'999');

1 COEFFICIENTS IS FILE,
 2 COEF_RECORD IS RECORD,
  3 C(13) IS FIELD (DEC FLOAT);

1 TIME_SERIES IS FILE,
 2 TS_RECORD (1:20) IS RECORD,
  3 (TS_CONS,TS_INV,TS_GDP,TS_VX,TS_PM) ARE FIELDS
    (DEC FLOAT);

1 LOCAL_EXOG IS FILE,
 2 EX_REC (1:30) IS RECORD,
  3 (II,GOV) ARE FIELDS (DEC FLOAT);

1 TR_IN IS FILE,
 2 TR_IN_RECORD (1:30) IS RECORD,
  3 (VM,PX) ARE FIELD (DEC FLOAT);

1 TR_OUT IS FILE,
 2 TR_OUT_RECORD (1:30) IS RECORD,
  3 (VX,PM) ARE FIELD (DEC FLOAT);
```

(Continued)

Figure 5-4. Specification of a reduced econometric model of a country.

```
1 LOCAL_SOL IS FILE,
 2 SOL_RECORD (1:30) IS RECORD
  3 (CONS,INV,GDP) ARE FIELDS (PIC'BB(6)9.V(6)9');
/ * * * * * * * * * * * * DATA PARAMETERS * * * * * * * * * * * * /
SIZE.SOL_RECORD=PD_SIM;
SIZE.TS_RECORD=PD_TS;
T IS SUBSCRIPT;
/ * * * * * * * * * * * * EQUATIONS * * * * * * * * * * * * /
/ * A1 * / CONS(T)=IF T>1 THEN C(1)+C(2)*GDP(T)+
C(3)*CONS(T-1)
        ELSE TS_CONS(T+DEL);
/ * A2 * / INV(T)=IF T>1 THEN C(4)+C(5)*GDP(T)+
C(6)*GDP(T-1)+C(7)*II(T)
        ELSE TS_INV(T+DEL);
/ * A3 * / GDP(T)=IF T>1 THEN CONS(T)+INV(T)+VX(T)+
GOV(T)-VM(T)
        ELSE TS_GDP(T+DEL);
/ * A4 * / VX(T)=IF T>1 THEN C(8)+C(9)*PX(T)+
C(10)*GDP(T-1)
        ELSE TS_VX(T+DEL);
/ * A5 * / PM(T)=IF T>1 THEN C(11)+C(12)*PM(T-1)+
C(13)*VM(T)
        ELSE TS_PM(T+DEL);
/ * * * * * * EQUATIONS DEFINED EXTERNALLY * * * * * * /
/ * E1 * / TR_IN_RECORD(T)=DEPENDS_ON(TR_OUT_RECORD(T));
```

Figure 5-4. (*contd.*)

description of the organization of the seven files follows. The syntax of data description is similar to that used in PL/1, except that it describes the file organization and not memory data structures. A file is a tree of arrays, specified depth-first level by level. The description of each level starts with the level number, the name of the structure, and its number of repetitions, followed by the definition of its constituents one level below. In the example presented, several of the variables repeat (from 1 to 20 and from 1 to 30 times). A repeating structure may be viewed as a vector, and repeating substructures are then matrices, with each repeating level adding a dimension to the respective array. The number of repetitions gives the size (or range) of the array along the respective dimension. It is necessary to provide an equation that defines the number of repetitions of each array that has variable size dimensions. Thus, SIZE.TS_RECORD = PD_TS means that the size or range of the lowest-order (right-most) dimension of the structure TS_RECORD is equal to PD_TS. Similarly, the number of repetitions of the local solution records—the number of periods of simulation—is given by the variable PD_SIM. T is declared to be a subscript that denotes the period of the simulation.

The specification in Figure 5-4 concludes with five equations for the interior variables, denoted A1 to A5, and an equation, E1, that relates external variables. The values of the variables for the first period (T = 1) come from the Time_series file. Otherwise they are defined by the respective expressions. The operator IF . . . THEN . . . ELSE selects the appropriate expression that applies in each case.

It is important to realize that the module specification closely resembles the original econometric model, as written in the textbook. It is easily modifiable because new equations can be put anywhere into the specification, since the statement order is irrelevant to the meaning of the specification. Finally, the programmer is relieved from describing implementation details, like input/output operations, loops, order of execution, and so on.

Interprocess Configuration

The Configuration Specification Language, CSL, defines flow of data between program modules. Objects of the language are modules and data sets (files) that the modules exchange. A target/source or consumer/producer relationship between a data set (file) and a module is represented by a directed edge between those objects. When the same file is produced by one module and consumed by another, then these two modules become connected via the file.

Two attributes of configuration nodes are worthy of mentioning here. A *module type* shows whether the module is:

- simple—an individually specified module (default);
- compound—a group of modules for which a configuration is defined separately; or
- interactive—a human communicating with the system through a terminal.

Data sets (files) have an *organization* attribute with the following values: sequential (default), indexed, mail, and post. A *sequential file* is exchanged as one entity. It can be consumed only after it has been entirely produced. Such a file may have only one producer, but any number of consumers. An *indexed file* has a variable denoted as a key and used to define (access) records in the file. There are no restrictions on the order or number of references to such a file made by producers and consumers. The MODEL compiler automatically incorporates in the generated programs code for modules to lock each other when updating critical data. A *mail file* is a collector of records. It is private to its consumer and therefore it can have only one consumer, but several producers. Records from different producers are accepted by the consumer in order of their arrival. A *post file* is a distributor of records to dynamically addressable data sets (files). The post file has one producer, and each of its records includes a key used as an address of a destination file. Therefore, it can have any number of edges connecting it to mail files.

Figure 5-5 shows a configuration that synthesizes the models of the Pacific Basin countries and the rest of the world. These models are the initial modules of a global parallel computation.

```
CONFIGURATION: PACIFIC_BASIN_MODEL
F: USA_EXOG, USA_TR_IN ORG: MAIL
   → M: USA
   → F: USA_SOL, TR_OUT ORG: MAIL;
F: JAP_EXOG, JAP_TR_IN ORG: MAIL
   → M: JAP
   → F: JAP_SOL, TR_OUT;
F: TWN_EXOG, TWN_TR_IN ORG: MAIL
   → M: TWN
   →F: TWN_SOL, TR_OUT;
F: PHI_EXOG, PHI_TR_IN ORG: MAIL
   → M: PHI
   → F: PHI_SOL, PHI_OUT;
F: THI_EXOG, THI_TR_IN ORG: MAIL
   → M: THI
   → F: THI_SOL, TR_OUT;
F: KRA_EXOG, KRA_TR_IN ORG: MAIL
   → M: KRA
   → F: KRA_SOL, TR_OUT;
F: WRLD_EXOG, TR_OUT ORG: MAIL
   → M: WRLD
   → F: WRLD_SOL, TR_IN ORG: POST;
F: TR_IN
   → F: USA_TR_IN,JAP_TR_IN,TWN_TR_IN,PHI_TR_IN,KRA_
TR_IN,THI_TR_N;
```

Figure 5-5. Configuration network for Pacific Basin model.

Typically, boundaries of modules are defined along functional divisions. In our example, the six countries and the world model form modules naturally. Processes are consumers or producers of their source or target files, respectively. Each country process (module) produces files of trade out (TR_OUT) and local solutions (SOL) and consumes a file of trade in (TR_IN). The world process (WRLD) has a target file of trades in (TR_IN) and a source file of trades out (TR_OUT).

Use of The Timer

The timer traces the branches in the generated module programs and evaluates their computation times. In this way it can report to the programmer the worst-case delays between input and output operations. These delays are then used to guide assigning module programs to individual processors. The delays can be used by the programmer in locating bottlenecks in the configuration graph and assessing the need for repartitioning of modules to reduce their inherent delays. The configuration can thus be viewed at that point as a PERT chart, or a network of queues and servers.

As an example, consider the configuration graph in Figure 5-5. It consists of a large parallel component containing six country modules and a single component with the world model. The Timer provides the worst-case delays between TR_OUT and TR_IN for each of the six country models, and the delay between TR_IN and TR_OUT for the world model. The critical path, that is, the longest delay in the cycle, is created by the USA model (which consists of 2000 equations) and the world model. If the number of available processors exceeds the number of modules, then to shorten the total computation time, the USA and world modules have to be further partitioned and their parts computed in parallel. If there are fewer processors than modules, then several models have to be allocated to a single processor (in multiprogramming mode). Several of the lowest-delay country models can be grouped in a single processor, as long as the total of their delay does not exceed the delay of the USA module. In this way it is possible to modify the configuration and the assignment of modules to processors in progressive steps that reduce total computation time.

THE OPERATION OF THE MODEL COMPILER

The compilation of an equational specification into an object code consists of four stages: (1) syntax analysis, (2) semantic analysis and checking, (3) scheduling of program events, and (4) generation of the program. The second and third stages, which are significant of our approach, are reviewed below.

Semantic Analysis and Checking

The compiler translates the specification into a directed graph. However, this graph is unlike other directed graphs that represent dependencies in the computation (for sequential program analysis, see Kuck et al. (1981), Warren (1983); for data-flow graphs, see Dennis (1980)). A new tool was developed termed an *array graph,* in which a node represents an entire array of data or equations and an edge an entire array of dependencies. An array data node represents the accessing, storing, or evaluation of an entire data array. The underlying graph of individual structure elements and their dependencies may be derived from the array graph based on the attributes of dimensionality, ranges, and forms of subscript expressions, which are given for each node and edge in the array graph.

A node A corresponding to an m-dimensional data or equation represents the elements from $A(1, 1, \ldots, 1)$ to $A(N1, N2, \ldots, Nm)$, where $N1 \cdots Nm$ are the ranges of dimensions 1 to m, respectively. Similarly, a directed edge represents all the instances of elemental dependencies among the data elements of the nodes connected by that edge. The dependencies show precedence relations imposed on the execution order of the respective implied procedural program subprocesses. There are several types of such relations. For example, a *data-dependency* precedence refers to the need to evaluate the independent variables of an equation before the dependent variable can be evaluated. *Data parameters* of a structure (such as size of a dimension) must be evaluated before evaluating the respective structure. Similarly, a *hierarchical* precedence refers to the need to receive the entire message before its components can be accessed or, conversely, the need to evaluate the components of the message before it can be sent out.

Use of data-dependency graphs to optimize programs, in particular for parallel execution, has been proposed recently in the literature (see, for example, Allen et al. 1983; Ferrante et al. 1984; Kuck et al. 1981; Waters 1983). The distinctive feature of the array graph of the MODEL language is the compact representation of data dependencies (a node represents entire array, not a single element) and the lack of control dependencies (flow of control is generated by the compiler).

From the country model specification, the compiler builds an array graph, a fragment of which is shown in Figure 5-6. Nodes of this graph represent arrays,

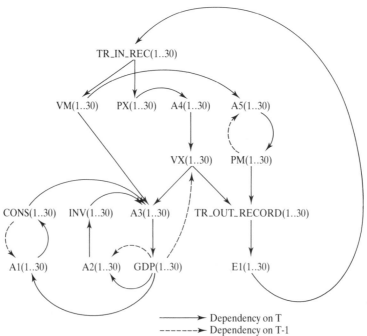

Figure 5-6. Fragment of the array graph for the specification in Figure 5-4.

like CONS, INV or GDP, and equations defining those arrays. Edges also represent arrays of dependencies, not a single dependency. For example, the edge between GDP and equation A4, shows that each instance T of equation A4 (and there are up to 30 of them, each defining a different element of the array VX) depends on the $T-1$ element of GDP.

The MODEL compiler recognizes that all the nodes in this fragment of the array graph have the same range, denoted by the global subscript T. This range is set by the value of SIZE.SOL_RECORD, defined by the data parameter equation. The dimensions of arrays other than SOL_RECORD or its descendants CONS, INV, GDP are therefore implicitly defined and no separate equation defining, say, SIZE.TR_IN_RECORD or SIZE.TR_OUT_RECORD is needed. This and other similar features of the MODEL compiler simplify specifying programs in the MODEL language.

Checking the specification and making corrections and additions may be regarded as inferring or propagating attributes from node to node. The following general types of checks and corrections take place.

1. Consistency of dimensionality and subscripting, sizes of dimensions, and data types of variables are checked by propagating them from node to node.
2. Data-description statements are generated for variables that have been referred to in equations but have not been declared by the programmer.
3. Equations are generated to equate an undefined target variable to the same-named source variable.
4. A set of linear algebraic equations is identified wherever a cycle is detected in the array graph. The adequate initial values, termination conditions and solving methods can be selected by the programmer or are supplied by the compiler by default.

Experience has shown that these checks are effective in locating 80–90 percent of the errors (not including syntax errors) in development of a program (Szymanski et al. 1984). The remaining errors are located by running the generated program with source data and examining the target data produced.

Scheduling Program Events

In composing a module specification, the programmer chooses natural and convenient data structures and equations. Typically, this choice does not correspond to the most efficient implementation. In addition, the programmer description of data is independent of the medium of the data and whether it is internal (in main storage), external (secondary storage), or exchanged (communication line carrying messages). It is up to the compiler to map the specification into an efficient procedural computer program.

The scheduling starts with creating a component graph that consists of all the maximally strongly connected components (MSCC) in the array graph and the edges connecting MSCCs. The component graph is therefore an acyclic directed graph. This graph is then topologically sorted. Next, the subscripts for each node in the component graph are determined. Iterations for these subscripts must bracket the respective nodes to define all the values of the elements in the structured variables.

The optimization of the schedule proposed in the MODEL compiler is based on merging scopes of iterations to enable elements of the same or related structures to share memory locations. Usually there are many ways in which components can be merged (for different dimensions), each corresponding to different total orderings of the component graph. The memory requirements of different candidate scopes of iterations serves as the criterion for selecting the optimal merging and corresponding total ordering of the schedule. The selection is equivalent to the NP-complete problem of finding a clique with the maximum weight of nodes in an undirected graph. Therefore, a heuristic is used.

The specification may contain circular dependencies for which no linear order of computation exists. In these cases, an iterative method is applied to find values of the variables. The programmer may also optionally designate a set of linear algebraic equations as a BLOCK (possibly, nested blocks) and provide initial values, convergence conditions, and the method of solution to be used. In the absence of such specifications, the compiler selects default conditions and generates the procedure for the iterative solution.

An edge can be disregarded in scheduling, if the dependency it represents is enforced by the loop in which both nodes belonging to the edge are nested. Those edges are marked by dashed lines in Figure 5-6. GDP$\rightarrow$A4 is an example of such an edge, because the appropriate fragment of the array graph can be enclosed in a loop iterating over T. After eliminating all such edges, the fragment still contains cycles. One such cycle consists of equations A1, A2, A3, and variables that those equations define (CONS, INV, GDP). These variables and equations would create a block of computation for which a numerical method of solving algebraic equations would be applied. Numerical aspects of the solution could be decided by the programmer or left to the compiler to provide for. In the latter case, the iterative Gauss–Siedel method is applied, because it is relatively easy to generate code for it. However, other methods are implemented as well.

The equation E1 is needed to show an external dependency (through other modules) of the input TR_IN_RECORD on the output TR_OUT_RECORD. It forms, with statements A4 and A5, another set of linear algebraic equations. The equations that specify in detail the external dependency are in some other modules in the global configuration. The cooperation of the CSL and MODEL compilers is necessary in designing and implementing a numerical solution to algebraic equations that spread over a group of modules. This is discussed further in the next section.

CONFIGURATION PROCESSING

The configuration description is first transformed into the configuration graph. Nodes of this graph are modules and files while edges represent consuming and producing relations. Then the graph is checked for correctness and consistency.

Cycles in the configuration graph are identified, and the programmer is warned that they constitute a necessary but not a sufficient condition for a deadlock (sufficient conditions are checked locally in each module).

The configurator also identifies groups of modules that can be run concurrently. Such groups form parallel components. Next, a component graph is created. Its nodes represent parallel components and edges show the implied sequential order of node execution. The component graph is used to generate a dependency matrix.

An exchange of data between modules executed in parallel can be either through a mail file or a pair of a post and mail files connected together. The MODEL compiler, when generating a program for a module, optimizes the use of the main memory assigned to data, often replacing the entire range of an array by a window—that is, by few elements. When such array has to be communicated to the other modules, only that window, few records at a time, can be sent out. Therefore, program optimization causes a producer to store or send as few records at a time as feasible. Similarly, a consumer has also to store and consume a minimum number of records at a time. When producer and consumer processes are concurrent, the post and mail files require a buffer for a limited number of records. This type of data exchange realizes the concept of a pipeline or a stream. The programmer is not involved in this aspect of program design but is warned if a file cannot be exchanged in this fashion.

The configurator would find for the econometric modeling configuration in Figure 5-5 that all the modules can be run in parallel. There are six simple cycles in the configuration (each country model is connected to the world model and vice versa). The records that are exchanged along those cycles are indexed by the same global subscript, T. An attempt to run those modules literally would lead to an immediate deadlock (each country module would wait for the communication from the world module and the world module would wait for messages from country modules). The MODEL compiler discovers the possibility of the deadlock through analysis of subscript expressions in the respective records and variables. The compiler issues a warning message to the programmer and proceeds to further interpretation of such specifications as defining a system of algebraic linear equations. The compiler produces an iterative procedure for solving those equations. At the beginning of execution, instead of waiting for communication, each module would start computations with some assumed initial values and then send out the results. After that, it would wait for communication from others. Such iterative solution carried over several modules, and not inside them, would terminate only if the global computation converged, or a prescribed number of iterations would be executed. Similarly like for algebraic equations nested in a single module, the numerical aspects of the solution can be defined by the programmer or set by default.

For the specification presented, the iterative solution was selected by default. For each iteration step in solving global equations there are solutions of local econometric models for each country. The user is not involved in designing mailboxes, addressing communication, or synchronizing iteration steps, since the only input required from the user is the configuration description as in Figure 5-4. All those and similar other implementation details are generated by the configurator.

The output of the configurator is in the form of two data structures. The first is a list of all the processes in the parallel application. For each process it includes commands for loading and creating the process, and parameters for input/output and for setting up the circuits needed by the module for communication with others. All circuits are restricted to one-way communications.

The second data structure produced by the configurator consists of a dependency matrix. There is a row and a column in the matrix for each module. There may be precedence relations between parallel components whenever sequential files are used for communication between them. The precedence relations will be marked at the intersection of the row and the column of the modules in the respective parallel components.

The output structures produced by the configurator are stored away in a configuration object file.

RUN-TIME ENVIRONMENT

The operating systems normally residing on the processors of the parallel architecture under consideration were augmented by the two programs:

- an interpreter for the input commands, operating under VMS on the front-end processor (FP); and
- a server for executing the commands received by the interpreter. Each associated processor (AP) runs its own copy of the server program under ELN operating system.

The run-time environment is illustrated in Figure 5-7. In the first step, identical server programs are loaded to each AP. Next, the entire application is started by running the interpreter program with the configuration object file in the FP. If the configurator were run on a different computer (e.g., a traditional sequential VAX), the configuration object file would have to be placed on a disk connected to the FP.

The interpreter first reads this file and then, as shown in Figure 5-7, repeatedly checks the dependency matrix to determine which modules are not further dependent on others and can therefore be scheduled for execution.

The interpreter also incorporates a scheduler, which collects information on the memory and CPU utilization in each AP. Based on this information the interpreter selects the AP that will be allocated to the respective ready-for-execution module. This will be accomplished by the interpreter sending commands to the respective server in an AP. The latter will load (from disk in the FP) and create the module, and set up its communications with other modules.

The interpreter will then wait for the notification of the termination of the process or other condition codes from the respective server. Such notifications are

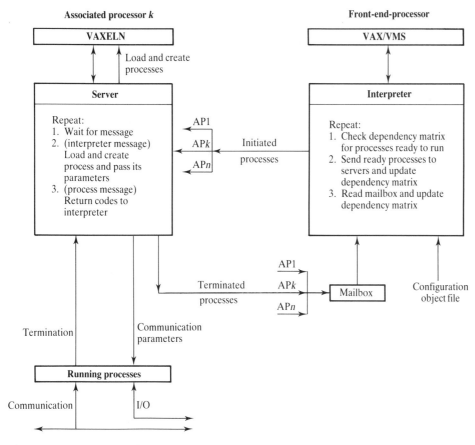

Figure 5-7. Run-time MODEL environment.

queued in a mailbox. The interpreter will be blocked while awaiting input in the mailbox.

The server is the counterpart of the interpreter in each AP. It awaits input commands from the interpreter, starts a module, and executes the command by calling the local operating system (VAXELN). The server also passes parameters to VAXELN on the circuits that need to be created for interprocess communications and on input/output devices that need to be connected to the initiated module. Finally, the server awaits a report of termination of any of the processes initiated by it. It then notifies the interpreter of the respective termination.

Additionally, the server evaluates performance of the respective AP. This includes evaluating available memory and CPU utilization, since the previous most recent initiation of a process in the AP.

The synchronization of modules is implemented (invisibly to the programmer) by blocking a module on "receive" if the input buffer is empty, and blocking a module on "send" only if the destination queue buffers are full.

CONCLUSIONS

The greatest challenge in parallel programming of scientific computations is to make effective use of the potential parallelism provided by hardware. The approach presented in this paper supports parallelism at high, interprocess level. It is derived from the programmers's partitioning of the problem into modules. The timer enables the programmer to evaluate the efficiency of the partitioning scheme at compilation time. The configurator provides the tool for synthesizing repartitioned and redesigned modules. Therefore, three cooperating components of the MODEL system—MODEL compiler, configurator, and timer—constitute an integrated software development system that supports rapid prototyping, modularization, and comprehensive consistency checking.

Use of an equational language for expressing computations shields the user from considering low-level implementation details, like describing input/output operations, loop structure, flow of control in the program, and so on. Compilation of specifications, including optimization and synchronization algorithms and customized code generators, provides the user with efficient implementation for a parallel computer. Only code generators would have to be rewritten if the system were moved to the different machine. As code generators form a separate and relatively simple part of the overall system, the MODEL approach offers high level of portability.

REFERENCES

Allen, J. R., K. Kennedy, C. Porterfield, and J. Warren (1983). "Conversion of control dependence to data dependence," in *Proceedings 10th ACM Symposium on Principles of Programming Languages,* pp. 24–26. ACM, New York.

Ashcroft, E. A. and W. W. Wadge (1977). "Lucid, a nonprocedural language with iteration," *Commun. ACM,* Vol. 20, No. 7, pp. 519–526.

Baron, J., B. Szymanski, E. Lock, and N. Prywes (1985). "An argument for nonprocedural languages," in *The Role of Language In Problem Solving—1* (ed. Robert Jernigan, Bruce W. Hamill, and David M. Weintraub), pp. 127–146. North-Holland, Amsterdam.

Chen, M. (1986). "A parallel language and its compilation to multiprocessor machines or VLSI," in *Proceedings 13th Annual ACM Symposium on Principles of Programming Languages,* pp. 131–139. ACM, New York.

Dennis, J. B. (1980). "Data flow supercomputers," *IEEE Computer,* Vol. 13, No. 2, pp. 48–56.

Ferrante, J., K. J. Ottenstein, and J. D. Warren (1984). "The program dependence graph and its use in optimization," in *Proceedings 6th International Conference on Programming. LNCS 167,* pp. 125–132. Springer-Verlag, Berlin.

Gana, J. L. (1978). "Automatic program generator for model building in social and engineering science," Ph.D. Dissertation, Department of Computer and Information Science, University of Pennsylvania, Philadelphia.

Hoffman, C. M. and M. J. O'Donnell (1982). "Programming with equations," *ACM Trans. Programming Languages and Systems,* Vol. 4, No. 1, pp. 83–112.

Klein, L. R. (1975). "The LINK model of world trade with application to 1972–1973," in *Quantitative Studies of International Economic Relations* (ed. P. Kenen). North-Holland, Amsterdam.

Kuck, D. J., R. H. Kuhn, D. A. Padua, B. Leasure, and M. Wolfe (1981). "Dependence graphs and compiler optimization," in *Proceedings 8th ACM Symposium on Principles of Programming Languages,* pp. 207–218. ACM, New York.

Prywes, N. (1984). "Distributed large scale computation with an application to world-wide econometric studies," *Large Scale Systems,* Vol. 7, No. 3. pp. 89–97.

Szymanski, B., and N. Prywes (1988). "Efficient handling of data structures in definitional languages," *Science of Computer Programming,* Vol. 10, No. 2, pp. 221–245.

Szymanski, B., N. Prywes, E. Lock, and A. Pnueli (1984). "On the scope of static checking in definitional languages," in *Proceedings ACM'84 Annual Conference: The Fifth Generation Challenge,* pp. 197–207. ACM, New York.

Szymanski, B., Y. Shi, and N. Prywes (1985). "Synchronized distributed termination," *IEEE Trans. Software Eng.* Vol. SE-11, No. 10, pp. 1136–1140.

Warren, J. (1983). "A hierarchical basis for reordering transformations," in *Proceedings 10th ACM Symposium on Principles of Programming Languages,* pp. 272–282. ACM, New York.

Waters, R. C. (1983). "Expressional loops," in *Proceedings 10th ACM Symposium on Principles of Programming Languages,* pp. 1–10. ACM, New York.

6

CACHE COHERENCE IN MIMD SYSTEMS: A PETRI NET MODEL FOR A MINIMAL STATE SOLUTION

Jean-Loup Baer and Claude Girault

INTRODUCTION

Advance in technology is the factor that has had the largest impact on the evolution of computer architecture.[1] However, most experts recognize that problems in the form of physical limiting features may appear by the end of the decade.[2] Thus, looking at the general-purpose uniprocessor as the common mode of computing might not hold true for very long, and investigating the design and efficient use of multiprocessors is becoming increasingly important. A second aspect of the technological impact is that two long-standing goals of computer designers—fewer main memory accesses and a better matching of processor cycle time and memory access time—have been achieved by extending the memory hierarchy to include a *cache* or fast buffer between the processor and the main memory.

Details of cache organization and their impact on performance are extensively covered in Smith.[3] They will be reviewed briefly in the next section. For the purposes of this introduction it is sufficient to know that caches are managed automatically by the hardware in a manner resembling that of the operating system features of a paging system. The main differences are that on a

The work of J.-L. Baer was supported in part by NSF Grants MCS-8304534 and DCR-8503250; the work of C. Girault was supported in part by CNRS-GRECO/C3-ATLAS.

cache miss to a line (often called block)—the equivalent of a page fault—there is no context-switch and that the miss ratio is a few percent, which is orders of magnitude greater than the page fault rate. These two differences stem from the fact that the access time ratio between primary memory and cache is 10 versus $>10^4$ in the secondary–primary memory case.

In this chapter we consider the design of the cache–primary memory interface in systems composed of several processors, each with their own local cache, connected via some switching structure to a shared main memory. Recent examples of such MIMD multiprocessors are the IBM 3084 and 3090[4] (4 processors) and S-1[5] (16 processors under design). Much more ambitious projects[6,7] envision several hundreds of processors, each with their own local caches. Systems in which each processor is a microcomputer with associated cache have been built for such applications as database transaction processing[8] or even general-purpose computations,[9] and multiprocessor-with-caches workstations are in production.[10,11]

The introduction of local caches in a multiprocessor gives rise to the *cache coherence* problem. Since several caches can contain a copy of a particular memory location, there must be means to prevent processors from simultaneously modifying their respective copies. Otherwise, inconsistencies would arise and the "database" would become incoherent. Similarly, a processor requesting a copy of a memory location should always receive the most up-to-date version. Because of the speed ratio mentioned above, the coherence solutions must not slow down the system too much and therefore hardware-based solutions are needed.

In recent years, the cache coherence problem has been studied extensively. The proposed solutions can be broadly divided into three categories:

- software-based solutions;
- solutions for shared-bus systems;
- directory-based solutions.

The first two cases restrict the generality of the solutions. The software solution enforces cache coherence by allowing only pure code and private data (if task migration is forbidden) to be loaded into a cache. The solutions for shared-bus systems (for a qualitative and quantitative comparative evaluation see Archibald[12]) take advantage of the fact that caches can "listen" to *all* the transactions on the bus. However, the shared-bus architecture limits this solution to a relatively small number of processors.

This paper deals with directory-based solution. The states of the lines whose main memory storage is controlled by some memory controller are known to that memory controller. In other words, the state information can be distributed among the memory controllers. The state of a line is encoded in a bit vector. In the first published solution of that type,[13] a bit-map, with one bit vector per main memory line, is attached to the memory controller. A complete state information is encoded in $(n + 1)$ bits, $g, e_0, e_1, \ldots, e_{n-1}$, where e_k indicates whether the line is present in the kth cache ($k = 0, \ldots, n - 1$) and g indicates whether the line is clean or dirty. Thus, if all e_i are 0 the line is in no-cache (state "Absent"), if $g = 0$

and one or more e_k is 1 then the line is present in one or more caches but has not been modified (state "Present+"), and if $g = 1$ then one and only one $e_k = 1$ and it indicates that the line is in cache k and has been modified (state "PresentM").

However, this solution is very expensive in terms of space and does not allow for easy expandibility in the number of processor–cache pairs. We have therefore introduced another state solution[14] in which the knowledge given to the controller is not quite complete but can be encoded in only two bits; moreover, the encoding does not depend on the number of processors and thus lends itself better to modular system building. The "two-bit" encoding defines four states: "Absent" and "PresentM" which have the same meaning as above, and "Present1" (present in exactly one cache and not mofified) and "Present*" (present in 0 or more caches and not modified). Since the information given by these states does not include the location of the owning caches, the memory controller might need to broadcast orders to all caches (e.g., for invalidation of a given line). This might unnecessarily disrupt caches that do not contain a copy of the line under consideration. It is for a similar reason (the absence of complete information) that a state such as "Present*" now exists. The existence of a separate "Present1" was justified by performance reasons but gave rise to "ghost" signals and rendered the protocols quite complex.

Archibald and Baer[14] have sketched the protocols needed between the processors and the memory controllers and have indicated for which range in the number of processor–cache pairs and for which degree of sharing the "two-bit" solution does not degrade the system unduly. More formal and more detailed models for these protocols are needed to ensure their correctness (e.g., absence of ghost signals). Moreover, these models help in establishing bounds for the hardware resources required at both the cache and controller levels. We present such a model based on Petri nets.

The remainder of this chapter is organized as follows. After a brief review of caches we describe succinctly and informally the hardware black boxes, their physical and logical interconnections, and a 3-state cache coherence protocol. Then we introduce the Petri Net model. The section on the Detailed Model is the heart of the chapter; the model of the cache coherence protocol is described in detail. After that we show where optimizations could be included and give some examples of refinements of the model and conclude on possible extensions and other applications of the nets.

CACHE MEMORIES

Cache memories are high-speed buffers placed between the processor and main memory to hold code and data currently in use by the processor. Access time to caches is typically of the order of 100 nsec, which is about 10 times faster than access to main memory. The management of caches follows the virtual-memory concept. However, the management is entirely provided by the hardware; this is required by the small difference in speed between cache and main memory accesses. The entities that are mapped from the memory into the cache are called *lines*. A memory reference is for a word (byte) within a line.

The basic operation of a cache and the choices that have to be made for its organization and management policies are best explained if we follow a memory reference, say to line a, from the processor. (The following explanation is slightly oversimplified; more relevant detail will be introduced in subsequent paragraphs.) The memory reference to a is first translated from a virtual to a real adddress (this translation and how it can be partially overlapped with access to the cache is beyond the scope of our discussion). The real address is then transmitted to the cache. The cache is (logically) divided into two parts: a directory used to identify the lines it contains and the data part which contains the contents of the lines. If a directory search for the referenced line is successful, we have a *cache hit*. Then the contents of the line b in the cache, which is the mapping of line a in memory, are either transmitted to the processor (read) or altered (write). If the search is unsuccessful—*cache miss*—the memory reference is then transmitted to main memory. The line a is then loaded in the cache (in b), at the expense of replacing another line, and the reference is submitted anew to the cache. A good measure of the performance of a cache is its *hit ratio,* which is the ratio of the number of cache hits to the total number of memory references.

An important design decision is the organization of the directory. At one extreme we can make the search very fast by constraining the mapping $a \rightarrow b$ to only one position. This is called direct mapping. At the other extreme, we can make the mapping completely general: we then have a fully associative map. Usually caches are organized in a set-associative fashion: the line a can be mapped into a small number of positions in the cache (2, 4, or 8 depending on the systems). This retains some of the generality of the fully associative concept and some of the simplicity of the direct mapping. In the remainder of this paper, we will abstract this organization and will deal only with the fact that we have either cache hits or cache misses; we will assume a fast searching mechanism but will not go into any more detail.

Another design choice is the write policy. When the processor performs an operation that modifies the contents of a line (a write), this modification can be done either in the memory only, or in the memory and the cache, or in the cache only. The *write-through* policy writes in both the cache and main memory (there exist variations in which write is performed only in main memory when there is a cache miss). In the *write-back* scheme, writes are performed solely in the cache (again there are variations, see Smith[3]). When a modified line is to be replaced to make room for another, its contents are then written back to memory. The advantages of write-through are simplicity and reliability, since the contents of main memory are always up-to-date. Those of write-back are mostly related to performance, since there are fewer writes to main memory. It is the method that is preferred for high-performance systems and the one we will use here. It implies that each line b in the cache must have a *modified* bit associated with it that indicates whether the line is clean (if its contents are identical to those of its corresponding a in main memory) or dirty (if its contents have been modified).

As noted earlier, on a cache miss the line that has to be loaded in the cache will in general displace a line already there. In the direct-map approach there is no choice as to which line to write-back. In a set-associative organization, there is a (limited) choice; hence, a *replacement algorithm* must be implemented. Whether the line chosen to be replaced is selected randomly (within the same set of course), or in FIFO (first-in-first-out) fashion, or according to a LRU (least-recently used) policy has little influence on the overall performance of the cache. Here we will assume a reasonable choice but will not show the implementation details. However, we will distinguish whether the line to be replaced is clean (no write-back necessary) or dirty (its contents must be sent back to memory).

Finally, we have to consider the effects of concurrent I/O and of multiprocessing. This will be dealt with in considerable detail later. At this point, we simply note that this requires that lines in the cache might be invalidated, for example, because the contents of their corresponding line in memory are modified by some I/O processing. This will be indicated by a *valid* bit associated with each line.

INFORMAL DESCRIPTION OF THE ARCHITECTURE AND PROTOCOLS

The Architecture

The multiprocessor architecture that we consider (Fig. 6-1) consists of the following.

- Processor-cache pairs P_i-C_i
- Primary memory modules M_j and associated controllers K_j
- An interconnection network

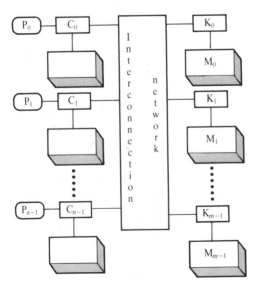

Figure 6-1. Multiprocessor architecture.

From the cache coherence protocols viewpoint, the following "black boxes" are of interest. The caches consist of:

- a directory containing the address tags (to recognize if a given line is in the cache), a valid bit, and a modified bit;
- a set of data values corresponding to the contents of the respective lines;
- a control unit that responds to the demands of the corresponding processor and to the messages from all controllers;
- FIFO queues for incoming and outgoing messages.

  The controllers consist of:

- a bit map (2 bits/main memory line) to encode the state of each line;
- a data queue sitting in front of the main memory—This queue will not intervene in a logical sense in the protocols;
- a control unit that manages the messages from all caches;
- FIFO queues for incoming and outgoing messages as well as a wait buffer (a small associative table) for messages in transit.

  The interconnection network will be modeled as a packet-switching network without redundant paths and without failures. This implies that packets might contain any combination of orders, addresses, status bits and data. Our constraints also imply that if A sends two messages to B these messages will always be received in the order in which they were sent. Furthermore, we assume that there are enough entries in the input–output queues of the controllers and enough buffering in the individual switches of the interconnection network that no message will ever be lost. We will return to the modeling of the interconnection network in the section on Extensions and Improvements.

  The Petri Net model reflects the underlying hardware structure. It consists of three nets interconnected by places modeling buffers or mailboxes. These three nets are:

- the L-net for processor-cache interaction;
- the K-net for the controller flow of actions;
- the G-net for the cache actions upon receiving messages from the controller.

In our modeling we have tried to expose as much parallelism as possible while at the same time taking into account the realities of hardware implementation. First, it is clear that the controllers and the caches can proceed in parallel. But, in addition, there is some potential concurrency in each of the hardware structures modeled by the Petri Nets. For example, the L-net is divided into two parts: one corresponding to access to the directory and one to access to the data. Concurrent access to a shared resource is restricted by semaphores (places in the net) but otherwise concurrent access is permissible. This allows not only pipelining but also "cache cycle stealing" by the G-net. Similarly, a memory controller can process concurrently requests for different lines, but two requests for the same line must be processed sequentially. Although the algorithms to process two requests for the same line are not overly difficult to model, the hardware implementations become quite complex for a very small gain—or even possibly a loss—in performance. In the same vein, we disallow concurrent reading or writing of the bit-map.

The Protocols

Detailed protocols will be given in the section on the Detailed Model. Here we explain the exchanges of control and data messages between caches and controllers as well as the role of the interconnection network. We begin by giving an informal overview as seen from a generator of memory references, that is, a processor. Recall that the controllers K_j keep the global states of the lines stored in the memory modules they control. This global state is either "Absent" (not cached anywhere), "PresentM" (present and modified in one cache), or "Present*" (present and clean in 0 or more caches). Furthermore, the caches know whether the lines they contain are valid and clean or dirty. A cache that contains a valid dirty copy of a line will be called the *owner* of that line.

There are four cases to consider, depending on a read or a write, and a hit or a miss. In addition, we have to give the protocol in case of a line replacement.

1. *Read hit.* No special action.
2. *Write hit.* If the line is already dirty, there is no special action (with respect to a uniprocessor). On the other hand, if the line is clean, the cache asks for permission to modify it (a REQUEST). This permission (a GRANT) will be given by the controller monitoring this line. This may entail a broadcast message to INVALIDATE the line, which might be present in other caches. A state change, to "PresentM", will occur.
3. *Read miss.* Once the replacement has been taken care of (see below), a read REQUEST is sent to the controller. If the line is not in state "PresentM", this request can be fulfilled immediately (GRANT and transmission of data). Otherwise this will require a PURGE of the owner (initiated by the controller). Once this is accomplished, the GRANT and transmission of data can be performed and the state becomes "Present*".
4. *Write miss.* We proceed (almost) as above if the line is in state "PresentM". If the line is in state "Present*" we broadcast an INVALIDATE signal before fulfilling the request. If the state is "Absent," a GRANT and the data can be transmitted immediately. In all cases the new state is "PresentM."
5. *Replacement.* If the line to be replaced is valid and dirty, a RETURN is sent to the controller indicating the replacement and writing-back the data. A state change to "Absent" takes place.

We do not elaborate yet on the underlying structure of the interconnection network. Each cache can send and receive messages to and from each controller. Several messages can proceed concurrently in the network with the usual conflicts being resolved at the network level. The mechanisms for broadcasts are assumed to be handled by the network itself. Our protocols are designed to be independent of the structure of the network, the only constraints being that messages sent from a source to a destination are received in the order in which they were sent.

Addressing in messages is handled as follows. If the destination is a controller, the high-order bits $\hat{a}$ of the address of the line a will suffice to select the memory controller (the remainder of the address will be denoted by $\bar{a}$). If the destination is a cache, the concatenation of the cache number and of the whole address of the line will be needed.

We can now proceed by describing the control message types and exchanges. Actual transfers of data (PUTs and GETs) will also be indicated. Unless otherwise specified, the source cache will be C_k and the memory controller will be K_x. In the tables that follow, those left-justified correspond to messages originating from a cache while those right-justified correspond to messages sent by a controller.

1. On a cache hit to a valid line for read or valid dirty line for write, there is no message emanating from the cache.
2. On a cache miss (in C_k) to line a, a READ REQUEST or a WRITE REQUEST is sent to K_x ($x = \hat{a}$). On a write hit on an unmodified line, a WRITE REQUEST is sent. These REQUESTs are messages of the form (k, a, m, s) sent by C_k to K_x, where m is the access mode, read or write, and s is the actual state of the line in C_k, valid or invalid. This is summarized by the table:

REQUEST	$m = w$	$m = r$
$s = i$	WRITE	READ
$s = v$	WRITE	N/A

3. On a cache miss, there might be a need to replace a valid line, say o. If o has been modified, a PURGE RETURN will be sent to K_y (y determined by $\hat{o}$) along with the data to write-back (PUT). Other uses of the RETURN messages and the format of the return table will be described later.
4. When C_k requests a line in state "PresentM," the controller K_x must broadcast a QUERY in order to retrieve the data. If C_k has sent a WRITE REQUEST then K_x broadcasts a PURGE QUERY. The owner of the line, C_l, will invalidate it and send the data (PUT) to K_x along with a PURGE RETURN message. If it was a READ REQUEST, K_x sends an UPDATE RETURN. The only difference with the previous case is that the line in C_l will remain valid and clean (rather than dirty). In both cases K_x will wait for the RETURN and accompanying data before sending a GRANT, and the data, to C_k.

When C_k requests a line that is not in state "PresentM," then there is no need for K_x to wait for any data. On a WRITE REQUEST and a line in state "Present*," an INVALIDATE QUERY is broadcast. On a READ

REQUEST and for a line in state "Absent," no additional message is necessary. In all cases, K_x can immediately send a GRANT to C_k.

A QUERY is broadcast to all caches except C_k. Each message is of the form $(h, x, \bar{a}, u)$, where $h \neq k$ is a destination cache and u is a parameter indicating whether the line can remain valid or not. This is summarized by the table below (with $m = w$ meaning the line was modified and $m = r$ that it was not):

QUERY	$m = w$	$m = r$
$u = i$	PURGE	INVALIDATE
$u = v$	WRITE	N/A

5. Obviously, if line a is not cached in C_k, the latter will ignore QUERYs. If C_k has a clean copy of a, it will not generate any RETURN. Therefore, RETURNs are generated by the control unit of a cache only for the lines it owns. A RETURN message is of the form (k, a, m, s) where $m = w$ is the modified bit and s is the desired new valid bit. A transfer of data (PUT) will take place. This is summarized as:

RETURN	$m = w$	N/A
$s = i$	PURGE	N/A
$s = v$	UPDATE	N/A

6. As just seen, RETURNs are of two kinds: those generated for replaced lines and those that are answers to QUERYs. In the first case, K_k will not generate more messages. In the second, a GRANT will be sent to the original requester. This will take the form of a $(k, x, \bar{a}, g)$ message where g indicates whether the grant is for read or for write.

GRANT	$m = w$	$m = r$
$s = i$	WRITE	READ
$s = v$	WRITE	N/A

As soon as K_x determines that a GRANT can be sent, a data transfer (GET) also takes place.

To close this section we show the messages generated when a cache C_k incurs a write miss on line a owned by cache C_l. The state of line a ("PresentM")

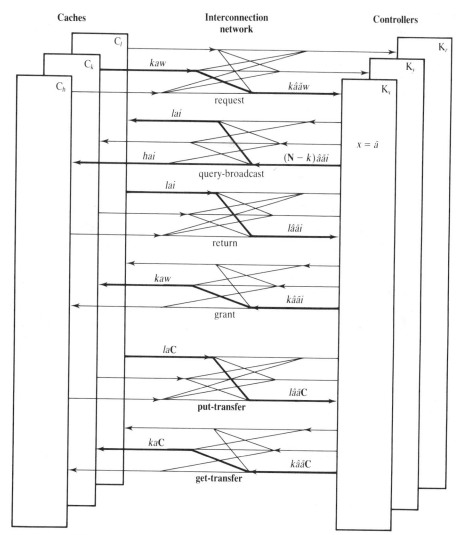

Figure 6-2. Network messages.

is known to the controller K_x ($x = \hat{a}$). The sequence of messages is also shown on Figure 6-2.

1. C_k sends a (k, a, w, i) WRITE REQUEST for the missing line a.
2. K_x broadcasts a PURGE QUERY ($N\text{-}k, x, \bar{a}, i$) to all caches but k ($\mathbf{N}$ is the set of all caches) since a is in state "PresentM."
3. C_l owns a; it answers with a (l, a, w, i) PURGE RETURN and in parallel writes back the line (via a $(l, a, \mathbf{C})$ PUT). ($\mathbf{C}$ is the contents of the line.)
4. After having received the RETURN, K_x sends a $(k, x, \bar{a}, w)$ WRITE GRANT to C_k along with data (a $(k, a, \mathbf{C})$ GET).

Moreover, if a dirty block o had to be replaced to make room for a, then C_k would also have generated a (k, o, w, i) PURGE RETURN along with a (k, o, C) PUT.

This high-level description does not convey the subtleties involved when several requests from various caches and/or controllers are interleaved, hence the need for the models of the next sections.

MODELING WITH PETRI NETS

Overview

We give now a top-down description of our model using an extension of Petri Nets[15] called *Predicate/Transition nets*[16-19] which use colored tokens, inhibitor arcs, and FIFO places.[16,20-22] These nets and corresponding notations will be described below.

In our model of a multiprocessor system, as depicted in Figure 6-1, colored tokens are associated with each cache and each controller. The colored tokens allow us to fold the general model—N identical cache subnets interconnected with M identical controller subnets—into a single concise description (Fig. 6-3). Two main sets of colors are used to distinguish individual caches and controllers:

$N = [0, \ldots, N-1]$ is the set of processor and cache numbers (notation C_h, C_k, C_l).

$M = [0, \ldots, M-1]$ is the set of memory module and controller numbers (notation K_x, K_y, K_z).

Other sets of colors are used for the values of control variables; several colored components may be gathered into compound tokens to denote messages or table entries.

A further refinement will yield the local and global cache nets (Figs. 6-4 and 6-5) and the controller net (Fig. 6-6).

Predicate/Transition Nets and Notations

Predicate/Transition nets (PTN) are an extension of the classical Petri nets (PN). Informally, a PN consists of a set of places corresponding to conditions that may hold in the system, a set of transitions representing events that may occur, and a set of directed arcs connecting (input) places to transitions and transitions to (output) places. Places may contain tokens that signify the holding of the corresponding condition. A PN has associated with it an initial marking (the number of tokens initially assigned to each place in the net). A transition may fire when all its input places contain a token. After firing, a token is removed from every input place and a token is added to every output place. The firing of a transition corresponds to the occurrence of an event. For example, in our model,

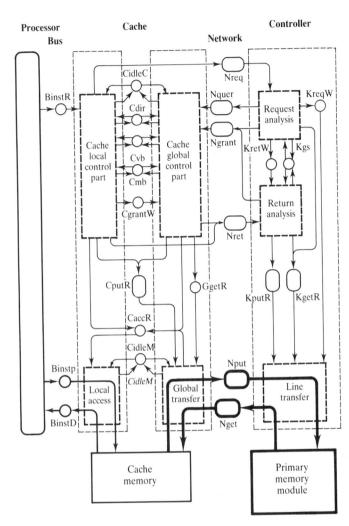

Figure 6-3. Complete model structure.

some places will be buffers with the tokens filling them being messages; the firing of a transition could correspond to the transmission of a message from a buffer in a cache to another in a controller.

Predicate/Transition nets extend PNs by associating an n-tuple of values— or colors in the case of colored PNs, which are a special case of PTNs—to each token. Now the places contain bags of colored tokens and arcs linking places and transitions are labeled. The labels are either sets of colors or free variables. The firing rule is modified in the sense that a transition can fire only if the input places contain one token of each color in the label of the corresponding input arc to the transition. Similarly, output places will be filled, after the firing, by one token of

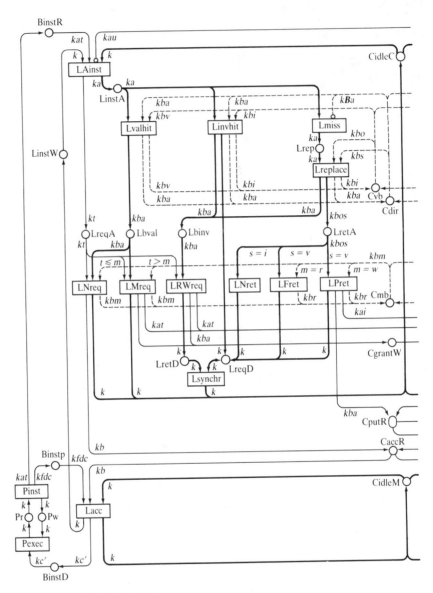

Figure 6-4. Cache local part.

each color contained in the label of the associated output arc. The rules for the free variable case are the same except that the free variable can be bound to any color of some set and places connected by arcs labeled with the free variable must possess (or will receive) tokens of that same color. For general PTNs, optional predicates can be associated with transitions to express restrictions on the colors allowed for binding variables.

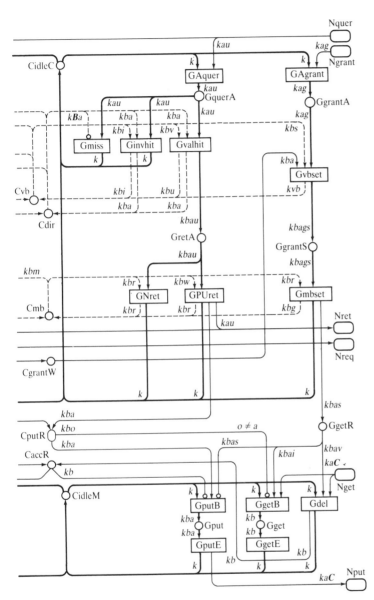

Figure 6-5. Cache global part.

To illustrate these concepts, consider Figure 6-7 which models the part of the cache access to check whether there is a hit or a miss (this figure assumes a single processor environment; more "colors" will be added in Figure 6-4 where we model a multiprocessor system). Here, a and b denote lines, s is the state of a line, and v and i are colors for valid and invalid states. The transition LAinst when fired has deposited an a token in place LinstA, indicating that a search for

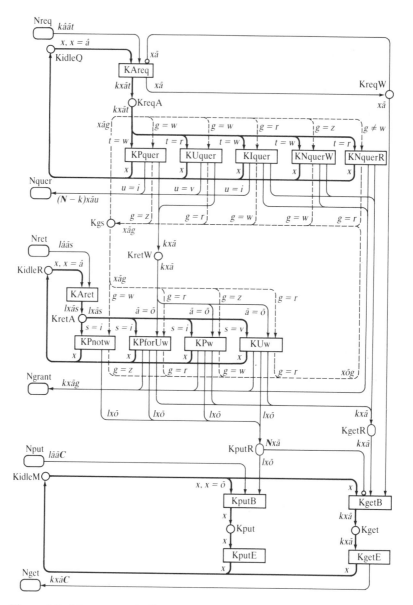

Figure 6-6. Memory controller.

the line b corresponding to a is required. Places Cdir and Cvb represent, respectively, the directory, and the valid bits for the cache. If there is an $a \rightarrow b$ mapping in Cdir, and if the valid bit associated with b is on, then transition Lvalhit will fire (this is indicated by the labels ba and bv, a simplified notation for (b, a) and (b, v), on the arcs from Cdir and Cvb to Lvalhit), removing the a

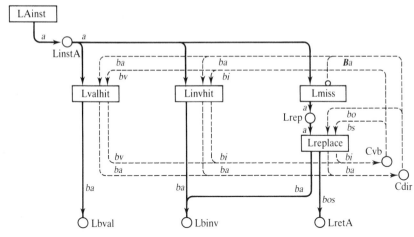

Figure 6-7. Modeling example.

token from LinstA, sending a (b, a) token in Lbval and putting back the original tokens in Cdir and Cvb. Note that tokens such as (b, v) might also be referenced as (b, s) with a predicate $v = s$ associated with the transition Lvalhit. If the mapping exists but the entry is invalid (label bi on the arc from Cvb), then transition Linvhit will fire. If the mapping does not exist—and this is indicated by the inhibitor arc from Cdir to transition Lmiss labeled $\mathbf{B}a$ whose meaning is that no a is matched by any element b in the set $\mathbf{B}$ of all entries in the cache—then Lmiss will fire. A line to be replaced in $\mathbf{B}$, say o, will be selected and that line will be come invalid.

In our model, inhibitor arcs are represented in the figures with a small circle at their connection with the transition. When an arc between an input place and a transition is an inhibitor arc, the firing rule of the transition is modified in the sense that for this place there must be no token present (of the color labeled by the inhibitor arc) for the transition to fire, with, of course, all other conditions as before.

Finally, we will use FIFO places, insuring that tokens are removed in the same order in which they were put in.

We will in addition use the following notation, easily translatable into available languages for verification tools,[23,24] to give a literal description of the model.

⟨transition⟩ ::= ⟨input part⟩⟨optional predicate part⟩
                                    "|"⟨transition-indent⟩">"⟨output part⟩
⟨input part⟩ ::= ⟨output part⟩ ::= ⟨part⟩
⟨part⟩ ::= ⟨label⟩"*"⟨place-ident⟩ | ⟨part⟩"+"⟨label⟩"*"⟨place-ident⟩
⟨optional predicate part⟩ ::= "[ ]"⟨Boolean expression⟩
⟨label⟩ ::= ⟨set of tokens⟩

Each label denotes the set of simple or compound tokens removed from or produced into the corresponding place by the transition. Sets are used for broadcasts. The Boolean expression denotes either an inhibitor arc or a supplementary condition for firing the transition. For example, the literal description of the transition Lmiss in Figure 6-7 is

$$a * \text{Linsta}[\ ](\mathbf{B}, a) * \text{Cdir} = 0 \mid \text{Lmiss} > a * \text{Lrep}$$

Complete Model Structure

The structure of the Petri Net of Figure 6-3 reflects the hardware organization. Each processor has its own cache memory; the cache controller is modeled by the *cache subnet.* Each primary memory module has an associated controller modeled by the *controller subnet.* Communication between a processor and its cache is by a private bus interface; in the model this is represented by a set of places prefixed by "B." Messages between caches and controllers transit through the interconnection network. In the model, these messages will be held in FIFO places prefixed by "N."

From the cache coherence viewpoint, it is sufficient to consider that a *processor* performs only one of two actions: either produces orders to access the cache, or consumes the results (data) delivered by the cache. The processor nodes in the net will be prefixed by "P." Orders produced by a processor will result in tokens being put in the "B" places. These places are FIFO, and this allows a pipelined processor to prepare several access orders in advance.

A *cache* consists of two separate units: a control unit and a memory unit. Each unit has a local component for the interface with the processor (prefix "L") and a global one (prefix "G") for the communication with the controllers. The common data structures are represented as sets of tokens in places prefixed by "C."

The control unit of C_k is idle when there is a k token in the place CidleC; this token also insures mutual exclusion between the actions of the local and of the global control parts. The local part of the unit analyzes the processor requests and communicates when necessary (for example on a cache miss) with the memory controllers (places Nreq and Nret). The global part monitors queries and grants (places Nquer and Ngrant) from the memory controllers and also sends return commands (in Nret) when needed.

The local and global control parts share the "address" information of the cache as follows.

- The place Cdir which contains the tags indicating whether a given line of memory is mapped in a line of the cache. This is represented by tokens (k, b, a) for all cache numbers k and all lines b in these caches.
- The place Cvb which indicates whether the contents of a line b are valid or not. This is modeled by tokens (k, b, s).
- The place Cmb which indicates whether the contents of a line b have been modified or not. This is modeled by tokens (k, b, m).
- The place CgrantW which receives a token from the local part when a permission for write is needed. This serves as a warning to the global part.

At initialization, the mapping in Cdir is undefined, all lines are invalid and, for convenience, all lines are clean. All cache controllers are idle.

Similarly the place CidleM controls the cache memory unit and the mutual exclusion between its local and global parts. The local part performs the actual load or store requested by the processor. The global part is active when data transfers from memory (place Nget) or to memory (place Nput) are to be done.

The one-way communication between the control and memory units of the cache consists of the following.

- The place CaccR which receives a token after the control recognizes a cache hit or after completion of the protocol for a cache miss. This token allows the memory unit to start processing in earnest the data transfer to/from the processor (place Binstp indicates additional parameters and BinstD holds the data).
- The FIFO place CputR which receives (k, b, a) tokens for lines to be transferred to memory.
- The places GgetR which receives a (k, b, a) token. The corresponding line being transferred from memory will then either be stored or ignored.

The primary *memory modules* are bank interleaved, that is, the higher bits of the address of a line determine the module in which it is stored. The lower bits of the address $\bar{a}$ determine the position of the line within the module.

The associated *controller* K_x is composed of a control unit and a memory unit. The control unit is divided into a request analysis unit and a return analysis unit. These two units can proceed concurrently but share all the information on the status of the lines controlled by K_x. In particular:

- The place Kgs is the representation of the bit map storing the states of the lines. It contains tokens of the form $(\bar{a}, g)$ with: $(g = w)$ for "PresentM," $(g = r)$ for "Present*," and $(g = z)$ for "Absent." Only one unit can access Kgs at a given time.
- Since we restrict the controller to process only one request for a given line at a time, there is a place, KreqW, which contains $\bar{a}$ tokens identifying these lines.
- Some of the protocols require queries to be sent to all caches. The request parameters will be held in the place KretW until the return analysis unit disposes of them.

Writes to the memory unit itself, that is, orders for transfers from a cache to the memory, are modeled by tokens $(k, x, \bar{a})$ in KputR while reads are similar tokens in KgetR.

DETAILED MODEL

We present now a detailed Petri Net model for the three-state cache coherence protocol. The three subnets—L-net, K-net and G-net—will be described in this order.

Local Instruction Processing by Caches

As noted previously, our model of the processor actions is limited to the orders it gives to its associated cache. The processing of these orders by the cache is shown in Figure 6-4. An access order by processor P_k to cache C_k for line a is represented by the transition Pinst putting a (k, a, t) token in place BinstR and a complementary token (k, f, d, c) in Binstp. The first token is used by the cache local control unit to access its directory and prepare the data access ($t = r$ for read, $t = w$ for write and exchange—in the case of a test and set type of instruction). The second token will be for the actual access (f is an access function—read, write, or exchange—d is a byte displacement with a, and c is a value in case of a store).

Note that at this time our model represents a simple sequential processor. When P_k is ready for a cache access, Pinst may fire. After the cache returns the desired value (or stores it), a token is put in BInstD, Pexec will fire, and P_k will be ready again. We have neglected the modeling of important internal actions that do not require the use of the cache, such as virtual address translation and effective address calculation that are embedded in the time between the firings of Pexec and Pinst. By making BinstR, Binstp, and BinstD be FIFO places, we can introduce pipelining. For our purposes, the processor action can be summarized by

$$k * \text{Pr} \mid \text{Pinst} > (k, a, t) * \text{BinstR} + (k, f, d, c) * \text{Binstp} + k * \text{Pw}$$

The local cache processing can be described in six steps of control followed by one step of access.

Step L1. The cache accepts the order (transition LAinst). The control unit of the cache must be idle, it must be waiting for a new access order and such an order must have been produced by P_k. In case of a concurrent request sent through the network, priority is given to that external request. This is modeled via an inhibitor arc issued from the place Nquer. The transition breaks the token into two parts. A token (k, a) used to access the cache directory (step L2) and a token (k, t) to check the access rights during the request analysis (step L5).

$$k * \text{CidleC} + k * \text{LinstW} + (k, a, t) * \text{BinstR} \mid \text{LAinst} > (k, a) * \text{LinstA}$$
$$+ (k, a) * \text{LreqA}$$

Step L2. This step checks whether the requested memory reference to a is in the cache, say in position b. Three cases are possible: (1) there is no mapping, that is, there is no (k, b, a) token in Cdir; (2) there is a mapping, that is a token (k, b, a) is present in Cdir and the mapping is valid, that is the token (k, b, s) in Cvb has a value for s of $s = v$; (3) as in (2) but the value for s is $s = i$, that is, the mapping is invalid. Note that in all three cases the contents of Cdir and Cvb are left untouched. These three cases translate into the following transition firings.

1. *There is a cache miss (transition Lmiss).* This is modeled by an inhibitor arc from Cdir with a set label $(k, \mathbf{B}(a), a)$ indicating the absence of a token

(k, b, a)($\mathbf{B}(a)$ represents the subset of the lines in the cache in which a could be mapped; thus it models the cache organization: direct mapping, set associative or fully associative). A token (k, a) is put in Lrep for the replacement algorithm (Step L3).

$$(k, a) * \text{LinstA} [ ] (k, \mathbf{B}(a), a) * \text{Cdir} = 0 \mid \text{Lmiss} > (k, a) * \text{Lrep}$$

2. *There is a valid hit (transition Lvalhit).* The next action will be to check the access rights (step L5).

$$(k, a) * \text{LinstA} + (k, b, a) * \text{Cdir} + (k, b, v) * \text{Cvb}$$
$$\mid \text{Lvalhit} > (k, b, a) * \text{Lbval} + (k, b, a) * \text{Cdir} + (k, b, v) * \text{Cvb}$$

3. *There is a hit but the line is now invalid (transition Linvhit).* This could have happened because of a PURGE, an UPDATE followed by an INVALIDATE, or an INVALIDATE. Since the line b is free there is no need for a replacement. Consequently, a (k, b, a) token is put in Lbinv to prepare for a REQUEST and a (k, b) token is put in LretD, since no analysis of the return of a replacement is needed (this will allow skipping of step L-4).

$$(k, a) * \text{LinstA} + (k, b, a) * \text{Cdir} + (k, b, i) * \text{Cvb}$$
$$\mid \text{Linvhit} > (k, b, a) * \text{Lbinv} + (k, b, a) * \text{Cdir} + (k, b, i) * \text{Cvb}$$

Step L3. This step models the replacement algorithm. The selection of the line o to be replaced by line a is not modeled explicitly but subsumed by the transition Lreplace. This transition puts a (k, b, a) token in Lbinv for a subsequent REQUEST (step L5), puts a (k, b, o, s) token in LretA for the potential write-back (step L4), replaces the (k, b, o) token in Cdir by a (k, b, a) token but at the same time places a (k, b, i) token in Cvb so that accesses to o and a will be respectively a miss and an invalid hit until a has been loaded.

$$(k, a) * \text{Lrep} + (k, b, o) * \text{Cdir} + (k, b, s) * \text{Cvb}$$
$$\mid \text{Lreplace} > (k, b, a) * \text{Linv} + (k, b, o, s) * \text{LretA} + (k, b, a) * \text{Cdir} + (k, b, i) * \text{Cvb}$$

Step L4. This step is performed only when a replacement is needed. The first task of this step is to determine whether line o has to be written-back. This decision is reached by examining the value of s in (k, b, o, s) and of m in the token (k, b, m) found in Cmb. There are three cases. At the completion of each of them a (k, b) token is sent to LretD to indicate the termination of this step. Also the token found in Cmb is reset to r (for convenience since its associated one in Cvb is invalid).

1. *Write-back (Transition LPret).* Line o is valid $(s = v)$ and modified $(m = w)$. A RETURN command is sent to K_y $(y = \hat{o})$ by placing a (k, o, i) token in Nret. At the same time, a (k, b, o) token is put in the FIFO place CputR, so that the actual data can be sent to the memory module y.

$$(k, b, o, v) * \text{LretA} + (k, b, w) * \text{Cmb}$$
$$\mid \text{LPret} > (k, o, i) * \text{Nret} + (k, b, o) * \text{CputR} + (k, b) * \text{LretD} + (k, b, r) * \text{Cmb}$$

2. *The line o is valid ($s = v$) and clean ($m = r$).* No interaction with memory is necessary since the line has global state "Present*."

$$(k, b, o, v) * \text{LretA} + (k, b, r) * \text{CMb} \,|\, \text{LFret} > (k, b) * \text{LretD} + (k, b, r) * \text{Cmb}$$

3. *No interaction with memory (Transition LNret).* Line o is invalid; this can happen at initialization time or after a PURGE or INVALIDATE.

$$(k, b, o, i) * \text{LretA} \,|\, \text{LNret} > (k, b) * \text{LretD}$$

Step L5. In this step we prepare potential REQUESTs to be sent to K_x. There are three possible cases: cache hit (with no REQUEST), cache miss with either a READ or WRITE REQUEST, and cache write hit on an unmodified line leading to a WRITE REQUEST.

1. *Cache hit with adequate rights (Transition LNreq).* If line b contains a valid copy of line a and the access request from the processor is read ($t = r$) or write on an already modified line ($t = m = w$) then all accessing is local. This is tested by the predicate $t < = m$. The (k, b, a) token in Lbval becomes a (k, b) token in CaccR, indicating to the memory unit of the cache that it has some work to do as soon as it becomes idle (cf. step L7). Similarly, the control unit is released for another access (token k in CidleC). The other data structures are left unchanged.

$$(k, t) * \text{LreqA} + (k, b, a) * \text{Lbval} + (k, b, m) * \text{Cmb} [\,] t < = m$$
$$| \text{LNreq} > (k, b) * \text{CaccR} + (k, b, m) * \text{Cmb} + k * \text{CidleC}$$

2. *Cache miss (Transition LRWreq).* In case of a cache miss as detected previously (token in Lbinv) either a READ REQUEST or a WRITE REQUEST must be sent to K_x. A (k, a, t) is placed in Nreq with t indicating read or write. A (k, b, a) token is moved to CgrantW for keeping the association between b and a when the data will be coming back (step G5). A k token is placed in LreqD for synchronization with the analysis step (step L4).

$$(k, t) * \text{LreqA} + (k, b, a) * \text{Lbinv}$$
$$| \text{LRWreq} > (k, a, t) * \text{Nreq} + (k, b, a) * \text{CgrantW} + k * \text{LreqD}$$

3. *Cache write hit on an unmodified line (Transition LMReq).* In this case, the controller has to give permission to the cache to write in that line (since copies of the same line might be in several other caches). This condition is tested by the predicate $t > m$ using the (k, t) token in LreqA and the (k, b, m) token in Cmb. The Write REQUEST command is similar to a cache write miss (except that we do not have to synchronize with the replacement algorithm). The grant analysis in the global part will determine whether the data transfer is necessary by testing the valid bit (step G5).

$$(k, t) * \text{LreqA} + (k, b, a) * \text{Lbinv} + (k, b, m) * \text{Cmb} [\,] t > m$$
$$| \text{LMreq} > (k, a, t) * \text{Nreq} + (k, b, a) * \text{CgrantW} + (k, b, m) * \text{Cmb} + k * \text{CidleC}$$

Step L6. This is simply a control step when both steps L4 and L5 have been needed.

$$k * \text{LreqD} + k^* \text{LretD} \mid \text{Lsynchr} > k * \text{CidleC}$$

Step L7. This step models the access to the memory part of the cache. It starts either immediately after the recognition of a cache hit with correct access rights or after a (maybe long) protocol involving a memory controller. It can occur concurrenly with parts of the replacement algorithm or write-backs of other lines.

Access starts when a token appears in CaccR (either from step L5 case 1 or from steps G5 or G8). An inhibitor arc from CaccR directed to the net modeling the cache global unit prevents any access to line b while it is read or written in the local unit. This is necessary so that the contents of the line are the same when access is granted and actually performed and prevents the line of being written back while it is accessed.

The transition Lacc performs the actual access to the data according to the parameters stored in Binstp. Results c' (the—partial—contents of the line in case of a read or dummy in case of a write) are stored in BinstD. A k token is put in LinstW to allow processing of a new P_k order and in CidleM to allow a data access by the cache local or global memory unit.

$$(k, f, d, c) * \text{Binstp} + (k, b) * \text{CaccR} + k * \text{CidleM}$$
$$\mid \text{Lacc} > (k, c') * \text{BinstD} + k * \text{LinstW} + k * \text{CidleM}$$

The processor is also put in the ready state.

$$(k, c') * \text{BinstD} + k * \text{Pw} \mid \text{Pexec} > k * \text{Pr}$$

Coherence Management by Memory Controllers

The role of a memory controller K_x is two-fold (refer to Fig. 6-6): one is to answer the requests from the caches for lines stored in the memory bank M_x and the other is to take care of the data sent by the caches either because it was asked by K_x or as the consequence of a replacement algorithm. Therefore, the controller is divided into a request analysis unit (available when a token x is present in KidleQ), a return analysis unit (token x in KidleR), and a memory unit for the interface with the memory module itself (token x in KidleM). The coherence management consists of two request steps, two return steps and two memory steps.

Step K1. Recall that the controller K_x controls the memory module which contains the lines a with $a = \hat{a}$, $\bar{a}$ and $x = \hat{a}$. In order to simplify the logic in the controller, we specify that only one request for a given line can be processed at a given time (this does not mean that requests for different lines cannot be processed concurrently). Thus, a small associative table KreqW is used to keep the identities of the lines that are processed by K_x. Before K_x accepts a new request, it checks that the given line is not already being acted upon, that is not in KreqW. If it is absent, the processing of the request starts by storing the line's identity in KreqW. The checking is modeled by an inhibitor arc from KreqW to the transition KAreq which, when it fires, signals the start of the decoding of the request.

The request itself is modeled by a $(k, \hat{a}, \bar{a}, t)$ token in Nreq, with t being the desired access type. This token is passed to KreqA.

$$(k, \hat{a}, \bar{a}, t) * \text{Nreq} + x * \text{KidleQ}[\,](x, \bar{a}) * \text{KreqW} = 0 \quad \text{and} \quad x = \hat{a}$$
$$|\text{KAreq} > (k, x, \bar{a}, t) * \text{KreqA} + (x, \bar{a}) * \text{KreqQ}$$

Step K2. In addition to managing the requests and returns, the controller keeps the global state of each line in its module. This state is stored in a bit-map modeled by the place Kgs. Because this bit-map is too large to fit in the same chip as the controller, it has to be considered as any off-chip memory. Hence concurrent access to it is forbidden. The indivisibility of transition firings adequately models this constraint.

There are five cases to consider, depending on the type of request (cf. the section "Protocols" earlier) and the global state g of the line.

The first two cases are when the request is for a line in state "PresentM" $(g = w)$. This implies that C_k incurred a cache miss. Only one copy of the line exists in some cache C_l. It has to be written back to memory before K_x can send a GRANT and the data to C_k. In order to do so either a PURGE or an UPDATE QUERY will be broadcast to all caches. At the same time, a token $(k, x, \hat{a})$ will be stored in an associative memory KretW, similar to KreqW, for the return analysis.

The broadcast command depends on whether a READ REQUEST $(t = r)$ or a WRITE REQUEST $(t = w)$ was sent when a cache miss was detected. The broadcast, to all caches except C_k, will be modeled by a set of tokens $(\text{N-}k, \hat{a}, \bar{a}, u)$ put in Nquer with $u = i$ for a PURGE $(t = w)$ and $u = v$ for an UPDATE QUERY $(t = r)$. This will be needed by the global part of the control unit of cache C_l during its analysis of the controller request (cf. Step G3). Depending on the value of t we have one of the following.

1. WRITE REQUEST (transition KPquer). We perform the operations outlined above with $u = i$. We also store a token in Kgs which will be used for the return analysis (cf. step. K4). We store an "Absent" state $(g = z)$, since it is conceptually what it should be at the return of the write-back.

$$(k, x, \bar{a}, w) * \text{KreqA} + (x, \bar{a}, w) * \text{Kgs}$$
$$|\text{KPquer} > (\text{N-}k, x, \bar{a}, i) * \text{Nquer} + (k, x, \bar{a}) * \text{KretW}$$
$$+ (x, \bar{a}, z) * \text{Kgs} + x * \text{KidleQ}$$

2. READ REQUEST (transition KUquer). We set $u = v$ and the state in Kgs to "Present*" $(g = r)$.

$$(k, x, \bar{a}, r) * \text{KreqA} + (x, \bar{a}, w) * \text{Kgs}$$
$$|\text{KUquer} > (\text{K-}k, x, \bar{a}, v) * \text{Nquer} + (k, x, \bar{a}) * \text{KretW}$$
$$+ (x, \bar{a}, r) * \text{Kgs} + x * \text{KidleQ}$$

In the other three cases there is no need for a write-back. A valid copy of the requested line exists in main memory. Therefore a copy of this data and permission to use it can be sent right away. However, the controller might have to concurrently broadcast an INVALIDATE QUERY if the line is in some state which implies potential sharing and the request is not a READ REQUEST.

We have decoupled, for modeling purposes, the messages indicating that the data is forthcoming (GRANT) and the actual sending of the data (PUT). The former is a READ or WRITE GRANT token in Ngrant; the latter will be taken care of by the memory unit and is prepared at this step by putting a $(k, x, \bar{a})$ token in KgetR. Depending on the request we have the following three cases.

1. *WRITE REQUEST on a line in state "Present*"* $(g = r)$. This can occur because of a write miss or a first write on a clean copy. An INVALIDATE is sent to all other caches (transition KIquer). A GRANT can be sent immediately, data is prepared, and the new state "PresentM" $(g = w)$ is stored.

$(k, x, \bar{a}, w) * KreqA + (x, \bar{a}, r) * Kgs$
$| \, KIreq > (N\text{-}k, x, \bar{a}, i) * Nquer + (k, x, \bar{a}, w) * Ngrant + (k, x, \bar{a}) * KgetR$
$$+ (x, \bar{a}, w) * Kgs + x * KidleQ$$

2. *No broadcast on a WRITE REQUEST (transition KNquerW).* When there is a WRITE REQUEST $(t = w)$ for a line that has not been accessed by any cache (state "Absent," $(g = z)$) the response of the controller is immediate: a GRANT i is sent, data is prepared, and the new global state can be stored as "PresentM" $(g = w)$.

$(k, x, \bar{a}, w) * KreqA + (x, \bar{a}, z) * Kgs$
$| \, KNquerW > (k, x, \bar{a}, w) * Ngrant + (k, x, \bar{a}) * KgetR$
$$+ (x, \bar{a}, w) * Kgs + x * KidleQ$$

3. *No broadcast on a READ REQUEST (transition KNquerR).* When there is a READ REQUEST $(t = r)$ for a line not in state "PresentM" $(g \neq w)$, we can proceed as above with a global state change to "Present*" $(g = r)$.

$(k, x, \bar{a}, w) * KreqA + (x, \bar{a}, g) * Kgs [\,] g \neq w$
$| \, KNquerR > (k, x, \bar{a}, r) * Ngrant + (k, x, \bar{a}) * KgetR$
$$+ (x, \bar{a}, r) * Kgs + x * KidleQ$$

Step K3. The transition KAret is similar to the transition KAreq except that it is triggered by RETURNs from the caches rather than by REQUESTs. These returns either are awaited as answers to PURGE or UPDATE QUERY messages or are spontaneously generated by the caches in the case of replacement algorithms (although these latter ones might become awaited if some request for them has been received while they were selected for replacement). The tokens modeling the RETURNs are of the form $(l, \hat{o}, \bar{o}, s)$ where l identifies the cache, $o = \hat{o}, \bar{o}$ the line, and s the new state for the line.

$$(l, \hat{o}, \bar{o}, s) * Nret + x * KidleR [\,] x = \hat{o} \, | \, KAret > (l, x, \bar{o}, s) * KretA$$

Step K4. This step performs the return analysis in the same sense that step K2 performed the request analysis. We consider four cases depending on whether the return was awaited or not, and on the type of command (cf. the RETURN table in "Protocols").

The first three cases correspond to awaited returns, that is, answers to PURGE or UPDATE QUERY messages. In these cases a $(k, x, \bar{a})$ token is present in KretW (recall transitions KPquer and KUquer). Thus, if the return for this line o is awaited a corresponding $(k, x, \bar{a})$ token is in KretW with $\bar{a} = \bar{o}$ and k identifying the requesting cache that is waiting. The state in the bit-map will allow to differentiate between a return from a PURGE and an UPDATE QUERY.

Once the return analysis has been performed, a GRANT can be sent to the requesting cache. The token $(k, x, \bar{a})$ can be moved from KretW to KgetR. In case the control and actual data messages are not in the same packet, we take care of the fact that the data might not yet have arrived by placing an $(l, x, \bar{o})$ token in KputR and an inhibitor arc from that place to transition KgetB, which sends the data to C_k. The token in KputR will be absorbed by KputB when the data is received from cache C_l. We have now the following three cases.

1. *Awaited message following an UPDATE RETURN (transition KUw).* This corresponds to state "Present*" $(g = r)$ and a valid line $(s = v)$. The state remains in state "Present*" since both C_k and C_l will have a copy of a.

$$(l, x, \bar{o}, v) * \text{KretA} + (x, \bar{o}, r) * \text{Kgs} + (k, x, \bar{o}) * \text{KretW}[\,] $$
$$= |\, \text{KUw} > (k, x, \bar{a}, r) * \text{Ngrant} + (k, x, \bar{a}) * \text{KgetR} + (l, x, \bar{o}) * \text{KputR}$$
$$+ (x, \bar{o}, r) * \text{Kgs} + x * \text{KidleR}$$

2. *Awaited message following a PURGE (transition KPw).* This corresponds to a line that has become invalid $(s = i)$ in cache C_l and a state that had been temporarily considered as "Absent" $(g = z)$. The state will be changed to state "PresentM" (g becomes w); C_k will have the only valid copy of a.

$$(l, x, \bar{o}, i) * \text{KretA} + (x, \bar{o}, z) * \text{Kgs} + (k, x, \bar{a}) * \text{KretW}[\,]\, \bar{a} = \bar{o}$$
$$|\, \text{KPw} > (k, x, \bar{a}, w) * \text{Ngrant} + (k, x, \bar{a}) * \text{KgetR} + (l, x, \bar{o}) * \text{KputR}$$
$$+ (x, \bar{o}, r) * \text{Kgs} + x * \text{KidleR}$$

3. *Replacement algorithm initiated while an UPDATE QUERY was sent by the controller for the same line (transition KPforUw).* This happens for parameters $s = i$ and a state "Present*" $(g = r)$. As shown earlier when explaining the transition Lreplace (step L3), cache C_l had immediately modified its directory after having selected o as the line to be replaced. When C_l received the UPDATE QUERY it ignored it because o was now invalid. Thus, the replacement must be considered as an anticipated answer to the QUERY. Note that a $(k, x, \bar{o})$ exists in KretW, so there is no real harm done; in fact, this is just a speed-up! The actions to be taken are similar to those above.

$$(l, x, \bar{o}, i) * \text{KretA} + (x, \bar{o}, r) * \text{Kgs} + (k, x, \bar{a}) * \text{KretW}[\,]\, \bar{a} = \bar{o}$$
$$|\, \text{KPforUw} > (k, x, \bar{a}, r) * \text{Ngrant} + (k, x, \bar{a}) * \text{Kget} + (l, x, \bar{o}) * \text{KputR}$$
$$+ (x, \bar{o}, r) * \text{Kgs} + x * \text{KidleR}$$

It remains to analyze the case when an unexpected return—a PURGE RETURN $(s = i)$ for a dirty replaced line—arrives at K_x. We are now in the situation where no corresponding token has been stored in KretW. This is checked implicitly by allowing the corresponding transition to fire only if the state is "PresentM" $(g = w)$, since all awaited RETURNs are for lines in state "Absent" or "Present*" as per step K2. This state is changed to "Absent" $(g$ becomes $z)$. Also, since data is forthcoming, an $(l, x, \bar{o})$ token is inserted in KputR. This cannot be overlooked, because a request for this line could be in progress concurrently and cannot be satisfied until the data has been written back.

$$(l, x, \bar{o}, i) * \text{KretA} + (x, \bar{o}, w) * \text{Kgs} \mid \text{KPnotw} > (l, x, \bar{o}) * \text{KputR}$$
$$+ (x, \bar{o}, z) * \text{Kgs} + x * \text{KidleR}$$

The last two steps are modeling the operations of the memory module per se. This module receives data to store from PURGE operations (PUT) and sends data to caches according to their requests (GET). Since these operations are not atomic and require adequate synchronization, we show how they are performed in two steps (begin: K5, and end: K6). A token x in KidleM prevents multiple accesses to the resource.

Step K5. The two transitions that activate the memory module differ by their synchronization conditions, which insure that the transfer of data that had to be written-back has been completed.

1. *Sending data to a cache (transition KgetB).* Recall that on a request for data by cache C_k a token $(k, x, \bar{a})$ was placed by the request analysis unit in KgetR. If a corresponding token $(l, x, \bar{a})$, sent by some cache $l \in N$, exists in KputR this means that some write-back for the same line is in progress. An inhibitor arc is used to prevent that the GET starts before the PUT is completed (i.e., before the actual write in memory is performed). As soon as the writing actually starts, the token in KputR will be removed but the unavailability of the memory unit prevents the GET of being started. As soon as the memory unit takes over control to send the data to the cache, another request for the same line can be accepted and the $(x, \bar{a})$ token is removed from the associative table KreqW. A token in Kget indicates the cache to which the line has to be sent as well as the fact that the memory is busy.

$$(k, x, \bar{a}) * \text{KgetR} + (x, \bar{a}) * \text{KreqW} + x * \text{KidleM} [\ ] (N, x, \bar{a}) * \text{KputR} = 0$$
$$\mid \text{KgetB} > (k, x, \bar{a}) * \text{Kget}$$

2. *Receiving data from a cache (transition KputB).* The line being transferred is represented by an $(l, \hat{o}, \bar{o}, C)$ token in Nput, where C is the contents of the line. An $(l, x, \bar{o})$ token exists in KputR, as explained previously, and it must be removed. A token is placed in Kput to indicate that the memory unit is busy.

$$(l, \hat{o}, \bar{o}, C) * \text{Nput} + (l, x, \bar{o}) * \text{KputR} + x * \text{KidleM} \mid \text{KputB} > x * \text{Kput}$$

Step K6. The last two transitions terminate the data management and free the memory unit.

1. *End of a write-back (transition KputE).* If a request is pending for that line, it can now proceed; that is, the memory unit will be activated at step K5 for a GET.

$$x * \text{Kput} \mid \text{KputE} > x * \text{KidleM}$$

2. *End of a transfer to a cache (from the controller's viewpoint; transition KgetE).* A $(k, x, \bar{a}, C)$ token is placed in Nget to denote that the contents C of line a must be transferred to cache k.

$$(k, x, \bar{a}) * \text{Kget} \mid \text{KgetE} > (k, x, \bar{a}, C) * \text{Nget} + x * \text{KidleM}$$

Global Transfer Management by Caches

In addition to answering the orders from its associated processor, a cache has to monitor the queries of the controllers and to interface with the interconnection network for the transfer of data. The global control unit needs to access the cache directory to answer the queries and the memory part of the cache for the data transfers.

The modeling of the global processing of the cache consists of three steps of query analysis and three steps of grant analysis in the control unit, and two steps of data transfers in the memory unit (cf. Fig. 6-5).

Step G1. At the arrival of a query message broadcast by some controller K_x, a token (k, a, u) is placed in Nquer with $u = i$ for a PURGE or INVALIDATE and $u = v$ for an UPDATE (cf. the QUERY table in "Protocols"). The transition GAquer will fire when the control unit is idle and will transfer the incoming token in GquerA.

$$(k, a, u) * \text{Nquer} + k * \text{CidleC} \mid \text{GAquer} > (k, a, u) * \text{GquerA}$$

Step G2. The query analysis starts by checking whether line a is mapped in some line b and if so what its local state is. We have the following three possible cases.

1. *Valid copy of a in the cache (transition Gvalhit).* In the case where a is mapped in the cache, modeled by the presence of a (k, b, a) token in Cdir, and the line is valid (token (k, b, v) in Cvb), then we need to change the local state to (k, b, u) in Cvb and prepare an eventual write-back for the return analysis by placing a (k, b, a, u) token in GretA.

$$(k, a, u) * \text{GquerA} + (k, b, a) * \text{Cdir} + (k, b, v) * \text{Cvb}$$
$$\mid \text{Gvalhit} > (k, b, a, u) * \text{GretA} + (k, b, a) * \text{Cdir} + (k, b, u) * \text{Cvb}$$

2. *Invalid copy of a in the cache (transition Ginvhit).* If line a had been previously valid in the cache and is invalidated without being replaced (for example, as a consequence of an instance of the previous case), then there is no need to answer the query, since for all practical purposes the line is not in the cache. The control unit can proceed with other tasks and the mapping of a is left unchanged.

$$(k, a, u) * \text{GquerA} + (k, b, a) * \text{Cdir} + (k, b, i) * \text{Cvb}$$
$$| \text{Ginvhit} > (k, b, a) * \text{Cdir} + (k, b, i) * \text{Cvb} + k * \text{CidleC}$$

3. *Line a is not in the cache (transition Gmiss).* This case is modeled by an inhibitor arc from Cdir (cf. step L2, case 1). Evidently no action is necessary.

$$(k, a, u) * \text{GquerA} [\,] (k, \mathbf{B}, a) * \text{Cdir} = 0 \,| \text{Gmiss} > k * \text{CidleC}$$

Step G3. In case of a valid hit, a return will occur depending on the value of the modified bit of line b. Thus there are two cases (after their respective completions, the control unit becomes idle).

1. *Line b has been modified (transition GPUret).* There is a (k, b, w) token in Cmb. A write-back of the line is always needed. This is modeled by a (k, a, u) token in Nret (cf. RETURN table in Section 3.2). At the same time this transfer of data is prepared by placing a (k, b, a) token in the FIFO place CputR to signal the cache memory unit. The modified bit is reset to r for consistency with an UPDATE QUERY. It is of no consequence in the case of PURGE since the line is now invalid.

$$(k, b, a, u) * \text{GretA} + (k, b, w) * \text{Cmb}$$
$$| \text{GPUret} > (k, a, u) * \text{Nret} + (k, b, a) * \text{CputR} + (k, b, r) * \text{Cmb} + k * \text{CidleC}$$

2. *Line b is clean (transition GNret).* The only query that could have been sent is INVALIDATE. The invalidation has been taken care of by transition Gvalhit.

$$(k, b, a, u) * \text{GretA} + (k, b, r) * \text{Cmb} \,| \text{GNret} > (k, b, r) * \text{Cmb} + k * \text{CidleC}$$

Step G3 completes the query analysis. The next three steps describe the grant analysis that is needed when the controller answers a previous request from the cache. The functions of the global control unit are to prepare the actual transfer of data and to notify the local control unit that it can proceed.

Step G4. This step is similar to step G1. Instead of a return token in Nquer, we have a grant token (k, a, g) in Ngrant, with the memory controller having set $g = r$ for a READ and $g = w$ for a WRITE (cf. the GRANT). The transition GAgrant moves the (k, a, g) token to GgrantA

$$(k, a, g) * \text{Ngrant} + k * \text{CidleC} \,| \text{GAgrant} > (k, a, g) * \text{GgrantA}$$

Step G5. A GRANT is always expected. When the cache made a request, a token (k, b, a) was placed in CgrantW (step L5). This token and the token in GgrantA are removed to place (k, b, a, g, s) token in GgrantS for the next step and a (k, b, v) token is placed in Cvb to validate the entry.

$$(k, a, g) * \text{GgrantA} + (k, b, a) * \text{CgrantW} + (k, b, s) * \text{Cvb}$$
$$| \text{GVbset} > (k, b, a, g, s) * \text{GgrantS} + (k, b, v) * \text{Cvb}$$

Step G6. This step terminates the grant analysis and stores the right access bit in Cmb.

$$(k, b, a, g, s) * \text{GgrantS} + (k, b, r) * \text{Cmb} \,| \text{Gmbset}$$
$$> (k, b, a, s) * \text{GgetR} + k * \text{CidleC}$$

The last two steps correspond to the management of the memory unit of the cache and are reminiscent of the similar actions at the memory controller level. Our modeling relies on a sufficient number of buffers for the line contents. Refined modeling of the interconnection network can take care of this assumption (see next section).

Step G7. The first part in the analysis of the data transfers depends on whether a line is written-back to memory, or is accepted from memory and stored, or whether finally its presence is immaterial. These three cases are distinguished by the presence of a (k, b, a) token in CputR or GgetR, and the validity of the line being transferred.

1. *Write-back of line b (transition GputB).* The presence of a token in CputR indicates that a write-back must be performed. A token is placed in Gput to that effect. However, there are two situations in which we want to wait for the transfer to take place. The first is when a PURGE for line a has arrived just after a local access to it by the processor. We want the access by the processor to have precedence, since there is no way to backtrack at that level. Therefore, we introduce an inhibitor arc from place CaccR. The second is when a WRITE REQUEST for (valid) line a has been followed by a PURGE to that same line. The data transfer for line a from the controller is in progress and must be completed (and the local access also done, since it will write into the line) before the (modified) line is sent back to the main memory module. This is modeled by an inhibitor arc from GgetR.

$$(k, b, a) * \text{CputR} + k * \text{CidleM}[\,](k, b, a, s) * \text{GgetR} = 0 \quad \text{and}$$
$$(k, b) * \text{CaccR} = 0 \mid \text{GputB} > (k, b, a) * \text{Gput}$$

2. *Transfer answering a cache miss (transition GgetR).* A (k, b, a, i) token in GgetR indicates that a cache miss (or an answer to a permission to write with an intervening PURGE) has occurred. The line transferred from the memory module—(k, a, c) token in Nget—is to be stored in the memory unit of the cache at the next step. However, it may happen that in the case of a replacement or a PURGE that the old contents of b, where a is to be loaded, have not been stored yet. Thus, an inhibitor arc delays the load in the cache while there remains a (k, b, o) token in CputR with $o = a$. This latter condition is important, because it avoids deadlock in the pathological case of the replacement for o—(k, b, o) token in CputR—being needed by the request for a—(k, b, a) token in CputR—while there is a simultaneous purge for a—another (k, b, a) token in CputR.

$$(k, b, a, i) * \text{GgetR} + (k, a, c) * \text{Nget} + k * \text{CidleM}[\,](k, b, a) * \text{CputR} = 0$$
$$\mid \text{GgetB} > (k, b) * \text{Gget}$$

3. *Transfer on a WRITE REQUEST for a write on clean line (transition Gdel).* This transfer is useless if the line is still valid. The (k, a, c) token in NGet is deleted and the cache memory unit can be released.

$$(k, b, a, v) * \text{GgetR} + (k, a, c) * \text{Nget} + k * \text{CidleM} \mid \text{Gdel} > (k, b) * \text{CaccR}$$
$$+ k * \text{CidleM}$$

Step G8. This step ends the processing in the memory unit and either sends the data in case of a PUT or stores it and activates the local unit in case of a GET.

1. Write-back (transition GputE). A token is placed in Nput.

$$(k, b, a) * \text{Gput} \mid \text{GputE} > (k, a, c) * \text{Nput} + k * \text{CidleM}$$

2. Store data in cache (transition GgetE). Now the local part can proceed.

$$(k, b) * \text{Gget} \mid \text{GgetE} > (k, b) * \text{CaccR} + k * \text{CidleM}$$

EXTENSIONS AND IMPROVEMENTS

There are two ways in which the models and the protocols can be extended: (1) build more parallelism and pipelining into the existing model and (2) design protocols with better performance. We give some examples of how this could be achieved but we do not dwell upon them in as much detail as in the previous section.

Pipelining in the Processor

Modifying the model to represent a pipelined processor is fairly simple. At the processor request level, it is sufficient to replace the places Pr, Pw, BinstR, Binstp, and BinstD by FIFO equivalents and to initialize Linstw with several tokens. But in order to be sure that instructions are not executing out of sequence, we stipulate that the pipe be stopped in the case of a needed interaction with memory (cache miss or permission to write). Thus, the pipelining is allowed to continue only when there is a valid hit. Note that this changes other parts of the local cache model; for example, we now have queues of requests for the cache memory unit (place CaccR must be a FIFO place) and a stage in the pipeline is devoted to dequeue these requests because the memory part of the cache can be accessed by only one request at a time.

There are other instances of pipelining and local (i.e., within a given unit) parallelism in our model. For example, the memory controllers can have requests for different lines in various stages of processing, the global parts of the caches can process queries and replacements at the same time, and even in the local part of the cache, replacement of dirty blocks and grant requests can proceed in parallel.

Interconnection Network

Concurrency is a major requirement in the interconnection network. In the model of the previous section, the network modeling was lumped into the "N" places (Nreq, Nret, etc.). A more detailed model is sketched here. We separate the cache-controller and the controller-cache communications by postulating two interconnection networks, one in each direction. Furthermore, we allow pipelin-

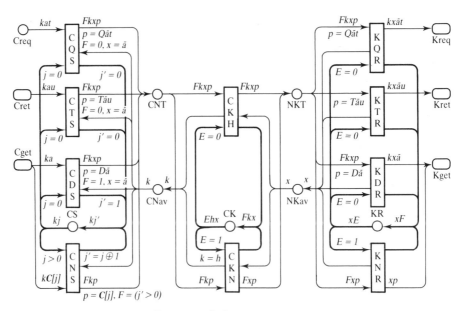

Figure 6-8. Cache to controller transmission.

ing of messages. These messages are either short (1 packet for an order) or long ($J + 1$ packets, 1 for the order and J, related to the line size, for data). Each packet carries a header bit F indicating whether this is the last packet in the message or not. The network itself (we show only the cache-controller network; the controller-cache would be modeled in the same fashion) is modeled as a sender unit, a transmission unit, and a reception unit (see Fig. 6-8).

Although we show only one transmission unit, it should be clear that it represents the whole switching structure between the sender units (cache controllers) and reception units (memory controllers). Another level of modeling would yield individual stages in a multistage interconnection network. A further refinement could show individual stages. The network can be seen as performing distribution and merging of messages from the sending units, an array of buffers represented by the places Creq, Cret, and Cput indexed by a cache number, to the reception units, another array of buffers (Kreq, Kret, Kput) indexed by controller numbers.

The sending unit's first task is to build the message by taking a token from either Creq, Cret (a short message), or from Cput (a long message) and to insert the appropriate F bits. In the case of a long message, the number of packets are counted modulo $J + 1$. The header packets are created by transitions CQS, CTS (Cache Request or Return Send if short) and CDS (Cache Data Send if long). These packets are of the form (F, k, x, p) with F being the termination bit, k the label of the sender cache, x the label of the destination controller, and p

depending on the type of message. If we have a request, p will be of the form $(Q, \bar{a}, t)$ with Q indicating a short Message and $t = r$ for a READ REQUEST or $t = w$ for a WRITE REQUEST (or permission to write). If we have a return, p will be of the form $(T, \bar{a}, a)$ with T indicating a short return message and $u = i$ for a PURGE or a replacement and $u = v$ for an UPDATE. If we have a data transmission (put), the p in the header will be $(D, \bar{a})$ with D for data. Following the header, in the case of a long message, are data packets of the form (F, k, p) with $p = C[j]$ being the contents of the jth word in the line $(j = 1, \ldots, J)$. The transmission of the data is performed by J firings of the CNS (Cache Network Send) transition.

The interface between the sending unit and the transmission unit is modeled through the two places CNT (Cache Network Tranmission) and CNav (Cache Network Available). The place CNT contains at most one (F, k, x, p) or (F, x, p) token per cache having sent a packet to transmit while the place CNav has one token per cache that is not transmitting.

The transmission unit computes the address of the destination, here a controller K_x although in the next level of refinement it could be another transmission unit (switch in the next stage). It allocates controllers to caches and performs the required transmission of the message, packet by packet. This is modeled as follows. The place CK contains tokens (E, h, x), one per controller K_x with h indicating which cache was last connected to K_x. New interconnections are allowed only when $E = 0$, that is when the previous message has been entirely transmitted. When this is true, the transition CKH may fire for any cache C_k requiring to transmit a header to K_x, this for any value of h in $(0, h, x)$. If $E = 1$, only transition CKN can fire and this for transmission from cache C_k where $k = h$ with C_h being the last cache which was connected to K_x. This insures that long messages are transmitted without interleaving of other messages.

Initially, all tokens in C_k have $E = 0$. When the header of the first message arrives at the transmission unit, transition CKH will fire, assuming that the controller can receive it (place NKav). The header bit F will be the new value for E and the cache identity k will be the value for h. If the message is short it will be transmitted directly to place NKT and the controller K_x will be "busy" until it has put the message in one of its internal FIFO queues. If the message is long, transition CKN will fire J times (until $E = 0$; i.e., until the header bit $F = 0$).

The reception unit works in a way very similar to the sending unit. Short messages are directed, via the Q, T, or D attributes of p, to either the Kreq or Kret queues (short messages for REQUESTs and RETURNs) or Kput queue (long messages for data).

The controller-cache network will be similar to the one just described except that it needs to include broadcasts. This could be modeled either by a special broadcast bus or by extending the functions of the transmission unit so that some transition fires only when all cache controllers are ready to receive. Although this might seem unrealistic, one should remember that at a lower level of modeling this latter condition translates simply into having the (two) switches in the next stage ready to receive.

Protocol Performance Improvements

The three-state protocol that we have described is not as efficient as one could hope for. There are many ways in which it could be improved. However, better performance, measured in terms of messages on the switch and/or amount of data transferred between caches and memory modules, does not come without a price: complexity in the state tables, or in the protocols, or in both.

A particular drawback in the current protocol is the need for broadcasts. The original solution to the cache coherence[13] did not have this problem, since the location of each copy of a line was known. But the price to pay, an $(n + 1)$-bit encoding of the state in the controller, is too extreme. However, there are a variety of schemes that can be used to minimize the number of broadcasts. We present one solution and allude to two others.

In most computations the amount of shared data is limited. Thus, many lines will be stored in only one cache. This fact can be encoded in the controller, with a fourth state that we call "Present1" (only one cache has a copy and it is clean).[14] We introduce two new message types. The first one is a new REQUEST, called MODIFY REQUEST, which is sent by a cache in an attempt to write a clean line for the first time. If the line is in state "Present1," the controller GRANTs the request without having to send the data and without broadcast, and changes the state to "PresentM." The second is a RETURN CLEAN message in case a clean line is being replaced. This allows a state change from "Present1" to "Absent." Thus, it appears that both our goals of limiting the number of messages (no broadcast) and the data transferred (no data in response to a REQUEST MODIFY, data that was discarded in our previous solution) have been attained at almost no price, since encoding of a fourth state comes for free in our two-bit table. The only additional complexity is two new message types and a very slightly more sophisticated local cache and memory controllers.

However, synchronization problems can arise because of these apparently trivial modifications. To ensure, correct protocols we must add more communication. This is best illustrated by the following example (see also Fig. 6-9).

Assume that at time t, a clean copy of line a is in cache C_i. The global state of a in K_x is "Present1." Now at time t, C_i decides to replace a and sends a RETURN CLEAN message to K_x to that effect. This message is going to be delayed on the network for some unknown reason (for example, many caches have requests or data to send to K_x) and will arrive at time T. In between, say at time t_1 (all times t_i will be less than T), cache C_j has a write miss on a. A WRITE REQUEST is sent to K_x and it arrives at t_2. Line a being in state "Present1," a broadcast INVALIDATE is sent, followed, say at t_3, by a GRANT and a change to state "PresentM." The INVALIDATE signal at C_i will be without effect because a has been replaced. When the GRANT arrives at C_j, a write is performed and a becomes dirty. Now, at t_4, C_j decides to replace a. A RETURN DIRTY is sent to K_x. Upon arrival at time t_5, the global state is changed to "Absent." To continue with this pathological case, assume that a new cache C_k requests a clean copy of a at time t_6. Since the global state is "Absent," this

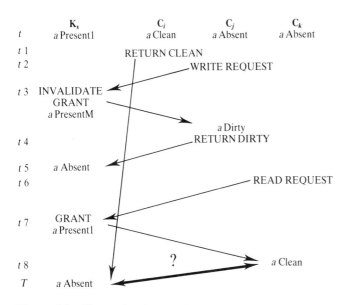

Figure 6-9. Ghosts signal example.

request is GRANTed immediately and the new global state becomes "Present1." Now, finally, the RETURN CLEAN from C_i arrives at time T. The controller seeing a RETURN CLEAN when the line is in state "Present1" changes the state to "Absent." But this is inconsistent, since a clean copy is cached in C_k. If, after time T, a new cache (or C_i or C_j for that matter) were to perform a WRITE REQUEST, the copy in C_k would not be invalidated, because the controller has an (erroneous) "Absent" global state.

There are several alternatives for remedying the situation. One of them is to require an acknowledgment on INVALIDATE. In the previous example, the RETURN CLEAN from C_i would play the role of this acknowledgement in the same way as a RETURN DIRTY plays it for a PURGE. Most often though, a specific ACKNOWLEDGMENT message would be needed. But in all cases we can see a slight increase in the traffic and the introduction of new message types. Whether this is justified to improve performance is an open question.

Another solution[25] to the limitation of broadcast is to encode more knowledge in the local cache. For example, we could have a local state indicating that, on a READ REQUEST, the line being loaded in the cache is the only one cached in the whole system. The permission to write could then be given locally with an accompanying message to the controller. However, it is easy to see that this will lead to race conditions.

Finally, we could strike a compromise between the 2-bit and the $(n + 1)$-bit encoding. For example, with $\log n$ bits we could indicate the location of the owning cache if the line is in state "Present1" or "PresentM," and the number of caches with copies of the line if in state "Present*." This would limit broadcasts and allow changes to state "Absent." The price is a larger encoding table and the design of a new protocol (on which we are actually working).

CONCLUSIONS

In this paper we have used a powerful modeling tool, Extended Petri Nets, to study the difficult problem of cache coherence in a multiprocessor system where the interconnection structure between processors and memory modules is not a single shared bus. The Petri Net modeling of the protocols is very valuable in understanding the difficulties that can arise in the synchronization and exchanges of messages, and in determining the hardware requirements of the caches and memory controllers.

By replacing the part of the model representing the memory controllers (K-net) by a simpler one modeling a shared bus, and by modifying the model of the cache interactions with the network (G-net) so that all bus transactions are considered (and most discarded), we could model a spectrum of shared-bus solutions (each solution corresponding to a pair K-net, G-net). Similarly, we could modify the G-net to include a "snooping" cache with a replication of the directory structure so that less message passing would exist between the L and G-nets (at the cost of a slightly more complex G-net). Finally, extensions to the memory controller with either the $\log n$ extra-status bits or the inclusion of an on-chip table keeping the ownership information for those lines most recently referenced could be modeled via modifications to the K-net only.

There are other applications to this model. First, we should be able to prove formally the correctness of this type of protocol. A serious effort in that direction has already begun.[26,27] Second, the model could be used as an entry point for a simulation program. Third, we could derive a Stochastic Petri Net[28-31] from the above Petri Net (with possible introduction of simplifying assumptions to facilitate the analysis). From the Stochastic Petri Net, we should be able to derive the optimal work periods for the caches. A comparison with the results of a simulation would provide some light on the use of Stochastic Petri Nets. Finally, the current model assumes that messages, that is, commands and data, always arrive at their destination. The model could be expanded to include acknowledgements and time-out mechanisms. Although this is not realistic for a shared-memory system, it is necessary if we want to extend the cache coherence paradigm to data coherence in networks. This exercise in modeling could lead to a useful tool for more complex protocol verification.

REFERENCES

1. Baer, J.-L. (1984). "Computer architecture," *Computer,* Vol. 17, No. 10, pp. 77–87.
2. Gerola, H. and R. Gomory (1984). "Computers in science and technology: Early indications," *Science,* Vol. 225, No. 4657, pp. 11–18.
3. Smith, A. J. (1982). "Cache memories," *Computing Surveys,* Vol. 14, No. 3, pp. 473–530.

4. Tucker, S. (1986). "The IBM 3090 System: An overview," *IBM Systems J.*, Vol. 25, No. 1, pp. 4–19.

5. Widdoes, L. C. (1980). "High-performance digital computer development in the S-1 project," *Proceedings IEEE Compcon,* 1980, pp. 282–291.

6. Gajski, D., D. Kuck, D. Lawrie, and A. Sameh (1983). "CEDAR: A large multiprocessor," *Computer Architecture News,* Vol. 11, March, pp. 7–11.

7. Gottlieb, A., R. Grishman, C. P. Kruskal, K. P. McAuliffe, L. Rudolph, and M. Snir (1983). "The NYU ultracomputer—Designing an MIMD shared memory parallel computer," *IEEE Trans. Computers,* Vol. C-32, No. 2, pp. 175–189.

8. Frank, S. J. (1984). "Tightly coupled multiprocessor systems speeds memory access times," *Electronics,* Vol. 57, No. 1, pp. 164–169.

9. Fielland, G. and D. Rodgers (1984). "32-bit computer system shares load equally among up to 12 processors," *Electronic Design,* Sep., pp. 153–168.

10. McCreight, E. (1984). "The Dragon Computer System. An early overview," Xerox Corp., Palo Alto, Ca.

11. Thacker, C., private communication.

12. Archibald, J. and J.-L. Baer (1986). "Cache coherence protocols: Evaluation using a multi-processor simulation model," *ACM Trans. Computer Systems,* Vol. 4, No. 4, pp. 273–298.

13. Censier, L. M. and P. Feautrier (1978). "A new solution to coherence problems in multicache systems," *IEEE Trans Computers,* Vol. C-27, No. 12, pp. 1112–1118.

14. Archibald, J. and J.-L. Baer (1984). "An economical solution to the cache coherence problem," *Proceedings 11th Int. Symp. on Computer Architecture,* pp. 355–362. IEEE Press.

15. Peterson, J. (1981). *Petri Net Theory and the Modeling of Systems.* Prentice-Hall, Englewood Cliffs, N.J.

16. Brams (1982). *Réseaux de Petri: Théorie et Pratique.* Masson, Paris.

17. Genrich, H. and K. Lautenbach (1979). "The analysis of distributed systems by means of predicate/transition nets," *Lecture Notes in Computer Science,* No. 70. Springer-Verlag, Berlin.

18. Genrich, H., K. Lautenbach, and P. Thiagarajan (1980). "Elements of general net theory," *Lecture Notes in Computer Science,* No. 84. Springer-Verlag, Berlin.

19. Jensen, K. (1981). "Coloured Petri Nets and the invariant method," *Theor. Comput. Sci.,* Vol. 14, No. 3, pp. 317–336.

20. Berthelot, G. and R. Terrat (1982). "Petri nets for the correctness of protocols," *IEEE Trans. Communications,* Vol. 30, No. 12, pp. 2497–2505.

21. Finkel, A. and G. Memmi (1983). "FIFO nets: A new model of parallel computation," *6th G.I. Conference on Theoretical Computing,* Dortmund, Jan. 1983.

22. Memmi, G. (1983). "Méthodes d'Analyse de Réseaux de Petri: Réseaux à Files et Applications aux Systèmes en Temps Réel," Thèse d'Etat, Université de Paris VI.

23. Kujansuu, R. and M. Lindqvist (1984). "Efficient algorithms for computing S-invariants for predicate/transition nets," *5th European Workshop on Application and Theory of Petri Nets,* Aarhus.

24. Vautherin, J. and G. Memmi (1984). "Computation of flows for unary predicate/transition nets," *5th European Workshop on Application and Theory of Petri Nets,* Aarhus.

25. Yen, W. C., D. W. Yen, and K.-S. Fu (1985). "Data coherence problem in a multicache system," *IEEE Trans. Computers,* Vol. C-34, Vol. 1, pp. 56–65.

26. Chatelain, C., C. Girault, and S. Haddad (1986). "Specification and properties of a cache coherence protocol model," *7th European Workshop on Application and Theory of Petri Nets,* Oxford.

27. Haddad, S. and C. Girault (1986). "Algebraic structure of flows or regular colored Petri nets," *Proceedings 7th European Workshop on Application and Theory of Petri Nets,* Oxford.

28. Molloy, M. (1982). "Performance modeling using stochastic Petri Nets," *IEEE Trans. Computers,* Vol. C-31, No. 9, pp. 913–917.

29. Natkin, S. (1980). "Réseaux de Petri stochastiques," Thèse de Doctorat 3ème Cycle, Université de Paris VI.

30. Holliday, M. and M. Vernon (1985). "A generalized timed Petri Net model for performance analysis," *Proc. Int. Workshop on Timed Petri Nets,* Torino, July 1985, 181–190.

31. Marsan, M. A., G. Chiola, and G. Conte (1985). "Generalized stochastic Petri Net models of multiprocessors with cache memories," *Proceedings 1st International Conference on Supercomputing Systems,* San Petersburg, Dec. 1985, pp. 690–696.

7

THE OPTIMIZATION OF A HIERARCHICAL MEMORY SYSTEM FOR HIGH-SPEED SCIENTIFIC COMPUTERS

J. A. Davis and A. V. Pohm

INTRODUCTION

In the last decade, technological advancements in the area of high-speed computing have broadened our vision of the set of tractable problems that can be effectively computed. Current Class VI systems (Table 7-1) have a typical scalar rating of around 20 MFLOPS and a nominal vector rating of 100 MFLOPS to 2 GFLOPS. However, the solution for some classes of problems, especially for applications in artificial intelligence and expert systems, will remain effectively intractable until high-speed computers can operate at rates that are several orders of magnitude faster than current systems, in the range of 10^{12} floating-point operations per second (1 TFLOP).

With each successive generation of hardware, performance improvements have been made in both processor and memory design; however, current systems, like their predecessors, are still constrained by the throughput of the memory system. Supercomputers operating at the 1 GFLOP rate may require a memory system to supply an operand every 10–20 nsec, for example. While it is quite feasible to build a small memory operating in that range, most scientific applications require massive amounts of memory, often more than 256 Mb. As an example of the careful attention paid to balancing memory bandwidth with processor speed, consider the Hitachi S-810 supercomputer.[1] Figure 7-1 shows the basic structure of the vector unit and its connections to main memory and

Table 7-1. Representative class VI systems

Computer	Vendor	Year	Rating (MFLOPS)	Memory (Mb)	Wordsize (bits)	Processors	Clock (nsec)
X-MP	Cray Research	1982	400–1600	8–64	64	1, 2, 4	9.5
Cray-2	Cray Research	1985	2000	128–256	64	4	4.1
S-810/20	Hitachi	1983	630	32–256	64	1	?
VP-400	Fujitsu	1985	1140	64	64	1	7
SX-2	NEC	1985	1300	128–256	64	1	6

extended storage. Figure 7-2 shows memory sizes and peak data transfer rates between memory and the vector unit. It is apparent that the S-810 achieves a high throughput by providing large, high-speed memory and high-capacity data channels. Of course, there are many other factors that affect the performance of supercomputers, including the degree to which a program can be "vectorized," data and control dependencies, pipeline startup delays, vector lengths, and so on. In this chapter we limit the scope of technological factors that impact throughput to those that relate to developing a high-speed memory module.

The size–speed paradox for memory design is well known: as memory systems become larger, the access time increases owing, in part, to increased interconnection delays.[2] There are two basic approaches to this problem.

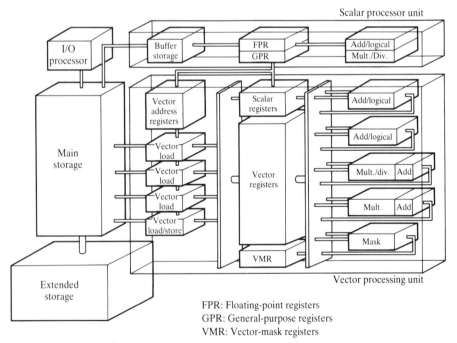

FPR: Floating-point registers
GPR: General-purpose registers
VMR: Vector-mask registers

Figure 7-1. The Hitachi S-810 supercomputer. (Reprinted from ref. 1 with permission from Elsevier Science Publishers, Amsterdam/New York.)

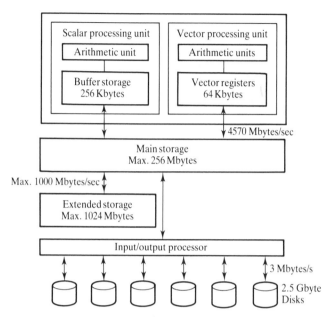

Figure 7-2. The Hitachi S-810 storage hierarchy. (Reprinted from ref. 1 with permission from Elsevier Science Publishers, Amsterdam/New York.)

1. *Faster technology.* The most obvious solution would seem to be to build larger, faster memory ICs, but there are several problems in this approach. First, there are physical limitations (e.g., the speed of light) that constrain what can be accomplished technologically. While we have not reached these limits yet, the rate of improvement is slowing down and the cost of achieving every small incremental improvement past some threshold becomes prohibitive. Second, higher-speed devices dissipate more heat, which often necessitates an elaborate cooling mechanism. Third, because high-speed devices consume more power and dissipate more heat, the density of the ICs is reduced, which increases the device interconnect delay time.

2. *Efficient organization.* A common approach to building fast memory systems is to use multiple interleaved memory modules, each module having an access time of about 40 nsec. The problem then becomes one of distributing memory accesses evenly through all modules so that data transfers can be performed in parallel. For example, a memory system composed of 64 interleaved modules should be able to provide 64 words every memory cycle. In practice, however, memory access patterns are application-dependent and it is difficult to distribute references so that *interference* does not occur.[3-7] The degradation in performance due to interference from randomly distributed requests is surprisingly large. As discussed in Hwang[8] and elsewhere, the effect of interference on memory bandwidth can easily be computed. With random requests made to M interleaved memory modules, we compute the *average*

bandwidth of the memory system by inspecting a string of K references. The probability that K is the length of a string of references to distinct memory modules is:

$$P(K) = \frac{K(M-1)}{M^K(M-K)}$$

The average bandwidth, $B(M)$, then becomes:

$$B(M) = \sum_{K=1}^{M} KP(K) = \sum_{K=1}^{M} \frac{K^2(M-1)}{M^K(M-K)}$$

As noted in Hwang,[8] $B(M)$ can be approximated by $M^{0.56}$. Thus, if we designed a system with $M = 64$ interleaved memory modules, the resulting bandwidth would be approximately the same as that of a system with 8 modules operating at full speed without interference. Therefore, although an interleaved organization does provide substantial speed improvement, there must still be an emphasis on improving the access time within the module.

The remainder of this chapter is concerned with optimizing the speed of a memory module within technological constraints by employing a hierarchical structure. The method developed will allow us to determine the optimal size of the first-level memory (the most critical) on the basis of the speed–size relationship for a given technology. The next section discusses important issues and tradeoffs for buffered memories and formulates a way to compute the effective access time for a multilevel hierarchy. The following section discusses the speed–size tradeoff for a given technology and computes the access time expressed in the speed–power product. Finally, we illustrate the results of the earlier sections for a hypothetical computer system.

HIERARCHICAL MEMORY STRUCTURE

In this section, we will review the structure of a linear multilevel memory hierarchy and the computation of the effective access time. Related factors such as the choice of replacement algorithm, formulation of the miss ratio, and determining the optimal number of levels in the hierarchy will be investigated.

Simply stated, the primary goal in building a memory hierarchy is to combine storage devices with differing speeds and capacities into a single storage unit in a way that optimizes access time with respect to size and cost. Our goal here is to minimize access time (rather than cost) while working within the physical constraints imposed by current technology. A simple block diagram for a three-level memory is shown in Figure 7-3. The first level in the hierarchy (closest to the CPU) provides the fastest access time, and each succeeding level is typically about 10 times slower and 10 times larger than the previous level. The goal is to reduce the effective access time of the entire hierarchy to that of the fastest level. This is possible when the stream of memory references has a high degree of *locality of reference,* so that all accessed words reside in level 1 memory. We make the following assumptions in subsequent discussions.

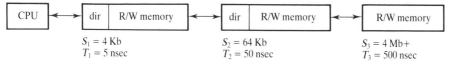

Figure 7-3. Three-level buffered (cache) memory hierarchy.

1. Each level in the hierarchy is separate and distinct, and is controlled by a separate cache directory. Each level may be built from different technology and will have a different *hit ratio*, size, and speed.
2. The hierarchy is *linear* in that the only path from a level K to the CPU is through all lower levels. Thus, the worst-case effective access time for the hierarchy is proportional to the summation of the access times for all levels between the CPU and the level containing the desired data.
3. The probability of finding the desired word in level K is given by the hit ratio, Hr_K. Note that Hr_J for a J-level hierarchy is 1.
4. The hierarchy is *fully nested*, so that a word found in level K of an N-level hierarchy is also present at all higher levels J, where $K < J \leqslant N$. Also, if a word is not found at level K, then it is not present in any lower level J, where $1 \leqslant J < K$.

The Structure of a Buffered Memory

A buffered memory usually consists of three major components: a directory, the data memory, and a priority update list (Fig. 7-4). The directory maintains a list

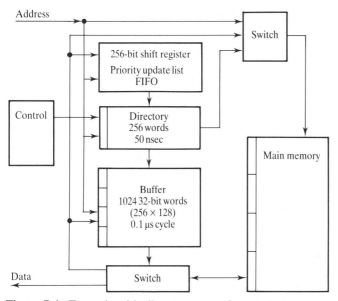

Figure 7-4. Example of buffered memory [A. V. Pohm and O. P. Agrawal, *High-Speed Memory Systems,* © 1983, p. 19 (A Reston Publication). Reprinted by permission of Prentice-Hall, Inc., Englewood Cliffs, N.J.]

of the addresses of words currently stored in the cache, and a flag for each word indicating whether it has been modified. Directories are usually implemented by a high-speed associative memory that can determine whether a word is resident in the cache in around 20–50 nsec. The data memory is simply the memory that is used to store the data. The priority update list refers to the hardware that selects the next word to be replaced when a new word is loaded into the cache.

There are four basic methods for mapping "user memory" into the cache address space.

1. *Direct mapping.* In the direct mapping scheme, each user memory address A maps into a cache address C such that $C = A$ modulo N, where N is the size of the cache. This method is simple and fast because the cache address can be directly determined from the physical address, and only one comparison is needed to determine if the desired word is at that location in the cache.

2. *Fully associative mapping.* In the fully associative organization, user data may reside anywhere in the cache. When a request for a word is presented to the cache, the user address is simultaneously compared to all cache entry tag fields. This method can provide a better access time than direct-mapped caches in cases where there is a high degree of contention between user memory address ranges for the same cache location. However, fully associative caches are more complicated and the search time is longer than for the direct-mapped cache.

3. *Set-associative mapping.* Set-associative mapping is a combination of direct mapping and fully associative mapping. In this scheme, words in the cache are organized in groups, and a user memory address A is mapped to group C such that $C = A$ modulo N, where N is the number of groups. At that point, all entries in the group are then compared to the user address in order to find a match. As noted in Hwang,[8] this compromise makes set-associative mapping popular.

4. *Sector mapping.* In the sector-mapping scheme, both user memory and cache memory are partitioned into sectors that contain several words. The relative placement of words within a sector remains the same; however, sectors may be located anywhere in the cache. When a request is made for a word that is not in the cache, the entire sector that contains the word is brought into the cache. The advantage of this organization is that the number of search tags is reduced and can therefore be searched quickly.

The choice of method of partitioning the cache is somewhat dependent on the pattern of memory references made by the user program. For our analysis, we have assumed the set-associative organization.

Another major factor relating to the performance of the system is the method used to select words in the cache for replacement. In the direct-mapped organization, there is no choice involved, but other organizations require that the cache logic control choose a word for replacement. There are several algorithms to choose from, including:

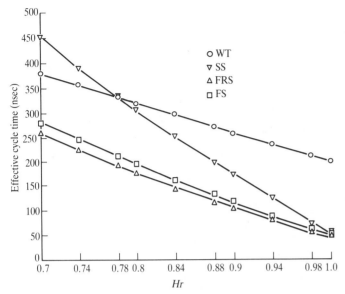

Figure 7-5. Effect of replacement algorithms on a 50 nsec buffer. Parameters: FR = 0.75, fraction reads; X = 0.25, fraction of words flagged; TDFR = 100 nsec, transfer time from memory to cache; TSRCH = 50 nsec, directory search time; TSRA = 300 nsec, main memory read time; TSWC = 750 nsec, main memory write cycle time; TSRC = 750 nsec, main memory read cycle time. [A. V. Pohm and O. P. Agrawal, *High-Speed Memory Systems,* © 1983, p. 34 (A Reston Publication). Reprinted by permission of Prentice-Hall, Inc., Englewood Cliffs, N.J.]

- Write Through (WT), or Store Through (ST)
- Simple Swap (SS), or Conflicting Usage Writeback (CUW)
- Flagged Swap (FS), or Flagged Conflicting Writeback (CUX)
- Flagged Register Swap (FRS)

The methods vary in complexity and performance. In Pohm,[9] the flagged swap algorithm is shown to provide good performance (Fig. 7-5), so we have chosen to use that method for replacement. A flow chart for the flagged swap is given in Figure 7-6. The flagged swap algorithm is also attractive because it can easily be modeled analytically for a variety of differing jobs by varying the parameters that specify the percentage of read operations and fraction of words modified.

Computing the Effective Access Time

In this section, we will derive a formula for computing the effective access time for a two- and three-level memory hierarchy. Referring to Figures 7-3 and 7-7, the memory hierarchy operates as follows.

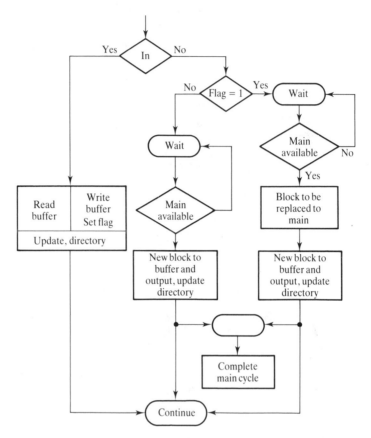

Figure 7-6. Algorithm for flagged swap replacement. [A. V. Pohm and O. P. Agrawal, *High-Speed Memory Systems,* © 1983, p. 40 (A Reston Publication). Reprinted by permission of Prentice-Hall, Inc., Englewood Cliffs, N.J.]

Search level 1. The CPU issues a read request for a word in the memory. The directory for the level-1 memory is searched, and if the word is found, it is returned to the CPU in one memory read (R_1).

Search level 2. If the word is not in level 1, the directory for level 2 is searched. If the word is in level 2, it must be copied to level 1 before passing it to the CPU in order to preserve the nesting rule. Before the words can be copied to level 1, one word currently located in level 1 must be discarded to make room for the new word. If the discarded word has been modified, then it must first be written back to level 2 (the nesting rule guarantees that there is room at level 2 for the word). Best-case timing for a level-2 read is $R_2 + W_1$, which is simply the time required to propagate the word from level 2 through level 1 to the CPU. Worst case is $(R_1 + W_2) + (R_2 + W_1)$, which includes the time needed to read a word from level 1 and write it to level 2.

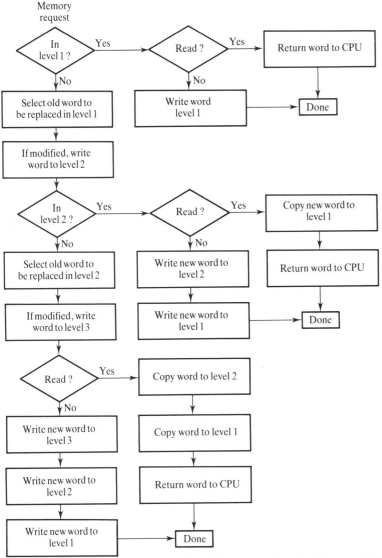

Figure 7-7. Operation of a three-level hierarchy. [A. V. Pohm and O. P. Agrawal, *High-Speed Memory Systems,* © 1983, p. 68 (A Reston Publication). Reprinted by permission of Prentice-Hall, Inc., Englewood Cliffs, N.J.]

Search level 3. If the word is not found in level 2, it is guaranteed to be in level 3. Before the word can be passed to the CPU, it must be copied to levels 2 and 1, replacing some other word, as described above. Best-case timing is $R_3 + W_2 + W_1$, which is the time needed to propagate the word to level 1. The worst case time is $(R_1 + W_2 + R_2 + W_3) + (R_3 + W_2 + W_1)$, which includes the time needed to replace a word in levels 1 and 2.

It can be seen that there are three key parameters that impact performance.

1. The probability of finding the desired word in a level (the hit ratio)
2. The ratio of reads to writes (memory write operations are typically slower)
3. The fraction of words that will need to be written to the next higher level during replacement (percentage flagged)

We can now formulate a method for computing the effective access time for a memory hierarchy. The effective access time (T_{eff}) for an n-level hierarchy is a function of the fault rate for each level such that

$$T_{\text{eff}} = \sum_{i=1}^{n} p_i \alpha_i$$

where p_i represents the "performance" of each level and α_i represents collected timing information. The performance can be described as a function of the input parameters that completely describe a level:

$$p_n = f(Fx_n, Hr_n, S_n, Tr_n, Tw_n, Ts_n, Rd_n)$$

where Fx = percentage of words flagged
    Hr = hit ratio
     S = size (in bits) of the memory
    Tr = read access time
    Tw = write cycle time
    Ts = directory search time
    Rd = percentage of accesses that are reads

Note that Tr, Tw, and Ts are determined by technology, and that Fx and Rd are determined experimentally. Our task is to balance S with Hr. A complete formulation for the effective access time for a two-level hierarchy is given by

$T_{\text{eff}} = Ts_1$ | level-1 directory search
                                                | level-1 hit:
$\quad + Hr_1(Tr_1 Rd_1 + (1 - Rd_1)Tw_1)$ | read/write level 1
                                                | level-1 miss:
$\quad + (1 - Hr_1)(Fx_1(Tr_1 + Tw_2)$ | replace old word in level 1
$\quad + Rd_1(Tr_2 + Tw_1)$ | copy new word to level 1
$\quad + (Rd_1 Tr_1 + (1 - Rd_1)Tw_1))$ | level-1 access

This can be easily extended to handle a three-level hierarchy:

$T_{\text{eff}} = Ts_1$ | level-1 directory search
                                                | level-1 hit:
$\quad + Hr_1(Tr_1 Rd_1 + (1 - Rd_1)Tw_1)$ | read/write level 1
                                                | level-1 miss:
$\quad + (1 - Hr_1)Ts_2$ | level-2 directory search
$\quad + (Hr_2 - Hr_1)(Fx_1(Tr_1 + Tw_2))$ | replace old word in level 1
$\quad + Rd_1(Tr_2 + Tw_1)$ | copy new word to level 1
$\quad + (Rd_1 Tr_1 + (1 - Rd_1)Tw_1)$ | level-1 access
                                                | level-2 miss

$$+ (1 - Hr_2)(Fx_2(Tr_2 + Tw_3)) \quad | \quad \text{replace old word in level 2}$$
$$+ Rd_2(Tr_3 + Tw_2) \quad | \quad \text{copy new word to level 2}$$
$$+ Fx_1(Tr_1 + Tw_2) \quad | \quad \text{replace old word in level 1}$$
$$+ Rd_1(Tr_2 + Tw_1) \quad | \quad \text{copy new word to level 1}$$
$$+ (Rd_1 Tr_1 + (1 - Rd_1)Tw_1) \quad | \quad \text{level 1 access}$$

The formulation for T_{eff} can be simplified by renaming the common subexpressions:

$$T_1' = Tr_1 * Rd_1 + Tw_1(1 - Rd_1)$$
$$T_2' = Fx_1(Tr_1 + Tw_2) + Rd_1(Tr_2 + Tw_1)$$
$$T_3' = Fx_2(Tr_2 + Tw_3) + Rd_2(Tr_3 + Tw_2)$$

If we write the hit ratio Hr_n as $1 - Mr_n$, the resulting expression for T_{eff} for a three-level hierarchy then becomes

$$T_{\text{eff}} = Ts_1 + T_1' + Ts_2 Mr_1 + T_2' Mr_1 + T_3' Mr_2 \qquad (7\text{-}1)$$

As an example, consider a three-level hierarchy with the following parameters:

Level 1	Level 2	Level 3
$Hr_1 = 0.90$	$Hr_2 = 0.98$	$Hr_3 = 1.0$
$Tr_1 = 50$ nsec	$Tr_2 = 300$ nsec	$Tr_3 = 1000$ nsec
$Tw_1 = 60$ nsec	$Tw_2 = 350$ nsec	$Tw_3 = 1000$ nsec
$Ts_1 = 50$ nsec	$Ts_2 = 50$ nsec	
$Rd_1 = 0.70$	$Rd_2 = 0.7$	
$Fx_1 = 0.50$	$Rx_2 = 0.50$	

We then compute:

$$T_1' = (50)(0.70) + 60 - (60)(0.7) = 53 \text{ nsec}$$
$$T_2' = (0.50)(50 + 350) + (0.70)(300 + 60) = 452 \text{ nsec}$$
$$T_3' = (0.50)(300 + 1000) + (0.70)(1000 + 350) = 1595 \text{ nsec}$$
$$T_{\text{eff}} = 50 + 53 + (50)(1 - 0.90) + (452)(1 - 0.90) + (1595)(1 - 0.98) = 185 \text{ nsec}$$

Thus, for these parameters, the effective access time for the hierarchy is 185 nsec, which is a reasonable performance improvement over level 2 or level 3 access times.

Hit Ratios as a Function of Cache Size

The probability of finding the desired word in the cache can be computed with a variety of analytical models. In general, the hit ratio will improve as the buffer becomes larger, up to the point where the entire data stream becomes buffer-resident. Increases in buffer size after that point do not improve performance. With most jobs, it is surprising how good the hit ratio is with relatively small buffers. For our analysis, we assume that the miss ratio is of the form

$$Mr = \frac{a_1}{(a_0 + W_b)^\alpha} \qquad (7\text{-}2)$$

and that the frequency of use of words by position in the buffer is

$$Z(f) = \frac{\alpha a_1}{(a_0 + fW_b)^{\alpha+1}}$$

where W_b is the size (in words) of a buffer that is f percent filled, and a_0, a_1, and α are appropriate constants that are determined experimentally.[9] Thus, for a completely filled buffer with W_b words, the incremental hit ratio is approximated by Eqn. (7-2). This approximation is known to have a good fit with experimental data when the constants are carefully chosen, as shown in Figure 7-8.[10,11] Both

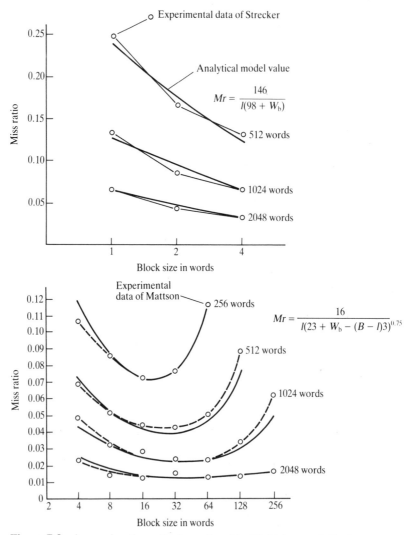

Figure 7-8. Approximation of miss ratio. [A. V. Pohm and O. P. Agrawal, *High-Speed Memory Systems,* © 1983, p. 69 (A Reston Publication). Reprinted by permission of Prentice-Hall, Inc., Englewood Cliffs, N.J.]

graphs show the close relationship between actual data and the approximation for Mr. In subsequent analysis, we assume that $\alpha \to 1$ and write the miss ratio for level i in terms of a memory containing C_i bits as

$$Mr_i = \frac{a_i}{C_i} \qquad (7\text{-}3)$$

Substituting Eqn. (7-3) into (7-1), the effective access time for a three-level hierarchy can be approximated by

$$T_{\text{eff}} = Ts_1 + T'_1 + Ts_2\frac{a_1}{C_1} + T'_2\frac{a_1}{C_1} + T'_3\frac{a_2}{C_2} \qquad (7\text{-}4)$$

Optimal Number of Levels

Typically, the number of levels in a hierarchy is determined by the cost of the memory system or concern for other factors such as system complexity. However, the number of levels can be treated as an unknown and optimized with respect to the effective access time of the hierarchy. In Chow,[12] two cases involving different system parameters are given and in both cases the optimal number of levels (N_{opt}) is proportional to the log of the size of the memory. Specially, Chow found

$$N_{\text{opt}} = \frac{\ln C_n}{(1 + \beta)}$$

where C_n is the capacity (size) of the hierarchy, and β is a constant of proportionality. For example, with $\beta \to 1$, the optimal number of levels for 10^6, 10^7, and 10^8 "words" is 7, 8, and 9, respectively.

For the remainder of the chapter, we have assumed a three-level hierarchy. The optimization techniques discussed in the next section are concerned mostly with the first-level memory, where the size–speed tradeoff is critical. In practice, the number of levels in the hierarchy is usually around four—even for large memory models—with the limiting factors being cost and reliability.

OPTIMIZING THE MEMORY HIERARCHY

In this section, we will demonstrate how the access time for a memory hierarchy can be optimized with respect to the size of the memory. As discussed in the Introduction, it is desirable to produce a memory system capable of providing an access time in the range of 5–10 nsec for relatively small block sizes (e.g., 100 words). The approach to optimizing the hierarchy centers around the following steps.

1. Formulate the effective access time for the hierarchy with the performance of each level (i.e., the miss ratio) expressed as a function of the size of the memory.
2. Formulate the access time for each level in the hierarchy expressed in terms of (a) the delay associated with driving signals onto and off the IC package and

(b) the access time characterized as a function of the speed–power product for a particular semiconductor technology.

3. Determine an optimal size for each level in the hierarchy. Note that size is a critical parameter in that larger memories will yield a better hit ratio, but they will also have more delay owing to an increased number of gates.

The effective access time for the hierarchy is given by Eqn. (7-4), and we will now compute the access time for individual levels in the hierarchy. The focus of the remainder of the paper is on the first-level memory, where the size–speed tradeoff is most critical. However, the same analysis can be used to determine the optimal sizes for subsequent levels in the hierarchy.

Deriving the Access Time for the First-Level Memory

The geometry for a level is shown in Figure 7-9. For the first level specifically, there are N_1 ICs for each bit position in a word, and each IC contains n_1 bits. Thus, the size of level 1 is $C_1 = N_1 n_1$ words, and each plane contains C_1 bits. In order to minimize IC interconnection delays, the memory is approximately organized as a $(\sqrt{N_1}/\sqrt{2}) \times \sqrt{2N_1}$ "square" array. One additional assumption is that packages will operate at the dissipation limit.

The access time for the first-level memory can be expressed as

$$T_1 = T_{ic} + (\sqrt{2N_1} - 1)T_w + T_{mux}$$

where T_{ic} is the cycle time for a memory IC, T_w is the wire delay per package, and T_{mux} is the multiplexer exclusive-or delay associated with line termination and bit correction. Note that the square geometry of the IC layout limits the worst-case delay to $2T_w\sqrt{N_1}/2$. We can further refine the formulation for T_1 by expressing T_{ic} in terms of a speed–power product (Δtp^{α} = constant) for a given technology, as shown by Vilkelis and Henle.[13] The cycle time for a memory IC then becomes

$$T_{ic} = T_{pk} + kn_1^{\alpha}$$

where T_{pk} is the delay driving into and off the package, and kn_1^{α} is the delay associated with the array of n_1 bits. The first-level memory access time T_1 is given by

$$T_1 = T_{pk} + kn_1^{\alpha} + (\sqrt{2N_1} - 1)T_w + T_{mux} \tag{7-5}$$

To find the minimum access time with respect to the number of bits per IC, we substitute $N_1 = C_1/n_1$ and solve $\partial T_1/\partial n_1 = 0$ to obtain

$$k\alpha n_i^{(\alpha-1)} - \frac{1}{2}\left(\frac{T_w\sqrt{2C_1}}{n_1^{3/2}}\right) = 0$$

$$n_1^{(\alpha+\frac{1}{2})} = \frac{\sqrt{C_1}}{\sqrt{2}}\frac{T_w}{k\alpha} \tag{7-6}$$

$$n_1 = \left(\frac{\sqrt{C_1}}{\sqrt{2}}\frac{T_w}{k\alpha}\right)^{2/(2\alpha+1)}$$

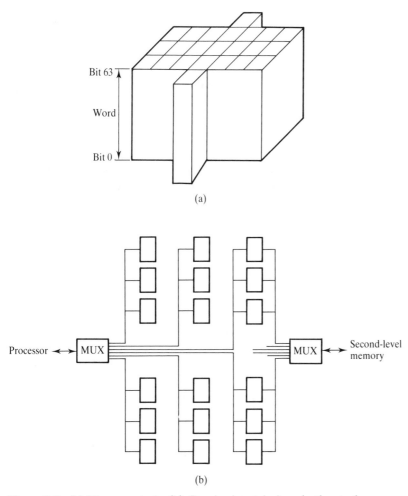

Bit 63

Word

Bit 0

(a)

Processor ←→ MUX ←→ MUX ←→ Second-level memory

(b)

Figure 7-9. (a) Memory stack. (b) One horizontal plane in the stack.

Substituting the optimum value for n_1 from Eqn. (7-6) into Eqn. (7-5), and using the identity $N_1 = C_1/n_1$, we obtain:

$$T_1 = T_{\text{mux}} + T_{\text{pk}} + k\left(\frac{\sqrt{C_1}}{\sqrt{2}}\frac{T_w}{k\alpha}\right)^{2\alpha/(2\alpha+1)}$$

$$+ T_w\left[\frac{2C_1}{(C_1/2)^{1/(2\alpha+1)}(T_w/k\alpha)^{1/(\alpha+\frac{1}{2})}}\right]^{1/2} - T_w$$

Rearranging terms:

$$T_1 = T_{\text{mux}} + T_{\text{pk}} + K_1(T_w^{2\alpha/(2\alpha+1)})(k^{1/\alpha}C_1)^{\alpha/(2\alpha+1)} - T_w$$

where

$$K_1 = (\alpha^{-2\alpha/(2\alpha+1)})(2^{-\alpha/(2\alpha+1)}) + (2^{(\alpha+1)/(2\alpha+1)})(\alpha^{1/(2\alpha+1)}) \qquad (7\text{-}7)$$

With collected constants, the expression for T_1 becomes

$$T_1 = T_{\text{is}} + K_2 C_1^\beta \qquad (7\text{-}8)$$

343

where:

$$T_{is} = T_{mux} + T_{pk} - T_w \tag{7-9}$$

$$K_2 = (T_w^{2\alpha/(2\alpha+1)})k^{1/(2\alpha+1)}K_1 \tag{7-10}$$

and

$$\beta = \frac{\alpha}{2\alpha + 1} \tag{7-11}$$

The formulation of the access time for the first level memory has now been optimized for minimum access time with respect to size. Selected parameters, such as T_w or α may be chosen to approximate current technology.

Determining the Optimal Size C_1

For simplicity, we assume that $Tr_i = Tw_i$ (i.e., $T_i = T'_i$), so that the effective access time for the hierarchy (Eqn. (7-4)) can be rewritten as

$$T_{eff} = Ts_1 + T_1 + Ts_2\frac{a_1}{C_1} + T'_2\frac{a_1}{C_1} + T'_3\frac{a_2}{C_2} \tag{7-12}$$

Substituting Eqn. (7-8) into Eqn. (7-12) yields

$$T_{eff} = Ts_1 + T_{is} + K_2C_1^\beta + Ts_2\frac{a_1}{C_1} + T'_2\frac{a_1}{C_1} + T'_3\frac{a_2}{C_2} \tag{7-13}$$

Note that the critical parameter with respect to the cycle time is the value of C_1. As C_1 is increased, the miss ratio is diminished but the delay is increased for the first-level memory. Optimizing with regard to the first level, one obtains

$$0 = \frac{\partial T_{eff}}{\partial C_1} = \beta K_2 C_1^{(\beta-1)} - \frac{a_1}{C_1^2}Ts_2 - \frac{a_1}{C_1^2}T'_2$$

$$C_1 = \left(\frac{a_1(T'_2 + Ts_2)}{\beta K_2}\right)^{1/(\beta+1)} \tag{7-14}$$

The optimal size for subsequent levels in the hierarchy can be determined using the same technique as used to find the optimal size for level 1. For example, the second-level memory is built from N_2 ICs and contains n_2 bits, and the access time is given by

$$T_2 = T_{is} + K_2C_2^\beta$$

where T_{is}, K_2, and β are defined in Eqns. (7-9), (7-10), and (7-11). Note that a different value for α will be chosen for level 2, reflecting a larger, slower memory. Assuming $Tr_2 = Tw_2$ (i.e., $T_2 = T'_2$), T_{eff} can be written as

$$T_{eff} = Ts_1 + T_1 + Ts_2\frac{a_1}{C_1} + T_{is} + K_2C_2^\beta\frac{a_1}{C_1} + T'_3\frac{a_2}{C_2}$$

Again, optimizing with regard to the second level, we obtain

$$0 = \frac{\partial T_{\text{eff}}}{\partial C_2} = \beta K_2 C_2^{(\beta-1)} \frac{a_1}{C_1} + T_3' \frac{a_2}{C_2^2}$$

$$C_2 = \left[\frac{a_2 T_3'}{\beta K_2 \dfrac{a_1}{C_1}} \right]^{1/(\beta+1)}$$

AN ILLUSTRATIVE EXAMPLE

In this section, we will determine the access time and size of the first-level memory for a typical three-level hierarchy (Fig. 7-3). Level-1 memory is described by parameters that approximate current best technology:

$$k = 4 \times 10^{-12}$$

$$T_w = 2 \times 10^{-10} \text{ sec/in}$$

$$\alpha = 0.75$$

$$a_1 = 100$$

$$T_{\text{pk}} = 1 \times 10^{-10} \text{ sec}$$

$$T_{\text{mux}} = 1 \times 10^{-10} \text{ sec}$$

We then compute intermediate constants:

$$\beta = 0.3$$

$$K_1 = 2.41$$

$$K_2 = 1 \times 10^{-10}$$

Assuming $T_2 = T_2' = 50$ nsec, and $Ts_2 = 50$ nsec, we can compute C_1 from Eqn. (7-14):

$$C_1 = \left[\frac{(100)(100 \times 10^{-9})}{(0.3)(1 \times 10^{-10})} \right]^{\frac{1}{1.3}}$$

$C_1 = 17\,716$ bits per plane, or words in level 1

From Eqn. (7-8), we compute the number of bits per IC:

$$n_1 = \left[\left(\frac{\sqrt{17\,716}}{\sqrt{2}} \right) \left(\frac{2 \times 10^{-10}}{(4 \times 10^{-12})(0.75)} \right) \right]^{\frac{2}{(2)(0.75)+1}}$$

$n_1 = 1092$ bits per IC

N_1 can be determined easily:

$$N_1 = \frac{C_1}{n_1} = 16 \text{ units}$$

From Eqn. (7-8), the access time for the first level memory is

$$T_1 = T_{is} + K_2 C_1^\beta$$
$$T_1 = (1 \times 10^{-10})(17\,716)^{0.3} = 1.8 \text{ nsec}$$

Thus, for the parameters assumed, an optimized first-level memory system would use approximately eight 1024-bit chips per bit position in the memory word and have a cycle time of around 2 nsec.

CONCLUSIONS

As access times for memories continue to decrease to the level at which gate and wire delay times are significant, it becomes crucial to optimize the memory with respect to speed and size. We have demonstrated one method that can be used to develop a memory hierarchy whose first level is of sufficient size and speed to support a high-speed supercomputer. The technique optimizes the chip and memory size for the first level of the memory hierarchy assuming that chip dissipation is a critical parameter. For current technology parameters, the first-level memory should involve 1024-bit IC chips in a 16 384-word memory.

ACKNOWLEDGMENTS

The authors would like to acknowledge the contributions of O. P. Agrawal and S. M. Sarwar to this chapter.

REFERENCES

1. Odaka, T., S. Nagashima, and S. Kawabe (1986). "Hitachi supercomputer S-810 array processor system," in *Supercomputers: Class VI Systems, Hardware and Software,* (ed. S. Fernback). Elsevier Science Publishing Company, New York.

2. Vacca, A. A. (1979). "Considerations for high-performance LSI applications," *Proceedings Spring COMPCON, 1979,* San Francisco, pp. 278–284.

3. Baskett, F. and A. J. Smith (1976). "Interference in multiprocessor computer systems with interleaved memory," *Commun. ACM,* Vol. 19, No. 6, pp. 327–334.

4. Cheung, T. and J. E. Smith (1984). "An analysis of the CRAY X-MP memory system," *Proceedings 1984 International Conference on Parallel Processors,* Chicago, pp. 499–505. IEEE Computer Society Press.

5. Hockney, R. W. and C. R. Jesshope (1981). *Parallel Computers: Architecture, Programming and Algorithms,* Adam Hilger, Bristol, UK.

6. Lawrie, D. H. and C. R. Vora (1982). "The prime memory system for array access," *IEEE Trans. Computers,* Vol. C-31, No. 5, pp. 435–442.

7. Yen, D. W. L., J. H. Patel, and E. S. Davidson (1982). "Memory interference in synchronous multiprocessor systems," *IEEE Trans. Computers,* Vol. C-31, No. 11, pp. 1116–1121.

8. Hwang, K. and F. A. Briggs (1984). *Computer Architecture and Parallel Processing.* McGraw-Hill, New York.

 9. Pohm, A. V. and O. P. Agrawal (1983). *High-Speed Memory Systems.* Reston Publishing Company, Reston, Va.

10. Mattson, R. L. (1971). "Evaluation of multilevel memories," *IEEE Trans. Magnetics,* Vol. MAG-7, pp. 814–819.

11. Strecker, W. D. (1976). "Cache memories for PDP-11 family computers," *Proceedings Third Annual Symposium on Computer Architecture, 1976,* New York, pp. 155–158.

12. Chow, C. K. (1974). "On optimization of storage hierarchies," *IBM J. Res. Dev.,* May 1974, pp. 194–203.

13. Vilkelis, W. V. and R. A. Henle (1979). "Performance vs. circuit package density," *Proceedings Spring COMPCON, 1979,* San Francisco, pp. 285–289.

8

TESTING TECHNIQUES FOR COMPLEX VLSI/WSI PROCESSING ARRAYS

F. Distante, M. G. Sami, and R. Stefanelli

INTRODUCTION

Testing of complex systems is becoming increasingly difficult: at the same time, its importance—always relevant—is nothing less than vital for such computing architectures (broadly classifiable as "supercomputing systems") as are dedicated to mission-critical applications or, at least, to applications that are very demanding in terms of credibility and reliability.

The problem has been made more difficult by the introduction of VLSI and now even of WSI devices. While complexity of internal functions makes "conventional" (structural) testing techniques very time-consuming and therefore quite costly, the low ratio of observation and control points (i.e., the external pins) in relation to such functions makes it very difficult to obtain an acceptable value of fault coverage.

A further point affecting a purely structural approach (which involves a close relationship between fault model, device description and test-pattern definition) derives from rapidly changing technology: that technologies forseen at the moment of system conception and at the time of actual implementation might be different. So usually are technologies and design rules adopted for different releases of the "same" device (i.e., characterized by identical functional description). It is obvious that an approach that allowed us to keep at least some of the test procedures unchanged, whatever the final implementation technology, would be more attractive.

"Behavioral" or "functional" testing approaches have been widely advocated in the past few years as interesting alternatives to structural testing techniques. Basically, behavioral testing was introduced for microprocessors (the first fairly complex integrated devices to be considered, since testing of very regular structures such as memories was practicable by ad hoc techniques). Behavioral testing[1-5] is based upon the description of a microprocessor's *instruction set* and, possibly, of its *control signals*, such as interrupt and so on. Testing aims at verifying whether the device is capable of correct operation, rather than at detecting the presence of possibly faulty parts. Some authors give a more restricted meaning to "functional" testing, adopting it for devices that are identified by a unique function or a limited set of functions (e.g., an ALU) but not by an instruction set; in that case again testing aims at verifying whether such functions are performed correctly.[6]

In ref. 7 the problem of behavioral testing was related to very complex devices—VLSI (or, possibly, wafer-scale) devices that can be described at a number of different abstraction levels by corresponding sets of "operators." A notable example of such a device would be an advanced "CISC-class" microprocessor endowed with a "silicon operating system," and whose behavior could be described at high level by a set of system primitives, at lower level by the set of "native" machine instructions used to implement the system primitives, and, at still lower level, by a set of microinstructions. The most relevant results achieved in ref. 7 allow us to state that a testing procedure for such a device can be designed at multiple abstraction levels, and that "optimum" test procedures for a lower level can be derived by suitably expanding an upper-level optimum testing procedure (optimality being defined with respect to error coverage and to testing ambiguity).

A particular instance of complex devices of great interest in the area of supercomputers is that of processing arrays: these structures, while already intrinsically important for classes of applications requiring supercomputing power (in particular, real-time signal processing), are potentially even more attractive because they are very well suited to VLSI or even WSI implementation. On the other hand, one of the main points that make processing arrays suitable for highly integrated implementation—the reduced number of I/O points as compared to the array's processing power—becomes a unfavorable factor as far as testing is concerned, since large sections of the device can be observed and/or controlled only in a very indirect way. This last fact will easily make the results of a test "ambiguous," allowing at least incorrect fault location or, worse, error masking and thus ultimately reliable testing.

It thus becomes necessary to identify an approach to testing of processing arrays that allows good coverage and reduces ambiguity without requiring unacceptably long testing times. Given the regularity of processing arrays, it appears reasonable to move towards dedicated or semidedicated techniques, rather then adopting totally general approaches. In particular, a limited amount of information on the internal structure may be quite useful in order to optimize all the figures of merit just outlined.

Liotta and Sciuto[8] presented a testing approach for a very particular class of processing arrays—namely, "pyramidal" arrays, dedicated to feature-extraction tasks in pattern recognition. These authors introduced some interesting concepts aimed at measuring the possibility of obtaining acceptable coverage and produced ambiguity figures. In fact, a two-level approach was suggested, first verifying the observability and controllability afforded at array level, and then proceeding to testing the individual processing elements in the array. The technique thus developed actually requires an intimate knowledge not only of the array interconnection structure but also of the communication interfaces (at least) of the single processing elements.

Here, after giving an overview of the general approach to behavioral testing of complex devices presented in ref. 7, we consider the case of systolic arrays. Some previous solutions are briefly examined, before we introduce a novel approach that is useful for the fault-tolerant array structure presented in ref. 9. There, an augmented interconnection structure is introduced in order to achieve reconfiguration in the presence of faulty processing elements. We will show that such an interconnection structure allows one to access independently all single processor elements (PEs), so that observability and controllability limits are those due to the intrinsic PE structure and are not degraded by the global system architecture. We will then define a testing strategy that keeps the overall testing time as low as possible; behavioral testing techniques will be used at the single-PE level, while only the structural information related to the interconnection network will be required at array level. Since the technique thus defined allows us not only to state whether the complete array is working but also to identify the single faulty PEs, it can also be used as a basis for static (production-time) reconfiguration of the array supported by the same interconnection network, thus ultimately enabling a better yield.

BEHAVIORAL TESTING: THE MULTIPLE-LEVEL APPROACH

Basically, the definition of behavioral testing for a "programmable" device, that is, a device characterized by a set of "instructions" or "operators" that it is capable of executing, is as follows.

> The aim is to demonstrate whether the device under test is capable of correctly executing all of its instructions, under all possible circumstances (e.g., in presence of specific control signals such as interrupts, etc.) and for any meaningful set of data.

A testing procedure will have to demonstrate the ability for correct execution for each of the various instructions. For each instruction in turn we will need a "test sequence" consisting of an initial "control" subsequence (possibly void) preloading all memories involved with suitable data, together with the instruction under test, and a final (possibly void) "observation" subsequence, making available to external observation all the results produced by the instruction under test. Whereas structural testing aims at identifying the set of faults that can occur in the given circuit, behavioral testing deals with errors rather than faults and it aims simply at verifying whether errors occur in any normal operation condition. Therefore, in particular, whenever structural redundancy masks some faults to the external observer, a no-error situation will be declared.

Such an approach is particularly attractive for user testing, since most often users do not have detailed information on the internal structure of complex VLSI devices, and moreover such structure is subject to changes with subsequent releases. It may be argued that behavioral testing of PEs yields a GO/NOGO type of result: this information, though, is more than adequate since no "repair" of faulty PEs is feasible, only substitution of the faulty ones with spares according to the fault tolerance strategy adopted.

Obviously, exhaustive testing would not be feasible. Consequently, several techniques have been presented that aim at definition of suitable testing procedures that allow us to "cover" the set of errors associated with instruction execution while requiring reasonably low processing time. A basic proposal on these lines was presented by Thatte and Abraham;[1] subsequently, several alternatives were presented, suggesting solutions as diverse as statistical testing,[10] and application-oriented testing.[4] In ref. 5 a formal approach was first introduced that allowed proof of the optimality of a given testing procedure with respect to two figures of merit, namely, error coverage and "ambiguity," defined as a measure of probability of either error masking or incorrect identification of errors. Instructions were described through the sequence of phases (corresponding to "microinstructions") involved in their execution, and the length of these sequences allowed evaluation of the complexity or, better, the "cardinality" of the instructions. It was proved that an ordering of instructions based upon their cardinality was the first step towards construction of optimum testing procedures, in which instructions of increasing cardinality were subjected to test.

Subsequent results[7] permitted a second, no less important, conclusion: that design of a testing procedure, considered as a succession of testing sequences related to all device instructions, can be independent of a technology-based fault model, and can thus be valid for different implementations of the same programmable device, as long as the definition of instructions remains unchanged. Obviously, the fault model—and therefore the technology—will reappear in the subsequent definition of the data sets to be used in conjunction with the testing sequences (in most instances the same instruction sequence will be repeated with a number of suitable data sets: this collection of data sets is here called a *data application*).

The introduction of very advanced CPUs or even of complex systems implemented as VLSI devices (such as dedicated arrays for signal processing) has increased the interest of a behavioral testing approach for a number of reasons. One is that the internal structure is of such complexity that structural testing would in any case be extremely time-consuming. More importantly, the ratio of control and observation points (i.e., the device pins) with increasing structural complexity becomes quite unfavorable when classical techniques are considered. Moreover, it may well be that a measure of internal redundancy has been added to achieve better production yield (it is well known that for larger chips yield tends to decrease): this makes it even more difficult for users to adopt classical structural testing techniques. On the other hand, the user needs to know only whether the device as a whole is performing correctly, not whether all its internal (possibly redundant) components are fault-free.

The adoption of "multiple abstraction levels" for description of such devices may often be a viable technique not only during the design phase (for which top-down approaches are by now well established), but also when the behavior of an existing device must be properly described. Consider, for instance, a VLSI systolic array, consisting of a number of identical PEs. Its behavior can be described as follows:

- at the highest (array) level, by a global command given to the whole array and involving a number of processing steps upon a full sequence of input data;
- at a lower (machine-instruction) level, by the sequence of elementary commands fed in parallel to all accessible PEs, together with single data;
- at a still lower level, by the sequence of microinstructions constituting each of the above commands.

It should be noticed that the number of observation and control points is the same at all three levels. Also, because the set of machine instructions is the same set that is used to make up the higher-level commands, passing to the second level does not introduce new actual possibilities of stimulating the device; the same is true for the microinstruction level (here, in fact, it is not even possible to execute single microinstructions in arbitrary fashion). What does vary is the granularity of observation, both as regards the values of results and as regards observation timing; at the highest level only the final results corresponding to the full input sequence will be compared for verification of correct operation, while at the machine-instruction level the results of a single processing step will be observed, and at the still lower level single-phase operation will be analyzed.

The problem then arises of whether testing procedures can be defined independently at different abstraction levels (in which case, obviously, it becomes necessary to identify an "optimum" abstraction level with respect to testing) or of identifying the relationships between testing procedures defined at different abstraction levels.

We summarize here the results presented in ref. 7 with reference to the most general case. We show how they can be applied to the specific case of systolic arrays in a later section.

Basically, a top-down approach to device description is envisioned: that is, a high abstraction level is considered first, then we proceed through subsequent refinements. It is assumed (as suggested above) that going from a high level of abstraction to lower ones, while increasing the detail of description, will not increase the number of observation and control points: this is obviously consistent with the assumption of a VLSI or WSI device. At any level, the device will be described by:

- a set of operators, each of which is defined by input and output operands and by the functions it performs;
- a set of sequencing information, detailing for each operator the phases through which operations are performed;
- a set of control and observation points.

Description of operators through a succession of phases (and of functions performed in such phases) allows us to evaluate the operator complexity and thus to associate with each operator a value of cardinality. When we pass from the description given at a high level of abstraction, l, to a more detailed description corresponding to level $l + 1$, each operator of level l will expand into a nonvoid set of operators of level $l + 1$. We denote this by

$$o_i^l \rightarrow \{o_{ij}^{l+1}\}$$

Assuming that a test procedure has been defined at level l, this will consist of a set of test sequences for all level-l operators; when we go to level $l + 1$, all operators in any given test sequence will independently expand into sets of level $l + 1$ operators. Let $A_i^l(o_i^l)$ be a test sequence for o, and let $\text{Ex}(A_i^l)$ be its expansion at level $l + 1$, defined as above. Sami et al.[7] demonstrated the following.

- For each operator contained in $\{o_j^i\}$ it is possible to find (at least) one test sequence contained in $\text{Ex}(A_i^l)$;
- Assuming that for o_i^l there are two different test sequences A_{i1}^l, A_{i2}^l of which A_{i1}^l is optimum, for each operator in the expansion of o_i^l it is possible to find in $\text{Ex}(A_{i2}^l)$ a test sequence that is not worse than any found in the expansion of $\text{Ex}(A_{i2}^l)$.

From the above, there arises the possibility of following a top-down approach in generation of test procedures: once an optimum level-l test procedure Pl has been found, optimum test procedures at level $l + 1$ can be found in the expansion of Pl—a fact that greatly reduces the environment (i.e., the set of alternative test procedures) in which the analysis must be performed.

So far, optimality of test procedures has been considered in a fairly abstract way; reference has been made to relative error coverage when comparing different test procedures belonging to the same abstraction level, but now there obviously arises the problem of relationships between coverage figures obtained at the various levels. Let us explore the problem of defining a "behavioral error" figure. Given the assumption that no information is available on structure and technology, error sets must again be defined with respect to device functionalities. Now, an error associated with execution of operator o^l may affect both "proper" functionalities (i.e., functionalities that appear in the nominal definition of o_i) and "improper" ones (those that do not appear in the nominal definition of the operator: we speak then of "improper" errors). Thus, for our previous example of a systolic array, a "wavefront load" array-level command will be associated with proper errors related to input buffers of the various PEs, but—owing, for example, to pattern sensitivity problems—it could also involve erroneous modification of other internal memories. Obviously, even "improper" functionalities must be improper only in relation to the given operator, but they must belong to the (larger) proper set of device functionalities that are taken into account when the device behavior is analyzed. This leads us to identify a "behavioral error coverage" figure, related to the set of faults that affect the behavior of the device rather than to the complete set of faults—a fact that, obviously, restricts the scope of testing and makes this approach suitable specifically for user testing rather than for manufacturing testing.

Clearly, by defining the behavioral coverage figure obtained through a given testing procedure as the ratio of identified errors with respect to the general set of possible errors, in a multiple-abstraction-level approach we can evaluate as many coverage figures as there are abstraction levels. We need to find out whether there is a relationship between the figures evaluated at the different levels and (possibly more important) we need to know, from this relationship, whether the coverage figures obtained are realistic or overly optimistic. In fact, if coverage appears to decrease with increasing level of detail, we conclude that high-level behavioral testing is not useful. It is evident, in fact, that the greater the detail of description, the nearer the error model gets to the structural fault model and thus the more realistic the error coverage figure becomes. An overly optimistic coverage figure may lead us to accept as correctly working a device that is actually faulty: thus, the high-level behavioral testing procedure ought to be followed (for all devices that have been found to be "acceptable") by lower-level testing procedures.

Now, it can be proved that, in order to achieve nondecreasing values of behavioral error coverage with increasing detail of description, the observability of functionalities that become "visible" with increasing detail must be as good as that of higher-level functionalities. Moreover, this holds only if functionalities are not redundant. This creates an obvious problem in the specific case of arrays of processing elements, such as systolic arrays, in which visibility of functionalities may be quite low: in fact, at the machine-instruction level there appear functionalities dealing with wavefront-loading into internal PEs that cannot (usually) be made directly observable at the external pins. Moreover, redundancy provided for fault-tolerance purposes (quite often present in such arrays) creates a further limitation to the "general" approach to behavioral testing: a solution can be reached by inserting observability at the single-PE level, but this in turn requires either good (ultimately, structural) knowledge of the PEs organization or else an augmented interconnection network. While some solutions in the first line will be briefly summarized in the next section, the section after that will deal in detail with the second type of approach, which can be adopted quite simply in arrays already provided with an augmented interconnection network for fault-tolerance purposes.

SOME APPROACHES TO TESTING
OF PROCESSING ARRAYS

In this section we will give a brief overview of different approaches to testing of array structures. We will consider only what are commonly denoted as "off-line" testing techniques, since our approach belongs to such a class.

Off-line testing differs from on-line testing in the fact that while the latter makes use of actual data (and possibly instructions) fed to the array during its normal computation, and is therefore concurrent with normal operation, the former implies use of ad hoc built sequences of data (and instructions) that will be processed by the array at testing time.

In the case of processing arrays, a third figure, heavily affecting time required for testing, must also be optimized in addition to error coverage and testing amgibuity: this is test parallelism.

If N being the number of cells in a rectangular array, the time required for testing is given by

$$T_{t_p} * \frac{N}{Pa}$$

where T_{t_p} is the time required to test a single cell and Pa is a positive integer $(1, \ldots, N)$ representing test parallelism.

As an example of some main lines of research, we will examine three different approaches to testing of arrays.

One approach consists in making use of the extreme regularity and repetitiveness of array architectures to achieve a sort of system-level self-testing, in which cells belonging to the same array test each other.

Preparata et al.[11] introduced the classical model for system-level fault diagnosis in distributed computer architectures. In this model, each unit in a set of $N > 2*t$ units is tested by at least t units (t-testability). The constraints of such an approach derive from the initial assumption that no more than t units are faulty in the system at the same time and that no two units test each other. The latter constraint was released by Hakimi and Amin,[12] who gave necessary and sufficient conditions on the connection assignments in such systems for unique identification of faulty units. The limit (t) of faulty cells accepted in both approaches derived from the fact that if a unit U and its t neighbors (performing the test) are faulty ($t + 1$ faulty units) it is not in any way possible to determine whether U is faulty. A crucial point is to determine how many of such cases of $t + 1$ faulty units are not diagnosable, since a strict application of such an approach to array structures limits the number of faulty cells to t irrespective of the number N of cells in the whole array.

Somani and Agrawal[13] define a "uniform open system" as a subsystem of $2*t + 1$ units consisting of its t neighbors at distance 1 and its t neighbors at distance 2 such that the total number of external edges is $t*(t - 1)$. The authors present an algorithm able to detect and locate up to $N*t/(2*t + 1)$ faulty units provided that the set of faulty units is acceptable. Acceptability of a set of faulty units implies that every uniform open system in the array contains no more than two faulty units.

A second possibility when implementing testing of array structures is to allow the array to operate upon test data sequences as it would upon actual data and then, in evaluating the results of computation, detect (and possibly locate) presence of faulty elements.

Elhuni et al.[14] considered the testing of two-dimensional arrays of combinatorial cells on the basis of results presented in ref. 15 concerning testing of ILA (iterative logic array) structures. The authors present an approach based on the idea of simultaneously testing cells at a given horizontal and vertical distance from each other. Two problems have to be faced: the difficulty of applying proper inputs to cells in an array of arbitrary dimensions and the need to propagate the effect of a fault to at least one observable output. To achieve such a goal, test sequences must be capable of regenerating themselves at the given horizontal and vertical intervals. Regeneration of test sequences means that while traveling through the array such sequences must periodically reconfigure themselves to their initial state. In this way, cells internal to the array may receive "external" data.

A cell in the array is characterized by a truth table (called a *flow table*[14]), which has a row for each x horizontal input and a column for each y vertical input. Each pair (x, y) is called a *state*. It is clear that if the flow table of a cell has m rows and n columns, to test an $N*M$ array we will need $MNmn(mn - 1)$ tests.[16] To achieve C-testability of two-dimensional arrays (meaning *constant testability*—i.e., the possibility of testing the array by a constant number of test vectors, independently of the number of cells), Elhuni et al.[14] prove that it is sufficient to add four rows and four columns (at most) to the state table of the basic cell of the array, so that given constraints on the transitions of an arbitrary cell are satisfied. Such constraints make sure that every pair of states is distinguishable, thus allowing a possible fault to propagate while passing through succeeding cells. They also show how, provided that the flow table is modified accordingly to the above, a $N*M$ array of combinational cells whose basic cell flow table has m rows and n columns can be tested in at most $(3m + 1)(3n + 1)(m + 4)(n + 4)$ steps. This is due to the fact that x inputs and y inputs are repeated every $(3m + 1)$ and $(3n + 1)$ cells at most and that the size of the modified table is at most $(m + 4)(n + 4)$.

As an example of a third possible approach, Liotta and Sciuto[8] presented a behavioral testing technique for array processors. Although applied to a pyramidal array architecture (PAPIA[18]), the approach is valid for a class of array processors characterized by given interconnection-network topologies, data-routing functions and instruction sets.

The proposed methodology exploits single-instruction multiple-data (SIMD) processing concepts to permit a formal and concise test strategy. This strategy is based on a functional model for the processing elements and the interconnection network. In the proposed approach, a systematic test-generation procedure is derived; its benefits consist in its independence of implementation detail, and

SIMD characterization that allows wavefront computation and a low order of testing complexity.

Testing is performed by sequences of instructions. These sequences are organized using two ordering criteria. The first criterion establishes the external observability and controllability of the instructions in the instruction set of each processing element. Concepts of frontier observability and controllability (either partial or complete) are then introduced and the whole set of instructions is partitioned into complete/partial observable/controllable classes. The second criterion uses instruction cardinality as a metric for evaluation of instruction complexity. This metric is used to combine instructions to form optimal test sequences.

The composition of a test sequence is based on two measures: fault coverage and ambiguity. Fault coverage is optimized by allowing only tested instructions to appear in a test sequence. Test ambiguity is minimized by subsequent refinements of fault coverage. This is achieved by increasing the complexity of a test sequence (adding tested instructions) and by defining a bounded error space (obtained from observability and controllability of each instruction in the sequence) for each test.

Single-cell test is possible following the "classical" behavioral testing techniques.[5,19] Cell-level instructions are thus ordered by increasing cardinality, and test sequences (and ultimately the cell-level test procedure) are designed following theorems presented in ref. 19.

A BEHAVIORAL TESTING TECHNIQUE FOR A CLASS OF FAULT-TOLERANT ARRAYS

As stated earlier, particular problems arise—concerning "credibility" of purely behavioral testing—when redundant arrays are considered. In fact, internal redundancy, adopted to achieve fault-tolerance through structural reconfiguration, further limits the confidence of high-level behavioral error coverage. In the present section, we introduce a technique that actually exploits part of the structural redundancy—namely, the *augmented interconnection network*—to enhance the confidence of behavioral testing. No structural information is necessary besides that concerning the augmented interconnection network itself.

We consider square $N * N$ arrays of processing elements, of the "wavefront-computation" type: actually, the technique can be extended without any difficulty to any rectangular array of the same class. Assuming computations to proceed in one wavefront direction only, the "nominal" array (i.e., an array without any fault-tolerance provisions) would have only $2 * N$ control points (the external inputs) and $2 * N$ observation points (the external outputs). Thus, while no PE would be directly observable and controllable, there would be $N^2 - 4 * N$ PEs that would be neither observable nor controllable directly, adding in a very considerable way to testing ambiguity (whatever the abstraction level chosen). Should redundant structures (allowing reconfiguration after fault) be adopted, if

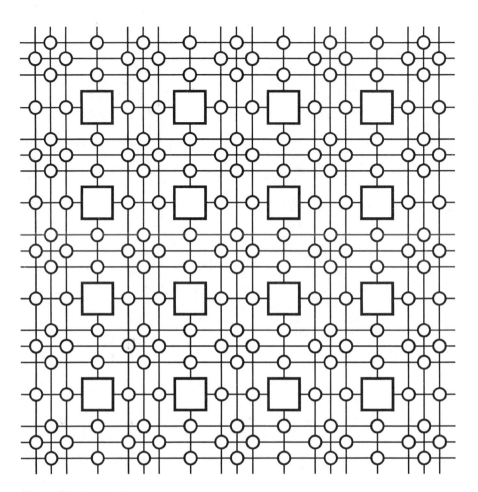

Figure 8-1. Fault-tolerant array.

their organization did not provide new access points to internal PEs, then obviously testing performances could not be improved; on the contrary, further fault masking would occur in dynamically (run-time) reconfigurable arrays.

Refer now to the basic structure represented in Figure 8-1: this is, again, a reconfigurable array, in which the basic interconnection structure has been substituted by an augmented interconnection network consisting of triple-switched busses between any pair of rows (columns) of PEs (details of the switch organization are given in Fig. 8-2).

The switched-bus technique has been advocated by other authors[20] for supporting reconfiguration of a systolic or wavefront array. The particular network represented in Figure 8-1 has been proved[9] to be capable of supporting fairly complex reconfiguration algorithms, leading to good probability of survival to faults with a reduced level of redundancy. Each switch can be positioned in

Figure 8-2. Switch organization for the fault-tolerant array.

one of the three states depicted in Figure 8-2. We assume the possibility of externally setting the state of individual switches during testing (such setting is performed by a host computer).

Actually, the network introduced consists of two distinct systems of busses and switches: two of the vertical busses and one of the horizontal busses only support transfers of data between horizontal inputs and outputs of interconnected PEs, while the remaining busses support "vertical" data transfers. We[21] have shown that some reconfiguration algorithms can be supported by different switched-bus strucures: while explicitly related to the organization in Figure 8-1, the present discussion can be easily extended to such networks.

The interconnection network here considered can be adopted for static (i.e., production-time) reconfiguration as well as for run-time reconfiguration. In this second instance, both self-reconfiguration (controlled by on-chip dedicated circuits) and host-driven reconfiguration could be envisioned. Now, if we consider production-time reconfiguration or host-driven reconfiguration, external testing of the array will be taken into account, and such testing needs to be capable not only of asserting whether the array as a whole is properly working but also of exactly locating the faulty PEs in order to confine them and introduce a suitable spare in the array operation. Moreover, concurrent multiple faults must be taken into account; that is, it is not possible to accept a stringent limitation such as "sequentiality in time" of failures.

All the above conditions might make other approaches to testing of arrays unacceptable whenever exact fault location was not guaranteed. Of course, the same would also be true for purely behavioral high-level testing. In fact, array-level behavioral testing could only indicate whether the device as a whole was properly operating, but it would not provide information sufficient to locate the faulty PEs. Rather, a suitable PE-level technique must be adopted: the testing procedure as a whole will do the following.

- It will first test the interconnection network—the busses and switches. It can hardly be expected to reach the single switch or bus segment, but the whole interconnection network is required to be working properly in order to support the reconfiguration algorithm (which provides only for faulty PEs). Thus, the constraint on this part of the testing procedure does not decrease its usefulness.

- It will properly set the switches so as to use the interconnection network to make single PEs visible externally for testing.

Then, assuming that an optimum machine-instruction-level test sequence has been already identified to test the single PE, we need to define an optimum algorithm by which the greatest number of PEs will be tested in parallel at each iteration. To this end, we must further assume that, in addition to the input/output pins of the various border PEs, the terminations of all busses can be reached by the external tester. While this possibility is obviously available for end-of-production testing, it may not be true for run-time (albeit off-line) testing. In the latter case, more often only "nominal" I/O terminations will be available, with redundant busses made acceptable through suitable multiplexing/demultiplexing. This would lead to inevitable decrease in test parallelism, but it would not otherwise invalidate the present discussion.

The second phase of the testing procedure will then consist in a sequence of switch settings or "configurations" performed by means of suitable external commands (the switches having already been proved to be correctly working). Each such command will make a subset of PEs directly controllable and observable from external pins, and all such PEs will be subject in parallel to PE-level testing. In this way, any faulty PE in the subset will be completely located. When the PE-level testing procedure has been completed, a new configuration command will be given and the net subset of PEs will be tested; this procedure will be iterated until all PEs have been tested and all faults thereby have been located.

Obviously, an algorithm for configuration sequencing is optimum if it allows minimization of the number of iterations. Another figure of merit is that of regularity for the topology of the subset under test at each iteration. This factor is mandatory if a general sequencing algorithm has to be created, and it is also related to the problem of actually setting the network switches without introducing an excessive burden on the control system.

Test of the Interconnection Network

Since switch configurations also are programmable by means of external commands, a behavioral approach is reasonable also for testing the interconnection network. Actually, we use a "mixed-mode" technique, exploiting a measure of structural information and affording a guarantee that the network itself (rather than simply its behavior) has been completely tested.

In this case, a test procedure will consist of a set of configuration commands (issued by a host computer) that will set all the switches in the network in given positions. In Figure 8-3 a possible test procedure comprising four different test actions is presented.

We assume that switches can be affected by three fault modes: stuck-at-0 (s-a-0), stuck-at-1 (s-a-1) (at the output pins of the switch), and stuck-at-state (s-a-state). Stuck-at-state means that the switch does not react to positioning

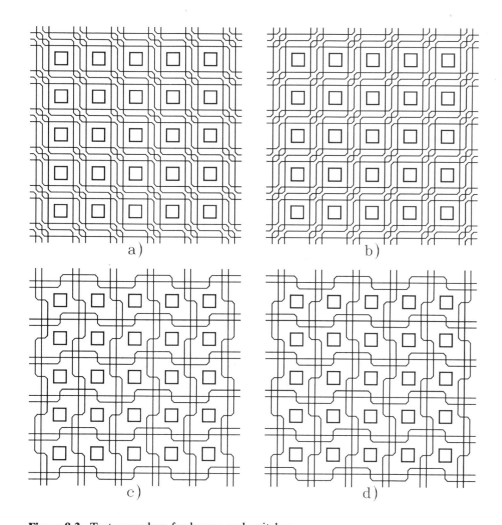

Figure 8-3. Test procedure for busses and switches.

commands. We also suppose that:

1. No two inputs can merge into a single output.
2. A single input cannot split into two outputs.

Comparing the test procedures presented in Figure 8-3 and the switch distribution around a PE (detailed in Fig. 8-4), it could be argued that it is in no way possible to test the s-a-state of switch A for path a–b. Actually a complete test of switch A is performed since if statements 1 and 2 are respected, the test action of Figure 8-3(c) will automatically test path a–b; s-a-0/1 of pin "b" will be controlled by the test action of Figure 8-3(d).

Another problem may concern testing of bus segments connecting PE pins

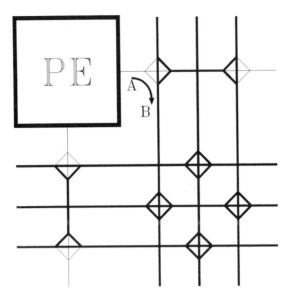

Figure 8-4. Details of connection of PEs to the interconnection network.

with the interconnection network and the possibility of s-a-0/1 of the pin of the switch performing such connection (pin "a" of switch A in Fig. 8-4). Such possible faults can be properly tested during the subsequent phase 2, that is, at the time of PE testing. It should be noticed that any such fault will be seen as though the interconnected PE is faulty. This is actually quite acceptable for the following reasons.

1. If the PE itself is faulty, it is logically disconnected from array operation and the directly connected lines will not support any data transfer.
2. If the PE itself is working properly but the directly connected lines are faulty or the input pin of the switch is affected by a s-a-0/1 fault, the PE must again be removed because otherwise its input–output data would be transferred over faulty lines.

It can easily be verified that our testing procedure gives complete coverage for single-fault occurrences; for multiple faults, data applications need to be designed so as to minimize the probability of error masking. Actually, occurrences of error masking are very limited; only a few peculiar distributions, not only of relative fault positions but also of fault types, would lead to such problems. We are at present studying optimization of test patterns in relation to this point.

Obviously, this approach does not provide any methodology for locating the fault. On the other hand, it has been already said that the whole interconnection network must work properly in order to suppport reconfiguration algorithms, so that error location (or the possibility of erroneous error location) loses its significance.

Testing of PEs

Consider the array structure represented in Figure 8-1. Suppose all "frontier" busses (i.e., all busses surrounding the array) have been removed, since such set of busses does not in any way affect the degree of observability or controllability of the internal cells of the array. If N is the number of cells in each row and column, we will have a total of $((N-1)+(N-1))*3 = 6N-6$ busses in the whole structure. Each bus provides two "external pins" (i.e., its terminals) so that the interconnection network will provide a total of $12N-12$ pins. If we also consider the external pins proper of the $4N$ boundary PEs, we obtain a total of $16N-12$ external pins.

It can easily be seen that

$$16N-12 < 4N2 \qquad \text{for } N > 3$$

which means that (as expected) not enough pins are available to simultaneously test all PEs. The maximum number of simultaneously testable PEs is given by the ratio

$$\frac{\text{Available external pins}}{\text{No. of pins per PE}}$$

that is, $(16N-12)/4 = 4N-3$. Hence, the whole array can be tested in trunc $(N^2/(4N-3)) \simeq N/4$ steps.

This is actually unrealistic, since two other factors have to be taken into account.

1. The external pins proper of the boundary PEs can be used only while testing such PEs.
2. Not only pin availability but also possible bus conflicts must be taken into account.

To consider the first factor, let us suppose that an initial step tests all boundary PEs. Cells still to be tested will then be $(N-2)^2$. We said that the external pins provided by the interconnection network are $12N-12$, so in this case the maximum number of simultaneously testable PEs will be $(12N-12)/4 = 3N-3$. Thus, the rest of the array will be tested in trunc$((N^2)/(3N-3)) \simeq N/3$ steps.

To avoid bus conflict, we assign a set of horizontal and vertical busses, respectively, to each row and column of cells of the array. The maximum number of busses that can be devoted to each column is

$$\frac{3(N-1)}{N} < 3 \tag{8-1}$$

On the other hand, column 1 and column N do not need any vertical bus to control and observe, respectively, their left (col. 1) and right (col. N) pins, as these are already external. As far as vertical bus requirements are concerned, these two columns behave as one. Then Eqn. (8-1) will change to

$$\frac{3(N-1)}{(N-1)} = 3 \qquad (8\text{-}2)$$

Assigning horizontal pins of PEs to vertical busses, three PEs per column (or, better, their horizontal pins) will be simultaneously controlled and observed. Extending the above to the rows, it follows immediately that avoidance of bus conflicts does not affect test parallelism, so that testing of the array can be performed in $N/3$ steps.

Provided the constraint of having at most three PEs under test per row and per column is satisfied, different topologies of PEs under test may be identified in the array. It has been said that regularity of the topology of the set of PEs under

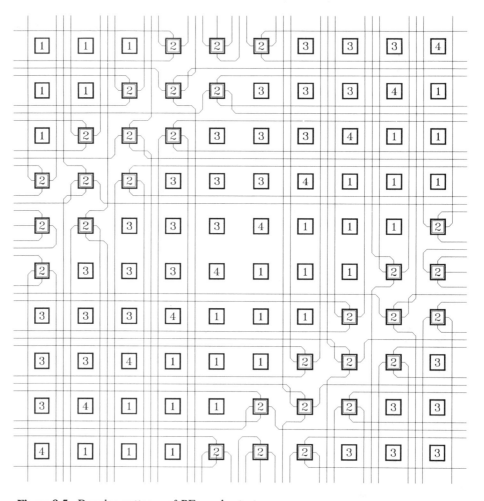

Figure 8-5. Regular patterns of PEs under test.

test is an important parameter. If regularity is kept, it will be possible to design an easy and iterative algorithm for switch positioning at each new step of the test that minimizes computational overhead. An example of such regular structure is given in Figure 8-5. The following rules are used to obtain it.

- in each row, three PEs are tested at each step; vertical input and output of the leftmost PE are transferred to the left-hand border, those of the rightmost PE go to the right-hand border, those of the center PE go, respectively, to the upper and to the lower border.
- For horizontal input and output of the three PEs in each column, rules are identical to the above ones with suitable transposition.

In Figure 8-5, a $10 * 10$ sample array is considered: four subsequent testing steps are necessary in this case (the numbers inside each PE denote the associated test step). In particular, Figure 8-5 shows the conditions at step 2, by highlighting PEs tested during step 2.

CONCLUDING REMARKS AND FURTHER DEVELOPMENTS

A technique that allows us to extend behavioral testing approaches to testing of processing arrays has been presented. Since in this case of such arrays a measure of error location is also necessary for achieving subsequent fault-tolerance through reconfiguration, the behavioral testing philosophy must be partially modified; the criterion presented here makes use of the augmented interconnection network used in a class of fault-tolerant processing arrays to give exact location of faulty PEs in the array.

Besides optimizing error coverage and confining test ambiguity at the level of individual PEs, the procedure here presented also optimizes the time required for testing the complete array.

The technique discussed here requires detailed structural information only on the interconnection network, while individual PEs need be represented only by behavioral information. At present, the definition of optimum testing procedure is being refined as regards data applications capable of minimizing the probability of error-masking when the interconnection network is tested.

A further line of development followed by the authors is extension of the present technique to on-line testing, performed at run time; then, in particular, the applicability of testing techniques to an array that has already undergone reconfiguration after faults has to be considered.

REFERENCES

1. Thatte, S. M. and J. A. Abraham (1978). "Methodology for functional level testing of microprocessors," *Proc. FTCS-8, Toulouse,* pp. 90–95.
2. Thatte, S. M. and J. A. Abraham (1979). "Test generation for general microprocessors architectures," *Proc. FTCS-9, Madison,* pp. 203–210.

3. Thatte, S. M. and J. A. Abraham (1980). "Test generation for microprocessors," *IEEE Trans. Computers,* Vol. C-29, No. 6, pp. 429–441.

4. Saucier, G. and R. Velazco (1981). "Microprocessor functional testing using deterministic test patterns," *Proc. EUROMICRO 7, Paris,* pp. 221–231.

5. Annaratone, M. and M. G. Sami (1982). "An approach to functional testing of microprocessors," *Proc. FTCS-12, Santa Monica,* pp. 158–164.

6. Kwok-Woon Lai (1981). "Functional testing of digital systems," PhD thesis, Carnegie-Mellon University, Pittsburgh.

7. Sami, M. G., M. Bedina, and F. Distante (1984). "A formal approach to computer-assisted generation of functional test patterns for VLSI devices," *Proc. ISCAS 84, Montreal,* pp. 19–23.

8. Liotta, L. and D. Sciuto (1985). "An approach to functional testing of array processors," *IAPR 85, Rapallo,* pp. 65–74.

9. Sami, M. G. and R. Stefanelli (1986). "Fault-tolerance and functional reconfiguration in VLSI arrays," *Proc. ISCAS 86, San Jose,* Vol. 2, pp. 643–648.

10. David, R., P. Thevenod-Fosse, and D. Jourdan (1981). "Etude du test aléatoire des microprocessuers," *Projet Pilote SURF, Rapport Final,* pp. 78–195, Convention I.R.I.A.

11. Preparata, F. P., G. Metze, and R. T. Chien (1967). "On the connection assignment problem of diagnosable systems," *IEEE Trans. Electronic Computers,* Vol. EC16, No. 6, p. 848.

12. Hakimi, S. L. and A. T. Amin (1974). "Characterization of connection assignment of diagnosable systems," *IEEE Trans. Computers,* Vol. C-23, pp. 86–88.

13. Somani, A. K. and V. K. Agrawal (1984). "System level diagnosis in systolic systems," *ICCAD '84, Port Chester,* pp. 445–450.

14. Elhuni, H., A. Vergis and L. Kinney (1986). "C-testability of two-dimensional arrays of combinatorial cells," *ICCAD 86,* pp. 74–76.

15. Parthasarthy, R. and S. M. Reddy (1981). "A testable design for iterative logic arrays," *IEEE Trans. Computers,* Vol. C-30, pp. 833–841.

16. Friedman, A. D. and P. R. Menon (1971). *Fault Detection in Digital Circuits.* Prentice-Hall, Englewood Cliffs, N.J.

17. Kautz, W. H. (1967). "Testing for faults in cullular logic arrays," *Proceedings 8th Annual Symposium on Switching Automata Theory,* pp. 161–174.

18. Cantoni, V., D. Ferretti, S. Levialdi and R. Stefanelli (1985). "PAPIA: A pyramidal architecture for image processing," *Proc. ARITH 7, Urbana.*

19. Bedina, M., F. Distante and M. G. Sami (1983). "A Petri-net model for microprocessor functional test," *J. d'electronique,* pp. 149–160.

20. Hedlund, K. (1986). "Reconfiguration strategy and technique in the WASP machine," *Proceedings IFIP Workshop on Wafer-Scale Integration, Grenoble,* pp. 89–97.

21. Sami, M. G. and R. Stefanelli (1986). "Fault-tolerant computing approaches," Internal Report 86-2, Department of Electronics, Politecnico di Milano.

PART THREE

Supercomputer Computations, Applications, and Performance Evaluations

---

9

SUPERCOMPUTERS AND MULTIPARAMETER SYSTEMS THEORY

John Jones, Jr.

INTRODUCTION

The main purpose of this work is to establish basic mathematical theory and algorithms applicable to the treatment of equations that arise in the study of multidimensional and multiparameter systems theory. The nature of such problems requires the use of larger-scale computers owing to the need for large storage capacity, large numbers of arithmetic computations, and the complexity of algorithms needed to solve such problems containing multiparameters. In the model simulation of highly complex and very large systems containing such multiparameters there are usually certain values of the parameters that have the property that small variations in these parameters lead to significant changes in the qualitative behavior of the solutions.

Examples of such behavior occur in the changes of parameters in large electrical networks that may cause overloads in parts of the circuit and eventually failure of the system, in fatigue in structural properties of materials in a region that may reflect overloads, and in failures or collapse in mechanical systems, and so on.

Such values of multiparameters need to be identified, since they are informative as to the nature and qualities of the performance of multiparameter systems near and at such parameters. These critical parameters may provide a connection between local and global properties of sets of solutions. Methods that analyze the behavior of solutions of nonlinear problems containing multiparameters are necessary because the number of nonlinear problems of interest for which one may find explicit solutions is very small.

The advancement in the computational capabilities of supercomputing systems has greatly enhanced our understanding of nonlinear problems and has also shown the complexity of even the most apparently simple nonlinear multiparameter systems. Such problems arise in the study of transport theory, optimal control theory, electrical network theory, filtering theory, stochastic processes, dynamic programming, dynamical systems, integral equations, reliability theory, CAD/CAM problems arising in the design of systems, and elsewhere.

In this chapter a development of the notion of various generalized inverses of matrices having multiparameter elements is first made; this is followed by a treatment of the basic notions of the equivalence and similarity of pairs of such matrices and solutions of sets of linear matrix equations; and finally solutions of nonlinear Riccati matrix differential equations whose coefficient matrices contain multiparameters are carried out. Algorithms are also established that are needed to program such problems. Examples are given that illustrate the techniques used.

COMPUTATION OF VARIOUS GENERALIZED INVERSES OF MULTIPARAMETER MATRICES

In this section a study is made of various generalized inverses of $m \times n$ multiparameter matrices. Methods of computing various generalized inverses are established. Methods used to compute such matrices avoid the classical approach for constant matrices of using the singular-valued decomposition of a matrix to compute the generalized inverse A^+ due to Penrose (1955).

Let capital letters denote $m \times n$ matrices belonging to a vector space of $m \times n$ matrices whose elements are polynomials in the multiparameters $\theta = (\theta_1, \theta_2, \ldots, \theta_n)$ with complex numbers as coefficients. The Moore–Penrose[7] (Penrose 1955) unique generalized inverse of any $m \times n$ constant matrix A is the unique matrix A^+ satisfying the following four conditions: (i) $AA^+A = A$; (ii) $A^+AA^+ = A^+$; (iii) $(AA^+)^* = AA^+$; (iv) $(A^+A)^* = A^+A$, where the symbol * denotes the conjugate-transpose of a matrix.

For any multiparameter matrix A, subscripts will denote the cases of the above equations; that is, A_1 satisfies condition (i), A_2 satisfies condition (ii), A_3 satisfies condition (iii), and so on, and in general $A_{1,2,3,4} = A^+$ satisfies all four conditions above. Various combinations of these four conditions are of use in applications. Penrose (1955) only considered the case of constant matrices, where $A_{1,2,3,4} = A^+$ is unique. In the case of multiparameter matrices, not all four conditions may be satisfied for any given matrix over the ring $R(\theta) = \mathscr{C}(\theta)$ of polynomials. Different applications require different combinations of the four conditions above, which is a feature that reduces computer time for certain classes of problems. For example, in the case of generalized Newton–Raphson methods for solving sets of nonlinear equations, $A_{1,2}$ is used instead of $A_{1,2,3,4}$.

Generalized Inverses A_1 of a Multiparameter Matrix A

Theorem 1. Let A be a multiparameter matrix of constant rank r, then the pair of augmented matrices

$$\begin{bmatrix} A & I \\ I & 0 \end{bmatrix}, \quad \begin{bmatrix} \bar{I} & R \\ C & 0 \end{bmatrix} \tag{9-1}$$

are equivalent over $R(\theta) = \mathscr{C}(\theta)$, where R, C are nonsingular (unimodular, i.e., $|R|$, $|C| \neq 0$) defined by

$$R = \begin{bmatrix} T \\ M \end{bmatrix}; \quad C = [SN] \tag{9-2}$$

such that

$$RAC = \begin{bmatrix} T \\ M \end{bmatrix} A[SN] = \begin{bmatrix} I_r & 0 \\ 0 & 0 \end{bmatrix} = \bar{I} \tag{9-3}$$

Proof. For any multiparameter matrix A having constant rank $r > 0$ there exist unimodular matrices R, C as above such that A can be reduced to (3), where A has rank r and I_r is an $r \times r$ identity matrix. Then

$$\begin{bmatrix} R & I \\ I & 0 \end{bmatrix}\begin{bmatrix} A & I \\ I & 0 \end{bmatrix}\begin{bmatrix} C & I \\ I & 0 \end{bmatrix} = \begin{bmatrix} RAC & R \\ C & 0 \end{bmatrix} = \begin{bmatrix} I & R \\ C & 0 \end{bmatrix} = \begin{bmatrix} I_r & 0 & T \\ 0 & 0 & M \\ S & N & 0 \end{bmatrix} \tag{9-4}$$

and the pair of matrices in Eqn. (9-1) are equivalent over $R(\theta) = \mathscr{C}(\theta)$.

Using a similar type of argument, the pairs of matrices

$$\begin{bmatrix} A^* & I \\ I & 0 \end{bmatrix}; \quad \begin{bmatrix} I_r & 0 & S^* \\ 0 & 0 & N^* \\ T^* & M^* & 0 \end{bmatrix} \tag{9-5}$$

are also equivalent over $R(\theta) = \mathscr{C}(\theta)$.

Theorem 2. Let A, R, C be as in Theorem 1 above, where the rank of A is r (constant) and R, C are unimodular matrices such that $RAC = \bar{I}$ given in Eqn. (9-3) above. Then for arbitrary matrices U, V, W of appropriate sizes, the matrix defined below is also an A_1 generalized inverse of A over the ring $R(\theta) = \mathscr{C}(\theta)$:

$$A_1 = C\begin{bmatrix} I_r & U \\ V & W \end{bmatrix}R \tag{9-6}$$

Proof. Let A be defined as in Eqn. (9-6) above, then we verify that $AA_1A = A$, namely,

$$AA_1A = R^{-1}\begin{bmatrix} I_r & 0 \\ 0 & 0 \end{bmatrix}C^{-1}C\begin{bmatrix} I_r & U \\ V & W \end{bmatrix}RR^{-1}\begin{bmatrix} I_r & 0 \\ 0 & 0 \end{bmatrix}C^{-1}$$

$$= R^{-1}\begin{bmatrix} I_r & 0 \\ 0 & 0 \end{bmatrix}C^{-1} = A \tag{9-7}$$

Theorem 3. Let A, R, C be given as in Theorem 1 above, then $[S \quad T] = A_1$ of A.

Proof. Making use of Eqns. (9-2), (9-3) we have

$$\bar{I} = \begin{bmatrix} I_r & 0 \\ 0 & 0 \end{bmatrix} = RAC = \begin{bmatrix} T \\ M \end{bmatrix}A[S \quad N] = \begin{bmatrix} TA \\ MA \end{bmatrix}[S \quad N] = \begin{bmatrix} TAS & TAN \\ MAS & MAN \end{bmatrix} \tag{9-8}$$

and $A = R^{-1}\bar{I}C^{-1}$. Then

$$C\bar{I}R = [S \quad N]\begin{bmatrix} I_r & 0 \\ 0 & 0 \end{bmatrix}\begin{bmatrix} T \\ M \end{bmatrix} = [S \quad O]\begin{bmatrix} T \\ M \end{bmatrix} = [S \quad T] \tag{9-9}$$

and

$$A[S \quad T]A = R^{-1}IC^{-1}[CIR]R^{-1}IC^{-1} = R^{-1}IC^{-1} = A \tag{9-10}$$

and $A_1 = [S \quad T]$ of A.

Generalized Inverses $A_{1,2}$ of Multiparameter Matrix A

Theorem 4. Let A have fixed rank r and R, C be given as in Theorem 1. Then $A_{1,2} = [S \quad T]$ of A.

Proof. Equation (9-8) implies that $TAS = I_r$ and so

$$[S \quad T]A[S \quad T] = S[TAS]T = SI_rT = ST \tag{9-11}$$

and $[S \quad T] = A_2$ of A. By results of Theorem 3 above, $[S \quad T] = A_1$ of A and hence $A_{1,2} = [S \quad T]$ of A.

Theorem 5. Let A have constant rank r and R, C satisfy the hypotheses of Theorem 2, and A_1, A_2 be A_1 generalized inverses of A, namely,

$$\tilde{A}_1 = C\begin{bmatrix} I_r & U_1 \\ V_1 & W_1 \end{bmatrix}R; \qquad \tilde{\tilde{A}}_1 = C\begin{bmatrix} I_r & W_2 \\ V_2 & W_2 \end{bmatrix}R \tag{9-12}$$

Then an $A_{1,2}$ of A is given by

$$A_{1,2} = \tilde{A}_1A\tilde{\tilde{A}}_1 \tag{9-13}$$

Proof. We verify that since $A_1\tilde{A}_1A = A$; $A\tilde{\tilde{A}}_1A = A$ that $AA_{1,2}A = A$ and

$A_{1,2}AA_{1,2} = A_{1,2}$. Consider the following:

$$AA_{1,2}A = A = A(\tilde{A}_1 A \tilde{\tilde{A}}_1)A = (A\tilde{A}_1 A)(\tilde{\tilde{A}}_1 A) = A\tilde{\tilde{A}}_1 A = A$$

$$A_{1,2}AA_{1,2} = (\tilde{A}_1 A \tilde{\tilde{A}}_1)A(\tilde{A}_1 A \tilde{\tilde{A}}_1) = (\tilde{A}_1 A \tilde{\tilde{A}}_1)(A\tilde{A}_1 A)\tilde{\tilde{A}}_1$$

$$= (\tilde{A}_1 A \tilde{\tilde{A}}_1)A_1 \tilde{\tilde{A}}_1 = \tilde{A}_1 (A\tilde{\tilde{A}}_1 A_1)\tilde{\tilde{A}}_1 = \tilde{A}_1 A \tilde{\tilde{A}}_1$$

$$= A_{1,2} \tag{9-14}$$

Theorem 6. Let A have constant rank r with R, C as given as in Theorem 2 above. Then the pair of matrices given below,

$$\text{(i)} \quad C\begin{bmatrix} I_r & 0 \\ V & 0 \end{bmatrix} R = A_{1,2}; \quad \text{(ii)} \quad C\begin{bmatrix} I_r & U \\ 0 & 0 \end{bmatrix} R = A_{1,2} \tag{9-15}$$

are each an $A_{1,2}$ of A for arbitrary U, V of appropriate size.

Proof. Verify for case (i) as follows:

$$\begin{cases} AA_{1,2}A = R^{-1}IC^{-1}C\begin{bmatrix} I_r & 0 \\ V & 0 \end{bmatrix}RR^{-1}IC^{-1} = R^{-1}\tilde{I}C^{-1} = A \\ A_{1,2}AA_{1,2} = C\begin{bmatrix} I_r & 0 \\ V & 0 \end{bmatrix}RR^{-1}\begin{bmatrix} I_r & 0 \\ 0 & 0 \end{bmatrix}C^{-1}C\begin{bmatrix} I_r & 0 \\ V & 0 \end{bmatrix}R = C\begin{bmatrix} I_r & 0 \\ V & 0 \end{bmatrix} \\ \qquad = A_{1,2} \end{cases} \tag{9-16}$$

Also for case (ii):

$$\begin{cases} AA_{1,2}A = R^{-1}\tilde{I}C^{-1}C\begin{bmatrix} I_r & U \\ 0 & 0 \end{bmatrix}RR^{-1}\tilde{I}C^{-1} = A \\ A_{1,2}AA_{1,2} = C\begin{bmatrix} I_r & U \\ 0 & 0 \end{bmatrix}RAC\begin{bmatrix} I_r & U \\ 0 & 0 \end{bmatrix}R = C\begin{bmatrix} I_r & U \\ 0 & 0 \end{bmatrix}\begin{bmatrix} I_r & 0 \\ 0 & 0 \end{bmatrix}\begin{bmatrix} I_r & U \\ 0 & 0 \end{bmatrix}R \\ \qquad = A_{1,2} \end{cases} \tag{9-17}$$

Generalized Inverses $A_{1,2,3}$ of Multiparameter Matrix A

Theorem 7. Let A have constant rank r and R, C be as in Eqns. (9-2), (9-3). Let $MT^* = 0$, then $[S \quad T] = A_{1,2,3}$ of A.

Proof. Let b be any column of T^*; we will first show that the equation $Ax = b$ has a solution x if and only if $Mb = 0$ and in this case the general solution x is given by $x = [S \quad T]b + Nz$, for arbitrary z of appropriate size.

Since R and C are nonsingular, $Ax = b$ has a solution $x \Leftrightarrow RAx = Rb$ has a solution $x \Leftrightarrow RACy = Ry$ has a solution y and

$$x = Cy \Leftrightarrow \begin{bmatrix} I_r & 0 \\ 0 & 0 \end{bmatrix}\begin{bmatrix} w \\ z \end{bmatrix} = \begin{bmatrix} T \\ M \end{bmatrix}b \text{ has a solution } y = \begin{bmatrix} w \\ z \end{bmatrix}$$

and

$$x = \begin{bmatrix} S & N \end{bmatrix} \begin{bmatrix} w \\ z \end{bmatrix} \Leftrightarrow \begin{bmatrix} w \\ 0 \end{bmatrix} = \begin{bmatrix} Tb \\ Mb \end{bmatrix} \text{ has a solution } \begin{bmatrix} w \\ z \end{bmatrix}$$

and $x = Sw + Nz \Leftrightarrow Mb = 0$ and $w = Tb$ and z arbitrary, $x = Sw + Nz \Leftrightarrow Mb = 0$ and $x = STB + Nz$, for z arbitrary.

The columns of N form a basis for $\mathcal{N}(A)$, the null space of A. This is seen by choosing $b = 0$ above, and the columns of N span $\mathcal{N}(A)$. The columns of N are linearly independent, since they belong to a nonsingular matrix C. Hence the columns of N form a basis for $\mathcal{N}(A)$.

Also, $\begin{bmatrix} S & T \end{bmatrix} = A_{1,2}$ of A by earlier results of Theorem 3. Let $\tilde{A} = \begin{bmatrix} S & T \end{bmatrix}$, then to show that $\begin{bmatrix} S & T \end{bmatrix}$ satisfies condition (iii) of Eqn. (9-1) we need to show that $(A\tilde{A})^* = A\tilde{A}$. In order to show the latter, it is sufficient to show that $(A\tilde{A})(A\tilde{A})^* = (A\tilde{A})$, since for the left-hand side $[(A\tilde{A})(A\tilde{A})^*]^* = (A\tilde{A})(A\tilde{A})^*$ holds and in that case $[A\tilde{A}]^* = A\tilde{A}$ must hold.

By hypothesis, $MT^* = 0$, and by the above argument using columns of T^* there exists a matrix X such that $AX = T^*$ and hence $X^*A^* = T$. Now, $\tilde{A} = \begin{bmatrix} S & T \end{bmatrix} = SX^*A^* = ZA^*$ for $Z = SX^*$, and $(A\tilde{A})(A\tilde{A})^* = A\tilde{A}\tilde{A}^*A^* = A[ZA^*]\tilde{A}^*A^* = AZ[A^*\tilde{A}^*A^*] = AZA^* = A\tilde{A}$. Thus $\begin{bmatrix} S & T \end{bmatrix}$ is an $A_{1,2,3}$ of A.

Generalized Inverses $A_{1,2,4}$ of a Multiparameter Matrix A

Theorem 8. Let $A \in \mathscr{C}^{m \times n}$ have rank r and R, C as in Eqns. (9-3), (9-4). Let $N^*S = 0$, then $\begin{bmatrix} S & T \end{bmatrix}$ is an $A_{1,2,4}$ generalized inverse of A.

Proof. Let d be any column of S. We will first show that the equation $A^*x = d$ has a solution x if and only if $N^*S = 0$ and that in this case the general solution x is given by $x = T^*S^*d + M^*z$, for arbitrary z of appropriate size.

Since R, C are nonsingular, R^*, C^* are also nonsingular and $A^*x = d$ has a solution x for d any column of $S \Leftrightarrow C^*A^*x = C^*d$ has a solution $x \Leftrightarrow C^*A^*R^*y = C^*d$ has a solution

$$x = R^*Y \Leftrightarrow \begin{bmatrix} I_r & 0 \\ 0 & 0 \end{bmatrix} \begin{bmatrix} W \\ Z \end{bmatrix} = \begin{bmatrix} S^* \\ N^* \end{bmatrix} d \text{ has a solution } \begin{bmatrix} W \\ Z \end{bmatrix}$$

and

$$x = R^* \begin{bmatrix} W \\ Z \end{bmatrix} \Leftrightarrow \begin{bmatrix} W \\ 0 \end{bmatrix} = \begin{bmatrix} S^*d \\ N^*d \end{bmatrix} \text{ has a solution } \begin{bmatrix} W \\ Z \end{bmatrix}$$

and

$$x = \begin{bmatrix} T^* & \vdots & M^* \end{bmatrix} \begin{bmatrix} W \\ Z \end{bmatrix} \Leftrightarrow N^*d = 0,$$

$W = S^*d$, $Z =$ arbitrary of appropriate size and $x = T^*W + M^*Z \Leftrightarrow N^*d = 0$ and $x = T^*S^*d + M^*Z$, for arbitrary Z of appropriate size.

The columns of M^* form a basis for $\mathcal{N}(A^*)$, the null space of A^*. The rest of the proof follows as in the case of $\mathcal{N}(A)$. We need to show that condition (iv) of Eqn. (9-1) holds for $[S \quad T]$. Suppose that $N^*S = 0$, then there exists an X such that $A^*X = S$, and $S^* = X^*A$. Also let $\tilde{A} = [S \quad T] = (A^*X)T = A^*Z$ for $Z = XT$. We must show that $[(\tilde{A}A)^*(\tilde{A}A)]$ is Hermitian. Since the second term is Hermitian, it is sufficient to show that $[(\tilde{A}A)^*(\tilde{A}A)] = [\tilde{A}A]$, for then the right-hand side $\tilde{A}A$ would be Hermitian.

Now

$$[(\tilde{A}A)^*(\tilde{A}A)] = (A\tilde{A}^*)(\tilde{A}A) = (A^*\tilde{A}^*)(A^*Z)A = (A^*Z)A = [\tilde{A}A]$$

so that $[\tilde{A}A]$ is Hermitian and $[S \quad T] = A_{1,2,3}$.

Generalized Inverses $A_{1,2,3,4}$ of a Multiparameter Matrix A

Theorem 9. Let $A \in \mathscr{C}^{m \times n}$ and $MT^* = 0$, $N^*S = 0$, and rank of $A = r$. Then $A_{1,2,3,4} = ST$ which is unique.

Proof. The conclusion follows immediately from Theorems 7 and 8 above. Such an inverse of $\tilde{A} = A_{1,2,3,4}$ is unique by the results of Penrose (1955).

The above result generalizes earlier results of Strang (1976) in which $A_{1,2,3,4} = A^+$ is obtained by using the singular-valued decomposition of A, where fully orthogonal matrices were used. In this work only row-orthogonal matrices R, and column-orthogonal matrices C were used to obtain $A_{1,2,3,4} = A^+$.

EXAMPLES

The following examples illustrate the above methods of computation of various generalized inverses of a matrix A that has constant rank r. Let

$$A = \begin{bmatrix} 1 & 1 & 1 \\ 1 & 1 & 1 \\ 1 & 1 & 1 \\ 1 & 1 & 1 \end{bmatrix}$$

From the augmented matrix, and performing elementary row and column operations, we get the following:

$$\begin{bmatrix} A & I \\ I & 0 \end{bmatrix} = \left[\begin{array}{ccc:cccc} 1 & 1 & 1 & 1 & 0 & 0 & 0 \\ 1 & 1 & 1 & 0 & 1 & 0 & 0 \\ 1 & 1 & 1 & 0 & 0 & 1 & 0 \\ 1 & 1 & 1 & 0 & 0 & 0 & 1 \\ \hdashline 1 & 0 & 0 & & & & \\ 0 & 1 & 0 & & \bigcirc & & \\ 0 & 0 & 1 & & & & \end{array}\right] \rightarrow \left[\begin{array}{ccc:cccc} 1 & 1 & 1 & 1 & 0 & 0 & 0 \\ 0 & 0 & 0 & -1 & 1 & 0 & 0 \\ 0 & 0 & 0 & -1 & 0 & 1 & 0 \\ 0 & 0 & 0 & -1 & 0 & 0 & 1 \\ \hdashline 1 & 0 & 0 & & & & \\ 0 & 1 & 1 & & \bigcirc & & \\ 0 & 0 & 1 & & & & \end{array}\right]$$

$$\rightarrow \left[\begin{array}{ccc:cccc} 1 & 0 & 0 & 1 & 0 & 0 & 0 \\ 0 & 0 & 0 & -1 & 1 & 0 & 0 \\ 0 & 0 & 0 & -1 & 0 & 1 & 0 \\ 0 & 0 & 0 & -1 & 0 & 0 & 1 \\ \hdashline 1 & -1 & -1 & & & & \\ 0 & 1 & 0 & & \bigcirc & & \\ 0 & 0 & 1 & & & & \end{array}\right] = \left[\begin{array}{c:c:c} I_r & 0 & T \\ \hdashline 0 & 0 & M \\ \hdashline S & N & 0 \end{array}\right]$$

$$A_{1,2} = [S \quad T] = \begin{bmatrix} 1 \\ 0 \\ 0 \end{bmatrix} [1 \ 0 \ 0 \ 0] = \begin{bmatrix} 1 & 0 & 0 & 0 \\ 0 & 0 & 0 & 0 \\ 0 & 0 & 0 & 0 \end{bmatrix} = A_1 = A_2$$

Next, making use of Gram–Schmidt process to make the rows of $\begin{bmatrix} T \\ M \end{bmatrix}$ orthogonal to each other and the columns of $[S \quad N]$ to be column-orthogonal to each other, we get from the above

$$\left[\begin{array}{ccc|cccc} 1 & 0 & 0 & 1 & 0 & 0 & 0 \\ 0 & 0 & 0 & -1 & 1 & 0 & 0 \\ 0 & 0 & 0 & -1 & 0 & 1 & 0 \\ 0 & 0 & 0 & -1 & 0 & 0 & 1 \\ \hline 1 & -\frac{1}{2} & -1 & & & & \\ 0 & 1 & 0 & & \bigcirc & & \\ 0 & -\frac{1}{2} & 1 & & & & \end{array}\right] \rightarrow \left[\begin{array}{ccc|cccc} 1 & 0 & 0 & 1 & 0 & 0 & 0 \\ 0 & 0 & 0 & -1 & 1 & 0 & 0 \\ 0 & 0 & 0 & -1 & 0 & 1 & 0 \\ 0 & 0 & 0 & -1 & 0 & 0 & 1 \\ \hline \frac{1}{3} & -\frac{1}{2} & -1 & & & & \\ \frac{1}{3} & 1 & 0 & & \bigcirc & & \\ \frac{1}{3} & -\frac{1}{2} & 1 & & & & \end{array}\right]$$

Then an $A_{1,2,4}$ of A is given by ST, that is,

$$A_{1,2,4} = ST = \begin{bmatrix} \frac{1}{3} \\ \frac{1}{3} \\ \frac{1}{3} \end{bmatrix} [1 \ 0 \ 0 \ 0] = \begin{bmatrix} \frac{1}{3} & 0 & 0 & 0 \\ \frac{1}{3} & 0 & 0 & 0 \\ \frac{1}{3} & 0 & 0 & 0 \end{bmatrix} = A_1 = A_2 = A_{1,2}$$

From the above we get

$$\left[\begin{array}{ccc|cccc} 1 & 0 & 0 & 1 & 0 & 0 & 0 \\ 0 & 0 & 0 & -\frac{1}{2} & 1 & -\frac{1}{3} & -\frac{1}{3} \\ 0 & 0 & 0 & -\frac{1}{2} & 0 & 1 & -\frac{1}{2} \\ 0 & 0 & 0 & -1 & 0 & 0 & 1 \\ \hline \frac{1}{3} & -\frac{1}{2} & -1 & & & & \\ \frac{1}{3} & 1 & 0 & & \bigcirc & & \\ \frac{1}{3} & -\frac{1}{2} & 1 & & & & \end{array}\right] \rightarrow \left[\begin{array}{ccc|cccc} 1 & 0 & 0 & \frac{1}{4} & \frac{1}{4} & \frac{1}{4} & \frac{1}{4} \\ 0 & 0 & 0 & -\frac{1}{3} & 1 & -\frac{1}{3} & -\frac{1}{3} \\ 0 & 0 & 0 & -\frac{1}{2} & 0 & 1 & -\frac{1}{2} \\ 0 & 0 & 0 & -1 & 0 & 0 & 1 \\ \hline \frac{1}{3} & -\frac{1}{2} & -1 & & & & \\ \frac{1}{3} & 1 & 0 & & \bigcirc & & \\ \frac{1}{3} & -\frac{1}{2} & 1 & & & & \end{array}\right]$$

$$A_{1,2,3} = \begin{bmatrix} 1 \\ 0 \\ 0 \end{bmatrix} [\tfrac{1}{4} \ \tfrac{1}{4} \ \tfrac{1}{4} \ \tfrac{1}{4}] = \begin{bmatrix} \frac{1}{4} & \frac{1}{4} & \frac{1}{4} & \frac{1}{4} \\ 0 & 0 & 0 & 0 \\ 0 & 0 & 0 & 0 \end{bmatrix}$$

and

$$A_{1,2,3,4} = \begin{bmatrix} \frac{1}{3} \\ \frac{1}{3} \\ \frac{1}{3} \end{bmatrix} \begin{bmatrix} \frac{1}{4} & \frac{1}{4} & \frac{1}{4} & \frac{1}{4} \end{bmatrix} = \begin{bmatrix} \frac{1}{12} & \frac{1}{12} & \frac{1}{12} & \frac{1}{12} \\ \frac{1}{12} & \frac{1}{12} & \frac{1}{12} & \frac{1}{12} \\ \frac{1}{12} & \frac{1}{12} & \frac{1}{12} & \frac{1}{12} \end{bmatrix}$$

The methods used in this chapter avoid the computation of eigenvalues of matrices to provide a numerical method of obtaining various generalized inverses of the Moore–Penrose (Penrose 1955) inverse.

For any constant matrix A, to obtain A_1, A_2, $A_{1,2}$ use can be made of Gaussian elimination with the variable pivot method. For further reduction to obtain $A_{1,2,3}$, $A_{1,2,4}$ we use a Gram–Schmidt process for obtaining column-orthogonal matrices and row-orthogonal matrices. Methods used avoid the lengthy singular-valued decomposition routines used by others to obtain $A = A_{1,2,3,4}$. For any multiparameter matrix A over $R(\theta) = \mathscr{C}(\theta)$ that has a fixed rank r there always exists at least an A_1, A_2, and an $A_{1,2}$ of A.

Consider the following *example* of a (1–2) weak generalized inverse of the matrix:

$$A(x, y) = \begin{bmatrix} x & y & x^2+y+1 \\ x^2y & xy^2 & x^3y+xy^2+xy \end{bmatrix}$$

Now, by making use of elementary row and column operations, we obtain

$$\begin{bmatrix} A(x,y) & I \\ \hline I & 0 \end{bmatrix} \rightarrow \left[\begin{array}{ccc|cc} x & y & x^2+y+1 & 1 & 0 \\ x^2y & xy^2 & x^3y+xy^2+xy & 0 & 1 \\ 1 & 0 & 0 & 0 & 0 \\ 0 & 1 & 0 & 0 & 0 \\ 0 & 0 & 1 & 0 & 0 \end{array} \right]$$

$$\rightarrow \left[\begin{array}{ccc|cc} x & y & x^2+y+1 & 1 & 0 \\ 0 & 0 & 0 & -xy & 1 \\ 1 & 0 & 0 & 0 & 0 \\ 0 & 1 & 0 & 0 & 0 \\ 0 & 0 & 1 & 0 & 0 \end{array} \right]$$

$$\rightarrow \left[\begin{array}{ccc|cc} x & y & y+1 & 1 & 0 \\ 0 & 0 & 0 & -xy & 1 \\ 1 & 0 & -x & 0 & 0 \\ 0 & 1 & 0 & 0 & 0 \\ 0 & 0 & 1 & 0 & 0 \end{array} \right] \rightarrow \left[\begin{array}{ccc|cc} x & y & 1 & 1 & 0 \\ 0 & 0 & 0 & -xy & 1 \\ 1 & 0 & -x & 0 & 0 \\ 0 & 1 & -1 & 0 & 0 \\ 0 & 0 & 1 & 0 & 0 \end{array} \right]$$

$$\rightarrow \left[\begin{array}{ccc|cc} 0 & y & 1 & 1 & 0 \\ 0 & 0 & 0 & -xy & 1 \\ 1+x^2 & 0 & -x & 0 & 0 \\ x & 1 & -1 & 0 & 0 \\ x & 0 & 1 & 0 & 0 \end{array} \right] \rightarrow \left[\begin{array}{ccc|cc} 0 & 0 & 1 & 1 & 0 \\ 0 & 0 & 0 & -xy & 1 \\ 1+x^2 & xy & -x & 0 & 0 \\ x & 1+y & -1 & 0 & 0 \\ -x & -y & 1 & 0 & 0 \end{array} \right]$$

$$\rightarrow \left[\begin{array}{ccc|cc} 1 & 0 & 0 & 1 & 0 \\ 0 & 0 & 0 & -xy & 1 \\ -x & 1+x^2 & xy & 0 & 0 \\ -1 & x & 1+y & 0 & 0 \\ 1 & -x & -y & 0 & 0 \end{array}\right] \rightarrow \left[\begin{array}{ccc|cc} I_r & 0 & 0 & 1 & 0 \\ 0 & 0 & 0 & -xy & 1 \\ -x & 1+x^2 & xy & 0 & 0 \\ -1 & xy & 1+y & 0 & 0 \\ 1 & -x & -y & 0 & 0 \end{array}\right]$$

$$\rightarrow \left[\begin{array}{c|c|c} I_r & 0 & T \\ \hline 0 & 0 & M \\ \hline S & N & 0 \end{array}\right]$$

Now a {1–2}-generalized inverse of $A(x, y)$ above is given by

$$S(x, y)T(x, y) = \begin{bmatrix} -x \\ -1 \\ 1 \end{bmatrix}^{(1\,0)} = \begin{bmatrix} -x & 0 \\ -1 & 0 \\ -1 & 0 \end{bmatrix} = A^-(x, y) = A_{1,2}(x, y)$$

where $A(x, y)A^-(x, y)A(x, y) = A(x, y)$, $A^-(x, y)A(x, y)A^-(x, y) = A^-(x, y)$. The null space $\mathcal{N}(A(x, y))$ is spanned by the vectors:

$$\begin{bmatrix} 1+x^2 \\ xy \\ -x \end{bmatrix}, \quad \begin{bmatrix} xy \\ 1+y \\ -y \end{bmatrix}$$

and the unimodular matrices $P(x, y)$, $Q(x, y)$ exist such that

$$P(x, y)A(x, y)Q(x, y) = \begin{bmatrix} 1 & 0 \\ -xy & 1 \end{bmatrix}\begin{bmatrix} x & y & x^2+y+1 \\ x^2y & xy^2 & x^3y+xy^2+xy \end{bmatrix}\begin{bmatrix} -x & xy & 1+x^2 \\ -1 & 1+y & x \\ 1 & -y & -x \end{bmatrix}$$

$$= \begin{bmatrix} 1 & 0 & 0 \\ 0 & 0 & 0 \end{bmatrix} = \left[\begin{array}{c|c} I_r & 0 \\ \hline 0 & 0 \end{array}\right]$$

The rank of $A(x, y)$ is 1 and the null space of $A^*(x, y)$ is spanned by the vector $\begin{bmatrix} -xy \\ 1 \end{bmatrix}$. Next consider an example of a set of equations:

$$\begin{bmatrix} x & y & x^2+y+1 \\ x^2y & xy^2 & x^3y+xy^2+xy \end{bmatrix}\begin{bmatrix} -x \\ -1 \\ 1 \end{bmatrix} = \begin{bmatrix} 1 \\ xy \end{bmatrix} = B(x, y)$$

where

$$A(x, y)X(x, y) = B(x, y) = \begin{bmatrix} 1 \\ xy \end{bmatrix}$$

and

$$A(x, y)A^-(x, y)B(x, y) = \begin{bmatrix} x & y & x^2+y+1 \\ x^2y & xy^2 & x^3y+xy^2+xy \end{bmatrix}\begin{bmatrix} -x & 0 \\ -1 & 0 \\ 1 & 0 \end{bmatrix}\begin{bmatrix} 1 \\ xy \end{bmatrix}$$

$$= \begin{bmatrix} 1 & 0 \\ xy & 0 \end{bmatrix}\begin{bmatrix} 1 \\ xy \end{bmatrix} = \begin{bmatrix} 1 \\ xy \end{bmatrix} = B(x, y)$$

and a consistency condition is satisfied, and the equation above has a general solution:

$$\begin{cases} X(x, y) = A^-(x, y)B(x, y) + [I - A^-(x, y)A(x, y)]Z(x, y) \\ X(x, y) = S(x, y)T(x, y)B(x, y) + N(x, y)Z(x, y) \end{cases}$$

for arbitrary $Z(x, y)$.

$$X(x, y) = \begin{bmatrix} -x & 0 \\ -1 & 0 \\ 1 & 0 \end{bmatrix} \begin{bmatrix} 1 \\ xy \end{bmatrix} + \left[I - \begin{bmatrix} -x & 0 \\ -1 & 0 \\ 1 & 0 \end{bmatrix} \begin{bmatrix} x & y & x^2 + y + 1 \\ x^2y & xy^2 & x^3y + xy^2 + xy \end{bmatrix} \right] Z(x, y)$$

$$X(x, y) = \begin{bmatrix} -x \\ -1 \\ 1 \end{bmatrix} + \left[I + \begin{bmatrix} x & 0 \\ 1 & 0 \\ -1 & 0 \end{bmatrix} \begin{bmatrix} x & y & x^2 + y + 1 \\ x^2y & xy^2 & x^3y + xy^2 + xy \end{bmatrix} \right] Z(x, y)$$

$$X(x, y) = \begin{bmatrix} -x \\ -1 \\ 1 \end{bmatrix} + \left[\begin{bmatrix} 1 & 0 & 0 \\ 0 & 1 & 0 \\ 0 & 0 & 1 \end{bmatrix} + \begin{bmatrix} x^2 & xy & x^3 + xy + x \\ x & y & x^2 + y + 1 \\ -x & -y & -(x^2 + y + 1) \end{bmatrix} \right] Z(x, y)$$

where

$$\begin{bmatrix} x & y & x^2 + y + 1 \\ x^2y & xy^2 & x^3 + y + xy^2 + xy \end{bmatrix} \begin{bmatrix} -x & 0 \\ -1 & 0 \\ 1 & 0 \end{bmatrix} \begin{bmatrix} x & y & x^2 + y + 1 \\ x^2y & xy^2 & x^3y + xy^2 + xy \end{bmatrix}$$

$$= A(x, y)A^-(x, y)A(x, y) = \begin{bmatrix} 1 & 0 \\ xy & 0 \end{bmatrix} \begin{bmatrix} x & y & x^2 + y + 1 \\ x^2y & xy^2 & x^3y + xy^2 + xy \end{bmatrix}$$

$$= \begin{bmatrix} x & y & x^2 + y + 1 \\ x^2y & xy^2 & x^3y + xy^2 + xy \end{bmatrix} = A(x, y)$$

Also

$$\begin{bmatrix} -x & 0 \\ -1 & 0 \\ 1 & 0 \end{bmatrix} \begin{bmatrix} x & y & x^2 + y + 1 \\ x^2y & xy^2 & x^3y + xy^2 + xy \end{bmatrix} \begin{bmatrix} -x & 0 \\ -1 & 0 \\ 1 & 0 \end{bmatrix} = A^-(x, y)A(x, y)A^-(x, y)$$

$$= \begin{bmatrix} -x^2 & -xy & -x^3 - xy - x \\ -x & -y & -x^2 - y - 1 \\ x & y & x^2 + y + 1 \end{bmatrix} \begin{bmatrix} -x & 0 \\ -1 & 0 \\ 1 & 0 \end{bmatrix} = \begin{bmatrix} -x & 0 \\ -1 & 0 \\ 1 & 0 \end{bmatrix} = A^-(x, y)$$

$$X(x, y) = S(x, y)T(x, y)b(x, y) + N(x, y)b(x, y)$$

and

$$Mb = [-xy \quad 1] \begin{bmatrix} 1 \\ xy \end{bmatrix} = [0] \quad \text{(consistency conditions)}$$

Brief History of Generalized Inverses of Multiparameter Matrices

The notion of a generalized inverse of a real or complex matrix has found many applications in many areas of multidimensional system theory. The interest in the theory of multidimensional systems and network problems and large-scale systems was indicated in an article by Bose and Mitra (1978) in which was introduced the notion of a generalized inverse of matrices whose entries belong to a polynomial ring or to the ring of integers. Using a reduction to Smith form, Bose and Mitra (1978) characterized those matrices that have a weak generalized inverse in the cases of the rings of integers and of polynomials in a single variable. For the general case of interest, that of polynomials in several variables, they only established partial results and left the solution open. Sontag (1980) gave a partial characterization for the case of polynomials in several variables. The main result of Sontag was that a generalized inverse requires the existence of a "Smith form" for the original matrix.

Let $R = \mathscr{C}(z_1, z_2, \ldots, z_n)$ denote the ring of polynomials in n-variables with complex coefficients. A weak generalized inverse (WGI) of a (not necessarily square) matrix $A(z_1, z_2, \ldots, z_n) = A(z)$ (also called a $(1, 2)$-generalized inverse of $A(z)$) is any matrix $B(z)$ such that the following equations hold:

$$A(z)B(z)A(z) = A(z), \qquad B(z)A(z)B(z) = B(z)$$

Results of Sontag (1980) established the equivalence of the statements:

a. $A(z)$ has a WGI;
b. there exist square unimodular (nonzero scalar determinant) matrices $P(z)$, $Q(z)$ over $R = \mathscr{C}(z)$ such that $A(z) = P(z)A_0Q(z)$, with

$$A_0 = \left[\begin{array}{c|c} I_r & 0 \\ \hline 0 & 0 \end{array}\right]$$

where I_r is the identity of order $r = \text{rank}[A(z)]$;
c. as a function of the complex variables $(z_1, z_2, \ldots, z_n)$ the rank of $A(z)$ is constant.

SIMILARITY AND EQUIVALENCE OF MATRICES

Denote by $\mathscr{C}^{m \times n}(\theta)$ the space of $m \times n$ matrices having elements belonging to the ring of polynomials in $\theta = (\theta_1, \theta_2, \ldots, \theta_n)$ with coefficients belonging to the field $\mathscr{C}$ of complex numbers and by $A^-(\theta) \in \mathscr{C}^{n \times m}(\theta)$ any generalized inverse of $A(\theta)$ that satisfies the equation $A(\theta)A^-(\theta)A(\theta) = A(\theta)$. The main purpose of this section is to establish the following results.

Theorem 10. Let $A(\theta) \in \mathscr{C}^{m \times k}(\theta)$, $B(\theta) \in \mathscr{C}^{1 \times n}(\theta)$ and $C(\theta) \in \mathscr{C}^{m \times n}(\theta)$. Then the following pair of matrices

$$\begin{bmatrix} -B(\theta) & 0 \\ -C(\theta) & A(\theta) \end{bmatrix}, \qquad \begin{bmatrix} A(\theta) & 0 \\ 0 & -B(\theta) \end{bmatrix}$$

are equivalent to each other if and only if the following equation

$$[I - A(\theta)A^-(\theta)]C(\theta)[I - B^-(\theta)B(\theta)] = 0$$

holds for some $A^-(\theta)$, $B^-(\theta)$ of $A(\theta)$, $B(\theta)$, respectively.

Proof. Let the Lyapunov matrix equation

$$A(\theta)X(\theta) - Y(\theta)B(\theta) = C(\theta)$$

have a solution pair $X(\theta)$, $Y(\theta)$ and $A^-(\theta)$, $B^-(\theta)$ exist, then multiplying the above equation termwise on the left-hand side by $(I - A(\theta)A^-(\theta))$ and termwise on the right-hand side by $(I - B^-(\theta)B(\theta))$ we see that

$$[I - A(\theta)A^-(\theta)] \cdot [A(\theta)X(\theta) - Y(\theta)B(\theta) = C(\theta)] \cdot [I - B^-(\theta)B(\theta)]$$

implies that the above equation holds. Now the equation

$$[I - A(\theta)A^-(\theta)] \cdot C(\theta) \cdot [I - B^-(\theta)B(\theta)] = 0$$

implies that the general solution of the Lyapunov equation above is given by

$$\begin{cases} X(\theta) = A^-(\theta)C(\theta) + A^-(\theta)Z(\theta)B(\theta) + [I - A^-(\theta)A(\theta)]W(\theta) \\ Y(\theta) = [A(\theta)A^-(\theta) - I]C(\theta)B^-(\theta) + Z(\theta) \\ \qquad + [A(\theta)A^-(\theta) + I]Z(\theta)B(\theta)B^-(\theta) \end{cases}$$

where $W(\theta) \in \mathscr{C}^{k \times n}(\theta)$ and $Z(\theta) \in \mathscr{C}^{m \times 1}(\theta)$ are arbitrary matrices.

Next, forming the nonsingular matrices,

$$\begin{bmatrix} Y(\theta) & I \\ I & 0 \end{bmatrix} \begin{bmatrix} -B(\theta) & 0 \\ -C(\theta) & A(\theta) \end{bmatrix} \begin{bmatrix} 0 & I \\ I & X(\theta) \end{bmatrix}$$

$$= \begin{bmatrix} A(\theta) & A(\theta)X(\theta) - Y(\theta)B(\theta) - C(\theta) \\ 0 & -B(\theta) \end{bmatrix}$$

and the pair of matrices above in Theorem 10 are equivalent to each other. The matrix equation of Theorem 10 above may be written as

$$A(\theta)[A^-(\theta)C(\theta)] + [I - A(\theta)A^-(\theta)]C(\theta)B^-(\theta)B(\theta) = C(\theta)$$

which shows that the Lyapunov equation above has a solution pair

$$\begin{cases} X(\theta) = A^-(\theta)C(\theta) \\ Y(\theta) = [A(\theta)A^-(\theta) - I]C(\theta)B^-(\theta) \end{cases}$$

In order to show that these matrices are the general solution of the matrix equation $A(\theta)X(\theta) - Y(\theta)B(\theta) = C(\theta)$, choose any solution pair $X_0(\theta) \in \mathscr{C}^{k \times n}(\theta)$, $Y_0(\theta) \in \mathscr{C}^{m \times 1}(\theta)$ such that $A(\theta)X_0(\theta) - Y_0(\theta)B(\theta) = C(\theta)$. Choose $W(\theta) = X_0(\theta)$, $Z(\theta) = Y_0(\theta)$. Then the general form of $X(\theta)$, $Y(\theta)$ given above for such choices of $W(\theta)$, $Z(\theta)$ implies that it represents the general solution and is

$$\begin{aligned} X(\theta) &= A^-(\theta)C(\theta) + A^-(\theta)Y_0(\theta)B(\theta) + [I - A^-(\theta)A(\theta)]X_0(\theta) \\ &= X_0(\theta) - A^-(\theta)[A(\theta)X_0(\theta) - Y_0(\theta)B(\theta) - C(\theta)] \\ &= X_0(\theta) \end{aligned}$$

and

$$Y(\theta) = [A(\theta)A^-(\theta) - I]C(\theta)B^-(\theta) + Y_0(\theta)$$
$$+ [A(\theta)A^-(\theta) - I]Y_0(\theta)B(\theta)B^-(\theta)$$
$$= Y_0(\theta) + [A(\theta)A^-(\theta) - I][Y_0(\theta)B(\theta) + C(\theta)]B^-(\theta)$$
$$= Y_0(\theta) + [A(\theta)A^-(\theta) - I] \cdot [A(\theta)X_0(\theta)B^-(\theta)]$$
$$= Y_0(\theta).$$

Theorem 11. If in addition to the hypotheses of the theorem above it is required that $A^-(\theta)C(\theta) = A(\theta)A^-(\theta) - IC(\theta)B^-(\theta)$, then the pair of matrices in the theorem above are similar to each other.

Proof. Choose $Z(\theta) \equiv 0$, $W(\theta) \equiv 0$,   then $Y(\theta) = X(\theta)$ and $A(\theta)[A^-(\theta)C(\theta)] - \{[A(\theta)A^-(\theta) - I]C(\theta)B^-(\theta)\}B(\theta) = C(\theta)$ and $A(\theta)X(\theta) - X(\theta)B(\theta) = C(\theta)$ and a similarity transformation may be constructed as in the proof of the earlier theorem above.

Theorem 12. Let the following Riccati matrix equation have a solution $X(\theta)$:

$$A(\theta)X(\theta) - X(\theta)B(\theta) + C(\theta) + X(\theta)D(\theta)X(\theta) = 0$$

where $A(\theta) \in \mathscr{C}^{m \times m}(\theta)$, $B(\theta) \in \mathscr{C}^{n \times m}(\theta)$, $C(\theta) \in \mathscr{C}^{m \times n}(\theta)$, $D(\theta) \in \mathscr{C}^{n \times m}(\theta)$, $X(\theta) \in \mathscr{C}^{m \times n}(\theta)$. Then the following pair of matrices belonging to $\mathscr{C}^{(m+n) \times (m+n)}(\theta)$ are similar:

$$\begin{bmatrix} -B(\theta) & D(\theta) \\ -C(\theta) & A(\theta) \end{bmatrix}, \quad \begin{bmatrix} X(\theta)D(\theta) + A(\theta) & 0 \\ D(\theta) & A(\theta) - D(\theta)X(\theta) \end{bmatrix}$$

Proof. Let $X(\theta) \in \mathscr{C}^{m \times n}(\theta)$ be any solution of the Riccati matrix equation above; then

$$\begin{bmatrix} X(\theta) & I \\ I & 0 \end{bmatrix} \begin{bmatrix} -B(\theta) & D(\theta) \\ -C(\theta) & A(\theta) \end{bmatrix} \begin{bmatrix} 0 & I \\ I & -X(\theta) \end{bmatrix}$$
$$= \begin{bmatrix} A(\theta) + X(\theta)D(\theta) & -X(\theta)B(\theta) - C(\theta) - X(\theta)D(\theta)X(\theta) - A(\theta)X(\theta) \\ D(\theta) & -B(\theta) - D(\theta)X(\theta) \end{bmatrix}$$

and the pair of matrices above are similar.

For example, $AX - XB = C$ where:

$$\begin{bmatrix} 1 & 1 \\ 1 & 0 \end{bmatrix} \begin{bmatrix} 1 & 0 \\ 0 & 2 \end{bmatrix} - \begin{bmatrix} 1 & 0 \\ 0 & 2 \end{bmatrix} \begin{bmatrix} 1 & 1 \\ 1 & 1 \end{bmatrix} = \begin{bmatrix} 0 & 1 \\ -1 & 0 \end{bmatrix}$$

and

$$A^- = B^- = \begin{bmatrix} \frac{1}{4} & \frac{1}{4} \\ \frac{1}{4} & \frac{1}{4} \end{bmatrix}, \quad X = \begin{bmatrix} 1 & 0 \\ 0 & 2 \end{bmatrix} = \text{solution}$$

The consistency condition: $(I - AA^-)C(I - B^-B) = 0$ holds and X also satisfies the equation $(I - AA^-)XB = (AA^- - I)C$ and also the equation $AX(I - B^-B) = C(I - B^-B)$.

EXAMPLES

The following examples illustrate various uses of the basic theory established earlier in this paper.

Example 1. Computation of various generalized inverses of a matrix. Given:

$$A(x, y) = \begin{bmatrix} x & x^2+1 \\ x^2y & x^3y+xy \end{bmatrix}$$

We first make use of elementary row and column operations of the following types: (i) interchange any two rows (columns) and (ii) for $i \neq j$ replace row (column) i by its sum with a (non-identically-zero polynomial) multiple of row (column) j such that these changes on the identity matrix preserve the unimodularity of such a transformation matrix that accomplishes these elementary operations. Such operations correspond to premultiplication or postmultiplication by a unimodular matrix whose determinant is a nonzero element of the ring $R(\theta) = \mathscr{C}(\theta) = \mathscr{C}(\theta_1, \theta_2, \ldots, \theta_n)$.

Consider the following augmented matrix and make use of the above types of elementary row and column operations:

$$\left[\begin{array}{cc|cc} x & x^2+1 & 1 & 0 \\ x^2y & x^3y+xy & 0 & 1 \\ \hline 1 & 0 & & \\ 0 & 1 & & \bigcirc \end{array}\right] \rightarrow \left[\begin{array}{cc|cc} x & x^2+1 & 1 & 0 \\ 0 & 0 & -xy & 1 \\ \hline 1 & 0 & & \\ 0 & 1 & & \bigcirc \end{array}\right]$$

$$\rightarrow \left[\begin{array}{cc|cc} x & x^2+1 & \dfrac{1}{x^2y^2+1} & \dfrac{xy}{x^2y^2+1} \\ 0 & 0 & -xy & 1 \\ \hline 1 & 1 & & \\ 0 & 1 & & \bigcirc \end{array}\right] \rightarrow \left[\begin{array}{cc|cc} x & 1 & \dfrac{1}{x^2y^2+1} & \dfrac{xy}{x^2y^2+1} \\ 0 & 0 & -xy & 1 \\ \hline 1 & -x & & \\ 0 & 1 & & \bigcirc \end{array}\right]$$

$$\rightarrow \left[\begin{array}{cc|cc} 1 & x & \dfrac{1}{x^2y^2+1} & \dfrac{xy}{x^2y^2+1} \\ 0 & 0 & -xy & 1 \\ \hline -x & 1 & & \\ 1 & 0 & & \bigcirc \end{array}\right] \rightarrow \left[\begin{array}{cc|cc} 1 & 0 & \dfrac{1}{x^2y^2+1} & \dfrac{xy}{x^2y^2+1} \\ 0 & 0 & -xy & 1 \\ \hline -x & 1+x^2 & & \\ 1 & -x & & \bigcirc \end{array}\right]$$

$$\rightarrow \left[\begin{array}{cc|cc} 1 & 0 & \dfrac{1}{x^2y^2+1} & \dfrac{xy}{x^2y^2+1} \\ 0 & 0 & -xy & 1 \\ \hline \dfrac{x}{(x^2+1)^2+x^2} & \dfrac{x^5+3x^3+2x}{(x^2+1)^2+x^2} & & \\ \dfrac{x^2+1}{(x^2+1)^2+x^2} & \dfrac{-x^4-2x^2}{(x^2+1)^2+x^2} & & \bigcirc \end{array}\right]$$

$$= \left[\begin{array}{cc|c} I_r & 0 & T \\ 0 & 0 & M \\ \hline S & N & \bigcirc \end{array}\right]$$

It is then see that

$$A_{1,2,3,4} = \frac{1}{[(x^2+1)^2+x^2]}\begin{bmatrix} x \\ x^2+1 \end{bmatrix}[1 \quad xy] \cdot \frac{1}{[x^2y^2+1]}$$

$$= \frac{1}{[x^2y^2+1]\cdot[(x^2+1)^2+x^2]}\begin{bmatrix} x & x^2y \\ x^2+1 & xy(x^2+1) \end{bmatrix}$$

$$A_1 = A_2 = A_{1,2} = \begin{bmatrix} -x \\ 1 \end{bmatrix}[1 \quad xy] = \begin{bmatrix} -x & -x^2y \\ 1 & xy \end{bmatrix}$$

$$A_{1,2,4} = \frac{1}{[x^2y^2+1]}\begin{bmatrix} -x \\ 1 \end{bmatrix}[1 \quad xy] = \frac{1}{x^2y^2+1}\begin{bmatrix} -x & -x^2y \\ 1 & xy \end{bmatrix}$$

$$A_{1,2,3} = \frac{1}{[(x^2+1)^2+x^2]}\begin{bmatrix} x \\ x^2+1 \end{bmatrix}[1 \quad xy] = \frac{1}{[(x^2+1)^2+x^2]}\begin{bmatrix} x & x^2y \\ x^2+1 & xy(x^2+1) \end{bmatrix}$$

An alternate way to compute $A_{1,2,3,4}$ for $A(x,y)$ above is as follows:

$$PAQ = \begin{bmatrix} 1 & 0 \\ -xy & 1 \end{bmatrix}\begin{bmatrix} x & x^2+1 \\ x^2y & x^3y+xy \end{bmatrix}\begin{bmatrix} -x & 1+x^2 \\ 1 & -x \end{bmatrix} = \begin{bmatrix} I_r & 0 \\ 0 & 0 \end{bmatrix} = \begin{bmatrix} 1 & 0 \\ 0 & 0 \end{bmatrix}$$

since $|P| = 1$, $|Q| = -1$, where P, Q are unimodular matrices. Then

$$A = P^{-1}\begin{bmatrix} I_r & 0 \\ 0 & 0 \end{bmatrix}Q^{-1} = P^{-1}\begin{bmatrix} I_r \\ 0 \end{bmatrix}[I_r \quad 0]Q^{-1}$$

$$A = \begin{bmatrix} 1 & 0 \\ xy & 1 \end{bmatrix}\begin{bmatrix} 1 \\ 0 \end{bmatrix}[1 \quad 0]\begin{bmatrix} x & 1+x^2 \\ 1 & x \end{bmatrix} \triangleq DC$$

$$A = \begin{bmatrix} 1 \\ xy \end{bmatrix} \cdot [x \quad 1+x^2]$$

where D, C are rank-1 matrices.

$$A_{1,2,3,4} = C^t(CC^t)^{-1}(D^tD)^{-1}D^t$$

$$A_{1,2,3,4} = \frac{1}{[(x^2+1)^2+x^2]}\begin{bmatrix} x \\ 1+x^2 \end{bmatrix} \cdot \frac{1}{[1+x^2y^2]}[1 \quad xy]$$

$$A_{1,2,3,4} = \frac{1}{[(x^2+1)^2+x^2]\cdot[1+x^2y^2]}\begin{bmatrix} x \\ 1+x^2 \end{bmatrix}[1 \quad xy]$$

$$= \frac{1}{[(x^2+1)^2+x^2]\cdot[1+x^2y^2]}\begin{bmatrix} x & x^2y \\ x^2+1 & xy(1+x^2) \end{bmatrix}$$

Example 2. Given, $A(x,y)$ below:

$$A(x,y) = \begin{bmatrix} x & y & x^2+y+1 \\ x^2y & xy^2 & x^3y+xy^2+xy \end{bmatrix}$$

Augmenting $A(x,y)$ as in Example 1 above and making use of elementary row and column operations on the augmented array, we obtain the following array:

$$\begin{bmatrix} x & y & x^2+y+1 & \vdots & 1 & 0 \\ x^2y & xy^2 & x^3y+xy^2+xy & \vdots & 0 & 1 \\ \hline 1 & 0 & 0 & \vdots & & \\ 0 & 1 & 0 & \vdots & \bigcirc & \\ 0 & 0 & 1 & \vdots & & \end{bmatrix}$$

$$\rightarrow \begin{bmatrix} 1 & 0 & 0 & \vdots & 1 & 0 \\ 0 & 0 & 0 & \vdots & -xy & 1 \\ \hline -x & 1+x^2 & xy & \vdots & & \\ -1 & x & 1+y & \vdots & \bigcirc & \\ 1 & -x & -y & \vdots & & \end{bmatrix} = \begin{bmatrix} I_r & 0 & 0 & \vdots & \\ 0 & 0 & 0 & \vdots & P \\ \hline & Q & & \vdots & \bigcirc \end{bmatrix}$$

Now

$$PAQ = \begin{bmatrix} 1 & 0 \\ -xy & 1 \end{bmatrix} \begin{bmatrix} x & y & x^2+y+1 \\ x^2y & xy^2 & x^3y+xy^2+xy \end{bmatrix} \begin{bmatrix} -x & 1+x^2 & xy \\ -1 & x & 1+y \\ 1 & -x & -y \end{bmatrix}$$

$$= \begin{bmatrix} 1 & 0 & 0 \\ 0 & 0 & 0 \end{bmatrix} = \begin{bmatrix} I_r & 0 & 0 \\ 0 & 0 & 0 \end{bmatrix}$$

and

$$A = P^{-1}\begin{bmatrix} I_r & 0 & 0 \\ 0 & 0 & 0 \end{bmatrix} Q^{-1} = P^{-1}\begin{bmatrix} I_r \\ 0 \end{bmatrix}[I_r \quad 0 \quad 0]Q^{-1}$$

$$A = \begin{bmatrix} 1 & 0 \\ xy & 1 \end{bmatrix}\begin{bmatrix} I_r \\ 0 \end{bmatrix} \cdot [I_r \quad 0 \quad 0]\begin{bmatrix} x & y & x^2+y^2+1 \\ 1 & 0 & x \\ 0 & 1 & 1 \end{bmatrix} \triangleq DC$$

$$A = \begin{bmatrix} 1 \\ xy \end{bmatrix}[x \quad y \quad x^2+y+1]$$

Now

$$A_{1,2,3,4} = C'(CC')^{-1}(D'D)^{-1}D'$$

$$A_{1,2,3,4} = \begin{bmatrix} x \\ y \\ x^2+y+1 \end{bmatrix}\left[[x \quad y \quad x^2+y+1]\begin{bmatrix} x \\ y \\ x^2+y+1 \end{bmatrix} \right]^{-1}$$

$$\cdot \left[[1 \quad xy]\begin{bmatrix} 1 \\ xy \end{bmatrix} \right]^{-1}[1 \quad xy]$$

$$A_{1,2,3,4} = \frac{1}{[x^2+y^2+(x^2+y+1)^2]} \cdot \frac{1}{[1+x^2y^2]}\begin{bmatrix} x & x^2y \\ y & xy^2 \\ x^2+y+1 & xy(x^2+y+1) \end{bmatrix}$$

Continuing from the above array, we get the following:

$$
\left[
\begin{array}{ccc|cc}
1 & 0 & 0 & \dfrac{1}{x^2y^2+1} & \dfrac{xy}{1+x^2y^2} \\
\hline
0 & 0 & 0 & -xy & 1 \\
\hline
-x & 1+x^2 & xy & & \\
-1 & x & 1+y & \bigcirc & \\
1 & -x & -y & &
\end{array}
\right]
$$

$$
\rightarrow
\left[
\begin{array}{c|cc|cc}
1 & 0 & 0 & \dfrac{1}{1+x^2y^2} & \dfrac{xy}{1+x^2y^2} \\
\hline
0 & 0 & 0 & -xy & 1 \\
\hline
\dfrac{x}{\Delta} & g(1+x^2) & k(xy) & & \\
\dfrac{y}{\Delta} & g(x) & k(1+y) & \bigcirc & \\
\dfrac{x^2+y+1}{\Delta} & g(-x) & k(-y) & &
\end{array}
\right]
$$

where $\Delta = x^2 + y^2 + (x^2 + y + 1)^2$; $k = (x^2 + 2y + 1)/\Delta$; $g = (x^3 + xy + 2x)/\Delta$. Thus, various generalized inverses of $A(x, y)$ can be obtained from the various arrays leading up to the last one above.

Example 3. Given, $A(s, z)$:

$$
A(s, z) =
\begin{bmatrix}
(s+1) & 1+z(s+1) & 0 & (s+1)z & z^2 \\
s & (sz+1) & -(s+1)(s+z) & sz & z^2 \\
0 & s(s+1) & (s+1) & s(s+1) & sz^2(s+1) \\
(s+1) & 1+z(s+1) & -(s+1)(s+z) & z(s+1) & z^2
\end{bmatrix}
$$

The purpose of this example is to analyze the rank of $A(s, z)$. Augment $A(s, z)$ to the right and below by an appropriate identity matrix to get the following array:

$$
\left[
\begin{array}{c|cccc|cccc}
1 & 0 & 0 & 0 & 0 & 1 & 0 & 0 & 0 \\
\hline
0 & -1 & -(s+1)(s+z) & -z & 0 & -1 & 1 & 0 & 0 \\
0 & -s(s+1)^2 & (s+1) & s(s+1)(1-z(s+1)) & 0 & -s(s+1) & 0 & 1 & 0 \\
0 & 0 & -(s+1)(s+z) & 0 & 0 & -1 & 0 & 0 & 1 \\
\hline
-z & 1+z(s+1) & 0 & z^2(s+1) & z^3 & & & & \\
1 & -(s+1) & 0 & -z(s+1) & -z^2 & & \bigcirc & & \\
0 & 0 & 1 & 0 & 0 & & & & \\
0 & 0 & 0 & 1 & 0 & & & & \\
0 & 0 & 0 & 0 & 1 & & & &
\end{array}
\right]
$$

By making use of elementary row and column operations it can be shown that

$$PAQ = \begin{bmatrix} 1 & 0 & 0 & 0 & 0 \\ 0 & 1 & 0 & 0 & 0 \\ 0 & 0 & (s+1) & 0 & 0 \\ 0 & 0 & 0 & s(s+1)(s+z) & 0 \end{bmatrix}$$

where P, Q are unimodular matrices. Thus the rank of $A(s, z)$ may be determined easily.

CONCLUSIONS

Most problems arising in applications contain several physical parameters that may vary over certain specified sets of values. Thus, it is important to understand the qualitative behavior of the system as the parameters vary. A good design for a system will always be such that the qualitative behavior does not change when the parameters are varied a small amount about the value for which the original design was made. However, the behavior may change drastically when highly nonlinear systems are subjected to large variations in the parameters. A change in the qualitative properties could mean a change in the stability of the original system, and thus the system may assume a state different from the original design. Hence, the values of the parameters, where this change takes place, are very critical to the simulation of a large complex multiparameter nonlinear problem. A knowledge of such values is absolutely necessary for the complete understanding of the behavior and reliability of the system.

In this chapter an attempt has been made to obtain solutions of matrix equations whose solutions are needed for computer simulation and computer-aided design (CAD) of systems and computer-aided manufacturing (CAM) which reflect the parameter values in the solution. Then a fine-tuning of such systems with multiparameters may be accomplished by various changes in these parameters and may thus allow for the design of robust solutions and also precision performance of adjusted parameter systems. These basic questions must be answered prior to the final design of complex systems and may require several computer simulation iterations to insure the desired reliability level of operation.

REFERENCES

1. Bose, N. K. and S. K. Mitra (1978). "Generalized inverse of polynomial matrices," *IEEE Trans. Automatic Control*, Vol. AC-23, pp. 491–493.

2. Cecioni, F. (1909). "Sopra operazoni algebriche," *Ann. Scuola. Norm. Sup., Pisa*, Vol. II, pp. 1–140.

3. Jones, John Jr., Charles R. Martin, and H. Undem (1984). "Solutions of higher order Riccati-type matrix equations," *Int. J. Systems Sci.*, Vol. 15, No. 9, pp. 1001–1010.

4. Jones John Jr. (1983). "Matrix equations over rings," *Math. Comput. Simul.*, Vol. 25, No. 6, pp. 489–492.

5. Mitra, S. K. (1973). "Common solutions to a pair of linear matrix equations $A_1 X B_1 = C_1$ and $A_2 X B_2 = C_2$," *Proc. Camb. Phil. Soc.*, Vol. 74, pp. 213–216.

6. Mitra, S. K. (1977). "The matrix equation $AXB + CXD = E$," *SIAM J. Appl. Math.*, Vol. 32, pp. 823–826.

7. Penrose, R. (1955). "A generalized inverse for matrices," *Proc. Camb. Phil. Soc.*, Vol. 52, pp. 17–19.

8. Rao, C. R. (1972). "Estimation of variance and covariance components in linear models," *J. Amer. Statist. Assoc.*, Vol. 67, pp. 112–115.

9. Rao, C. R. and S. K. Mitra (1971). *Generalized inverse of matrices and its applications*, Wiley, New York.

10. Sontag, E. D. (1980). "On generalized inverses of polynomial and other matrices," *IEEE Trans. Automatic Control*, Vol. AC-25, No. 3, pp. 514–517.

11. Strang, G. (1976). "Linear algebra and its applications," Academic Press, New York, Chapter 3.

10

SUPERCOMPUTER APPLICATIONS IN MODELING AND IMAGE PROCESSING FOR SPACE AND EARTH SCIENCES

Milton Halem, Barbara H. Putney, Judith E. Devaney, P. J. Camillo, R. J. Gurney, Hudong Chen, William H. Matthaeus, Don J. Lindler, Sara R. Heap, James P. Strong, H. K. Ramapriyan, James J. Little, and Michael J. McAnulty

INTRODUCTION

Satellite observing systems are producing spectral images of the Earth's surface and atmosphere, flux measurements of particles and fields in the extraterrestrial media, and spectra of objects from the far reaches of the universe. In many cases, the full information content from these data can only be inferred by their assimilation with other data into detailed models that simulate the physical processes occurring in nature. In other cases, the data themselves require intensive computational processing to reveal structures not readily apparent from standard processing. In both cases, space and Earth scientists are turning to the power of supercomputers to address the modeling and image processing computational requirements.

In the first part of this chapter, we describe some of the modeling applications of remotely sensed data and explore ways in which evolving supercomputing technologies make these applications possible. Each section in this part represents a current modeling study that relies on the potential of the supercomputer architectures.

The first section explains the need for an accurate gravity model that will be used when TOPEX/Poseidon altimeter data become available in the early 1990s. In order to derive global estimates of sea height, a 5-fold greater radial accuracy of the satellite's position will be needed. It is shown that a 17-fold improvement in speed over a scalar processor of the IBM 3081 has been obtained by the exploitation of the vector processing capabilities of a CYBER 205. Future vector processors of more power will make it possible to achieve the desired accuracies in reasonable times.

In The EOS era, remotely sensed data of the heat and soil moisture balance will become available on a global basis. As a precursor to global modeling of land surface processes, the second section develops a hillslope model for a catchment basin. The model is adapted to the NASA Massively Parallel Processor (MPP) because the physics ideally matches the architectural structure of the vertically uncoupled physical process in the model. This enables the achievement of speeds nearly comparable to what could be done with serial processors when they group a dozen or so processing elements devoted to a single vertical profile. However, it is then shown that a 500-fold increase on the MPP can be attained when the full 16 000 processors are used, or potentially a 1000-fold increase on a 64 000 processor Connection Machine.

At the forefront of fluid modeling theory is a new algorithm known as *cellular automata*. This is essentially a statistical-mechanical flow model that can be used to simulate large-scale gas dynamics. Previous numerical models attempted to solve the Navier–Stokes equation, making use of finite differences equations; however, the cellular automata theory relies on simpler mathematics and has the potential to dramatically increase the efficiency of many types of modeling problems. The third section of the first part presents a new extension of the cellular automata theory to the solution of magnetohydrodynamics. The extension will hopefully enable the investigators to study the interplanetary media as a plasma fluid.

In the second part of this chapter, the use of parallel processing for image analysis is addressed. For images to be of scientific value, their resolution must be sharp enough to resolve the details desired by the investigator. The first section discusses how parallel programming techniques are used to restore astronomical images that have been blurred by imperfections in the sensor instruments.

Tracking the motion of objects in image pairs by detecting local differences between the two images is another application that is shown to be practical for parallel computers. With a traditional serial computer, the matching and correlation processes can take hours or even days, compared to a few seconds on the MPP. The second section of this part presents an algorithm for image-matching techniques and shows how such image pairs obtained from synthetic-aperture radar instruments aboard NASA's Space Shuttle have been correlated to track ice floe motion.

The next section discusses the potential for programming a computer to see objects. Included are the problems involved in vision tasks, such as edge detection and vision levels, and an analysis of a current project underway on the Connection Machine to implement vision modules.

The chapter concludes with an analysis of the limitations of implementing parallel graphics algorithms on a massively parallel processor. This includes an explanation of how graphics are implemented on parallel machines as well as a discussion of the potential for animation.

The sections in this chapter each explore particular applications that made innovative use of supercomputer resources. Together, this chapter helps explain why such new architectures and algorithms are necessary to extract the maximum informational value from data produced by advanced spaceborne sensors.

Modeling of Physical Processes

PRODUCING AN ACCURATE GRAVITY MODEL ON A CYBER 205 VECTOR SUPERCOMPUTER*

The TOPEX/Poseidon Mission

The TOPEX/Poseidon satellite project requires a radial accuracy of 13 centimeters in the orbit of the TOPEX/Poseidon satellite that is to be launched in the early 1990s. In order to achieve this accuracy, a more precise gravity model is required. The Geodynamics Branch at Goddard Space Flight Center has been working to achieve this goal using the CYBER 205 computer and has produced the GEM-T1 model. Traditionally, this is an expensive computer problem involving long runs and large matrices. The software systems required are the GEODYN, SOLVE, and ERODYN programs. Redesign of the software for the vector computer has been completed. Comparison timings have yielded an improvement factor of 90 : 1 (CPU + I/O) over the IBM 360/95 for the creation of normal equations and 38 : 1 (CPU + I/O) over the IBM 3081 for the inversion of a 1921×1921 matrix. Even on the CYBER 205, this solution requires hundreds of hours, making the task impossible on the traditional sequential computers.

In 1982, Goddard Space Flight Center in Greenbelt, Maryland, obtained a CDC CYBER 205 vector computer. Previously, the Geodynamics Branch had been using the IBM 360/95 to determine gravity models, station positions, polar motion constants, and other geodetic parameters. That computer had served for many years and was long overdue for retirement. The speed of the 360/95 with thin-film memory was about the same as the IBM 3081. The models required for precise geodetic work required large amounts of CPU time and memory for the 360/95. It took 3+ hours to create the normal equations needed for solutions even when they were made on the size of the model and the numerical integration stepsize.

Therefore, the idea of a supercomputer was well received. This would be a pioneering effort that was required to further the desirable modeling. This paper will describe the software evolution on the CYBER 205 that has resulted in the preliminary gravity model, GEM-T1, required by the TOPEX/Poseidon satellite project in order to meet its scientific objectives. The technique employed to

---

* This section was contributed by Barbara H. Putney.

determine the gravity model for TOPEX/Poseidon is to express the geopotential as a harmonic expansion of C and S coefficients to degree and order that can be sensed by the TOPEX/Poseidon satellite. Existing satellite data are processed, removing all known errors and then extracting the gravity spherical harmonic coefficients from the residuals, using a combined least-squares estimation.

TOPEX/Poseidon is a joint venture initiated in 1987 by NASA and the Centre National d'Etudes Spatiales. It is an oceanographic satellite to be launched by rocket in the early 1990s. The primary goal of the TOPEX/Poseidon mission is to increase understanding of ocean dynamics by making precise and accurate observations of the oceanic topography for several years. These measurements will contribute towards the following.

- Determination of the general circulation of the ocean and its variability through combining topography, measurements of the internal density field of the ocean, and models of ocean circulation
- Tests of the ability to compute circulation from the forcing by winds
- Studies of the nature of ocean dynamics
- Calculation of the transport of heat, mass, nutrients, and salt by the oceans
- Determination of the geocentric oceanic tides
- Investigation of the interaction of currents with waves

In order to achieve these goals, the orbit of TOPEX/Poseidon has to be known to 13 cm in the radial direction. Using previously existing gravity models, it is currently estimated that the error would be 60 cm. The largest orbital errors in the current state-of-the-art orbit determination are caused by the errors in the gravity model. Consequently, it was determined that a better gravity model needed to be pursued. To meet the required accuracy, the gravity model sigmas had to be reduced by at least a factor of 2. This would necessitate a rework of about 1000 satellite arcs (5–30 days each) using the most up-to-date models and parameters. Currently, in the GEM-T1 model, there are 580 arcs from 17 satellites. State-of-the-art models were used for polar motion and Earth's rotation, precession and nutation of the Earth, Earth and ocean tidal perturbations, planetary ephemerides, and measurement modeling. For the first time, the computer did not constrain the use of the proper numerical step size and model. Because the computer runs were relatively short, the field could be created and tested in nine months instead of the several years it had taken in the past. The model thus far is the best satellite-only model that has ever been produced. In addition, some solved tidal constituents appear to be improved. The CYBER 205 has made this possible.

GEODYN, SOLVE, and ERODYN

The GEODYN software system provides state-of-the-art orbit determination and geodetic parameter estimation capabilities. Using a fixed-integration-step, high-order Cowell integrator, GEODYN numerically integrates satellite orbits in Cartesian coordinates and the force model partial derivatives. The forcing function includes a spherical harmonic representation for Earth gravitation, solar radiation pressure, Earth atmospheric drag, and dynamical Earth and ocean tides. Satellite observation modeling includes Earth precession and nutation, polar motion and Earth rotation, and tracking stations displacements due to solid tides and ocean loading. Tracking measurement corrections are provided for tropospheric and parallactic refraction, annual and diurnal aberration, antenna axis displacement and center of gravity of the satellite offset. Dynamic editing is performed as the Bayesian least-squares estimator is iterated to solution convergence. Estimated parameters include measurement and timing biases, and tracking station coordinates, as well as orbit state and parameters and all the above-mentioned models. The normal equations formed within GEODYN are output to a file for inclusion in large parameter estimations and error analyses.

The SOLVE program selectively combines and edits the least-squares normal equations formed by the GEODYN program or elsewhere to form solutions of parameters such as the gravity field, tracking station coordinates, polar motion, Earth rotation, ocean tides, and other geodetic parameters. A linear shift on the right-hand side of the normal equations can be performed. Other SOLVE capabilities include dynamical suppression of parameters based on numerical stability, application of weights to individual matrices or C-matrices when combining, and carrying out a partitioned Cholesky decomposition to compute optionally (a) the parameter solution, (b) the parameter solution plus standard deviations, or (c) the parameter solution plus a full variance/covariance matrix, as the user requires. The ERODYN program is the companion error analysis program that answers the question of what effect on the solved-for parameters do the errors on the unsolved-for parameters produce. Propagating the errors throughout the orbit is another option of the program, as is eigenvalue/eigenvector capability. This program uses the normal matrix from GEODYN or SOLVE. The state transition matrix and partials are obtained from GEODYN, thereby making it totally compatible and dependent on the other software.

At this time, all three packages are operating on the CYBER 205. They are in different stages of optimization for the vector computer. SOLVE and ERODYN are more naturally suited for a large vector computer because they are largely composed of matrix operations. The most heavily used program, GEODYN, is not a natural vector program, so that its conversion had to be handled differently.

Conversion of Software

The CYBER 205 vector computer can be thought of as two computers in one, a scalar processor and a vector processor. Vector lengths can be 65 000 64-bit words and operations that use vector lengths greater than 1000 make efficient use of the vector processor. Clearly, the name of the game is to write the required algorithm using long vectors. It is necessary that the same operation be done with all elements of a vector; however, it is not required that all results be stored.

Another technique used is to gather the elements required for an operation into a temporary vector, and scatter the results back into the original vector. A doubly efficient mathematical expression is called a *linked triad*. This construct contains two vectors and one scalar to be combined using two different operations of addition/subtraction and multiplication. Since one obtains twice as many instructions per second with this construct, it is highly desirable to formulate the algorithm with this in mind. The CYBER 205 can have two or four pipelines. In the vector processor, a vector is distributed to the pipelines, thereby making a four-pipeline machine. The programmer does not have to consider this architecture when writing the code, since the compiler distributes the vectors according to the particular machine architecture. Another major consideration is that of data handling. Programs that were formerly CPU-bound may now become I/O-bound. There are special I/O techniques that are used to optimize the I/O. One of them uses the pager (The CYBER 205 has a virtual operating system.) Another is buffered I/O. It has been necessary to employ these techniques to optimize the large transfer of data in and out of the software.

Redesign of GEODYN

It was determined that the GEODYN orbit determination program needed to be redesigned and rewritten to take advantage of the vector hardware. GEODYN can be used in many different ways, turning models on and off, solving for many or few parameters, using data, or simply integrating an orbit. The software traditionally used dynamic array lengths and pointers to take care of the size of the particular problem user, and this concept needed to be maintained. The large parameter normal equation creation was easily vectorizable. This type of run had traditionally been the largest and longest of the runs, although not the most typical. The most typical runs are orbit determination runs solving for fewer than 10 parameters. Traditionally, the program processes the satellite observations chronologically. Most often, the data are received one pass at a time, and one pass of data can contain several thousand observations. It was therefore decided to process the data one pass at a time, making the definition of a pass as long as practicable, since many values of the integrator have to be stored to accommodate this design. All models needed to be able to work on the data one pass at a time when the run did not solve for a large number of parameters. In the case of the large parameter estimation, the long vectors should be the variational equations for those parameters. Therefore, the program has to work in two different modes depending on the type of run. In addition, several models that are very time-consuming needed to be redesigned to use as much of the vector processor as possible. The recursive geopotential evaluator and the solid Earth and ocean perturbation are two such models. Since the CYBER 205 requires a front-end machine (Amdahl V-7), and the startup and initialization of the software is not vectorizable, and since several data sets have to be searched to obtain the data needed for a particular run, the program was divided into two programs, GEODYN IIS, the front-end part, and GEODYN IIE, the Cyber part, with two

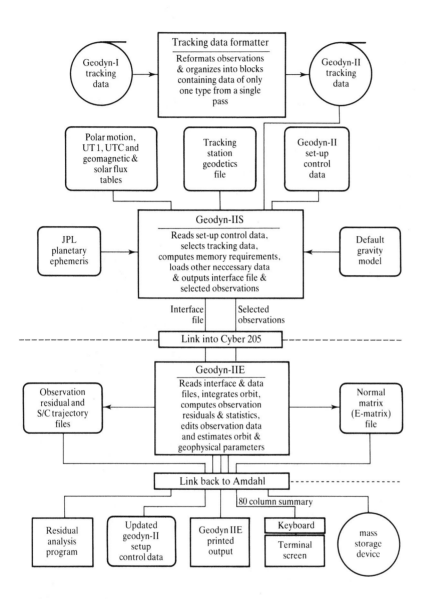

Figure 10-1. GEODYN-II flow diagram.

interface files created and passed to GEODYN IIE from GEODYN IIS (see Fig. 10-1). GEODYN IIS always runs on the front-end. GEODYN IIE is coded to run on the front-end or on the CYBER 205. To accomplish this, one master source file is maintained for GEODYN IIE with a merger of the sequential and vector code and a program to create the front-end or CYBER 205 programs. This allows more portability of the code and is highly desirable.

SOLVE and ERODYN

Both SOLVE and ERODYN are much more natural candidates for a vector computer. Both deal with large matrices and always contain large "do" loops. The matrix inversion routines needed to be vectorized, aiming to use as many linked triads as possible. The Cholesky decomposition, as it is coded, is divided into three parts: the part necessary to compute the solution, the part necessary to compute the standard deviations, and the part necessary to compute the complete inverse. The first two parts have been put into linked triad form, making them very fast on the Cyber. In addition, it has always been necessary to partition the solution for lack of memory on the computer. This is still true even though the CYBER 205 has 4 million words of memory. It was discovered that the I/O required for the partitioning and reading of the matrices in and out of the programs was taking more time than the inversion. On the CYBER 205, the programs are I/O bound. Normal FORTRAN I/O on the Cyber has a maximum blocking factor of 24 times 512 words. This is insufficient for the large I/O problem, so special packages have been developed. The ones employed are Q7BUFIN and Q7BUFOUT, which allow several large pages (65 000+ words) to be moved in and out at a time. In addition, there are several channels that can be used simultaneously for even larger data motions. These codes now have a large quantity of specialized Cyber code. It is intended that a single source be created, as was done in the GEODYN program that can run on the front-end in standard FORTRAN.

Comparison Timings

The TOPEX/Poseidon gravity modeling effort presented the first large-scale problem to be solved by the Geodynamics Branch using the GEODYN II system and the SOLVE program on the CYBER 205 computer.

Three different satellite data types were used in the TOPEX/Poseidon solution: optical, laser, and Doppler data. Of the three, only the Doppler data are dense. Therefore, when solving for large numbers of parameters, both the optical and laser arcs were very efficient. Figure 10-2 shows the running-time relationship between the number of parameters estimated and the number of observations in the satellite arc. Interestingly, the curve on one arc behaves almost linearly as the number of parameters is increased instead of showing the expected quadratic relationship that is experienced on a scalar machine when creating normal equations. The Doppler runs take approximately ten times longer since they contain ten times the number of observations.

An actual comparison of the creation of a normal matrix on the IBM 360/95 yielded a CPU improvement of 97 times on the CYBER 205, and an overall improvement of 90 times. The solution of a 1921×1921 matrix inversion yielded a CPU improvement of 77 times over the IBM 3081 and an overall improvement of 38 times. When estimating the GEODYN portion of the preliminary gravity model on the CYBER 205 and on the IBM 3081, the true value of the vector

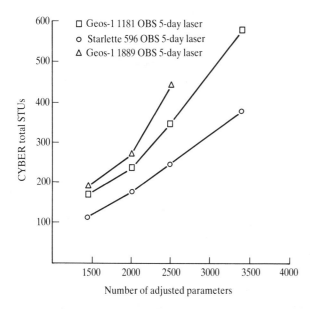

Figure 10-2. Computer time required for generation of normal by GEODYN-II.

processor can be observed. Three types of runs were made, the orbit convergence runs, the normal matrix generation runs, and the solution-testing runs. Table 10-1 compares the running times for the three types of runs on the IBM 3081 and the CYBER 205.

A totally dedicated IBM 3081 would have needed nine months to complete this task, while the dedicated CYBER 205 needed only 17 days. The solution was actually completed in about four months. In addition, some of the runs would have taken more than six hours on the 3081 and it is questionable whether the solution would be possible on that computer.

Results

The GEM-T1 gravity model was produced as a preliminary model for the TOPEX mission. It appears to be the best satellite-only gravity model that has been created. The CYBER 205 has made it possible to include and solve for parameters that could not be included previously owing to computer constraints.

Table 10-1. Running times

Type of GEODYN run	Factor	Hours 3081	Hours 205
Orbit conversion of 580 arcs	6.5	1156	178
Normal equations of 580 arcs	90	3960	44
Testing solutions in 720 arcs	6.5	718	110
Totals in hours	17.6	5834	332

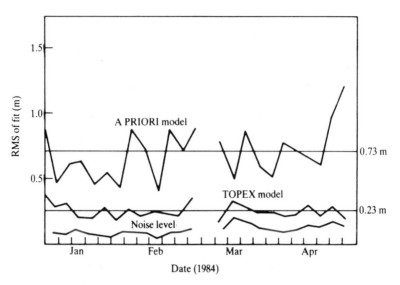

Figure 10-3. Precision orbit computations for the STARLETTE satellite using the May 1986 TOPEX/Poseidon Earth gravity model.

The GEM-T1 model contains geopotential coefficients to degree and order 36 as well as a subset of 66 ocean tidal coefficients for the long-wavelength components of 12 major tides and 5-day averaged Earth rotation and polar motion parameters for the 1980 period onwards. It contained data from 17 different satellites with almost 800 000 observations, half of which were from third-generation satellite laser-tracking systems. Many tests on the absolute value of the new model have demonstrated a large improvement in this field over previous fields even though surface gravity, altimeter, and satellite-to-satellite tracking data have not yet been included in the model. The final model will have coefficients to degree and order 50, as well.

One striking improvement is that of the observation residual fit improvement for the Starlette satellite. As can be seen in Figure 10-3, the RMS of fit using the best-known gravity field for the Starlette satellite prior to GEM-T1 averaged 0.73 m. Using the GEM-T1 model, the RMS of fit drops to 0.23 m. Starlette data were included and such a dramatic improvement was very surprising therefore. Starlette is a good geodetic laser satellite with a perigee height of 810 kilometers.

What does this mean to TOPEX/Poseidon? The radial error of the TOPEX/Poseidon orbit is now predicted to be sub-20 cm RMS level as a result of this model. It is anticipated that the rest of the improvement will come much more slowly.

Future Plans for TOPEX/Poseidon

For TOPEX/Poseidon, it is intended that the rest of the data be introduced, and that the models be improved in the data processing. Gradually, the a priori

TOPEX/Poseidon field will be determined prior to launch. Some resonant coefficients will probably need to be adjusted with the early TOPEX/Poseidon data. The early improvement in the gravity field resulting from the GEM-T1 model is very encouraging.

For the software, GEODYN II needs to be completed as far as having the GEODYN I capability. Data simulation and satellite-to-satellite tracking as well as some models, such as Earth's albedo and general relativity, are not yet included. The SOLVE and ERODYN programs are not yet fully I/O-optimized for the CYBER 205. It is anticipated that a follow-on computer to the CYBER 205 may be at Goddard in the 1990 timeframe. It therefore becomes essential that the machine-specific code currently in the software be minimized. GEODYN II operates on an IBM machine as well as on the Cyber. It is prudent that the SOLVE and ERODYN programs do so as well. The use of standard FORTRAN is another way to aim towards portability of software. In addition, the software will continue to evolve to support other new and old missions and scientific objectives that the Geodynamics branch will require in the area of state-of-the-art modeling and orbit determination.

Acknowledgments

The software described in this section is the work of many people. The GEODYN program was designed and written by Thomas V. Martin, William F. Eddy, and David D. Rowlands of EG&G Washington Analytical Services Center, Inc. The SOLVE and ERODYN programs were developed lately by Ronald H. Estes and W. David Wildenhain while they were employed by Business and Technological Systems, Inc. Both were under contract to NASA for the software development. The TOPEX/Poseidon model GEM-T1 is the work of a large team of NASA and contractor support and is described in "An Improved Model of the Earth's Gravitational Field GEM-T1," NASA Technical Memorandum No. 4091, published in July 1987 at Goddard Space Flight Center in Greenbelt, Maryland. The figures included in this paper are from that report, as is much of the material presented. In particular, the software section of that document was a joint effort of Thomas V. Martin and myself. I thank the entire group for making this a good team effort. I also thank the NASA Space and Earth Sciences Computing Center at Goddard Space Flight Center for the cooperation we received in getting this job done.

A SIMD IMPLEMENTATION OF A HILLSLOPE WATER FLOW MODEL*

The Watershed Model Description

We have implemented a physically based numerical model of heat and moisture flow in layered soil on the Massively Parallel Processor (MPP), as a precursor to a

---

* This section was contributed by Judith E. Devaney, P. J. Camillo, and R. J. Gurney.

model of complete catchment. Moisture flow within a catchment includes evaporation, overland flow, flow in unsaturated soil, and flow in saturated soil. Because of the empirical evidence that moisture flow in unsaturated soil is mainly in the vertical direction, flow in the unsaturated zone can be modeled as a series of one-dimensional columns. This initial version of the Hillslope model includes evaporation and a single column of one-dimensional unsaturated zone flow. This case has already been solved on an IBM 3081 computer and has now been mapped to the MPP architecture. With only 0.085 percent of the MPP processing elements being utilized in the one-dimensional case, the MPP required 10 sec to solve the same case that the IBM solved in 4 sec. Extension to the two-dimensional case on the MPP should involve only minimal additional computation time.

One important part of the global hydrological system is a catchment, which separates rainfall into three parts: evaporation; overland flow, which goes directly to a stream; and infiltration, which flows at a much slower rate vertically through the soil to a saturated zone, where the water then flows horizontally and merges into the stream or is stored as ground water. A catchment model involves four components: evaporation, overland flow, flow in unsaturated soil, and flow in saturated soil. If we are to understand the way in which spatial variations of hydrological parameters affect the water balance of a catchment, including evaporation, runoff, erosion, and transport of minerals, we have to model explicitly the flow both over and within a hillside.

Several researchers have written Hillslope models (Eagleson 1970; Freeze 1971). All of these have had limitations, mainly because they could not be executed in a reasonable amount of time. This computer limitation is much reduced if a parallel processor is used, as it is possible to write the model so that a solution can be obtained at many points simultaneously.

The first stage of the work is to verify that such a model may be executed efficiently on a parallel processor. To this end, we have encoded and tested a model that already exists (Camillo et al. 1983) on a serial computer—an IBM 3081—and that contains two of the four previously identified components: evaporation and unsaturated flow. We have transferred this model to the MPP to verify the accuracy of the parallel computations. We have also estimated the computational efficiency of the full catchment model in a parallel machine versus that of the equivalent model on a serial machine, if such a serial model were to be successfully created.

In this section, we discuss the physics of the one-dimensional model, the method of solution, and its adaptability to the parallel architecture.

The complete soil model is described by Camillo et al. (1983). The soil moisture profile in the unsaturated zone is the solution of the continuity equation

$$\frac{\partial \theta}{\partial t} = -\frac{\partial q_m}{\partial z} \tag{10-1}$$

where $\theta(z, t)$ is the volumetric soil moisture (water volume/soil volume) at depth z at time t, and q_m is the vertical soil moisture flux, modeled by Philip and de

Vries (1957) as follows:

$$q_m = k - D_\theta \left(\frac{\partial \theta}{\partial z} \right) \tag{10-2}$$

K is the hydraulic conductivity, and D_θ is the moisture diffusion coefficient, which depends on soil moisture θ, the soil matric potential ψ, and other physical constants. K and ψ are estimated with the parameterization

$$k(\theta) = k_s \left(\frac{\theta}{\theta_s} \right)^{2b+3} \tag{10-3a}$$

$$\psi(\theta) = \psi_s \left(\frac{\theta}{\theta_s} \right)^{-b} \tag{10-3b}$$

in which θ_s, K_s, and ψ_s are moisture content, conductivity, and potential at saturation (Clapp and Hornberger 1978). The value of b depends on soil texture.

The temperature profile in the soil may be modeled with Fourier's equations and represents one option in the serial version. However, we have chosen to implement the computationally simpler, yet physically adequate, force-restore equations (Lin 1980). The surface and deep soil temperatures, T_s and T, are modeled by

$$\frac{\partial T_s}{\partial t} = \frac{2G}{a} - \frac{2\pi}{\tau} (T_s - \bar{T}) \tag{10-4a}$$

$$\frac{\partial \bar{T}}{\partial t} = \frac{G}{a\sqrt{365\pi}} \tag{10-4b}$$

$$a = \sqrt{\lambda c \tau / \pi} \tag{10-4c}$$

where G is the soil-surface heat flux, λ and c are, respectively, the soil thermal conductivity and heat capacity, and τ is the length of day. $\bar{T}$ is the temperature at the depth at which fluctuations are seasonal rather than diurnal. For most soils, this depth is about 2 m. The conductivity and heat capacity are modeled as functions of soil moisture and soil type with the de Vreis (1975) model.

To solve these equations for θ, T_s, and $\bar{T}$, boundary conditions must be supplied for moisture and temperature both at the air/soil interface and in the bottom layer of the profile. In principle, either the fluxes q_θ and G or the variables θ and T could be specified. In the model, surface heat and moisture fluxes are computed to model the effects of the environment (i.e., rainfall, evapotranspiration, radiation, etc.) on the profile evolution. At the bottom of the moisture profile, a choice of flux or moisture boundary condition is used. One can specify constant moisture, a downward moisture flux equal to the hydraulic conductivity of the bottom layer, or any constant value.

The energy balance equation provides the surface fluxes

$$G = R + LE + H \tag{10-5}$$

All fluxes are positive downward. G is the heat absorbed by the soil, R is the net radiation flux, LE is the evapotranspiration energy flux, and H is the sensible heat. After finding the solution, the surface moisture flux q_θ is set equal to E, and G is used in the force-restore equations.

The net radiation R is divided into average short- and long-wavelength components

$$R = R_{short} + R_{long} \tag{10-6}$$

Either or both components may be estimated or measured. All four options are allowable within the computer program, with standard models such as the Brunt model for long-wave radiation being available as options to estimate either or both components.

A standard model for the latent heat flux under neutral atmospheric stability is explained by Eagleson (1970) as

$$LE = -\frac{\rho c_p k^2 \bar{U}_a}{\Gamma \ln^2(z/z_0)}(e_s - e_a) \tag{10-7}$$

where ρ is the density of air, c_p is the air specific heat, k is the von Karman constant (0.4), z_0 is the surface roughness, U_a is the wind velocity at height z averaged over a suitable time period ($\sim$1 hour), e_a is the vapor pressure at height z, e_s is the vapor pressure at the soil surface, and Γ is the psychometric constant (0.61808 mbar K^{-1}). This may be expressed as

$$LE = -C_1 \bar{U}_a(e_s - e_a) \tag{10-8a}$$

where

$$C_1 = \frac{\rho c_p k^2}{\Gamma \ln^2(z/z_0)} \tag{10-8b}$$

Input to the program includes the constant C_1 and both U_a and e_a as functions of time.

The sensible heat flux H in the continuity equation is calculated by

$$H = -\Gamma C_1 \bar{U}_a(T_s - T_a) \tag{10-9}$$

The terms of the heat balance equations are functions of the surface temperature T_s and the meteorological variables e_a, U_a, and T_a.

Method of Solution

The continuity equations (10-1 and 10-4) are solved by calculating the spatial derivatives of the moisture fluxes and then computing the time integral using numerical methods.

The soil is divided into N layers of varying thicknesses, Δz_i, where N and Δz_i are input variables. At a specified time, the moisture fluxes at the $N - 1$ interior boundaries are calculated by evaluating Eqn. (10-2). The surface and bottom fluxes are computed by evaluating the boundary condition equations at the top and bottom boundaries. This gives the flux at the $N + 1$ layer boundaries, and the derivative, with respect to depth, is approximated for the ith layer by

$$\frac{\partial q_m}{\partial z} = \frac{q_{m_{i+1}} - q_{m_i}}{\Delta z_i} \tag{10-10}$$

The continuity equations (10-1 and 10-4) are of the form

$$\frac{d\mathbf{y}}{dt} = \mathbf{f}(t, \mathbf{y}) \tag{10-11}$$

In this context, the vector $\mathbf{y}$ represents the state of the system and $\mathbf{f}(t, \mathbf{y})$ represents the model equations. The state vector, $\mathbf{y}$, has $N + 2$ elements: soil moisture, θ_i, in each of N layers, T_s (the surface soil temperature), and T (the deep soil temperature). The first N elements of $\mathbf{f}$ are Eqn. (10-10), and f_{n+1} and f_{n+2} are the right-hand sides of the force-restore equations (10-4a and 10-4b).

IBM SOLUTION

The equations described above were solved with double-precision, floating-point arithmetic on the IBM 3081 utilizing an Adams–Bashforth predictor–corrector method (Booth 1957; Teddington 1958). This solution is described in Camillo et al. (1983). In summary, for comparison purposes, the IBM version predicted the new value of the state vector $\mathbf{y}(p)(t + \Delta t)$ in terms of the backward differences of the derivatives, recalculated the derivatives from the model equations, then obtained the corrected value of the state vector $\mathbf{y}(c)(t + \Delta t)$.

The difference between $\mathbf{y}(p)$ and $\mathbf{y}(c)$ is a reliable estimate of the error, and the software determined whether each element of this difference lay within a user-specified window. If all differences were smaller than this window, the integration step size (Δt) was doubled, leading to increased computational efficiency. If any difference was too large, the step size was halved. This halving and doubling required no reevaluation of the model equations. The values of the four backward differences for the new integrator time (whether for halving or doubling of the integration time step) were calculated as linear combinations of the four back values for the old integrator time.

MPP SOLUTION

Double precision was not available on the MPP, so the method of solution had to be somewhat restructured to obtain the required accuracy in single-precision floating-point. The same Adams–Bashforth predictor–connector was used in the MPP solution. However, the equations were rederived in terms of the ordinates (i.e., the derivatives) instead of the backward differences. This eliminated many subtractions that would cause loss of accuracy, but retained the mathematically identical equations. The new equations are

$$\mathbf{y}(p)(t + \Delta t) = \mathbf{y}(t) + (\Delta t / 720)[1901\mathbf{f}(t) - 2774\mathbf{f}(t - \Delta t) \\ + 2616\mathbf{f}(t - 2\Delta t) - 1274\mathbf{f}(t - 3\Delta t) + 251\mathbf{f}(t - 4\Delta t)]$$

$$\mathbf{y}(c)(t + \Delta t) = \mathbf{y}(t) + (\Delta t / 720)[251\mathbf{f}(t + \Delta t) \\ + 646\mathbf{f}(t) - 264\mathbf{f}(t - \Delta t) + 106\mathbf{f}(t - 2\Delta t) - 19\mathbf{f}(t - 3\Delta t)]$$

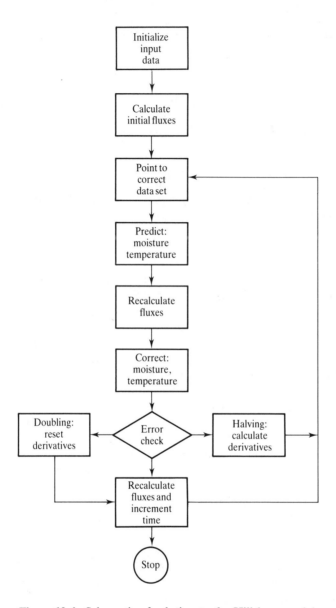

Figure 10-4. Schematic of solution to the Hillslope model.

where $\mathbf{f}(t + \Delta t)$ is the model evaluated with the predicted state vector, and Δt is the current integrator time step size.

The difference between $\mathbf{y}(p)$ and $\mathbf{y}(c)$ was used as an estimate of the error. A schematic of this solution is shown in Figure 10-4. Doubling of the time step was accomplished by saving the previously calculated derivatives and using them.

Thus, maximum accuracy could be retained. Where the time step could be doubled because the errors were small enough but there were insufficient back-derivatives, doubling was postponed until there were sufficient back data. When the error window checks required that the time step be halved, three of the required derivatives for the predictor–corrector were available, and two were missing. The Runge–Kutta method was used to calculate these needed derivatives. This combination of numerical techniques maintained the highest possible precision for the calculations. It also provided the most stable numerical approach, in that the predictor–corrector kept watch on the errors at each time step; the Runge–Kutta method ensured that all the derivatives were calculated to the same accuracy. The only disadvantage was that ten additional evaluations of the model equations were required for any time step that required halving.

The Runge–Kutta method was also used to calculate the initial values needed to start the predictor–corrector.

Although this restructuring of the solution required more calculations than the IBM version, the fact that the same calculations are done on many pieces of data at the same time, as well as the Boolean nature of the error-window checks, make the Hillslope model an ideal application for a single-instruction multiple-data (SIMD) architecture such as the MPP.

THE MPP COMPUTING ENVIRONMENT

As can be seen from Figure 10-5, the MPP consists of several parts that can be roughly divided into a serial processing segment (the main control unit, or MCU,

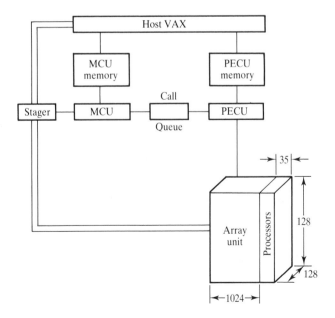

Figure 10-5. Block diagram of MPP.

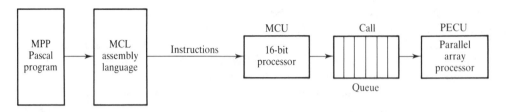

Figure 10-6. MPP Pascal system flowchart.

and its associated memory), a parallel processing segment (the processing element control unit, or PECU, and its associated memory, along with the array unit, or AU, which consists of memory and processors configured into a 128-by-128 array), and a staging memory for parallel data transfers between the MPP and the host (VAX 11/80) (Devaney 1985; Potter 1985).

Scalar calculations are performed in the MCU. This is a special-purpose microcoded 16-bit processor that has a 16-bit hardware multiplier. Parallel calculations are performed with the 16 384 bit-serial AU processors. A total of 1024 bits of memory are available to each processor. The MPP is a single-

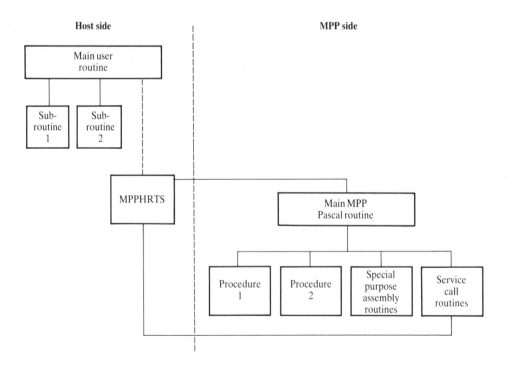

Figure 10-7. Hillslope model programming routines.

instruction multiple-data machine, hence, identical operations are performed on each PE at the same time.

The MCU is programmed via MCL assembly language. The PECU is programmed via PEARL assembly language. A high-level language, MPP Pascal, is compiled into MCL assembly language. Parallel computations are initiated in the PECU by calls to routines in PECU memory from MCL. A call queue exists so that the MCU can stack up to 15 calls, which the PECU can process in turn (see Fig. 10-6). A VAX language front end and subroutines are needed to handle initialization, input and output to disk, as well as to interface with the MPP-HOST run time system (MPPHRTS) that accesses the MPP. The Hillslope model was written with a VAX FORTRAN front end and subroutines, an MPP Pascal main routine and procedures, and some special-purpose assembly routines (see Fig. 10-7).

MAPPING THE HILLSLOPE MODEL TO THE MPP ARCHITECTURE

The initial mapping of the Hillslope model to the MPP primarily involved determining the scalar and parallel components of the calculations. Calculations both within the layers of the Hillslope and at the boundaries are required at each time step of the model integrations. The calculations within the Hillslope are identical at each layer, so they were arranged to be performed simultaneously in the MPP array unit. These parallel values consisted of soil moisture, temperature, depth, layer thicknesses, fluxes, derivatives, and backward differences, as well as predicted and corrected values (see Fig. 10-8). Because the model was set up with

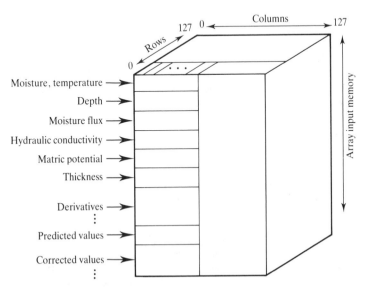

Figure 10-8. Values for the soil layers are arranged in parallel so that an individual PE is dedicated to the processing of a single "cell" of soil. In this initial one-dimensional version of the Hillslope model, only 14 of the 16 384 processing elements were used.

a view to extension to a two-dimensional model, each row in the AU was to represent one vertical column in the Hillslope, with the components of the row representing its layers. This initial version of the model was designed with 14 soil column layers to match the IBM calculations. Thus, in this one-dimensional rendition, only part of the first row of the AU was used for each parallel array of data. In addition, since the temperature and moisture values constitute the state vector (**y**) and thus require the same type of computations, they were placed together in the first row of the AU. While this is initially wasteful in terms of the computational power of the MPP, it facilitates the extension to a two-dimensional model, which will use the other rows and hence the full capabilities of the MPP.

The boundary conditions involve only single values at the top and bottom of the soil column modified with scalar input data, so they may be more efficiently evaluated serially with the MCU. Thus, implementing the model on the MPP involved scalar and parallel calculations as well as communication between the scalar and parallel components for boundary-condition values. The MPP architecture is very efficient at passing scalar values back and forth between the MCU and the AU because it has a register designed for this purpose. Two special-purpose assembly routines were written to take advantage of this. One took a user-specified row and column in a parallel array and placed a given scalar value there. Another took a user-specified row and column in a parallel array and retrieved a value into a scalar in the MCU. These were used in the boundary-condition calculations.

Data initialization on the MPP, therefore, involved initialization of parallel arrays as well as scalar data. These arrays were initialized in FORTRAN arrays and scalars on the VAX and transferred to the MPP scalars and arrays via the DR780 and DR11b buffers. The capability of the stager to permute the data bits between the VAX and AU was used to change the format of the floating-point data from the VAX to the MPP format while the data were being transferred between the VAX and the MPP. Because of this, parallel data transmission between the VAX and the MPP appeared transparent. Explicit bit swapping of scalar integer data between the VAX and MCU to accommodate the two separate integer formats was still necessary, however, as these values were transmitted across the DR11b, which has no data-permuting capability.

Special-purpose routines were written to enable the information in the parallel arrays to be output to the VAX. These routines passed parallel arrays into predefined VAX FORTRAN arrays. MPP Pascal-callable VAX FORTRAN routines were written that could write out the data in these arrays for user examination of intermediate and final results.

The next step in mapping the Hillslope model to the MPP architecture involved implementing the physical model equations in MPP Pascal.

MPP Pascal has a predefined data type called a PARALLEL ARRAY, whose dimensions match those of the MPP Array Unit. Parallel calculations are accomplished by defining variables of this data type and then using them in calculations. All the arithmetic and standard functions are available for use as operators on this parallel data type. In addition, predefined row and column indices enable references to user-specified portions of the parallel array. Masked assignments to portions of an array are possible through the use of the "WHERE" statement. For example:

```
WHERE (ROW_INDEX=0) DO
    A := B;
```

These instructions would move all elements of row 0 of parallel array B into the same locations of parallel array A.

Transfer of information between rows and columns of the arrays is handled via a SHIFT operation in MPP Pascal. This provided the access to the nearest neighbor or NEWS network of the PEs in the AU. Thus, derivatives could be calculated for each soil layer in parallel.

The predicted and corrected state vector values (soil moisture and temperature) involve a calculation of the type

$$\Delta t * \sum W_i * t_i$$

where W_i represents the derivatives for each layer, and t_i represents the constant scalar coefficients in the predictor or corrector equation.

By assigning the derivatives to individual parallel arrays so that ith-order derivatives for each layer are stored in the first row of the ith parallel array, the above calculation can be solved for each layer with a series of parallel operations. $W_i * (t_i * \Delta t)$ involves only multiplication of a parallel array by a scalar, as the coefficients of the predictor equation would be the same for each layer with the same-order back derivatives. The remaining sums can be done for each layer in parallel. Once the predicted and corrected values of each layer are available, their differences can be calculated simultaneously. Comparisons with user-input error windows can be done all at once with simple Boolean tests on the parallel arrays. Recalculation of the derivatives for each layer can then be done in unison with the model equations.

There are additional calculations needed at each layer and each time step in order to include the dependencies of the heat and moisture fluxes on the moisture and temperature profiles through the column.

These involve the matric potential, the hydraulic conductivity, the moisture fluxes as well as their derivatives, and temperatures. Special calculations must be done at the boundaries to include the effects of the air–soil interface at the top as well as the effects of saturated soil at the bottom of the column.

The matric potential and hydraulic conductivity calculations involve only parallel computations. They both depend on calculations of the type

$$\texttt{result} := a * A^b$$

where a and b are scalars and A is a parallel array (which is the same for both the matric potential and hydraulic conductivity). A parallel version of this was calculated by multiplying out "A^b" using the log product (A^n can be calculated with $\log_2$ multiplications (see Devaney 1985) rule, and then multiplying by "a".

The savings in time achieved by doing the calculations in parallel will be considerable as the model is extended to more dimensions. The derivatives (Eqn. (10-10)) are also easily available through parallel operations, as the change between layers can be obtained easily through the "shift" operator, and the thickness of each layer is stored in a parallel array. The same is true of the fluxes. Computation of thermal parameters involved mixing some scalar values with information from various points in parallel arrays and storing the results back in the parallel arrays. Here is where the special-purpose routines were used. Simple "get" and "put" routines were written to get/put a value out of/into a user-specified row and column in a parallel array. This could be done quickly using the special capabilities of the MPP architecture. Moreover, as the needed scalar computations were being done, parallel operations could be performed concurrently in the AU.

MINIMIZING THE PROGRAM EXECUTION TIME BY USING THE CAPABILITIES OF THE MPP THROUGH MPP PASCAL

The multiprocessing capabilities of the MPP are easily available through MPP Pascal. Scalar calculations are performed in the MCU. Parallel calculations are performed in the AU. The scalar MCU and parallel array unit calculations are done simultaneously, except when the MCU is expecting a scalar result from the AU. This would be the case, for example, when doing maximum, minimum, or sum operations on a parallel array. MPP Pascal produces a code that runs in the MCU and makes calls to library and special-purpose routines that run in the AU. The call queue enables the MCU to stack its calls (including register transfer data for each call) to the AU. Thus, a parallel operation, such as an assign, in MPP Pascal translates to a single call by the MCU to the AU to begin processing. The MCU is then free either to do scalar calculations or to send another parallel operation request to the AU. By recognizing that the MCU is a serial processor, it becomes apparent that sending requests to the AU parallel operations and then doing scalar operations in the MCU allows the scalar and parallel calculations to be done concurrently.

This feature of the MPP was used extensively in the boundary-condition calculations to reduce program execution time. It proved to be the single most important tool for reduction of program running time. Other techniques involved setting up masks at initialization time and reusing them instead of regenerating them with "WHERE" statements, and using temporary storage for results of functions that were to be used in multiple calculations.

Results of the Model

The model implementation was tested using data from March 8, 1973, from a bare-soil site in Phoenix, Arizona. All components of the energy balance (Eqn. (10-5)) were measured or estimated for a 24-hour period. In addition, many other parameters, such as the soil thermal and hydraulic parameters, could be estimated from data taken at the site.

Table 10-2. Mean and RMS of the difference between the hourly values of surface variables as computed by the IBM and MPP versions of the model

	Surface moisture, θ_s (volumetric)	Surface temperature, T_s (°C)	Soil heat flux, G(W m^{-2})	Latent heat, LE(W m^{-2})	Sensible heat flux, H(W m^{-2})
Mean	0.0	−0.003	0.25	0.13	0.05
RMS	0.005	0.046	3.2	2.6	1.1

The physics modeled on the MPP has been modeled with an identical equation set in a FORTRAN-coded program on a serial processor—an IBM 3081. This model has been intensively tested (see Gurney, R. J. and Camillo, P. J. (1984). "Modeling Daily Evapotranspiration Using Remotely Sensed Data," *J. of Hydrology,* vol. 69, pp. 305–324), and its successful application was used as a basis for debugging the MPP version. The data described here were used to calibrate the serial program, and the results were compared with the measured evaporation and surface temperatures and moisture. The procedure is described in detail in Camillo et al. (1983).

Briefly, we have used the measured net radiation [R in Eqn. (10-5)], and micrometeorological data to drive the model, which calculates surface soil moisture, surface temperature, and soil heat flux (G), latent heat flux (LE), sensible heat flux (J), and the remaining fluxes in Eqn. (10-5). The computed and measured quantities agreed well, giving confidence in the correctness of the code.

The MPP and IBM results are compared in Table 10-2. If d_1 is the difference between the IBM and MPP variable on the hour, then the mean and RMS in Table 10-2 are defined in the usual way:

$$\text{Mean} = \frac{1}{N} \sum_{i=1}^{N} d_i$$

$$\text{RMS} = \sum_{i=1}^{N} \frac{d_i^2}{N-1}$$

where $N = 24$. These comparisons were made for 0–0.5 cm soil moisture, θ_s; surface temperatures, T_s; soil heat flux, G; latent heat flux, LE; and sensible heat flux, H.

The IBM and MPP values for surface soil moisture and temperature are virtually identical, with the errors in Table 10-2 less than the minimum allowed in the predictor–corrector integrator. The RMS errors in the fluxes are small enough that they could never be measured directly. These numbers are also smaller than the smallest value each flux has during the day, and they are about 1 percent of the corresponding largest value. Therefore, from a physical point of view, the differences are insignificant. From a programming point of view, each hourly difference in the fluxes is what would be expected, given the differences in the temperatures.

The serial-processor version is not identical to the MPP version for timing purposes, because it has additional options not used here. There are also differences in implementation, such as the fact that the serial version used IBM double-precision extensively. The MPP implementation also has unique features, such as using the processor AU and the MCU simultaneously. It also does many more calculations whenever the time step is halved. This makes precise timing comparisons difficult. However, as an indication, the serial program took 4 sec to run these data on the IBM 3081, while the parallel Pascal version took 10 sec to produce essentially identical results on the MPP, even though the MPP was using only 14 of the 16 384 processing elements. The MPP version could deal with many more than the 14 soil layers with very little additional time, while the addition of extra layers adds time to the serial processor run approximately linearly. Thus, it may be seen that the "break-even" points in timing between the two machines occur when the model has approximately 35 layers. The complete Hillslope model, already described briefly in the Introduction, will have many more layers than this, and so it is clearly advantageous, from a timing point of view, to implement it on the MPP.

On a SIMD machine, we have coded a one-dimensional hydrological model of the surface energy, moisture balance, and moisture flow in the unsaturated zone, as a precursor to a complete catchment model. All previous attempts to code a catchment model on a serial machine have been unsuccessful owing to time or space constraints.

We have shown that it is feasible to use the MPP for numerical models, such as this one, and that the parallel architecture makes such calculations more efficient when the physical model includes modeling the same processes at many different points in space.

MAGNETOHYDRODYNAMIC CELLULAR AUTOMATA: THEORY AND POTENTIAL FOR APPLICATIONS TO MASSIVE PARALLELISM*

Cellular Automata

Properly constructed cellular automata can exhibit long-wavelength behavior essentially identical to that of hydrodynamics. Extension of the hydrodynamic results to more complex systems such as magnetohydrodynamics is discussed here. New variables and nonhydrodynamic forces on fluid elements can be handled by augmenting the number of microscopic degrees of freedom. Modification to the hydrodynamic microscopic streaming rules must take into account

---

* This section was contributed by Hudong Chen and William H. Matthaeus.

This work was supported in part by the National Science Foundation under Grant ATM-8609740 and in part by the Goddard Space Flight Center under the auspices of the Directors Discretionary Fund and the Solar Terrestrial Theory Program.

required symmetry properties of the macroscopic system. The magneto-hydrodynamic model described here uses two vector degrees of freedom on a hexagonal lattice with 36 allowed particle states per cell. The model allows computation of both Lorentz force and magnetic induction effects. The rules are entirely local, so the model is well suited to massively parallel computations.

A cellular automaton (CA) is a discrete-time dynamical system consisting of a set of cells on a lattice, a definition of the state of the system in terms of one or more integer quantities defined at each cell, and a set of local rules for simultaneously updating the state of all the cells (Wolfram 1983, 1986; Frisch et al. 1986). After the introduction of the CA concept by von Neumann (1966), early uses were found in a number of diverse areas (see Wolfram 1983), including studies of "lattice gases" (Hardy and Pomeau 1972) that displayed properties akin to hydrodynamics. The viewpoint emerged (Pomeau 1984; Margolus 1984; Wolfram 1986) that CAs with built-in microscopic randomness and carefully designed conservation laws might exhibit macroscopic features of a variety of physical systems, and that, in effect, such CAs might represent an alternative method for the solution of the relevant differential equations.

Recently Frisch, Hasslacher, and Pomeau (1986) (cited hereafter as FMP) showed that a particular class of CAs known as hexagonal lattice gases evolves, in the incompressible limit, according to the two-dimensional hydrodynamic equations. This discovery has raised interest in a number of CA-related questions. Do CA models such as FHP that have been examined principally on the basis of lattice gas theory actually work in practice? How good is the theory (Hardy and Pomeau 1972; Wolfram 1983, 1986; Hatori and Montgomery 1987; Gatignol 1975) on which the models are based? Questions such as these are currently being studied, especially by direct tests of computational precision (d'Humieres et al. 1985; Dahlburg et al. 1987) using lattice gas hydrodynamic codes.

A more subtle question (Orszag and Yakhot 1986) is whether CA algorithms are now or ever will be competitive with classical numerical methods for solution of hydrodynamic or other partial differential equations. In principle, CAs have a lot going for them. Encouraging computational features (Wolfram 1986; FHP) include lack of roundoff and numerical instability errors, since only integer or Boolean operations need be performed during the main update cycle. Moreover, in a pure CA model, updates depend only on information available at the cell being updated; that is, the dynamics are completely local. This largely eliminates the computational inefficiencies inherent in handling large data structures using other algorithms that demand random or delocalized "scatters" and "gathers." Thus, CAs with the local property are ideally suited for implementation on current vector and parallel computers. For example, when implemented on machines with highly parallel architectures such as the GSFC Massively Parallel Processor (Dorband 1986), a local CA algorithm should keep almost all the processors busy with independent Boolean computation or fast communication with nearest neighbors, leading to the possibliity of speed-up factors of hundreds or perhaps thousands over a CRAY-1 running the same algorithm.

It is not entirely clear whether estimates (Ôrszag and Yakhot 1986) of unfavorable Reynolds-number scaling of CA timings relative to timings of classical methods will pertain to CA implementations that are both highly parallel and efficient at bit-serial manipulations. Specifically, in the estimates of Orszag and Yakhot the "work" W and "storage" S are computed for CA and classical methods on the same footing. Large numerical factors in favor of the CA timings may multiply these estimates, solely on the basis of differences in bit versus floating-point speed per operation and the number of such operations required per cell update. In addition, floating-point word size must grow to maintain precision when the Reynolds number becomes arbitrarily large, whereas CAs will always use bits. Perhaps most important when considering extremely parallel architectures is the possibility that W/S for a parallel CA ought to be compared with W for a classical method such as Fourier spectral analysis that probably does not adapt to the parallel environment nearly as well.

Here we will discuss another area of current interest, namely the development of CAs for systems related to hydrodynamics. Specifically, we are concerned with magnetohydrodynamics (MHD) (Cowling 1976) in the same plane two-dimensional geometry (Fyfe et al. 1977) as used in the FHP hydrodynamic model. The two-dimensional incompressible MHD equations (Cowling 1976; Fyfe et al. 1977) may be written as

$$\rho\left(\frac{\partial \mathbf{v}}{\partial t} + \mathbf{v} \cdot \nabla \mathbf{v}\right) = -\nabla \mathbf{p} + \mathbf{J} \times \mathbf{B} + \nu \nabla^2 \mathbf{v} \tag{10-12}$$

$$\frac{\partial \mathbf{B}}{\partial t} + \mathbf{v} \cdot \nabla \mathbf{B} = \mathbf{B} \cdot \nabla \mathbf{v} + \mu \nabla^2 \mathbf{B} \tag{10-13}$$

where $\mathbf{B}$, $\mathbf{v}$, $\mathbf{J}$, $\mathbf{p}$, ρ, μ, and ν are the magnetic field, velocity field, electric current density, pressure, mass density, resistivity, and viscosity, respectively. For incompressible flow $\nabla \cdot \mathbf{v} = 0$ and $\rho = $ constant, while the pressure is determined from the Poisson equation that results from computing the divergence of (10-13). In the relevant two-dimensional (x, y) geometry, $\mathbf{v}$ and $\mathbf{B}$ lie in the x–y plane and depend only on those coordinates and time. The magnetic potential $\mathbf{A}_z$ is related to $\mathbf{B}$ by $\mathbf{B} = \nabla \times \mathbf{A}_z e_z$ where $\mathbf{z} = \mathbf{x} \times \mathbf{y}$. The electric current density is $\mathbf{J} = \nabla \times \mathbf{B} = -\nabla^2 \mathbf{A}_z$. The hydrodynamic model considered by FHP is simply recovered from the above by setting $\mathbf{B} = 0$ everywhere.

The extension of CA modeling to MHD is potentially an important one, since MHD is a central dynamical model in studies of astrophysics, space physics, and laboratory fusion plasma physics. In the following, we describe the MHD model and the problems inherent in applying CA methods to it. We develop physical motivations for alleviating the difficulties and present an algorithm for local CA computation of the MHD equations. The algorithm represents a generalization of the hexagonal lattice gas approach that may be useful for a variety of systems in addition to MHD.

Hydrodynamic CA and Vector Potential–Based MHD CA

The hexagonal lattice gas model (Frisch et al. 1986) consists of a regular hexagonal grid tiling the simulation domain, with dynamical particles residing at the vertices. Allowed particle states are labeled by an index that controls direction of particle motion; each of six index values represent particle motion or "streaming" in one of the six natural directions on the lattice. At most, one particle resides in each state, so no more than six particles simultaneously inhabit a cell. With lattice spacing and particle speed set to unity, particles stream at each discrete time level from one cell vertex to an adjacent one. Upon arrival at a cell, collisions occur with other inhabitants of the cell, governed by scattering rules (Frisch et al. 1986; Wolfram 1986) that conserve total particle number and momentum at the cell. The Fermi-type exclusion property is preserved by the dynamics. The macroscopic velocity **v** and particle number n are suitably defined as averages over the microstate.

Using lattice kinetic theory, FHP showed that this simple system obeys the two-dimensional incompressible hydrodynamic equations when the Mach number of the flow (essentially v since the "sound speed" is $O(1)$) is low and the density is less than 3. While the details of this demonstration are somewhat involved, one can easily understand heuristically why the model works. The collisions produce randomness at the short wavelengths and high frequencies while conserving momentum. The particles transport momentum as they move from cell to cell. Provided that density irregularities are smoothed out rapidly enough and the macroscopic state of the system "forgets" the microscopic geometry, the macrostate should reflect conservation of momentum, which is just what the Navier–Stokes equation implies. The real trick is that the choice of the hexagonal grid ensures (Frisch et al. 1986; Wolfram 1986) that the pressure tensor has the correct rotational properties at low Mach number, so the underlying hexagonal geometry is properly forgotten by the coarse-grained macroscopic quantities.

In seeking to generalize the FHP model to MHD, it would appear that the basic mechanism for momentum transport can be carried over from the purely hydrodynamic model and that one needs to concentrate on modeling the behavior of the magnetic field **B** and the effect of the Lorentz force **J** × **B** on the motion of fluid elements. The first model that addressed this problem was given by Montgomery and Doolen (1987), who chose to consider that magnetic behavior in terms of the magnetic vector potential, A_z, which obeys

$$\frac{\partial A_z}{\partial t} + \mathbf{v} \cdot \nabla A_z = \mu \nabla^2 A_z \tag{10-14}$$

Montgomery and Doolen introduced new states on the lattice labeled by a "vector potential quantum" σ that takes on values ± 1 and 0, for a total of 18 states per cell. By adopting vector-potential-conserving scattering rules, they were able to show that the model obeys Eqn. (10-14) in appropriate limits. However, because there is no back-reaction of the vector potential states on the motion of particles, there is no acceleration of fluid elements due to a Lorentz force. Consequently, it was suggested by Montgomery and Doolen (1987) that the Lorentz force could be incorporated as an external force, computed as needed from the macroscopic state of the vector potential by the relation $\mathbf{J} \times \mathbf{B}$ written as $-\nabla A_z \nabla^2 A_z$. The resulting model cannot be updated locally and therefore falls outside the realm of "pure" CA MHD.

Without activating the externally computed Lorentz force, the vector potential in the above model behaves essentially as a passive scalar. In our own investigations in this area (Chen and Matthaeus 1987), an even simpler passive scalar model was formulated for the behavior of A_z. Using only six states per hexagon, particles are "colored" by a passive label σ that may have the values 0 or 1. There is no influence whatsoever of the color on the particle motions or on the nature of the collisions. As in the Montgomery and Doolen model, the macroscopic A_z is related to the microstate by $nA_z = \sum_{a,\sigma} \sigma f_a^b$, where f_a^b is the particle distribution function and a labels the velocity quantum, but now σ refers to the particle color and not to additional states.

Upon considering how passive A_z models might be modified to allow microscopic computation of a quantity whose ensemble average effect is the Lorentz force, one is led to consider differences between nearest cell neighbor of quantities related to σ and therefore to A_z. This appears to be very difficult and probably impossible to accomplish. The principal difficulty seems to be that while one can find microscopic quantities A_1 and A_2 such that $\langle A_1 \rangle = \nabla A_z$ and $\langle A_2 \rangle = \nabla^2 A_z$, the estimate of the Lorentz force $-\langle A_2 A_1 \rangle$ will always be plagued by noise, especially since CAs need typically to be run in parameter regimes for which the means are smaller than the fluctuations. Conceptually, the problem is that the vector potential formulation, while fine for a passive scalar problem, suffers from the attempt to represent MHD physics that intrinsically has a vector character. Even if the macroscopic behavior of a scalar is known accurately, the microscopic information concerning its derivatives is likely to be nonlocal, so vector information is not available when it is needed.

Two-vector CA Transport

The vector nature of MHD referred to above is made clear by considering the structure of Eqns. (10-12) and (10-13), neglecting pressure and dissipation, in terms of the Elsasser (1950) variables $\mathbf{z}^{\pm} = \mathbf{v} \pm \mathbf{B}/\rho^{1/2}$. From $\partial \mathbf{z}^{\pm}/\partial t \approx \mathbf{z} \cdot \nabla \mathbf{z}^{\pm}$ it is easily seen that the relevant nonlinearities, including Lorentz force, appear as a generalization of advection, wherein the two combinations, of $\mathbf{v}$ and $\mathbf{B}$ "stream" in each other's "velocity field." Consequently, it would seem necessary to treat $\mathbf{B}$ on more equal footing with $\mathbf{v}$ to achieve a local MHD CA model.

In the model, we describe how (Chen and Matthaeus 1987) particles move on a hexagonal grid on which each particle occupies a state labeled by two vectors, $\hat{\mathbf{e}}_a$ and $\hat{\mathbf{e}}_b$, where as usual (Frisch et al. 1986) $\hat{\mathbf{e}}_a = (\cos 2\pi a/6,$

$\sin 2\pi b/6$), $\hat{\mathbf{e}}_b = (\cos 2\pi b/6, \sin 2\pi b/6)$ and both a and b run from 1 to 6. No more than one particle in each cell may occupy a state with a specified a and b, so that, at most, 36 particles may simultaneously reside in a cell. Let N^b ($=0$ or 1) denote the particle population at a certain location and define $f^b \equiv \langle N_a^b \rangle$ to be the ensemble-averaged particle distribution. At each time level, the noncollisional component of particle motion (i.e., "streaming") consists of motion to the adjacent cell in the direction $\hat{\mathbf{e}}_a$ with probability $1 - |P_{ab}|$. Alternatively, with probability $|P_{ab}|$, the particle moves to the adjacent cell in the direction $\hat{\mathbf{e}}_b$ $P_{ab}/|P_{ab}|$. This leads to a kinetic equation (Wolfram 1986) for the slow time scale evolution of the tensor distribution function $f_a^b(x, t)$,

$$\frac{\partial f_a^b}{\partial t} = -\{(1 - |P_{ab}|)\hat{\mathbf{e}}_a + P_{ab}\hat{\mathbf{e}}_b\} \cdot \nabla f^b + \Omega_{ab} \tag{10-15}$$

where Ω_{ab} represents the effect of collisions that modify f_a^b.

The macroscopic number density, fluid velocity field, and magnetic field will be designated as n, $\mathbf{v}$ and $\mathbf{B}$, respectively, and will be related to the microstate by the relations

$$n = \sum_{a, b} f_a^b \tag{10-16}$$

$$n\mathbf{v} = \sum_{a, b} \{(1 - |P_{ab}|)\hat{\mathbf{e}}_a + P_{ab}\hat{\mathbf{e}}_b\}f_a^b \tag{10-17}$$

$$n\mathbf{B} = \sum_{a, b} \{Q_{ab}\hat{\mathbf{e}}_b + R_{ab}\hat{\mathbf{e}}_a\}f_a^b \tag{10-18}$$

The 6×6 time- and space-independent matrices $\mathbf{P}$, $\mathbf{Q}$, and $\mathbf{R}$ need to be determined to specify the model. We also adopt the convention that all allowed collisions must preserve n, B, and v at each cell (Chen and Matthaeus 1987).

So far, the model has not at all been specialized to treat MHD, but there are already some local physics built into the above definitions. It is convenient to think of $\hat{\mathbf{e}}_a$ as the quantum mainly associated with momentum transport. This is exact when the effects of the new quanta $\hat{\mathbf{e}}_b$ are turned off by setting $P_{ab} = 0$. When $P_{ab} \neq 0$, the effect of the "magnetic quanta" $\hat{\mathbf{e}}_b$ is to deflect the particle motion, in a way that depends not only on the choice of the matrix elements of $\mathbf{P}$, $\mathbf{Q}$, and $\mathbf{R}$, but also on the local distribution of particles over the various $\hat{\mathbf{e}}_b$ states. In fact, it is clear from Eqn. (10-15) and the collision symmetries that the macroscopic particle density n must move in the "deflected" velocity field defined by Eqn. (10-17) in order that the continuity equation,

$$\frac{\partial n}{\partial t} + \nabla \cdot (n\mathbf{v}) = 0 \tag{10-19}$$

be satisfied.

Before specifying the matrix elements, the net effect of deflection is too complex to intuit, but it is clear that if f_a^b varies in space, the level of deflection will also vary. Fluid elements will experience a force. The nature of this force will be determined by selecting the matrix elements, which are, at this point, 108 in number. Elementary principles of rotational invariance reduce this number considerably. By requiring that the behavior of the system be locally invariant under both proper and improper rotations, we conclude that **P**, **Q**, and **R** must be circulant (Wolfram 1983) matrices, and that P_{ab}, Q_{ab} and R_{ab} depend only on $|a - b|$. There remain 12 coefficients in these matrices that must be selected to specify the nature of the forces on the fluid elements and the equation of motion of the field **B**. While we have in mind in the next section to specialize to an MHD model, it is noteworthy that variations of the subsequent developments may allow similar CA modeling of other hydrodynamic-like systems involving two vectors, such as motion of a fluid in a gravitational field.

MHD CA Model

Specialization to MHD is achieved by consideration of further symmetries of **P**, **Q**, and **R** that are implied by the structure of Eqns. (10-12) and (10-13). First, notice that the Lorentz force is unchanged by the transformation $B \rightarrow -B$. We wish to have this macroscopic transformation correspond to the microscopic transformation $\hat{\mathbf{e}}_b \rightarrow \hat{\mathbf{e}}_b$, so that $\hat{\mathbf{e}}_b$ will act as the magnetic quantum in the same way that $\hat{\mathbf{e}}_a$ controls undeflected momentum transport. To achieve this, imagine that $B \rightarrow -B$ everywhere while $\hat{\mathbf{e}}_b \rightarrow -\hat{\mathbf{e}}_b$, but that neither **v** nor $\hat{\mathbf{e}}_a$ are affected. Upon consideration of Eqns. (10-17) and (10-18), one can see that this requires $P_{ab} \equiv -P_{ab} + 3$ to ensure that the velocity is unchanged, while $Q_{ab} \equiv Q_{ab} + 3$ and $R_{ab} = -R_{ab} + 3$. Combined with the rotational and reflectional symmetries from the previous section, we are left with just six independent coefficients, chosen to be P_{aa}, P_{aa+1}, Q_{aa}, Q_{aa+1}, R_{aa} and R_{aa+1}. One can also verify that this choice of symmetry is consistent (Chen and Matthaeus 1987) with qualitative behavior of typical particles in model sheared magnetic and velocity fields. The symmetries of the Lorentz force and field line stretching (Chen and Matthaeus 1987) are thus accounted for in the above symmetry considerations. With these choices, the transformation $\hat{\mathbf{e}}_b \rightarrow -\hat{\mathbf{e}}_b$ will cause $B \rightarrow -B$ without changing **v** while the transformation $\hat{\mathbf{e}}_a \rightarrow -\hat{\mathbf{e}}_a$ will lead to $v \rightarrow -v$ without modifying **B**.

Before presenting the results from the kinetic theory treatment of this model, the nature of the allowed collisions should be specified. In order to preserve n, **B**, and **v**, we have found that the vector sum of the $\hat{\mathbf{e}}_a$ quanta and the $\hat{\mathbf{e}}_b$ quanta for all particles involved in a collision must be 0. This is a generalization of a similar result for the 2- and 3-body collisions used by FHP (1986; Wolfram 1986). Thus, 2-body collisions of the form

$$(a, b) + (a + 3, b + 3)(a', b') + (a' + 3, b' + 3) \qquad (10\text{-}20)$$

are permitted where a, b, a', and b' are any integers from 1 to 6 (sums treated as mod 6). Similarly, 3-body collisions are only possible when

$$(a, b) + (a + 2, b + 2) + (a + 4, b + 4)$$
$$(a', b') + (a' + 2, b' + 2) + (a' + 4, b' + 4) \qquad (10\text{-}21)$$

Higher-order collisions can be generated by applying the above rules (10-20) and (10-21) to cells with total occupation numbers greater than 3 provided that the Fermi exclusion rule is not violated.

Following the usual procedure (Frisch et al. 1986; Wolfram 1986; Montgomery and Doolen 1987), we argue that the collisional time and space scales are well-enough separated from the fluid scales that the CA system is always locally near to an equilibrium state determined only by the dynamically important conservation laws that characterize the collisions. In the present case, this leads to a Fermi–Dirac distribution with three Lagrange multipliers. The distribution (Chen and Matthaeus 1987) is expanded for low Mach number and magnetic field strength and the resulting approximate distribution is used in the kinetic equation (10-15) along with the definitions of the macroscopic quantities (10-16)–(10-18) to deduce equations of motion for $n\mathbf{v}$ and $n\mathbf{B}$. After a considerable amount of algebra (which nonetheless would have been much more tedious had the symmetry conditions not reduced the number of undetermined coefficients from 108 to 6), equations having the same general form as the MHD equations emerge. These are

$$\frac{\partial(nv)}{\partial t} = -C_1 \nabla \frac{n}{6} - C_2 \nabla \cdot [nG(n)\mathbf{v}\mathbf{v}]$$

$$+ C_3 \nabla \cdot [nG(n)\mathbf{B}\mathbf{B}] + C_4 \nabla [nG(n)\mathbf{v}^2] + C_5 \nabla [nG(n)\mathbf{B}^2] \quad (10\text{-}22)$$

and

$$\frac{\partial(nB)}{\partial t} = -D_1 \nabla \cdot [nG(n)\mathbf{v}\mathbf{B}]$$

$$+ D_2 \nabla \cdot [nG(n)\mathbf{B}\mathbf{v}] + D_3 \nabla [n\mathbf{v} \cdot \mathbf{B}] \quad (10\text{-}23)$$

where $G(n) = (18 - n)/(36 - n)$ and C_1, C_2, C_3, C_4, C_5, D_1, D_2, and D_3 are rational functions of the six independent streaming coefficients in the matrices $\mathbf{P}$, $\mathbf{Q}$, and $\mathbf{R}$.

To bring Eqns. (10-22) and (10-23) as closely as possible into correspondence with Eqns. (10-12) and (10-13), the remaining streaming coefficients must be determined according to the constraints $D_3 = 0$ (for no sources of $\nabla \cdot \mathbf{B}$), $C_1 > 0$ (for nonnegative pressure), $C_2 = C_3 = D_1 = D_2 > 0$ (so that the various terms in Eqns. (10-12) and (10-13) are represented with the correct relative weighting) and $|P_{ab}| < 1$ (for a probabilistic interpretation of the streaming). These give four equations and four inequalities that restrict allowed values of streaming coefficients P_{aa}, P_{aa+1}, Q_{aa}, Q_{aa+1}, R_{aa} and R_{aa+1}. We have found numerical solutions to the constraints that indicate the existence of continuous ranges of allowed parameters, all of which have $P_{aa} < 0$. One solution is $P_{aa} = -1/3$, $P_{aa+1} = +2/9$, $Q_{aa} = 1/2$, $Q_{aa+1} = 0.065$, $R_{aa} = 0$ and $R_{aa+1} \approx -0.232$.

Having solved the constraint equations, the final result for the macroscopic behavior of the MHD CA model is

$$\frac{\partial(nv)}{\partial t} = -C_2\nabla \cdot [nG(n)(\mathbf{vv} - \mathbf{BB})]$$

$$-\nabla\left[C_1\frac{n}{6} - nG(n)(C_4\mathbf{v}^2 + C_5\mathbf{B}^2)\right] \qquad (10\text{-}24)$$

$$\frac{\partial(nB)}{\partial t} = -C_2\nabla \cdot [nG(n)(\mathbf{vB} - \mathbf{Bv})] \qquad (10\text{-}25)$$

For the above solution, we have found $C_1 = 1.7$, $C_2 = 1.09$, $C_4 = -C_5 = C_2/2$. For $|\mathbf{v}| \ll 1$ and $|\mathbf{B}| \ll 1$, corresponding to low Mach number flow, the density will exhibit only small fluctuations about a uniform constant value (Frisch et al. 1986; Wolfram 1986) so that the factors of n in various terms cancel and the factor $C_2G(n)$ may be used to rescale the relationship between microscopic and macroscopic time (Frisch et al. 1986). This leads to a set of dynamical equations essentially identical to incompressible MHD. All numerical solutions to the constraints that we have found have the property that $C_4 = -C_5 = C_2/2$, leading to an exact representation of the Lorentz force in Eqn. (10-24).

There are several additional properties of the model that are discussed elsewhere (Chen and Matthaeus 1987) in greater detail. For example, while $\nabla \cdot \mathbf{B} = 0$ is not exactly enforced in the model, it is expected to decay in time from an initial value that may be present due to noise in the initial conditions (Dahlberg et al. 1987). The sound speed is $c_s \approx \sqrt{C_1/6}$, so the incompressible limit should not be much more difficult to achieve than in the hydrodynamic case, since many allowed values of the parameters have $C_1 = O(1)$. Moreover, DC levels of magnetic field are easily incorporated by simply establishing a nonzero spatially averaged value for $\mathbf{B}$ in the initial conditions; conservation of $\mathbf{B}$ by collisions ensures it will be time-independent, provided that boundary conditions are appropriate. As in the hydrodynamic case (Frisch et al. 1986), boundary conditions are easy to implement by direct intervention at the boundary with suitable adjustments to $\hat{\mathbf{e}}_a$ and $\hat{\mathbf{e}}_b$ populations.

Discussion of Cellular Automata

We have shown that generalizations of the FHP hydrodynamic CA to include fluid-like systems with two transported vectors can be achieved by defining an additional microscopic vector quantum, adjusting the streaming algorithm to account for macroscopic forces through microscopic particle deflection and then determining the nature of the additional vector and the nonhydrodynamic force on the fluid elements by symmetry considerations and a set of constraint equations. The basic framework of the model may likely be carried over to a number of fluid-related models, such as those with externally applied non-hydrodynamic forces. The idea of multidirectional streaming has some precedent in the recent one-dimensional CA model of Boghosian and Levermore (1987). The present approach is successful in establishing, through use of lattice kinetic theory, that a local MHD CA is feasible. All information used in the MHD model to update a cell state is available at each time level solely from the particle population presently at the cell, or from information carried by streaming to adjacent cells. Thus, efficient implementation in parallel computational environments is possible. We currently have plans underway to test the algorithm on the Massively Parallel Processor at NASA/GSFC, in collaboration with J. Dorband, E. Seiler, and L. Klein.

Acknowledgment

Helpful discussions with J. Dorband, L. Klein, T. Vachaspati, S. Wolfram, and D. Montgomery are gratefully acknowledged.

Image Processing for Remote Sensor Observations

RESTORING BLURRED ASTRONOMICAL IMAGES WITH THE MPP*

Image Degradation

We describe a method for algebraic image restoration, capable of treating images of astronomical objects. For a typical 500×500 image, direct algebraic restoration would require the solution of a $250\,000 \times 250\,000$ linear system. We use the block iterative approach to reduce the problem to solving 4900 121×121 linear systems. We have implemented the algorithm on the Goddard Space Flight Center's Massively Parallel Processor, which can solve a 121×121 system in approximately 0.04 sec. Here, we show examples of our results for various astronomical images.

The discrete model of linear image degradation is specified by the equation:

$$b = Hx + n \qquad (10\text{-}26)$$

where b and x are the pixel values of the degraded and original undegraded images stacked into column vectors, H is a matrix constructed from the impulse response (or point-spread function) of the degradation, and n is an unknown additive noise vector. The object of restoration is to determine x, given b and

---

* This section was contributed by Don J. Lindler and Sara R. Heap.

possibly information on the properties of n. If the point spread function used to construct H is not known for the given optical-detector configuration, it must be estimated from the blurred image b. The point-spread function is most easily estimated from point sources (i.e., stars) on the blurred image.

Since H may be ill-conditioned or singular, and only the statistical properties of the noise are known, there are many solutions for x that satisfy Eqn. (10-26). The success of a restoration therefore depends on the ability to model and apply to the restoration, known or assumed properties of the desired solution, such as positivity or smoothness.

Some advantages of algebraic image restoration are the following.

1. The point spread function may be spatially variant.
2. If a constrained least squares method is used, the applied constraints may be varied from pixel to pixel to make maximum use of the known image properties.
3. Missing or bad pixel values in the blurred images can be easily handled without directly attempting to repair their values.
4. Noise properties can vary from pixel to pixel.

The main disadvantage of algebraic image restoration is the size of the linear system. For a 500×500 pixel image, H is a $250\,000 \times 250\,000$ matrix. Even with the most powerful computers available (including the MPP), a direct solution of the system would be impossible. In the next section, we describe a technique—the block iterative method, of solving large linear systems.

The Block Iterative Restoration Algorithm

BLOCK JACOBI ITERATION

In most astronomical images, the point-spread function has a much smaller spatial extent than the image, so it is appropriate to work on the image locally. We therefore divide the image into blocks and restore each block separately, using values from the previous iteration as estimates of the unblurred image values outside the block. In most instances, the blurred image is a good choice for the starting or zeroth iteration. This type of iteration is called block Jacobi or group Jacobi iteration (Young 1971) and can be formulated in matrix notation as follows.

Consider the blurred image, b, divided into m blocks of equal size B_i, $i = 1, \ldots , m$:

$$
B = \begin{vmatrix}
B_1 & B_2 & \cdots & & \\
& B_{i-1} & B_i & B_{i+1} & \\
\cdots & \cdots & \cdots & \cdots & \\
& & & B_{m-1} & B_m
\end{vmatrix}
$$

Stack the elements of each block and place them into a vector:

$$B = \begin{vmatrix} B_1 \\ B_2 \\ \cdots \\ B_m \end{vmatrix}$$

Ignoring the noise for now, we write the system as

$$HX = B$$

where H is partitioned into blocks

$$H = \begin{vmatrix} H_{11} & H_{12} & \cdots & H_{1m} \\ H_{21} & H_{22} & \cdots & H_{2m} \\ \cdots & \cdots & \cdots & \cdots \\ H_{m1} & H_{m2} & \cdots & H_{mm} \end{vmatrix}$$

and X contains the restored values, blocked in the same manner as B. If the image were divided into blocks of n pixels each, then the block H_{ij} would have size $n \times n$. The block Jacobi method can now be written as

$$H_{ij}X_i^{r+1} = B_i - \sum_{j=1, j \neq i}^{m} H_{ij}X_j^r \tag{10-27}$$

$i = 1, \ldots, m$, and where X_i^r is the stacked values for iteration r of block j. If we define the vector on the right-hand side of Eqn. (10-27) as $B\,\mathrm{MOD}_i$ (i.e., the blurred image less contributions from outside the block as estimated from the previous iteration of the undegraded image), the linear system for block i can now be written as

$$H_{ii}X^{r+1} = B\,\mathrm{MOD}_i \tag{10-28}$$

Using the block Jacobi method, we can reduce the problem to solving m smaller systems of size $n \times n$ of the form

$$Hx = b \tag{10-29}$$

where H is H_{ii} for block i; x is x_i^{r+1} for block i, iteration $r + 1$; and b is $B\,MOD_i$ for block i.

The solution for block i now requires the solution of an $n \times n$ linear system. For example, to restore a 100×100 pixel image divided into $m = 100$ blocks, each of size, $n \times n = 10 \times 10$, the largest system to be solved would have H_{ii} of size 100×100. Since solutions of linear systems require on the order of n^3 operations, the block approach compares favorably to the direct solution of the $10\,000 \times 10\,000$ system. For a spatially invariant point-spread function, the problem is further reduced because H_{ii} will be identical for all $i = 1, \ldots, m$.

If a constrained least-squares approach is used to solve the linear system, the solution will converge to acceptable results even with a block size as small as the full-width at half-maximum (FWHM) of the point-spread function. Overlapping the blocks (accepting only the central portion for the next iteration) gives faster convergence or may produce convergence when no overlap results in divergence.

IMAGE CONSTRAINTS

The block Jacobi method reduces the restoration to solution of many smaller linear systems, but it does not address the ill-conditioned nature of H or the presence of noise in the blurred image. An ill-conditioned matrix means that small changes in b, caused by noise, yield large changes in the solution $x = H^{-1}b$. In this section, we show how constrained solutions can handle these problems.

In most images, the data vary smoothly except at isolated points or edges. For example, an image of a star field will vary smoothly, except at locations of individual stars. We can make use of this image property, smoothness, by applying a constrained least squares fit. Specifically, we minimize a linear operator $\|Qx\|$ (i.e., The sum of the squares in Qx), where Q is a matrix designed to control smoothness or other characteristics of the image (Twomey 1963; Philips 1962). For example, we can control smoothness in the one-dimensional case by minimizing the second difference in the solution subject to some other constraint. If the statistical properties of the noise are known, we could minimize the second difference such that the norm of $\|Hx - b\| = \|n\|$; that is to say, the difference of the blurred image and the solution reconvolved with the point spread function should have the same properties as the noise. In this case (minimize the second difference), Q would have the form

$$Q = \begin{vmatrix} 0 & 0 & & & & & \\ -1 & 2 & -1 & & & & \\ & -1 & 2 & -1 & 0 & & \\ \cdots & \cdots & \cdots & \cdots & \cdots & \cdots & \cdots \\ & & & & -1 & 2 & -1 \\ & & & & & 0 & 0 \end{vmatrix}$$

We use the method of Lagrangian multipliers, sometimes called the method of undetermined multipliers, to make the constrained least-squares fit. The solution of x is then given by (Andrews 1977):

$$x = (H^{T}H + \gamma Q^{T}Q)^{-1}H^{T}b \qquad (10\text{-}30)$$

where γ is the reciprocal Lagrangian multiplier. The value of γ can be iteratively selected to control the amount of constraint in the solution. The solution using Lagrangian multipliers places no restrictions on the form of Q. This flexibility allows the development of a variety of constraints depending on the known properties of the image.

Figure 10-9 shows the application of this constrained least-squares filter for a test case (a point source) with different values of γ_2. The subscript 2 is used to indicate that the constraint is the minimum second difference. Note in Figure

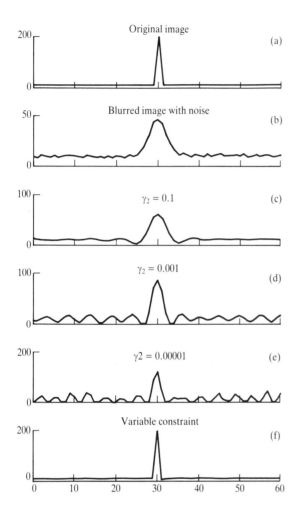

Figure 10-9. Effect of Lagrangian multipliers. (a) Original image; (b) image blurred with Gaussian PSF ($\sigma = 2.0$ pixels) and noise added ($\sigma = 1$ DN); (c) restoration with $\gamma_2 = 0.1$; (d) restoration with $\gamma_2 = 0.001$; (e) restoration with $\gamma_2 = 0.00001$; (f) restoration with $\gamma_2 = 0.1$ with constraint removed at the point source.

10-9(c), with the largest value of γ_2, that noise in the solution has been suppressed. However, the width of the point-source profile is almost as wide as the blurred profile. Also, some ringing in the restored profile is evident. Restored values on each side of the profile drop significantly below the background level. These problems result because the second difference is large at the location of a point source. We therefore remove the second-difference constraint at the point source by setting the rows of Q corresponding to the point-source location to zero. Figure 10-9(f) shows a restoration of the same test image when the second-difference constraint is not applied at the point source. A significant improvement is apparent.

A direct extension of the method to two-dimensional images is to minimize the Laplacian at each point. The Laplacian operator has a value at each pixel equal to four times the pixel value minus the values of the four immediate neighboring pixels. We use the subscript ⌉ to indicate the presence of the

Laplacian constraint. As before, we set rows of the matrix Q to zero when the Laplacian constraint is not appropriate (i.e., edges or point sources).

The constraint need not be binary: we can vary the amount of constraint between no constraint to full constraint for any pixel, simply by multiplying the appropriate row in Q by a constant factor running from 0 to 1.

Another useful constraint is to minimize the difference of x from a trial solution (i.e., minimize $\|p - x\|$). The solution using Lagrangian multipliers is given by Twomey (1963):

$$x = (H^T H + \gamma_t I)^{-1}(H^T b + \gamma_t p) \qquad (10\text{-}31)$$

where p is the trial solution, I is the identity matrix, and γ_t is the reciprocal Lagrangian multiplier. The subscript, t, will be used to identify the constraint as minimization of the solution from a trial solution. Some possible choices for the trial solution, p, are a constant value (i.e., all zeros) or the blurred image itself. In either case, the ill-conditioned nature of H can be avoided and reasonable solutions obtained.

Multiple image constraints can be applied simultaneously:

$$x = (H^T H + \gamma_a Q^T Q + \gamma_b Q^T Q + \cdots + \gamma_t I)^{-1}(H^T b + \gamma_t p) \qquad (10\text{-}32)$$

where a different value of γ can be selected for each constraint.

Selection of the reciprocal Lagrangian multipliers is done by trial and error with the evaluation of γ by visual inspection of the results for various values of γ or by examination of the difference of blurred image and the solution is reconvolved with the point-spread function. The difference should have the same properties as the noise.

MISSING OR BAD DATA VALUES

A problem occurs when trying to restore images with missing or bad data values (i.e., cosmic ray hits or bad charge-coupled device columns). If these defects are not taken into account in the restoration, their bad values will propagate to a larger portion of the output solution. (To some extent, every point in the solution depends on all other values in the blurred image.)

One method of handling bad pixels is to attempt to repair them before restoration by interpolating from neighboring values. This approach is successful only if the repair is accurate. An alternative method is to make no attempt at prior repair but handle them in the restoration process. In this approach, the restored image will have more data values than the blurred image, and the linear system is underdetermined and, therefore, singular (i.e., no direct inverse exists). To ignore defective pixels, we set the corresponding rows in matrix H to zero.

This method of implementation (as opposed to removing row H creating a nonsquare underdetermined system) allows us to keep the matrix H square and decrease the complexity of implementation. Keeping H square in no way alleviates the problem of singularity. However, the method of constrained least-squares solution does alleviate the problem of singularity and produces reasonable solutions.

Implementation of the Algorithm on the MPP

The procedure for block iterative restoration described earlier is actually carried out over three computers. We use our laboratory VAX 750 with Gould DeAnza image display for interactive analysis of the blurred and restored images. We then use a local area network to copy the blurred image and point-spread function from the laboratory computer over to the MPP VAX 780 host computer. We use the latter machine to prepare input to the MPP, invoke the MPP, and reconstruct the output from the MPP into restored images. Preparation mainly involves dividing the various images (blurred image, constraint image, and trial solution) into blocks of 11×11 pixels, stacking them into vectors, and formatting them for access by the FORTRAN driver. Reconstruction of MPP output is the reverse procedure. The MPP itself is saved for the computer-intensive tasks of matrix multiplication and solution of the linear systems. These tasks will be described in some detail later in this section.

The primary software system that we use for interactive image analysis is Interactive Data Language (IDL, Research Systems Inc., Denver, Colo.). We have installed IDL on the MPP VAX-host as the user's high-level language to guide the restoration. The following IDL statements constitute the complete set of commands to restore an image.

```
IDL>   setblur,BLUR, PSF,11,7
IDL>   setgamma, .001, .001
IDL>   setcon, C.
IDL>   settrial, TRIAL
IDL>   dnext, X.
---    MPP ----
IDL>   bresult, X
```

In this example, the degraded image is represented by the variable, BLUR, and the point-spread function, by PSF. The procedure, setblur, stipulates a block-size of 11 and step-size of 7 (i.e., the blocks overlap, and only the central 7×7 portion of a block is retained). C is an image controlling the constraint for each pixel, varying from 0.0 (no constraint) to 1.0 (full constraint) for each pixel. The two reciprocal Lagrangian multipliers, γ_7 and the γ_l, are both set to 0.001. TRIAL is the trial solution and X is the first estimate of the restored image. The routine, DNEXT, invokes the next iteration. The last statement reads in the output from the MPP stored in the file, "OUT.TMP," into the variable X.

Typically, one iteration takes a few minutes of CPU-time when the VAX/MPP is not bogged down with other users. This time does not include wait-time for the MPP, overhead in transferring the data, and so on. Since it is possible to examine an image while the MPP task invoked by DNEXT is running, the turn-around time is short enough that interactive work is a reasonable proposition. For restoration, it is essential: the eye can spot minute, but, systematic, imperfections in the restored image as well as catch glaring errors.

The majority of the execution time required in the block iterative restoration is matrix multiplication and solving the linear systems of equations. In the following two sections, we show how these operations can be efficiently mapped into the MPP architecture and that the Parallel Pascal language allows easy implementation.

Experiments show that a block-size of 11×11 pixels is suitable for restoring most of the astronomical images that we have worked with. This block-size results in matrix equations of size 121×121. These matrices map conveniently onto the 128×128 MPP array.

Solution of linear systems is accomplished by Gaussian elimination with no pivoting. The constrained least-squares technique gives the system enough stability that pivoting is not required. The Parallel Pascal code, which follows, will solve a linear system of size up to 127×127. The variables A, ROWI, and COLI are 128×128 floating-point arrays; ROW-INDEX and COL-INDEX are 128×128 integer arrays; ROWFLAG and COLFLAG are 128×128 Boolean arrays; and I and M are scalar integers.

```
1.    for I := 0 to M-1 do
2.         begin
3.              ROWFLAG := (ROW_INDEX=I);
4.              COLFLAG := (COL_INDEX=I);
5.              rowbroad(A,COLI,128,COLFLAG);
6.              where ROWFLAG do A := A/COLI;
7.              colbroad(A,ROWI,128,ROWFLAG);
8.              where not ROWFLAG do A :=
                      A-ROWI*COLI;
9.         end;
```

We now explain the code, using a 6×6 array of processors with a 4×4 matrix system as an example. The code will solve the system $Bx = y$ where B is an $M \times M$ matrix and x and y are M-element vectors. Initially, B and y are stored in variable A as follows.

Initial A

B11	B12	B13	B14	0	y1
B21	B22	B23	B24	0	y2
B31	B32	B33	B34	0	y3
B41	B42	B43	B44	0	y4
0	0	0	0	0	0
0	0	0	0	0	0

Upon completion, A will contain the solution x along with the original matrix reduced to the identity matrix by Gaussian elimination:

Final A

```
1   0   0   0   0   x1
0   1   0   0   0   x2
0   0   1   0   0   x3
0   0   0   1   0   x4
0   0   0   0   0   0
0   0   0   0   0   0
```

Lines 1 and 2 begin a loop on each row and column of the input matrix. For example, at the beginning of the third pass through, the loop (i.e., $I = 2$), A has the form:

A (after completing 2 columns)

```
1   0   *   *   0   *
0   1   *   *   0   *
0   0   *   *   0   *
0   0   *   *   0   *
0   0   0   0   0   0
0   0   0   0   0   0
```

Where an asterisk indicates an arbitrary value.

Line 3 generates a Boolean array with a value of 1 in each element of row I. For I equal to 2, ROWFLAG would contain:

ROWFLAG

```
0   0   0   0   0   0
0   0   0   0   0   0
1   1   1   1   1   1
0   0   0   0   0   0
0   0   0   0   0   0
0   0   0   0   0   0
```

ROWFLAG is set to 1 where ROW_INDEX has a value of I. ROW_INDEX is a Parallel Pascal variable containing the row number of each processing element. ROW_INDEX has the form

ROW_INDEX

```
0   0   0   0   0   0
1   1   1   1   1   1
2   2   2   2   2   2
3   3   3   3   3   3
4   4   4   4   4   4
5   5   5   5   5   5
```

Line 4 creates the Boolean variable COLFLAG containing 1s in column I. It is computed in the same way as ROWFLAG with COL_INDEX containing the column number of each processor.

```
              COLFLAG
        0   0   1   0   0   0
        0   0   1   0   0   0
        0   0   1   0   0   0
        0   0   1   0   0   0
        0   0   1   0   0   0
        0   0   1   0   0   0
```

The routine, rowbroad, in line 5 broadcasts each value in column I, specified by COLFLAG, along its corresponding row 128 times. If A has the form:

```
                       A
    A00    A01    A02    A03    A04    A05
    A10    A11    A12    A12    A14    A15
    A20    A21    A22    A23    A24    A25
    A30    A31    A32    A33    A34    A35
    A40    A41    A42    A43    A44    A45
    A50    A51    A52    A53    A54    A55
```

The result stored in COLI is

```
                     COLI
    A02    A02    A02    A02    A02    A02
    A12    A12    A12    A12    A12    A12
    A22    A22    A22    A22    A22    A22
    A32    A32    A32    A32    A32    A32
    A42    A42    A42    A42    A42    A42
    A52    A52    A52    A52    A52    A52
```

In line 6, the WHERE statement in Parallel Pascal allows a masked operation to be performed. Only the processors with a value of 1 in ROWFLAG will perform the specified operation. In this case, the division of A by COLI will only be done for row I. Since COLI contains $A(i, i)$ in all positions of row I, this statement divides row I (or equivalently equation I) by the value $A(i, i)$. This leaves the new value of 1.0 in position $A(i, i)$.

In line 7, the values in row I are broadcast along their respective columns, giving

```
                     ROWI
    A20    A21    A22    A23    A24    A25
    A20    A21    A22    A23    A24    A25
    A20    A21    A22    A23    A24    A25
    A20    A21    A22    A23    A24    A25
    A20    A21    A22    A23    A24    A25
    A20    A21    A22    A23    A24    A25
```

This copies equation I of the system (normalized so that $a(i, i) = 1.0$) into each row of ROWI.

Line 8 subtracts equation I, scaled by $A(I, J)$, from each other row, or equation, J (except $J = I$). This results in values of 0 in column I except at $A(I, I)$, which contains a 1. After completing the loop for $I = 2$, A will have the form

A (after completing
I equal to 2)

1	0	0	*	0	*
0	1	0	*	0	*
0	0	1	*	0	*
0	0	0	*	0	*
0	0	0	0	0	0
0	0	0	0	0	0

Upon completion of the loop for all I, the original matrix B is reduced to the identity matrix and the last column of variable A contains the solution x.

The inverse of a matrix can be obtained with the addition of the following two lines of code inserted between lines 5 and 6:

```
5.1    where COLFLAG do A=0;
5.2    where ROWFLAG and COLFLAG do A := 1;
```

These two lines add less than 0.01 seconds to the solution. Upon completion of the Gaussian elimination, the inverse of the original matrix B will be stored in A instead of the identity matrix.

MATRIX MULTIPLICATION

The second computationally intensive task is matrix multiplication. For each block restored, two multiplications of matrices of size 121×121 are required. On a VAX 11/750, each multiplication would require 40 sec of CPU time. This is reduced to only 0.3 sec on the MPP.

The Parallel Pascal code that follows will multiply two matrices A and B of size M and place the result in C. The code is presented without detailed explanation. It is important to note, though, that during each floating-point operation, all processors are fully utilized for 128×128 matrices. A, B, and C are 128×128 floating-point arrays, and $I, M,$ ROWFLAG, COLFLAG, ROW_INDEX, and COL_INDEX are the same as before.

```
1.    C := 0;
2.    for I := 0 to M-1 do
3.       begin
4.             ROWFLAG := (ROW_INDEX=I);
5.             COLFLAG := (COL_INDEX=I);
6.             rowbroad(A,COLI,128,COLFLAG);
7.             colbroad(B,ROWI,128,ROWFLAG);
8.             C := C+ROWI*COLI;
9.    end;
```

This algorithm for matrix multiplication takes 0.03 sec to multiply two 121×121 matrices, and 0.04 sec to invert a linear system of the same size. A typical image (512×512 pixels) requires the solution of about 5000 linear systems of size 121×121. Consequently, one iteration (block size of 11×11 pixels, step size of 7 pixels in both line and sample directions, spatially varying constraints) takes approximately 8 MPP-minutes. On a VAX 11/750, the identical procedure would take more than 3 CPU-days!

Application of the Algorithm

One question which may prove crucial to the understanding of the origin of quasars is "What kind of galaxy plays host to a quasar?" The difficulty in answering this question, of course, is that the host galaxy is extremely hard to get at. It only appears as faint fuzz around the quasar, if it is visible at all.

Because of this difficulty, the approach that has been used up until now is an indirect one. One assumes a model galaxy, convolves that model with the point-spread function (PSF) as defined by stars on the image, and compares that convolution with the observation. One then varies the parameters of the model (type of galaxy, central surface brightness, scale length, ratio of quasar to host luminosities) until an adequate fit is achieved or until it is clear that no adequate fit is possible under the given assumptions.

Our approach is just the opposite. We deconvolve the quasar image, making only one assumption—that the center of the galaxy contains a point source—and then examine the deconvolved image to ascertain the parameters of the underlying galaxy. As described earlier, we use the method of constrained least-squares, applying two constraints simultaneously, one involving smoothness in the restored image (Eqn. 10-30), the other involving deviation from a trial solution (Eqn. 10-31). The smoothness constraint is certainly appropriate for the host galaxy and background sky. It is emphatically not appropriate for the nucleus (quasar), since that, by definition, is a point-source. This is where the algebraic approach is so useful: it allows us to have local control of the constraints. We apply the smoothness constraint (minimize the Laplacian) and trial solution constraint (trial solution = sky background) to all the pixels in the image except at the location of the quasar.

As an example, we work with a CCD image of Quasar $2130 + 099$ obtained by Tim Heckman at the 4-meter telescope at CTIO. Quasar $2130 + 099$, otherwise known as II Zwicky 136, is a relatively nearby quasar with a redshift of only 0.06. Figure 10-10(a) shows a contour plot of the observed image at its lowest count levels. Not only can we see the galaxy extending 0.5 arcmin across the sky, but we can see two protrusions from the nucleus that look like spiral "stumps" if not full spiral arms. What we seek, then, from deconvolution of Q2130 + 099 is not so much to enhance the resolution as it is to remove the veiling of the host galaxy by the quasar. Ideally, we would like to suck up all the flux from the quasar (nucleus) into a single pixel, so that we can look at what is around it. Figure 10-10(b) shows a contour plot of the restored image at the same

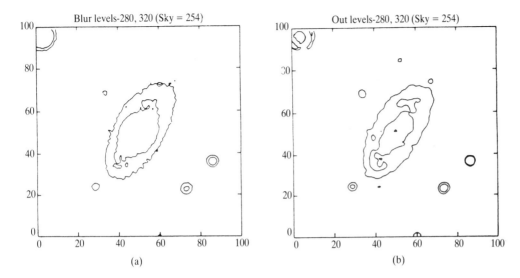

Figure 10-10. Contour plots of Quasar 2130 + 099. (a) The original image. The maximum count (at the nucleus of Q2130 + 099) is 21 900 counts/pixel. (b) The restored image. The count level at the nucleus (the quasar) is now 324 000 counts/pixel. Both images have a plate scale of 0.6 arcsec per pixel; thus, both span a 1 arcmin × 1 arcmin field. The two contour levels are at 280 and 320 counts/pixel; the average sky level is 254 counts/pixel.

contour levels as before. Now the spiral arms are more prominent and fully developed.

Figure 10-11 shows a cross-sectional plot of the restored image. It shows the Q2130 + 099 for what it is: an exceedingly bright nucleus (324 000 counts/pixel) embedded in a galaxy whose surface brightness falls off exponentially with increasing distance from the center—a brightness distribution typical of spirals. We therefore fit the brightness distribution of Q2130 + 099 to the Freeman law for spirals,

$$\mu(r) = \mu_0 + 1.087 \frac{r}{r_0}$$

to obtain a central surface brightness for the host-galaxy, $\mu_0 = +20.9$ mag/arcsec^2, and a scale length, $r_0 = 5.0$ arcsec. Converting to the B-filter, we obtain $\mu_0(B) = 21.3$ mag/arcsec^2 for Q2130 + 099. Converting from angular to linear measure (assuming $H_0 = 100$ km s^{-1} Mpc^{-1} and $q_0 = 0$), we obtain $r_0 = 4.1$ kpc. These values are typical of spirals, which have $\mu_0 = 21.6 \pm 0.3$, $r_0 = 2$–10 kpc. We conclude that the identification of the host-galaxy of Q2130 + 099 as a normal spiral is well established.

Another problem dealing with the past history of the universe is the question "How have galaxies evolved over cosmological time?" This question boils down to a comparison of the properties of nearby galaxies (short light-travel-time) vs. those far away (long light-travel-time).

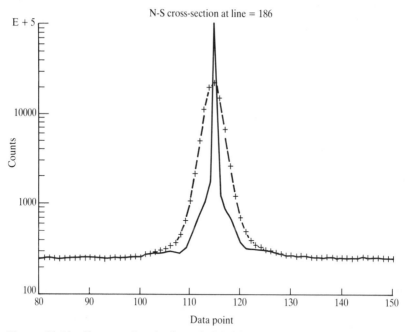

Figure 10-11. Cross-sectional plot of Q2130 + 099. The solid line shows the restored image. (The maximum count actually goes off-scale to 324 000 counts.) The crosses show the original (blurred image), while the dashed curve shows the result on convolving the restored image with the point-spread function.

The difficulty in answering this question is in detecting and measuring distant galaxies. At large distances, galaxies cannot be distinguished from stars, and they are exceedingly faint—perhaps 1 percent of the background sky brightness or less. The problem of contrast against the background sky is compounded by atmospheric blurring, which lowers the surface brightness of an object, sometimes below the detection threshold. Besides these problems caused by the Earth's atmosphere is another kind of difficulty—that of confusion. More distant galaxies have a higher surface density, and galaxy images start to overlap one another.

Can deconvolution help? On the one hand, the answer would appear to be yes. The process of deconvolution works to concentrate the flux of an object into fewer pixels, thus tending to push the object above threshold for detection. Also, deconvolution tends to separate overlapping objects, thereby counteracting the confusion problem. On the other hand, deconvolution can exacerbate noise in an image and may lead to spurious detections. Experiments with computer-generated fields indicate that deconvolution should help. Below, we describe an experiment with an actual image of a faint-galaxy field.

We made use of two CCD deep-sky pictures of a galaxy field obtained by Tony Tyson (Bell Labs) at the 4-meter telescope at CTIO. The two pictures are

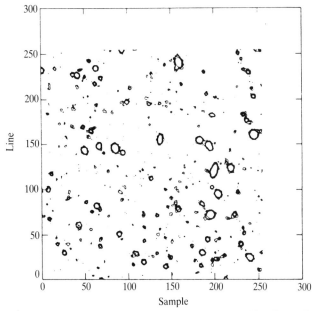

Figure 10-12. A CCD deep sky image obtained by Tony Tyson (Bell Labs).

Image	$\langle$Sky$\rangle$	σ (single pixel)	σ (3 × 3 average)
T2	3010	± 5.5	±2.8
T1	3010	±17.5	±6.6
T1R	3010	±11.6	±7.6

of the same field, which covers a 2.5 × 2.5 arcmin region of the sky (Fig. 10-12). One is a median-average of six exposures slightly offset from one another and re-registered before median filtering (called T2), and the other is one of the six exposures (T1). We deconvolved T1 with rather high smoothing constraints ($\gamma_1 = 0.01$, $\gamma_t = 0.01$) to produce a restored image, T1R. We compare T1 and T1R to see which provides the more sensitive and reliable detections. We use T2 to define the list of objects in the field. We also use it to evaluate the reliability of a detection: any detection on T1 or T1R not also detected on T2 is judged a spurious detection.

The sky background (in counts per pixel) of the three images have characteristics shown in Figure 10-12. The σ's should be interpreted rather loosely, because the histogram of fluxes does not have a Gaussian flux distribution. (Recall that T2 was generated via a nonlinear filter, and T1R was generated with smoothing constraints applied. The smoothing constraint causes the noise to clump together to form a mazy pattern on the image.)

Table 10-3.

Picture	Threshold	Total found	Spurious	
			Isol.	Mult.
T2	11.4	252	0	0
T1	26.2	135	1	23
T1R	30.3	139	3	3

We used a straightforward algorithm for detection. An object is detected at pixel = (i, j) if it meets two criteria: (1) it is a local maximum, that is, pixels immediately surrounding (i, j) are fainter, and (2) the average count-level in a 3×3 box centered on (i, j) exceeds some user-set threshold. We used a threshold (given in the table above in counts above sky), which corresponds to a 4σ detection. The total number of detections on T1 and T1R is about the same. However, the number of valid detections on T1R is significantly higher.

In Table 10-3, we distinguish between two types of spurious detections: "detections" of isolated objects not in T2, and multiple detections of a single object on T2. On T1, there were 23 cases in which a single object (on T2) was tagged as multiple. Thus, T1R produced 133 valid detections, while T1 gave only 111 valid detections. The main reason for the improvement on T1R is that the

Figure 10-13. Voyager images of Jupiter (top) and Ganymede (bottom). The observations are shown at left, the restorations at right.

deconvolution actually smoothed out some of the irregularities in T1, thereby suppressing noise that could be mistaken for a signal. Deconvolution may actually help more than is evident from the table. The three cases where T1R produced multiple detections may, in fact, be multiple; i.e., deconvolution may have resolved the object into a cluster of individual galaxies.

IMAGES OF SOLAR SYSTEM OBJECTS

The left-hand side of Figure 10-13 shows images of Jupiter (top) and Ganymede (bottom) taken by Voyager. A point-spread function was constructed using an image of a star taken with Voyager. The images on the right show the restoration after two iterations with a constant constraint with γ_7 and γ_t set to 0.03 (selected by visual examination of results with various values for the reciprocal Lagrangian multipliers). The improved resolution in the images on the right will be important for analysis of weather patterns on Jupiter and study of planetary detail with images from the Hubble Space Telescope.

MASSIVELY PARALLEL CORRELATION TECHNIQUES FOR DETERMINING LOCAL DIFFERENCES IN PAIRS OF IMAGES*

Image Correlation Techniques

The advent of parallel architectures such as that of the Massively Parallel Processor (MPP) has made it possible to apply computationally intensive cross-correlation techniques to obtain high-resolution results from large images in the detection of local differences between pairs of images. The speed of the MPP has been essential in this work. This chapter presents the results obtained thus far at the Goddard Space Flight Center in applying massively parallel cross-correlation techniques on the MPP to automatically determine elevation and ice floe movement from pairs of synthetic-aperture radar (SAR) images obtained from space by detecting local differences.

This chapter describes two ongoing efforts at the Goddard Space Flight Center that employ correlation techniques to determine local differences in images using computationally intensive algorithms on the MPP. Both efforts involve analysis of synthetic-aperture radar (SAR) images taken from radar sensors on the Space Shuttle and the SEASAT spacecraft. The first is the development of an algorithm for the automated analysis of stereo image pairs to determine elevation information. The second is the development of automated

---

* This section was contributed by James P. Strong and H. K. Ramapriyan.

techniques to determine the relative movement of ice in sequential pairs of images of Arctic ice floes.

Stereo analysis requires the determination of local displacements between images caused by terrain elevation, while ice floe tracking requires the determination of local translation and rotation. Local correlation techniques are used in both tasks, but the ice-tracking problem requires a significant amount of processing using global cross-correlation techniques. With local correlation, it is necessary to match a reference or template neighborhood in one image with various candidate matching neighborhoods within a search area in the other. Once the relative locations of matching neighborhoods in the two images ("disparity" in stereo analysis and "displacement" in tracking) are known, elevation maps or motion-vector diagrams can easily be computed. The number of calculations for local correlation operations is proportional to the product of the area of the neighborhoods, the number of candidate neighborhoods, and the number of points in the image where the matching is to be performed (or the required resolution). As will be discussed in later sections, both efforts require that all pixels in the two images be matched. With images of 512×512 pixels, one has on the order of 10^{11} calculations. The resulting computation load can be handled in a reasonable amount of time only with very high-speed computers. The massively parallel architecture of the MPP is ideally suited to solving the above problem.

The sections below describe how these two tasks are being implemented on the MPP. The next section describes the implementation of the stereo matching algorithm. The following section describes the requirement differences between stereo matching and ice floe tracking, and the final section describes how the ice-floe algorithm is presently being implemented.

Stereo Matching

During October 1984, the Space Shuttle *Challenger* was flown with a Shuttle Imaging Radar instrument (SIR-B). One of the experiments during this mission was to obtain overlapping images of an area of the Earth viewed from multiple incidence angles. Any two of these images form "pseudostereo pairs." Through a suitable geometric model, based on the distance between corresponding pixels in the two images and the spacecraft (slant range), surface elevations can be computed. Manual analysis of stereo pairs is both tedious and time-consuming. Analysis of large areas can take months to complete. This section reports on an automated algorithm developed on the MPP to match corresponding points in SIR-B image pairs. This algorithm can match pixels in 512×512 images within 50 sec. The same task performed manually may require up to 2 work days with results of much lower resolution.

DIFFICULTIES IN STEREO MATCHING
The major difficulties in matching corresponding pixels in the two images are as follows.

1. Different brightness levels in the two images

2. Local distortions of the image

3. Low-contrast areas and noise

Items 1 and 3 apply equally to radar images of sea ice. The first difficulty is often obviated by the use of normalized correlation functions for matching gray level or edge images. The second is inherent in stereo analysis because of the different viewing angles. It occurs most severely in regions of rapidly changing terrain and creates a horizontally stretched or compressed area surrounding corresponding pixels in one image relative to the other. Because of the large off-nadir viewing angles and difference in viewing angles required to achieve reasonable elevation accuracy, this problem is particularly acute in radar images. Thus, the basic clue used to determine the elevation also makes its determination more difficult.

Any techniques for correcting local distortions must take into account the fact that the distortion function can have a broad band of spatial frequencies. For example, the distortion function for a mountain range would have low frequencies, but added to these would be high frequencies caused by rock formations making up the surface. When a human observer fuses two images seen through a viewer, the low-frequency information is used to obtain an initial fusion in which the eyes are brought into alignment (a technique used for automatic focusing of some cameras); then, high-frequency information brings out a detailed perception of depth. The progression from low to high frequency suggests that a hierarchical approach for detecting matching pixels would be appropriate. With this approach, an initial match is performed on low-frequency information in an image, and increasingly higher frequencies are then incorporated to obtain the final matching of corresponding pixels.

Even with no local distortion, errors can occur due to noise, spatial periodicities, and low contrast in the image. One way of reducing errors in general is to provide redundancy by computing matches at nearly every pixel in the image. Then, surface continuity constraints can be used to correct for local elevation discontinuities due to noise. Matching at nearly every pixel is a formidable task on standard serial computers. However, the architecture of the MPP is well suited to the local neighborhood operations required for matching pixels. The following sections discuss the matching technique developed for the MPP and results obtained using the MPP algorithm. To aid in the discussion, one image is labeled the "reference" image and the other the "test" image. All operations are performed on the test image. The matching algorithm implemented on the MPP is an example of what has been termed the Hierarchical Warp Stereo technique explored initially by Marr and Poggio (1979) and pursued later by Quam (1984). Both techniques are iterative, starting with low resolution and increasing the resolution with each iteration. The MPP algorithm consists of the following steps.

1. Preprocessing of the test image

2. Determination of matches

3. Removal of "bad match" areas in the disparity function

4. Smoothing the resulting disparity function

5. Warping the test image

Steps 2 through 5 are repeated for each iteration. The following subsections discuss each of these steps in detail.

PREPROCESSING OF THE TEST IMAGE

Because of the viewing geometry, the resolutions of the two SIR-B images are different in the stereopsis direction. Thus, a linear scale change is applied to the test image so that its resolution is the same as that of the reference image. This operation is implemented using a linear warping function in the stereopsis direction. The test image can, in the same operation, be translated to reduce the absolute value of the maximum disparity between the two images. Translation is effected by adding a constant value to the warping function. When this is done, the size of the initial search area can be reduced. The initial warping function is incorporated into the net disparity function when determining elevations.

DETERMINATION OF MATCHES

For each reference image pixel, a match is performed between a neighborhood surrounding that pixel (the "template") and neighborhoods within a search area in the test image. At each iteration of the algorithm, the sizes of all neighbourhoods are reduced, allowing higher-resolution matches at each step. The location of the center pixel within each neighborhood in the test image relative to the location of the reference pixel is the disparity value associated with that neighborhood.

The measure used for matching neighborhoods is the normalized mean and variance correlation given by

$$\text{match score } (k) = \frac{\sum (X_i - \bar{X}) \times (Y_{i-k} - \bar{Y}_k)}{\text{SQRT}(\sum (X_i - \bar{X})^2) \times \text{SQRT}(\sum (Y_{i-k} - \bar{Y}_k)^2)}$$

where X_i and Y_{i-k} are gray levels of the ith pixels within the template neighborhood and the kth in the search area, respectively. The values $\bar{X}$ and $\bar{Y}_k$ are the mean values computed over the template and Kth search area neighborhoods. For each pixel in the reference image, the match score for all neighborhoods within the search area is computed. The pixel at the center of the neighborhood with the highest correlation value or match score is selected as the matching pixel. The resulting disparity function is, therefore, made up of integer values.

REMOVAL OF "BAD MATCH" AREAS IN THE DISPARITY FUNCTION

If the stereopsis dimension in the stereo image pairs corresponds to the slant range between ground points in the images and the spacecraft, it can be proved that the slope of the disparity function must be between −1 and +1. Therefore, a simple test for a bad match is to observe adjacent values of the disparity function and determine whether there is a jump of more than 1 pixel.

The human visual system appears to have the capability of interpolating surfaces over areas where bad matches occur. This process is emulated in the

MPP algorithm by interpolating the disparity function across all areas where a bad match has been detected. Interpolation is performed using iterative-solution partial differential equations similar to those used in heat flow problems (with disparities in the place of temperatures). To perform the interpolation, two-dimensional partial differential equations are applied to solve for the disparity in the bad-match regions, assuming that the bordering pixels surrounding the bad match area are constrained to be at the computed good disparity values (constituting the boundary conditions). The equations used for obtaining the interpolated disparity at pixel $[i, j]$ at iteration $t + 1$ from the values at iteration t are as follows:

$$D(i, j, t + 1) = D(i, j, t) + \frac{d(D(i, j, t))}{dt}$$

where

$$\frac{d(D(i, j, t))}{dt} = \frac{\partial^2(D(i, j, t))}{\partial_1^2} + \frac{\partial^2(D(i, j, t))}{\partial_j^2}$$

The second partial differential equations reduce to

$$\frac{d(D(k, j, t))}{dt} = D(i, j + 1, t) + D(i, j - 1, t) + (D(i + 1, j, t)$$

$$+ D(i - 1, i, t) - 4D(i, j, t)$$

when it is assumed that the two-dimensional grid increments are unity. The number of iterations required to reach the final solution is dependent on the sizes of the bad-match regions.

SMOOTHING THE RESULTING DISPARITY FUNCTION
After interpolation, the disparity function is smoothed to obtain a more continuous warping function with fractional pixel values rather than integer values. Smoothing is performed on the MPP by averaging over a neighborhood proportional in size to the neighborhood used to obtain the disparity function.

WARPING THE TEST IMAGE
The smoothed disparity function is used as a one-dimensional distortion function to "geometrically correct" the test image in the stereopsis direction. The warped image values are obtained by resampling the test image using linear interpolation.

The matching algorithm has been tested on overlapping SIR-B images with incidence angles of 25 and 42 degrees taken over a plateau region in Northern India at its border with Bangladesh. The signal-to-noise ratio is high almost everywhere in these two images. The results of the matching algorithm on these images are illustrated in Figures 10-14 through 10-17. Figures 10-14(a) and 10-14(b) show the reference and test images. Viewing Figures 10-14(a) and (b) stereoptically, one can observe the plateau region and the river valley around it. Figure 10-15(a) is the reference image again and Figure 10-15(b) is the test image after it has been warped during the matching process. If one views Figures

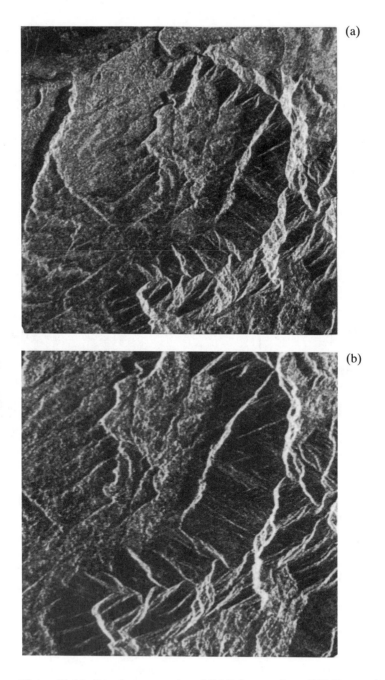

Figure 10-14. Pseudostereo pairs of SAR images from SIR-B experiment. (a) Reference image. (b) Test image.

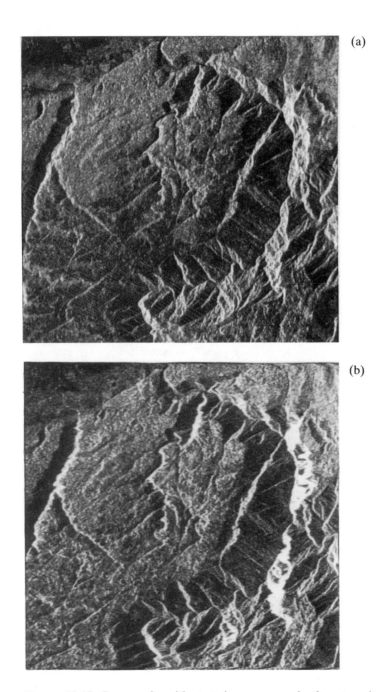

(a)

(b)

Figure 10-15. Same pair with test image warped after two iterations of matching algorithm.

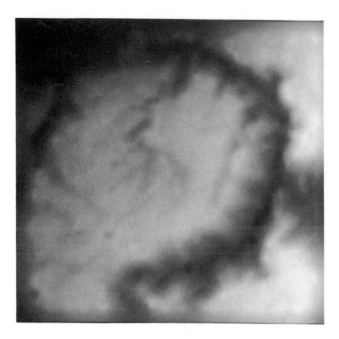

Figure 10-16. Disparity function after second iteration. Dark areas indicate low elevation; light areas indicate high elevation.

10-15(a) and 10-15(b) stereoptically, virtually no depth is perceived, because the warped test image matches the reference image very well. Two iterations of matching and warping were used to obtain this image, the first with 25×25 templates and the second with 13×13 templates. Further iterations with 10×10 templates or smaller yielded too many discontinuities. This indicates that for many areas in the particular SIR-B images used, there is insufficient information in neighborhoods smaller than about 10 pixels square to produce good correlation.

Figure 10-16 is the two-dimensional disparity function derived during the matching process. Dark areas in this image represent pixels in the reference image that are to the right of their corresponding pixels in the test image. In the light areas, the opposite is true. The disparity function is approximately linearly proportional to the actual elevations in the images with the dark areas in Figure 10-16 corresponding to low elevations and the lighter areas to higher elevations. In Figure 10-17, a three-dimensional perspective view is presented of the disparity function. In generating this view, the disparity function was treated as a two-dimensional surface illuminated by a light source at approximately the location of the Shuttle radar sensor about 42 degrees from vertical. One can easily identify the plateau region and river valleys corresponding to those seen in the original stereo pairs.

Figure 10-17. Perspective view using disparity function as an elevation surface and light source of location of spacecraft.

Differences Between Stereo Matching and Ice Motion Detection

Stereo images are usually taken from two different viewpoints. Although the SIR-B images were taken at different times, objects on land are stationary and any local distortions between the two images are due to elevation variations only. On the other hand, sea-ice images from the SEASAT spacecraft were taken from as close to the same viewpoint as possible. Any local differences are due to motion of ice floes. Specific differences in the resulting images are summarized as follows.

1. Ice-floe images are obtained from the same viewpoint and the elevation variations over the ice floes are small in relation to the range resolution. A specific floe in one image will appear the same in the other image except for translation and rotation unless the rotation is large. (Large rotations could change the amount of radar-reflected energy to the spacecraft owing to different orientations of the surface features relative to the viewing direction).

2. In stereo image pairs, the disparity between corresponding pixels is only in one dimension (the stereopsis direction). The magnitude of the disparity is limited by the overall elevation differences within the image. In ice images, motion is two-dimensional and the magnitude depends primarily on the time lapse between observations. In stereo images, the maximum disparity is typically only a small fraction of the image size as compared to ice motion, which is observed to be up to half the image size for the sample SEASAT image pairs with which we are experimenting.

3. In stereo analysis, there is usually a one-to-one correspondence between pixels in one image and those in the other when the surface is continuous. In ice floe images, however, this is not the case because ice floes can break up and open water can appear or disappear between images. Thus, in stereo analysis, local distortions make correlation more difficult to obtain, but there is no rotation, and search areas are small. With ice images, the lack of small-scale distortions makes correlation much easier. However, rotation must be taken into account, and the search areas can be extremely large. The next section discusses our present approach to incorporating rotation into the matching algorithm and to managing large search areas.

Matching of Ice Floes in Sea Ice Images

In 1978, a synthetic aperture radar imaging experiment was flown aboard the SEASAT spacecraft. Radar images of Arctic ice floes were obtained every few days over the same area. On the basis of these images, it was verified that ice motion could be measured through time sequential SAR imagery (Leberl et al. 1983). However, in order to perform this task on a daily basis on a large number of images, some form of automated analysis must be developed. The work described in this section reflects our initial efforts in implementations of algorithms.

Because large translations and rotations are possible between images, the stereo analysis algorithm described in the previous section cannot immediately be applied. Our approach is to measure ice motion in two steps. The first involves global correlation between both images to match significant ice floes and determine their translation and rotation. Using these results, the test image is geometrically corrected or warped to the extent that the stereo matching algorithm can then be applied for final matching. The following describes our current effort in this task.

GLOBAL CORRELATION FOR DETERMINING TRANSLATION AND ROTATION

This approach makes use of the fact that sea-ice images are generally made up of individual ice floes—many of which are of significant size and are not distorted between images. Consider the global cross-correlation function computed over the entire reference and test images. Ice floes of sufficient size that are translated with respect to each other without rotation in the two images will create local peaks in the cross-correlation function at locations corresponding to the amount of translation. If, for a given peak, the test image is translated by an amount corresponding to the location of that peak, the areas contributing to it will be exactly overlapped. Local correlation or differencing techniques can then be applied to isolate or detect these areas. If this process is then repeated for each local peak in the cross-correlation function, all ice floes that are translated with respect to each other in the two images without rotation will be detected. A two-dimensional displacement function can then be built up by storing the horizontal and vertical translation values at each pixel within the detected regions. To account for rotation, this process is repeated for various rotation angles. A summary of these steps follows.

1. Perform global cross-correlation between the reference and test image.
2. Find each local peak in the global cross-correlation function.
3. For each local peak, translate the test image by an amount corresponding to the location of the peak.
4. Using local correlation or local differencing, detect the regions contributing to that peak.
5. In the displacement function, store the appropriate translation values at the pixels within these regions.
6. Remove these regions from both images.
7. Rotate the test image by an incremental amount.
8. Repeat steps 1 through 7 until the total range of possible rotation angles has been covered. The removal of the "detected" regions from the image at each step should increase the chances of detecting local peaks caused by smaller regions in the global correlation function in later iterations. This algorithm can also be applied to edge images obtained from the test and reference images to increase the chances of finding local peaks in the cross-correlation function.

Although this algorithm is computationally intensive, the global cross-correlations can be performed efficiently on the MPP using two-dimensional fast Fourier transforms. The main advantage of the global cross-correlation function is that it can efficiently detect large displacements of ice floes.

After the global correlation step, the displacements of most of the significant ice floes will have been detected. Thus, one will have a resulting displacement function where each pixel in significant ice floes has a vertical and horizontal translation value stored. (The amount of detected rotation and translation of a given ice floe is used to compute the horizontal and vertical translation of each of its pixels.) The translation values of pixels outside of the significant ice floes can be computed using the interpolation techniques described in the stereo matching section with the translation values at the edge of the significant ice floes providing the boundary values.

Using the displacement function as a two-dimensional distortion function, the test image can now be geometrically corrected or warped to match the reference image more closely. Thus, for the second step of the algorithm, the detected ice floes in the test image have been "derotated" and translated close enough to their positions in the reference image that the stereo matching algorithm may now be applied to refine the matching of the detected regions and to match areas that were undetected in the first step.

Preliminary Results of Image Correlation

In Figures 10-18(a) and 10-18(b), the test image has been translated and the reference image rotated by an amount determined visually such that one of the significant ice floes is overlapped in the two images. This is equivalent to the results that are expected in the area of that ice floe after the warping operation is completed as a result of the global correlation step. Application of the stereo matching algorithm (modified for two-dimensional matching) gives the result shown in Figure 10-19(a), which shows a low value for the horizontal translation (dark), and similarly in Figure 10-19(b) for the vertical translation within the ice floe. In addition, Figure 10-20 shows the "match scores" used to determine these translations. It indicates high scores or good matches within the ice floe.

The stereo matching and sea-ice tracking algorithms are computationally intensive, involving hundreds of billions of arithmetic operations. However, both are well matched to massively parallel architectures such as the MPP. Results obtained from the stereo matching task indicate that high-resolution products can be obtained automatically with such architectures at speeds several orders of magnitude faster than can be obtained manually. For instance, the results shown in Figures 10-16 and 10-17 for a 512×512 image requiring two cycles of the algorithm can be obtained in less than 50 sec. The results shown in Figure 10-18 were obtained in approximately 10 sec. The sea-ice tracking problem is more difficult than the stereo matching algorithm. However, initial experiments indicate that our approach should produce accurate results. The amount of processing required, however, indicates that it is only through parallel algorithms and the availability of massively parallel architectures that this task can be performed on an operational basis.

VISION MODULES ON THE CONNECTION MACHINE*

Vision on the Connection Machine

Computational vision requires enormous computing power. The bandwidth of a typical camera is 60 Mbits/sec. To get the most out of such a signal, we need a processor architecture with high throughput as well as flexible communication.

* This section was contributed by James J. Little.

Support for the A. I. Laboratory's artificial intelligence research was provided in part by the Advanced Research Projects Agency of the Department of Defense under Office of Naval Research Contract N00014-85-K-0214 and under Contract DACA76-85-C-0010.

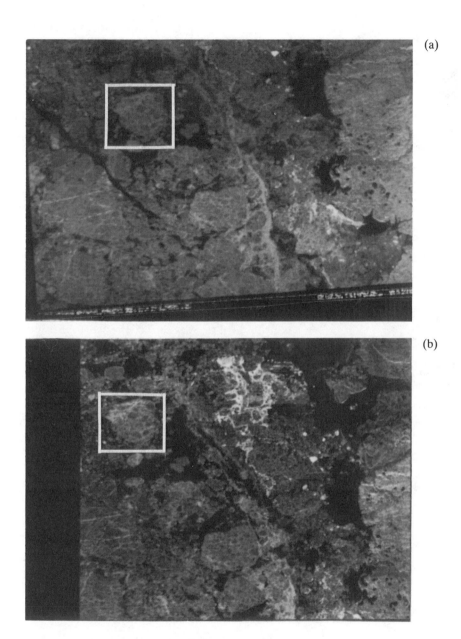

Figure 10-18. Time sequential pairs of ice floe images. Reference image (a) rotated and test image (b) translated such that a particular significant ice floe in both images overlap each other.

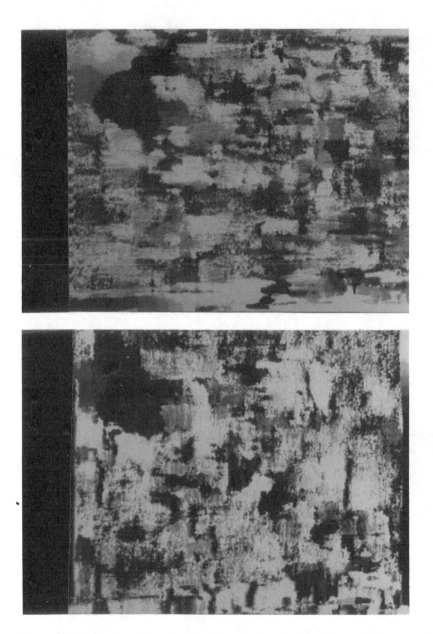

Figure 10-19. Horizontal and vertical translation function. Large dark areas indicate low or no translation at the overlapping ice floes.

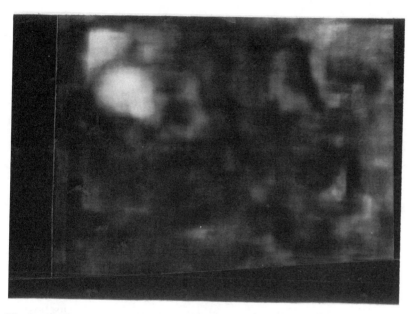

Figure 10-20. Match score values. Brightness shows good matches within overlapping ice floes.

Vision has several stages, proceeding from an image to a symbolic description of the scene. Many modules in early vision, such as edge detection, binocular stereo, motion analysis, and color, have an inherent spatial parallel component. Middle vision constructs image elements from the output of early vision, and computes spatial relations among them. The outputs of these modules can be combined, by high-level vision modules, to form rich symbolic descriptions of the scene. The implementation of generic vision modules demonstrates the ability of the Connection Machine to solve vision problems easily and rapidly, using a variety of interesting aspects of the communication structure of the machine.

The Connection Machine is a powerful fine-grained parallel machine that has proven very useful for implementation of vision algorithms. Among the existing vision systems on the Connection Machine are binocular stereo (Drumheller and Poggio 1986) and optical flow detection (Little and Bulthoff 1986). In implementing these systems, several models using the Connection Machine have emerged, since the machine provides a variety of communication modes. The Connection Machine implementation of algorithms can take advantage of the underlying architecture of the machine in novel ways. We describe several common, elementary operations that recur throughout this discussion of parallel algorithms. Algorithms used in modules at many levels in vision are presented. These illustrate a wide range of methods for using the Connection Machine for vision.

The Connection Machine (Hillis 1985) is a parallel computing machine

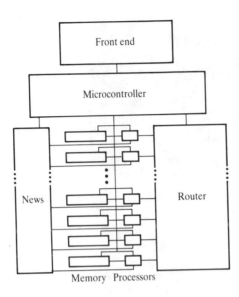

Figure 10-21. Block diagram of the connection machine.

having between 16K and 64K processors, operating under a single instruction stream broadcast to all processors (Fig. 10-21). It is a single-instruction multiple-data (SIMD) machine, because all processors execute the same control stream. Each of the processors is a simple 1-bit processor, currently with 4K bits of memory. There are two modes of communication among the processors: first, the processors are connected by a mesh of wires into a 128×512 grid network (the NEWS network, so-called because of the four cardinal directions), allowing rapid direct communication between neighboring processors; and, second, the router, which allows messages to be sent from any processor to any other processor in the machine. The processors in the Connection Machine can be envisioned as being the vertices of a 16-dimensional hypercube (in fact, it is a 12-dimensional hypercube; at each vertex of the hypercube resides a chip containing 16 processors).

Figure 10-22 shows a four-dimensional hypercube; each processor is

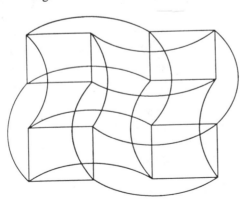

Figure 10-22. Four-dimensional hypercube.

connected by four wires to other processors. Each processor in the Connection Machine is identified by a unique integer in the range $0 \cdots 65535$, its hypercube address, imposing a linear order on the processors. This address identifies the processor for message-passing by the router. Messages pass along the edges of the hypercube from source processors to destination processors. In addition to local operations in the processors, the Connection Machine can return to the host machine the result of various operations on a field in all processors; it can return the global maximum, minimum, sum, logical AND, and logical OR of the field.

To manipulate data structures with more than 64K elements, the Connection Machine provides *virtual processors*. A single physical processor operates as multiple virtual processors by serializing operations in time, and dividing the memory of each processor accordingly. This is otherwise invisible to the user. The number of virtual processors assigned to a physical processor is denoted by the *virtual processor ratio* (VP ratio), which is always ≥ 1. When the VP ratio is greater than 1, the Connection Machine is necessarily slowed down by that factor, in most operations. The host for the 16K Connection Machine at the MIT AI Lab is a Symbolics 3640 Lisp Machine. In this paper, we assume a 64K Connection Machine. Connection Machine programs utilize Common Lisp syntax, in the language *Lisp (Lasser 1986). Statements in *Lisp programs are compiled and manipulated in the same fashion as Lisp statements, contributing significantly to the ease of programming the Connection Machine. An excellent introduction into programming concepts for the Connection Machine is in (Hillis and Steele 1986).

Many vision problems are best solved by a combination of several communication modes on the Connection Machine. The design of these algorithms takes advantage of the underlying architecture of the machine in novel ways. There are several common, elementary operations that recur throughout this discussion of parallel algorithms: routing operations, scanning, and distance doubling.

Memory in the Connection Machine is attached to processors, each of which, has, at present, 4K bits of local memory. Local memory can be accessed rapidly. Memory of processors nearby in the NEWS network can be accessed by passing it through the processor on the path between the source and destination. At present, NEWS accesses in the machine are made in the same direction for all processors—that is, to read in one processor, using NEWS access, say, the North, and, in the next, the South, requires two separate accesses. The *router* on the Connection Machine provides parallel reads and writes among processor memory at arbitrary distances and with arbitrary patterns. It uses a packet-switched message-routing scheme to direct messages along the hypercube connections to their destinations. This powerful communication mode can be used to reconfigure completely, in one parallel write operation, taking one router cycle, a field of information in the machine. The Connection Machine supplies instructions so that processors can concurrently read and concurrently write a memory address, but since these memory references can cause significant slowdown, we will usually only consider exclusive read, exclusive write (EREW) instructions (Cook 1980). We will usually not allow more than one processor to access the memory of

$$Processor\text{-}number = [0 \quad 1 \quad 2 \quad 3 \quad 4 \quad 5 \quad 6 \quad 7]$$
$$A = [5 \quad 1 \quad 3 \quad 4 \quad 3 \quad 9 \quad 2 \quad 6]$$

$$Plus\text{-}scan(A) = [0 \quad 5 \quad 6 \quad 9 \quad 13 \quad 16 \quad 18 \quad 21]$$
$$Max\text{-}scan(A) = [0 \quad 5 \quad 5 \quad 5 \quad 5 \quad 5 \quad 9 \quad 9]$$

Figure 10-23. Examples of *plus-scan* and *max-scan*.

another processor at one time. However, in histogramming, we will take advantage of combiners when we can guarantee few and evenly spaced collisions. The Connection Machine can combine messages at a destination, by various operations, such as logical AND, inclusive OR, summation, and maximum or minimum.

The *scan* operations are a powerful set of primitive operations (Blelloch 1986). These operations can be used to simplify and speed up many algorithms. They directly take advantage of the hypercube connections underlying the router and can be used to distribute values among the processors and to aggregate values using associative operators. Formally, the scan operation takes a binary associative operator $\oplus$, with identity 0, and an ordered set $[a_0, a_1, \ldots, a_{n-1}]$, and returns the set $[0, a_0, (a_0 \oplus a_1), \ldots, (a_0 + a_1 + \cdots + a_{n-2})]$. This operation is sometimes referred to as the data-independent prefix operation. Binary associative operators include minimum, maximum, and plus. Figure 10-23 shows the results of scans using the operators *maximum* and *plus* on some example data.

The four scan operations *plus-scan*, *max-scan*, *min-scan*, and *copy-scan* are implemented in microcode and take about the same amount of time as a routing cycle. The *copy-scan* operation takes a value at the first processor and distributes it over the other processors. These scan operations can take segment bits that divide the processor ordering into segments. The beginning of each segment is marked by a processor whose segment bit is set, and the scan operations will start over again at the beginning of each segment. Figure 10-24 shows some examples.

Versions of the *scan* operations also work using the NEWS addressing

$$Processor\text{-}number = [0 \quad 1 \quad 2 \quad 3 \quad 4 \quad 5 \quad 6 \quad 7]$$
$$A = [5 \quad 1 \quad 3 \quad 4 \quad 3 \quad 9 \quad 2 \quad 6]$$
$$SB \ (segment \ bit) = [1 \quad 0 \quad 1 \quad 0 \quad 0 \quad 0 \quad 1 \quad 0]$$

$$Plus\text{-}scan(A, SB) = [0 \quad 5 \quad 6 \quad 3 \quad 7 \quad 10 \quad 19 \quad 2]$$
$$Max\text{-}scan(A, SB) = [0 \quad 5 \quad 5 \quad 3 \quad 4 \quad 4 \quad 9 \quad 2]$$
$$Min\text{-}scan(A, SB) = [MX \quad 5 \quad 1 \quad 3 \quad 3 \quad 3 \quad 3 \quad 2]$$
$$Copy\text{-}scan(A, SB) = [0 \quad 5 \quad 5 \quad 3 \quad 3 \quad 3 \quad 3 \quad 2]$$

Figure 10-24. Examples of segmented *scan* operations. MX is the maximum possible value.

scheme—we will call these *grid-scans*. These allow one to sum, take the maximum, copy, or number values along rows or columns of the NEWS grid quickly.

For example, *grid-scans* can be used to find for each pixel in an image the sum of a $2m \times 2m$ square region centered at the pixel. This sum can be determined for all pixels by executing a *plus-scan* along the rows. Each pixel then gets the result of the scan from the processor m in front of it and m behind it, and by subtracting these two values, each pixel has the sum in its neighborhood along the row. We now execute the same calculation on the columns, giving each element the sum of its square. The whole calculation requires only a few *scans* and routing operations and runs in a time that is independent of the size of m. We will see several other uses of the scan operations later.

DISTANCE DOUBLING

Another important primitive operation is *distance doubling* (Wyllie 1979; Lim et al. 1987), which can be used to compute the effect of any binary, associative operation, as in *scan*, on processors linked in a list or a ring. For example, using *max*, *doubling* can find the extremum of a field contained in the processors. Using message-passing on the router, *doubling* can propagate the extreme value to all processors in the ring in $O(\log N)$ steps, where N is the number of processors in the ring. Each step involves two send operations. Typically, the value to be maximized is chosen to be the cube-address (a unique integer identifier) of the processor. At termination, each processor connected in the ring knows the label of the maximum processor in the ring, hereafter termed the *principal processor*. This serves to label all connected processors uniquely and to nominate a particular processor (the *principal*) as the representative for the entire set of connected processors. At the same time, the distance from the *principal* can be computed in each processor. Figure 10-25 shows the propagation of values in a ring of eight processors. Each processor initially, at step 0, has an address of the

Step	0	1	2	3	4	5	6	7
	1	2	3	4	5	6	7	0
0	4	1	5	2	11	12	19	3
	2	3	4	5	6	7	0	1
1	4	5	5	11	12	19	19	19
	4	5	6	7	0	1	2	3
2	19	19	12	19	19	19	19	19
	0	1	2	3	4	5	6	7
3	19	19	19	19	19	19	19	19

Figure 10-25. Distance doubling. Upper entry is the address; the lower entry is the value.

next processor in the ring, and a value that is to be maximized. At the termination of the ith step, a processor knows the addresses of processors $2^i + 1$ away and the maximum of all values within $2^i - 1$ processors away. In the example, the maximum value has been propagated to all 8 processors in $\log 8 = 3$ steps.

Vision Tasks

We catalog a set of vision tasks common to many approaches to early and middle vision. Early-vision algorithms exhibit *spatial parallelism,* in which an operation is applied to all pixels in unison, in a spatially homogeneous computation. The classic example is filtering of convolution. A large class of regularization computations (Poggio 1985a) can be cast in this framework, when the input data lie on a regular mesh. These spatially parallel computations are easily mapped into operations using only NEWS accesses. When regular, but not spatially homogeneous operation is necessary, scan operations can be used to produce simple, efficient algorithms. Notably, scans in grid directions can also be used to make more efficient some spatially homogeneous computations such as region summing. Finally, tasks requiring arbitrary, diverse communications among elements can utilize the power of the router. There are natural classes of operations which map easily into the different communication modes of the Connection Machine. We will first describe edge detection, which, in most, but not all, aspects is a spatially parallel operation. These algorithms assume an initial mapping of processors to pixels in the image array.

Edge Detection

Edge detection is an important first step in many low-level vision algorithms. It generates a concise, compact description of the structure of the image, suitable for manipulation in higher-level interpretation tasks. There are many edge detectors in the literature, but all share common aspects of spatial parallelism. Here we will analyze the Connection Machine implementation of Marr–Hildreth edge-detection and Canny detection schemes.

FILTERING

A fundamental operation in vision processing is filtering the input image, both to remove noise and to select an appropriate spatial scale. Typically, filtering is accomplished by convolution with a filter of bounded spatial extent, often a Gaussian. We have implemented a variety of methods for computing the Gaussian convolution of an image.

An interesting, simple implementation of Gaussian convolution relies on the binomial approximation to the Gaussian distribution (for details, see Little et al. 1987). The algorithm uses a kernel $y[n]$ given by $y[-1] = 1/4$, $y[n] = 0$ otherwise, and requires only the operations of integer addition, shifting, and local communications on the two-dimensional mesh; it could be implemented on a two-dimensional mesh architecture much simpler than the Connection Machine.

The binomial approximation is very simple to implement on a 1-bit processor such as the Connection Machine. Such a convolution amounts to a processor adding 1/2 of its own value to 1/4 of the sum of two of its neighbors, say, north and south, or east and west. The scaling can be accomplished simply by right shifting, or possibly reading from the neighboring processors with a 1-bit offset in the field address. Because a two-dimensional Gaussian convolution is separable into two one-dimensional convolutions, this can be used to implement an approximation to convolution of a two-dimensional signal with a two-dimensional Gaussian filter. To approximate a Gaussian distribution with standard deviation σ, $m = 2(\sigma)^2 - 1$ iterations are needed. This approach is especially suited to the fine-grained architecture of the Connection Machine, where, at present, a multiplication is much more expensive than an addition. Convolution with a Gaussian filter can also be approximated by iterated convolution with a uniform (boxcar) filter of width N and height $1/N$. To approximate a Gaussian with standard deviation σ, $(12\sigma^2 - 1)/(N^2 - 1)$ iterations are required. The boxcar approximation is useful when σ is large. In addition, there is a fast implementation using *grid-scans*. The edge-detection method finds edges at the zero-crossing of the image convolved with $\nabla^2 * G(\sigma)$. This filter is often approximated by the difference of Gaussians $G(\sigma_1) - G(\sigma_2)$, $\sigma_1 \le \sigma \le \sigma_2$. On the Connection Machine, it is easy to compute $\nabla^2 * G(\sigma)$ by convolving with $G(\sigma)$, and then filtering with the discrete Laplacian. Zero-crossings in $\nabla^2 * G_1(\sigma) * I$ are found by examining the sign bits of neighboring processors, using NEWS accesses.

BORDER FOLLOWING

Border following uses the more flexible communication abilities of the router of the Connection Machine. In our analysis, we consider two parameters, n, the number of curves in the image, and m, the number of pixels on the longest curve. Each pixel in the Connection Machine can link up with the neighbor pixels in the curve, by examining its 8-neighbors in the grid, in negligible time. Higher-vision modules need a unique tag or pointer to refer to a curve as a unit; this is the problem of computing connected components. Further, the label should be known by all the pixels in the curve. So, each pixel on the curve must be labeled with a unique identifier for the curve. *Doubling* permits the pixels on the curve to select a label, the address of the *principal processor,* for the curve, and to propagate that label throughout the curve in $O(\log m)$ steps.

Then the total number of curves can be computed by selecting the principal processors, and *enumerating* them using a *scan* operation. The *enumerate* operation returns the number of curves (n).

RECONFIGURING FOR OUTPUT

At this point, the curves have been linked, labeled uniquely, and counted. The structure constructed so far is sufficient to support most operations on curves for image understanding, so all processing after this is for output only. This goes against our guideline of keeping all information in the Connection Machine, but is an interesting example of restructuring data in the machine. To output the pixels from the Connection Machine, the points on the curves should be numbered in order to create a stream of connected points. The curve-labeling step, using *doubling,* can be augmented to record the distance from the *principal processor,* as well as its label, during label propagation, for only a slight increase in message length. We can find the length m of the longest curve by one global maximum operation.

A simple method suggested by Guy Blelloch lets us assign an index to each point on an edge, so that the points can be ordered in a stream for output from the Connection Machine. Each edge *sends* its length to the processor whose address is the index of the edge. Then, a *plus-scan* on the set of processors representing these edge lengths generates the starting location, in the stream, of the first point in each edge. This value is *sent* to the first point (the principal point) in the edge, which broadcasts it to the points in the edge, using *doubling.* Each point constructs an index for itself from its location in the edge and the stream location of the first point. Ranking the pixels by this method takes $O(\log m)$ *sends,* for doubling, two routing operations, and a *scan.*

The ordered pixels then *send* their (x, y) values to the address given by the rank, in one operation, with no collisions. The (x, y) coordinates of the pixels on the curve will be in sequential order in the processors by cube address. The computations needed for border following depends on the log of m, the length of the longest curve, and the log of n, the number of curves in the image; typically, both are proportional to n, in an $n \times n$ image.

Canny Edge Detection

The Canny edge detector is often used in image understanding (Canny 1986). It is based on directional derivatives, so it has improved localization. Implementing the Canny edge detector on the Connection Machine involves implementing the following.

1. Gaussian smoothing $G * I$
2. Directional derivative $\nabla(G * I)$
3. Nonmaximum suppression
4. Thresholding with hysteresis

Gaussian filtering and computing directional derivatives are local operations as described above. Nonmaximum suppression selects as edge candidates those pixels for which the gradient magnitude is maximal in the direction of the gradient. This involves interpolating the gradient magnitude between each of two pairs of adjacent pixels among the pixels' eight neighbors, one forward in the gradient direction, one backward. This is accomplished in constant time using the NEWS network.

Thresholding with hysteresis is used to eliminate weak edges due to noise. Two thresholds on gradient magnitudes, *low* and *high,* are computed, based on an estimate of the noise in the image intensity. The nonmaximum suppression step has selected those pixels for which the gradient magnitude is maximal in the direction of the gradient. In the thresholding step, all selected pixels with gradient magnitude below *low* are eliminated. All pixels with values between *low* and *high* are considered as edges if they can be connected to a pixel above *high* through a chain of pixels above *low*. All others are eliminated. This is essentially a spreading activation operation; it requires propagating information along curves.

HISTOGRAMMING

Esimating the gradient magnitude distribution can be performed by histogramming that value. There are several ways this can be implemented on the Connection Machine.

Gradient magnitudes can be quantized for the histogram bucket size, for m buckets. Sorting the gradient magnitudes configures the data thus:

$$\cdots k, k, k, k, k+1, k+1, k+1, \ldots$$

Each processor determines whether it is a lower bound between elements with value k and the elements with value $k + 1$, for all k. A boundary processor sends its cube address to location H_k in the histogram table. To convert this table into a histogram, each H_i subtracts H_{i-1}, or the appropriate lower value when i was not represented in the image. A *copy-scan* can fill in empty elements to simplify this differencing operation.

Histogramming in m buckets by *counting* involves stepping from $0 \le i \le m$, selecting processors where intensity $= i$, and counting the number of selected processors (H_i), using global counting operations. This needs m counting operations. When m is less than 64, this can be more efficient than histogramming by sorting.

Finally, when only one value in the distribution is needed, say, finding the kth percentile, estimation via probing can be used. Here, a binary search on a set of m values is performed in $O(\log m)$ global counting operations, until the value i, $0 \le i \le m$ is found for which k percent of the values are $\le i$. For $m = 256$, this requires only 8 counting operations.

We can also histogram by *sending* a 1 from each pixel to the processor associated with its intensity value. Since the router can sum many messages arriving at a processor in the message-passing cycle, the only computation needed is the routing cycle. Many pixels could attempt to write to one histogram value; then there would be many collisions. However, the routing hardware incurs little penalty for having up to 32 collisions per destination. A randomizing strategy becomes feasible, to minimize the number of collisions. We can allocate a contiguous block of processors for each value in the histogram. For a 256×256 8-bit image, a block is 256 processors per value. Each pixel computes a random value r, $0 \le r \le 255$. The pixel *sends* its location $i \times 256 + r$, where i is intensity value. The votes are summed on arrival, using combiners in the router. Then the votes are tallied using a *plus-scan* operation, with segment-bits set at the beginnings of blocks. After the scan, the last element in a block contains the appropriate histogram value. When the a priori distribution of intensities is known, the sizes of blocks can be tailored to it. One *send* operation can collect the values into the histogram.

PROPAGATION

In thresholding with hysteresis, the existence of a *high* value on a connected curve must be propagated along the curve, to enable any *low* pixels to become *edge* pixels. This requires a number of operations depending on the length of the longest segment above *low,* which will be connected to a *high* pixel. Only pixels above *low,* which survive nonmaximum suppression, are considered. Each pixel can, in constant time, find the one or two neighboring pixels with which it forms a connected line, by examining the state of all 8 neighbors in the NEWS network. All pixels above *high* are marked as *edge* pixels. Using *doubling,* propagating a bit to indicate the *edge* property, changes this dependence to $O(\log m)$. For most practical examples, propagating in the NEWS network is faster than using the asymptotically optimal *doubling* procedure.

INTERPOLATION

The output of feature-based stereo algorithms is a set of sparse disparity measurements in the image. Constructing a surface description from these measurements is an interpolation problem (Grimson 1981). Multigrid methods (Terzopoulos 1986) have been applied to interpolation on the Connection Machine and have shown favorable speed-ups (McBryan 1986).

Middle Vision

Before edges and other features of images can be used for high-level processes such as recognition, they must be grouped into "chunks" and their spatial relations computed. Marr's (1982) "primal sketch" contains such structural elements. Ullman (1984) describes "visual routines" that perform these tasks. Labeling points in an edge with a unique label resembles more the constructive tasks of middle vision than early vision. The boundaries between the stages are sometimes blurred. The connected component algorithm described below assembles and labels two-dimensional regions. In the context of "visual routines," this is "region coloring." For computing spatial relations, the tools of computational geometry are used. A variety of geometrical algorithms were designed for the Connection Machine, including several convex hull algorithms and a Voronoi diagram algorithm. Another important task in middle vision is integrating information from many visual sources. One approach toward integration, suggested by Poggio (1985b), uses coupled Markov random fields (Geman and Geman 1984). This approach allows formulation of smoothness constraints on the individual modules, and compatibility constraints on their coupling, as well as explicitly dealing with discontinuities. Its implementation on the Connection Machine exhibits speed-ups of several orders of magnitude from a serial machine.

CONNECTED COMPONENT LABELING

A fast practical algorithm for labeling connected components in a two-dimensional image array using the Connection Machine has been developed by Lim et al. (1987). The algorithm has a time complexity of $O(\log N)$ where N is the number of pixels. The central idea in the algorithm is that propagating the largest or smallest number stored in a linked list of processors to all processors in the list takes $O(\log L)$ time, where L is the length of the list using *doubling*.

In the algorithm (see Lim et al. (1987) for more details), the label of a connected (4-connected) component is the largest processor address (i.e., processor ID) of the processors in the set. The complexity of the algorithm is measured in terms of N, the length of the longest boundary in the image. The whole algorithm takes $O(\log N)$ routing cycles on the Connection Machine.

We have devised a connected component algorithm utilizing *scan* operations along grid-lines. In each phase of this algorithm, the label of a region, as specified by the processor with maximum cube-address, is propagated left, right, up, and down, with a *max-scan* operation. The number of phases of this algorithm depends on the complexity and the alignment of figures in the image. Its worst-case behavior originates from an image containing long ellipsoidal regions, oriented along diagonals.

CONVEX HULL

There are four planar convex-hull algorithms that have been suggested for the Connection Machine. As with serial convex-hull algorithms, which one is the most practical will depend on the specifics of the problem. We will describe each one briefly. All of these algorithms for m points require $O(m)$ processors.

The first algorithm is based on a concurrent read exclusive write (CREW) PRAM algorithm described in Aggarwal et al. (1985). Since the Connection Machine does not perform well on concurrent reads, we have shown elsewhere that their algorithm can be modified to work with exclusive reads and *scans* (Blelloch and Little 1987). This algorithm for m points has the optimal asymptotic time bound of $O(\log m)$. Although this algorithm has the best asymptotic bound of the algorithms we mention, it has a large constant and therefore might not be the most practical algorithm.

The second is a parallel version of the QUICKHULL method (Preparata and Shamos 1985). This algorithm can be implemented using a small constant number of router cycles and scans per step (Blelloch and Little 1987). As with the serial QUICKHULL, for m hull points, this algorithm runs in $O(\log m)$ steps for well-distributed hull points, and has a worst-case running time of $O(m)$.

The third is a parallel version of Graham's sequential algorithm (Preparata and Shamos 1985) and requires $O(\log^2 m)$ routing cycles for m points (Little 1986). The final algorithm is a parallel version of the Jarvis march algorithm (Preparata and Shamos 1985), requiring only a few arithmetic operations, plus a global maximum computation per hull point (Little 1986). Although this algorithm requires $O(m)$ steps for m hull points, it may be the most practical for some applications, since the constant is small and m is often small.

VORONOI DIAGRAMS

Aggarwal et al. (1985) describe an $O(\log^3 N)$ algorithm for computing the Voronoi diagram of N points in parallel using the CREW (concurrent read exclusive write) model. For $N = 1000$ this is 1000 steps, each of which needs at least one routing cycle. Since the Connection Machine has the NEWS network, a set of mesh connections among the processors, a brushfire method can be easily implemented, which propagates the label of the closest point through the NEWS mesh.

In the proposed algorithm, each pixel in the mesh is labeled with the (i, j) location of the point closest to its (x, y) coordinate, which we may take to be its center. The result of this labeling is accurate only at the grid-spacing. For the L_1 and L_∞ metrics, propagation is simple. By using 4-connected or 8-connected neighbors, we can make the arrival time of a propagated label be identical to its L_1 or L_∞ distance. In the Euclidean metric, we must propagate the (x, y) of a point as well as its index. The algorithm for the Euclidean metric is described in detail by Little (1986).

High-Level Vision

The image structures identified by middle vision are used in high-level vision, for example, in recognition. Common routines needed by model-based vision include geometric transformation of three-dimensional models of objects and computing the visible portions of the object from particular viewpoints. We describe an abstract problem, triangle visibility, to highlight how such tasks might be solved on the Connection Machine. Recognition is often posed as a matching problem, between features of a known model and computed image features. An outline of a method for performing graph matching identifies some ways to use the Connection Machine for this problem.

Certain systems in vision need to determine visibility of scene elements. For example, let the input be a set of m opaque triangles in three-dimensional space, selected at random with each coordinate in some range. Find the vertices of the triangles that are visible from the origin.

The problem can be parallelized over the set of triangles or the set of vertices. Even though there are three times as many vertices, the description of a triangle is larger, and the increased communication cost outweighs the reduction in elements. A triangle *shadows* all vertices that lie in the triangular cone formed by the origin and the edges of the triangle and that are behind the plane containing the triangle. The volume in space defined by this criterion is described by four linear inequalities from the bounding half-spaces. Each triangle, in a preprocessing step, generates the four plane equations. A vertex can then be tested for visibility by evaluating these equations for its (x, y) coordinates.

Our formulation uses multiple copies of the m triangles. We assume $m \ll 64\text{K}$. The problem can be parallelized by copying the triangles k times in the memory (64K) of the Connection Machine, where $k = 65\,536/m$. This divides the machine into k subsets of processors. The description of the triangle i is computed in processor $k \times i$. Segment bits are set in these processors. The descriptions of all m triangles can be *copy-scanned* to replicate them k times. During computation, triangles 0 through m occupy processors 0 through m (cube address), and so forth. The k copies of triangle i are then *sent* to the processors $j \times m + i$, $j \leq k$. Then, the triangles are in k blocks of m, in consecutive order. Each triangle processor will handle up to $n = (ceiling(3m^2/65\,536))$ points. The vertices of the triangles are divided into blocks of n points. The points are *sent* to the sets of triangles against which they are to be tested. The first n points are sent to processors $0, \ldots, n-1$, the next n to processors $m, \ldots, m+n-1$, and so forth. We assume $n \leq m$, which is true when $m \leq 21\,845$. The preprocessing filter, described later, will almost certainly reduce the number of active triangles below this.

Segment bits are inserted at the beginning of each set of triangles. In each testing step, the description of the point at the beginning of each set of points is *copy-scanned* across the set of triangles. All triangles test the active points in parallel. Then, the descriptions of the points are *sent* to the next lower processor in the block of m. The first point is complete, and is eliminated. This brings a new point to the beginning of each section of triangles, ready to be copied to all the triangles in the next step. There are $n = (ceiling(3m^2/65\,536))$ steps.

Many of the triangles in this example are themselves completely occluded by larger triangles. We suggest a first filtering step so that small triangles that are occluded by large triangles can be eliminated before the problem is partitioned into groups. Each triangle is projected onto a projection plane, anywhere in the visible region, orthogonal to a line of sight from the origin. Then, the projection plane is subdivided into a $k \times k$ grid. Each triangle can determine all squares it covers completely. At the intersection points in this grid, each triangle determines its z-value. Each triangle should cover, on average, one-sixth of the rectangles. Now, each triangle generates a copy of itself for each rectangle it covers; choose k so that

$$\frac{k^2}{6} * m \leq 65\,535$$

where m is the number of triangles, so that each triangle–rectangle pair can be allocated to a processor. For 1000 triangles, k is 18. The triangle–rectangle pairs contain the *zmin, zmax* of each triangle in that rectangle. Organize the processors contiguously by rectangle. Then *scan* the triangles to find the minimum of the *zmax* covering the rectangle. Eliminate all triangles which are completely enclosed in a rectangle and whose *zmin* is greater than this *zmax*; these triangles cannot be seen. This should significantly reduce both the number of triangles, and, consequently, the number of vertices. Then, the number of iterations of the triangle-point process should be significantly smaller.

GRAPH MATCHING
The problem is to compute the list of the occurrences of (an isomorphic image of) a small graph H as a subgraph of a larger graph G. We will outline a method to

distribute the matching process among the processors of the Connection Machine. A similar solution for object recognition is described by Harris and Glynn (1986). We use dynamic allocation of processors to matchings. A partial matching is contained in a processor. At each step in the graph matching algorithm, a matching (processor) acquires the information necessary to determine all legal successors. It then finds processors to continue with the new matchings, and is then returned to the pool of free processors. The information concerning the graphs can be stored in several ways in the memory of the Connection Machine. We can store the adjacency list for a vertex G as a bit vector in a processor. The graph G can be stored, with many copies, throughout the Connection Machine. Each matching processor can access these copies randomly, so that contention among the processors is minimized. The description of the smaller graph H can be stored in each matching processor, as well as the partial matching it is expanding. A more detailed discussion of a scheme for performing graph matching can be found in Little (1986).

There are many difficult problems in performing a combinatorial search on a parallel machine. Nodes in the search tree are accessing many different sections of the graph structures. By distributing the graph data through the machine, with many copies, random routing strategies can reduce data contention. A further difficulty is maintaining sufficient free processors to explore completely a subtree in the search tree (to prevent blocking), while at the same time using sufficient processors to make progress. Wah et al. (1985) discusses many of these issues, which are mostly independent of the processor architecture.

Schemes for allocating processors to tasks are described by Hillis (1985). The total throughput of this algorithm can be measured in terms of the number of partial matchings generated in each step. The critical factor in this problem is to control the number of active matchings so as to allow expansion, without creating blocking. The process should monitor itself to record the average number of successors at each level, allowing good control of allocation.

Conclusions

We have identified several powerful communication patterns that allow us to use the Connection Machine to design efficient algorithms for vision. The powerful communication methods permit construction of extended image structures in logarithmic time. Schemes can easily arrange data in the Connection Machine so that rapid distribution of information using the scan mechanism allows efficient algorithms. These algorithms represent a subset of those currently designed for or implemented on the Connection Machine. Other general algorithms for vision, such as minimum-cost path, are described by Little (1986).

We have described the algorithms in terms of fundamental operations of the Connection Machine. We will give a brief outline of the comparative running times of the primitives we have been discussing. Let us take as a time unit the time for a 1-bit operation. The actual time required by this operation will change as the Connection Machine evolves. In these units, then, accessing the memory of a neighboring processor via the NEWS network takes 3 units per bit. Global operations, such as logical OR and logical AND, need less than 50 units. Counting all active processors requires 200 units. Routing and scanning uses 500 units. Adding 16-bit quantities takes 20 units, while multiplying them takes 250 units. The relative speed of these operations may change in future versions of the Connection Machine. In another document (Little 1986), we give more detailed descriptions of these algorithms and their running times on the present machine. In actual time, for example, our present implementation of Canny edge detection, operating on a 256×256 image, from image to linked edge pixels, takes less than 50 msec. Many of the other algorithms described above achieve similar times, and show speed-ups of several orders of magnitude over present implementations on serial computers.

LIMITATIONS OF INHERENTLY PARALLEL GRAPHICS ALGORITHMS*

Graphics on Parallel Computers

We discuss several alternative strategies for rendering a canonical graphic data structure onto a raster display mapped on a mesh-connected computer (MCC). The controlling variables are the number M of primitives in the data structure, the maximum projected area dA of the primitives, and the expected time R to route data. Problems addressed include the limited local memory of MCC processors, the lack of local indexing within a processor, and the size of the MCC array, generally 1/16 of a standard video display.

Mesh-connected machines originally arose to meet the requirements of two-dimensional system calculations, and, particularly in the case of the Massively Parallel Processor (MPP) built by Goodyear Aerospace for NASA, for global image processing, which involves local, loosely coupled processes that are highly parallel. It is not clear that computer vision or computer graphics, each of which deals with an abstract structure at one end and a parallel data array at the other (Pavlidis 1982), are as well suited, although certain of their operations are indeed highly suited for some sort of parallelism.

This section studies the applicability of a typical graphics procedure under the constraints that (a) the database be a standard canonical graphic model; (b) the procedure fit the constraints of an existing machine; and (c) animation may be possible. At this writing, it is primarily a design document, although much of what is discussed is in the process of implementation.

---

* This section was contributed by Michael J. McAnulty.

GRAPHICS REQUIREMENTS

Graphic rendering is the process of making a picture from a computer data structure. In the very simple case that the structure is a square array of color values, this process is trivial—a raster copy. Interesting graphics renders from data structures that are at once more flexible and abstract, and the rendering process consists of making explicit the geometry that is implicit in the model data structure. We consider here a single canonical representation—representation of the surfaces of objects as connected triangle primitives, planar patches in three dimensions. For simple objects with no environment, only a few hundred primitives may be necessary to represent the scene, although for more complete scenes that may include terrain, the number of primitives quickly moves into the thousands.

The end result of a graphics computation is to assign a color value to each picture element (pixel). In simplified form, this requires explicit use of the position of the light source(s) and the surface normal of the patch that projects onto the pixel. The latter is not obtainable until the patch has been transformed into some world coordinate system, where the patches connect edgewise to form surfaces. To change the viewed orientation requires a 4×4 matrix of numbers for a three-space change, necessary to compute the new normal, followed by a 4×2 projection transformation; and these must be applied to each primitive for each new frame. Animation of a limited sort involves the ability to apply such a transformation to each primitive in the model, rerender it, and do this at rates of up to 30 frames/sec. Where more than one primitive projects to a pixel, it must be determined which primitives are occluded by (are behind) which. We leave aside questions of partial occlusion (aliasing), shadowing, transparency, and many other concerns of highly competent graphics.

MESH-CONNECTED COMPUTER (MCC)

The target architecture of this work is the single-instruction multiple-data stream (SIMD) organization exemplified by, among others, the MPP built for NASA. The important distinguishing features of this machine that are of importance here are that the processors (PEs) are bit-serial, the amount of local storage in a PE is approximately 1000 bits with another 2000 available in a secondary store, and each PE may pass data to or from each of its four-neighbors. There are 16 384 PEs arranged in a 128×128 array. (Useful picture resolutions begin at 512×512.) The array is driven by the main control unit (MCU), which also may communicate with a host fileserver and, important to our work, may send data to all PEs simultaneously—a broadcast function.

Finally, the PE instruction set is quite limited, and local indexing into the PE memory is not possible. This would appear to make such common algorithmic data structures as vectors, stacks, and queues difficult to implement. As is shown later, the implementation of these is, in fact, straightforward, but must always fully calculate worst-case operations that assume the maximum amount of data. The graver challenge lies in making sure that no PE need ever exceed that maximum amount; this is particularly important when it is realized that the local memory may store only sixty 16-bit quantities, and a single triangular patch requires 10 of these for its definition.

Planar Patch Strategies

The simplest of graphics-rendering algorithms are highly uncoupled and data-parallel. Two extremes define the space of most such procedures.

STRATEGY A—BROADCAST HALF-SPACES

In this strategy, each element of the model, a triangular patch, is transformed and then broadcast to the entire array, one edge at a time. Each edge is formulated as a simple linear constraint so that each PE may calculate whether it is inside or outside the edge. After three edges have been broadcast, only those PEs whose grid coordinates lay on the "inside" of all three edges remain awake to accept a color and depth value. If a PE accepts a pixel value and already has one, that with the shallower depth is retained (Z-buffer technique). The purest and most literate exposition of this strategy is exemplified by the Pixel-Planes machine developed by the Chapel Hill group (Fuchs et al. 1985).

MPP limitations impinge on the success of this strategy in several ways. First, to maintain a true animation rate of near 30 Hz, only 300 or so patches can be transformed and broadcast. Second, if one will live with a reduced animation rate, the primary memory of the main control unit, where broadcasts originate, is somewhat limited and must contain not only data, but all array software as well as the model-management and transforming software. If the model cannot be kept here in its entirety, then speed of transfer to a host will, if required for every frame, further vitiate performance. Each PE (each pixel) tests independently of all others in parallel, so that the rendering time for any patch is independent of its area. This is a major advantage for large patches, but for smaller patches, the objection that "most PEs are not doing useful work (i.e., are not transforming data)" (Hummel and Rojer 1985), may be raised. However, this objection might also be leveled at sequential search processes, where all probes but the last do not provide the answer.

Strategy A results in a very simple and elegant PE program with no requirement for data-passing between PEs. Further, the array memory requirement is small enough that a large picture may be folded onto the array, an edge broadcast once, and the half-space and depth tests applied as many times as there are segments folded onto the array. Thus, a 512×512 picture would place 16 layers into the memory, allowing about 60 bits per layer (pixel), easily sufficient to hold a depth and color. For models whose number M of primitives is small, this is the strategy of choice, and allows considerable extra effects to be applied (Fuchs et al. 1985). For those with very many primitives, however, such as terrain or highly detailed and curved objects, the requirement of traversing and transforming the entire model sequentially for each frame is burdensome.

STRATEGY B—SCAN-GENERATION IN THE ARRAY

At one extreme end from Strategy A, this strategy moves the abstract model, as a collection of triangular patches, out into the array, and allows array elements to generate the pixels upon which they will project. This requires that, if a PE calculates, at most, one patch, each of the pixels it generates must be communicated to its proper location in the raster map. The time this takes is proportional to dA, the size of the largest projected patch, since a process can only generate one pixel at a time; however, the time it takes to route a pixel value must also be considered.

There are aesthetic advantages to this strategy, the greatest being that the model is put into the array once, so that further broadcasts for new frames need only send transformation parameters. The transformations are calculated in parallel, and scan generation may, to some degree, proceed in parallel as well. A later section describes a representative algorithm for scan-generation, and suggests some interesting SIMD programming considerations at this level. The array is, in general, underutilized, unless the number of primitives approaches 16 000. No PE should hold more than one primitive (unless there are more than the array capacity, of course) since it will then need to generate twice as many pixels, taking twice the time.

The generalized, free-for-all routing required interacts with the pixel-generation process in this way. A single cycle of pixel generation would require a maximal routing distance of 128 (measure of the array) if it were not for contention. That is, there is not a one-to-one mapping between generated pixels and processors, so that a simple array sort cannot easily be adapted to the problem. Several different pixels may wind up in a single PE (there may be many overlapping patches). Routing and generation cannot be easily overlapped, so that if two generation cycles run in tandem, the array has twice as many packets to route. Thus, a naive organization would alternate generation and routir₃ steps, allowing each to complete. This is proportional to $dA * R$, where R is the time to perform a complete routing of pixel locations and values (packets).

STRATEGY C—BEST OF BOTH WORLDS

During an initial broadcast of primitives, each PE that lies within a patch stays awake to receive the three-space parameters of that patch (three vertices and lighting information). This will amount to about 160 bits. Each PE retains the parameters of ALL patches that impinge on it. Each PE now calculates the plane of each of its patches, in turn; selects that with the shallowest depth; and calculates a pixel value for itself.

When transformation coordinates for the next frame are broadcast, they are applied to all copies of all resident patches. These are then projected to the image plane (the array). The effect of this will be that certain PEs lose patches as well as gain them. (We use the simplistic rule that if the center of a pixel lies within a patch, the whole pixel lies within it.) PEs that recalculate their membership in a patch, and are no longer in it, may simply delete it.

Discovering that a PE has gained a new patch is more complex. We may, before transforming, determine for a PE and a primitive whether any of its edges, in fact, run through it, and count the number of corners that lie inside the edge. This may be done by testing each of the pixel's corners with respect to the edge. If, after transformation, an edge includes more corners, then the PE into which that edge has moved, is passed the primitive. This may appear to become cumbersome as primitives become smaller, but the determining factor is rather the number of primitives within a PE, not the multiplicity of edges. Corners are even less straightforward, but we are forced to defer further consideration because of the following consideration.

The number of primitives held within a PE is at most six, and a model of any reasonable complexity cannot guarantee that, at some orientation, some pixel will not intersect more than six patches. Overflowing onto the secondary memory, while not catastrophic, is cumbersome. Simply eliminating the deeper patches from full PEs may indeed prove catastrophic and the determination of which primitives to reload into which PEs is not a practicable task. If local memory were more forgiving, this would be the strategy of choice, providing that movement of the edges from one frame to the next were only a very few pixels in extent. Routing of primitives is then controlled and bounded, there is no dependence upon the patch size dA, and the only determining proportionality is the number of patches that may overlap.

STRATEGY D—MINIMAL DATA

As presented, strategy D requires a processor to retain an unpredictable number of patches, and the maximum capacity of local memory is six of these, or 16 if recourse is made to the stager array. Further, no allowance has been made for temporary storage of edges. If, instead of full patch parameters, only vertices were stored in the array, and only in those pixels they project to, it might be possible to generate all derived quantities within the array. One possible mechanism is for each vertex to diffuse itself outward until two vertices' effusions meet, at which point elements between the two might relax themselves according to some constraint that could be linear or of higher order. This relaxation fits well the original objective of the MCC.

It is necessary to assign each vertex a unique identifier, and the vertex must then carry a list of identifiers of all other vertices with which it shares an edge. This is because an effusing vertex will encounter many others from other surfaces in the model, and should not try joining except with true neighbors. In order to carry this out, each vertex must effuse its own identifier, as well as the identifiers of several neighbors, and, in a unique labeling of vertices, this may, for high M, require 10–15 bits for each identifier. As is common in a SIMD environment, every vertex packet must be as long as possible, so that any intermediate PE may hold perhaps no more then 16 such packets. Paper simulations suggest that, even if some mechanism for halting effusions can be formulated, the number of effusing packets a single PE must hold is not controllable.

STRATEGY E—OPTIMIZE STRATEGY B

The second pure strategy of pushing the entire model onto the array, scan generating and routing, required time proportional to $dA * R$, the time required to scan, generate, and route, respectively. The multiplicative relation probably cannot be removed, but there remains the fairly simple expedient of reducing dA and R. The first reduction can be achieved by subdividing the model's patches, and the second by ensuring that the pixels generated by each PE do not have to travel very far. Subdivision is straightforward, if laborious, and is assumed to be performed prior to loading on the array. All patches must be ordered by area, and then the largest split and its parts exchanged into the sorted list. This continues until the list attains some desirable length that will utilize the array without flooding it. Flooding of the array occurs if it is too densely packed with primitives, as is described next.

This relates to the second component of the strategy, which is to locate each primitive on or near some PE that it will actually project to, so that the routing distance will be on the order of sqrt(dA). This can, of course, be done during the first load of the model, as with previous schemes, but requires that each new frame cycle moves those primitives that no longer lie in their projection on the array. This presents an interesting routing problem, which we are pursuing further, in which a primitive has no unique destination; under a naive routing scheme, contention for destinations is possible, since only one primitive should occupy a PE; and if a primitive cannot occupy any of its intended destinations because of previous occupancy, it will settle for something nearby. The term "flooding" describes a situation in which contention for destinations is high.

Algorithmic Considerations

The topics in this section address, in part, the feasibility of operations mentioned earlier. In a standard sequential environment, most of these are taken for granted. In a situation that does not provide local indexing, they cannot be. Some very weak timing estimates are provided, based upon the 10 MHz clock of the MPP. Although no arithmetic analyses are done, empirical elementary timings (Faiss 1987) for 16-bit quantities place addition at $3.2\,\mu$sec, multiplication at $16.3\,\mu$sec, and division at about $30\,\mu$sec. To apply a full geometric transformation to a vertex requires about 0.5 msec. The dependence upon operand length is because the PEs are bit-serial. To route a single bit between PEs or to swap within a local memory takes about four clock cycles. As will become apparent in the following sections, aggregate operations from sorts to indexed accesses to array routes all appear to cluster about 1 msec. This is substantial, since any of the strategies involves many such aggregate operations and the video constraint allows only 30.

LOCAL INDEXED ACCESS

Let a contiguous section of local memory be subdivided into N pieces of $B + 1$ bits each, or a total of $L = N(B + 1)$ bits in length. Suppose that we wish to access the Ith piece of this array, where I is a local index register. Since all units must access the same address at the same time, then the accessed data must eventually reside at a common address, which means moving or copying it from the array of pieces to some common register. This may be effected by broadcasting, in turn, the values $1, \ldots, N$. At each broadcast, processors compare this number with their own I-register. Those processors that test equal copy the data into a common register from the array piece currently pointed to for all processors (this is a global instruction), while other processors temporarily disable themselves. This operation, in general, will require a B-bit copy for each value $1, \ldots, N$, so that such an access takes time proportional to L. This amounts to about 0.3 msec, if the entire memory is used.

LOCAL SORTING

Let a contiguous section of local memory be subdivided into N pieces of $B + 1$ bits each. One bit indicates whether the piece is occupied by data or not. Calculate the sorting key of the first piece and place in T, where the key will take on a very large value if the piece is empty. For pieces $2, \ldots, N$, calculate the key value from the piece, compare with T, swap each piece if its key value is smaller than T and place this value into T. Now repeat the entire process beginning with the second piece, ignoring the first which now has the smallest key value associated with it.

This is just a selection sort, and will take time proportional to N^2. In the normal world, the expected frequency of the exchanges is highly data-dependent. The worst case, where all N pieces contain data and are in reverse order, will require $(B + 1) * N(N - 1)/2$ single-bit exchanges. For an MPP processor with six patches of 160 bits each, this amounts to about 1 msec, or 2400 exchanges requiring four cycles of 0.1 μsec each. In the SIMD world, the worst case is always to be expected. If a single processor at any step requires an exchange, all other processors must wait for it, and it is difficult to see how the exchange can be deferred, since its effect may be critical to the next step, and is address-bound in any event.

Total sorts are seldom required in the strategies presented, since lists are maintained one element at a time, so that such maintenance is perhaps a more realistic estimate. That is, at any step, either a piece is emptied or a new set of data is put into the last piece. If a piece at position J is emptied, then the first $J - 1$ passes involve no exchanges, and the Jth to Nth passes will each involve exchange of a single piece, as the now-empty piece will be bubbled to the end. If a new piece receives data, it will do so at the end position, and this may simply be swapped toward the front of the array, so that the number of exchanges is, at most, $N - 1$, as with the deletion, and this adds about 0.04 msec to the time required simply to perform comparisons. On the average ($N/2$ swaps), this time is closer to 0.02 msec, so that insertion or deletion from the array, with its rearrangement after the operation, will require about 0.12 msec.

MANAGING OTHER DATA STRUCTURES LOCALLY

As can be seen from the discussion of local sorting, any management procedure must be exhaustive. That is, the sort has no data dependencies that affect its timing, except in unusual circumstances. However, exhaustive sorts are not always required. If pieces are removed from or added to the array one at a time, rearrangement consists of moving a single piece that is out of order in an otherwise ordered array. In the case of a deletion, a piece now evaluates to a high key value, and if a conditional exchange is swept from the front of the array, the empty piece will wind up near the end with the other empty ones. In the case of an addition, if it is always made at the end, then it should be swept forward from the end of the array. In either case, this amounts to, in the aggregate (and unexpected) worst case, $B * N$ bit exchanges, which, in the current choice of parameters, amounts to about 0.4 msec, and since a forward sweep and a backward sweep must be done separately, rearrangement may occupy 0.8 msec.

Consider stack management, maintaining the stack as growing from one end of the array. In a push operation, the item to be added is in a temporary register. All processors begin searching their stacks from the bottom, simply querying the occupied bit. At each comparison, those that find an empty piece copy the temporary into that piece, while the others mark it occupied, and then turn themselves off. This requires a one-bit register to indicate either that a processor has successfully stored its operand or that it has not, and is thus still active. A pop operation is similar but moves from the other end of the array. In either case, this amounts to $B * N$ bit transfers (or about 1000) at the assumed rate of four cycles each, or 0.4 msec. This is because the most general case is that stacks will be of widely varying sizes, so that, at each piece, at least one processor is likely to require a data transfer from the temporary to the top of the stack.

SCAN-CONVERTING A PATCH

Scan-conversion is the process of generating the coordinates of each covered pixel from the patch parameters. One direct procedure traverses each raster line that touches the patch in, say, the x direction from one side of the patch to the other, generating each pixel address in turn.

More specifically, determine the minimum and maximum y-values among the vertices, this determines which x-lines need be traversed. Place the vertex containing the minimum y into A, and now choose from the two remaining vertices that with the lesser x value and call it B. (Recall that the original vertices have now been projected onto the image plane.) For each value beginning at YLOW, intersect the line connecting A and B with the line Y = current-scanline. Count up (in X) from this intersection in pixel-sized increments until an intersection with the line connecting A with the remaining undistinguished vertex C is reached. If Y should eventually reach B before C (B is lower), replace the starting line with that connecting B and C. If the scan line reaches C first, then replace the finish line with that connecting B and C. Continue in this fashion until $Y >$ YHIGH.

```
/* stylized pseudo-algorithm for scan conversion */

/*=====preparatory phase=====*/
/* vertices projected to three-two-dimensional
 points A,B,C. reorder. */
 if (A.Y>B.Y) then swap(A,B);
 if (A.Y>C.Y) then swap(A,C);
        /* now min-y point in A*/
 if (B.X>C.X) then swap(B.C);
        /* upper-left point now in B*/
/* directional increment dx/dy for each edge */
/* at this point all values are scaled up to include
four fractional bits*/
 DAB=(B.X-A.X) div (B.Y-A.Y);
 DAC=(C.X-A.X) div (C.Y-A.Y);
 DBC=(C.X-B.X) div (C.Y-B.Y);

 CY=trunc(A.Y+1);
/*CX,CY are on pixel centers*/
 SX=A.X+(CY-Z.Y)*DAB;'
 FX=A.X+(CY-A.Y)*DAC;
        /* start, finish lines*/

 CX=trunc(SX);
/*trunc simple zeroes fractional bits*/

 YHIGH=B.Y;
 if (YHIGH<C.Y) then begin
            YHIGH=C.Y;
            YMID=B.Y;
            end
       else
            YMID=C.Y;

/*=====iterative phase=====*/

  while (CY <= YHIGH) do
    begin
      CX=CX+1;
      if (CX>FX) then
        begin
          CY=CY+1:
          /*start new scan line*/
          if (CY>= YMID) then
```

```
        /*replace start or finish*/
        begin
!         if (YMID=C.Y) then begin
!           /*replace finish line*/
!             DFX=DBC;
!             FX=DFX*(CY-C.Y);
!                 end
!             else begin
!             /*replace starting line*/
!             DBX=DBC;
!             BX=DBX*(CY-B.Y);
                end;
            else
    /*start new scan line; start & finish still ok*/
                    begin
*                       SX=BX+DBX;
*                       CX=trunc(SX);
*                       FX=FX+DFX;
                    end
        else /*still on same line, send it*/
            {route CX,CY,Z, value}
```

As presented, the algorithm does not handle the cases where *Dxx* may be infinite (an edge is horizontal or nearly so), and practitioners of Parallel Pascal will note that the conditionals would need to be reworked. It is a parallel algorithm in the spirit of Parallel Pascal, or APL for that matter, since all capitalized variables are array variables with unique locations in the memory planes. At each pixel iteration (step along a scan line), some processor is likely to require changing scan lines. This entails a change in its Y-coordinate and a new intersection with the current starting edge, as well as a test to see whether the starting or finishing edge needs to be updated. The work to simply change a line is labeled "*" in the left margin, that required to change a start or finish line is labeled "!" For a general situation, at least one processor is likely to require both at each elementary cycle, so that the exceptional computation will have to be performed *dA* times in general.

If we call the height $(YHIGH - A.Y)$ of the tallest patch H, this will generally be about $2*\mathrm{sqrt}(dA)$. If the algorithm is run only to where $CY >= $ YMID and those processors go to sleep until everyone gets there, and then everyone is restarted from YMID, including updating start or finish lines, then all the work labeled "!" is done totally in parallel exactly once rather than dA times. The number of times the elementary cycle is run may now grow to $2dA$ at worst. This suggests a candidate rule of thumb that may be stated in the vernacular: *If exceptional work* (*not common to all processors*) *cannot be done in the beginning, consider deferring it until the end.* If we apply the same thinking to each scan line, however, for the exceptional work labeled "*", a worst-case number of elementary cycles will be $H*dA$, and that work will need to be done H times, anyway.

A SOURCE-OBLIVIOUS ROUTING ALGORITHM

The routed packets include destination addresses (x and y at 10 bits each), a depth value of 16 bits, and color information of 10 bits for a total of 46, to which we add one to designate full or empty (empty packets may be ignored by the receiver). Each PE maintains four buffers, each of length BUFLEN, for packets that must be routed north, east, south, or west. Given the data requirements of the scan-conversion algorithm presented here, BUFLEN is limited to 2, although PEs without a primitive inside could hold a BUFLEN of 4, if we wished to complicate the algorithm.

In addition to packets, two other messages are sent. A prospective destination informs its sender of a full buffer in the direction of the prospective transfer, under the assumption that the packet to be transmitted is likely to continue in the same direction. A buffer is full even though the destination may be hoping to rid it of one packet during the prospective routine. This is a conservative approach, and may be contrasted to one in which every sender sends, and is then passed a positive or negative acknowledgment indicating whether the destination was able to receive the packet or not. This, however, requires a ripple of acknowledgment signals across the entire array. They may, of course, be one bit in length, with each beat of the ripple taking about 3 μsec, or 0.5 msec total for the ripple.

The routing proceeds by cycling direction D through N, E, S, W repeatedly until no PE has any packets left in any buffers. At each direction, each prospective destination sends a single bit to its prospective sender to indicate whether its buffer in direction D is full. If so, an empty packet will be sent. Then each PE sends (and receives), confident that it has room for a new packet, or that none will be sent. Each destination PE redetermines the direction of the new packet, based on the relationship of the destination to that PE's location and the status of the buffers. The preferred direction is calculated by comparing DX with DY, either of which may be negative, and choosing the larger in magnitude provided that either there is buffer space available or it will be the next direction of transfer, in which case the packet stays in the communication buffer (a software area, the actual communication structure is a single bit).

This and more intelligent procedures are about to undergo closer study, and rather a lot of study is necessary. However, some lower bound on timing is possible and informative. It should take a minimum of four clock cycles to transfer one bit, at 0.1 μsec, or about 20 μsec for one packet to travel one pixel. For one packet to go the maximum distance would require 2.5 msec, which is substantial, and if contention is high, this could double or triple. If expected lengths of travel are small, on the order of 10, then with a contention factor of 5 (which seems large) each full routing should take less than 1 msec.

In considering Strategy E, the compromise, it should be noted that not only do dA, the number of cycles of the scan-generator, and R, the expected routing time, enter into the determination of frame time, but so, too, does M, the number of primitives, since the more PEs that are producing pixels, the greater the possibility for contention. While smaller dA alone implies both shorter frame time (fewer generate cycles) and shorter routing time (less distance to travel), it also tends to increase contention (greater routing time). Although an analytical treatment of these relations may prove possible, they seem more directly amenable to simulations that have been started, but not completed, at this time.

Discussion of Graphics Algorithms

Graphics algorithms, as with most computation in general, rely heavily upon rather precise numbers. This is due in part to the fact that precise numbers are one of the most accessible data structures implemented by most computers. It is reasonable to consider the redesign of algorithms to lessen their dependence upon numbers, particularly when confronted with an architecture that does not directly support these data types. The size of the MPP and its anticipated descendants suggest that we investigate some analogy to coarse encoding (Ballard 1986), in which the precision of a quantity is distributed over several low-precision units.

It is well known that, particularly in animation, the changes from one frame to the next are generally small, so that a next frame is "predictable" from the current one, a convenience termed *time-coherence* that is seriously underutilized. We have incorporated some limited use of this, to the extent that, while the transformation is still done at full precision for each frame, it is at least done in parallel in Strategy E, and the amount of communication is kept minimal by moving patches as close to their projections as possible.

The major perceived limitation of the MPP appears to be the limited depth of each PE. Several investigators in the MPP Working Group think alternatively, that more PEs would alleviate the need for greater depth. Our view is that if array size is increased, the maximum routing length increases also, while if an oversize square problem is instead folded over onto a smaller array, utilizing several depth layers, then the maximum routing distance remains constant plus some small amount to go between levels in PE memory planes. Since most of our proposed strategies go to some pains to minimize routing, this is not a major issue. However, the compromise embodied in Strategy E (local scan-generation) was made necessary simply because the more direct Strategy C, which avoided scan-generation, could not contain necessary data. However, Strategy E depends most directly upon M, and the more PEs available, the higher M may be, and the lower dA may be.

Reducing the dependence upon precision, as discussed in the first paragraph of this section, is one form of rethinking algorithms. We are still highly conditioned by our sequential background, and most procedures described here rely upon terms from that background. An alternative form of representation of a model, rather than as a data base of canonical primitives, is as a functional specification for generating primitives (Wainer (1989)). Integrating such specifications into the more structured world of interacting graphic components is still a thorny challenge.

Finally, integration of any algorithm into an operationally competent system addresses the title topic, limitations. In this discussion, little attention has been paid to the fact that the only direct way to handle images that are larger than the array is to fold them onto it and hope that sufficient memory planes are available. For highly competent models, such as true terrain and surroundings, the generated image is a window, often small, onto the model, so that only a portion of it is used at any time. The question of what to do with primitives that currently are not in the scene, but may be eventually, adds another order of magnitude to the memory limitation.

REFERENCES

Aggarwal, A., B. Chazell, L. Guibas, C. O'Dunlaing, and C. Yap (1985). "Parallel computational geometry," *Proc. 25th IEEE Symp. Found. of Computer Sci.,* pp. 468–477.

Andrews, H. C. and B. R. Hunt (1977). *Digital Image Restoration,* pp. 148–149. Prentice-Hall, Englewood Cliffs, N.J.

Ballard, D. H. (1986). "Cortical connections and parallel processing: Structure and function," *Behavioral and Brain Sci.,* Vol. 9, pp. 67–120.

Blelloch, G. (1986). *Parallel Prefix vs. Concurrent Memory Access,* Technical report (in preparation). Thinking Machines Corporation, Cambridge, Mass.

Blelloch, G. and J. Little (1987). "Parallel solutions to geometric problems on the scan model of computation," Third Annual Symposium on Computational Geometry, 1987.

Boghosian, D. and D. Levermore (1989). "A cellular automaton for Burgers' equation," forthcoming.

Booth, A. D. (1957). *Numerical Methods.* Academic Press, New York.

Camillo, P. J., R. J. Gurney, and T. J. Schmugge (1983). "A soil and atmospheric boundary layer model for evapotranspiration and soil moisture studies," *Water Resources Res.,* Vol. 19, p. 371.

Canny, J. F. (1986). "A computational approach to edge detection," *IEEE Trans. Pattern Anal. Machine Intelligence,* Vol. 8, No. 6, pp. 679–698.

Chen, H. and W. Matthaeus (1987a). *Fluids,* forthcoming.

Chen, H. and W. H. Matthaeus (1987b). *Phys. Rev. Lett.,* forthcoming.

Chen, H., and W. H. Matthaeus (1987c), forthcoming.

Clapp, R. B., and G. M. Hornberger (1978). "Empirical equations for some soil hydraulic properties," *Water Resources Res.* Vol. 14, p. 601.

Cook, S. A. (1980). "Towards a complexity theory of synchronous parallel computation," *Int. Symp. Ueber Logic und Algorithmic zu Ehren vo Proffessor Ernst Specker, Zurich.*

Cowling, T. G. (1976). *Magnetohydrodynamics,* Adam Hilger, Bristol, UK.

Dahlburgh, J., D. Montgomery and G. Doolen (1987). "Noise and compressibility in lattice gas fluids," Dartmouth College preprint.

Devaney, J. E. (1985). " The MPP—A totally different approach to programming," presented at the 1985 IEEE Computer Society Workshop on Computer Architecture for Pattern Analysis and Image Data Base Management, November 1985, Miami Beach, Florida. IEEE Computer Society Order No. 622, IEEE Catalog No. 85CH2229-3.

de Vries, D. A. (1975). "Heat transfer in soils, heat and mass transfer in the biosphere," *Scripa,* Washington, D.C.

d'Hummieres, D., P. Lallemand and T. Shimomura (1985). Los Alamos National Lab. preprint LA-UR-85-4051.

Dorband, J. (1986). Private communication.

Drumheller, M. and T. Poggio (1986). "Parallel stereo," *Proc. IEEE Conference on Robotics and Automation*," San Francisco.

Eagleson, P. S. (1970). *Dynamic Hydrology*. McGraw-Hill, New York.

Elsasser, W. (1950). *Phys. Rev.*, Vol. 179, p. 183.

Faiss, R. O. (1987). "The Goodyear SIMD processors: insights gained from 20 years of usage," *Proc. 1987 Multiprocessor and Array Processor Conference III* (*MAPCON III*). Society for Computer Simulation, San Diego.

Freeze, R. A. (1971). "Three-dimensional, transient, saturated unsaturated flow in a groundwater basin," *Water Resources Res.* Vol. 7, p. 929.

Frisch, U., B. Hasslacher, and Y. Pomeau (1986). *Phys. Rev. Lett.*, Vol. 56, p. 1505.

Fuchs, H. et al. (1985). "Fast spheres, shadows, textures, transparencies, and image enhancements in pixel-planes," *Computer Graphics* Vol. 19, No. 3, pp. 111–120. [SIGGRAPH-85 Conference Proceedings]

Fyfe, D., D. Montgomery, and G. Joyce (1977). *J. Plasma Phys.*, Vol. 17, p. 369.

Gatignol, R. (1975). "Theorie cinétique des gaz a répartition discrète des vitesses," *Lecture Notes in Physics*, No. 36. Springer-Verlag, New York.

Geman, S. and D. Geman (1984). "Stochastic relaxation, Gibbs distributions, and the Bayesian restoration of images," *IEEE Trans. Pattern Anal. Machine Intelligence*, Vol. 6.

Grimson, W. E. L. (1981). *From Images to Surfaces*. MIT Press, Cambridge, Mass.

Hardy, J. and Y. Pomeau (1972). *J. Math. Phys.*, Vol. 13, p. 1042.

Harris, J. G. and A. M. Glynn (1986). "Object recognition using the connection machine router," *Proceedings IEEE 1986 Conference on Computer Vision and Pattern Recognition*, pp. 134–139.

Hatori, T. and D. Montgomery (1987). "Transport coefficients for magnetohydrodynamic cellular automata," Dartmouth College preprint.

Hillis, D. (1985). *The Connection Machine*, MIT Press, Cambridge, Mass.

Hillis, D. and G. L. Steele (1986). "Data parallel algorithms," *Commun. ACM*, Vol. 29, No. 12, pp. 1170–1183.

Hummel, R. A. and A. Rojer (1985). "Connected component labelling in image processing with MIMD architectures," NYU Courant Institute of Mathematical Sciences—Computer Science Division, TR-173.

Lasser, C. (1986). "The complete *Lisp manual." Thinking Machines Corporation, Cambridge, Mass.

Leberl, F., J. Raggam, C. Elachi, and W. Campbell (1983). "Sea ice motion measurements from SEASAT SAR images," *J. Geophys. Res.*, Vol. 88, No. C3, pp. 1915–1928.

Lim, W., A. Agrawal and L. Nekludova (1987). "A fast parallel algorithm for labeling connected components in image arrays," *International Conference on Computer Vision*.

Lin, J. D. (1980). "On the force-restore method for prediction of ground surface temperature," *J. Geophys. Res.* Vol. 85, p. 3251.

Little, J. J. (1986). "Parallel algorithms for computer vision," AIM-928, MIT AI Laboratory.

Little, J. J., and H. Bulthoff (1986). "Parallel computation of optical flow," AIM-929, MIT AI Laboratory.

Little, J. J., G. Blelloch, and T. Cass (1987). "Parallel algorithms for computer vision on the Connection Machine," International Conference on Computer Vision, 1987.

Margolus, N. (1984). *Physica* (Amsterdam), Vol. 10D, p. 81.

Marr, D. and T. Poggio (1979). "A computational theory of human stereo vision," *Proc. Roy. Soc. London*, pp. 301–328.

Marr, D. (1982). *Vision*. W. H. Freeman, San Francisco.

McBryan, O. A. (1986). "Numerical computation on massively parallel hypercubes," *Proceedings of the 1986 Hypercube Conference, SIAM*.

Montgomery, D. and G. Doolen (1987). *Phys. Lett. A*, in press.

Orszag, S. and V. Yakhot (1986). *Phys. Rev. Lett.*, Vol. 56, p. 1691.

Pavlidis, T. (1982). "Algorithms for graphics and image processing," pp. 1–3. Computer Science Press, Rockville, Md.

Philip, J. R. and D. A. de Vries (1957). "Moisture movement of porous materials under temperature gradients," *EOS Trans. AGU* Vol. 38, p. 222.

Philips, D. L. (1962). "A technique for the numerical solution of certain integral equations of the first kind," *J. ACM*, Vol. 9, pp. 84–97.

Poggio, T. (1985a). "Early vision: From computational structure to algorithms and parallel hardware," *Computer Vision, Graphics, and Image Processing*, Vol. 31.

Poggio, T. (1985b). "Integrating vision modules with coupled MRGs," MIT Artificial Intelligence Laboratory working paper 285.

Pomeau, Y. (1984). *J. Phys. A.*, Vol. 17, p. L415.

Potter, J. L. (1985). "The massively parallel processor." MIT Press, Cambridge, Mass.

Preparata, F. P. and M. I. Shamos (1985). *Computational Geometry—An Introduction*. Springer-Verlag, New York.

Quam, L. (1984). "Hierarchical warp stereo," *Proceedings, Image Understanding Workshop*, pp. 149–155.

Teddington, A. (1958). *Modern Computing Methods*. Philosophical Library, New York.

Terzopoulos, D. (1986). "Image analysis using multigrid relaxation models," *IEEE Trans. Pattern Anal. Machine Intelligence*, Vol. 8, No. 2, pp. 129–139.

Twomey, S. (1963). "On the numerical solution of the Fredholm integral equations of the first kind," *J. ACM*, Vol. 10, pp. 97–101.

Ullman, S. (1984). "Visual routines," *Cognition*, Vol. 18.

von Neumann, J. (1966). "Theory of self-reproducing automata," (ed. A. W. Burks). University of Illinois, Urbana.

Wah, B. W., G. Li, and C. F. Yu (1985). "Multiprocessing of combinatorial search problems," *IEEE Computer*, Vol. 18, No. 6, pp. 93–108.

Wainer, M. S. (1989). "Generating fractal surfaces on general-purpose mesh-connected computers," *IEEE Trans. Computers* (forthcoming).

Wolfram, S. (1983). *Rev. Mod. Phys.*, Vol. 55, p. 601.

Wolfram, S. (1986). *J. Stat. Phys*, Vol. 45, p. 471.

Wyllie, J. C. (1979). "The complexity of parallel computations," TR-79-387, Department of Computer Science, Cornell University, Ithaca, New York.

Young, D. M. (1971). *Iterative Solution of Large Linear Systems*, pp. 434–437. Academic Press, New York.

11

SUPERCOMPUTER APPLICATIONS OF THE HYPERCUBE

John Apostolakis, Clive Baillie, Robert W. Clayton, Hong Ding, Jon Flower, Geoffrey C. Fox, Thomas D. Gottschalk, Bradford H. Hager, Herbert B. Keller, Adam K. Kolawa, Steve W. Otto, Toshiro Tanimoto, Eric F. Van de Velde, J. Barhen, J. R. Einstein, and C. C. Jorgensen

INTRODUCTION

In this chapter, we survey some of the early applications of hypercubes to computationally intense problems—mainly science and engineering fields. Our presentation is biased by our experience at Caltech, although the many commercial hypercubes from Ametek, Floating Point Systems, INTEL, and NCUBE are rapidly broadening the use of hypercubes. In the next section we summarize the current status of C^3P, the Caltech Concurrent Computation Program, whose work is described in the succeeding five sections. The first of these has a general overview, which is expanded in the book by Fox.[1] It describes the hypercube and its place in a taxonomy of parallel machines; the general issues concerning the uses of the hypercube are illustrated, and several applications listed in Table 11-1 are sketched. Caltech research in the area of automating decomposition of problems, aimed at aiding the software development task, is also reviewed.

The other four sections give an in-depth discussion of several Caltech hypercube applications concerning the multigrid approach to partial differential

The work of the first 13 authors was supported in part by Department of Defense Grants DE-FG03-85ER25009 and DE-AC03-85ER40050, in part by the Parsons and System Development Foundations, and in part by the office of the program manager of the Joint Tactical Fusion Office. Grants from Sandia and IBM also supported some of this research.

equations, the quantum chromodynamics theory of high-energy physics, geophysics, and the Kalman filter used in multitarget tracking. The final section covers the pioneering Oak Ridge research on the use of the commerical NCUBE as a controller for a robot. This is a real-time application—rather different from the "number-crunching" of the previous sections.

THE CALTECH CONCURRENT COMPUTATION PROGRAM (C^3P)

The original hypercube ideas were developed at Caltech with the first major ·hardware—the Cosmic Cube with 64 nodes—being completed in 1983 by Chuck Seitz in the Caltech Computer Science Department.[2] Starting in 1981, we have built up a research group—now called C^3P—whose emphasis is an application-oriented approach to fundamental issues in computation. We built two generations of hypercubes, the Mark II and Mark III, as part of C^3P to provide sufficient parallel computing resources to support many users. We finished this phase of our work in November 1988 when the 128 node Mark IIIfp hypercube shown in Figure 11-3 was completed. This powerful parallel computer will have 0.5 Gbyte of memory and a peak performance of over one GFLOPS. In Figure 11-4 we show a commercial NCUBE, in which a board contains 64 single-chip CPUs, each with 11 communication channels and 0.5 Mbyte of memory. Our 512-node NCUBE is now operational, as is a 1024-node system installed in SANDIA's new computer science division. Our two major machines will be our backbone resource for our research that is centered on the philosophy of

Solution of real problems on real hardware with real software

which is illustrated by our original physics calculations.[3,4]

We are phasing out the in-house hardware component of C^3P as parallel processing technology is being successfully transferred to industry.[5] Another crucial part of C^3P is the user community: currently some twenty research groups at Caltech's Campus and the Jet Propulsion Laboratory in various fields of computational science and engineering. C^3P provides these users access to parallel computing hardware and software as well as financial support for students and postdoctoral researchers developing applications and algorithms. The research groups are motivated by both the future promise of parallel computing and the near-term possibility of using existing machines to solve major computational science projects. This production use of parallel computers is possible because we stress powerful machines and our philosophy ensures that we implement full problems and do not get misleading answers from incomplete implementations. The final component of C^3P is a central group to address the computer science and computer engineering issues. Here, for instance, we develop necessary systems software; an effort that is still and perhaps even more necessary with the commercial machines. We also develop fundamental algorithms and research issues such as neural networks both for the assignment problems discussed later and as part of an attractive approach to parallel artificial intelligence.

Finally, we stress that even our theoretical work is closely based on the results of the Caltech user's group, where by now over 100 separate hypercube codes have developed. As illustrated in Table 11-1, these cover a very wide range of algorithms and disciplines. For more general information, we refer the reader to our recent C^3P annual reports,[6,7] and also the proceedings of the hypercube conferences.[8,9,10] Details of some of these applications are given in the next section.

Table 11-1. Current parallel algorithms and applications within the Caltech Concurrent Program ongoing or completed in 1986–87

Biology and computation and neural systems (CNS)				
Number	**Status**	**Name**	**Lead personnel**	**Report or HCCA3 Abstract**
1	I	Structural simulations of neural networks using a general-purpose neural-network simulator	J. Bower (f), M. Nelson W. Furmanski U. Bhalla, M. Wilson	$(C^3P$-404, 405)
2	I	Back-propagation algorithms for character recognition and computer games	C. Koch (f), E. Felten J. Hutchinson, S. Otto	(A261)
3	I	Pattern recognition by neural networks on hypercubes	A. Ho, W. Furmanski	(A207)
4	I	Collective stereopsis	R. Battiti	(A16, C^3P-420)
5	B	Mapping the human genome	G. Fox (f), L. Hood (f), W. Furmanski	
6	B	Modeling complex neurons	W. Furmanski, C. Koch (f)	
Chemistry and chemical engineering				
7	I	Integration of coupled sets of ordinary differential equations from chemical reaction dynamics	P. Hipes T. Mattson M. Wu A. Kuppermann (f)	$(C^3P$-347) (A85)
8	B	Polymer simulations	H-Q. Ding W. Goddard (f)	(A262)
9	B	Concurrent optimization and dynamical simulation in chemical engineering	A. Skjellum M. Morari (f)	
10	B	Quantum lattice system for high T_c superconductivity and Monte Carlo simulation	H-Q Ding W. Goddard (f)	

Table 11-1. *Continued*

Number	Status	Name	Lead personnel	Report or HCCA3 Abstract
Engineering				
11	C	Ray tracing on the hypercube	J. Goldsmith (j) J. Salmon	(C^3P-295, 384, 403) (A73)
12	I	Plasma simulations on the Mark III	P. C. Liewer (j), R. W. Gould (f), V. K. Decyk (UCLA), J. D. Dawson (UCLA)	(C^3P-460) (A108)
13	I	Vortex dynamics	A. Leonard (f) F. Pepin, K. Chua	(A131)
14	I	Synthetic-aperture radar (SAR) analysis on the hypercube	J. Kim, G. Fox (f) G. Aloisio, N. Veneziani (Italy) J. Patterson (j), B. Zimmerman (j), C. Wu (j)	(C^3P-468)
15	I	Flux-corrected transport on the NCUBE	D. Walker G. Montry (Sandia)	
16	I	Parallel free-language hydrodynamics	R. Williams	(A189) (C^3P-424, 465)
Geophysics				
17	I	Finite-element wave propagation	E. Clayton (f)	(C^3P-408) (A264)
	I	Normal modes of the Earth	T. Tanimoto (f)	(C^3P-408)
18	I	Finite-element flow modeling	R. Gurnis, B. Hager (f),	(A189)
19			A. Raefsky, G. Lyzenga (j)	(C^3P-408, 463)
Physics				
20	I	Lattice gauge theory with fermions on the hypercube	J. Apostolakis, C. Baillie H-Q. Ding, J. Flower S. Otto, G. Fox (f) R. Gupta (Los Alamos)	(A184) (C^3P-450, 411)
21	B	Random lattice calculations	T. W. Chiu	(A183)
22	C	Two-dimensional melting	M. Johnson (IBM)	(C^3P-268)
23	I	Nonlocal path integral Monte Carlo for helium	M. Cross (f)	(A177)
24	I	$N \log N$ algorithm for astrophysical particle dynamics	J. Salmon M. Warren	(A164)
25	I	The hypercube for astronomical data analysis	P. Gorham T. Prince (f)	(A215)
26	I	Multichannel Schrödinger equation	T. Barnes D. Kotchan (Toronto)	

Table 11-1. *Continued*

Number	Status	Name	Lead personnel	Report or HCCA3 Abstract
		General algorithms and numerical analysis		
27	C	LU decomposition of banded matrices and the solution of linear systems	D. Walker, T. Aldcroft A. Cisneros, G. Fox (f), W. Furmanski	(A4) (C^3P-348)
28	C	Optimal matrix algorithms and communication strategies for homogeneous hypercubes	G. Fox (f) W. Furmanski	(C^3P-314, 329, 386) (A265)
29	I	Adaptive multigrid on the Mark III	E. Van de Velde	(C^3P-406, 447)
30	I	Finite-element methods in coherent parallel C	E. Felten, R. Morison S. Otto	(A56)
31	C	Communication strategies for network simulations	G. Fox (f) W. Furmanski	(C^3P-405)
32	C	A concurrent implementation of the prime factor algorithm	J. Kim G. Fox (f) G. Aloisio N. Veneziani (Italy)	(A6) (C^3P-468)
33	C	Concurrent tracking algorithms with Kalman filters	T. Gottschalk I. Angus	(A186) (C^3P-387, 388, 398) (C^3P-478-481)
34	I	Concurrent $\alpha - \beta$ search techniques for computer chess	E. Felten S. Otto	(C^3P-383) (A268)
35	C	Shift register sequence random number generators on the hypercube	T-W. Chiu	(A182)
36	B	Transaction analysis on the NCUBE	A. Frey, R. Mosteller (IBM)	
37	I	Branch-and-bound algorithms	E. Felten	(A239)

Notes:

Status	Report Label	Affiliation
I In Progress	(C^3P – XXX) C^3P Document Number	(f) Caltech Faculty
B Beginning	(AXXX) HCCA3 Abstract Number	(j) Jet Propulsion Laboratory
C Complete		

C^3P Documents may be obtained from C^3P Requests; Caltech Concurrent Computation Program, 206-49; California Institute of Technology; Pasadena, CA 91125. HCCA3 refers to Third Hypercube Conference (ref. 10) whose proceedings are published by ACM.

THE HYPERCUBE AS A SUPERCOMPUTER

The Hypercube as a Concurrent Computer

Figure 11-1(a) displays some key characteristics of *concurrent computers* and indicates those of the *hypercube*. Curiously enough, the hypercube is named after its topology, shown in (b)—one of its least important characteristics! The hypercube has *large* (or perhaps better *medium*) *grain size*; it consists of many entities or *nodes* each of which is a complete computer capable of containing a significant portion of the problem (e.g., with a memory that is typically at least 0.5 Mbyte per node). All the memory on the hypercube is *distributed*—that is, associated with a particular node. Nodes can access data stored on other nodes by sending requests (messages) to other nodes. Such requests are most efficient if handled with a direct hardware link, but messages can be forwarded by intermediate nodes so that any node can communicate with any other. The current machines have been designed with rather general purpose nodes, but there is no reason why one should not optimize the nodes to a particular task, say, to be a LISP engine. The hypercube is MIMD: each node can operate asynchronously with separate instruction streams. MIMD (multiple-instruction multiple-data) should be distinguished from SIMD (single-instruction multiple-data), in which each node is driven by the same instruction stream. The SIMD architecture is most natural for fine-grain size machines.[11]

Coarse	vs.	Fine grain size
Distributed	vs.	Shared memory
MIMD	vs.	SIMD
General-purpose	vs.	Specialized nodes

The hypercube

(a) Choices in concurrent computers

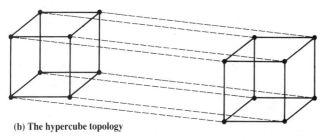

(b) The hypercube topology

Figure 11-1. Some key characteristics of concurrent computers and the properties of the hypercube, in which 2^p computers at the corner of a cube in p dimensions are connected along the edges of the cube.

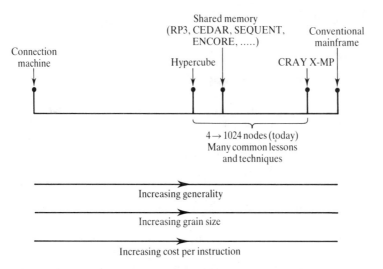

Figure 11-2. A comparison of the generality, grain size, and cost effectiveness of various computers. The scale is approximate and by no means linear.

The hypercube naturally supports a message-passing programming environment and one typically uses a LAPMP—large asynchronous processes with message passing—model. These issues will be discussed further later. The explicit hypercube topology is a good topology for current technology. It can be built relatively cheaply and seems to offer a rich enough interconnect to allow the majority of problems to perform well. The purpose of the following two sections is to demonstrate this in detail. Here we note two useful features of the hypercube. First the maximum distance between any two nodes is $\log_2 N$ where N is the number of nodes. Thus, any message-passing overheads tend to be small and, even if forwarding is important, to grow slowly with N. Second, the hypercube topology includes within it all relevant mesh topologies, and so problems needing mesh connectivity can use direct links in a hypercube. However, the crucial characteristic of the hypercube is its grain size and this is emphasized in Figure 11-2. The hypercube has many characteristics similar to those of other concurrent computers, in particular, shared memory machines, of comparable node (grain) size. In particular, there are many common lessons and techniques for the hypercube, RP3, BUTTERFLY, ENCORE, and SEQUENT shared-memory machines and even multiheaded ETA and CRAY supercomputers. The connection machine with 65 536 very small SIMD nodes is really quite distinct from the hypercube discussed here even though its topology is close to being hypercubic! Figure 11-2 should not be taken very quantitatively. For instance, we classify the CRAY X-MP as more "general" than the hypercube. This is based on the greater ease, on the CRAY compared to the hypercube, of using *existing* FORTRAN codes with reasonable performance. We believe that the MIMD hypercube will have good performance on a wide variety of irregular problems ill-suited to the CRAY's vector unit. However, one currently needs to program the hypercube from scratch to realize this performance. We have deliberately placed the distributed- and shared-memory medium grain size machines close together on the scale of Figure 11-2; these two classes of machine have many similarities.[12] Most of the discussion in this paper applies to any medium or large grain size machine; for instance, lessons from our hypercube research will allow the development of good codes for multiheaded ETA and CRAY computers.[5] The recently announced AMETEK S2010 should exhibit many of the essential features of the hypercube but with a lower-dimension interconnect.[13,14] This illustrates the relative unimportance of the topology for the hypercube.

Our goal is the development of the best possible cost/performance in a supercomputer of general applicability. We do not know how to define "general"; pragmatic definitions could be "problems running on CRAYs today," or, nearer home, "large problems of interest to Caltech scientists and engineers." Our current work has used hypercubes that are cost-effective but they have not been supercomputers, that is, not capable of peak performance comparable to the best CRAY can offer. However, this seems to be changing and there are now several hypercubes offering supercomputer performance.

In Figure 11-3 we show the Mark III hypercube constructed at Caltech's Jet Propulsion Laboratory. Each node is two PC boards with two 68020 microprocessors, 4 Mbytes of memory and a WEITEK floating-point enhancer. A 128-node Mark IIIfp system has gigaflop peak performance and a total of 0.5 Gbyte of memory.

Currently, one of the best commercial hypercubes for scientific and engineering compatibility is the NCUBE shown in Figure 11-4. Each node has a custom chip with performance comparable to the VAX11/750 and eleven built-in communication channels; the node is completed with six memory chips. A 2048 node NCUBE system offers approximately 0.25 GFLOPS performance with 1 Gbyte memory. In 1988, the new INTEL iPSC/2, FPS T-series and AMETEK S2010 also offer supercomputer performance.

In each case, at a cost of approximately 2 million dollars, one achieves performance very competitive with the current CRAY X-MP and CRAY-2 supercomputers. Note that the hypercube architecture naturally gives you *large* memory with high computational power. This is needed in most major scientific and engineering applications requiring supercomputers.

Why the Hypercube Works

Here we briefly review the essential issues determining the performance of a hypercube on a given problem. It will turn out that the key criterion is that the problem be *large*, in a sense that one can quantify.[1,15] The material in this section is covered in more detail in Refs. 1, 4, 15, and 16.

In Figures 11-5 and 11-6, we illustrate the use of a 16-node concurrent computer to solve a very simple problem—the solution of Laplace's equation,

$\nabla^2 \phi = 0$, in two dimensions. The sample problem has 256 grid points in a 16×16 mesh at which the potential $\phi(i, j)$ is to be determined. As shown in Figure 11-5, we suppose that a simple iteration (relaxation) algorithm is to be used to solve this problem. This is *not* the best way of solving this particular algorithm. However, similar albeit more sophisticated iterative techniques are probably the best approach to large three-dimensional finite-difference or finite-element calculations. Thus, although the simple example in Figure 11-5 is not "real" or interesting itself, it does illustrate important issues.

Use of the hypercube for this class of problem involves *domain decomposition*. The computational solution consists of a simple algorithm

$$\phi(i, j) = \tfrac{1}{4}[\phi(i + 1, j) + \phi(i - 1, j) + \phi(i, j + 1) + \phi(i, j - 1)] \qquad (11\text{-}1)$$

(a)

Figure 11-3. (a) A 32-node Mark III hypercube without floating-point enhancement. (b) The basic node board of the Mark III hypercube. (c) The WEITEX XL-based floating-point enhancement PC board to be added to each node of the Mark III hypercube.

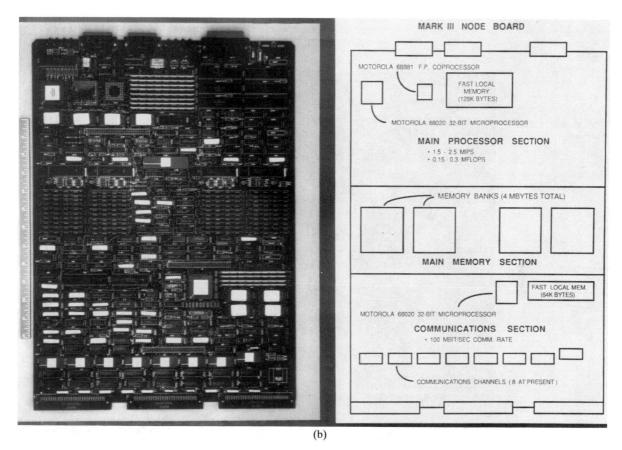

MARK III NODE BOARD

MOTOROLA 68881 F.P. COPROCESSOR

FAST LOCAL
MEMORY
(128K BYTES)

MOTOROLA 68020 32-BIT MICROPROCESSOR

MAIN PROCESSOR SECTION
• 1.5 - 2.5 MIPS
• 0.15 - 0.3 MFLOPS

MEMORY BANKS (4 MBYTES TOTAL)

MAIN MEMORY SECTION

FAST LOCAL MEM.
(64K BYTES)

MOTOROLA 68020 32-BIT MICROPROCESSOR

COMMUNICATIONS SECTION
• 100 MBIT/SEC COMM. RATE

COMMUNICATIONS CHANNELS (8 AT PRESENT)

(b)

Figure 11-3. (contd.)

applied to each point of the dataset. We get concurrency by applying Eqn. (11-1) simultaneously in different parts of the underlying data domain. This is a very simple but key idea. We can consider a typical problem as "an algorithm applied to a dataset." We achieve concurrency by leaving the algorithm unchanged and executed sequentially within each node; rather, we divide up the underlying dataset. One attractive feature of this method is that it can be extended to very large machines. A $100 \times 100 \times 100$ mesh with 10^6 points is not an atypical problem; nowadays, we divide this domain into perhaps 64 parts—clearly such a problem can be divided into many more parts and use future machines with very many nodes.

Returning to the toy example in Figure 11-5, we associate a 4×4 subdomain with each processor. Let us examine what any one node is doing; this is illustrated in Figure 11-6. We see that, in this case, an individual processor is solving the "same" problem—Laplace's equation with an iterative algorithm—as a sequential computer. There are two important differences.

**CALTECH/JPL CONCURRENT
SUPERCOMPUTER NODE**

(c)

Figure 11-3. (contd.)

- The concurrent algorithm involves different geometry—the code should not address the full domain but rather a subset of it.
- The boundary conditions are changed. Referring to Figure 11-6, one finds conventional boundary conditions

$$\phi \; is \; known$$

on the left and bottom edges of the square subdomain. However, on the top and right edges, one finds the unusual constraints

Please communicate with your neighboring nodes to update points on the edge.

For this class of problem, the hypercube and sequential codes can be quite similar; they "only" differ in the geometry and boundary-value modules. We have found it relatively easy to develop codes that run either on concurrent or on sequential machines depending on input data. Typically, we have developed such code from scratch and not modified sequential code; the latter is not usually

(a)

(b)

Figure 11-4. The commercial NCUBE/10 hypercube. (a) Cabinet that can hold up to 1024 nodes configured as a 10-dimensional hypercube. (b) Basic board containing 64 nodes.

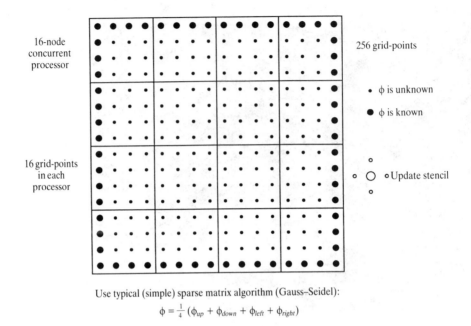

16-node
concurrent
processor

16 grid-points
in each
processor

256 grid-points

• φ is unknown

● φ is known

Update stencil

Use typical (simple) sparse matrix algorithm (Gauss–Seidel):

$$\phi = \frac{1}{4} \left(\phi_{up} + \phi_{down} + \phi_{left} + \phi_{right} \right)$$

Figure 11-5. A simple use of the hypercube configured as a two-dimensional mesh to solve Laplace's equation.

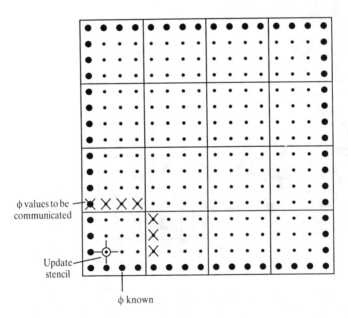

φ values to be communicated

Update stencil

φ known

Figure 11-6. The problem seen by the bottom left processor in the algorithm of Figure 11-5.

492

structured in an appropriately modular fashion to allow direct conversion to concurrent form.

Figure 11-6 and the novel boundary condition cited above make it clear that communication is associated with the edge of the region stored in each node. We can quantify the effect of this performance of a hypercube by introducing two parameters t_{calc} and t_{comm} to describe the hypercube hardware.

t_{calc} The typical time required to perform a generic calculation. For scientific problems, this can be taken as a floating-point calculation

$$a = b * c \quad \text{or} \quad a = b + c$$

t_{comm} The typical time to communicate a single word between two nodes connected in the hardware topology.

The parameters t_{calc} and t_{comm} are not precisely defined and depend on many parameters, such as size of message length for t_{comm} and use of memory or registers for t_{calc}. The overhead due to communication depends on the ratio τ given by

$$\tau = \frac{t_{comm}}{t_{calc}} = 1.5 \rightarrow 3 \tag{11-2}$$

where we have quoted the value for our initial Cosmic Cube and Mark II hypercubes with which we have the most experience. For problems similar to those in Figure 11-5, we have implemented code and measured the performance of the hypercube. We can express the observed speed-up S as

$$S = \frac{N}{1 + f_C} \tag{11-3}$$

where the problem runs S times faster than a single node on a hypercube with N nodes. f_C is the fractional concurrent overhead which in this problem class is due to communication. As the latter is an edge effect, one finds that

$$f_C = \frac{0.5 \, t_{comm}}{n^{1/2} \, t_{calc}} \tag{11-4}$$

($\sim 1/n^{1/2}$ for the Cosmic Cube or Mark II Caltech/JPL hypercubes), where one stores n grid-points in each node with $n = 16$ in the example of Figures 11-5 and 11-6. In Eqn. (11-4), $n^{1/2}$ is the ratio of edge to area in two dimensions. We see that f_C will be ≤ 0.1 in this example, that is, the speed-up will be ≥ 90 percent of optimal, as long as one stores at least 100 grid-points in each node. This is an example of how one can quantify the importance of the problem being *large*. On a machine with N nodes, the hypercube performs well on two-dimensional problems with at least 100 grid-points in each node.

One can generalize Eqn. (11-4) by introducing, in general, fractional, *system dimension d* associated with any problem.[15] In terms of grain size n and dimension d,

$$f_C = \frac{\text{constant} \, t_{comm}}{n^{1/d} \, t_{calc}} \tag{11-5}$$

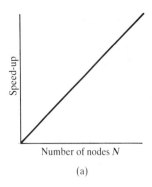
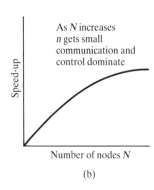

Figure 11-7. The speed-up on a hypercube as a function of the number of nodes for two circumstances: (a) fixed grain size—problem size proportional to number N of nodes; and (b) fixed problem (domain) size—grain size proportional to $1/N$.

for a concurrent computer with

$$d_c = \text{dimension of (the topology of) the computer} \geq d \qquad (11\text{-}6)$$

For the hypercube, $d_c = \log_2 N$ is large and Eqn. (11-6) is satisfied for most problems, and this explains why a rich topology allows the concurrent computer to perform well.

From Eqn. (11-5), we see that the overhead f_C only depends on the grain size and so that the speed-up S is linear with N for extrapolation at constant grain size. This is contrasted in Figure 11-7 with an extrapolation of a fixed problem to machines with an increasing number N of nodes. In the latter case, $n \propto 1/N$ decreases and the importance of control and communication overheads increase; the speed-up when plotted against N eventually levels off. It is our impression that one typically builds larger machines to solve larger problems and that the approximately fixed grain size extrapolation (S linear with N) is most appropriate.

In many problems, there are other degradations in the performance of current computers and we have reviewed these in Refs. 1, 15, and 16. Apart from communication, load imbalance is often a significant issue. One needs to parcel out work to the nodes so that each has approximately the same amount of computation. This was trivially achieved in Figure 11-5 by ensuring that each node processes an equal number of grid points. We have shown that one can view load balancing as an optimization problem and apply a variety of techniques, of which simulated annealing[15] and neural networks[17] are the most attractive. We are currently building the load balancer as a dynamic utility on the hypercube and have reviewed this work elsewhere.[18,19] We will return to this issue after the next section.

Science on the Hypercube at Caltech

MOTIVATION

A reasonable extrapolation of current technology should allow the construction of *large grain size* concurrent computers whose performance will be several orders of magnitude greater than that of current (1980s) supercomputers. More specialized *fine grain size* machines, such as the current Connection Machine, will lead to even greater performance for some problems.[11] At Caltech, we have adopted a somewhat unusual but practically effective approach to developing the scientific uses of concurrent machines and "proving" the general viability of the hypercube. The research program was based not upon a general theoretical framework, but rather upon experiment; we supplied the necessary support to allow leading computational scientists to use hypercubes, going beyond "try-out" algorithms to solve significant problems. This approach has had the advantage of ensuring that "complete" programs were developed so that performance could be assessed without neglecting possible hidden sequential bottlenecks that would reduce the overall performance. In the previous section, we suggested that a broad range of problems will be capable of realizing this performance by obtaining a speed-up comparable to the number of nodes. Future machines may well have upwards of 10^5 nodes, but the simple idea of domain decomposition should be extendable to such machines as long as the problem is large enough—in the language of the previous section, as long as $n^{1/d}$ is larger than a value around 5.

In the rest of this section, we describe some of the Caltech work on the hypercube that we summarized earlier. Further details may be found in our annual reports.[6,7]

THE HYPERCUBE IN BIOLOGY

Neural Circuit Simulation

There is growing interest in the use of simulation in biological research. One such application involves the study of large systems of neurons. These can either be "real" neurons when simulating the brain, or "applied" or "theoretical" neurons that comprise computational circuits of the type discussed in Hopfield[20,21] and the section Neural Networks (p. 566). The concurrent decomposition issues in simulating such systems are very similar to those involved in the simulation of an array of electronic components such as those in a chip. The best algorithms depend upon the nature of the circuit, but in all cases the hypercube can be an excellent circuit simulator. In the case of "real" brain simulations, this conclusion is not surprising; nature's computer, the brain, is a kind of distributed memory "concurrent computer." It should be expected that a general-purpose distributed-memory concurrent computer like the hypercube can be applicable to its simulation.

An earlier surprise in using the hypercube was its effectiveness not only in short-range (nearest-neighbor) problems like that of Figure 11-5 but also in long-range (full-interconnect) cases. In fact, long-range algorithms correspond to *system dimension* $d = 1$ and the overhead is proportional to the inverse of the grain size.[1,4,15] Many neural simulations can be thought of as fully connected—in fact, if on average each neuron is connected to l others, then if $l \gg N$, the number of nodes, the system will have system dimension $d = 1$, irrespective of its geometry. Cases with $l \leq N$ may require the special load-balancing techniques outlined in the preceding and following sections; a very difficult case with $l = 4$ and random connectivity is discussed in Fox.[22] The application of the hypercube to robotics and load balancing will be described in a later section.

Protein Dynamics

An important area of scientific computation in biology and chemistry involves the dynamics of large protein molecules. This is treated as a particle-dynamics problem in which the concurrent implementation depends on the range of the force. Short-range-force problems can be treated similarly to the methods of Figure 11-5, but in the protein case, since the interatomic electrical forces are long-range, one can usually employ the very efficient long-range algorithm mentioned above even though we may typically ignore the screened potential of atoms that are widely separated. In fact, the implementation issues are not very different from those in a circuit simulation; a protein forms a "circuit" whose elements are the atoms and whose connection is defined by the interatomic force. This is an example of the general equivalence given by the theory of *complex systems*.[15]

THE HYPERCUBE IN CHEMISTRY

Chemical Reactions

The hypercube has been employed by Kuppermann[23] in the implementation of a major new algorithm for the detailed simulation of three-I and four-body chemical reactions. This simulation includes several components. The first involves the solution of a finite-element problem treated by spatial decomposition of the type described in the previous section. Current Caltech applications of finite-element problems, using conjugate gradient and multigrid methods on the hypercube, are described in Fox,[1] Lyzenga,[24] and Flower.[25] The latter uses automatic decomposition methods to assign nodal points optimally to the individual processors in the hypercube. The major part of Kuppermann's calculation involves the solution of a coupled-channel Schrödinger equation; this uses the logarithmic derivative method and is dominated by the inversion of an $M \times M$ matrix, where M is the number of channels. The Gauss–Jordan algorithm was implemented on the hypercube for this application and performs with high efficiency.[26] Interesting values of M go up to 1000 and such large problems can profitably use hypercubes with several thousand nodes. Independently of this project, we have investigated a wide range of matrix algorithms on the hypercube, including full, banded, and sparse matrices for both equation solving, matrix multiplication, and eigenvalue determination.[1,26–29] Typically, matrix algorithms decompose well on the hypercube, with their performance being governed by Eqn. (11-5) with system dimension $d = 2$.

THE HYPERCUBE IN ENGINEERING

Chaos

Two groups have used the hypercube at Caltech to determine the dimension of data sets;[30] in one case this corresponded to experimental plasma data and in another to trajectories (strange attractors) coming from the solutions of ordinary differential equations.[31,32] As reviewed in Fox[1] this problem, involving the calculation of a correlation function, is well handled by a variation of the full interconnect algorithm.

Computational Fluid Dynamics

In general, computational fluid dynamics uses an elaboration of the techniques we have described for the solution of partial differential equations. The importance of turbulent flow introduces some important new issues. Investigations have examined flow at high Reynold's number using vortex methods. Here the solution of the differential equations is exchanged for a study of the dynamics of independent vortices. These vortices effectively interact with a long-range force, and so one can use the full interconnect (long-range-force) method to achieve a hypercube implementation of high efficiency.[33]

The dynamic nature of the irregularities produced by turbulence poses algorithmic challenges even for sequential machines. It is natural to use an underlying mesh that changes or adapts as the solution changes. Work is under way on such an adaptive mesh on the hypercube, making use of the multigrid solution method.[34] An aim is to combine both the mesh adaption and the hypercube decomposition into a single step, since both need similar optimization methods. Note that the need for adaptive meshes implies that, even on a sequential machine, the user can only be concerned with the local problem. This renders the transition to the hypercube particularly natural, as domain decomposition has already been enforced by the locally adapting mesh. This work is described in the next section.

Earthquake Engineering

The partial differential equation methods described have applications throughout many disciplines. At Caltech, they are being used to solve finite-element problems arising in many structural analysis problems including those occurring in earthquake engineering and at the Jet Propulsion Laboratory in the analysis of spacecraft structures.

Convolutional Decoding

Convolutional decoding is used in communication, as between a spacecraft and Earth, to decrease the incidence of undetected errors with minimum increase in the volume of information to be transmitted. The Viterbi algorithm is a well-known method of convolutional coding whose complexity increases exponentially with the number of states. It has been shown that the structure of this algorithm is formally identical to that of the Fast Fourier Transform (FFT), and both FFT[1] and Viterbi decoding[35,36] can use the hypercube very efficiently. The hypercube topology exactly matched that needed by these algorithms. The Viterbi decoding is sufficiently simple that realistic use of it could benefit from a specialized node optimized for this problem.

Ray Tracing in Computer Graphics

Ray tracing is a technique used to render computer graphics images of three-dimensional models. It is time-consuming but leads to very realistic images. The picture is divided into a two-dimensional mesh of pixels and several rays are run through each pixel. These rays are propagated according to the laws of optics, and interact with the environment by refraction and reflection. Two kinds of decompositions are relevant here. The calculation is rather easily decomposed, since each pixel is independent and each processor can run rays independently. One must use the *scattered* decomposition for the pixels to achieve load balance, because pixels near a complicated part of the picture will take longer to process than those in a "dull" background. The scattered decomposition has shown itself useful in matrix algorithms[1,27,28,37] and finite-element problems.[38] One "scatters" the basic entities of the problem (pixels, matrix elements, nodal points) over the hypercube so that each node gets a part of "the action." This can be viewed as a statistical method of load balancing.[19,38] Whereas the pixels can be handled in a relatively simple fashion, the databases describing the model for the image can be very large and in general require a different decomposition. This issue has to be handled by more general load-balancing methods and is a topic of current research.[19,39] It is expected that the hypercube will still perform well even when the database is decomposed; the pixel decomposition leads to negligible inefficiencies of 1–2 percent. This application motivated the development of an advanced multitasking system for the hypercube.[40]

GEOPHYSICS

The use of the hypercube in geophysics at Caltech is particularly pleasing, as the group of Clayton and Hager have been able to use the hypercube on a day-to-day basis for many different applications.[24,41,42] This is described in more detail later.

Seismic Waves

The example given under Why the Hypercube Works is typical of the application of the hypercube to the study of seismic waves. These are typically solved by finite-difference methods that work as well on the hypercube for the fourth-order differencing as for the standard second-order approximation.[1,16] New applications being explored include nonuniform media for which the optimal methods use a mixture of numeric and partially analytic methods. This leads to irregularities in the computational complexity per grid point and nontrivial load balancing issues.

Geodynamics

Finite-element methods as discussed earlier have been employed with a preconditioned conjugate gradient iterative solver.[24] The study of the Earth's mantle is reduced to one of thermal convection in an incompressible medium. Three-dimensional problems require large memory to yield good efficiencies, for reasons that can be seen from Eqn. (11-5). Whereas systems with (*system*) dimension 2 need about 100 points per node to obtain good efficiencies, the change from $n^{-1/2}$ to $n^{-1/3}$ in Eqn. (11-5) requires that three-dimensional problems need about 1000 points per node to get good speed-ups.

Normal Modes and Tomography

Two types of geophysical calculations use the hypercube in a different fashion—each node independently calculates *part* of the answer. In tomography, ray tracing is used to propagate acoustic waves through the Earth. The propagation time is sensitive to the structure of the Earth, which is obtained by inversion from the observed timing data. In a normal-mode analysis, a set of synthetic seismograms is compiled for a given model of the Earth and a particular earthquake is source parameters. The signal is analyzed into separate modes for each eigenfrequency of the Earth and each mode is calculated separately on a single processor node. These applications are characterized by, essentially, 100 percent concurrent efficiency.

PHYSICS

Computational Astrophysics

One particularly interesting problem involves a study of the evolution of the universe on the hypercube.[43] This employs the "particle-in-the-cell" (PIC) algorithm, which involves both particle dynamics (galaxies evolving under Newton's laws) and a mesh-based algorithm. The galaxies are "smeared" to derive a mass density on a mesh, and then the FFT is used to calculate the long-range component of the gravitational potential. This reduces a problem of complexity N_g^2 to one that is $N_g \log N_g$, where N_g is the number of galaxies in the simulation. PIC codes involve an interesting conflict between the cell and particle decompositions. These may not be simultaneously load-balanced.

In many cases, this presents no serious problem as the easily load-balanced FFT dominates the poorly balanced particle stage. Further investigation of a reformulation of the problem using a (galaxy) clustering algorithm to replace the FFT is under way.[44] This approach has the same $N_g \log N_g$ calculational complexity and should be easier to load-balance.[45]

High-Energy Physics

Lattice gauge theory calculations were an early motivator of the hypercube research at Caltech and have been a central theme of our hypercube used at Caltech.[46] Roughly, twenty separate lattice gauge calculations have been performed on the hypercube, and most of these have been published.[6] The theory is very complex, but this application makes use of the hypercube at high efficiency, even for small volumes (e.g., $4 \times 4 \times 4 \times 16$ four-dimensional mesh) in each node, when the surface-to-volume ratio is high. The regularity of the current numerical formulations leads to rather straightforward concurrent decompositions. This work is described in more detail under Lattice Gauge Theories on Hypercubes.

Condensed Matter

The regular nearest-neighbor Monte Carlo algorithm encountered in the lattice gauge theory is neatly complemented by some of the condensed-matter Monte Carlo calculations performed on the hypercube. In the study of the melting of a two-dimensional solid, an irregular "almost-nearest-neighbor" problem is involved, and one needs a subtle algorithm to both get efficiency and satisfy the constraint of detailed balance.[47] A Monte Carlo study of a long-range force problem—a two-dimensional gas—requires a very different algorithm from that for the long-range dynamics problem. Detailed balance implies that only one particle can be updated at a time and care is required to ensure that one can decide efficiently which particle to update on the hypercube.[48]

Granular Physics

An intuitively appealing application of the hypercube involves simulation of wind-driven and gravity-driven motion of a collection of sand grains. The conventional continuum approximations are not used, but rather each grain is moved separately in accordance with Newton's laws. This method is intrinsically *very* time consuming and is perhaps only worth pursuing if one believes that computer performance will increase substantially in the future. This is a particle dynamics problem and the sand grains interact by contact only, and define an irregular but "pure" nearest-neighbor algorithm. The time required to calculate the grain–grain force is typically so large that the node-to-node communication costs are negligible. Load imbalance represents the only serious impact on efficiency, although, in practice, even this is a minor problem. It is amusing to note that the initial hypercube implementation had an efficiency ε of 3 and a speed-up of 200 on a 64-node hypercube. One part of the calculation involves the determination of which sand grains touch. This was implemented on a single node as a search of a list of all N_g (number of grains), requiring a time of order N_g^2. The concurrent algorithm is implemented with a spatial decomposition, which means that this step only needs to search the local and neighboring nodes. Such a search takes a time of order $(N_g/N)^2$ on the hypercube and results in a "free" speed-up of order N^2! Of course, this was a case in which the sequential algorithm was intrinsicaly poor and should also have used a spatial decomposition (or more pompously a *geometric hashing*) method. When the concurrent implementation is referred to this improved sequential algorithm, the efficiency assumes a more sensible value—somewhat less than unity owing to load imbalance.[49]

OTHER APPLICATIONS

Tracking Algorithms

Recently, we have investigated a class of tracking algorithms in which several (N_0) objects are followed by Kalman filters.[50,51] In the case that the objects are close, the association of measurements with objects requires the high internode communication bandwidth of machines like the hypercube. The tracking used our concurrent sorting algorithm to dynamically optimize the assignment of objects to nodes. The performance of the hypercube depends initially on the complexity of the filter—the more sophisticated filter will lead to more computation and less overhead concurrent f_C. Even for a simple filter, we find good performance as long as $N_0 \gtrsim 4N$ for N_0 objects decomposed over N nodes. This work is described in more detail under Multiple-target Track Initiation on a Hypercube.

Computer Chess

We have developed a rather complete computer chess program that runs on the NCUBE hypercube. The nature of the α–β search method of the game tree for chess makes good concurrent algorithms hard. One can only find out "sequentially" which are the useful lines to investigate. However, there is parallelism that increases as one explores deeper in the tree; this implies that we can make use of more processors either as the time allocated per move increases or the speed of the processor nodes increases.[53] This may be a general feature of some real-time problems. The latest version of the program, as reported at the Third Hypercube Conference, has achieved a speed up of 100 on a 256-node NCUBE.[54]

Time Warp

A collaboration between Jefferson at UCLA and a group at JPL has constructed a major concurrent event-driven simulation package on the Mark II hypercube.[55] This uses the time-warp algorithm, which allows simulation rollback to within a node to cope with lack of synchronization between the nodes. Interesting speed-ups have been obtained on a war-game application and the results are now being evaluated.[56]

Software

We will make some brief remarks about the software environment on the current hypercubes. Further information may be found in Seita,[2] Fox,[1] and Walker,[57] and the vendor-specific data for the various commercial machines.

The general software model for using the hypercube was illustrated under Why the Hypercube Works. Node code is constructed with a conventional high-level language (dominantly C with some FORTRAN in the case of Caltech) augmented by a subroutine library to allow communication between the nodes. This implements the LAPMP—large asynchronous processes with message passing—programming model introduced under The Hypercube as a Concurrent Computer.

The current (commercial and in-house Caltech) hypercubes have operating systems that are currently "just" communication libraries. These have more or less flexibility, with the more flexible systems having lower performance— that is, higher values of t_{comm}.[58] As shown, there are many similarities between the sequential and concurrent codes for a given problem. The latter involve different geometry and different boundary condition modules. We have implemented the so-called CUBIX extension to the communication library, which makes the node I/O and system environment "look like" a traditional UNIX process.[59] This makes it easier to generate code that, with the appropriate switches, will run on either concurrent or sequential machines.

Currently, we are developing a more powerful environment in which one has several objects or processes running in each node[40] and an optimizer determines how best to assign objects to nodes so as to balance the load and minimize the communication between processes.[60] This optimizer is itself a concurrent algorithm running as one or more of the processes in each node.[18] Currently, the neural-network approach appears to be the most attractive choice for the concurrent optimizer.[17]

The features of the old and new schemes are indicated in the current program environment:

- user chooses objects (process), that is, subdomains of dataset;
- user assigns objects to nodes of computer;
- user writes code to control object;

and the dynamic load balancing environment:

- computer generates objects;
- computer dynamically assigns objects to nodes;
- user still has to write the code to control a general object.

We believe that we may be able to extend our optimization techniques to both choose objects and generate the code for them from conventional sequential code.[17]

Conclusions

The scientific applications described under Science on the Hypercube have been fully implemented on a hypercube and give speedups that are within 20 percent of optimal. We believe that this illustrates the broad applicability of the hypercube to science and engineering. At Caltech, we see that the next step is to produce and use hypercubes with supercomputer performance, and this is now technically possible with the NCUBE commercial machine and the new (1988) FPS, INTEL, and AMETEK models with vector add-on boards. The lessons from our research show that one need "only" build machines with a comparable $t_{comm}/t_{calc} \sim 2$ to our current hardware to achieve speed-ups comparable to the number of nodes.

The lack of good software—both at the operating system and application level—is the main issue holding back the development of parallel computers. We hope to extend our work to develop useful "parallel supercomputer software tools" on the basis of our experience using "real parallel machines" to solve "real problems."

THE DESIGN OF A PORTABLE PARALLEL MULTIGRID ALGORITHM FOR THE HYPERCUBE

Introduction

By incorporating coarser grids in the solution process, multigrid methods turn simple relaxation operators into very powerful tools for the solution of (mainly elliptic) partial differential equations. Using multigrid methods, the solution of many problems can be found with an operation count proportional to the number of unknowns. Another important advantage of the multigrid strategy is the easy adaptability to many distinct circumstances, for example, boundary conditions, irregular regions, nonlinearities. In contrast, the conjugate gradient method,[61] for example, may require the development of a new preconditioner for each new problem. Based on the multigrid strategy, it is thus possible to build a software environment supporting many different applications. While it is unrealistic to expect the development of a general-purpose solver (as, say, for systems of ordinary differential equations), duplication of effort can be avoided in such an environment. This is even more important when the use of parallel computer architectures is considered. In this case, the parallel aspects of the multigrid program can remain hidden from the application.

While the implementation of the algorithms reflects our goal of developing a general-purpose multigrid environment, we focus on just one class of very important realistic problems at this time:

Solve the Dirichlet boundary value problem

$$-\Delta u + g(x, y, z, u) = f(x, y, z)$$

on a tetrahedron Ω.

Primary issues we address with this class of problems are: parallelism, the computational complexity of three space dimensions, local grid refinement, and nonlinearity.

In the next section, we give a brief introduction to the multigrid method and its convergence theory. We also introduce other concepts we used in the development of our multigrid algorithms. After that, the key issues of parallel multigrid are discussed and an overview of existing parallel multigrid programs is given. The remaining sections present our current algorithms and some preliminary results.

Multigrid Algorithms: Theoretical Background

For an extensive introduction and bibliography regarding multigrid algorithms and their convergence theory, we refer to the papers by Trottenberg and Stüben, Hackbusch, and Brandt.[62] We briefly repeat here those concepts directly related to our work.

Ordinary relaxation methods, like Gauss–Jacobi or Gauss–Seidel, reduce the high-frequency error components very well. The bad overall convergence of these methods is due to the behavior of low-frequency components. The boundary between high and low frequencies is determined by the grid on which the problem is discretized. Typically, wavelengths less than twice the grid spacing are defined to be high-frequency with respect to the particular grid. Hence, some low frequencies of one grid are high frequencies of another (coarser) grid. The general idea of the multigrid method is to reduce the high-frequency errors on fine grids and the low-frequency errors on coarse grids, each time using the same relaxation operator. The property that determines the quality (in a multigrid context) of such a relaxation is quantified by the "smoothing factor," loosely defined as the worst factor by which high-frequency error components are reduced each relaxation sweep. Typically, 2–3 relaxation steps reduce amplitudes of the high-frequency components by a factor of 10.

The two-grid iteration is an important first step in the derivation of the multigrid method (and in its convergence theory). We assume that the continuous problem is discretized on a coarse and a fine grid; furthermore, we assume that an exact solver is available for the coarse discretization. The two-grid process for linear problems starts with an initial guess on the fine grid, smoothing it by applying the chosen relaxation method a number of times. When smoothed, the defects of the fine grid are projected down (restricted) to the coarse grid. Because the error was smooth, the restriction well approximates the fine-grid defects. After solving (exactly) the defect equation on the coarse grid, the solution on the fine grid is corrected by adding the interpolation of the coarse-grid solution values, which are approximations for the fine-grid errors. Nonlinear problems can be handled by the above Defect Correction Scheme using an obvious linearization and Newton iteration. A more direct technique, the Full Approximation Scheme, is preferable, however. In this case, the initial guess on the fine grid is smoothed by applying a number of nonlinear relaxation steps. Because the defects are not sufficient to find (an approximation for) the error, both the right-hand side and the solution are restricted. The coarse grid solved, the restriction of the fine-grid solution is subtracted from the coarse solution; the result is interpolated and used to correct the fine-grid approximation. The convergence of both the defect correction and the full-approximation two-grid scheme is treated rigorously in Hackbusch.[62]

A two-grid method is converted into a multigrid method by recursively substituting a number of two-grid iterations for the exact coarse solver in the above two-grid scheme. (One iteration replacing the exact solver is termed a V-cycle, two iterations a W-cycle.) The coarsest grid in this process can many times be solved by letting the relaxation process converge (SOR). For some problems, however, particularly those occurring in a continuation process (see below), the coarse-grid relaxation will not converge. It is then necessary to provide an exact solver for the coarsest grid.

The above multigrid method can still be greatly improved by providing a good initial value for the fine-grid solution. An easy and very effective way to get such an initial value is to solve the second-finest grid with a multigrid method and project the solution found to the finest grid. This idea can, of course, be repeated and leads to the Full Multigrid method: starting with a solution on the coarsest grid, projecting it to the next level, and so on. In Figure 11-8, a Full Approximation Scheme multigrid algorithm for a simple Poisson equation is displayed in an informal programming language notation.

The main attraction of the multigrid method is potentially very fast convergence: after fine tuning, one Full Multigrid sweep usually suffices to obtain the accuracy required. Fine tuning the algorithm involves choosing the right relaxation, restriction, and interpolation operators, as well as choosing the appropriate iteration parameters (V or W cycle, number of relaxations before and after the coarse grid correction). The above choices should be guided by the particular application at hand. Once the property of convergence in one sweep is obtained, the number of arithmetic operations needed is slightly more than a constant times the number of unknowns in the finest grid. This follows from the observation that the work on level $i - 1$ is roughly 8 (i.e., 2^3) times less than the work on level i (this is not true for $i = 1$ because the coarsest grid solver is likely to be more expensive).

Even better performance can be obtained through the application of local grid-refinement techniques: refining only some parts of the computational domain can reduce the number of arithmetic operations without sacrificing accuracy.[62,63] Even for linear problems, it is then crucial to use the Full Approximation Scheme, because the coarse grids should approximate the solution of the problem (at least in those areas that are not covered by finer grid patches). If the decision whether and where to construct finer grid patches is made during the computations (and is based on intermediate results), the refinement algorithm is said to be adaptive. (The term adaptive is also used for the much simpler strategies that determine at run time the iteration parameters.)

Many problems contain a free parameter(s) in their formulation. A typical example would be the viscosity or Reynolds number in fluid dynamics. It is then often important to calculate the behavior of the solution as the parameter changes. For some values, the solution can only be found by using an extrapolation technique on known neighboring solutions. This is particularly the case when the problem has bifurcation points and the solution to the problem is no longer unique. A very successful technique of this kind is pseudo-arclength continuation. It is outside the scope of this chapter to introduce these problems. For a full exposition, we refer to Bolstadt,[64] Chan,[65] and Hackbusch.[62] We note, however, that the coarse grids play a crucial role in combining continuation and multigrid.

Finally, we introduce the problem of combining domain decomposition and

```
multigrid iteration (level)
{
    if (level=0)
        solve the coarsest level
    else
        relax (level) nr1 times

        construct the level-1 problem by
            projecting level solution to level-1 (as
            initial guess)
            projecting level right hand side to
            level-1
                and adding 7-point operator of initial
                guess

        if (level ←1)
            solve the coarsest level
        else
            multigrid iteration (level-1) nm times

        subtract restriction of level solution from
        level-1 solution
        add interpolation of level-1 result to level
        solution

        relax (level) nr2 times
}
full multigrid iteration (numlevels)
{
    initialize equation on coarsest grid

    solve the coarsest level

    interpolate level 0 solution to level 1 (as
    initial guess)

    for level=1 to numlevels-2
        multigrid iteration (level) nf times
        construct the level+1 problem (by
        discretizing)
        interpolate level solution to level+1 (as
        initial guess)
    multigrid iteration (numlevels-1) nf times
}
```

Figure 11-8. The full approximation scheme embedded in a full multigrid algorithm.

multigrid methods. Given an elliptic system defined on the union of two domains Ω_0 and Ω_1 with a nonempty intersection, the boundary of Ω_0 can be split into two parts Γ_0^E and Γ_0^I, the latter part lying inside domain Ω_1. Analogously, the boundary of Ω_1 is split in two parts. Assume that the boundary-value problem of the given system can be solved exactly on each domain and that some initial guess is provided for both domains. The following procedure, which is to be repeated in an iterative fashion, is known as Schwarz's alternating method (boundary values on Γ_0^E and Γ_1^E remain untouched):

interpolate guess on Ω_0 to boundary Γ_0^I;
solve Dirichlet problem on Ω_1;
interpolate guess on Ω_1 to boundary Γ_0^I;
solve Dirichlet problem on Ω_0.

This iteration is shown[66] to converge to the solution on the total domain for Laplace's equation (the proof relies on the maximum principle). The convergence of the numerical analogue is proven in Miller.[67] In Oliger[68] it is shown that the combination of Schwarz's method and a relaxation method is equivalent to a block Gauss–Seidel relaxation scheme, whose convergence is shown both theoretically and experimentally. The convergence rate is shown to depend on the area of overlap between the domains. Moreover, Schwarz's iteration has been successfully applied to more general problems in the context of composite mesh methods to solve problems on irregular domains.[69,70] Under Implementation Details we display the results of some numerical experiments that confirm the convergence for three-dimensional nonlinear problems decomposed into many domains. An apparent disadvantage of Schwarz's method is its very slow convergence, unless the overlapping region is substantial. The naive combination of Schwarz's method with a multigrid solver also exhibits this behavior. A more direct approach, however, avoids the necessity for large overlapping regions.[69] In this case, the same multigrid method is used on both domains, but Schwarz's principle is used in every relaxation step. Hence, new boundary values from the neighboring region are used as soon as they are available.

Parallelizing Multigrid: General Issues

The implementation of a serial multigrid program can proceed in a very structured way: each of the operators (smoothing, interpolation, restriction, coarsest grid operator) can be independently developed. Once they are available, they can be put together into an easy-to-read recursive program. A straightforward way to parallelize such a multigrid program is to parallelize each of the operators: grids are mapped in a suitable way over the processors and corresponding communication primitives take care of processor boundary effects.[71–74] The (parallel processing) efficiencies thus obtained are very high and probably unbeatable. This parallelization method does suffer a number of disadvantages however, ranging from the practical to the fundamental.

An important practical consideration is that all of the operations need to be parallelized. In a sufficiently general multigrid package, such as we describe below, the number of operations can be high (one hundred and up). In most instances the changes necessary are straightforward but bug-prone (loop indices, communication calls at processor boundaries, and so on). This is especially the case when special grid-to-processor mappings are used. A parallelization strategy that does not involve changing these operators at all is thus highly desirable to cut down in development and "transportation" time (between different machines and/or operating systems).

The programs parallelized as above are very synchronous in nature: the parallel program basically proceeds like the serial program, doing one macro operation (e.g., a relaxation) at a time. Each operation is carried out in parallel, while the processors are in loose synchronization with each other (every communication call being a synchronization point). There are definite advantages to this mode of operation: a very simple, but extremely efficient communication system like the "Crystalline Operating System"[75] is sufficient to implement the program; the results of the parallel and serial versions are identical (provided suitable relaxation methods like Red–Black Gauss–Seidel are used); subtle synchronization bugs like race conditions and deadlock are virtually eliminated. On the negative side, the distribution of the problem over the processors and the problem itself must be very regular; locally adaptive grid refinement strategies are difficult to achieve, as are dynamic load-balancing techniques; overlapping communication and computation is impossible.

The most fundamental problem remains with the handling of the coarsest grid. In this simple parallelization strategy, one usually repeats the smoothing step until convergence. From a parallel computation point of view this is acceptable, although efficiency problems occur on machines with inefficient communication systems: if convergence on the coarsest grid is slow, many (inefficient) iterations may be necessary. While relaxation until convergence works fine in many instances, problems are known, particularly when doing continuation, where the coarse grid iteration diverges.[64,65,76] It is then necessary to provide a parallel direct solver for the coarsest grid. This is a rather cumbersome task, even if such a solver is already available. The data structures required by the latter (probably a coefficient matrix distributed in some definite way over the processors and compatibly distributed solution and right-hand-side vectors) are likely to be totally different from the data structures involved in the rest of the multigrid program. Suitable mappings (in both directions) between these two data structures have to be developed. These operators and the direct solver involve complicated communication patterns. This makes the total program complicated, big, and hardly portable (across architectures and/or operating systems). It is not even clear whether reasonable efficiencies can be obtained.

Another approach in the parallelization of multigrid algorithms is presented by Hoppe.[77] This method, based on macro data flow, is asynchronous and can hence more easily accommodate local grid refinement and irregular decompositions. It also has the ability to overlap communication and computation. The problems on the coarsest grid (direct solver) remain unsolved, however.

In the remainder of this paper, we present a parallel multigrid method that addresses the issues raised above: Communication operations and references to them are localized in a small number of routines, making the program reasonably portable. The method is potentially asynchronous and fully MIMD; as a result it is feasible to overlap communication and computation and to include dynamic load balancing (if necessary). Coarse grids are handled adequately without the need for a parallel direct solver; hence, continuation problems can be handled. The major part of our exposition will be concerned with a serial multigrid solver, indicative of the fact that the algorithm is designed to produce easily parallelized and portable code.

Target Problems and Their Discretization

Although most of our code is independent of the specific equations solved, we do target specific problems, namely nonlinear elliptic equations of the form:

$$-\Delta u + g(x, y, z, u) = f(x, y, z)$$

on a tetrahedron Ω (a brick). Currently only Dirichlet boundary conditions are handled. A prototypical application would be reaction–diffusion equations. (See Implementation Details later for actual g and f functions we have used.)

These problems exhibit many features to ensure that the method and the code can easily be modified and enhanced to include a wide application range. In the meantime, we can study issues regarding effectiveness of parallelization, convergence, refinement strategies, error estimates, and the like, with a relatively small code. The crucial aspects of the problems we consider are their nonlinearity and their three-dimensional character.

The nonlinearity of the problems requires us to use the Full Approximation Scheme. This is, however, a rather simple high-level enhancement to a Defect Correction Method and the issues regarding their parallelization do not basically differ. (Note that also the incorporation of local grid refinement already presumes the use of the Full Approximation Scheme.) A more crucial consequence of the nonlinearity is the need to handle the coarse grids properly. This means allowing the method to use much coarser grids than desirable from a parallel computation point of view and providing a good coarsest-grid solver. The method should also allow continuation so that parameter-dependent problems can be addressed.

The three-dimensional character of our problems is rather unimportant for the logic and the mathematics of the algorithm, although it does introduce a higher degree of complexity in the implementation. There are two major trouble spots related to three dimensions. First, communication efficiency effects are more pronounced than in two dimensions because surface-to-volume ratio is the key factor rather than perimeter-to-area. Three-dimensional grids also have a much larger connectivity: each grid element can have up to 26 neighbors (6 along sides, 12 along edges, 8 at the vertices). The other issue is the difficult topology of general objects. For example, an operation occurring rather frequently in our multigrid method is the intersection of the surface of one object with another object. We decided not to address issues like these for now and allow only bricks in our programs. This simplification allows us to study all other aspects with a much smaller code.

The multigrid operators we currently use are based on the simplest discretizations possible for the given problem. This choice is also dictated by the practical consideration of keeping the code as small as possible during development. To increase the order of approximation later, we only need to add the appropriate sequential routines, not changing anything in the communication structure of the program. A consequence of this low-order approximation is that at this time we cannot handle problems with severe singularities in the solution. The relaxation operator is based on the following second-order discretization: the Laplacian is approximated by a seven-point operator (three-dimensional analog of the five-point operator); the right-hand side is evaluated at the center point; the nonlinear term $g(\mathbf{x}, u)$ is approximated at the center of the difference star by

$$g(\mathbf{x}, u) \approx g(\mathbf{x}, u_{\text{old}}) + g_u(\mathbf{x}, u_{\text{old}})(u - u_{\text{old}})$$

In an obvious way this discretization leads to a Jacobi and Lexical or Red–Black Gauss–Seidel relaxation procedures. The projection operators between fine and coarse grids are similarly based on the lowest-order approximations possible: the restriction uses straight injection of the fine grid values to the coarse grid points, and the interpolation is trilinear.

A Parallel Multigrid Method

The logical structure of our parallel multigrid solver is completely determined by a sequential multigrid algorithm that incorporates local grid refinement and domain decomposition. The inclusion of local grid refinement in a multigrid algorithm introduces a whole array of questions: How are the boundaries of the fine grid patches determined? How does one handle overlapping fine grid patches? How do the coarser and the finer grid patches interact? How does it affect the restriction and interpolation operators? Once these and other issues are resolved, we use this sequential algorithm to develop a fully parallel multigrid algorithm. The convergence of algorithm II is assured to a large extent by the theory summarized above (although, as indicated, some important questions remain unanswered). Algorithm I should be regarded as an heuristic shortcut, presented for completeness and as an introduction to the second, more complicated algorithm.

DATA STRUCTURES
A (regular rectangular) grid is defined by two main attributes: a certain region of space (which we arbitrarily restrict to be brick-shaped) and the grid spacings in x, y, and z directions used to discretize the region. The brick is defined by the coordinates of a reference point $(rfpx, rfpy, rfpz)$ and the positive lengths

(lx, ly, lz). The grid spacings are defined by (hx, hy, hz) and (somewhat superfluously) by the integers (nx, ny, nz) for the number of grid spacings in each direction.

On every grid a number of grid functions are defined, used for the representation of solution, right-hand side and other quantities (depending on the application). The definition of a grid function includes the grid attributes mentioned above and memory to store the values of the quantity it represents (see also next section).

In a multigrid algorithm without local grid refinement, the set of grids in the algorithm is ordered by a simple "fine/coarse" relationship. This linear ordering allows us to define the "level" of a grid. Typically, the level 0 grid (the coarsest) has grid spacings twice the size of the level 1 grid. There is a similar relation between the grid spacings at level i and $i + 1$. An appropriate way for us to represent such a linearly ordered set is a doubly linked list.[78] Thus, the grid data structure contains a pointer (possibly a null pointer) to a fine and to a coarse grid. This structure of grids connected in a doubly linked list is called an *Lgrid*.

Local grid-refinement attempts to economize on the number of floating-point operations by introducing only finer levels in those regions of the computational domain that need it. (We glance over the difficult task of detecting such regions.) With local grid refinement we introduce another relation in the set of grids. This relationship we call the "parent/child" relation, characterized by the fact that the region of a child covers only part of the parent region. Children of the same parent may have intersecting regions. As a result, children of children of the same parent ("cousins") may have intersecting regions. The parent/child relation induces a forest structure on the set of grids: the set is the union of a number of trees, each grid without a parent being the root of one tree. (We note that a tree structure of grids was first introduced by Berger[79] in the context of hyperbolic equation solvers.) To represent this structure, each grid contains an array of pointers to child grids.

With both relations active in the set of grids, we need to impose a number of restrictions on the fine/coarse and parent/child relations:

A child grid and its parent must be of equal coarseness.

This assumption is not restrictive in any way, it just insures that between directly linked grids only one relation is active. As a result, the children do not contain any extra information (with respect to the parent). It is hence reasonable to let the data of the parent and the child share their memory space. Algorithm II (below) relies on this possibility.

The child of a grid cannot have a coarser grid and must have a finer grid.

A set of grids with the two relations satisfying the above assumptions must consist of a forest of trees with Lgrids at the vertices. It is thus natural to talk about a parent/child relation between Lgrids. Moreover, within one tree, the notion of "level" of a grid remains meaningful: children and their parent are at the same level; the higher the level, the finer the grids. We call such a tree of Lgrids a

TLgrid. Finally, to make the notion of a level of a grid independent of a particular TLgrid, we assume that

The coarsest grid in a TLgrid structure is at level 0.

The data structures discussed so far are sufficient for a complete representation of all the data associated with a domain-decomposed local-refinement multigrid algorithm. For our algorithms, it is necessary, however, to provide more links between the grids. This necessity is inferred from the observation that grids on overlapping regions are not necessarily directly linked (e.g., the "cousins" example mentioned above). Another reason is that the current data structure is dominated by the parent/child relation rather than the linear fine/coarse relation on which the multigrid method relies.

The necessary extra links are provided in the following structure. All grids (across all trees) on the same level are collected in a circular linked list, which we call a *Cgrid*. No particular order is prescribed. A Cgrid thus collects the information of one particular level in one structure. There is a slight complication, however. Because child grids are on the same level as their parents both parent and child grids could end up in the same Cgrid structure. Since the children only duplicate information, only the parent is kept in the Cgrid structure and the children are ignored. (Note that this is only possible when data of children and parent share the same memory, which has the effect of keeping children and parent automatically up to date whenever one of the "family" changes.) An array of pointers to these Cgrids is kept (the pointer points to any grid of the Cgrid). This array, which we call an *ACgrid*, is indexed by the level.

ALGORITHM I

We present two different algorithms using the above data structures. The first one is based on the TLgrid structure and allows only one TLgrid (no forest). It does have many drawbacks which, however, are remedied by the more complicated algorithm of the next subsection.

This algorithm starts out with a full multigrid procedure on the Lgrid at the root of the tree. The values obtained on the finest grid of this Lgrid are used as boundary and initial values for a full multigrid on each of the children. This projection of boundary and initial values to the child Lgrids is repeated recursively in the TLgrid structure until the tree is exhausted.

The main advantage of this method is the simplicity of its logical structure. However, numerically it does not have enough drawbacks to make us reject it as a robust and reliable general-purpose method (it works well on many specific examples, though). The weaknesses of this strategy are apparent from a few simple observations: The results of the child Lgrids are never used by the parent Lgrid. Because of this, the changes due to better approximation in the child region cannot influence the domain exterior to the child region. That is acceptable for hyperbolic problems that have a maximum radius of influence (in finite times); for elliptic problems we have no such guarantee. A related disadvantage is that child grids with overlapping regions never exchange any information.

ALGORITHM II

To address the difficulties of algorithm I, we need to introduce more interaction between the many grids. It turns out, however, that the extra operators necessary for this more difficult algorithm are needed anyway for the parallelization of even algorithm I. As a result, the extra development time necessary for this algorithm (in a parallel environment) is negligible.

In fact, the description of the algorithm can be very short on a high level: just do a normal full multigrid algorithm substituting Cgrids for grids. That is, each time a multigrid program without grid refinement would ask for a relaxation of the grid at level i, we perform a relaxation of the Cgrid at level i. The ACgrid structure is clearly adequate for this task. This algorithm works for a single TLgrid as well as for a forest of TLgrids. It is necessary, however, to specify what is meant by the relaxation of a Cgrid or by the interpolation and restriction between two Cgrids.

The definition of the relaxation operator for a Cgrid follows immediately from Schwarz's alternating method. The grid patches of the Cgrid are smoothed one at a time using some relaxation method. Between grid smoothings, there is now an extra step: for all grids that intersect the region of the last smoothed grid, the boundary values must be updated. The circular list representation is an adequate structure to perform this operation. The order in which the grid patches are relaxed is not defined, nor is the order in which boundary values are exchanged. On numerical grounds, some orderings may be preferable and are easily implemented (in the sequential version of the program).

The restriction operation is quite easily defined as well. Only the fine/coarse relationship is involved; it is never necessary to operate between child and parent as they are on the same level. When a Cgrid is restricted to a coarser level, all member grids execute the restriction operator to their coarser grids. The latter are guaranteed to exist (on levels different from zero) because of the third assumption above (all TLgrids in the forest start at level 0). An ambiguity is left in this definition: consider two grids with intersection regions such that their coarser grids have the same parent. In this case, memory is shared at the coarse level. The result of the restriction in the intersection is then dependent on the order in which the restriction is executed. Some order may, once again, be preferable on numerical grounds.

The interpolation operator (from coarse to fine) between two Cgrids requires careful consideration. First of all, the grids involved in the interpolation need to be determined. This is slightly tricky when there are parent grids in the coarse Cgrid. In this case, it is the grid one level finer than the child itself that needs to receive the interpolated values. The finer grid is guaranteed to exist by the second data structure assumption. Another complication is important even if no parent grid is present in the Cgrid. The values interpolated to the fine grid boundary are used as "local Dirichlet boundary conditions" in the subsequent relaxation process on the fine Cgrid. This is correct if the fine grid lies completely in the interior of a coarse parent grid. However, if the fine grid boundary intersects the exterior boundary of the computational domain, a serious error occurs: instead of the available exact exterior boundary values, the interpolation of a coarse grid discretization is used by the fine grid. To remedy this problem, the interpolation step must be followed by an extra step to correct the values of fine grid points on the exterior boundary.

To complete the definition of our multigrid algorithm, we must specify the coarsest grid procedure. When the ACgrid structure consists of only one TLgrid, there is just one coarsest grid and any direct solver can be used. We currently use a standard Gaussian elimination procedure with partial pivoting, embedded in a Newton iteration (to handle the nonlinearity). With multiple TLgrids, the coarsest level Cgrid consists of several grids defined on intersecting regions. We use the above direct solver in combination with Schwarz's method: after every Newton iteration, boundary values are exchanged between intersecting grids in the same way as is done during the relaxation step discussed above. The convergence of the iteration on this coarsest level will be slow unless the intersection of the regions involved is big. This is no problem, however: once we go to finer levels we refine the coarse grids only locally and in such a way that the intersections decrease in size. On the finer levels, these smaller overlaps are sufficient because the domain-decomposed multigrid is less sensitive to their size.

THE PARALLEL ALGORITHM

To parellelize the above algorithm, the forest of TLgrids is distributed over the processors. On each processor only a number of TLgrids are active. On any particular processor, only those computations related to the active grids are done. Inactive grids participate in the local processing only through communication routines and use (almost) no further resources of the processor. Whenever the algorithm requires an operation on a Cgrid, each processor performs the operation on the active grids of the particular Cgrid. The fundamental data communication that takes place is the exchange of boundary value information. Only when an exchange between an active and an inactive grid takes place (in the relaxation process or in Schwarz's method on the coarsest grids) is physical communication necessary (between two active grids, a simple in-memory copy suffices). The parallel program differs from the sequential one only in the order in which the boundary values are exchanged. In fact, the ambiguity that was left in the definition of the operations on a Cgrid is the source of parallelism.

We left open the possibility of assigning more than one active TLgrid per processor. This could be useful, for example, in future parallel operating systems that provide the possibility for dynamic load balancing. (Such a system is currently under development.[43]) Load balancing could be achieved by shuffling TLgrids between processors.

As sketched above, the TLgrids are still in some synchronization: all TLgrids proceed to the next level at about the same time (after a boundary exchange). This is not strictly necessary if we allow each TLgrid to proceed even when new boundary information is not available for some grids. This can be accommodated in the current data and program structure. The numerical implications of such a strategy are not clear, however.

Grid Function Operations

The data structures and algorithms discussed in the previous section constitute the highest-level part of the actual code. Although the actual program size of this part is rather small, it contains all logical control of the algorithm. The bulk of the code (about 7500 lines of C) handles operations on grid functions, which represent the discretization of a function on a rectangular grid. These operations contain the details of the actual computations and as a result most of the computing time is spent in these routines. They are usually very simple from a logical point of view (typically three nested loops) but require special attention to implement them efficiently.

The most straightforward grid function operations are those that involve only grid function or grid functions defined on the same grid. Operations like this include initialize to zero, initialize with the discretization of an arbitrary continuous function, initialize the boundary, interpolate a grid function, find the linear combination of two functions. Also included in this package are I/O routines to write out grid functions in user-readable form (for debugging purposes). We also have versions to write and read grid functions to and from files, used to ship data between machines. We are also developing software to display these graphically. Beside these general-purpose operations, also the specific relaxation operators are implemented as routines of this type. The somewhat more complicated operations involve operations on pairs of grid functions defined on different grids. The previously discussed coarse-to-fine and fine-to-coarse projections are such operations: they act on pairs of functions defined on the same region but at different coarseness levels.

More important from a parallel computation point of view is the boundary-value exchange operation, which is used between grid functions on different regions but at the same coarseness level (although this is not enforced). This routine interpolates the first grid function at grid points of the second that lie on the intersection of the first region with the boundary of the second region. This is done in several stages: first, it is determined whether the two regions have an intersection at all (this is a quick test since we only allow bricks as regions). Consequently, we check for each boundary element (sides, edges, and vertices) of the second region whether it has an intersection with the first region. If it does, those grid points lying on the intersection get their value by interpolation from the first grid function. This operation has three variants. The version described above acts on two active grids, that is, grids active in the same processor. In the "send" variant, the second grid (which needs the boundary values) is inactive. In this case, one or more message buffers are filled with the values resulting from the interpolation and sent to the appropriate processor. The "receive" variant, with inactive first and active second grid function, reads the buffers and actually updates the values at the boundary points of the second grid. These two routines, of course, form the fundamental communication operation of the parallel multigrid algorithm.

Up to now we have ignored the fact that grid functions are used to approximate continuous functions. Given a rectangular grid, this approximation can be done in a variety of ways. The most obvious fashion is to store the value at every grid point. Alternatively, some piecewise polynomial approximation might be used (as in a conventional finite-element approach). We assume such an approximation operator as given. Most operations defined on grid functions are consistent (in some loosely defined way) with operations on the continuous functions—that is, the operation on the grid function approximates the operation on the continuous function. This presents no fundamental problems on simple rectangular grids. With (forests of) TLgrids a more flexible way to approximate functions (e.g. the solution of the problem) is introduced. It is more difficult to keep consistency in this case: in some areas of the computational domain the continuous function is approximated multiple times (because of overlapping grids). This introduces some ambiguity when calculating global quantities like norms. As an example, we discuss the calculation of the L-2 norm of a function approximated on a forest of TLgrids. We use this to compute the L-2 norm of the defects or the L-2 distance between numerical solutions and known exact solutions of sample problems. These quantities give us an idea of the global accuracy obtained (see Preliminary Results). Computation of norms is likely to gain importance when adaptive grid refinement is incorporated in the algorithm.

On any node of a TLgrid, only the finest grid is used to approximate the continuous function. Subregions covered by child grids should use the finest region of the child grid. From this observation, a recursive procedure to calculate the norm follows. (This can also be considered a recursive definition.) To describe the procedure, we refer to the squares of the norms as the norms (this makes it possible to add and subtract them easily). On the leaves of the TLgrid tree, we calculate the norm on the finest grid. On other nodes of the tree we do the same but perform a correction for every child. The norm of the function on the child grid is subtracted and the norm obtained on the finest level of the child is added. The norm of the TLgrid function is the result obtained at the finest grid of the root of the TLgrid. Note that this definition is ambiguous when child grid regions intersect: the result depends on the order in which the children are visited. This seems unavoidable since the same function is approximated by two different approximations in those regions. The problem becomes even more pronounced when several TLgrids are involved. We can calculate the norm on each using the above procedure and then make some allowance for intersections. The heuristic shortcut we make is to sum the norms on each TLgrid, weighed by a factor based on the volume of the region of each root Lgrid. (Calculating the norm on the intersection and subtracting it, is impractical because, in general, the grids are not aligned with the intersection.) In spite of the conceptual problems related to their precise definition, norms as defined (be it ambiguously) remain an important tool to help in the fine tuning of the method.

Implementation Details

One important implementation detail is already apparent throughout the previous sections: the data-structuring concepts require a programming language to support them. In addition, this programming language should be available and well supported on a wide variety of machines. Hence our choice for the C language.[80] We have more reasons to reject FORTRAN as a viable language for this project: The recursive nature of the multigrid method can be expressed clearly in a language like C. Converting to iterative form (as is necessary in standard FORTRAN) quickly leads to unreadable code. Furthermore, dynamic memory allocation is absolutely necessary to write a sufficiently general solver.

The algorithm as presented is largely architecture-independent. Only one assumption has been made: The architecture is sufficiently coarse-grained to accommodate one or more substantially sized TLgrids on every processor. Our current code runs on the ELXSI 4.2 BSD UNIX system, using the process-creation primitives and the file-management facilities of the operating system to implement parallelism. We are currently working on a hypercube version of the method, our first target machine being the Mark III. It is clear that our program, for realistically sized problems, requires both large memory and fast processing capabilities. So it is very important to keep the software running on the most up-to-date hardware (this is why we emphasize portability so vigorously). New hypercube developments toward larger nodes are thus very important, as are developments in other parallel architectures.

Preliminary Results

The flexibility of the proposed method makes a complete study of its numerical properties dependent on a whole array of parameters: dimensions of coarsest and finest grids, number of domain decompositions, number of relaxations, coarse grid iterations, location of local grid refinement patches, and so on. A complete numerical study, which is part of our research goals, is thus necessarily lengthy and complicated. In this paragraph, we only display the results of some preliminary tests that focus on aspects of Schwarz's method. When measuring errors, we use the L-2 norm as introduced in under Grid Function Operations earlier.

For our tests, we used sample problems with known exact solution (so that we can compute the errors), given by the equation (let $\mathbf{x} = (x, y, z)$*

$$-\Delta u + g(\mathbf{x}, u) = 0.0$$

on the unit cube, with

$$g(\mathbf{x}, u) = \alpha(\alpha + 1.0)u \, \|\mathbf{x} - \mathbf{x}_0\|^{-2}$$

With appropriate Dirichlet boundary conditions, this problem has the exact solution

$$u(\mathbf{x}) = \|\mathbf{x} - \mathbf{x}_0\|^{\alpha}$$

For the first example displayed, we used $\mathbf{x}_0 = (-1.0, -1.0, -1.0)$ and $\alpha = -1.0$. The singularity is then well outside of the computational domain (the current low-order discretization cannot handle these) and the nonlinear term vanishes

---

* We thank E. Doedel for suggesting this.

Table 11-2. Error as a function of the number of Schwarz's iterations (8 domain decompositions, $\alpha := -1.0$)

| Iteration | Domain size | | | |
	0.9	0.8	0.7	0.6
0	1.39559E − 01	1.55394E − 01	1.61288E − 01	1.83455E − 01
1	2.11007E − 02	5.97013E − 02	7.22526E − 02	1.19548E − 01
2	2.52749E − 03	1.78556E − 02	2.94255E − 02	7.90276E − 02
3	8.10437E − 04	4.95463E − 03	1.15123E − 02	5.23084E − 02
4	9.12753E − 04	1.40296E − 03	4.44968E − 03	3.45955E − 02
5	1.02534E − 03	4.06280E − 04	1.71109E − 03	2.28632E − 02
6	1.12174E − 03	1.28376E − 04	7.23667E − 04	1.50997E − 02
7	1.20569E − 03	5.14863E − 05	4.86900E − 04	9.96716E − 03
8	1.27818E − 03	3.06001E − 05	4.81701E − 04	6.57556E − 03
9	1.34008E − 03	2.49936E − 05	5.01235E − 04	4.33553E − 03

(Laplace equation). The second and third examples are fully nonlinear with $\alpha = -2.0$ and the singularity at $(-1.0, -1.0, -1.0)$.

In Tables 11-2 and 11-3, the unit cube is decomposed in eight overlapping cubes of equal size and we have varied the length of the cube edges between 0.6 and 0.9. Because each domain in the table is discretized on a $4 \times 4 \times 4$ grid, the discretization is worse with large subdomains (larger grid spacings). Schwarz's method, on the other hand, performs better as the subdomains increase in size (larger overlap). In both examples, eight subdomains of size $0.8 \times 0.8 \times 0.8$ perform best to reduce the total error. Table 11-4 displays the performance of the coarsest grid iteration when the domain is split into 27 cubes, with edge length varying between 0.4 and 0.8. The results indicate a decrease in size of the error during the first few iterations for all size regions. In terms of global convergence, size 0.6 wins out. Note that no high accuracies are to be expected from the

Table 11-3. Error as a function of the number of Schwarz's iterations (8 domain decompositions, $\alpha := -2.0$)

| Iteration | Domain size | | | |
	0.9	0.8	0.7	0.6
0	5.44560E − 02	6.09656E − 02	6.25710E − 02	7.09305E − 02
1	8.28574E − 03	2.42759E − 02	2.81116E − 02	4.58872E − 02
2	1.76018E − 03	7.52022E − 03	1.14027E − 02	3.02216E − 02
3	2.37666E − 03	2.22964E − 03	4.42367E − 03	1.99719E − 02
4	2.83465E − 03	7.91031E − 04	1.76597E − 03	1.32214E − 02
5	3.17104E − 03	3.98776E − 04	9.36878E − 04	8.77503E − 03
6	3.43819E − 03	2.94308E − 04	8.28388E − 04	5.84871E − 03
7	3.65291E − 03	2.66356E − 04	8.64128E − 04	3.92527E − 03
8	3.82544E − 03	2.58748E − 04	9.01650E − 04	2.66317E − 03
9	3.96381E − 03	2.56659E − 04	9.28399E − 04	1.83784E − 03

Table 11-4. Error as a function of the number of Schwarz's iterations (27 domain decompositions, $\alpha = -2.0$)

Iteration	Domain size			
	0.8	0.6	0.5	0.4
0	7.31317E − 02	9.18533E − 02	9.42970E − 02	1.04715E − 01
1	2.15004E − 02	6.19962E − 02	6.94091E − 02	9.15469E − 02
2	5.82431E − 03	3.91540E − 02	5.04038E − 02	8.23760E − 02
3	2.10856E − 03	2.39051E − 02	3.61915E − 02	7.52550E − 02
4	2.49153E − 03	1.43657E − 02	2.58814E − 02	6.91973E − 02
5	2.88837E − 03	8.58298E − 03	1.85071E − 02	6.39765E − 02
6	3.14300E − 03	5.14748E − 03	1.32657E − 02	5.93757E − 02
7	3.33146E − 03	3.14586E − 03	9.55143E − 03	5.53403E − 02
8	3.48360E − 03	2.01651E − 03	6.92382E − 03	5.17771E − 02
9	3.61069E − 03	1.41577E − 03	5.06670E − 03	4.86671E − 02

domain iteration because only very coarse discretizations are used. In all three examples, the decomposition with largest overlaps initially converges fastest, but the maximum accuracy attained is less than with the other decompositions owing to loss of convergence in the remaining iterations. This seems to be an effect of exchanges between nonneighboring domains, in other words: there is a limit to how much overlap is beneficial.

Overall convergence rates are slow. These, however, do not measure the real effectiveness of Schwarz's procedure within a multigrid context. In fact, we never run the procedure to convergence. For the above examples (8 and 27 decompositions) we obtained good results with a multigrid that does no exchanges at all on the coarsest level: the direct solver is applied once to each of the regions separately (of course, exchanges take place on the finer levels). Apparently, the direct solver in this case is enough to reduce the low-frequency error components while the high frequencies are taken care of by the smoothing operators. This is difficult to measure directly. Using full multigrid on the same example with 1, 8 (edge 0.6) and 27 (edge 0.4) domains, we obtained comparable global accuracies (comparing instances of about equal number of unknowns). In other examples, we noted slightly lower accuracy when using more domains.

Conclusions

The software presented provides an environment to examine in a systematic way many issues related to parallel multigrid in three dimensions. Among the many numerical analysis aspects needing further investigation, both experimentally and theoretically, we mention optimal order of discretization and appropriate relaxation and projection operators for a wide variety of applications, influence of asynchronous boundary-value exchanges, convergence of multigrid domain decomposition schemes, optimal grid sizes, and criteria for adaptive grid refinement. The numerical issues cannot be isolated from the parallel computation issues, however. For example, the more adaptive the algorithms are, the more crucial an issue dynamic load balancing becomes.

LATTICE GAUGE THEORIES ON HYPERCUBES

Introduction

Gauge theories are ubiquitous in elementary particle physics: the electromagnetic interaction between electrons (QED) is based on the gauge group $U(1)$, the strong force between quarks and gluons is believed to be explained by quantum chromodynamics (QCD) based on $SU(3)$, and there is a unified description of the weak and electromagnetic interactions in terms of the gauge group $SU(2) \times U(1)$. The strength of these interactions is measured by a coupling constant. This coupling constant is small for QED, so very accurate analytical calculations can be performed using perturbation theory. However, for QCD the coupling constant appears to increase with distance, so that perturbative calculations are only possible at short distances. In order to solve QCD at a longer distances, Wilson[81] introduced lattice gauge theory in which the space-time continuum is discretized onto a lattice, which is typically hypercubic, and the resulting system is numerically simulated by computer. Variables representing quarks are placed on the sites of the four-dimensional lattice and on the connecting bonds or links between the sites reside other variables that represent gluons. In the case of QCD, these gluon variables are actually $SU(3)$ matrices.

In practice, the quantum mechanician is not really interested in the properties of a gauge theory in a finite box, so the space-time volume that the lattice represents should be made as large as possible. This requirement, coupled with the four-dimensional nature of the lattice and the large number of degrees of freedom at each site and link, makes for large memory demands on the computer. Lattice gauge theory Monte Carlo simulations often contain 10^6–10^7 degrees of freedom. As a result of the Monte Carlo algorithm, the answers have statistical uncertainties and interesting physical properties tend to have unfavorable signal-to-noise ratios. Thus, very long runs, updating a large number of variables, are necessary, which further increases the demands upon the computer. As a result, lattice gauge theories have provided strong motivation for the development of high-performance advanced-architecture computers, like hypercubes.

Most of the work on lattice gauge theory has been directed towards solving lattice QCD and thus deriving the hadron mass spectrum from first principles. This would confirm QCD as the theory of the strong force. Other calculations have also been performed; in particular, confinement of quarks has been demonstrated and the properties of QCD at finite temperature and/or finite baryon density have been investigated. Unfortunately, in order to simulate lattice QCD on a computer one must integrate out the quark variables (because they are fermions), leaving a high nonlocal fermion determinant for each flavor of quark. Physically, this determinant arises from closed quark loops. The simplest way to proceed is to ignore these quark loops and work in the so-called quenched approximation with no flavors of quark present. (This may be valid for heavy quarks.) However, to investigate the physically more realistic fully interacting QCD, with the inclusion of dynamical quarks, we must go beyond the quenched approximation and tackle the problem of the fermion determinant.

Monte Carlo

A Monte Carlo algorithm is used to simulate numerically a lattice gauge theory. This cycles through all the links, randomly changing their values until they settle down into physically correct configurations. In other words, Monte Carlo algorithms generate a chain of configurations, U, which are distributed with a probability proportional to $e^{-S(U)}$, where S is the action for the theory under study. Various statistical correlations between the link variables are evaluated and averaged over many such configurations to yield the desired physical properties of the gauge theory. As an example, the force between quarks is related to the average value of large loops of links, that is, products of link matrices along closed paths. There are five popular methods for generating such chains: Metropolis, pseudo heat bath, microcanonical, Langevin, and hybrid.

METROPOLIS

In the Metropolis method[82] one proposes small changes in the configurations, and accepts these changes with a probability

$$\text{prob} = \min\left(1, \frac{P(U' \to U)e^{-S(U')}}{P(U \to U')e^{-S(U)}}\right) \qquad (11\text{-}7)$$

Here U' is the trial configuration, $P(U - U')$ is the probability of proposing the change given that one is at U, and $P(U' \to U)$ is the reverse probability. If these two probabilities are equal, as they are in most programs for pure gauge QCD (no quarks), then changes that lower the action are always accepted, while those that increase it are accepted only conditionally. Typically, the trial changes are made on a single site or link variable, and many trials (10–30) are made before moving on the next site. This is an extremely simple method for implementing for a local action.

PSEUDO HEAT BATH

Ideally one would like to make a change to a link or site variable by drawing from a probability $e^{-S(U')}$. This is the heat bath method, which can be implemented straightforwardly for $SU(2)$.[83] For $SU(3)$, it is more efficient to update the three $SU(2)$ subgroups in turn using the $SU(2)$ heat-bath algorithm[84] than to use the direct $SU(3)$ heat-bath method.[85] This variation is referred to as the pseudo heat-bath method. It is more complicated to code than the Metropolis algorithm, but is faster because it is applied only once to each link.

MICROCANONICAL

The Metropolis and pseudo heat bath algorithms move through configuration space stochastically. Microcanonical algorithms, in contrast, move deterministically through configuration space. Here, one enlarges the configuration space by adding fictitious momenta canonical to the degrees of freedom one wants to study, and then solves Newton's equations.[86,87] In practice this means solving coupled partial equations using difference approximations.

LANGEVIN

The Langevin method, like the microcanonical, involves introducing a fictitious time and solving a differential equation for the motion of the configuration, although it is stochastic. Schematically, the equation is[88]

$$\frac{dU}{d\tau} = -\frac{dS(U)}{dU} + \eta \tag{11-8}$$

where τ is the fictitious time, and η is Gaussian noise. The first term on the rhs is a drag term that pushes the action towards its minima, while the noise term ensures the correct exponential distribution about these minima. Once again, difference appoximations are used to solve the differential equations.

HYBRID

Microcanonical algorithms have the advantage of moving quickly through configuration space, but often do not sample all of it. Langevin algorithms, on the other hand, move more slowly through configuration space but are erdogic. Hybrid algorithms[89] use microcanonical evolution to move quickly through configuration space, but occasionally update some of the fields with a heat bath. These algorithms interpolate between microcanonical and Langevin, and are probably optimal.

The Metropolis and pseudo heat-bath methods are exact, while results from the microcanonical, Langevin, and hybrid methods must be extrapolated to zero step size. These approximate algorithms can, however, be made exact as follows.

GUIDED EXACT

After some number of steps using one of the approximate algorithms, the entire change in the lattice is accepted or rejected according to the Metropolis criterion give above.[90,91] Here, however, the forward and backward probabilities, $P(U \rightarrow U')$ and $P(U' \rightarrow U)$, are not equal and must be included. The aim is to make the probability of acceptance high, and thus explore configuration space quickly, by tuning the so-called guiding algorithm.

Fermions

With the exception of the heat bath algorithm, all of the above Monte Carlo algorithms can also be used to simulate dynamical fermions. In fact, the approximate algorithms have been developed specifically for the inclusion of dynamical fermions. The time needed to run these algorithms scales naively with the volume of the lattice, while for the exact algorithms the time scales as the square of the volume. Nevertheless, the exact algorithms remain of interest, since they yield fewer systematic errors. With the inclusion of dynamical fermions, the action is nonlocal, so that the variation in the action when the fields are changed is not simple to evaluate. One needs to calculate the product of the inverse of a sparse matrix with a vector for each step in the algorithms. This is the most time-consuming part of the program. To do this inversion, the method of conjugate gradients is used.

We shall now discuss some of the work done on lattice gauge theory on the hypercube at Caltech—a complete list is displayed in Table 11-5—and then go on to outline work that will be done on various high-performance concurrent computers in the future.

Table 11-5. Lattice gauge theory research at Caltech using the hypercube

Authors	Project	Hypercube	Reference
Brooks, Fox, Otto Randeria, Athas, Debenedictis, Newton, Seitz	Glueball mass	Mk I 4-node	152
Otto, Randeria	Glueball mass, modified action	Mk I 4-node	153
Otto, Stack	Static quark potential (meson) $12^3 \times 16$ lattice	Mk I 64-node	46
Otto, Stolorz	Glueball mass, enhanced statistics $12^3 \times 16$ lattice	Mk I 64-node	154
Fucito, Soloman	Chiral symmetry breaking, mass spectrum, finite temperature deconfinement, pseudofermions	Mk II 64-node	136–141
Patel, Otto, Gupta	Monte Carlo renormalization group, nonperturbative β-function	Mk I 64-node	155
Flower, Otto, Martin	Finite-temperature deconfinement, 4 light quark flavors by Langevin	Mk II 32-node	Unpublished
Flower, Otto	Energy density, heavy meson	Mk II 32-node	142
Flower, Otto	Scaling of static quark potential (meson), 20^4 lattice	Mk II 128-node	144
Kolawa, Furmanski	Glueball mass ($SU(2)$) Hamiltonian "loop" formalism	Mk II 32-node	143
Stolorz, Otto	Microcanonical renormalization group	Mk I 64-node	156
Flower	Restoration of rotational symmetry	Mk II 128-node	145
Flower	Static quark potential (baryon),	Mk II 128-node	146
Flower	20^4 lattice Energy density (baryon)	Mk II 32	147
Baillie, Ding	Quark potential (meson)	Mk III 32-node	In progress
Baillie, Brickner, Gupta	QCD with fermions	Connection machine	In progress

Past Lattice Gauge Theory Calculations at Caltech

THE QUARK POTENTIAL

The first QCD calculation on the original Caltech/JPL hypercube[46] measured the quark potential in order to demonstrate that quarks are confined. (This calculation has recently been repeated using a much bigger lattice on the Caltech/JPL Mark II hypercube.[92]) Figure 11-9 shows the result: the mutual potential energy of a pair of quarks, plotted as a function of their separation distance. At large separation the behavior is linear, implying quark confinement. This is a QCD analog of the Coulomb force law between electrons (in QED). The error bars represent statistical errors due to the Monte Carlo algorithm. This computation was performed on a $12^3 \times 16$ lattice mapped onto a six-dimensional hypercube (64 nodes). The hypercube was mapped onto a $4 \times 4 \times 4$ three-dimensional mesh. As a result, each node was responsible for the update or evolution of a $3^3 \times 16$ sublattice of the entire problem. The concurrent efficiency of the computation was measured as 95 percent. The 5 percent inefficiency is accounted for by a 2 percent loss due to load imbalance and a 3 percent loss due to communication overhead. It is significant that this low communication overhead is not due to the short range of interaction between the degrees of freedom. In fact, most of the variables in the $3^3 \times 16$ sublattice are communicated at least once during an update cycle. The overhead is low because of the proportionally greater amount of computation required for each variable.

We can quantify these remarks by noting that the communication component of the concurrent overhead for this problem on the Caltech/JPL Mark I

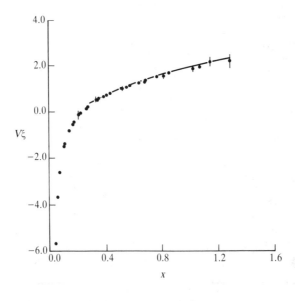

Figure 11-9. The heavy quark potential result as described by Otto.[46]

and II hypercubes follows the relation

$$f = \frac{1}{\varepsilon} - 1 = \frac{0.25}{n^{1/3}} \qquad (11\text{-}9)$$

Where $n = 3^3 \times 16$ is the grain size. In order to elaborate this point, let us consider a lattice gauge theory calculation for $SU(m)$ gauge theory. The calculation involves multiplication of $m \times m$ matrices and has an associated computational cost proportional to m^3; the communication cost is proportional to the number of matrix elements or m^2. Thus, we find using the notation introduced earlier

$$\frac{1}{\varepsilon - 1} \propto \frac{1}{m} \frac{1}{n^{1/3}} \frac{t_{\text{comm}}}{t_{\text{calc}}} \qquad (11\text{-}10)$$

and decreases as m increases. The measured value in Eqn. (11-9) corresponds to the case $m = 3$.

This quark potential calculation was performed in the quenched approximation, corresponding to heavy quarks. It is currently being repeated for light quarks using a new algorithm for dealing with dynamical fermions.[93]

BARYONS ON THE LATTICE

A detailed study of heavy baryons (three quarks bound together) has also been performed via Monte Carlo lattice gauge theory on the hypercube.[94] Studying the off-axis quark potential, the effect of the discrete rotational symmetry of the Euclidean lattice on physical parameters such as the string tension was assessed. At $\beta = 6.1$ these are of order 15 percent but seem insignificant at $\beta = 6.3$. The heavy baryonic potential was caclculated and yields a string tension comparable to that observed in mesonic Monte Carlo calculations as well as that derived from Regge slopes and relativized hadronic models. It is suggested that the effects of string vibrations are small in the range $x \lesssim 0.5$ fm. The baryonic energy density was also studied and strongly supports the dual superconductor model of confinement as well as suggesting that the baryonic strings meet at a single central point rather than joining the quarks pairwise. The evidence for this is displayed as a contour plot of the chromoelectric and chromomagnetic field distributions in the neighborhood of the quarks making up the baryon in Figures 11–10(a) and (b), respectively.

THE "WALKING PROGRAM"

It is useful to discuss here an important method of structuring the QCD calculation in order to simplify the application code. As is the case in much practical programming, there is a right way and a wrong way to write the code. The issue of concern relates to the previously mentioned loops. The fundamental variables of the calculation are matrices and a loop is a product of these matrices along some closed path through the lattice. On a distributed-memory machine such as the hypercube, the encoding of these can become quite difficult, because

a)

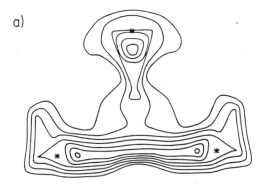

b)

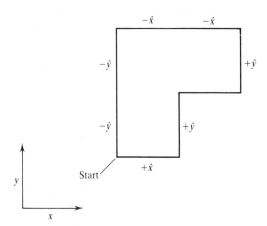

Figure 11-10. Contour plot of the field distributions for the observable $Q(2, 2, 3; 4)$ from Flower.[94] (a) Chromoelectric; (b) Chromomagnetic.

the loop can overlap more than one processor subdomain. Explicitly keeping track of where a given loop crosses processor boundaries is a daunting task, especially in four dimensions!

An effective way to deal with this problem is to devise a walking program for the calculation of loops. Figure 11-11 shows how to describe the shapes of arbitrary loops. A loop is specified by a string of symbols, each of which gives the

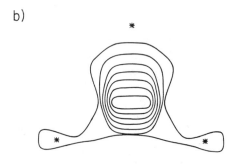

Figure 11-11. The loop corresponding to the walker string $(+\hat{x}, +\hat{y}, +\hat{x}, +\hat{y}, -\hat{x}, -\hat{y}, -\hat{y}, -\hat{y})$.

direction for a single step along the loop. The loop shown in specified by the string $(+\hat{x}, +\hat{y}, +\hat{x}, +\hat{y}, -\hat{x}, -\hat{x}, -\hat{y}, -\hat{y})$. To compute the loop, we feed the walker routine a starting location and this string as input. The walker reads the first entry of the string, takes a step through the lattice in that direction, and sets a matrix "answer" equal to the matrix it finds there. It then reads the next string entry, steps in that direction, and multiplies the matrix it finds there. It then reads the next string entry, steps in that direction, and multiplies the matrix it finds there by "answer." This process continues until the end of the string is reached. At this point, the walker will have walked completely around the loop and "answer" will finally contain the desired result. The walker travels around the loop, carrying the partial answer along with it.

The beauty of this technique is twofold. First, given a general walker routine, loops of all sizes and shapes are handled with equal ease. All that is required is to construct the appropriate string for the loop. Second, this algorithm translates quite easily into a parallel environment. All that needs to be added is a check, at each step, to determine whether a processor boundary is being crossed. If so, the partial result and the remaining string are passed to the appropriate processor. Once a processor passes along its work in this manner, it checks to see whether any work requests (consisting of partial answers and strings) have entered its domain. If so, it processes them. Since the loops close, we are ensured that, once the dust settles, the loop answers will reside in their correct processors, that is, the final answer will end up in the processor that contains the start of the loop.

The parallel walker program allows computation of loops of arbitrary shape and size to proceed, simply by specifying loops strings. Since the entire QCD calculation is based on loops, the routine allows the high-level coding to be transparent to issues involving processor boundaries.

Future Lattice Gauge Theory Calculations at Caltech

A great number of lattice gauge theory calculations have been performed in the quenched approximation. Recently, many algorithms have been invented to deal with dynamical fermions, and tested on small lattices. What one would like to do now is realistic simulations of QCD with and without quarks on larger lattices, calculating the hadron mass spectrum, the properties at finite temperature and/or finite baryon density, the quark potential, and so on, to see the effect of the quark loops. These calculations are all extremely computationally intensive.

In the near-term future at Caltech, we will be involved in three main lattice gauge theory projects. First, in collaboration with R. Gupta, G. Kilcup, and S. Sharpe, we are using a guided hybrid Monte Carlo algorithm to investigate QCD with Wilson and Susskind fermions, looking at both the finite-temperature phase transition and the quark potential. Second, we are testing a mixed Metropolis/Langevin algorithm for dealing with dynamical fermions, developed at Caltech, with a view to using it for the quark potential calculation. Finally, we are using a pure gauge QCD code developed at Caltech as one of the benchmarks for performance evaluation of advanced architecture computers.

GUIDED HYBRID MONTE CARLO—FINITE TEMPERATURE AND QUARK POTENTIAL

R. Gupta, G. Kilcup, and S. Sharpe developed a CRAY code that analyzes QCD with dynamical Susskind fermions using an exact guided hybrid Monte Carlo algorithm.[95] C. Baillie took this code and changed the implementation of the fermions from Susskind to Wilson. The entire code runs at over 100 MFLOPS on the CRAY X-MP. This will be the first exact algorithm for Wilson fermions.

Gupta[95] presents tests of the hybrid Monte Carlo algorithm with Susskind fermions and results for the finite-temperature phase transition on 4^4 and 4×6^3 lattices. The acceptance in the global Metropolis step can be tuned and kept large without having to make the hybrid step size prohibitively small. Evidence is found for a first-order phase transition at $m = 0.1$.

Recently, we have obtained preliminary results from the Wilson fermion version of the hybrid Monte Carlo algorithm running on CRAYs at both SDSC and Los Alamos. On a 4×6^3 lattice we find evidence for a first-order phase transition at approximately $\varkappa = 0.156$. We are also looking at the quark potential on a 8^4 lattice, measuring up to 4×4 Wilson loops.

MIXED METROPOLIS/LANGEVIN—QUARK POTENTIAL

Many calculations have been made of the quark potential in the quenched approximation (one of high accuracy was done at Caltech).[92] These are consistent with the expected behavior for the string tension, but there are discrepancies. Hence, there is considerable interest in re-doing these calculations with the effects of dynamical fermions included.

We intend to calculate the quark potential for a fully interacting QCD and pseudofermion system using a mixed Metropolis/Langevin algorithm developed at Caltech for hypercubes.[93] This algorithm uses the standard multi-hit Metropolis algorithm to update the gauge fields and second-order Langevin to evolve the fermions. The algorithm is approximate because detailed balance is violated. We have done tests with free fermions which show that the error can be minimized by tuning the step size in the Langevin equation. We have also done a preliminary run at $\beta = 6.1$ in order to compare our results with those obtained in the quenched approximation.[92] However, for this value of β we find that we have crossed over into the deconfined phase, which emphasizes the importance of including fermions. We are now running at lower values of β to determine whether they are in the confined phase and if so to measure the string tension.

PERFORMANCE EVALUATION OF ADVANCED ARCHITECTURE COMPUTERS

Recently, a number of advanced-architecture computers have become commercially available. These new machines promise better cost–performance than traditional computers, and some of them have the potential of competing with current supercomputers, such as the CRAY X-MP, in terms of maximum performance. Caltech is involved in an ongoing project to evaluate a broad range of advanced architecture computers using a number of complete scientific application programs.[5,96] The computers to be evaluated include

- distributed-memory machines such as the NCUBE, INTEL iPSC, and Caltech/JPL hypercubes, the FPS T-series, and the MEIKO computing surface;
- shared-memory, bus-architecture machines such as the Sequent Balance and the Alliant FX/8;
- very long-instruction-word machines such as the Multiflow Trace 7/200;
- "traditional" supercomputers such as the CRAY X-MP and CRAY-2;
- SIMD machines such as the TMC Connection Machine 2 (CM-2).

QCD is one of the 11 application codes from a number of scientific disciplines selected as benchmarks.[5,96]

In Table 11-6 we give some preliminary results for the update phase of the QCD program for a number of different computers. It is interesting to note that for this application the speed of a single NCUBE processor is approximately the same as for a VAX 11/750, which in turn is comparable to the speed of a SUN 3/160 with 68881 floating-point chip. An early version of the C* compiler was used in obtaining the CM-2 results for the QCD update; future versions of it are expected to produce more efficient code. Meanwhile we have preliminary results for *LISP and PARIS versions of the code, based on timings for performing $SU(3)$ matrix multiplication only. In the last column of Table 11-6 we list the maximum performance in MFLOPS for the code running on the largest available machine (1024 processors for the NCUBE, and 65 536 processors for the CM-2).

We expect to extend our performance analysis work further to include more

Table 11-6. Timings in seconds of the pure gauge QCD update phase on a $2 \times 2 \times 2 \times 2$ lattice for several computers

Machine	Time/sweep (sec)	KFLOPS/processor	MFLOPS/machine
SUN3/160 + 68881	3.14	101.9	
VAX 11/750 VMS	2.75	116.4	
CRAY X-MP	0.026	12 300.0	
NCUBE	2.59	123.6	126.6
NCUBE (C)	4.18	76.6	78.4
CM-2 (C*)	52.70	0.38	24.9
CM-2 (*LISP)	>23.6	<0.85	<55.5
CM-2 (PARIS)	>2.0	<16.0	<1048.6

Note that on CM-2 lattice is stored with 1 site/processor; on other machines there are 16 sites/processor. These timings are for a single sweep through the lattice, and were found by averaging over 10 sweeps. The last column gives the maximum performance for the largest available version of the concurrent machines. All codes are written in FORTRAN unless stated otherwise. Except for the CM-2 results, the code has not been optimized or customized for the target machines. In particular, the code on the CRAY X-MP has not been vectorized yet. The CRAY timings were performed by Wayne Pfeiffer at SDSC.

applications and machines. We also intend to develop detailed performance models of the machines studied.

In conclusion, the future looks bright for Caltech in lattice gauge theory. We will perform several important calculations during the forthcoming year, utilizing both traditional and advanced architecture computers.

APPLICATIONS OF THE HYPERCUBE IN GEOPHYSICS

Introduction

Many subdisciplines of geophysics are at the point where access to facilities for very large-scale computations is a necessity. The simple zeroth-order problems involving flat layered structures, uniform material properties, and two dimensions have been solved; frontier research involves the effects of realistic lateral variations in material properties and three dimensions. For the most part, these problems are not amenable to solution by analytic techniques; numerical methods are required. The expense of these methods has up to now made solution of many important problems in geophysics prohibitively expensive.

The rapid development of concurrent processors holds the promise of the feasibility of achieving massive computational power for those problems that can be solved with reasonable efficiency on parallel machines. Fortunately, many important problems in geophysics lend themselves to fairly straightforward decomposition in parallel computers with a hypercube architecture. We describe here research in progress at Caltech in solving real geophysical problems on hypercubes. The examples we discuss are in the fields of seismology, both using the finite-difference and normal-node approaches, and in numerical modeling of geodynamics problems, particularly simulations of mantle convection.

Finite-Difference Wave Simulation

The simulation of seismic waves in complicated Earth models requires the use of direct numerical solutions. These methods are far more expensive than the traditional semianalytic techniques that have been used for media that vary only with depth. However, the ability to model all types of wave phenomena (diffractions, surface waves, head waves, etc.) justifies the increased expense in many cases.

A typical application of numerical modeling is in the simulation of strong motion waves due to earthquake sources. The presence of basins filled with low-velocity sediments causes reverberation and amplification of the waves. The shape of the basins determines where the largest ground motions will occur. These effects require numerical procedures to simulate them.

Unfortunately, the size of even the largest supercomputers is inadequate for three dimensional simulations. Realistic models need several gigabytes of memory to span the region of interest. Also, since the algorithms tend to do few calculations per memory reference, the methods are ill-suited to machines that have slow memory relative to the processor speed.

The wave simulations, however, are well-suited to computers in which the memory and CPU are distributed. These highly-parallel machines can be exploited to maximum efficiency by dividing the region to be modeled into subregions that reside in separate memories, and that are updated by separated CPUs. Each subregion is independent except for perimeter elements that require knowledge of the solution in the neighboring subregions. However, the inter-processor I/O associated with the border elements can be minimized if a sufficient number of solution points are contained in each subregion. Consequently, the wave simulation calculations are expected to perform more efficiently on coarse-grained parallel machines rather than fine-grained machines. Here, coarse- and fine-grained refer to the number of individual processors that make up a machine of a particular net memory size and computational power.

For wave simulation problems there are three numerical schemes that have been applied. These are the finite-difference (FD), finite-element (FE), and pseudo-spectral (PS) methods. These methods differ in the manner in which the spatial derivatives are approximated. The FD and FE methods differ in their derivation, but in the end produce localized operators for estimating the spatial derivatives. The PS methods use Fourier transforms to approximate the derivatives. They require the fewest points per wavelength (hence reducing the memory requirements for a given physical problem), but need several two- or three-dimensional Fourier transforms of the entire model region for each time update. The interprocessor I/O overhead appears to be higher for the PS methods than for either the FD or FE method, when applied to distributed systems.

In this section, we shall focus on the FD method applied to hypercube-architecture computers. This method has the simplest and most direct decomposi-tion. The FE method can be expected to give a similar level of performance. It is discussed in the next section in the context of viscous-flow problems.

To illustrate decomposition of the FD algorithm, we consider the simple two-dimensional acoustic wave equation

$$P_{tt} = v^2(P_{xx} + P_{zz})$$

where P is the pressure field and v is the wave velocity. A straightforward application of second-order approximations of the derivatives leads to the following explicit system:

$$P_{i,j}^{n+1} = 2P_{i,j}^n + P_{i,j}^{n-1} + \frac{v_{i,j}^2 \Delta t^2}{h^2} [p_{i+1,j}^n + P_{i-1,j}^n + P_{i,j-1}^n + P_{i,j+1}^n - 4P_{i,j}^n]$$

where h is the spatial grid size, and Δt is the time step. Here $P_{i,j}^n = P(t = n\,\Delta t, x = ih, z = jh)$. The solution is solved by marching in time from initial conditions (i.e., the source) specified at $t = 0$. Two memory planes, each spanning the full x and z extent of the model, are required to do the time extrapolation. A straightforward algorithm consists of an outer loop over time and an inner loop(s) over space. Unfortunately, this algorithm requires that the entire spatial region be swept for each time-step.

To modify this algorithm to exploit a distributed system, we divide the model into subregions, which we will, for convenience, take to be squares of $N \times N$ sample points. The FD stencil given by the formula above indicates that only nearest-neighbor points are required for the time update. Consequently, the formula can be applied in unmodified form to all interior points of each subregion. The only modification necessary is for the perimeter elements. We have found that adding an extra row of perimeter "pseudo" elements to each subregion makes the decomposition the simplest. The extra elements contain copies of the appropriate solution points in the neighboring processors. If this is done, then the FD formula can be applied to each subregion without modification (i.e., the subroutine from the equivalent sequential program is kept intact). The additional step that is now necessary is an I/O exchange operation to update the extra perimeter elements.

The I/O overhead is proportional to the number of perimeter elements, which for $N \times N$ subregions is $4N$. However, if the machine is capable of independent asynchronous communication with its neighbors, this factor reduces to N. The number of computational operations is proportional to N^2, leading to a net relative overhead (I/O to computation) of $1/N$. Table 11-7 gives the overhead for a two-dimensional implementation of the acoustic wave equation. The overhead is determined by relative timings of a problem running in one processor (no overhead) compared with a problem that is four times the size, running in four processors. The timings were done on Caltech's Mark II hypercube, running under the CrOS operating system. Larger problems involving more processors give similar results.

It is left as an exercise to the reader to show that for CPUs that can support asynchronous I/O the I/O overhead can be overlapped with the interior computations. This involves a slight reordering of the calculations. This trick is used for higher-order ID schemes that require more extra bordering elements. Note, however, that a fourth-order scheme can be implemented with no more storage requirements than a second-order scheme. Our current production runs use a fourth-order scheme.

Table 11-7. Overhead dependence on subregion size for the acoustic problem

Subregion size	Overhead
10×10	10%
20×20	5%
40×40	0%

Finite-Element Modeling in Geodynamics

Finite-element calculations of continuum mechanics problems are useful in a wide range of fields in geophysics where the geometry or physics of a problem suggests or requires a wide range in material properties, in mesh geometries, or in resolution. Examples include numerical simulations of the state of stress near oil wells, of the flow of glaciers and large ice sheets, and of the buildup and release of stress due to viscoelastic creep around fault zones.

On geological timescales, the rocks in the Earth's deep interior respond to stress by undergoing slow, creeping flow. The resulting thermal convection is the ultimate cause for surface plate motions and geologic activity. Numerical simulations play a key role in unraveling the physics of these processes, since the relevant rheologies and temporal and spatial scales are difficult to scale to the laboratory. The finite-element method is well suited for carrying out these simulations, since it is capable of providing adequate resolution where needed and can also handle large variations in material properties.

FE applications typically lead to the need to form and solve a matrix equation of the form $\mathbf{Ax} = \mathbf{b}$, where $\mathbf{A}$ is an assembly of element "stiffness" matrices, $\mathbf{x}$ is the vector of nodal displacements, and $\mathbf{b}$ is the "force" vector (see, e.g., Zienkiewicz[97]). (For the problems of greatest interest to us, which include the effects of stress-dependent rheologies, $\mathbf{A}$ itself is a function of the solution $\mathbf{x}$, and the equation must be solved iteratively 5–10 times to reach convergence.) The equation can be solved either by "direct" means such as Gaussian elimination, or by iterative techniques, such as conjugate gradient or multigrid. Iterative techniques fit naturally into the hypercube architecture.

It is of interest to estimate the storage and CPU cost needed to solve this equation.[98] Consider a brick p nodes by q nodes by r nodes, with $p \geq q \geq r$ ($r = 1$ corresponds to two dimensions). Each element has NEN nodes, each node has $NDOF$ degrees of freedom, and the problem has NSD spatial dimensions. The storage and CPU requirements for direct solution and iterative solution by the conjugate-gradient (CG) technique described below are given in Table 11-8, assuming quadrilateral elements. Ranges in storage for the conjugate-gradient technique depend upon the number of geometrically distinct elements that must be stored. In most of our applications, the geometries are not all different, but come in clumps with identical structures, so the lower limits in storage are more usually appropriate.

One problem in estimating CPU costs for an iterative algorithm is in estimating the total number of iterations required. Our experience, incorporated in these estimates, had been that approximately $p \cdot NDOF$ iterations are required for well-conditioned problems.

From Table 11-8 it is clear that direct solution techniques are not competitive in three dimensions, either in storage or CPU cost. Even in two dimensions, for large problems, iterative techniques appear preferable. For problems with stress-dependent rheology, iterative techniques are even more attractive; less-accurate intermediate solutions are required because the entire problem must be iterated upon several times.

Table 11-8. Complexity of various steps in direct and iterative solution methods

	General	2-D	3-D
Direct Stor.	$DNOF^2pq^2r^2$	$4pq^2$	$9p^2q^2r^3$
Indirect Cost	$1/2NDOF^3pq^3r^3$	$4pq^3$	$14pq^3r^3$
Iter. Stor.	$(1 \rightarrow pqr)NSF \cdot NEN(NSD \cdot NEN + 1)/2$ $+ NDOF \cdot pqr$	$(20 \rightarrow 70)pq$	$(28 \rightarrow 360)pqr$
Iter. Cost	$(NDOF \cdot NEN^2 + 5)NDOF^2p^2qr$	$150p^2q$	$1800p^2qr$

The question then becomes whether iterative solution of the FEM equations is feasible on a hypercube. The answer is that decomposition of the finite-element problem is simple, straightforward, and, if sufficient memory is available in each processor, efficient. The basic approach is to map adjacent regions of the physical domain into adjacent processors. As in the finite-difference case, efficient decomposition requires that the ratio of effective surface area to volume of the mesh in each processor be small, that is, that many calculations be done for exchange of information between processors. Load balancing among processors for grids of irregular shapes can be solved by the "scattered decomposition" technique,[38] in which a stencil of processor assignments is repeated over the grid.

To address the efficiency of the concurrent decomposition of iterative algorithms, we consider the specific case of the conjugate-grading technique discussed by Lyzenga.[24] This procedure consists of the following algorithm:

Initialize $(k = 0)$: $\mathbf{r}^{(0)} = \mathbf{p}^{(0)} = \mathbf{b} - \mathbf{A}\mathbf{x}^{(0)}$
Iterate over k
  1. $\alpha_k = (\mathbf{r}^{(k)} \cdot \mathbf{r}^{(k)})/(\mathbf{p}^{(k)} \cdot \mathbf{A}\mathbf{p}^{(k)})$
  2. $\mathbf{x}^{(k+1)} = \mathbf{x}^{(k)} + \alpha_k \mathbf{p}^{(k)}$
  3. $\mathbf{r}^{(k+1)} = \mathbf{r}^{(k)} - \alpha_k \mathbf{A}\mathbf{p}^{(k)}$
  4. $\beta_k = (\mathbf{r}^{(k+1)} \cdot \mathbf{r}^{(k+1)})/(\mathbf{r}^{(k)} \cdot \mathbf{r}^{(k)})$
  5. $\mathbf{p}^{(k+1)} = \mathbf{r}^{(k+1)} + \beta_k \mathbf{p}^{(k)}$
  6. If not converged, $\mathbf{k} = \mathbf{k} + 1$

This algorithm consists of two types of operations: vector dot products and the matrix–vector product, such as $\mathbf{A}\mathbf{p}^{(k)}$. If local basis functions are used in the finite-element discretization, the contributions to $\mathbf{A}$ interacting with any given node are only from neighboring nodes. Thus, both the dot product and matrix–vector product can be done in parallel and require minimal communication between processors.

For simplicity, assume that each processor has assigned to it an $N \times N$ portion of a two-dimensional elasticity problem. For each iteration, each processor must do $12N^2$ operations (defined as multiplication plus addition) associated with the three dot products, $12N^2$ operations associated with the three vector additions, and $72N^2$ operations associated with the matrix–vector product (each node is connected via shape functions to nine neighbors, including itself, each with $NDOF = 2$). Total communications require sending three scalar contributions to global dot products (negligible), receiving two global scalars (negligible), and communicating $8N$ contributions to $\mathbf{Ap}^{(k)}$ from adjacent processors, one for each side and each degree of freedom. So long as N is large, the ratio of communication to computation, $1/(12N)$ is small and the decomposition is efficient.

For three-dimensional problems, $81N^3$ operations for dot products, $81N^3$ operations for vector additions, and $2187N^3$ operations for the matrix–vector product are required for each iteration. About $72N^2$ communications are needed, giving an inefficiency of $\sim 1/32N$ for large N. (It should be pointed out, however, that for processors that only have enough memory to store three-dimensional problems with relatively small N [say, $N = 5$], a surprising fraction of nodes are on the surface [98 out of 125].) Substantial memory per node is required for efficient computation.

Lyzenga[24] used the Mark II hypercube to demonstrate that the conjugate-gradient algorithm runs with the expected efficiency for two-dimensional problems. Useful tests of three-dimensional efficiencies required processors with more memory per node than is available on the Mark II.

APPLICATION TO NORMAL-MODE DATA ANALYSIS

The interior structure of the Earth is mainly investigated by seismic waves. At the long-wavelength, long-period end, geophysicists have observed oscillations of the Earth as a whole—the normal modes of the Earth. There are more than 1000 modes identified so far, and most of the modes have periods longer that about 100 sec. We can classify modes as spheroidal and toroidal motions, which are the normal modes of a spherically symmetric sphere. Strictly speaking, the Earth is not a spherically symmetric sphere, as is evident from the existence of oceans, mountains, and various other topographic features. Thus, normal modes of the Earth are not purely spheroidal or toroidal in a rigorous sense. But in the long-wavelength range, because the oscillations are only sensitive to large-scale average properties of the Earth, the Earth seems almost a spherically symmetric body with a slight perturbation from it. As we attempt to observe modes for shorter wavelengths, however, the effect of deviation from spherical symmetry becomes larger and we find more and more complications.

In the long-period range, geophysicists have had success in recovering structure by using perturbation theory for a slightly heterogeneous sphere. Now geophysicists can see roots of continents that penetrate a few hundred kilometers into the Earth and also the gross structure beneath the mid-oceanic ridges where plates pull apart. Further progress calls for extending the analysis to shorter periods.

There are two aspects of the perturbation approach that can benefit from the use of concurrent algorithms. The first aspect is the calculation of eigen-frequencies and eigenfunctions for a zeroth-order spherically symmetric Earth model. The second aspect is the application of concurrent algorithms to the large-scale least-squares inversion problem. These two aspects are elaborated in the following sections.

Computation of Eigenfrequencies and Eigenfunctions

We need to calculate eigenfrequencies and eigenfunctions of spheroidal and toroidal nodes of the zeroth-order Earth model in order to evaluate the terms in the perturbation expansion. Each type of motion consists of a range of horizontal wavelengths. Horizontal wavelength is represented by angular order l and azimuthal order m of vector spherical harmonics, but for a spherically symmetric sphere, normal modes for a given l make up degenerate modes ($2l + 1$-fold degeneracy from $m = 1$ to $m = l$). The whole problem of computing normal modes breaks up into two-point boundary-value problems for different l and the two different types of motion.[99]

Let us first take the case of toroidal oscillations and explain some details. The displacement of a toroidal oscillation is given by

$$u_r = 0$$

$$u_\theta = W(r) \frac{1}{\sin \theta} \frac{\partial Y_l^m(0, \phi)}{\partial \phi} \tag{11-11}$$

$$u_\phi = -W(r) \frac{\partial Y_l^m(0, \phi)}{\partial \theta}$$

and the equation for $W(r)$ is simply a second-order ordinary differential equation. In the above expression, Y_l^m is a spherical harmonic function. We ordinarily solve this by introducing another function $T(r)$, which is related to shear stress by

$$\sigma_{r\theta} = T(r) \frac{1}{\sin \theta} \frac{\partial Y_l^m}{\partial \phi} \tag{11-12}$$

and

$$\sigma_{r\phi} = -T(r) \frac{\partial y_l^m(0, \phi)}{\partial \theta} \tag{11-13}$$

Then the equations to be solved are two first-order ordinary differential equations given by

$$\frac{dW}{dr} = \frac{1}{r} W(r) + \frac{1}{\mu} T(r) \tag{11-14}$$

$$\frac{dT}{dr} = \left(\frac{(l - 1)(l + 2)\mu}{r^2} - \rho\omega^2 \right) W(r) - \frac{3}{r} T(r) \tag{11-15}$$

where $\mu(r)$ is rigidity, ρ is density, and ω is the (angular) eigenfrequency. The boundary conditions are given by $T = 0$ at the surface of the Earth and also at the core–mantle boundary, which is at about the depth of 2890 km. This is because the Earth's surface is a free surface bounded by air and also the outer core is known to consist of molten material. The core–mantle boundary is then a solid–liquid boundary where shear stress must vanish.

The two equations (11-14) and (11-15), with two boundary conditions, $T = 0$ at both ends, is the problem to solve. Note that only the angular order l appears in the above equations and the azimuthal order m does not show up, which is the direct consequences of degeneracy. Modes with the same l possess the same eigenfunction $W(r)$.

Each l gives us a different problem to solve and for the period range larger than 100 sec we must obtain solutions up to about $l = 100$, that is to say, we must solve an independent two-point boundary-value problem 100 times. The computer code for this problem requires less than 100 Kbyte memory and thus can be handled by a modest processor. It is clear that the number of processors directly enhances the performance of the computation. We plan to extend the method to higher frequency in the near future, up to about 30 sec period. Then the maximum range of l will be about 600. The advantage of the use of a concurrent algorithm in this problem is obvious.

In the case of spheroidal modes, the displacement is given by

$$u_r = U(r) Y_l^m$$

$$u_\theta = V(r) \frac{\partial Y_l^m}{\partial \theta} \tag{11-16}$$

$$u_\phi = V(r) \frac{1}{\sin \theta} \frac{\partial y_l^m}{\partial \phi}$$

Self-gravitation becomes important for this type of problem and, along with displacements, the gravitational potential perturbation

$$\psi = P(r) y_l^m$$

must also be obtained simultaneously. The basic equations are three second-order differential equations for $U(r)$, $V(r)$, and $P(r)$, which can be transformed to six first-order differential equations

$$\frac{d\mathbf{y}}{d\mathbf{r}} = \mathbf{A}\mathbf{y}$$

where $\mathbf{A}$ is a six by six coefficient matrix and $\mathbf{y}$ is the eigenfunction vector. Boundary conditions are obtained from the free surface condition and regularity at the center of the Earth, $r = 0$.

Computer code for this problem is also of modest size, but obviously slightly larger than the case for toroidal modes. The current size of the program requires about 200 Kbyte of memory, thus requiring processors with resonable memory.

APPLICATION TO LEAST-SQUARES ALGORITHM

The inversion of seismograms for the structure of the Earth is done by using the relation

$$u_{\text{obs}} = u_{\text{theoretical}} + \frac{\partial u_{\text{theoretical}}}{\partial v} \delta v$$

where u_{obs} is the observed seismogram, $u_{theoretical}$ is the theoretical seismogram for a zeroth-order Earth mode, and the last term represents the correction due to unknown structure which has seismic velocity δv; δv is a function of r, 0, and ϕ, and is the quantity we want to solve for.[100,101]

This problem can be written in the form $\mathbf{Ax} = \mathbf{b}$, where $\mathbf{b}$ is the difference between data and theory, $(u_{obs} - u_{theoretical})$, $\mathbf{A}$ is obtained from $\partial u_{theoretical}/\partial v$, and $\mathbf{x}$ is a solution vector for δv. $\mathbf{A}$ is ordinarily a matrix with about 10^5 rows and 10^3 columns in our problems. One way to solve this problem is to apply the least-squares method, that is to solve $\mathbf{A}^T\mathbf{Ax} = \mathbf{A}^T\mathbf{b}$.

The most time-consuming step in solving such problems is the step to obtain $\mathbf{A}^T\mathbf{A}$ and $\mathbf{A}^T\mathbf{b}$ from data. For a given data value u_{obs}, we compute its theoretical value $u_{theoretical}$ and $\partial u_{theoretical}/\partial v$ and evaluate their contributions to $\mathbf{A}^T\mathbf{A}$ and $\mathbf{A}^T\mathbf{b}$. We let each processor take care of each data value, compute $u_{theoretical}$ and $\partial u_{theoretical}/\partial v$, and calculate the contribution to $\mathbf{A}^T\mathbf{A}$ and $\mathbf{A}^T\mathbf{b}$. The increase in number of processors directly enhances the speed. After obtaining these two matrices, however, existing scalar machines are able to solve $\mathbf{A}^T\mathbf{Ax} = \mathbf{A}^T\mathbf{b}$ for reasonable problem sizes. But since most of our computation is spent in getting $\mathbf{A}^T\mathbf{A}$ and $\mathbf{A}^T\mathbf{b}$, a concurrent algorithm is quite useful for our problems.

MULTIPLE-TARGET TRACK INITIATION ON A HYPERCUBE

Introduction

Track initiation for a multiple-target scenario is one of the classic problems of automated surveillance systems. Given a general model for allowed trajectories and data from some sensor system, the number of targets is to be determined and estimates of the states of these targets are to be made. In it barest form, a central issue in multiple object tracking is the assignment problem:

> Given a collection of (nearby) candidate trajectories and a set of new data values, how should the measurements be assigned to specific tracks?

The practical realities of false alarms (detector hits not associated with real tracks) and missed detections provide further complications for this already difficult problem.

Surveys of various techniques for multiple-target tracking are given by Blackman[102] and Bar-Shalom.[103] Among the many schemes for track initiation, two extremes are "track splitting" and "optimal assignment." In the track-splitting approach, all plausible track ↔ data pairings are allowed, so that a single track can spawn a large number of candidates for closely spaced data. (The implicit assumption in this approach is that false tracks created early in the algorithm will die out as more data are gathered.) In the optimal-assignment approach, all feasible track ↔ hit associations subject to certain constraints are examined over some number of data frames, but only that specific assignment which minimizes a global cost function is retained. In either case (and for all intermediate algorithms, such as those of Barniv[104] and Washburn[105]), the computational requirements of multiple-target track initiation can be enormous.

We examine the question of track initiation for a typical surveillance application: detection of nearly simultaneous multiple-missile launches using infrared measurements from a staring satellite in geosynchronous orbit. The next section provides a brief description of the target trajectories and the Kalman filter formalism that is used to estimate the state of a single target. Further details of these issues are provided in Gottschalk.[50,51] A sequential track-splitting solution for the track-initiation problem is then developed in the subsequent section.

The central part of this work concerns implementation of the track-initiation algorithm on a concurrent computer. Issues in the concurrent decomposition are discussed and a summary of the concurrent algorithm is given. The concurrent calculation has been done on the Caltech Campus/JPL Mark II and Mark III hypercubes. Various aspects of concurrent versus sequential performance on the Mark II are presented.

Preliminaries: Single Target Tracking

In an inertial frame, the acceleration vector for a boosting rocket may be written as

$$\mathbf{a}(t) = \frac{-g}{r^3}\mathbf{r}(t) + \mathbf{a}_b(t) \tag{11-17}$$

where the first term is simply gravity and the second term is a time-dependent thrust term. For purposes of this work, this thrust component is taken from the model presented by Latimer[106] with variations of order 10 percent in the model parameters used to generate random threats.

Measurements of booster positions are assumed to be provided by a satellite in geosynchronous orbit, so that a number of additional complications such as the Earth's rotation should, in principle, be included. However, as is demonstrated in Gottschalk,[51] these effects are inconsequential for the track-initiation problem. Instead, measurements will be given by simple projections of the booster trajectory onto a uniform pixel array in the inertial launch frame. To be definite, the projections measure the "z" and "x" components of the position vector, with the z axis normal to the Earth at the launch site. Measurements are assumed to be made at fixed time intervals Δt (typically 5 sec).

Tracking of boosters with variable acceleration characteristics is done using a simple, linear Kalman filter formalism (see, e.g. Gelb[107]). Conceptually, this is a nine-state filter model, with position, velocity, and acceleration in each of three Cartesian projections as independent degrees of freedom. However, with the inertial-frame simplifications of the preceding paragraph, the model reduces to three disjoint three-state models, each describing motion in a single dimension.

For the one-dimensional tracking problem, the state vector is simply

$$\mathbf{x}(t) \equiv [x(t), n(t), a(t)]^{\mathrm{T}} \tag{11-18}$$

and the system model is given by the canonical form

$$\mathbf{x}(t + \Delta t) = \Phi[\Delta t]\mathbf{x}(t) + \mathbf{u}(t) \tag{11-19}$$

where $\mathbf{u}$ is a random perturbation and Φ is the transition matrix for the deterministic part of state evolution. It is shown in Gottschalk[51] that a constant acceleration approximation,

$$\Phi[\Delta t] \equiv \begin{bmatrix} 1 & \Delta t & \Delta t^2/2 \\ 0 & 1 & \Delta t \\ 0 & 0 & 1 \end{bmatrix} \tag{11-20}$$

is adequate for tracking the slowly accelerating booster. The observation of the state at time t is simply the measurement of position corrupted by noise

$$z = H\mathbf{x}(t) + v \tag{11-21}$$

where

$$H \equiv [1 \quad 0 \quad 0] \tag{11-22}$$

is the projection matrix.

To use the standard Kalman filter formalism, the dynamic covariance

$$Q \equiv E[\mathbf{u} \quad \mathbf{u}^T] \tag{11-23}$$

and the measurement covariance

$$R \equiv E[v^2] \tag{11-24}$$

must be specified. This last term is estimated by

$$R = f_M \frac{\Delta l^2}{12} \tag{11-25}$$

where Δl is the cell width of the pixel array (typically 0.5 km) and $f_M \approx 2$. The dynamic covariance matrix is parameterized as

$$Q = \text{diag}[Q_x, Q_v, Q_a] \tag{11-26}$$

In Gottschalk,[51] values for these parameters were determined by optimization of tracking performance for extremely small detection cell sizes (e.g. $\Delta l \approx 1$ m). As is shown,[51] the simple filter model of Eqns. (11-18) to (11-26) is quite adequate in the sense that the innovations

$$y(t_{k+1}) \equiv z(t_{k+1}) - Hx[k + 1 \mid k] \tag{11-27}$$

are dominated by measurement errors for sensor cell sizes $\Delta l > 0.5$ km. (In Eqn. (11-27), $x[k + 1 \mid k]$ represents the predicted state of the system at time $t_k + 1$, given measurements through time t_k.)

Sequential Multiple-Target Tracking

Given an adequate model for following a single trajectory, the major problem of multiple-target tracking becomes one of assigning new measurements as possible

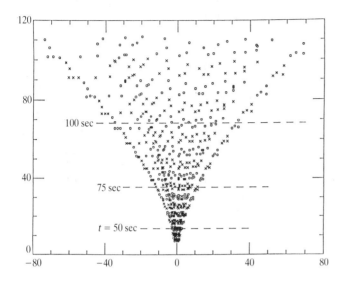

Figure 11-12. Pixel hits for 40-target example.

extensions of existing tracks. The complexity of this assignment problem can be appreciated by considering the time-integrated pattern of pixel hits for a typical multiple-target threat illustrated in Figure 11-12. The data points in this plot represent pixel hits for a simulated 40-booster launch at $\Delta t = 5$ sec sighting intervals, with alternating symbols used for successive sightings. The individual launch sites are scattered with a $2\,km \times 2\,km$ window, and launch times are generated at random within a 2 sec window beginning at $t = 0$. The first sightings in Figure 11-12 are recorded for $t = 40$ sec and the last sightings are at $t = 120$ sec. To help clarify the nature of target motion, the dashed lines in Figure 11-12 show the mean vertical positions of detector hits at $t = 50$, 75, and 100 sec.

From examinations of the detector hits for various simulated threats, it is clear that objects do not move much until about 30 sec after launch. A trivial track file initialization for Figure 11-12 is done using two consecutive data sets beginning at 30 sec. Each observation in the second sighting initiates a track, with booster position estimates given by the coordinates of the observation. The horizontal velocity of each track is initially set to zero and the vertical velocity is given by the average value determined from the first two frames of data. The initial covariance matrix for the Kalman filter is to set to a (large) scalar multiple of the identity matrix.

Subsequent data sets are used to extend and/or split tracks in a straightforward manner. Specifically, an individual measurement $z_j(k + 1)$ at time $t_k + 1$ extends an existing track x_l if

$$|y_{j,\,l}| \equiv |z_j - Hx_1[k + 1 \mid k]| \le d_{cut} \qquad (11\text{-}28)$$

where d_{cut} is an association cutoff parameter (typical values are 1.5–2.5 km).

Every track ↔ hit pairing that satisfies Eqn. (11-28) is used to define a new track for the next time-frame. The philosophy behind this all-neighbors approach is quite simple. Without imposing additional constraints on the allowed behavior of real trajectories, the actual nature of the threat cannot be determined from only a few frames of data. The gating prescription of Eqn. (11-28) is loose enough to ensure that nearly all true tracks will be accepted—at the expense of a very large number of false tracks at early times.

In fact, without some sort of track-pruning prescription, the number of candidate tracks accepted by the gating scheme of Eqn. (11-28) rapidly grows out of control, particularly for the (frequent) case of nearby real tracks. This problem is dealt with by introducing an additional algorithm to delete any new tracks that are "equivalent" to tracks already in the data file. Two tracks x_l and x_j formed in the track ↔ hit association algorithms are said to be equivalent if

$$|Hx_j[k \mid k] - Hx_l[k \mid k]| \le d_{\text{merge}} \qquad (11\text{-}29)$$

and

$$|Hx_j[k + l \mid k] - Hx_l[k + l \mid k]| \le d_{\text{merge}} \qquad (11\text{-}30)$$

where d_{merge} is a cutoff. That is, present and predicted measurements for equivalent tracks agree within the specified resolution. If two tracks are equivalent, only one is kept in the track file.

The track extension/compression scheme defined by Eqn. (11-30) is easily implemented in a straightforward, recursive manner. All unique track extensions of the track data file prior to time step t_k are formed using data received at time t_k, with the new track file formed in this manner serving as input for data at the next time step. Note that only the *present* track file need be stored (fading memory filter).

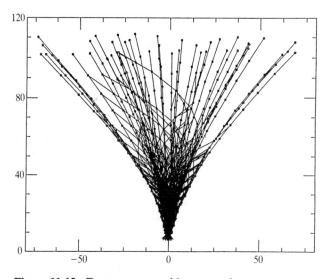

Figure 11-13. Forty-target tracking example.

Figure 11-13 illustrates typical track-initiation results for this sequential, all-neighbors algorithm. The data values for this example are as shown in Figure 11-12. In addition, line segments have been drawn for each track extension.

$$x_l[k \mid k] \rightarrow x_{j,\,l}[k+1 \mid k+1] \tag{11-31}$$

satisfying Eqns. (11-28) to (11-30). The results shown in Figure 11-13 are calculated for $d_{\mathrm{cut}} = 1.8\,\mathrm{km}$ and $d_{\mathrm{merge}} = 0.8\,\mathrm{km}$. For the first few scans after initialization, the data points in Figure 11-12 are sufficiently close together that very many track $\leftrightarrow$ hit associations satisfy Eqn. (11-28), leading to very large candidate track files (e.g., Fig. 11-13 has 409 candidate tracks after processing data at $t = 65\,\mathrm{sec}$). This initial combinatoric confusion begins to die at about $t = 80–90\,\mathrm{sec}$, and the number of plausible tracks decreases rapidly. At the last time-frame, the number of candidate tracks is 45. The results in Figure 11-13 also clearly show some of the spurious candidate tracks that are temporarily accepted by the loose gating in Eqn. (11-28).

Concurrent Multiple-Target Tracking

Two general features of the sequential multiple-target tracking example of the preceding section are particularly significant in decomposing the problem for concurrent computation.

1. At intermediate times, the track file can have a very large number of potential tracks.
2. At early times, when the actual tracks are close together, most tracks can be paired with most data according to Eqn. (11-28).

This suggests a decomposition in which the candidate track file at each time step is distributed across the cube, with each node receiving the full data set (pixel hits) at each time step. The track $\leftrightarrow$ hit association is an inherently parallel task that is ideally suited for this decomposition. The only difficulty in generalizing the sequential code involves the compression of duplicate tracks according to Eqns. (11-29) and (11-30). While each node can trivially compress its own local track file, the compression of identical tracks that are not in the same node would seem to require nontrivial node-to-node communications and comparisons.

To solve the global track-compression problem, it is first useful to make two simple observations.

1. Track compression need not be complete. The point of track elimination according to Eqns. (11-29) and (11-30) is simply to prevent "combinatoric explosions" of the track file. A few duplicate entries cause no real problem.
2. Only pairs of tracks that are physically nearby in the coordinate system of Figures 11-12 and 11-13 are candidates for compression.

These remarks suggest that the compression problem in the concurrent implementation can be solved by expanding the problem to include the extra task of *sorting* candidate tracks across the cube. A convenient sorting key for this purpose is the *horizontal* (x) coordinate of Figures 11-12 and 11-13. If locally extended/compressed tracks from the nodes are sorted and redistributed after each new set of data is processed, then identical tracks from different nodes at the end of one step in the algorithm are likely to end up in the same node at the start of the next step. That is, the compression of identical tracks from different nodes is simply deferred for one time step.

The concurrent track initialization algorithm thus has the following simple, recursive form.

1. At the beginning of a time step, each node has its own local track file, either from track initialization or from the output of the previous time step.
2. Each node receives the complete pixel data set and performs (local) track extensions and compressions as in the sequential algorithm.
3. The local track files are then sorted and redistributed across the cube.

As is discussed in more detail below, it is trivial to arrange the cube-wide communications of step (3) in such a manner that the number of tracks per node is roughly constant at the end of the redistribution. That is, the algorithm naturally incorporates simple load balancing.

The global sorting of track files is done using a simple generalization of the algorithm presented by Felten.[52] The 2^d nodes of a d-dimensional hypercube are first mapped onto a one-dimensional ring topology using the standard CrOS III algorithms.[1] Global sorting across the cube is done with respect to the node ordering implied by this mapping. The sorting procedure involves two basic elements: (1) local sorting of lists within a single node using standard algorithms,[108] and (2) merging of the sorted lists for pairs of nodes connected by a communications channel. The merging algorithm is straightforward. The two ends of a communication channel are designated "high" and "low" according to the ordering implied by the ring mapping. The high end sends a copy of the lowest elements of its sorted list and receives a copy of the highest elements from the low end, inserting these elements into its own list as necessary. An initial loop of merges on all hypercube channels is done to create a roughly sorted configuration, and successive left–right merges along the ring decomposition are then repeated until the sorting has been completed.

The actual data structures in the track file are somewhat lengthy and these elements are *not* swapped back and forth during the sorting process. Rather, the structures involved in sorting consist of the sorting key (horizontal position) of a track and two integer pointers to the node and location within the node of the actual track structure. Redistribution of the track structures according to the outcome of the sorting exercise consists of three parts.

1. Determination of destinations ("tickets") for the individual items in the sorted list
2. Communication of the ticket for a track to the node which contains that track
3. Redistribution of the actual tracks according to the tickets

The first step in trivial. A simple communication loop is performed to transmit the number of tracks in each node to all other nodes. Given this global portrait of the cube contents, each node can calculate destination nodes for its subset of the globally sorted list, with destinations chosen so that the new number of tracks per node is approximately constant (load balancing).

The cube-wide communications in steps (2) and (3) are done using the *crystal_router* algorithm.[109] Given a list of data items within a node and new destinations for these items, the *crystal_router* provides an optimal scheme for transmitting the data "from here to there." Briefly, a loop is performed on the $N_{chan} = d$ communications channels of a d-node hypercube and, for each channel, a loop is made over the data elements within each node. Let l indicate the present channel of the communications loop. If the lth bit of the destination processor (ticket) agrees with the lth bit of the present node, the data remains in that node (i.e., the data is already in the correct half of the cube with respect to the lth channel). If the present and intended locations of the data item disagree in the lth bit, the data item is transmitted out along the channel. At the end of the loop on communication channels, a given item is in the correct half of the cube with respect to all communications channels—meaning that it has arrived at its proper destination.

The two-fold use of the *crystal_router* in this work was, in fact, the first practical application of this communication scheme by the Caltech Concurrent Computation Program.

Evaluations of Concurrent Performance

The concurrent algorithm of the previous section has been implemented on the Caltech/JPL Mark II and Mark III hypercubes. This section contains some simple investigations of performance on the Mark II. All results in this section are for the specific data-set shown previously in Figures 11–12 and 11-13. (The rather low value of 40 targets in this example was selected so that the entire sequential program could be run on a single node of the Mark II, thus allowing meaningful timing comparisons.)

Total track file sizes and cumulative CPU times for the sequential and concurrent calculations are shown in Figure 11-14. For the first few data sets after initialization, the hypercube track files are seen to be substantially larger than those for the sequential problem. For example, at $t = 55$ sec,

$$N_{tracks} = 310 \; (sequential) \tag{11-32}$$

$$N_{tracks} = 415 \; (4\text{-}node \; hypercube) \tag{11-33}$$

$$N_{tracks} = 1375 \; (32\text{-}node \; hypercube) \tag{11-34}$$

This initial duplication of tracks in the concurrent program is as expected from the discussion in the previous section. At early times, the tracks and data in Figures 11-12 and 11-13 are sufficiently tightly bunched that duplicate tracks in separate nodes occur rather frequently. From the timing results in Figure 11-14, it is seen that the four-node hypercube program is indeed almost 4 times faster than

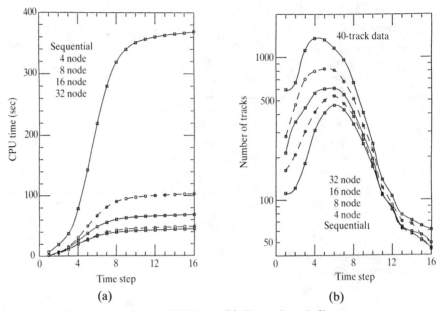

Figure 11-14. (a) Cumulative CPU time. (b) Sizes of track files.

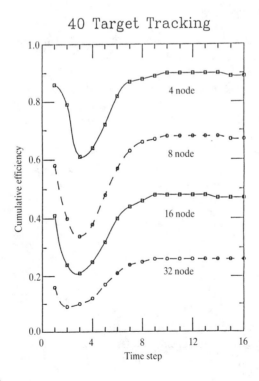

Figure 11-15. Forty-target tracking.

the sequential algorithm, while the increase in cube size from 16 nodes to 32 nodes results in essentially no additional decrease of total execution time. This last result is not particularly surprising, as one would expect good performance only if the total number of tracks is rather larger than the number of nodes in the hypercube.

A canonical measure of hypercube efficiency is given by the ratio

$$\varepsilon \equiv \frac{t[sequential]}{N \times t[N\text{-}node\ concurrent]} \tag{11-35}$$

The numerator in Eqn. (11-35) is the total CPU time for the sequential calculation and the denominator is the execution time on a hypercube, scaled by the number of nodes. Efficiency results for 4-, 8-, 16-, and 32-node Mark II concurrent calculations are shown in Figure 11-15. The rather pronounced dips in all of these curves are again simple results of track duplications at early times in the processing (the hypercube programs *indeed* do more work). Provided that the number of true tracks is significantly larger than the number of nodes in the hypercube (e.g., the 4-node calculation), the efficiency of the hypercube implementation is seen to be rather good.

It is in fact instructive to examine the origins of inefficiencies in the hypercube program in more detail. With reference to the definition of efficiency in Eqn. (11-35), there are two obvious contributions to $\varepsilon > 1$.

1. Sorting and redistribution are entirely "overheads" in that the sequential calculation does not require these tasks.
2. The concurrent calculation can have internal load imbalances in that all nodes must wait for the slowest node to complete its track extensions before sorting and redistribution can begin.

Figure 11-16 presents results for these two sources of inefficiencies for 4-, 8-, 16-, and 32-node Mark II configurations.

The top half of Figure 11-16 shows the *cumulative* fractions of hypercube CPU time "wasted" in the sorting and distribution aspects of the concurrent calculation. In association with these communications costs, it is useful to define a communications efficiency,

$$\varepsilon_{comm} \equiv 1 - \frac{t_{sort/comm}}{t_{tot}} \tag{11-36}$$

so that, by the end of the calculations,

$$\varepsilon_{comm}[4\text{-}node] \approx 0.90 \tag{11-37}$$

with rather smaller communications efficiencies for higher-dimensional hypercubes. It is worth noting that the amount of CPU time spent in sorting and redistribution is almost stable as the number of nodes is increased (e.g., $t_{comm} \approx 12$ sec for 4 nodes and $t_{comm} \approx 12.5$ sec for 16 nodes). The decrease in ε_{comm} for increasing hypercube dimension instead reflects the *decrease* in the track-extension CPU times as this work is distributed among more and more nodes.

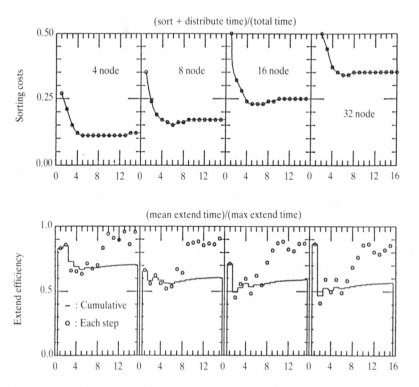

Figure 11-16. Forty-target hypercube tracking.

Although the track files are approximately balanced at the start of each step in the concurrent algorithm, the actual time spent in extending and compressing track files can vary substantially from node to node (e.g., five well-spaced tracks would require five passes through the gating and Kalman filter algorithm, while five highly clustered tracks could generate 25 such track extensions). A simple measure of this particular inefficiency is given by the ratio

$$\varepsilon_{\text{load}} \equiv \frac{\text{mean[extend/compress time]}}{\text{max[extend/compress time]}} \tag{11-38}$$

where the maximum and average are evaluated over all nodes in the hypercube. The numerator in Eqn. (11-38) thus measures the time that would be spent in a perfectly balanced track extension, while the slowest node's time (the de-nominator in Eqn. (11-38)) determines the actual CPU time spent in the hypercube program. Cumulative and per-time-step results for the efficiencies in Eqn. (11-38) are shown in the bottom half of Figure 11-16.

Combining results from Figures 11-15 and 11-16 leads to the amusing conclusion that

$$\varepsilon_{\text{total}}[4\text{-}node] > \varepsilon_{\text{comm}}[4\text{-}node] \times \varepsilon_{\text{load}}[4\text{-}node] \tag{11-39}$$

That is, the net efficiency of the 4-node calculation is significantly better than that expected from examinations of the various contributions. After some thought, this pleasant result is recognized as simply a new occurrence of a phenomenon noted in some previous hypercube applications.[1] Consider the specific task of removing duplicate tracks from a list of N candidates. This nominally requires $O(N^2)$ evaluations of Eqns. (11-29) and (11-30). In the sequential algorithm, all possible comparisons are made, while the d-dimensional hypercube examines only smaller, local sublists for the comparisons. That is,

$$N_{\text{compare}}[sequential] \gg N_{\text{compare}}[concurrent] \qquad (11\text{-}40)$$

$$n^2 \gg d \times \left(\frac{N}{d}\right)^2 \qquad (11\text{-}41)$$

where the second line is a crude but instructive estimate. The additional algorithm/decomposition efficiency implied by Eqns. (11-40) and (11-41) is the origin of the result in Eqn. (11-39). Indeed, if a sufficiently large tracking problem were run on the cube (e.g., 100 tracks on a four-node hypercube), one would expect $\varepsilon_{\text{Total}} > 1$.

Concluding Remarks

This work has demonstrated that a track-splitting approach to multiple-target track initiation can be successfully implemented on a hypercube. The additional costs of sorting and communications in the concurrent algorithm are essentially compensated by the net algorithmic efficiency of Eqns. (11-40) and (11-41). The overall concurrent efficiency of Eqn. (11-35) is quite large, *provided* that the total number of targets in the tracking example is significantly larger than the number of nodes.

Most of the obvious avenues for improvement in the track-initiation procedure of this work require improvements in the sequential algorithm. For example, the constant-acceleration linear Kalman filter model of Eqns. (11-18) to (11-21) should be replaced by a nonlinear extended filter that more accurately describes the dynamics of accelerating boosters. Given this better model, the covariance information of the filter could be used to decrease the association gate size in Eqn. (11-28) as more and more measurements are associated with a track. While this precision tracking would allow earlier rejection of spurious tracks in Figure 11-13, the net cost would be a significant increase in the CPU time of the filter/extend phase of the algorithm. However, this increased work load for the sequential algorithm implies even greater efficiencies for the concurrent implementation (the sorting costs *and* load imbalances in Fig. 11-16 would both decrease). As the underlying sequential tracking formalism is made more realistic, the advantages of the concurrent computation algorithms can only increase.

ADVANCES IN CONCURRENT COMPUTATION FOR MACHINE INTELLIGENCE AND ROBOTICS

Introduction

Intelligent robots operating in unstructured, and perhaps hostile, environments will require enormous onboard computing power and flexibility. These requirements are driven by the need to solve repeatedly a variety of highly complex mathematical problems such as online planning; sensor fusion to keep track of the positions, courses and identities of all "objects" and potential threats in a constantly changing world model; navigation; dynamics and coordinated control of one or more effectors. A fundamental consideration is the system's capability to achieve operational responses in hard real-time, and in a semiautonomous decision environment characterized by severe constraints on size, weight, and power consumption.

In support of these objectives, a new generation of message-passing concurrent computers with hypercube architecture, designed from the ground up for optimal implementation in VLSI, has recently been investigated.[110,111] The hypercube hardware, developed by NCUBE Corporation, contained 64 processors in our initial implementation. The number of processors that can currently be accommodated within a single enclosure of approximately $0.5 \, m^3$ is 1024, each designed to operate at speeds comparable to that of a VAX 11/780. This hypercube is shown in Figure 11-4.

Several architectural characterizations make the hypercube attractive for robotics and machine intelligence uses. The first advantage is communication time between nodes, where it offers an excellent tradeoff with respect to wiring complexity (design cost). Second, the hypercube is the perfect network for one of the most important of all computational algorithms, the fast Fourier transform (FFT), which is used in machine intelligence applications such as sensor signal processing. Third, the hypercube is a superset of most of the other candidate networks. For example, a grid of any dimension can be mapped onto a hypercube by "ignoring" an appropriate set of interconnections. Fourth, the hypercube is the most densely connected network that is also scaleable to thousands of processors. For example, in order to double the number of processors in a system, it is only necessary to add one communication channel to each node. Finally, a hypercube looks topologically identical from the point of view of each node: there are no corner versus edge, or root versus leaf nodes, as there are in regular grids or trees. This symmetry is particularly attractive for simplifying the dynamic reconfiguration of the system.

While VLSI-based computers, such as the NCUBE hypercube, possess great advantages in power, flexibility, and compactness, new methodologies must be developed to use them as effectively as possible, in meeting the special requirements of intelligent robotics concerned with time-critical applications. The aim of this section is to provide an overview of our initial experiences in this area, focusing on multiprocessor load-balance, mobile robotics, and neural networks.

Scheduling and Load Balancing

Load-balancing algorithms[112,113] are required for dealing explicitly with the allocation of resources in concurrent computation ensembles. The goal is to minimize the overall execution time by evenly distributing the task loads across the system, while minimizing the interprocessor communication requirements inherent to message-passing algorithms. The difficulty in solving this problem lies in the conflict of constraints over a configuration space that grows exponentially with the number of tasks. In particular, the goal of minimizing interprocessor communication, to avoid saturation effects that degrade performance, requires that tasks be "clustered" on few, adjacent processor nodes; on the other hand, to best utilize the resources of all the processors requires that tasks be spread out over all nodes.

The load-balancing problem is closely related to multiprocessor scheduling, a subject that has been studied extensively[114] over the past twenty years and for which excellent reviews can be found in the literature.[115] Major difficulties arise when the number of tasks required by a particular algorithm exceeds the number of available processors, and/or when the interconnection topology of the task graph, as obtained from the precedence constraints, differs from the interconnection topology of the computation ensemble.[111] Optimal schedules are in general extremely difficult, if not impossible to obtain, since for an arbitrary number of processors, unequal task execution times and nontrivial precedence constraints, the problem is known to be NP-complete.[116]

THE ROSES SCHEDULER

To address the scheduling problem, we have developed over the last two years a prototype system named ROSES.[111,117,118] We assume that one is given a set of tasks $\{e \mid e = 1, \ldots, E\}$, each task having an expected time-length $L(e)$. There are specified precedence constraints among the tasks. A goal exists. To reach that goal, the entire set of tasks must be completed, in any sequence compatible with the precedence constraints. The tasks are to be performed on a set of identical concurrent processors $\{p \mid p = 1, \ldots, P\}$. Each processor can handle only one task at a time; thus, preemption is not allowed. The sooner the goal is reached, the better—that is, the objective is to determine an optimum or near-optimum schedule.

The problem is NP-complete, since the number of precedence-satisfying schedules to be considered, in a complete search, generally grows faster than polynomially with such complexity indicators as the number of tasks. Despite the NP-completeness, ROSES quickly achieves near-optimum solutions. It does this by combining heuristic techniques for handling time complexity, with special instances of abstract data structures to handle space complexity. In other words, ROSES uses powerful heuristic techniques for optimizing the sequences in which to consider possible schedules, and uses carefully chosen abstract data structures to store and access the information needed to construct and evaluate new schedules efficiently. The needed information includes, for example, the original constraints of the problem, the choices available to each vertex of the search tree, the current tasks-on-processors status in a schedule being constructed and evaluated, and the knowledge (about past-considered schedules) that ROSES accumulates as it investigates more and more alternatives.

Currently, ROSES *assumes* a *simple* nonpreemptive scheduling approach. Once a task is assigned to a processor, it is processed there without interruption until finished. Whenever there is a processor free to be assigned a task, an individual assignment is made, either for that processor to start a particular new task, or for that processor to idle until it is possible (and favorable) for it to start a new task.

For "bookkeeping" purposes, each successive assignment is given an ordinal number called a base-point index. That index correlates an entire set of descriptors, including (among other things) the time of assignment, the processor to be assigned, and pointers indicating which tasks are "available" (have their precedence constraints satisfied) at the time of assignment. The base point corresponds to a vertex of the search tree. For a not-yet-completed schedule having fixed assignments up to (but not including) a given base point, one may vary the schedule from that point onward by changing the task assignment to the processor associated with that base point.

At each base point, all tasks ready to be assigned (because their precedence requisites are satisfied) constitute a "set of alternatives" (or A-set). The A-set is constructed and updated in such a way as to continually satisfy the precedence constraints. Choosing a task from an A-set is guided by heuristics—"soft evidence" that a particular choice is favorable—combined with branch- and bound-type considerations. At each base point, ROSES calculates several strict lower bounds on the further time needed to complete all tasks; and if that time is "uninteresting" compared to the best solution time previously found by ROSES, then the search backtracks to an earlier base-point vertex.

ROSES searches for a solution in an enhanced depth first way that combines graph-theoretic "impasse detection" techniques (e.g., time bounds), powerful heuristics, and abstract data structures. Some simple examples of time-bound considerations, of heuristics, and of the implementing data structures, are given below.

Time-bound considerations can be associated with two overall lower limits.

T_0, the minimum time-to-goal calculated by assuming that there are no precedence constraints, but that the number of processors remains fixed at P. This limit is just the sum of all task-lengths, divided by the number of processors.

T_∞, the minimum time-to-goal calculated by assuming that the precedence constraints do apply, but that the number of processors is infinite. T_∞ is just the critical length for *any* precedence-chain of tasks in the problem.

A concept related to T_∞, and used in the heuristics as well as in the branch-and-bound considerations, is the critical path length to goal, $f(e)$, starting with task e. Specifically, $f(e)$ denotes the length of the longest precedence-chain starting with task e. Its use in one of ROSES' key heuristics is as follows. At every base-point, the most-favored task to be assigned, of all those in the A-set, is the task with largest $f(e)$ value. Schedules that involve the most-favored choice are investigated first; schedules involving less-favored choices are investigated later. Furthermore, this heuristic is extended in a way that causes ROSES to completely exclude consideration of some irrelevant schedules. This exclusion can be explained in terms of a "delay" function, Δ. Suppose that a given partially-constructed schedule has a base-point index b at which task e was the most favored of all available tasks; and suppose that instead of assigning task e at b, the schedule does not assign it until a later base-point, $b + \delta$. Then $\Delta(e) = \delta$ is the "delay function" for this task and schedule. ROSES excludes from consideration all schedules with delay functions $\Delta(e)$ greater than δ_M, where δ_M is an input parameter. Thus, the condition $\Delta(e) > \delta_M$ is a cause for backtracking.

Another important time-bound consideration leads to backtracking. Suppose that, at a given base point, the only available task has an $f(e)$ such that the already expended time, when added to $f(e)$, exceeds the total start-to-finish time of a completed schedule (solution) previously found by ROSES. Then the unfinished schedule deserves no further investigation; backtracking is called for.

In the case of an idling choice, it may be that the minimum total idling time implied for all processors (as calculated with the help of the data structures) is such as to bring the lower limit of the schedule's completion time to a value above that of an earlier-found solution. In that case, ROSES abandons consideration of the current incomplete schedule, and backtracks so as to modify the schedule starting from an earlier vertex (base point).

One example of a ROSES data structure is the double linked list describing the task graph, that is, the tasks and their precedence constraints. Each task is described in terms of indices labeling the vertices of the graph. Note that the task-graph vertices imply AND gates, in contrast to the search-tree vertices, which are OR vertices. The data structure describing tasks consists of a series of quartets. Each quartet consists of (a) the vertex-index corresponding to the task's tail (its start), (b) the vertex-index corresponding to the task's head (its end), (c) a pointer to the previous quartet with same tail but different head (fan-out list), and (d) a pointer to the previous quarter with same head but different tail (fan-in list). This structure makes it easy to service requests such as: find the set of all tasks with head-vertex h. Details of ROSES can be found elsewhere.[111,118]

SIMULATED ANNEALING

Recent years have seen a major advance in the area of combinatorial optimization. Based on an analogy with the behavior of condensed matter at low temperatures, a new optimization methodology (referred to as "simulated annealing") has been proposed[119] that uses techniques suggested by statistical mechanics to find global optima of systems with large numbers of degrees of freedom. Simulated annealing can best be understood in terms of discrete-time Markov chains with a finite state space,[120] since the configuration space C underlying combinatorial optimization problems is in general a countable and finite set. For an irreducible, aperiodic, and recurrent Markov chain with stationary k-step transition probabilities $P_k^{i \to j}$ between configurations i and j, it is known that a stationary probability distribution Π_j exists. It is defined as the limit

$$\Pi_j = \lim_{k \to \infty} P_k^{i \to j}, \quad i, j \in C$$

The basic idea is then to construct a function $\Pi(\theta)$ defined on C which, in the limit $\theta \to 0$, will differ from zero only for those configurations that are the global minima. One must thereafter determine the appropriate conditions that the configuration-generation function and the configuration acceptance criterion (e.g., the Metropolis criterion; see, for example, Barhen[121]) must satisfy (i.e., recurrence, aperiodicity, irreducibility) to guarantee that $\Pi(\theta)$ is indeed the stationary probability distribution of the Markov chain induced by the simulated annealing. From such a construction, it is then easy to demonstrate that the annealing algorithm will generate asymptotically, and with probability 1, a global solution of the combinatorial optimization problem.

Simulated annealing is an attractive alternative for static load balancing of hypercube multiprocessors. A simple illustrative example is presented below. A more sophisticated treatment, based on a neural network formalism, has also been published recently.[121] Consider a d-dimensional hypercube with $N_H = 2^d$ identical nodes indexed by n; consider furthermore a set of communicating processes indexed by i and having cardinality N_T. Let n_i denote the processor on which task i is currently located. To induce processes to use efficiently all system resources, we formalize the static load-balance concepts as follows.

We assume that each node of the homogeneous ensemble has K resource capacities [e.g., CPU in cycles/sec; communication channels in bytes/sec] R_k, with $k = 1, \ldots, K$. Let r_{ik} represent the requirement of task i for resource k. The average load per node for resource k is then simply

$$\Lambda_k = \frac{1}{N_H R_k} \sum_i r_{ik} \tag{11-42}$$

The actual load of node n is

$$\lambda_{nk} = \frac{1}{R_k} \sum_i r_{ik} \, \delta_{nn_i} \tag{11-43}$$

where δ denotes the Kronecker symbol. The load balance constraints can then be expressed as

$$|\lambda_{nk} - \Lambda_k| \leq \varepsilon_{nk} \tag{11-44}$$

where ε_{nk} are real positive constants that characterize the system's throughput requirements. Hence, the contribution to the objective function is given by

$$E_\lambda = \frac{w_\lambda}{2} \sum_n \sum_k \left[\sum_i x_{ik} \, \delta_{nn_i} - \bar{x}_k \right]^2 \Delta_{nk} \tag{11-45}$$

where x_{ik} and $\bar{x}_k$ refer to r_{ik}/R_k and to $(\sum_i x_{ik})/N_H$, respectively, and where Δ_{nk} is an appropriate step function.

The contribution to the objective function from message passing can be expressed as

$$E_\mu = \frac{w_\mu}{2} \sum_n \frac{1}{b_n} \sum_i \sum_{j \neq i} D^{j \to i} \sum_{m \neq n} H_{nm} \, \delta_{nn_i} \, \delta_{mm_j} \qquad (11\text{-}46)$$

where b_n refers to the effective bandwidth of link n, $D^{j \to i}$ denotes the total length of messages between processes j and i, and H represents the Hamming distance matrix on the hypercube. To account for fixed overheads at each node during the computation, we must add the following term:

$$E_\psi = \frac{w_\psi}{2} \sum_n (\rho R_n + \sigma S_n + \tau T_N) \qquad (11\text{-}47)$$

In Eqn. (11-47), R_n, S_n, and T_n denote, respectively, the number of messages received, sent, and in transit at node n, and ρ, σ, and τ correspond to overheads per message measured on the actual hypercube.

Precedence constraints are also included in the objective function via the expression

$$E_\pi = \frac{w_\pi}{2} \sum_i \sum_{j \neq i} \sum_n \sum_m \pi_{ij}(n, m) \, \delta_{nn_i} \, \delta_{mm_j} \qquad (11\text{-}48)$$

The function $\pi_{ij}(n, m)$ in Eqn. (11-48) includes not only the "logical" precedence constraints requirements, but also the temporal effects induced by spatial distribution and message-propagation delays.

The solution of the static load-balancing problem corresponds to the minimization of the function

$$E_H = E_\lambda + E_\mu + E_\psi + E_\pi \qquad (11\text{-}49)$$

To illustrate these issues, we now address some of the practical considerations related to the scheduling and load-balancing of robot-related algorithms on a concurrent computer. To fix the ideas, we consider in the following the solution of the inverse dynamics equations of a manipulator arm. This problem was chosen because it is relatively "simple," while exhibiting the nonlocal communication and structural irregularity characteristics of interest.

EXAMPLE: NEWTON–EULER INVERSE DYNAMICS

Several state-of-the-art formalisms are currently available to efficiently solve the inverse dynamics problem of serial link manipulator. The aim is to calculate the forces or torques based on known motion. In the Newton–Euler formalism the equations for each link are written in link-fixed coordinate systems in order to simplify the calculation of the inertia tensors. A set of recurrence relations allow the angular velocities, angular accelerations, and linear accelerations at the center-of-mass of each link to be successively calculated from the base to the end effector. Net forces and torques acting on each link's center-of-mass are then obtained. Forces and torques acting at the joints are subsequently calculated in a recursion from the "hand" to the base. Joint actuator torques or forces are determined from a knowledge of the orientation of each joint. Detailed derivations can be found in Luh and Lin's seminal papers.[122,123]

For the sake of brevity, we include here (in Table 11-9) only our proposed partition of the equations of motion into a set of tasks, since it differs from Luh's. In the nomenclature for Table 11-8, all vectors are generally expressed in the ith coordinate system: $\mathbf{w}_i$ = angular velocity of link i; $\dot{\mathbf{w}}_i$ = angular acceleration of link i; $\ddot{\mathbf{p}}_i$ = linear acceleration of link i; $\mathbf{F}_i$ = net force acting on link i; $\mathbf{\Gamma}_i$ = net torque acting on link i about the center-of-the-mass; $\mathbf{p}_i^*$ = origin of the ith coordinate system with respect to the $(i-1)$th; $\mathbf{r}_i^*$ = position of center-of-mass of link i; $\mathbf{J}_i$ = inertia tensor about center-of-mass of link i; $\mathbf{A}_i^{i-1}$ = frame transformation matrix from $(i-1)$th to ith coordinate systems (denoted as $\mathbf{A}_i^-$ in the table); by analogy, $\mathbf{A}_i^+$ will denote the frame transformation $\mathbf{A}_i^{i+1}$; $\mathbf{f}_i$ = force exerted on link i by link $i-1$; $\mathbf{\gamma}_i$ = moment exerted by link $i-1$ on link i.

Typical initial conditions are $\mathbf{w}_0 = \dot{\mathbf{w}}_0 = 0$; $\mathbf{p}_0 = g\mathbf{z}_0$, thereby absorbing gravity into the initial acceleration to reflect the simplified form of the force balance equation

$$\mathbf{f}_i = \mathbf{F}_i + \mathbf{A}_i^+ \mathbf{f}_{i+1} \tag{11-50}$$

Initial conditions for the backward recursion are obtained from the specification of $\mathbf{f}_{N+1}$ and $\mathbf{\gamma}_{N+1}$, the external force and moment exerted on the hand. The joint actuator torques or forces are simply (omitting friction)

$$\mathbf{\tau}_i = \tilde{\mathbf{\gamma}}_i \mathbf{A}_i^- z_{i-1}$$

or

$$\phi = \tilde{\mathbf{f}}_i \mathbf{A}_i^- z_{i-1} \tag{11-51}$$

Table 11-9. Robot inverse dynamics computational tasks nomenclature (Newton–Euler formalism, six-link manipulator)

Task no.	Rotational link	Prismatic link
1–6[a]	$\mathbf{w}_i = \mathbf{A}_i^-(\mathbf{w}_{i-1} + \mathbf{z}_{i-1}\dot{\mathbf{q}}_i)$	$\mathbf{w}_i = \mathbf{A}_i^-\mathbf{w}_{i-1}$
7–12	$\mathbf{w}_i = \mathbf{A}_i^-(\dot{\mathbf{w}}_{i-1} + \mathbf{z}_{i-1}\ddot{\mathbf{q}}_i + \mathbf{w}_{i-1} \times \mathbf{z}_{i-1}\dot{\mathbf{q}}_i)$	$\dot{\mathbf{w}} = \mathbf{A}_i^-\dot{\mathbf{w}}_{i-1}$
13–18	$\mathbf{V}_i^{(1)} = \mathbf{w}_i \times (\mathbf{w}_i \times \mathbf{p}_i^*)$	$\mathbf{V}_i^{(1)} = \mathbf{w}_i \times (2\mathbf{A}_i^- \mathbf{z}_{i-1}\dot{\mathbf{q}}_i + \mathbf{w}_i \times \mathbf{p}_i^*)$
19–24	$\ddot{\mathbf{p}}_i = \mathbf{A}_i^-\ddot{\mathbf{p}}_{i-1} + \mathbf{w}_i \times \mathbf{p}_i^* + \mathbf{V}_i^{(1)}$	$\ddot{\mathbf{p}} = \mathbf{V}_i^{(1)} + \mathbf{A}_i^-(\ddot{\mathbf{p}}_{i-1} + \mathbf{z}_{i-1}\ddot{\mathbf{q}}_i) + \dot{\mathbf{w}}_i \times \mathbf{p}_i^*$
25–30	$\mathbf{V}_i^{(2)} = \mathbf{w}_i \times [\mathbf{w}_i \times \mathbf{r}_i^*]$	
30–36	$\mathbf{F}_i = m_i[\mathbf{V}_i^{(2)} + \dot{\mathbf{w}}_i \times \mathbf{r}_i^* + \ddot{\mathbf{p}}_i]$	
37–42	$\mathbf{\Gamma}_i = \mathbf{J}_i + \dot{\mathbf{w}}_i \times (\mathbf{J}_i\mathbf{w}_i)$	
43–48	$\mathbf{V}_i^{(3)} = \mathbf{\Gamma}_i = (\mathbf{p}_i^* + \mathbf{r}_i^*) \times \mathbf{F}_i$	
49–54[b]	$\mathbf{f}_i = \mathbf{F}_i + \mathbf{A}_i^+\mathbf{f}_{i+1}$	
55–60	$\mathbf{V}_i^{(4)} = \mathbf{p}_i^* \times (\mathbf{f}_i - \mathbf{F}_i)$	
60–66	$\mathbf{\gamma}_i = \mathbf{A}_i^+\mathbf{\gamma}_{i+1} + \mathbf{V}_i^{(3)} + \mathbf{V}_i^{(4)}$	

[a] $\dot{\mathbf{q}}_i$ and $\ddot{\mathbf{q}}_i$ are the first and second time derivations of the generalized coordinates.
[b] The joint index i runs from 1 to 6 for tasks 1 to 48, and from 6 to 1 for tasks 49 to 66.

Table 11-10. Processor load balance for the solution of the inverse dynamics equations of the Stanford Manipulator

Item			This work		Luh (1982)[123]
Processors	1	2	3^a	4^b	6
Load^c	1	0.96	0.95	0.61	0.37
Speed-up	1	1.96	1.96	3.22	2.56

^{a} We allocate an order-2 cube, but schedule tasks on three nodes only.

^{b} Asymptotic domain (critical length exceeded): using more than 4 processors for this simple example wastes resources.

^{c} Load factor for most-unbalanced node in system.

The processor utilization results, shown in Table 11-10, refer to the most unbalanced node and are given for two, three, and four processors. Table 11-10 shows that there is substantial improvement in performance over previously reported results.[122] This improvement is particularly significant, in light of the fact that NCUBE nodes are much more pwowerful (by at least one order of magnitude) than the processors used in the previous study,[123] which the load-balance results do not explicitly reflect. This combined effect should open the possibility for real-time control of flexible manipulators having many more than six degrees of freedom.

The fundamental role of task scheduling and load balancing in achieving good concurrent computation efficiencies for irregular robotics problems of the type discussed above cannot be overemphasized. Therefore, it is important to provide well-defined benchmarks against which the performance of available codes can be tested. As a first step in that direction, we have carried out a comparison between the recent results of Kasahara and Narita,[124] the original work of Luh and Lin,[123] ROSES, and simulated annealing (with and without message-passing overheads). To provide a fair basis for comparison, we have assumed that each processor has the same performance parameters as the ones used by Luh and Lin, and by Kasahara (40 μsec for a floating-point add, 50 μsec for a floating-point multiply, rather than the 2 μsec associated with the NCUBE processor design). Furthermore, instead of using task partition of Table 11-9 and the cost estimates for the general form of the equations,[125] we adopt the task-partition and "specialized" costs given by Luh and also used by Kasahara. The results of the comparison are summarized in Table 11-11 and in Figure 11-17. The importance of properly accounting for message-passing overheads is emphasized in Figure 11-18.

Mobile Robots

To provide a context for the subsequent discussion, we first describe the particular machine that is being developed as a testing ground for our research results: the Hostile Environment Robotic Machine Intelligence Experiment Series (HERMIES).[126] We then summarize our progress in the development of

Table 11-11. ROSES benchmark results—solution of the Newton–Euler inverse dynamics equations for the Stanford 6-DOF Manipulator using the parameters of Kasahara[124]

Number of processors	Luh (1982)[123] (msec)	Kasahara (1985)[124] (msec)	ROSES (determin.) (msec)	Simulated annealing[a] (msec)	Optimal schedule (msec)
1	24.80	24.83	24.80	24.83	24.80
2	—	12.42	12.43	12.41	12.40
3	—	8.43	8.49	—	8.43
4	—	6.59	6.67	6.63	6.38
5[b]	—	5.86	5.88	—	5.67
6	9.7	5.73	5.78	—	5.67
7	—	5.69	5.67	—	5.67
8	—	—	5.67	—	5.67

[a] No overheads.
[b] Beginning of asymptotic domain; optimal schedule on any processor would equal the critical path of the graph.

VERTEX, a virtual-time operating system for robotics applications of the hypercube.

THE HERMIES-II ROBOT

HERMIES is a self-powered mobile robot system comprising a wheel-driven chassis, dual manipulator arms, on-board distributed processors, and a directionally controlled sensor platform. The HERMIES-IIB model (see Fig. 11-19) is propelled by a dual set of independent wheels having a common axle alignment and driven by separate direct-current (dc) motors.

The on-board computer and electronic equipment are located in an

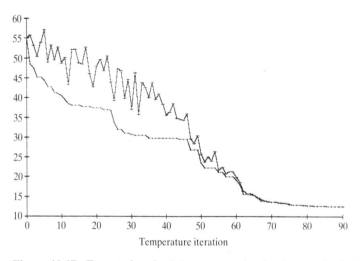

Figure 11-17. Expected and minimum energies for hypercube load balance performance via simulated annealing.

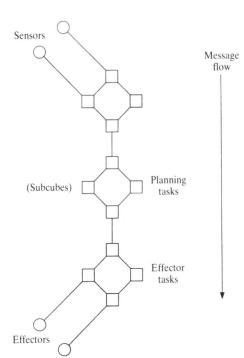

Sensors

Message
flow

(Subcubes)

Planning
tasks

Effector
tasks

Effectors

Figure 11-18. Primary
message flow for a robotics
application of hypercubes.

enclosure mounted above the drive chassis, and the dual-arm manipulator torso is located above the computers and electronics. The manipulators are currently five degrees of freedom units and will be upgraded to seven degrees of freedom in HERMIES-III. The torso assembly for the arms also includes a shoulder pitch motion for each arm. Currently, sonar-scan data are preprocessed on board HERMIES for navigation planning. A ring of five sensors, each of which consists of a phased array of four Polariod transceivers, allows for a narrow effective beamwidth. Motor drives for the sensor pan-tilt control are high-speed dc servodrives that permit the sonar ring to be stepped quickly. The dc servodrive of the tilt platform has been designed to accommodate not only the sonar array, but also an infrared range detector and dual miniature charge-coupled-device (CCD) color cameras.

A major objective in the design of HERMIES-IIB was to increase the degree of self-contained autonomy; that is, dependence on off-board immobile computers has been reduced by using VME and IBM-AT backplanes in combination. The VME system, which includes several Motorola 68020 microprocessors, provides all control and sensor data interfacing. The VME system also serves as a data gateway to the AT backplane, which houses a fourth-order (sixteen nodes) hypercube parallel computer based on the NCUBE Corp. 32-bit node processor chip. Future HERMIES models will have up to 128 nodes onboard. The hypercube host processor serves as the supervisory robot control engine. The onboard hypercube provides a processing speed in excess of 16 VAX/11-780s and is being used to implement world models, sensor-processing

Figure 11-19. The Hermes IIB Model Robot

560

algorithms (e.g., vision), navigation, and manipulation kinematics and dynamics algorithms. The VME system facilitates onboard integration of a reasonably high-performance computer vision system using DataCube Corp. expansion boards, which provides $512 \times 512 \times 8$ color resolution and traditional image-processing functions. It is believed that HERMIES-IIB represents one of the most computationally powerful mobile robots in existence today. An application involving the use of HERMIES in conjunction with neural-network algorithms for sensor interpretation and near-optimal autonomous navigation has recently been described.[127,128]

Virtual-Time Operating-System Shell

While the distributed-memory architecture of a hypercube leads to its scaleability to very large numbers of processors, this same feature causes a difficulty in rapid response to environmental events, especially for applications in which the timing of effector actions is important. The difficulty arises because of the considerable, and indeterminate, time involved in the overhead of message passing, at least in presently available machines. For this reason, the planning task must send its commands to effector tasks well in advance of the times at which the effectors must act. Once commands have been sent, they are out of reach and cannot be changed directly, as may be required by unpredictable events.

HYPERCUBE COMMUNICATION IN A ROBOTICS APPLICATION

Communication between the hypercube and external sensors and effectors is most efficient when there is a direct I/O channel between each sensor and the node that processes its raw data, and a direct channel between each effector and the node that directly controls it. The NCUBE computer can be equipped with special I/O boards that provide such an arrangement for serial sensor data and control signals.

A general problem in utilizing a message-passing multiprocessor for any application, including robotics, is the mapping of tasks onto nodes so as to minimize message passing and the time required to complete tasks. The time required to pass a message between two nodes varies directly with the number of links separating them. It will therefore often be natural to take advantage of the hypercube's configurability into subcubes by mapping hierarchical robotics tasks onto subcubes of appropriate sizes. Then the relatively high rates of message passing often required between low-level subtasks will take place between neighboring nodes. A message sent to the top of a task's hierarchy will cause a "ripple" of messages through the lower levels of that hierarchy.

Message passing in a hypercube is handled by the operating system (OS), which resides on each node. For the NCUBE computer this OS is named VERTEX. Message passing is by direct memory access and uses a VERTEX protocol implemented through interrupts.

MESSAGE PASSING IN TIME-CRITICAL ROBOTICS APPLICATIONS

When an autonomous robot incorporating a message-passing computer performs actions in a time-critical setting, or on moving objects, there is the general requirement that the planning task sends command messages to an effector task well in advance of the times at which these commands are to be carried out. (Here we assume, for purposes of clarity, a single centralized "planner," or planning task.) The minimum lead time for the planner's command is that required for all calculations by, and message-passing between, the effector subtasks, prior to the command signal to the external device. However, the time required for nonsynchronous message passing is indeterminate to at least some extent for all hypercube computers presently known to the authors. Messages can be delayed at any node by the processing of other messages on other serial channels, or by delays in assigning buffer space. Unusual circumstances such as the migration of tasks (see below) can cause much longer delays, also of indeterminate extent. Therefore, there is normally a requirement for "planning ahead"—sending command messages safely in advance so as to allow for "maximum" possible delays in communication. Planning ahead involves the projection into the future of the "world model," such as the future positions of moving objects, and the like.

Given the requirement for planning ahead, there will normally exist at each node of an effector task a queue of input messages. It is also useful for efficiency that such queues exist, so that a node may begin to process a new message immediately on completing the previous one.

When unpredictable changes take place in the environment, they are sensed and interpreted by the sensor task(s) and communicated to the planner (see Fig. 11-18), which in many cases will then have to change its previous plans. If messages implementing these plans had already been sent to effector tasks (through planning ahead), they would have to be corrected or canceled. To do so would also require the correction or cancellation of any and all ripple messages sent within the effector subcube as a result of the original command. In some cases the rate of progress of such corrections through the effector subcube would not be sufficiently rapid to prevent the undesired external action from taking place. Therefore, a facility is required for emergency communication with the node directly linked to the external device (the "controller" node).

It is obvious that such corrections, cancellations, and emergency messages must be handled by the operating system itself. For if a correction/cancellation arrives at the input queue of a node while its "mate," the message to be corrected/cancelled, is still in that queue, the operating system can make the necessary changes transparently to the application process. An emergency message must interrupt a running process; this, too, must be a function of the operating system.

AN EXAMPLE: CONTROLLING A ROBOT ARM IN THE PRESENCE OF MOVING OBSTACLES

As an example of an autonomous robot operating in time-critical fashion in an unpredictable environment, we consider the control of a robot arm in the presence of moving obstacles. Suppose that sensor tasks "observe" the motions of the obstacles and send their projected future paths to the planner. The planner generates the arm trajectory so as to achieve the desired goal(s) while avoiding the obstacles.

For purposes of illustration, we assume the following simple model for trajectory generation. The planner defines the trajectory by specifying a series of "via points" (which are multidimensional positions through which the arm must pass) and a time for each via point. The planner sends messages containing pairs (via point, time) to the effector-task hierarchy. The top-level effector task converts the via points into the corresponding sets of joint angles, and generates for each joint angle a spline of cubic functions, one for each path segment between a pair of via ports, in such a manner that angular velocity and acceleration are continuous at the via points. (For simplicity of illustration, constraints representing the limits of the arm's work space and of its angular accelerations are neglected here.) In this manner, velocities and accelerations, though not explicitly given by the planner, are implicit in its choice of via points and times. Lower-level effector tasks, perhaps one for each joint, evaluate the cubic functions at sufficient numbers of intermediate points on each path segment to provide the required path-update rate, and use these points for control of the joints.

A simplified diagram of the computer tasks, and of the messages between them, is then the following:

Sensor tasks
$\downarrow$
   Messages: projected paths of obstacles as functions of future time
$\downarrow$
Planner task: plans path to goal, avoiding obstacles
$\downarrow$
   Messages: via points: (position, time) of arm
$\downarrow$
Effector task, high-level: converts via points to joint angles, calculates cubic-spline coefficients
$\downarrow$
   Messages: (cubic coefficients, times) for segments between via points
$\downarrow$
Effector tasks, low-level: evaluates cubic functions and controls effectors

We now consider what must be done when unexpected changes in the motions of the obstacles require changes of plans. For brevity, we will call the effector tasks simple "E-high" and "E-low." We note that the higher up a task is on the diagram above, the further ahead of real time it is working. Suppose that at the moment the planner "recognizes" the change and "decides" to alter the via points starting with no. 7, the following conditions hold (the path segment from via point i to point j will be denoted ij).

• The planner has already sent via points through no. 11 to task E-high.

- Task E-high has already sent sets of coefficients for segments through 78 to task E-low.
- The effector itself is between via points 5 and 6.

The following diagram indicates these conditions. (A task's input message queue is shown directly above the task.)

Planner—working on via points beyond no. 11 Input queue: via points 10, 11
↓

E-high (Effector task, high-level)—working on segment 89
↓

Input queues: (coefficients, times) for segments 67, 78
↓

E-low (Effector tasks, low-level)—working on segment 56
↓

Command signals to effector (all joints) for path point within segment 56.

The following actions must take place, if time permits. The planner must send to task E-high messages correcting the via points 7 through 11. Points 10 and 11, not yet utilized by task E-high must "roll back" to recalculate the cubic coefficients for segments 67, 78, and 89. Correction messages for the first two of these segments must be sent to tasks E-low.

In order for task E-high to calculate the coefficients for a segment, it requires the values of the angular position, velocity, and acceleration at the segment origin, the position at the terminus, and the times of the two via points. Two kinds of items must be saved so that all necessary variables may be retrieved. (a) If input messages are saved temporarily, positions and times can be retrieved. (b) The velocity and acceleration for via point n are results from task E-high's calculation for segment $n - 1, n$. They constitute a local "state" vector, used for the calculation for segment $n, n + 1$. These state vectors must also be saved temporarily.

NONCONSERVATION OF TEMPORAL LOGIC IN DYNAMIC MULTIPROCESSOR SYSTEMS

In time-critical applications, it is generally important that messages arriving at a node be processed in a particular order (temporal logic), which is not necesarily that of their arrival at the node. Possible reasons of the arrival of messages out of order include the following.

- Messages may arrive from two or more nodes which differ in their processing loads and therefore "think about the future" at different rates.
- Communication delays, arising from the traversal of additional links or from the temporary busy-ness of an intermediate node en route, may affect some messages more than others.
- Tasks may need to migrate in the event of a hardware failure, or if dynamic load balancing is employed. Task migration would cause considerable message

delays. (Alternatively, task migration might necessitate clearing and restarting of the message trains.)

Thus, there is a requirement for the node's operating system properly to order messages in the input queue, as indicated by time-stamps in the message headers.

NECESSARY EXTENSIONS TO THE NODE OPERATING SYSTEM

The discussion above indicates the necessity of adding to the node's operating system (OS) (VERTEX in the case of NCUBE computer) a shell which (on the basis of codes included in message headers) implements cancellation messages and the restoration of temporal logic by ordering messages in the input queue according to their time-stamps.

If, on arrival at its destination node, a cancellation or correction message finds its "mate" in the input queue, the shell actions are: for the cancellation message, to discard it with its mate; for the correction message, to discard it after substituting its data for that of its mate.

Several types of emergency messages are needed. One type causes the shell to trap a particular message upon its (later) arrival and discard it, or, if it is too late to do so, to interrupt the running process and schedule an appropriate alternate such as a "stop" program. Another type of emergency message simply causes an interrupt and "stop." A requirement for the use of emergency messages is that the planner "knows" the locations of the controller node(s).

POSSIBLE ACTIONS WHEN CANCELLATION/CORRECTION MESSAGES ARRIVE TOO LATE

When a cancellation/correction message arrives too late—i.e., when its mate has already been processed—one or more of several possible actions may be taken, depending on the application and the amount of time available before a deadline, including the following.

- *For cancellation*: emergency trap of any output message(s) at the controller node
- *For a correction*: emergency trap of any output message(s) at the controller node, followed by recalculation with the corrected input data
- *For either*: a procedure that compensates for the error
- Message notifying the planner

Recalculation, discussed in the example above, requires these additional functions for the OS shell.

- Temporarily save input messages after processing, for possible retrieval.
- Temporarily store vectors, for possible retrieval.

A general discussion of all these possibilities is beyond the scope of this chapter. In the same vein, the analogy of such operating system requirements to "time-warp" functions[55,151] is discussed elsewhere.[129]

WORK IN PROGRESS

The virtual-time (VT) shell in its present form includes new versions of the following time-warp functions: ordering of messages in an input queue by time-stamp; cancellation (anti-) messages; the saving of previous input and output messages and state vectors; roll-back. Correction messages are implemented. Also, processes that require more than one input message are scheduled to run upon the arrival of the last of the set. Message headers identify source and destination nodes, length, and type of message, and include codes that specify the shell functions.

This completed part of the VT shell, with appropriate modifications for the NCUBE, has been added to VERTEX, to form the new VIRTEX environment.

The question of how to adapt virtual-time concepts to real-time robotics applications in an optimal manner poses considerable theoretical and practical problems, which we are starting to investigate. In particular, we intend to investigate the integration of the VIRTEX shell with hard-real-time scheduling algorithms.

In the nearer term, functions to be added to the shell include the following.

- Emergency messages.
- "Clean-out of over-ridden messages.
- A delay procedure for cases in which changes are necessary and actions can be put off into the future.
- Implementation of commands to be executed at specified time increments after an awaited signal—that is, at "virtual times." (For example, the command to do action A at time $tO + tA$, action B at time $tO + tB, . . . ,$ where tO is as yet unknown.) The signal might be an environmental event, the (future) time of which is unpredictable. In certain applications such commands could be utilized for precalculation of effector parameters, allowing more rapid action once the signal arrives.

Finally, we plan to construct a suitable test bed to exercise thoroughly and with random timings all functions of the VIRTEX.

Neural Networks

Over the last decade, there has been an increasing interest in artificial neuromorphic systems (ANS), defined as adaptive dynamical systems modeled on the general features of biological networks, that can carry out useful information processing by means of their state response to initial or continuous input. One motivation for this interest is found in the fundamental theoretical contributions of Grossberg, Cohen, and Carpenter in the areas of associative learning, adaptive pattern recognition, and cooperative–competitive decision making by neural networks.[130] In the same vein, Hopfield and Tank have shown that applicability of neuromorphic techniques to the solution of the combinatorially complex "traveling salesman problem."[21] Work at Oak Ridge National Laboratory and at the Jet Propulsion Laboratory/Caltech is providing significant advances in the design stability and storage capacity of nonlinear continuous neural networks.[131] In the area of hardware implementation, major achievements have resulted from the efforts of Hecht-Nielsen, Mead, and others.[132] This situation provides a strong incentive to explore the development of parallel neuromorphic algorithms for machine-intelligence applications.

A. AUTONOMOUS ROBOT NAVIGATION

One particularly appealing area is in the application of neural networks to sensor-interpretation problems encountered by autonomous mobile robots.[128,133] For an autonomous robot to function in dynamic environments, it must depend heavily on sensor data. Unfortunately, owing to sensor inaccuracies and processing speed limitations, current methods of pattern recognition and image processing are not well suited to rapidly changing perspectives of a navigating robot. Taking sonar as an example, sonar distance ranging is subject to a variety of uncertainties affected by temperature, specular reflection, absorbency, and positioning inaccuracies. Nevertheless, navigation decisions about the shapes and boundaries of objects must be made from changing and limited perspectives. Data from potentially many sensor and information sources must be combined, balancing multiple weak constraints in order to arrive at global conclusions about a particular spatial environment.

Our current research focuses on the use of reconstructed spatial information for sensor uncertainty and navigation planning. Briefly described, the method proceeds as follows. Neural states are defined in terms of a degree of certainty that three-dimensional obstacle boundaries are present in volumetric cubes mapped by phased-array sonar returns. (See Figs. 11-20 to 11-22 for a simplified two-dimensional description of this process.) Several simulated room environments are configured in the laboratory and explored by HERMIES II.[134] Location uncertainties are stored in a neural network using a modified Hebbian learning rule applied to a partitioning of the room's volume. After learning a series of potential room configurations from slightly different positions, the robot is presented with a partial sensor graph representing a single line-of-sight perspective from one point in an unidentified room. A threshold-limited associative-recall criterion is used to regenerate a best-fit reconstruction of the three-dimensional parts of the room that are out of the line of sight. This information is then used by a newly developed navigation method to plan a potential path between the robot's current location and an arbitrarily selected room area.

At present, the robot is represented by a single volumetric cell, although extensions to irregular shape and manipulator dynamics are being explored. The room, however, can be of arbitrary complexity limited only by the computational power of the supporting computer system.

The simulated neural network has been implemented in C on a 64-node NCUBE hypercube computer. The program calculates potential room-pattern matches by broadcasting a sonar line-of-sight distance vector to a whole series of

Real environment

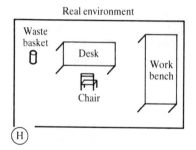

Sensor sonar graph environment

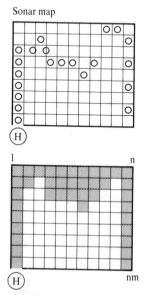

(H) = Hermies robot location

Figure 11-20. The robot environment.

Sonar map

1   n

nm

Sonar map as
nm states where
a dark space is a state of 1 and
a light space is a state of 0

Figure 11-21. A state representation of a sonar map.

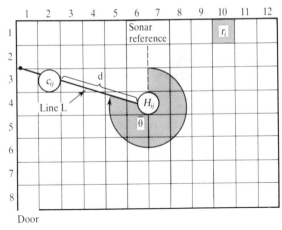

H_{ij} = robot location
r_i = spatial region in room
L = line through c_{ij} from H_{ij}

then: $\begin{cases} v_{3,1} \to 1 \\ v_{3,2} \to 1 \end{cases}$ turned on by return c_{ij}

Figure 11-22. A graphic representation of a sonar map. H_{ij} = robot location; r_i = spatial region in room; L = line through c_{ij} from H_{ij}. $v_{3,1} \to 1$, $v_{3,2} \to 1$, turned on by return c_{ij}.

nodes simultaneously. Each node then performs a best-fit reconstruction of potential three-dimensional patterns and broadcasts the result back to a controller board that serves as the interface between the robot and the external processor. Threshold values are increased in the nodes until only a single pattern is returned. This pattern is then used as the most probable three-dimensional environment for the robot path planner. Although not yet applied, a second set of nodes simultaneously calculates a cross-associative verbal label for the same pattern that is being regenerated. These labels will eventually be used to feed an expert system (CLIPS) currently used to control higher-order robot planning under a rule-based system.

In order to minimize memory problems associated with scaling up volumetric representations, a calculation-intensive method for determining network weights is explored instead of storing and maintaining large interconnection matrices.

This method does not maintain a large weight matrix in memory but rather maintains only a set of vectors corresponding to average pattern classes identified during learning. The actual weight connecting any two elements is then calculated at the time of recall. Using these weights, the sum of the products of the vector used to cue recall and the connection weights biases the state change of the simulated neuron. The actual value regenerated uses a standard sigmoid function to calculate an estimated value for the vector of recalled values.

B. STRATEGIC DEFENSE APPLICATIONS

Space battlefield platforms for strategic defense missions will require enormous onboard computing power and flexibility, including the ability for faster than real-time responses in a semiautonomous decision-making environment characterized by severe constraints such as size, weight, power, and the like.

We are currently simulating[135] on the NCUBE hypercube complex neural networks, in order to explore their practical applicability for solving real-world SDI problems. This will allow us to qualitatively test and evaluate neuromorphic algorithms in such areas as irregular simulations (Battle Management/C^3), multisensor integration, learning, associative memory, and fast optimization. This general area of research also directly addresses numerous issues involved in the more fundamental question of intelligent computers built around large-scale parallel architectures. Our research aims at modeling such specialized computers on the hypercube to assess the feasibility of potential electronic or optical implementations.

CONCLUSIONS

Some of the most challenging computational problems facing scientists and engineers today arise in the area of intelligent systems. Future robot designs, in particular, will emphasize dynamic processes requiring complex calculations to be performed onboard. Concurrent processing based on VLSI technology, and hypercube supercomputers specifically, are achieving this high efficiency within the limited physical space allowed by autonomous systems.

REFERENCES

1. Fox, G. C., M. A. Johnson, G. A. Lyzenga, S. W. Otto, S. K. Salmon, and D. Walker (1988). *Solving Problems on Concurrent Processors.* Prentice-Hall, Englewood Cliffs, N.J. [The Software Supplement to the book is edited by I. Angus, G. Fox, J. Kim, and D. Walker.]

2. Seitz, C. L. (1985) "The Cosmic Cube," *Commun. ACM*, Vol. 28, p. 22.

3. Athas, W., E. Brooks, E. DeBenedictis, R. Faucette, G. Fox, M. Johnson, S. Otto, C. Seitz, J. Stack, and P. Stolorz (1984). "Pure gauge $SU(3)$ lattice theory on an array of computers," *Phys. Rev. Lett.*, Vol. 52, p. 2324.

4. Fox, G. C. and S. Otto (1984). "Algorithms for concurrent processors," *Physics Today* (May 1984) [Caltech report C^3P-71]

5. Walker, D. W., P. Messina, and C. F. Baillie (1988). "Performance evaluation of scientific programs on advanced-architecture computer," in *Proceedings of the Third Conference on Hypercube Concurrent Computers and Applications* (ed. G. C. Fox). ACM, New York.

6. Fox, G. C. (1986). "Annual report of the Caltech Concurrent Computation Program 1985–86," *Hypercube Multiprocessors 1987* (ed. M. T. Heath), p. 353. SIAM, Philadelphia. [Caltech report C^3P-290B]

7. Fox, G. C. and P. C. Messina (1987). "The Caltech Concurrent Computation Program annual report 1986–1987," Caltech report C^3P-487.

8. Heath, M. T. (1986). "Hypercube multiprocessors 1986," edited by M. T. Heath—proceedings of Hypercube Conference, September 1985 Hypercube Conference, SIAM, Philadelphia.

9. Heath, M. T. (1987). "Hypercube multiprocessors 1987," ed. M. T. Heath. SIAM, Philadelphia.

10. Fox, G. (1988). "Hypercube multiprocessors 1988," *Proceedings of the Third Conference on Hypercube Concurrent Computers and Applications* (ed. G. C. Fox). ACM, New York.

11. Fox, G. C. (1988). "What have we learnt from using real parallel machines to solve real problems," in *Proceedings of the Third Conference on Hypercube Concurrent Computers and Applications* (ed. G. C. Fox). ACM, New York.

12. Fox, G. C. (1987). "Domain decomposition in distributed and shared memory environments I," *Lecture Notes in Computer Science* (ed. C. Polychronopoulos). Springer-Verlag, New York [Caltech report C^3P-392]

13. Dally, W. and C. Seitz (1986). "A VLSI architecture for concurrent data structures," Ph.D. Dissertation, California Institute of Technology, Pasadena, Calif. [*J. Distributed Systems* Vol. 1, p. 187.]

14. Seitz, C., W. C. Athas, C. M. Flaig, A. J. Martin, J. Siezovic, C. S. Steele, and W-K. Su (1988). "The architecture and programming of the AMETEK 2010," in *Proceedings of the Third Conference on Hypercube Concurrent Computers and Applications* (ed. G. C. Fox). ACM, New York.

15. Fox, G. C. and S. W. Otto (1986). "Concurrent computation and the theory of complex systems," in *Hypercube Multiprocessors, 1986* (ed. M. T. Heath), p. 244. SIAM, Philadelphia. [Caltech report C^3P-255]

16. Fox, G. (1985). "The performance of the Caltech hypercube in scientific calculations: A preliminary analysis," in *Supercomputers—Algorithms, Architectures and Scientific Computation* (ed. F. A. Matsen and T. Tajima) University of Texas Press, Austin. [Caltech report C^3P-161]

17. Fox, G. C. and W. Furmanski (1986). "Load balancing by neural network," CALT-68-1408, unpublished. [C^3P-363]

18. Fox, G. C., A. Kolawa, and R. Williams (1986). "The implementation of a dynamic load balancer," in *Hypercube Multiprocessors, 1987* (ed. M. T. Heath), p. 114. SIAM, Philadelphia. [Caltech report C^3P-328]

19. Fox, G. C. (1986). "A review of automatic load balancing and decomposition methods for the hypercube," in *IMA Volumes in Mathematics and its Applications*, Vol. 13. Springer-Verlag, New York. [Caltech report, C^3P-385]

20. Hopfield, J. (1982). "Neural networks and physical systems with emergent collective computational abilities," *Proc. Natl. Acad. Sci. USA*, Vol. 79, p. 2554.

21. Hopfield, J. J. and D. N. Tank (1985). "Neural computations of decisions in optimization problems," *Bio. Cyb.*, Vol. 52, p. 141.

22. Fox, G. C. (1986). "A graphical approach to load balancing and sparse matrix vector multiplication on the hypercube," in *IMA Volumes in Mathematics and its Applications*, Vol. 13. Springer-Verlag, New York. [Caltech report C^3P-327B]

23. Kuppermann, A. and P. G. Hipes (1986). *J. Chem. Phys.* Vol. 84, pp. 55–62.

24. Lyzenga, G. A., A. Raefsky, and B. H. Hager (1985). "Finite elements and the method of conjugate gradients on a concurrent processor," in *Proceedings of The 1985 ASME International Computers in Engineering.*" ASME. [Caltech report C^3P-164]

25. Flower, J. W., S. W. Otto, and M. C. Salama (1987). "A preprocessor for finite element problems," in *Proceedings, Symposium on Parallel Computations and Their Impact on Mechanics, ASME.* [Caltech report C^3P-292]

26. Hipes, P. and A. Kuppermann (1986). "Gauss–Jordan inversion with pivoting on the Caltech Mark II hypercube," in *Proceedings of the Third Conference on Hypercube Concurrent Computers and Applications* (ed. by G. C. Fox). ACM, New York. [Caltech report C^3P-347]

27. Aldcroft, T., A. Cisneros, G. C. Fox, W. Furmanski, and D. Walker (1988). "A banded matrix LU decomposition on the hypercube," Caltech report C^3P-348c. In *Proceedings of the Third*

Conference on Hypercube Concurrent Computers and Applications (ed. G. C. Fox). ACM, New York.

28. Fox, G. C. and W. Furmanski (1988). "Matrix," in *Proceedings of Third Conference on Hypercube Concurrent Computers and Applications* (ed. G. C. Fox). ACM, New York. [Caltech report C^3P-386]

29. Fox, G. C., A. J. G. Hey, and S. Otto (1985). "Matrix algorithms on the hypercube I: Matrix multiplication" *Parallel Computing*, Vol. 4, p. 17. [Caltech report C^3P-206]

30. Grassberger, P. and I. Procaccia (1983). *Physica*, Vol. 9D, p. 189.

31. Lorenz, J. and P. D. Noerdlinger (1987). "Analysis of strange attractors on the hypercube," unpublished Caltech report C^3P-400.

32. Theiler, J. T. (1987). "An efficient algorithm for estimating correlation dimension from a set of discrete points," *Phys. Rev. A*, Vol. 36, p. 4456.

33. Chua, K. and A. Leonard (1987). "Three dimensional vortex methods and the vortex reconnection problem," *Bull. Amer. Phys. Soc.*, to be published.

34. Van de Velde, E. F. and H. B. Keller (1987). "The parallel solution of nonlinear elliptic equations," Caltech report C^3P-447.

35. Pollara, F. (1985). "Concurrent Viterbi algorithm on a hypercube," in *Proceedings of the 23rd Annual Allerton Conference on Communication Control and Computing* (ed. B. Hajek and D. C. Munson Jr.). University of Illinois. [Caltech report C^3P-208]

36. Pollara, F. (1986). "Concurrent Viterbi algorithm with trace-back," in *Advanced Algorithms and Architectures for Signal Processing*: SPIE Proc. Vol. 696, p. 204. [Caltech report C^3P-462]

37. Fox, G. C. (1984). "Square matrix decomposition: Symmetric, local, scattered." [Caltech report C^3P-97]

38. Morison, R. and S. Otto (1986). "The scattered decomposition for finite elements," *J. Sci. Comput.* Vol. 2. [Caltech report C^3P-286]

39. Goldsmith, J. and J. Salmon (1988). "A hypercube ray-tracer," in *Proceedings of the Third Conference on Hypercube Concurrent Computers and Applications* (ed. G. C. Fox). ACM, New York.

40. Salmon, J., S. Callahan, J. Flower, and A. Kolawa (1987). "The MOOSE status report," May 6, 1987, unpublished Caltech report C^3P-427.

41. Frankel, A. and R. W. Clayton (1985). "Finite difference simulations of seismic scattering: Implications for propagation of short-period seismic waves in the crust and models of crustal heterogeneity," *J. Geophys. Res.* Vol. 91, p. 6465. [Caltech report C^3P-203]

42. Nour-Omid, B. and K. C. Park (1987). "Solving structural mechanics problems on the Caltech hypercube machine," *Computer Methods Appl. Mech. Eng.* Vol. 61, p. 161.

43. Salmon, J. and C. Hogan (1986). "Correlation of QSO absorption lines in universes dominated by cold dark matter," *Monthly Notices Roy. Astron. Soc.* Vol. 221, p. 93. [Caltech report C^3P-211]

44. Salmon, J. and M. Warren (1988). "An $O(N \log N)$ hypercube N-body integrator," in *Proceedings of the Third Conference on Hypercube Concurrent Computers and Applications* (ed. G. C. Fox). ACM, New York.

45. Barnes, J. and P. Hut (1986). "A hierarchical $O(N \log N)$ force calculation algorithm," *Nature*, Vol. 324, p. 446.

46. Otto, S. and J. Stack (1984). "The SU(3) heavy quark potential with high statistics," CALT-68-1113, *Phys. Rev. Lett.*, Vol. 52, p. 2320. [Caltech report C^3P-67]

47. Johnson, M. A. (1986). "Concurrent computation and its application to the study of melting in two dimensions," PhD. thesis, Caltech. [Caltech report C^3P-268]

48. Fucito, F. and S. Solomon (1985). "Monte Carlo parallel algorithm for long range interactions." *Computer Phys. Commun.* Vol. 34, p. 225. [Caltech report C^3P-79A]

49. Werner, B. T. (1987). "A physical model of wind-blown sand transport," Caltech PhD. dissertation; unpublished Caltech report C^3P-245.

50. Gottschalk, T. D. (1986). "Booster trajectory calculations," Caltech report C^3P-387.

51. Gottschalk, T. D., I. G. Angus, and G. C. Fox (1986). "Hypercube tracking: A preliminary status report," Caltech report C^3P-388.

52. Felten, E., S. Karlin, and S. W. Otto (1985). "Sorting on a hypercube," Caltech report C^3P-244.

53. Felten, E., R. Morison, S. Otto, K. Barish, R. Fatland, and F. Ho (1987). "Chess on the hypercube," in *Hypercube Multiprocessors* (ed. M. T. Heath), p. 327. SIAM, Philadelphia. [Caltech report C^3P-383]

54. Felten, E. W. and S. W. Otto (1988). "Chess on a hypercube," in *Proceedings of the Third Conference on Hypercube Concurrent Computers and Applications* (ed. G. C. Fox). ACM, New York.

55. Jefferson, D. and B. Beckman (1985). "Implementation of time warp on the Caltech hypercube," *SCF Conference on Distributed Simulation, San Diego.* [Caltech report C^3P-141]

56. Jefferson, D. (1988). "The time warp operating system," *Proceedings of the Third Conference on Hypercube Concurrent Computers and Applications* (ed. G. C. Fox). ACM, New York.

57. Walker, D. W. and G. C. Fox (1988). "A portable programming environment for concurrent multiprocessors," presented at the *Twelth IMACS World Congress on Scientific Computation, July 1988, Paris.* [Caltech report C^3P-496]

58. Kolawa, A. and S. Otta (1986). "Performance of the Mark II and INTEL Hypercubes," in *Hypercube Multiprocessors, 1986* (ed. T. Heath), p. 272. SIAM, Philadelphia. [Caltech report C^3P-254]

59. Salmon, J. (1986). "CUBIX—Programming hypercubes without programming hosts," in *Hypercube Multiprocessors, 1987* (ed. M. T. Heath) p. 3. SIAM, Philadelphia. [Caltech report C^3P-378]

60. Koller, J. (1988). "A Dynamic load balancer on the Intel hypercube," in *Proceedings of the Third Conference on Hypercube Concurrent Computers and Applications* (ed. G. C. Fox). ACM, New York.

61. Concus, P., G. H. Golub, and D. P. O'Leary (1976). "A generalized conjugate gradient method for the numerical solution of elliptic partial differential equations," in *Sparse Matrix Computations* (ed. J. R. Bunch and D. J. Rose). Academic Press, New York.

62. Hackbusch, W. and U. Trottenberg (1981). "Multigrid methods," *Lecture Notes in Mathematics* No. 960. Springer-Verlag, New York.

63. Bank, R. E. (1981). "Multilevel iterative method for nonlinear elliptic equations," in *Elliptic Problem Solvers* (ed. M. Schultz) pp. 1–16. Academic Press, New York.

64. Bolstadt, J. H. and H. B. Keller (1986). "A multigrid continuation method for elliptic problems with folds," *SIAM J. Sci. Stat. Comput.,* Vol. 7, pp. 1081–1104.

65. Chan, T. F. and H. B. Keller (1982). "Archlength continuation and multigrid techniques for nonlinear elliptic eigenvalue problems," *SIAM J. Sci. Stat. Comput.,* Vol. 3, pp. 173–193.

66. Schwarz, H. A. (1869). "Ueber einige abbildungsaufgaben," *Jour. f. die reine und angew. Math.,* Vol. 70, pp. 105–120.

67. Miller, K. (1965). "Numerical analogs to the Schwarz alternating procedure," *Numerische Mathematik* Vol. 7, pp. 91–103.

68. Oliger, J., W. Shamarock, and W-P. Tang (1986). "Convergence analysis and acceleration of the

Schwarz alternating method," CLaSSic-86-12, Center for Large Scale Scientific Computing, Stanford University.

69. Linden, J. (1981). "Mehrgitterverfahren fur die Poisson-Gleichung in Kreis und Ringgebiet unter Verwendung lokaler Koordinaten," Diplomarbeit, Institut fur Angewandte Mathematik, Universitat Bonn.

70. Starius, G. C. (1977). "Composite mesh difference methods for elliptic boundary value problems," *Numer. Math.*, Vol. 28, 242–258.

71. Chan, T. F. and R. Tuminaro (1986). "Implementation of multigrid algorithms on hypercubes," *Proceedings of the Second Conference on Hypercube Multiprocessors*, ref. 9.

72. McBryan, O. and E. Van de Velde (1985). "Parellel algorithms for elliptic equations," *Commun. Pure Appl. Math.*, Vol. XXXVIII, pp. 769–795.

73. McBryan, O. and E. Van de Velde (1985). "Hypercube algorithms and implementations," *Proceedings of the 2nd SIAM Conference on Parallel Processing for Scientific Computation, Norfolk.* SIAM, Philadelphia.

74. Thole, C. (1985). "Experiments with multigrid on the Caltech hypercube," GMD internal report.

75. Johnson, M. A. (1986). "The specification of CrOS III," unpublished Caltech report C^3P-253.

76. Dinar, N. and H. B. Keller (1985). "Computations of Taylor vortex flows using multigrid continuation methods," Caltech Appl. Math. Report. *Journal of Fluid Mechanics.*

77. Hoppe, H. C. and H. Muhlenbein (1986). "Parellel adaptive full multigrid methods on message based multiprocessors," *Parallel Computing*, Vol. 3.

78. Wirth, N. (1976). *Algorithms + Data Structures = Programs.* Prentice-Hall, Englewood Cliffs, N.J.

79. Berger, M. and J. Oliger (1984). "Adaptive mesh refinement for hyperbolic partial differential equations," *J. Comp. Phys.* Vol. 53, pp. 484–512.

80. Kernighan, B. W. and D. M. Ritchie (1978). *The C Programming Language,* Prentice-Hall, Englewood Cliffs, N.J.

81. Wilson, K. G. (1974). *Phys. Rev.*, Vol. D10, p. 2445.

82. Metropolis, N., A. W. Rosenbluth, M. N. Rosenbluth, A. H. Teller, and E. Teller (1953). *J. Chem. Phys.*, Vol. 21, p. 1087.

83. Creutz, M. (1980). "Monte Carlo study of quantized $SU(2)$ gauge theory," *Phys. Rev.*, Vol. D21, p. 2308.

84. Cabibbo, N. and E. Marinari (1982). "A new method for updating $SU(N)$ matrices in computer simulations of gauge theories," *Phys. Lett.*, Vol. 119B, p. 387.

85. Pietarinen, E. (1981). "String tension in $SU(3)$ lattice gauge theory," *Nucl. Phys. B.*, Vol. 190, p. 349.

86. Callaway, D. and A. Rahman (1983). "Lattice gauge theory in the microcanonical ensemble," *Phys. Rev.*, Vol. D28, p. 1506.

87. Polonyi, J. and H. W. Wyld (1983). "Microcanonical simulation of fermionic systems," *Phys. Rev. Lett,* Vol. 51, p. 2257.

88. Parisi, G. and Y. Wu (1981). "Perturbation theory without gauge fixing," *Sci Sin.*, Vol. 24, p. 483.

89. Duane, S. (1985). "Stochastic quantization vs. the microcanonical ensemble: getting the best of both worlds," *Nucl. Phys. B*, Vol. 257, p. 652.

90. Scalettar, R. T., D. J. Scalapino, and R. L. Sugar (1986). "New algorithm for the numerical simulation of fermions," *Phys. Rev.*, Vol. B34, p. 7911.

91. Duane, S., A. D. Kennedy, B. J. Pendleton, and D. Roweth (1987). "Hybrid Monte Carlo," preprint FSU-SCRI-87-27.

92. Flower, J. W. and S. W. Otto (1986). "Scaling violations in the heavy quark potential," *Phys. Rev.,* Vol. D34, p. 1649.

93. Flower, J. W. (1987). "Lattice gauge theory on a parallel computer," PhD. Thesis, California Institute of Technology.

94. Flower, J. W. (1987). *Nucl. Phys. B,* Vol. 289, p. 484.

95. Gupta, R. (1987). "The hybrid Monte Carlo algorithm and the chiral transition," invited talk at the 1987 meeting on Field Theory on a Lattice, Seillac, France.

96. Baillie, C. F. and E. W. Felten (1987). "Benchmarking concurrent supercomputers," in *High Performance Computer Systems,* ed. E. Gelenbe, pub. Elsevier, Amsterdam [Caltech report C^3 p. 453].

97. Zienkiewicz, O. C. (1977). *The Finite Element Method.* McGraw-Hill, Chichester, U.K.

98. Winget, J. M. (1984). "Element-by-element solution procedures for nonlinear transient heat conduction analysis," Caltech PhD thesis.

99. Takeuchi, H. and M. Saito (1972). "Seismic surface waves," *Methods Computat. Phys.,* Vol. 11, pp. 217–295.

100. Woodhouse, J. H. (1983). "The joint inversion of seismic waveforms for lateral variations in Earth structure and earthquake source parameters," in *Proceedings of the Enrico Fermi International School of Physics,* Vol. LXXXXV (ed. H. Kanamori and E. Boschi) pp. 366–397. North-Holland, Amsterdam.

101. Tanimoto, T. (1984). "Waveform inversion of mantle Love waves: The born seismogram approach," *Geophys. J. R. Astr. Soc.,* Vol. 78, pp. 641–660.

102. Blackman, S. S. (1986). *Multiple-Target tracking with Radar Applications.* Artech House.

103. Bar-Shalom, Y. (1978). "Tracking methods in a multitarget environment," *IEEE Trans. Automatic Control,* Vol. AC-24, p. 618.

104. Barniv, Y. (1985). "Dynamic programming solution for detecting dim moving targets," *IEEE Trans. Aerospace Electron. Systems,* Vol. AES-21, p. 144.

105. Washburn, R. B., T. Kurien, A. L. Blitz, and A. S. Willsky (1984). "Hybrid state estimation approach to tracking for airborne surveillance radars," ALPHATEH report TR-180.

106. Latimer, J. H. (1985). "An implementation of a powered flight model," MITRE report WP-26469.

107. Gelb, A. (1974). *Applied Optimal Estimation.* MIT Press, Cambridge, Mass.

108. Knuth, D. E. (1973). *The Art of Computer Programming, Vol. 3: Sorting and Searching.* Addison-Wesley, Reading, Mass.

109. Fox, G. C. and W. Furmanski (1986). "Communications algorithms for regular convolutions on a hypercube," in *Hypercube Multiprocessors, 1987* (ed. M. T. Heath), p. 223. SIAM, Philadelphia. [Caltech report C^3P-329]

110. Barhen, J. and J. Palmer (1986). "The hypercube in robotics and machine intelligence," *Comp. Mech. Eng.,* Vol. 4, No. 5, p. 30.

111. Barhen, J. and E. C. Halbert (1986). "ROSES: An efficient scheduler for precedence-constrained tasks on a hypercube multiprocessor," in *Hypercube Multiprocessors '86* (ed. M. T. Heath), Part III, Chap. 2, pp. 123–147. SIAM—Society for Industrial and Applied Mathematics, Philadelphia.

112. Chow, Y. C. and W. H. Kohler (1979). "Models for dynamic load balancing in a heterogenous multiple processor system," *IEEE Trans. Comput.,* Vol. C-28, p. 354.

113. Tantawi, A. N. and D. Towsley (1985). "Optimal static load balancing in distributed computer systems," *J. ACM,* Vol. 32, No. 2, p. 445.

114. Coffman, E. G. (1976). *Computer and Job Shop Scheduling Theory.* Wiley, New York.

115. Graham, R. L., E. L. Lawler, J. K. Lenstra, and A. H. G. R. Kan (1979). "Optimization and

approximation in deterministic sequencing and scheduling: A survey," *Annals Discrete Math.,* Vol. 5, p. 169.

116. Garey, M. R. and D. S. Johnson (1979). *Computers and Intractability: A Guide to the Theory of NP-Completeness.* Freeman, San Francisco.

117. Barhen, J. (1985). "Robot inverse dynamics on a concurrent computation ensemble," *Proceedings 1985 International Computers in Engineering Conference,* Vol. 3, pp. 415–429.

118. Barhen, J., P. C. Chen, and E. C. Halbert (1987). "ROSES: A robot operating system expert scheduler," ORNL/TM-9987. Oak Ridge National Laboratory.

119. Kirkpatrick, S., C. Gelatt, and M. Vecchi (1983). "Optimization by simulated annealing," *Science,* Vol. 220, p. 671.

120. Romeo, F., A. Sangiovanni-Vincentelli, and C. Sechen (1984). "Research on simulated annealing at Berkeley," *Proc., IEEE ICCD-84,* pp. 652–657.

121. Barhen, J. (1986). "Combinatorial optimization of the computational load balance for a hypercube supercomputer," *Proceedings Fourth Symposium on Energy Engineering Science,* pp. 71–80. DOE-CONF 8605122, Argonne National Laboratory.

122. Luh, J. Y. S., M. W. Walker, and R. P. Paul (1980). "On-line computational scheme for mechanical manipulators," *J. Dyn. Syst. Meas. Contr.,* Vol. 102, p. 69.

123. Luh, J. Y. S. and C. S. Lin (1982). "Scheduling of parallel computation for a computer controlled mechanical manipulator," *IEEE Trans. Syst. Man. Cyb.,* Vol. SMC-12, p. 214.

124. Kasahara, H. and S. Narita (1985). "Parallel processing of a robot arm control computation on a multiprocessor system," *IEEE J. Robot. Autom.,* Vol. RA-1, No. 2, p. 104.

125. Barhen, J. (1987). "Hypercube ensembles: An architecture for intelligent robots," in *Special Computer Architectures for Robotics and Automation* (ed. J. Graham), Chap. 8, pp. 195–236. Gordon and Breach, New York.

126. Weisbin, C. R., J. Barhen, and W. R. Hamel (1987). "Research and development program for the Center for Engineering Systems Advanced Research," ORNL/TM-10232, Oak Ridge National Laboratory.

127. Burks, B. L. et al. (1987). "Autonomous navigation, exploration and recognition using the HERMIES-IIB robot," *IEEE Expert,* Vol. 2, No. 4, p. 18.

128. Barhen, J., W. B. Dress, and C. C. Jorgensen (1988). "Applications of concurrent neuromorphic algorithms for autonomous robots," in *Neural Computers* (ed. R. Eckmiller), pp. 321–333. NATO ASI, Springer-Verlag, New York.

129. Einstein, J. R., J. Barhen, and D. Jefferson (1987). "Virtual-time operating system functions for robotics applications on a hypercube," in *Hypercube Multiprocessors 1987* (ed. M. T. Heath), pp. 100–108. SIAM, Philadelphia.

130. Grossberg, S. (1987). *The Adaptive Brain,* North-Holland, Amsterdam (in press, 1987).

131. Guez, A., V. Protopopescu, and J. Barhen (1988). "On the design, stability, and capacity of non-linear neural networks," *IEEE Trans. Syst. Man. Cyber.,* Vol. 18, No. 1, p. 80.

132. Candill, X. X. (1987). *Proceedings IEEE First International Conference on Neural Networks,* San Diego (June 1987).

133. Jorgensen, C. C. (1986). "Neural network navigation using hypercube computers," presented at the *Second Conference on Hypercube Multiprocessors.*

134. Jorgensen, C. C., W. R. Hamel, and C. Weisbin (1986). "Exploring autonomous robot navigation," *BYTE Magazine,* September 29–October 1.

135. Barhen, J., V. Protopopescu, N. Toomarian, and M. Clinard (1987). "Concurrent neuromorphic algorithms for optimization of the computational load of a hypercube supercomputer," *Proc. IEEE-ICNN-1,* Vol. 4, pp. 687–696.

136. Fucito, F., R. Kinney, and S. Solomon (1984). "On the phase diagram of finite temperature QCD in the presence of dynamical quarks," *Nucl. Phys. B,* Vol. 248, p. 615. [Caltech report C^3P-333].

137. Fucito, F. and S. Solomon (1985). "The Chiral symmetry restoration transition in the presence of dynamical quarks," *Phys. Rev. Lett.,* Vol. 55, p. 2641. [Caltech report C^3P-331]

138. Fucito, F., C. Rebbi, and S. Solomon (1985). "Finite temperature QCD in the presence of dynamical quarks," *Nucl. Phys. B,* Vol. 253, p. 727. [Caltech report C^3P-332]

139. Fucito, F. and S. Solomon (1985). "A concurrent pseudo fermion algorithm," *Computer Phys. Commun.,* Vol. 36, p. 141. [Caltech report C^3P-118]

140. Fucito, F. and S. Solomon (1985). "On the order of the deconfining transition for finite temperature QCD in the presence of dynamical quarks," *Phys. Rev. D,* Vol. 31, p. 1460. [Caltech report C^3P-334]

141. Fucito, F., J. M. Moriarty, C. Rebbi and S. Solomon (1986). "The hadronic spectrum with dynamical fermions," *Phys. Lett. B,* Vol. 17, p. 235. [Caltech report C^3P-341]

142. Flower, J. W. and S. Otto (1985). "The field distribution in $SU(3)$ lattice gauge theory," *Phys. Lett.,* Vol. B160, p. 128. [Caltech report C^3P-178]

143. Furmanski, W. and A. Kolawa (1987). "Yang–Mills vacuum: An attempt at lattice loop calculus," *Nucl. Phys. B,* Vol. 291, p. 594. [Caltech report C^3P-335]

144. Flower, J. and S. Otto (1986). "Scaling violations in the heavy quark potential," *Phys. Rev.* Vol. 34, p. 1649. [Caltech report C^3P-262]

145. Flower, J. (1986). "Baryons on the lattice—I. Rotational symmetry," CALT-68-1369, Caltech report C^3P-319.

146. Flower, J. (1986). "Baryons on the lattice—II. Static potential," CALT-68-1377, Caltech report C^3P-361.

147. Flower, J. (1986). "Baryons on the lattice—III. Energy density," CALT-68-1378, Caltech report C^3P-362.

148. Barhen, J. (1986). "An intelligent machine operating system for hypercube ensemble architectures, *Proceedings DOE/CESAR Workshop on Planning and Sensing for Autonomous Navigation,* pp. 61–83. ORNL/TM-9987, Oak Ridge National Laboratory.

149. Barhen, J., N. Toomarian, and V. Protopopescu (1987). "Optimization of the computational load of a hypercube supercomputer onboard a mobile robot," *Appl. Optics,* Vol. 26, No. 23, p. 5007.

150. Scalapino, D. J. and R. L. Sugar (1981). "A method for performing Monte Carlo calculations for systems with fermions," *Phys. Rev. Lett.,* Vol. 46, p. 519.

151. Jefferson, D. (1985). "Virtual time," *ACM Trans. Programming Lang. Sys.,* Vol. 7, No. 3, p. 405 [and references therein].

152. Brooks, E., G. Fox, S. Otto, M. Randeria, W. Athas, E. Debenedictis, N. Newton, and C. Seitz (1983). "Glueball mass calculations on an array of computers," *Nucl. Phys.,* Vol. B220 [FS8].

153. Otto, S. and M. Randeria (1983). "Modified action glueballs," *Nucl. Phys. B,* Vol. 255, p. 579. [Caltech report C^3P-330]

154. Otto, S. and P. Stolorz (1985). "An improvement for glueball mass calculations on a lattice," *Phys. Lett. B,* Vol. 151, p. 428 [Caltech report C^3P-101, C^3-343]

155. Patel, A., S. Otto, and R. Gupta (1985). "The non-perturbative β-function for $SU(2)$ lattice gauge theory," *Phys. Lett. B,* Vol. 159, p. 143. [Caltech report C^3P-216]

156. Stolorz, P. (1986). "Microcanonical renormalization group for $SU(2)$," *Phys. Lett. B,* Vol. 172, p. 77.

12

STOCHASTIC PETRI NETS AS A TOOL FOR THE ANALYSIS OF HIGH-PERFORMANCE DISTRIBUTED ARCHITECTURES

M. Ajmone Marsan, G. Chiola, and G. Conte

INTRODUCTION

Understanding the effectiveness of the different software/hardware architectural alternatives is a crucial point in the design of supercomputers, and in general of any high-performance distributed computing system. Owing to the growing complexity of such systems, the design process can no longer be committed uniquely to the "feeling" of the architecture designers, but must be supported by a well-established quantitative methodology. A lot of theoretical and practical work has been done in the last years in the field of performance evaluation, but, as outlined by Ferrari,[1] the world of performance-evaluation specialists has suffered since its emergence from a sort of insularity in the large computer science community. The impact of these techniques on the system design process has thus been minimal and sporadic.

The classical methodologies of performance evaluation have the goal of assessing and comparing different computer installations in order to either identify and remove the possible bottlenecks of a given system, or predict the effectiveness of upgraded configurations. This approach is often supported by measurements performed on real systems (monitoring) in order to extract significant parameters. In the case of supercomputing and of distributed systems with tight performance requirements, the quite different objective of performance evaluation is the quantitative assessment of the design alternatives arising after the first definition stages. Modeling techniques are thus compulsory, and the approach is effective only if the designer has confidence in the modeling techniques and in the analysis methodology.

From this point of view, performance-evaluation techniques should be no longer considered a bizarre discipline cultivated by eccentric people, but one of the basic elements that form the knowledge of a system designer. On the other side, a lot of effort is needed from the specialists to offer efficient methodologies and tools to cope with the problems encountered by the system designers. We aim to make some contribution in this direction.

Performance Analysis and Stochastic Petri Nets

The establishment of a methodology for performance analysis is based, first, on the choice of the level of detail at which the system has to be described, and, as a consequence, of the modeling tool to be used. As an example, if the adequacy of a piece of hardware to accomplish a given task has to be evaluated, the best choice could be to model the system as a set of logic gates and to use a simulator to perform the analysis.

The second choice that must be made is related to the "stimuli" to which the system must be submitted in order to obtain the desired answers; in the vocabulary of performance analysis this is called "workload." If the knowledge of the final application is very deep, traces of deterministic temporal sequences of significant events can be used as workload. In other cases, the complex phenomena that take place in the system can be described by means of probabilistic assumptions. The latter approach has some advantages: not all the details of the system behavior need to be known to perform the analysis, as may happen in the early design steps; furthermore it is possible to obtain performance indices using analytical or numerical techniques instead of simulation; architectural choices can be ordered by considering classes of applications instead of specific cases.

Performance evaluation of computer systems using analytic approaches has for a long time been based on the theory of stochastic point processes, and in particular of some special classes of stochastic processes that are easier to handle from a mathematical point of view. The best-known and most widely used example of such a class is provided by Markov processes[2-5] (including Markov chains as a subclass). However, the development and the solution of analytical models of computer system performance based on stochastic processes require a fairly deep knowledge of the underlying theory.

Performance models based on the theory of queues[6-8] have become very popular because they allow some features typical of the behavior of a computer system to be described in a simple graphical manner, and because they can be translated into a stochastic process model, and analyzed as such. Moreover, for a wide class of queueing models, closed-form solutions have been computed and are readily available. Much of the difficulty inherent in the use of stochastic processes can thus be overcome if suitable classes of queueing models can be used.

Unfortunately, however, not all the features typical of the operation of computer systems (and in particular of parallel computer systems) lend themselves to a neat description in terms of the subclass of queueing systems for which closed-form solutions are known. Examples of the features that cannot easily be handled with queueing models are simultaneous resource possession, synchronization, blocking, and splitting of customers.

Recently, a new class of stochastic models has been used for the performance evaluation of distributed architectures. These models are generally known under the name stochastic Petri nets.[9-15] They are obtained by introducing a stochastic time measure into classical Petri net models.[16-18] Stochastic Petri nets allow those features that are difficult to handle with queueing systems (blocking, synchronization, splitting of customers, and the like) to be described simply, but they do not offer a gamut of closed-form results that can readily be utilized. Thus, the analysis of a stochastic Petri net model involves its translation into a stochastic process model, and its solution with classical tools. However, the advantage of the graphical representation of the system operations is maintained, and the translation into a stochastic process model, as well as its solution, can be automated by a suitable computer tool.

A further advantage of stochastic Petri net models is their precise and unambiguous description of the system operations, and the possibility of using a Petri net-based approach in several different phases of the system design, namely, specification, verification, performance analysis, and automated implementation. This has the advantage of integrating the performance evaluation step into the design process, as is not always the case at present.

Analysis of a Multiprocessor Architecture with Cache Memories

As a significant example of the use of stochastic Petri nets for the analysis of complex architectures, we discuss the effectiveness of different policies for the loading and unloading of the cache memories' content in a multiprocessor environment.

Cache memories[19] have long been used as an effective tool for performance improvement of computer systems. Indeed, it often happens that the performance of a computer is limited by the memory access time rather than by the CPU speed. On the other hand, using large, high-speed primary memories that match the CPU speed could result in excessive cost or even be unfeasible. A smaller size, high-speed cache memory can then be interposed between the CPU and the primary memory, this faster memory being loaded with the information that is most frequently accessed by the CPU.

Many large, medium, and even small computers today have cache memories, and in the near future cache memories will be common also in one-chip microcomputers. It thus seems natural that multiprocessor computer

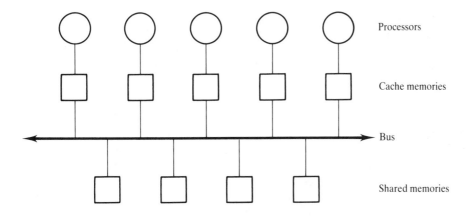

Figure 12-1. Single-bus multiprocessor architecture with private cache memories.

systems should be designed using cache memories. A sketch of the organization of a multiprocessor architecture using caches is presented in Figure 12-1. Each CPU (or processor) has direct access to a private cache memory, while the main memory is comprised of several blocks that can be accessed through an interconnection network, and that are shared among processors. The availability of cache memories is in this case even more important than in a single processor system, because of the phenomenon of memory interference among processors and of contention for the use of the interconnection network. In this chapter we restrict our attention to multiprocessor architectures in which the interconnection network is made of one global bus linking all processors and memories. In this case, the memory interference problem does not exist, but the contention for the bus may be severe.

Several different policies have been proposed for the dynamic loading and unloading of the cache memory content.[19] Here we consider the copy-back and write-through policies with and without buffering. In the former case, main memory lines are loaded into the cache when needed, and the lines discarded to make room are copied back to the main memory, possibly through the use of buffers. In the latter case, write operations are performed on the main memory as well as on the cache, so that discarded lines need not be copied back in the main memory.

A copy-back strategy in a multiprocessor environment raises the problem of maintaining consistency among caches and main memory. A number of cache-consistency protocols have been devised to deal with this problem,[20] and Petri net techniques have already been proposed both for their validation[21] and for their performance evaluation.[22] However, since this chapter is intended to provide a tutorial on the use of stochastic Petri nets, rather than a thorough study of cache memories, we do not consider this issue. For the sake of simplicity, we concentrate on hardware and architectural problems, without explicitly modeling the consistency algorithms.

OVERVIEW OF PN DEFINITIONS
AND NOTATION

A Petri net with inhibitor arcs (PN)[17] comprises a set of places P, a set of transitions T, and three functions defined on the set of transitions. The input, output, and inhibition functions ($I(.)$, $O(.)$, and $H(.)$) map transitions on "bags" (or multisets, i.e., sets with multiplicity) of places. In the graphical representation of PNs, places are drawn as circles and transitions as bars. The input and output functions are represented with directed arcs from places to transitions and vice versa, with the multiplicity written as a number close to the arc (the number 1 is omitted). The inhibition function is represented with small-circle-headed arcs connecting a transition t_i to every place p_j contained in $H(t_i)$. We denote by $i_j(t_k)$, $o_j(t_k)$, and $h_j(t_k)$ the multiplicity of input, output, and inhibitor arcs connecting p_j and t_k.

Places may contain tokens, drawn as black dots. The state of a PN is defined as the number of tokens contained in each place. The PN state is usually called the PN marking, and is a bag of places M; it can be convenient to represent the marking M with a p-tuple (where p is the number of places of the PN) $(m_1, \ldots, m_p)$, where m_i is a natural number representing the multiplicity of place p_i into the marking M.

A formal definition of PN is thus the following:

$$PN = (P, T, I(.), O(.), H(.), M_0) \qquad (12\text{-}1)$$

where M_0 is the initial marking of the net.

In Figure 12-2 a very simple example of a Petri net is depicted, representing a tightly coupled two-processor system with a shared memory. Places p_1 and p_2 represent two processors running concurrently on private memories. Transitions t_1 and t_2 represent the issuing of an access request for the shared memory. Transitions t_3 and t_4 represent the start of the shared memory access from processors 1 and 2, respectively. The inhibitor arc connecting p_3 to t_4 gives priority for the shared memory access to processor 1, when both processors issue an access request (one token is present both in p_3 and in p_4). Place p_6 represents the condition in which the shared memory is free, thus acting as a semaphore that guarantees exclusive access. Transitions t_5 and t_6 model the end of a memory access, after which the common memory is released, and the processor resumes its running.

A transition t_i is said to be *enabled* by marking M iff $I(t_i)$ is contained in M and for each $p_j \in H(t_i)$ (i.e., for each j such that $h_j(t_i) > 0$) $m_j < h_j(t_i)$. Any enabled transition t_i into marking M_j can fire, changing the state of the PN to marking $M_k = M_j - I(t_i) + O(t_i)$ (i.e., removing as many tokens as the multiplicity of the input arcs of t_i from, and adding as many tokens as the multiplicity of the output arcs into, the corresponding places). In this we say that M_k is *one-step reachable* (and actually reached) from marking M_j by firing transition t_i. The firing of transition t_i may disable other (previously enabled) transitions that are said to be in conflict with t_i.

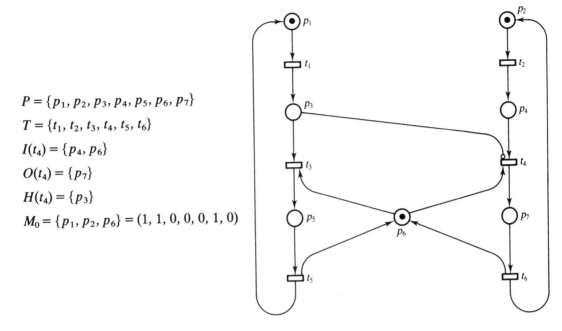

$P = \{p_1, p_2, p_3, p_4, p_5, p_6, p_7\}$

$T = \{t_1, t_2, t_3, t_4, t_5, t_6\}$

$I(t_4) = \{p_4, p_6\}$

$O(t_4) = \{p_7\}$

$H(t_4) = \{p_3\}$

$M_0 = \{p_1, p_2, p_6\} = (1, 1, 0, 0, 0, 1, 0)$

Figure 12-2. A Petri net representing a two-processor system.

A marking $M_{(k)}$ is said to be reachable from marking $M_{(1)}$ iff there exists a sequence of markings $M_{(1)}, M_{(2)}, \ldots, M_{(k)}$ such that, for every pair of consecutive markings $M_{(n)}, M_{(n+1)}$ the marking $M_{(n+1)}$ is one-step reachable from marking $M_{(n)}$ by firing some enabled transition.

The reachablility set (RS) $R(M_0)$ of the PN is the set of all markings reachable from M_0, including M_0 itself. If, for every marking $M \in R(M_0)$, m_p is less than or equal to some natural number k, then place p is said to be *k-bounded*. If there exists a number K such that all places of the PN are K-bounded, then the PN itself is said to be *K-bounded*.

The reachability graph (RG) $G(M_0)$ of the PN is the directed graph whose vertices are the elements of $R(M_0)$, and whose arcs (i, j) indicate that M_j is one-step reachable from M_i.

The incidence matrix $\mathbf{C}$ of a PN defined as in (1) has entries $c_{jk} = o_j(t_k) - i_j(t_k)$. The vector $\mathbf{i}$, integer solution of the matrix equation $\mathbf{C}^T\mathbf{i} = \mathbf{0}$ is a *place invariant* (P-invariant) of the PN. Similarly, the vector $\mathbf{j}$, solution of the matrix equation $\mathbf{Cj} = \mathbf{0}$ is a *transition invariant* (T-invariant) of the PN. Invariants define structural properties of the PN. The scalar product between a P-invariant and any marking $M \in R(M_0)$ yields a constant, the *token count* of the invariant. The linear equation resulting from this scalar product will be indicated as a *marking invariant* (M-invariant).

The reachability graph of our example net of Figure 12-2 is shown in Figure 12-3. The incidence matrix and the three minimal-support P-invariants are as

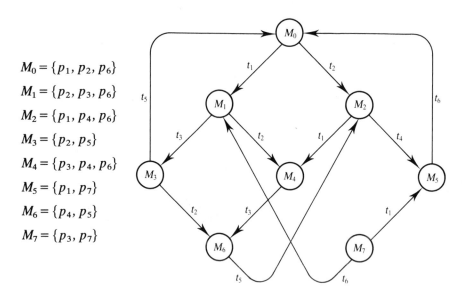

$$M_0 = \{p_1, p_2, p_6\}$$
$$M_1 = \{p_2, p_3, p_6\}$$
$$M_2 = \{p_1, p_4, p_6\}$$
$$M_3 = \{p_2, p_5\}$$
$$M_4 = \{p_3, p_4, p_6\}$$
$$M_5 = \{p_1, p_7\}$$
$$M_6 = \{p_4, p_5\}$$
$$M_7 = \{p_3, p_7\}$$

Figure 12-3. Reachability graph for the PN in Figure 12-2.

follows:

	t_1	t_2	t_3	t_4	t_5	t_6	i_1	i_2	i_3
p_1	-1				1		1		
p_2		-1				1		1	
p_3	1		-1				1		
p_4		1		-1				1	
p_5			1		-1		1		1
p_6		-1	-1		1	1			1
p_7				1		-1		1	1

By multiplying the P-invariants for the initial marking we obtain:

$$m_1 + m_3 + m_5 = 1$$
$$m_2 + m_4 + m_7 = 1$$
$$m_5 + m_6 + m_7 = 1$$

The first two M-invariants state that the tokens representing the two processors are preserved during shared-memory accesses, while the last one proves that the access to the shared memory is actually exclusive, since no more than one token can be shared among p_5 and p_7. The fact that the net is covered by P-invariants (all places belong to at least one P-invariant) also implies boundedness (in this case the net is 1-bounded).

TIMED PETRI NETS (TPN)

The most natural way of introducing time into a PN is based on its interpretation as a system model in which, given a situation (marking), some time must elapse before an event occurs (i.e., a transition fires). The event is the final result of some activity that is performed by the system when it is in the situation specified by the marking. Time is thus naturally associated with transitions, indicating that they can fire some time after they become enabled. The choice of associating time with transitions is the most frequent in the literature on timed PN (TPN),[23] and the resulting models are known as *timed transition PN* or TTPN.

From TTPN it is possible to derive either analytical or simulation models of the system under investigation. The derivation of a simulation model from a TTPN poses mainly implementation problems, and some packages exist for this purpose.[24-26] The derivation of an analytical model from a TTPN may be more complex, and present subtle theoretical problems. In this chapter we consider only the issues related to TTPN analysis, and do not discuss the problems concerning their simulation.

Traditionally, timing in a TTPN was specified either in a deterministic or in a stochastic manner. In the former case, times are defined to be constant, and the TTPN analysis can be performed using an algebraic approach. Timing constraints in this case usually change the qualitative behavior of the model with respect to the underlying untimed PN. In the latter case, transition firing delays are defined to be random variables with given probability distributions,[27,28] so that the TTPN can be viewed as a graphical representation of a stochastic process, which can be analyzed using a probabilistic approach. The qualitative behavior of the model does not change with respect to the underlying PN, provided that delay distributions have unlimited support.[29]

When random firing delays are used, it is necessary to further separate the cases of discrete- and continuous-time distributions. Some results concerning the integration of deterministic transition firing delays into TTPN with geometrically distributed timing have been published.[30,31] In the first case[30] the deterministic delays are restricted to be equal to the step of the geometric distribution, whereas, in the second case,[31] arbitrary deterministic times are allowed.

STOCHASTIC PETRI NETS

TTPN in which firing delays are defined to be random variables with continuous probability distributions are generally called *stochastic Petri nets*.

TTPN With Exponential Timing (SPN)

Several authors independently proposed the association of random, exponentially distributed firing delays with PN transitions as a simple, but useful technique for augmenting a PN model with timing. In the earlier works,[9,27,28] the authors mainly considered the association of a (possibly marking-dependent) firing rate with each transition in the net. The resulting models were called *stochastic PN* (SPN). Consider an SPN with a marking M in which several transitions are simultaneously enabled. The model semantics is such that the transition with which is associated the shortest delay will fire first. The SPN reaches then a new marking M' in which transitions that were already enabled in a previous marking, but did not fire, may still be enabled. Because of the memoryless property of the exponential distribution that yields a residual life distribution equal to the distribution of the firing delay itself, it can be assumed that the activity associated with each transition is restarted in any new marking. This assumption is valid even if the semantics of the model implies that activities are continued; indeed, the restarting of the activity associated with a transition is not "felt" by the model.

A formal definition of an SPN is thus the following:

$$SPN = (P, T, I(.), O(.), H(.), M_0, L) \qquad (12\text{-}2)$$

where $(P, T, I(.), O(.), H(.), M_0)$ is the PN associated with the SPN, and

$$L = \{l_1, l_2, \ldots, l_n\} \qquad (12\text{-}3)$$

is the set of *marking-dependent* firing rates associated with the PN transitions.

Owing to the memoryless property of the exponential distribution of firing delays, SPN are isomorphic to continuous-time Markov chains (CTMC).[28] In particular, a K-bounded SPN can be shown to be isomorphic to a finite MC. The MC associated with a given SPN can be obtained using the following rules.

1. The MC state space S corresponds to the reachability set $R(M_0)$ of the PN associated with the SPN $(M_i \leftrightarrow i)$
2. The transition rate from state i (corresponding to marking M_i) to state j (M_j) is obtained as

$$q_{ij} = \sum_{k:\, t_k \in E_{ij}} l_k \qquad (12\text{-}4)$$

where E_{ij} is the set of transitions enabled by marking M_i whose firing generates marking M_j.

Using these rules, it is possible to obtain an algorithm that automatically derives from the SPN description the state transition-rate matrix of the isomorphic CTMC.

An SPN is said to be *ergodic* if it generates an ergodic CTMC. A sufficient condition for an SPN to be ergodic is that the initial marking M_0 is reachable from any $M \in R(M_0)$. If the SPN is ergodic, it is possible to compute the steady-state probability distribution on markings, solving the usual matrix equation:

$$\pi Q = 0 \qquad (12\text{-}5)$$

with the additional constraint:

$$\sum_i \pi_i = 1 \qquad (12\text{-}6)$$

where $\mathbf{Q}$ is the infinitesimal generator whose elements are obtained as explained before, and π is the vector of the steady-state probabilities.

From the steady-state distribution π it is possible to obtain quantitative estimates of the behavior of the SPN. For example:

- *Probability of a particular condition* of the SPN. If in the subset $A \subset R(M_0)$ the particular condition is satisfied, the required probability is given by:

$$P\{A\} = \sum_{i \in A} \pi_i \qquad (12\text{-}7)$$

- *Expected value of the number of tokens in a given place.* If $A(i, n)$ is the subset of $R(M_0)$ for which the number of tokens in place p_i is n, and the place is k-bounded, then the expected value of the number of tokens in p_i is given by

$$E[m_i] = \sum_{n=1}^{k} [nP\{A(i, n)\}] \qquad (12\text{-}8)$$

- *Mean number of firings in unit time.* If A_j is the subset of $R(M_0)$ in which a given transition t_j is enabled, then the mean number of firings of t_j in the unit time is given by

$$f_j = \sum_{i:\, M_i \in A_j} \left(\pi_i \frac{l_j}{\displaystyle\sum_{k:\, t_k \text{ enabled in } M_i} l_k} \right) \qquad (12\text{-}9)$$

If we assume that the transitions of the example in Figure 12-2 are associated with the firing rate vector $L = [1, 1, 10^3, 10^3, 1, 1]$ (running and access times are equal, while the arbitration time for the access to the shared resource is three orders of magnitude shorter), we can label the reachability graph of Figure 12-3 with these firing rates, obtaining the infinitesimal generator of the continuous-time Markov Chain:

$$\mathbf{Q} = \begin{bmatrix}
-2 & 1 & 1 & 0 & 0 & 0 & 0 & 0 \\
0 & -1001 & 0 & 1000 & 1 & 0 & 0 & 0 \\
0 & 0 & -1001 & 0 & 1 & 1000 & 0 & 0 \\
1 & 0 & 0 & -2 & 0 & 0 & 1 & 0 \\
0 & 0 & 0 & 0 & -1000 & 0 & 1000 & 0 \\
1 & 0 & 0 & 0 & 0 & -2 & 0 & 1 \\
0 & 0 & 1 & 0 & 0 & 0 & -1 & 0 \\
0 & 1 & 0 & 0 & 0 & 0 & 0 & -1
\end{bmatrix}$$

The steady-state solution of this chain yields the following marking probabilities:

mark	M_0	M_1	M_2	M_3	M_4	M_5	M_6	M_7
prob	0.1997	0.0004	0.0004	0.1995	10^{-6}	0.1998	0.2003	0.1998

The limitation of SPN is that the graphical representation of systems rapidly becomes difficult when system size and complexity increase. Moreover, the number of states of the associated MC grows very fast with the dimensions of the net. SPN can thus be used only to model systems of limited size.

SPN With Immediate Transitions (GSPN)

Generalized stochastic Petri nets (GSPN) were introduced in refs. 12 and 32 in order to try to cope with the problem associated with the explosion of the number of MC states by defining two types of transitions: timed transitions and immediate transitions. An exponentially distributed firing time is associated with timed transitions, whereas immediate transitions are defined to fire in zero time with priority over timed transitions. We adopt the convention of drawing timed transitions as white boxes, and immediate transitions as black bars. Firing rates are obviously associated only with timed transitions, and they may depend on the GSPN marking.

A formal definition of a GSPN is thus as in Eqn. (12-2) where now the array L contains firing rates in the case of timed transitions, and weights in the case of immediate transitions.[32]

Several transitions may be simultaneously enabled in a marking. If the set of enabled transitions E comprises only timed transitions, then the enabled timed transition t_i ($t_i \in E$) fires with problability

$$\frac{l_i}{\sum\limits_{k:\, t_k \in E} l_k} \qquad (12\text{-}10)$$

exactly as in the case of SPN. If E comprises both immediate and timed transitions, then only immediate transitions can fire (with priority over timed ones). If E comprises zero or more timed transitions and only one immediate transition, then this is the one that fires. When E comprises several immediate transitions, Eqn. (12-10) can still be used, but now the firing probability is a ratio of weights. The association of weights with immediate transitions requires the identification of sets of immediate transitions that may be in conflict with each other, called extended conflict set (ECS).[32] The identification of ECS can be implemented based on structural and linear invariant techniques.[32] Consistency checks for the correct probabilistic definition of probabilities through the use of ECS are performed with a structural analysis of the underlying PN, based on the notion of *confusion*.[32]

By examining the GSPN behavior as a function of time we can easily realize that it is equivalent to the time behavior of a stochastic point process (SPP) $\{X(t), t \geq 0\}$ with a finite state space. A one-to-one correspondence exists between GPSN markings and SPP states. Sample functions, representing a possible behavior sequence of the SPP, may present "multiple discontinuities" due to the sequential firing of one or more immediate transitions. The process is observed to spend a nonnegative amount of time in markings enabling timed transitions only, while it transits in zero time through markings enabling immediate transitions. We call *tangible* a state (or marking) of the former type and *vanishing* a state (or marking) of the latter type.

GSPN applications allow the following assumptions to be made.

- The reachability set is finite.
- Firing rates do not depend on time parameters.
- The initial marking is reachable with a nonzero probability from any marking in the reachability set. No marking (or group of markings) exists that "absorbs" the process.
- No infinite path of vanishing markings can be followed when walking through the reachability graph.

Disregarding, for the time being, the concept of time, and focusing our attention on the set of states the process enters because of a transition (note that the word "transition" in this context indicates a change of state due to the firing of a transition of the net) out of a given state, we can observe that an embedded Markov chain (EMC) can be recognized within the SPP. The behavior specifications listed previously are sufficient for the computation of the transition probabilities of the EMC. The EMC can then either be solved numerically for steady-state probability, or, more conveniently, be *reduced* to comprise tangible states only, as shown in refs. 12 and 32. The numerical steady-state solution of the reduced EMC is computationally less expensive to perform, since the state transition matrix is (usually) substantially smaller than the one of the original EMC. The reduction procedure is possible because the analyst is interested only in the timed part of the SPP. The immediate part of the SPP contributes to the specification of its behavior but has no direct impact on the evaluation of performance estimates.

Using this technique, we can analyze GSPN models of systems that are too complex to be studied by means of SPN. This is possible for two reasons: first, since immediate transitions have priority over timed transitions, the number of reachable markings in a GSPN is smaller than in a topologically identical SPN. Second, vanishing markings can be removed from the SPP, thus further reducing the state space, and generating a Markov-chain model whose solution is easier to compute.

In our example of Figure 12-2, if we define the two transitions t_3 and t_4 to be immediate and the other four transitions to be exponentially timed with rate 1, we obtain the GSPN of Figure 12-4. Its reachability graph is shown in Figure 12-5(a), from which we can see that marking M_4 of the PN RS of Figure 12-3 is no longer reachable, owing to the priority mechanism defined on immediate transitions. In Figure 12-5(b) the tangible RG of the GSPN is depicted, in which vanishing markings are collapsed into state-transition arcs.

Since M_4 was the only marking in which the inhibitor arc connecting p_3 and t_4 played a role in the enabling conditions of t_4, this arc has no effect in the GSPN of Figure 12-4 and can thus be removed without changing the behavior of the

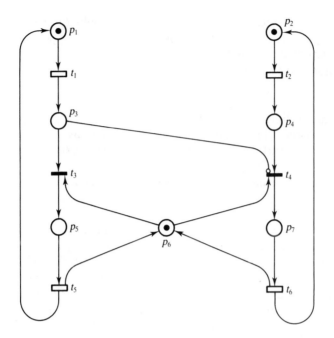

Figure 12-4. GSPN model of the multiprocessor system.

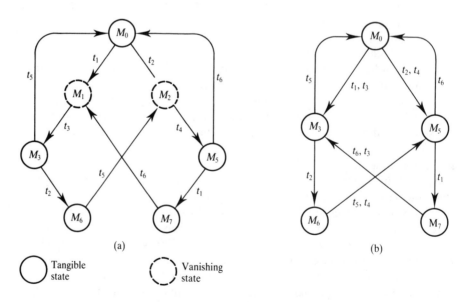

Figure 12-5. (a) Reachability of the GSPN in Figure 12-4. (b) Tangible reachability graph.

model. Notice, therefore, that in the GSPN the two processors behave identically and can thus be considered statistically equivalent.

In GSPN models, exponentially distributed firing times coexist with firing delays that are deterministically equal to zero. Even though immediate transitions increase the modeling power of GSPN with respect to SPN with all exponentially timed transitions, this does not represent a significant extension of the type of firing-time distributions available in the model.

FOLDING OF A GSPN MODEL

Parallel systems are often designed using a modular approach, so that their architecture comprises several replicas of identical units that cooperate for the solution of a single problem.

The models of systems of this type must separately describe each module replica, in order to correctly represent the parallelism of computations. In some cases it is mandatory that each module be distinguished from others: for example, when the individual behavior of each module must be analyzed, when the parameters of the various modules are different, or when a different workload is applied to each module. More frequently, the individual representation of each module is not necessary, and it can be traded off for an increased simplicity in the model.

In the case of GSPN, the existence of several identical modules in the system is reflected by the presence of as many identical subnets that are properly interconnected. When the modules need not be distinguished for the computation of the relevant performance figures, it is often possible to exploit the GSPN symmetry to construct compact models. This process is called *folding*, since its initial step is the construction of a GSPN in which the identical subnets are folded onto each other. The compact model is then completed by inserting in the net the elements that in the original model interconnect the subnets.

Again using the two-processor system as an example, we can see that the model of Figure 12-4 is composed of two identical subnets that describe the behavior of each processor and that are interconnected by the subnet that represents the shared memory. It is then easy to fold onto each other the two processor subnets and then to insert into the model the shared-memory representation. By so doing we obtain the GSPN in Figure 12-6.

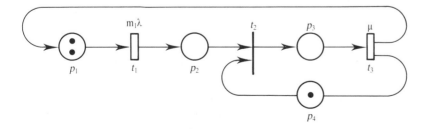

Figure 12-6. Folded GSPN model of the multiprocessor system.

Place p_1 contains tokens that represent "thinking" processors, that is, processors running on their private memories. Transition t_1 models the shared-memory access request issued by a thinking processor. Hence it is exponentially timed, and fires at a load-dependent rate equal to $m_1\lambda$, where m_1 is the number of tokens in p_1, and $\lambda = 1$ is the rate at which each thinking processor issues a memory request. Place p_2 contains tokens representing processors that have issued a memory request, but have not yet started their access. Place p_4 may contain a token representing the free shared memory. The immediate transition t_2 models the start of access, and place p_3 may contain a token representing a processor accessing the shared memory. Transition t_3 with firing rate $\mu = 1$ models the access time.

Note that in this folded model the two processors are not distinguishable any more: we have obtained a more abstract and more compact model, that in fact is the GSPN representation of an M/M/1/2/2 queue. Indeed, processors can be viewed as customers of a "service center" constituted by the arbitration mechanism for the access to the shared memory. Using queueing terminology, place p_2 acts as a queue, and place p_3 represents a Markovian single server.

As a final remark, it is important to stress that while the construction of a detailed GSPN model of a complex system is fairly easy, the development of compact models based on the folding approach, may in some instances be nontrivial, and require experience and ingenuity.

SPN with Generally Distributed Firing Times

Two papers have dealt with the extension of SPN to arbitrarily distributed firing times.[13,29] In the first paper,[13] the authors define extended SPN (ESPN), and classify transitions in the three following categories.

- *Exclusive transitions*: for all markings that enable an exclusive transition t_i, this is the only enabled transition.
- *Competitive transitions*: for all markings enabling a competitive (nonexclusive) transition t_i, all enabled transitions are in conflict with t_i (their firing disables t_1).
- *Concurrent transitions*: for some marking enabling a concurrent (nonexclusive) transition t_i, some enabled transition is not in conflict with t_i (its firing does not affect the enabling of t_i).

It is then possible to show that the SPP underlying an ESPN is semi-Markov, provided that with all concurrent transitions is associated an exponentially distributed firing time, and that the firing policy of all competitive transitions is such that, when they become enabled, the new firing delay is resampled from the distribution associated with the transition. Exclusive and competitive transitions can be associated with arbitrarily distributed firing delays. The steady-state distribution of the semi-Markov process underlying an ESPN is then obtained with standard techniques.

In the second paper,[29] subsequently expanded in ref. 34, a deeper analysis of transition firing policies is presented. Under the *race* policy, all enabled transitions sample a firing delay when a new marking is entered, and the minimum sampled delay determines both the transition that fires, and the sojourn time in the marking. The distributions that are sampled by each transition can be either the distributions of the transition firing delay (race with *resampling* or RR), or the distributions of the remaining time to fire, counting the time for which the transition was enabled either since its last firing (race with *age memory* or RA) or since it has become enabled (race with *enabling memory* or RE).

In the case of resampling, the SPP underlying the SPN is semi-Markov by definition, whereas in the cases with memory the SPP in a Markov process with partly discrete and partly continuous state-space. Solution techniques are presented in refs. 29 and 34 in the case of phase type distributions.[35] The expanded modeling capability is paid for with increased complexity of the state-space of the underlying Markov-chain model.

SPN with Deterministic and Exponential Firing Times (DSPN)

An extension of GSPN models that allows firing delays of timed transition to be either constant or exponentially distributed random variables, has been considered.[14,36]

The resulting class of models is called DSPN, where the D stands for deterministic transition timing and the S stands for stochastic (exponentially distributed) transition timing. The formal definition of a DSPN is again similar to Eqn. (12-2), but now the array L contains the transition rates of exponential transitions, the weights of immediate transitions, and the firing delays of deterministic transitions. In order to distinguish the two timed transition types, we draw exponential transitions as white boxes and deterministic transitions as black boxes.

The firing policy entailed by DSPN is race with enabling memory (RE). Local preselection among conflicting activities can be implemented using random switches of immediate transitions as in GSPN. The definition of the firing policy is important because deterministic transitions can be disabled before their firing delay has elapsed, thus allowing, for instance, the easy modeling of communication protocol timeouts.

APPLICABILITY CONDITIONS

In order to keep the underlying stochastic model reasonably simple, some restrictions must be observed in the use of deterministic firing times.

In the cases of exclusive and competitive transitions, a constant firing delay can be used freely. If we restrict all DSPN markings to enable at most one deterministic concurrent transition, then the model solution becomes fairly simple, and it can be obtained using the technique described in the next section.

Note that this constraint can often be checked a priori (i.e., before generating the reachability graph) by analyzing the M-invariants covering the input places of the deterministic transitions.

The restriction of no more than one deterministic transition enabled in each marking is a sufficient condition to maintain the DSPN reachability graph structure independent of time constraints. This nice property can be exploited to use classical PN analysis techniques like linear algebra for invariant computation.

ANALYSIS OF DSPN

Under the condition of at most one deterministic concurrent transition enabled in each marking, it is possible to map the DSPN on a semi-Markov process,[2,3,37] using an approach quite similar to the "embedded Markov chain" (EMC) technique discussed by Kleinrock[6] for the analysis of M/G/1 queueing systems. Indeed, it is possible to define a discrete-time Markov chain by sampling the continuous-time process at the instants of deterministic transition firing if a deterministic transition is enabled, and at the instants of firing of any exponential transition otherwise. For the sake of convenience in explanation, we further distinguish two classes of concurrent deterministic transitions: *independent* transitions, which cannot be disabled by the firing of another transition, and *preemptable* transitions, which can.

When either no deterministic transition, or an exclusive deterministic transition is enabled in a given marking M_i, this marking trivially maps into state S_i of the EMC. The average sojourn time in S_i is $1/\Lambda_i$ if no deterministic transition is enabled in it, where Λ_i is the sum of the firing rates λ_k of all transitions t_k enabled in M_i; the state transition probability $P\{S_i \rightarrow S_j\}$ is λ_k/Λ_i if there exists a transition t_k enabled in M_i whose firing changes the marking to M_j.

When an independent deterministic transition t_d is enabled in marking M_i, together with some exponential transitions, the next state of the EMC is sampled only at the instant of firing of t_d; that is, the EMC state evolution does not account for the marking changes due to the firing of exponential transitions during the enabling interval τ_d of t_d, but "delays" those possible state changes to the instant of firing of the deterministic transition; the state transition probability of the EMC is then computed using the Chapman–Kolmogorov equation.

In the case of either a competitive transition or a preemptable deterministic transition t_d, the next state of the EMC is sampled either at the instant of firing of t_d, or at the instant in which t_d is disabled. We can compute the probability of actually firing t_d by studying the transient evolution of the stochastic part of the process during the time interval t_d.

A solution technique for this class of models considering only one deterministic transition at a time is presented in refs. 14 and 36. From the steady-state solution of the EMC it is possible to compute the steady-state probability distribution of the DSPN by weighting the state probabilities with the mean sojourn times, and converting the probabilities of states enabling concurrent deterministic transitions with a conversion matrix $\mathbf{C}_d$ that accounts for the difference between $E[M_i]$, the average sojourn time in the DSPN marking and $E[S_i]$, the average sojourn time in the EMC state.

The EMC transition probability matrix, the state mean sojourn times, and the probability conversion matrix, can all be computed efficiently using truncated Taylor series expansion of matrix exponentials. The steady-state solution algorithm for DSPN enabling no more than one deterministic concurrent transition in each marking has been embedded into a computer package for the analysis of GSPN models,[26,38] allowing an automated analysis of DSPN with several hundreds of markings in their reachability set.

A SIMPLE EXAMPLE

To clarify the use of the solution technique outlined in the previous section, we illustrate its application to our usual two-processor example. If we take the GSPN model of Figure 12-6 and substitute for the exponential transition t_3 a deterministic one with firing time $\tau = 1$, we obtain the DSPN in Figure 12-7. The motivation for this change is that, while the interrequest times can easily be imagined to be stochastic (owing to the imprecise knowledge of the actual programs that are running on the processors), a memory access is usually an activity of fixed duration, determined by the speed of the clock of the processors, and the number of bytes to be read or written. The DSPN in Figure 12-7 can thus be viewed as a more realistic model (a second approximation) of the system under study. More generally, this model is the DSPN representation of an M/D/1/2/2 queue.

The applicability conditions for the analytical solution of the model are satisfied, since the only deterministic transition (t_3) can be enabled only once, as proved by the M-invariant $m_3 + m_4 = 1$. The reachability graph generated by the DSPN in Figure 12-7 is the same as that of the GSPN in Figure 12-6, and is shown in Figure 12-8(a). It contains three tangible markings labeled T_1, T_2, and T_3, as well as one vanishing marking labeled V. The possible transitions among markings are represented by arrows labeled with the letters "e," "i," and "d," to specify whether the transition that causes the change of marking is exponential (t_1), immediate (t_2) or deterministic (t_3). The vanishing marking can be removed from the RG, obtaining the reduced RG of Figure 12-8(b).

Assume for notational convenience that markings are partitioned into two classes MD and ME depending on the fact that t_d is enabled or not in them, and reordered so that the states $S_i \in MD$ of the EMC come first. The infinitesimal

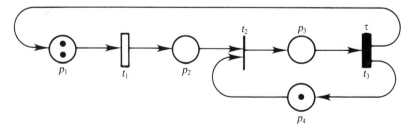

Figure 12-7. DSPN model of the M/D/1/2/2 queue.

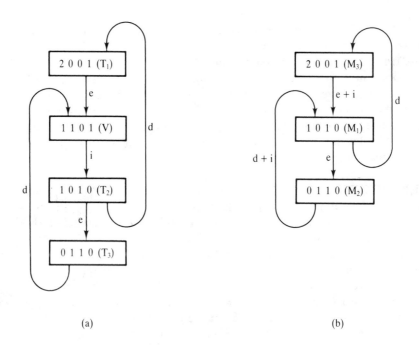

(a)   (b)

Figure 12-8. (a) Reachability graph of the DSPN in Figure 12-7. (b) Reduced reachability graph of the DSPN in Figure 12-7.

generator matrix $\mathbf{Q}$ of the exponential part of the net is easily obtained as

$$\mathbf{Q} = \begin{bmatrix} -\lambda & \lambda & 0 \\ 0 & 0 & 0 \\ 2\lambda & 0 & -2\lambda \end{bmatrix}$$

Note the reordering of the tangible markings: $S_1 \leftrightarrow M_1 = T_2$, $S_2 \leftrightarrow M_2 = T_3$, and $S_3 \leftrightarrow M_3 = T_1$, needed because $MD = \{T_2, T_3\}$ and $ME = \{T_1\}$. Clearly, the deterministic transition can never be preempted.

Figure 12-9 depicts the idea of the construction of the EMC from the reduced reachability graph. The EMC transition probability matrix $\mathbf{P}$ can be computed as shown in refs. 14 and 36. In our case the matrices $\mathbf{Q}'$ (subset of $\mathbf{Q}$ representing the exponential transitions that can be enabled when the deterministic transition is enabled) and $\mathbf{\Delta}_3$ (possible state changes after the firing of the deterministic transition t_3) are

$$\mathbf{Q}' = \begin{bmatrix} -\lambda & \lambda & 0 \\ 0 & 0 & 0 \\ 0 & 0 & 0 \end{bmatrix} \qquad \mathbf{\Delta}_3 = \begin{bmatrix} 0 & 0 & 1 \\ 1 & 0 & 0 \\ 0 & 0 & 1 \end{bmatrix}$$

where $\mathbf{\Delta}_3(3, 3)$ is equal to 1 by definition, since the deterministic transition is not enabled in S_3. The first two rows of the EMC transition probability matrix can be

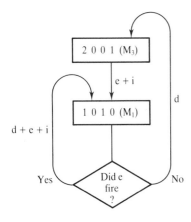

Figure 12-9. Sketch of the
construction of the EMC.

obtained by taking the corresponding rows of the matrix $\exp(\tau \mathbf{Q}')\mathbf{\Delta}_3$. The third
line of **P**, which refers to a state in which the deterministic transition is not
enabled, derives simply from matrix **Q** through the deletion of the elements of
the main diagonal and the normalization to 1 of the remaining elements. Using
this procedure, we obtain in this case

$$\mathbf{P} = \begin{bmatrix} 1-x & 0 & x \\ 1 & 0 & 0 \\ 1 & 0 & 0 \end{bmatrix}$$

where $x = e^{-\lambda \tau}$.

From a sample path we could see that from markings M_2 and M_3 we always
jump to marking M_1, whereas from M_1 we can jump either to M_3 (if the
deterministic transition fires before the exponential one) or to M_2. This latter
jump is not recorded by the EMC, but the return to M_1 generates the element
$P(1, 1)$.

The steady-state "visit" probabilities of the EMC can easily be computed in
this case, obtaining the following closed form expression:

$$\boldsymbol{\pi}' = \left[\frac{1}{1+x}, 0, \frac{x}{1+x} \right]$$

It is clear from Figure 12-9 that the time spent in state S_1 by the EMC
(which in this case is deterministically equal to τ) must be redistributed between
markings M_1 and M_2. In fact, the EMC never visits state S_2, while the
continuous-time process does visit marking M_2. The average fraction of time
spent in M_1 by the continuous-time process while the EMC visits state S_1 is
obtained as

$$c = \frac{1}{\tau} \int_0^\tau e^{-\lambda \tau} d\tau = \frac{1 - e^{-\lambda \tau}}{\lambda \tau}$$

The steady-state probability distribution of the continuous-time process is then obtained as

$$\pi = \frac{1}{\gamma}[\gamma_1, \gamma_2, \gamma_3]$$

where:

$$\gamma_1 = \pi_1' \tau c$$

$$\gamma_2 = \pi_1' \tau (1 - c)$$

$$\gamma_3 = \pi_3'/2\lambda$$

$$\gamma = \gamma_1 + \gamma_2 + \gamma_3$$

MODELS OF MULTIPROCESSORS WITH CACHE MEMORIES

The performance of single-processor computer systems using cache memories has been studied by several researchers.[19,39] Fewer results exist in the multiprocessor case.[40,41] Even if results obtained using trace-driven simulation may more closely reflect the locality of accesses of real programs, the use of analytical models has the advantage of providing results that more clearly show the influence of the parameters on the overall performance.

In this section, we illustrate the use of DSPN to model several different load/unload policies in the two-memory-level multiprocessor system in Figure 12-1. In the following we use the term "load" to indicate the transfer of one line from the main memory into the cache, "copy" to indicate the write-back operation (i.e., the transfer of the content of one line from the cache to the main memory), and "write" to indicate write-through (i.e., the write operation of one word directly into the main memory). The times required to complete these operations are denoted by τ_l, τ_c, and τ_w, respectively.

Copy-Back

The simplest cache-updating policy (copy-back or write-back) is described by the DSPN in Figure 12-10 in the case of a three-processor system. In this case, when a miss (a reference to a memory cell that is not present in the cache) occurs, a line is discharged from the cache and copied into the main memory, then the line containing the requested word is moved into the cache (we do not consider throughout this chapter the impact of the policy for the selection of the line to be replaced).

Both the load and the copy operations require the use of the bus, so that the processor remains idle or blocked until the desired line is loaded into the cache. The marking of the DSPN shown in Figure 12-10 represents the system when all the processors are active (one token in p_1, p_4, and p_7) and the bus is idle (a token in p_{10}). We describe the behavior of processor 1, since the same considerations apply to the others. The firing of t_1 models a cache miss, and hence a request for a data transfer from the cache to the main memory and vice versa through the

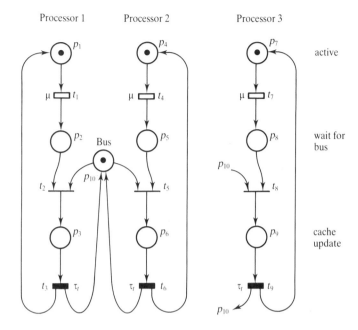

Processor 1   Processor 2   Processor 3

active

wait for
bus

cache
update

Bus

Figure 12-10. DSPN model of the copy-back policy in the case of three processors.

interconnection network. If the time interval between two cache misses is assumed to be a random variable with exponential distribution and mean $1/\mu$, then μ is the firing rate of t_1. The firing of t_2 models the beginning of the transfer operation: a token is moved to p_3, thus enabling t_3. The delay associated with this transition models the time required to perform the line replacement into the cache; if τ_c is the time needed to copy a line into the main memory and τ_l is the time required to load a line from it, $\tau_i = \tau_l + \tau_c$ is the total delay. This value is fixed and therefore the time delay associated with t_3 is a constant. In the model in Figure 12-10 the behavior of each processor is modeled by a subnet like the one already described; place p_{10}, which models the availability of the bus, is shared among the subnets.

The graphical complexity of the model increases only linearly with the number of processors, but very soon the explosion of the reachability graph makes the solution of the model no longer affordable. If all processors are assumed to behave in a statistically identical manner, a simpler model can be used, folding the DSPN in Figure 12-10 as shown in Figure 12-11. In this case the number of processors is represented by the number of tokens in p_1 in the initial marking (3 in Fig. 12-11). The firing rate of t_1 is marking dependent, equal to $m_1\lambda$ to model multiple independent exponential requests. Each token in p_2 models a processor requesting line replacement into the cache, and the presence of a token in p_3 denotes that a cache line is being replaced.

In order to improve the efficiency of the multiprocessor system, it is

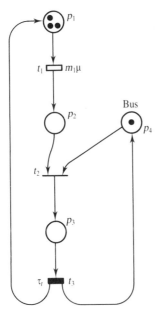

Figure 12-11. Folded version
of the DSPN in Figure 12-10.

necessary to reduce the time interval during which each processor is idle.
Different cache updating policies can be conceived to obtain this goal. Many of
these policies, such as write-through (with and without buffering), copy-back with
buffering, copy-back of the modified lines only, and read-through can be easily
described using DSPN models.

Write-Through

The DSPN in Figure 12-12 models the write-through policy in a single processor
system. In this case, when the processor needs to write a memory cell, the
operation is done directly on the main memory (as well as on the cache, if the
corresponding line is also there). Using this technique, the line replacement, in
the case of a miss-on-read, consists only in loading the requested line.

In the DSPN in Figure 12-12 the presence of a token in p_1 models the
processor active state; two transitions are thus enabled, the firing of t_1 models the
occurrence of a miss-on-read, the firing of t_2 the request for a write operation.
The chain $p_1-t_1-p_2-t_3-p_4-t_5$ models the processor behavior, like each subnet in
Figure 12-10, the only difference being in the time delay associated with timed
transitions. μ_r represents the rate of a miss-on-read and therefore $1/\mu_r$ is the
mean time delay associated with t_1, and τ_l (the time needed to load a line) is
associated with t_5 (no write operation is needed). The chain $p_1-t_2-p_3-t_4-p_5-t_6$
models the write-through operation. The firing of t_2 represents the write request;
then, if the bus is available, a token moves to p_5. The presence of a token in p_5
models the write operation into the main memory (and into the cache if

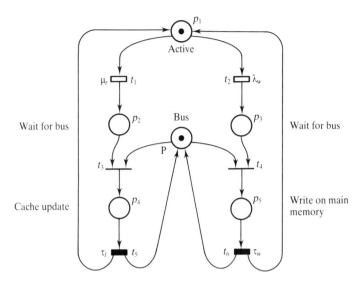

Figure 12-12. DSPN model of the write-through policy (single processor).

necessary). λ_w denotes the firing rate of t_2, and τ_w is the delay associated with t_6, representing the time needed to write a single word into the main memory.

The same net can be used to model compactly a multiprocessor system. In this case the number of processors in the system corresponds to the number of tokens in p_1 in the initial marking; the firing rates of t_1 and t_2 must be set to $m_1\mu_r$ and $m_1\lambda_w$, respectively.

Buffering

An improvement of the efficiency of a cache system can be obtained by introducing a pool of high-speed buffers associated with each processor to temporarily hold the information to be transferred to the main memory. The increase in hardware complexity is justified by the reduction of the processor idle time, both in the copy-back and write-through policies.

WRITE-THROUGH WITH BUFFERING

In this case the buffer temporarily holds the words that must be written into the main memory. The processor need not wait for the completion of the operation in order to resume its activity. The DSPN model of write-through with buffering, in the case of one processor, is shown in Figure 12-13. The net is similar to the previous one; places p_7 and p_8 and transition t_7 are added. In the initial marking, p_8 contains as many tokens as the number of buffers available to the processor. When a token moves to p_3, t_4 is enabled only if one of the buffers is available; in this case we assume that the processor becomes active as soon as t_4 fires. A null

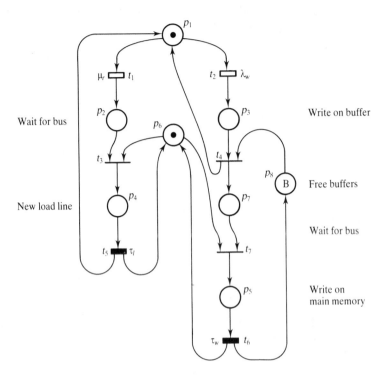

Figure 12-13. DSPN model of the write-through policy with buffering (single processor).

delay is associated with t_4, since the time needed to write into the buffer is considered part of the normal CPU operation. The updating of the main memory takes place later on, as soon as the bus is available.

In the case of a multiprocessor system, the detailed DSPN model is composed of as many subnets (like that in Fig. 12-13) as there are processors in the system; place p_6, representing the bus, is shared among subnets. This net becomes soon very hard to solve, so that it becomes mandatory to develop compact models. The folding of the DSPN is not straightforward, because different buffers are associated with each processor. Figure 12-14 shows a compact DSPN that can model a system with P processors, each one with a pool of two buffers. The chain p_1–t_1–p_2–t_3–p_4–t_5 in Figure 12-13 is split, in the net in Figure 12-14, into three different chains. The first one (p_1–t_1–p_2–t_{11}–p_3–t_3) models the behavior of processors with no pending write request into their buffer. The other two parallel chains model the behavior of processors in the cases of one and two pending requests, respectively. The firing of t_2, t_5, and t_8 models the write requests; the firing of the first two transitions moves the token representing a processor to the next chain at the right, putting a new request in queue, without interrupting the processor activity. The firing of t_8 moves the processor to a wait state (place p_{10}) because no more buffers are available. The firing of t_2, t_5, and t_8

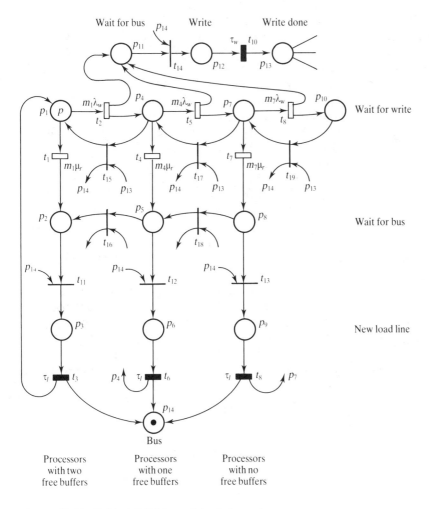

Figure 12-14. Folded DSPN model of the write-through policy (P processors, 2 buffers each).

moves a token into p_{11} where the write requests are queued, waiting for the bus. When the bus is available, the write operation can take place (a token in p_{12}). At the end of write, the token moves to p_{13}, thus enabling a subset of immediate transitions selected among t_{15}, t_{16}, t_{17}, t_{18}, and t_{19}. The firing of one of these transitions models a buffer release by moving the token representing the corresponding processor one chain to the left. A random switch is defined so that the probability of firing of each transition is proportional to the number of tokens present in its input place; in this way an equally likely random selection of which buffer to release is implemented.

COPY-BACK WITH BUFFERING

A similar performance improvement can be obtained using buffers to temporarily store the lines to be copied back into the main memory. The write operation into the auxiliary memory (the buffer) can be very fast and is not delayed by any contention for the interconnection network. The new line requested can then be loaded into the cache and the processor immediately resumes its activity. The update of the main memory can be performed subsequently.

Two different policies can easily be analyzed using DSPN models. The first one is shown in Figure 12-15 in the case of one processor. In this case, the delay associated with t_3 models the time required to write the old line into the buffer and to copy from the main memory the new one. The bus is not released, and while the processor resumes its activity the old line is copied from the buffer into the main memory (the associated delay is modeled by t_4). As in the previous cases, a direct extension to a multiprocessor model can be obtained using as many subnets (like that in Fig. 12-15) as there are processors.

An alternative solution to the copy-back policy with buffering that tries to reduce the processor idle time in the case of a multiprocessor configuration, is shown in Figure 12-16. In this case the copy-back operation is not performed immediately after the replacement of the old line into the cache, but the bus is released and can be used by other processors to perform the replacement, thus reducing their idle time. The effectiveness of this policy depends of course on the number of buffers, that is, on the number of lines that can be stored temporarily. The pending load requests can have priority over copy requests. The priority can

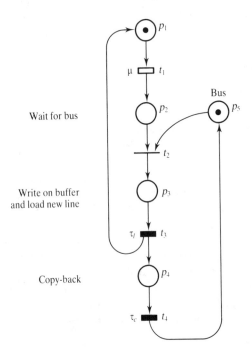

Figure 12-15. First DSPN model of the copy-back policy with buffering; the bus is kept after the completion of the load operation and the copy-back of the buffer content is immediately started (single processor).

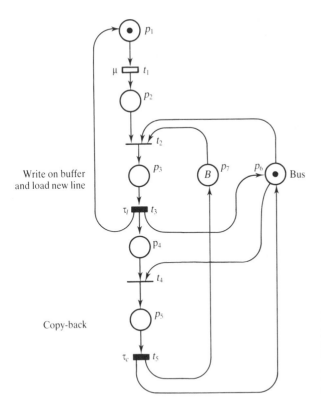

Write on buffer
and load new line

Copy-back

Figure 12-16. Second DSPN
model of the copy-back
policy with buffering; the
bus is released between the
load and copy operations
(single processor).

easily be modeled in the DSPN by adding proper inhibitor arcs such that only
t_2-type transitions can fire when both t_2-type and t_4-type transitions would be
enabled. The size of the buffer is modeled by the initial marking of p_7.

Copy-Back of the Modified Lines and Read-Through

Two other policies can be introduced to limit the processor idle time. The first
one associates a flag with each line of the cache; the flag is set when a word in the
line is modified, so that the copy-back operation is needed only for flagged lines.
All the above DSPN models of copy-back can be easily modified to introduce this
mechanism. As an example, consider the model in Figure 12-10. In this case the
sequence p_3–t_3 can be modified as shown in Figure 12-17. The probability
distribution associated with the random switch models the probability that at least
one write operation has taken place in the line to be discharged.

The read-through policy anticipates the read of the word needed by the
processor with respect to the cache update, thus further reducing the idle time of
the processor. DSPN models of systems using this mechanism can be built easily.

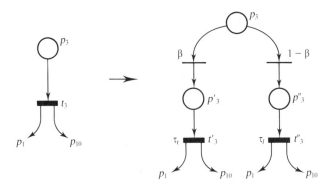

Figure 12-17. Transformation of a subnet in Figure 12-10 to model the copy-back operation of modified lines only.

NUMERICAL RESULTS

As an example of application of the above models to the performance evaluation of multiprocessors with cache memories, we consider the buffered write-through policy, as modeled by the compact DSPN in Figure 12-14. This choice was made because, in a multicache environment, write-through is thought to alleviate consistency problems. It thus seems that actual implementations of cached multiprocessor systems should use this policy, unless some special consistency protocol is implemented in the bus definition.[20] Parameters of the model are the following.

1. Number of processors P
2. Number of write buffers available to each processor
3. Miss ratio α
4. Instruction workload, that is, the percentage of read, write, and fetch memory accesses
5. Main memory access time for word write τ_w
6. Transfer time τ_l to load a cache line from the main memory
7. Bus-assignment policy between load and write requests

Following Smith[19] we set the instruction workload to 35 percent read, 15 percent write, and 50 percent fetch. Normalizing the processor cycle time to 1, the rate of transitions t_2, t_5, and t_8 (write memory-request rate) becomes $\lambda_w = 0.15$. This normalized rate depends only on the instruction workload and determines an upper bound of $1/0.15 \approx 6.67$ on the achievable speed-up in a write-through cached system with respect to the main memory access time. The firing rate of transitions t_1, t_4, and t_7 is set to $\mu_r = 0.85\alpha$, that is, the probability of performing a nonwrite memory access multiplied by the cache miss ratio.

In order to reduce the number of free parameters, we also set $\tau_l = 8\tau_w$, and consider only the case in which processors have two write buffers each. The bus-assignment policy is assumed to be random with equally likely probability for

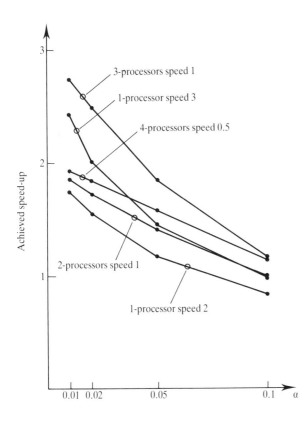

Figure 12-18. Achieved speed-up as a function of the cache miss ratio for systems with potential speed-up of 2 and 3.

each request in the queue, independently of its kind (either cache load or buffer write). To implement this policy, immediate transitions t_{11}, t_{12}, t_{13}, and t_{14} are grouped into a random switch, each one with a firing probability proportional to the number of tokens in its input place.

Figure 12-18 and Figure 12-19 depict the overall achieved speed-up of different systems versus the cache miss ratio α. This performance figure is defined to be the overall processing power (the mean number of active processors) times the speed of any processor in the system. The relative processor speed is defined as the ratio between the main memory access time and the processor cycle time. The potential speed-up of a multiprocessor system is the number of processors times their speed. In Figure 12-18 it is possible to compare the achieved speed-up of a single processor system with speed 2, with that of a two-processor system with speed 1, or even with the achieved speed-up of a four-processor system with speed 0.5. Such a comparison shows that many slow processors always yield better performance than a single faster processor with the same potential speed-up. Moreover, Figure 12-19 shows that a four-processor system composed of processors with cycle time equal to the main-memory access time yields better performance than a single processor running six times faster, in the case of a cache miss ratio greater than 1.7 percent. Note that our comparisons are made for

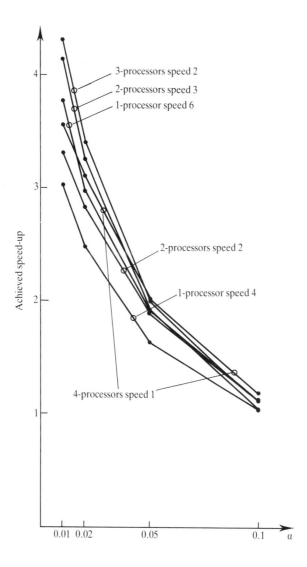

Figure 12-19. Achieved speed-up as a function of the cache miss ratio for systems with potential speed-up of 4 and 6.

the same value of the cache miss ratio α in systems with different numbers of processors and the same potential speed-up. If the partitioning of the total workload among processors results in task sets that have similar locality characteristics in memory accesses, and that do not share a large amount of memory, then it is reasonable to say that equal cache miss ratios entail a constant total cache size. Instead, if the work-load partitioning does not satisfy the above requirements, a larger but slower total cache is needed for a greater number of processors in order to achieve the same miss ratio. In the latter case, our results can still be used for a comparison at constant total cache size, but the curves corresponding to different numbers of processors must be read for different values of the abscissa, and the actual value of the cache miss ratios must be extracted from the workload.

Table 12-1. Definition of performance figures

PP (processing power)	$E\{m_1\} + E\{m_4\} + E\{m_7\}$
BU (bus utilization)	$Pr\{m_{14} = 0\}$
#WQ (mean number of write queued)	$E\{m_{11}\}$
#UB (mean number of used buffers in system)	$E\{m_4\} + E\{m_5\} + E\{m_6\} + 2E\{m_7\}$
	$+ 2E\{m_8\} + 2E\{m_9\} + 2E\{m_{10}\}$
#PFB (mean number of processors with full buffer)	$E\{m_{10}\}$
#PWM (mean number of processors waiting on miss)	$E\{m_2\} + E\{m_5\} + E\{m_8\}$

In Table 12-1 are defined some other interesting performance figures easily obtainable from the steady state probability distributions of tokens in the places of the DSPN model. Table 12-2 shows the numerical values of these performance figures in the case of a four-processor system with processor speed 1, and with different size of write buffers. Notice the excellent bus utilization (77.5 percent) and processing power (89 percent) of the system with two buffers per processor in the case of cache miss ratio $\alpha = 0.01$.

The steady-state solution of DSPNs with deterministic timing requires the computation of the steady-state probability distribution of an embedded Markov chain (EMC) whose transition probability matrix can be obtained with a matrix exponential algorithm. This part of the solution can be computationally very heavy, and the CPU time grows very fast with the number of markings. The construction of the EMC requires about 20 minutes of CPU time on a VAX/780 in the case of four processors (which yields 458 tangible markings) using a package for DSPN analysis,[26] while the other solution steps take less than one minute of CPU time. For this reason, we also tried an approximate DSPN model with all exponential timing. The results reported in Table 12-3 (obtained in less than one minute of CPU time each) show that exponential times lead to a fair

Table 12-2. Performance indices computed in the case of four-processor systems

α	#B	PP	BU	#WQ	#UB	#PFB	#PWM
	0	2.899	0.635	0.441		0.878	0.025
0.01	1	3.402	0.741	0.998	1.193	0.314	0.053
	2	3.56	0.775	1.444	1.852	0.125	0.073
	0	2.526	0.731	0.667		1.051	0.076
0.02	1	2.951	0.844	1.529	1.483	0.489	0.160
	2	3.101	0.886	2.371	2.592	0.243	0.235
	0	1.755	0.886	1.059		1.330	0.300
0.05	1	1.959	0.967	2.362	1.888	0.77	0.600
	2	2.009	0.988	3.682	3.557	0.428	0.877
	0	1.088	0.969	1.241		1.416	0.703
0.1	1	1.165	0.997	2.488	1.883	0.785	1.233
	2	1.183	0.999	3.533	3.351	0.363	1.635

Table 12-3. Performance indices computed in the case of a four-processor system with two buffers, assuming exponential timing

α	PP	BU	#WQ	#UB	#PFB	#PWM
0.01	3.409	0.743	1.814	2.060	0.265	0.094
0.02	2.936	0.840	2.549	2.586	0.403	0.262
0.05	1.953	0.957	3.400	3.153	0.540	0.843
0.1	1.195	0.992	3.222	2.953	0.449	1.543

approximation of the processing power and of the bus utilization (with maximum error of 5 percent), while they are unreliable for the prediction of buffer utilization.

CONCLUSIONS

In this chapter we have described stochastic Petri net models suitable for the performance analysis of complex computing systems. As an example of the effectiveness of these tools, we have applied DSPN to the development of models for the description and the analysis of multiprocessor systems comprising cache memories. The most commonly used policies for the loading and unloading of the cache information have been considered, presenting both detailed and compact DSPN models. The models that we have presented do not incorporate all the details of the multiprocessor behavior, but they are examples of modeling of a specific function.

The goal of the examples was to demonstrate the effectiveness of SPN models in the ranking of different architectural solutions. Since high performance is the main reason for developing supercomputers, in the design phase it is frequently necessary to select the best solution among different alternatives. The answer to this type of question requires the development of models allowing different policies or mechanisms (often at the hardware level) exercised by workloads (defined at the software level) normally known only very imprecisely. This imprecision makes the stochastic approach the only viable alternative.

SPN models can be used to represent the system at many different levels of detail, from hardware/software interaction[42] down to hardware components,[33] but only a careful selection of the level of detail required to model the specific function under study can yield nets of reasonable complexity, and whose solution can be obtained with limited effort. When applying SPN techniques, the modeler very soon experiences the importance of representing into the nets only the functions that are significant at the chosen level of abstraction.

Finally, it must be observed that an effective performance analysis methodology relies on the availability of tools facilitating the model construction and verification and automating the solution techniques. In the case of SPN, such tools must give the user the possibility of describing the net graphically, and of defining both parameters and performance figures at the same net level. All the details concerning the construction of the reachability graph, the solution of the Markov chain, and so on, need not be presented to the user, who only needs to set up the SPN and then issue a "solve" command. This approach has been followed in the implementation of GreatSPN, a graphical SPN package for a UNIX-based workstation.[38]

REFERENCES

1. Ferrari, D. (1986). "Considerations on the insularity of performance evaluation," *IEEE Trans. Software Eng.*, Vol. SE-12, No. 6, pp. 678–683.

2. Feller, W. (1966). *An Introduction to Probability Theory and Its Applications*. Wiley, New York.

3. Cinlar, E. (1975). *Introduction to Stochastic Processes*. Prentice-Hall, Englewood Cliffs, N.J.

4. Kemeni, G. and J. L. Snell (1960). *Finite Markov Chains*. Van Nostrand, Princeton, N.J.

5. Karlin, S. and H. M. Taylor (1975). *A First Course in Stochastic Processes*. Academic Press, New York.

6. Kleinrock, L. (1975). *Queueing Systems Volume I: Theory*. Wiley, New York.

7. Trivedi, K. S. (1980). *Probability and Statistics with Reliability, Queueing, and Computer Science Applications*. Prentice-Hall, Englewood Cliffs, N.J.

8. Sauer, C. H. and K. M. Chandy (1981). *Computer System Performance Evaluation*. Prentice-Hall, Englewood Cliffs, N.J.

9. Symons, F. J. W. (1980). "Introduction to numerical Petri nets, a general graphical model of concurrent processing systems," *A.T.R.*, Vol. 14, No. 1, pp. 28–33.

10. Florin, G. and S. Natkin (1985). "Les reseaux de Petri stochastiques," *TSI,* Vol. 4, No. 1, pp. 143–160.

11. Molloy, M. K. (1982). "Performance analysis using stochastic Petri nets," *IEEE Trans. Computers,* Vol. C-31, No. 9, pp. 913–917.

12. Ajmone Marsan, M., G. Balbo, and G. Conte (1984). "A class of generalized stochastic Petri nets for the performance analysis of multiprocessor systems," *ACM Trans. Computer Systems,* Vol. 2, No. 1, pp. 93–122.

13. Dugan, J. B., K. S. Trivedi, R. M. Geist, and V. F. Nicola (1984). "Extended stochastic Petri nets: Applications and analysis," in *Proc. PERFORMANCE '84, Paris, France*. North-Holland, Amsterdam.

14. Ajmone Marsan, M., and G. Chiola (1986). "On Petri nets with deterministic and exponential transition firing times," in *Proc. 7th European Workshop on Application and Theory of Petri Nets, Oxford, England*.

15. Prisgrove, L. A. and G. S. Shedler (1986). "Symmetric stochastic Petri nets," *IBM J. Res. Develop.,* Vol. 30, No. 3, pp. 278–293.

16. Agerwala, T. (1979). "Putting Petri nets to work," *IEEE Computer,* Vol. 12, pp. 85–94.

17. Peterson, J. L. (1981). *Petri Net Theory and the Modeling of Systems*. Prentice-Hall, Englewood Cliffs, N.J.

18. Reisig, W. (1985). *Petri Nets: an Introduction*. Springer Verlag, New York.

19. Smith, A. J. (1982). "Cache memories," *ACM Computing Surveys,* Vol. 14, No. 3, pp. 473–530.

20. Sweazey, P. and A. J. Smith (1986). "A class of compatible cache consistency protocols and their support by IEEE Futurebus," in *Proc. 13th Ann. Symp. on Computer Architecture, Tokyo, Japan*.

21. Baer, J. L. and C. Girault (1985). "A Petri net model for a solution to the cache coherence problem," in *Proc. 1st Int. Conf. on Supercomputing Systems, St. Petersburg, Fla.*

22. Vernon, M. K. and M. A. Holliday (1986). "Performance analysis of multiprocessor cache consistency protocols using generalized timed Petri nets," in *Proc. Performance '86 and 1986 SIGMETRICS Joint Conference, Raleigh, NC,* pp. 9–17.

23. *Proceedings of the International Workshop on Timed Petri Nets.* Torino, Italy, 1985.

24 Dugan, J. B., A. Bobbio, G. Ciardo, and K. S. Trivedi (1985). "The design of a unified package for the solution of stochastic Petri net models," in *Proc. Int. Workshop on Timed Petri Nets.* Torino, Italy.

25. Leszak, M. and H. P. Godbersen (1985). "DEAMON: A tool for performance-availability evaluation of distributed systems based on function nets," in *Proc. Int. Workshop on Timed Petri Nets.* Torino, Italy.

26. Chiola, G. (1985). "A software package for the analysis of generalized stochastic Petri net models," in *Proc. Int. Workshop on Timed Petri Nets.* Torino, Italy.

27. Natkin, S. (1980). "Les reseaux de Petri stochastiques et leur application a l'evaluation des systèmes informatiques," These de Docteur Ingegneur, CNAM, Paris, France.

28. Molloy, M. K. (1981). "On the integration of delay and throughput measures in distributed processing models," PhD Thesis, UCLA, Los Angeles, Calif.

29. Ajmone Marsan, M., G. Balbo, A. Bobbio, G. Chiola, G. Conte, and A. Cumani (1985). "On Petri nets with stochastic timing," in *Proc. International Workshop on Timed Petri Nets,* pp. 80–87. Torino, Italy.

30. Molloy, M. K. (1985). "Discrete time Petri nets," *IEEE Trans. Software Eng.,* Vol. SE-11, No. 2, pp. 417–423.

31. Holliday, M. A. and M. K. Vernon (1985). "A generalized timed Petri net model for performance analysis," in *Proc. Int. Workshop on Timed Petri Nets.* Torino, Italy.

32. Ajmone Marsan, M., G. Balbo, G. Chiola, and G. Conte (1987). "Generalized stochastic Petri nets revisited: random switches and priorities," in *Proc. Int. Workshop on Petri Nets and Performance Models,* pp. 44–53. Madison, Wis.

33. Ajmone Marsan, M., G. Balbo, and G. Conte (1986). *Performance Models of Multiprocessor Systems,* MIT Press, Cambridge, Mass.

34. Ajmone Marsan, M., G. Balbo, A. Bobbio, G. Chiola, G. Conte, and A. Cumani (1989). "The effect of execution policies on the semantics and analysis of stochastic Petri nets," *IEEE Trans. Software Eng.,* Vol. SE-15, No. 7, July.

35. Neuts, M. F. (1981). *Matrix Geometric Solutions in Stochastic Models.* Johns Hopkins University Press, Baltimore, Md.

36. Ajmone Marsan, M., and G. Chiola (1987). "On Petri nets with determinisitic and exponentially distributed firing times," in *Advances on Petri Nets '87* (ed. G. Rozenberg), pp. 132–145. Springer-Verlag, New York.

37. Howard, R. A. (1971). *Dynamic Probabilistic Systems.* Wiley, New York.

38. Chiola, G. (1987). "A graphical Petri net tool for performance analysis," in *Proc. 3rd Int. Workshop on Modeling Techniques and Performance Evaluation, Paris, France.*

39. Rao, G. S. (1978). "Performance analysis of cache memories," *J. ACM,* Vol. 25, No. 3, pp. 378–395.

40. Goyal, A. and T. Agerwala (1984). "Performance analysis of future shared storage systems," *IBM J. Res. Develop,* Vol. 28, No. 1, pp. 95–108.

41. Patel, J. H. (1982). "Analysis of multiprocessors with private cache memories," *IEEE Trans. Computers,* Vol. C-31, No. 4, pp. 296–304.

42. Ajmone Marsan, M., G. Balbo, G. Chiola, and G. Conte (1987). "Modeling the software architecture of a prototype parallel machine," in *Proc. 1987 SIGMETRICS Conference, Banff, Alberta, Canada.*

INDEX

Adams–Bashforth
    predictor-connector
    403
Adaptable architectures
    92–3
    current research trends
    93–4
    feasibility of 101
    projects survey 95
Advanced-architecture
    computers,
    performance
    evaluation of 528–
    30
Algebraic image
    restoration 421–2
Algebras 231–3
ALGOL-60 226
Alliant FX/8 529
APL 248
Application ring 254, 258–
    9
Architectural adaptation
    19–28, 93
Architectural improvement
    8
Architectural level 8
Architectural optimization
    19
Arithmetic pipelines 40–1
Array graphs 283–5
Array systems 33
    aligned-memory 35–6
    bit-parallel 81–5
    bit-serial 85–91
    classification 34–6
    industrial 81–91
    local-memory 35

memory organization
    35–6
Artificial intelligence 329
Artificial neuromorphic
    systems (ANS) 566
Assertive programming
    271–2
Astrophysics 499
Asynchronous parallel
    computing
    structures 49–67
Augmented
    interconnection
    network 357

Baryons study on
    hypercube 525
Behavioral error 353, 354
Behavioral testing 349,
    357–65
    multiple-level approach
    350–4
    processing elements
    357–65
Binocular stereo 451
Bit-parallel array system
    35
Bit-serial array system 34
Block iterative restoration
    algorithm 422–37
    application of 432–7
    implementation on MPP
    427–32
Block Jacobi iteration
    422–4
Border following 457
BSP supercomputer 83

Buffer memory 49, 333–5
Buffer size and
    performance effect
    339
Buffered multistage delta
    networks 263–4
Buffering 601–4
    copy-back policy with
    604–5
    write-through policy
    with 601–3

C 252
Cache coherence 292–328
    detailed model 309–21
    directory-based solution
    293
    problem of 293
    protocols 289–302
    solution categories 293
    three-state protocol 309
Cache controller 309
    subnet 308
Cache cycle stealing 297
Cache directory,
    organization of 295
Cache global transfer
    management 318–
    21
Cache hit 295, 311, 312
Cache instruction
    processing 310–13
Cache memory 16–18,
    294–6, 598–601
    multiprocessor
    architecture analysis
    580–1

Cache miss 293, 295, 310, 312
Cache nets 302
Cache organization 292
Cache performance 295
Cache protocol performance improvements 324–6
Cache size, and hit ratios 339–41
Cache subnet 308
Cache to controller transmission 322–4
Cache updating policy 598–600
Caltech Concurrent Computation Program 481–4
Caltech/JPL Mark I hypercubes 524–5
Caltech/JPL Mark II hypercubes 524–5, 545
Caltech/JPL Mark III hypercubes 545
Canny edge detector 458–9
Catchment model 400
CDC-ETA 70
Cellular automata 412–21
Chaining 40–1
Chemical reactions 496
Chess program 501
CHoPP supercomputer 106–53
  active task 116
  architectural mechanisms 109
  assembly language 141–2
  automated DC testing 142
  branch instructions 113
  closed-loop design system 142
  computing node 110–11
  conflict-free memory 114–16
  custom design tools 148–50
  data-dependency structures 130–1
  demonstration unit packaging scheme 144–5
  design and simulation using SCALD 138–41
  design management structure 150–1
  design philosophy 141
  experiences with SCALD 146–7
  external I/O devices 111
  factory support 147
  FETCH & ADD instruction 134
  Fetch and Add instructions 122
  frequent branching 126–31
  functional block diagram 110
  Get/Put interactions 120–2
  high-level logic design 143
  indivisible instructions for shared data 122–3
  instruction execution 124
  instruction issue rate 125–6
  instruction parcels 112, 113
  interaction of functional units and registers 111–14
  interboard wiring 145–6
  intertask communications 119
  intertask synchronization instructions 113
  job control 123
  large simulations 151–2
  Livermore Loops 123–4, 126, 128–32, 134–6
  load and store memory reference instructions 113
  memory latency 124–5
  memory location structure 114
  memory protection 123
  off-the-shelf parts 143–4
  performance estimates 135–7
  prepare-to-branch instruction 114
  principles of operation 108–19
  printed circuit board layout system 150
  program interrupt 118
  programming units 116
  Realfast hardware accelerator 152–3
  register-to-register computational instructions 113
  SCALD simulation program 151
  Send/Receive instruction 120–2
  sequential code 126
  simulation to replace hardware prototypes 142–3
  slot 116
  state diagram 117
  structures likely to vectorize 131–3
  structures not likely to vectorize 133–7
  superinstruction layout 112
  task 116–19
  task creation 119
  task-manipulation hardware 117
  task management 119
  task manager 110–11, 116
  task manager control instructions 113
  task preemption 118
  task slot 116
  task swap 118
  task synchronization 119, 120–2
  task termination 118, 119
  unavailable register 118
  user-coded primitives 148
CIVIC compiler 133
Class VI systems 329
Coherence management 313–18
Columbia Homogeneous Parallel Processor. See CHoPP supercomputer

Concurrent computers, 485
Condensed matter 500
Conditional branching 45–7
Configuration processing 286–8
Connection Machine 448–65, 529
  block diagram 452
  border following 457
  convex-hull algorithms 461
  distance doubling 455–6
  edge detection 456, 458–9
  gradient magnitude distribution 459
  graph matching 463–4
  high-level vision 462
  histogramming 459
  labeling connected components 461
  memory 453
  middle vision 460
  NEWS network 454–5, 460, 462, 465
  principal processor 455, 457, 458
  processor instructions 453
  programming 453
  reconfiguring for output 457–8
  scan operations 454–5
  virtual processors 453
  vision tasks 456
  Voronoi diagrams 462
Connectors 226
Continuity equations 402–3
Continuous-time Markov chains (CTMC) 586
Contract 277
Control Data-ETA 71
Control signals 349
Convex-hull algorithms 461
Convolutional decoding 497–8
Cooperative computation 277
Copy-back policy 598–600
  of modified lines and read-through 605–10

with buffering 604–5
Cosmic Cube 19
Cost optimization 5
CRAY X-MP 80–1, 133, 136, 137, 223, 228, 529
CRAY-1 40, 44, 45, 77–80, 413
CRAY-1-S 222
CRAY-2 222, 223, 529
CREW 461, 462
Crystal router algorithm 545
CSL (Configuration Specification Language) 273, 274–6, 281
CYBER-205 vector computer 4–7, 18–19, 74–5, 391, 396
  conversion of software for 393–4
Cycle sum test 252

Data algebras 240
Data application 351
Data-dependency graphs 284
Data-driven computation 234, 239
  disadvantage of 237
Data-flow architectures 94–5, 99
Data-flow graphs 28–9, 94, 283
Data-flow principle 28–32
Data-flow program scheme 31
Data-flow ring 254, 259–60
Data-flow supercomputers, prospects for 101–2
Data parameters 284
Date-driven dataflow 226
DEC MicroVAX II minicomputer 145
DEC VAX-11/780 89
Demand-driven computation 234
  disadvantages of 238
Demand-driven dataflow 226
Demand packet 256
Demand ring 254, 256–8

Denied requests handling 61–2
Denied resource table 60–1
Dennis machine, cell block architecture 99
Design improvement 8
Design level 7
Design optimization 9
De Vreis (1975) model 401
Dirichlet boundary conditions 513, 517
Dirichlet boundary value problem 503
Distance doubling 455–6
Distributed array processor (DAP) 89–91
DO-loops 31–3, 49, 90–1
Dynamic computer (DC) groups 54
Dynamic fermions 522, 525, 527, 528
Dynamically partitionable system level of adaptation 19, 23–8

Eager controller 259–60
Earth science 499
  Hypercube applications 530–5
  inversion of seismograms 537–8
  normal-mode data analysis 535
Earthquake engineering 497
Eazyflow engine 226, 227, 238–9
  architecture 252–5
  interconnection topology 262–4
  multilayered 262–4
  submachines 254–63
Econometric modeling 276–83
Edge detection 456, 458–9
Eduction rings 254
Effective access time 335–9
Eigenfrequencies, calculation for Earth model 536–7
Eigenfunctions, calculation for Earth model 536–7

ELXSI 4.2 BSD UNIX system 517
Embedded Markov chain (EMC) 589, 594–5, 609
Emitter-coupled logic (ECL) 158
Energy balance equation 401
Enhanced computational parallelism 93
Equational programming 272
Equivalent semantics 251–5
ERODYN program 393, 396, 399
Error-window checks 405
Estimate table 59
ETA-10 supercomputer 75–7
Expert systems 329, 569
Extended conflict set (ECS) 588

Fault-tolerant arrays 357–65
  switch organization 359
FIFO (first-in-first-out) 296
Fifth-generation computing systems (FGCSs) project 223–4
Finite-difference wave simulation 530–2
Finite-element modeling 533–5
Finite sequences 247
Flagged swap algorithm 335
Flagged swap replacement 336
Flip permutations 88
Floating-point addition pipelines 72
Floating-point operation 222
Floating-point pipelines 72
Flow table 356
Fluid dynamics 497
Folding process 591–2
Force-restore equations 401

FORTRAN 89, 137, 155, 159, 160, 162, 167, 170, 172, 174–6, 191, 192, 194, 207, 399, 411, 517
Function definitions 228

Galaxies, host to quasars 432–7
Ganymede 437
Gather 49
GEM-T1 gravity model 391–9
Generalized inverses of multiparameter matrices 370–80
GEODYN 392–3, 394
GEODYN I 399
GEODYN II 396, 399
GEODYN IIE 394, 395
GEODYN IIS 394, 395
Geodynamics 499
  Hypercube applications 533–5
Geophysics, Hypercube applications 530–5
G-net 297, 326
Gradient magnitude distribution 459
Granular physics 500
Graph matching 463–4
Graphics algorithms 465–77
  local indexed access 470–1
  local management of other data structures 472
  local sorting 471
  planar patch strategies 467–70
  scan-conversion 472–5
  source-oblivious routing 475–6
  time-coherence 476
Graphics requirements 466
Gravity model GEM-T1 391–9
GreatSPN 611
GSFC Massively Parallel Processor 413

Heat balance equations 402

Heat-bath method 521
HERMIES mobile robots 557–61, 567
Hexagonal lattice gas model 415
Hierarchical Warp Stereo technique 439
High-energy physics 499–500
Hillslope water flow model 399–412
Histogramming 459
Hit ratios 295
  and cache size 339–41
Hitachie S-810 supercomputer 329–30
Hybrid algorithms 522
Hydrological system 400
Hypercube
  four-dimensional 452
  MK.3 228
Hypercube applications 480–577
  biology 495–6
  chemistry 496
  concurrent computation advances 550–70
  earth science 530–5
  engineering 497
  geodynamics 533–5
  geophysics 498–9, 530–5
  issues determining performance of 487–94
  lattice gauge theory 520–30
  multiple-target tracking 538–49
  normal-mode data analysis of the earth 535
  physics 499–500
  science 495
  software environment 501–2
  see also Machine intelligence; Multigrid algorithms; Robotics

IBM 360/95 391, 396
IBM 3080 224
IBM 3081 391, 396, 397, 400, 403

IBM 3084 293
IBM 3090 293
Ice floes
    global correlation 446–8
    image correlation 448
    matching in sea ice
        images 446
    motion detection 445–6
    tracking 438
    translation and rotation
        446–8
ID 235
if-then-else-fi 235, 237,
    242, 257, 261
ILA (iterative logic array)
    structures 356
Illiac-IV 83
Image constraints 424–6
Image correlation
    ice floes 448
    techniques 437–8
Image degradation 421–2
Image processing 421–77
Image restoration 421–4
    missing or bad data
        values 426
Improper errors 354
Improper functionalities
    353, 354
Indexed file 281
Industrial architectures,
    evolution of 70–81
Infinite sequences 247
Insert packet 260
Instruction-level adapta-
    tions 94
Instruction pipelines 40,
    44–9
    major causes of disrup-
        tions 44
Instruction set 349
Integrated circuits 139, 144
Inter-element com-
    municator 58
Interconnection networks
    289–302, 321–3, 359
    testing 360–2
ISWIM 240–2
Iteration 242

Jupiter 437

Kartashev dynamic com-
    puter 95

KL1 (Kernel Language 1)
    223
K-net 326

Lagrangian multipliers
    424–6
Langevin algorithms 522
Langevin method 522
Laplace program 249
Laplacian operator 425–6
Large-scale integration
    (LSI) 92–3, 101,
    158
Latent heat flux under
    neutral atmospheric
    stability 402
Lattice gauge theory 520–
    30
    future calculations at
        Caltech 527–8
    past calculations at Cal-
        tech 524–7
    walking program 525–7
Lattice kinetic theory 415
Least-squares algorithm
    537–8
Limited memory band-
    width 45
LINEAR MODEL 126
LINK project 276–7
Linked triad 394
Lisp 235, 453
Livermore Loops 123–4,
    126, 128–32, 134–6,
    173
L-net 297
Load-balancing algorithms
    551
Lorentz force 416
LOW RISC 224
LRU (least-recently used)
    policy 296
Lucid 239–51, 253, 258,
    261, 264, 265
Lyapunov matrix equation
    381

Mach number 415
Machine intelligence 550–
    70
Magnetohydrodynamic
    cellular automata
    412–21

Mail file 281
Mailbox 161
Mapping methods for user
    memory 334
Markov chains 554
Markov process 579
Marr-Hildreth edge-
    detection scheme
    456, 457
Massively Parallel Proces-
    sor (MPP) 88–9,
    390, 399, 403–5
    architecture 407–10
    array unit 408
    computing environment
        405–7
    data initialization 408
    implementation of block
        iterative restoration
        algorithm 427–32
    restoring blurred astro-
        nomical images
        421–37
    techniques for determin-
        ing local differences
        in pairs of images
        437–48
Master control registers
    (MCU) 90
Mathematical libraries 172
Mathematical semantics
    226, 230–3
Matrix multiplication 431–
    2
Matrix similarity and
    equivalence 380–7
Maximally strongly con-
    nected components
    (MSCC) 285
Medium-scale integration
    (MSI) 158
Memory-access operation
    optimization 9–18
Memory bandwidth 73
Memory conflicts 54–62
Memory controllers 306,
    313–18
Memory interleaving 9–10
Memory management,
    hybrid scheme 261–2
Memory modules 309
Memory overlap 11–16
Memory storage schemes
    36

Memory systems
    access time for first-level
        342–4
    access time optimization
        341–5
    average bandwidth 332
    hierarchical 329–47
    hierarchy optimization
        341–5
    linear multilevel hier-
        archy 332
    optimal number of levels
        341
    optimal size for sub-
        sequent levels 344–5
    optimal size of hierarchy
        344
    size-speed paradox for
        330–2
    three-level hierarchy 337
Merge nodes 29–32
Mesh-connected computer
    (MCC) 466
Metropolis method 521
Metropolis/Langevin algo-
    rithm 527, 528
Microcanonical algorithms
    522
Microprogramming level
    of adaptation 19,
    20–2, 25–8
MIMD (multiple-
    instruction multiple-
    data) systems 292–
    328, 485
Miss ratio 340
MODEL compiler 276,
    281, 283–7
MODEL configurator 274
MODEL equational lan-
    guage 276, 277
MODEL language specifi-
    cation 279
MODEL system 273–6
MODEL timer 282–3
Modeling of physical proc-
    esses 391–421
Modules 272, 273
Monte Carlo algorithm
    521, 524, 527, 528
Monte Carlo calculations
    500
Monte Carlo lattice gauge
    theory 525

Moore–Penrose unique
    generalized inverse
    370
MPP Pascal 410–12
Multicomputer systems
    49–52
Multidimensional system
    theory 379
Multiflow Trace 7/200,
    529
Multigrid algorthims 503–
    20
    data structures 510–14
    full approximation
        scheme embedded
        in 506
    grid function operations
        515–16
    implementation of 507,
        516–17
    parallel multigrid solver
        510–14
    parallelization 507–9,
        514
    preliminary results 517–
        19
    target problems and
        their discretization
        509–10
    theoretical background
        504–7
Multiparameter matrices
    generalized inverses of
        370–80
    history of 379–80
Multiparameter systems
    theory 369–88
Multiple abstraction levels
    352
Multiple operations, op-
    timization of 18–
    19
Multiple-target tracking
    538–49
    concurrent 543–9
    sequential 540–3
Multiprocessor architec-
    ture 296–8
    stochastic Petrie net
        analysis 580–1
Multiprocessor scheduling
    551
Multiprocessor systems
    53–67

Navier–Stokes equation
    222, 415
Nested iteration 244
Neural circuit simulation
    495–6
Neural networks 566–70
Newton–Euler inverse
    dynamics 555–7
Non-consecutive locations
    of consecutive data
    words in the same
    data vector 47–9
Non-memory access oper-
    ation optimization 9
Non-release of redundant
    resources 95
Nonnullary variable 241
Nonpointwise functions
    245
Nonpointwise operator 235
Nonstrict conditional ex-
    pressions 242
Nonstrict operator 235
Nullary variable 241

Operational models 233–4
Operational attributes
    234–6
Operator nets 226, 228,
    230–3, 239–51
Operators 226
Optical flow detection 451
Optimization methodology
    553–5

PADS (Programmer Ad-
    vanced Debugging
    System) 160, 171
Page address registers 56
Page requests handling 57–
    8
PARALLEL ARRAY 408
Parallel computation 224–
    6
Parallelization 9
PEER (Program Execu-
    tion Evaluation
    Routine) 171
Perfect interleaving for
    multiprocessor 62,
    67
Perfect interleaving for
    uniprocessor 62–3

Performance analysis and stochastic Petri nets 579–80
Performance evaluation of advanced-architecture computers 528–30
Performance improvement 7–67
    levels of 7–8
Petri nets
    complete model structure 308–9
    definitions and notation 582–4
    extensions 321, 326
    model 297
    modeling with 302–9
    timed 585
    timed transition 585–8
    see also Stochastic Petri nets 578
Physical processes, modeling of 391–421
Piped dataflow 236
Pipeline systems 33
    classification 40–9
    dynamic 41
    on-line feeding of temporary results to pipeline stages needing them 43–4
    operation sequence 43
    pipeline length 43
    redistribution of pipeline resource 44
    time of operation in a stage 43
Pipelined multiprocessors 41–4
Pipelined processor 321
Pipelines 9, 93
    arithmetic 40–1
    industrial multiprocessors 70–81
    see also Instruction piplines
Planar patch strategies 467–70
Pointwise operator 235
POP-2 240
Post file 281
PRAM algorithm 461

Predicate/transition nets (PTN) 302
Predictably heedless operator 236
Processing arrays 348–66
    approaches to testing 355–7
Processing elements
    behavioral testing 357–65
    testing techniques 363–5
Processor operating system 56, 57
Program weight 59
Prolog 223, 224
Proper functionalities 353
Protein dynamics 496
Prototype architectures 91–9
Pseudo heat-bath method 521
Pyramidal array architecture (PAPIA) 356
Pyramidal arrays 350

Quark potential 528
Quasars, host galaxy 432–7
QUICKHULL 461

Ray Trace Simulation 178
Ray tracing 498, 499
Realfast hardware accelerator 152–3
Reconfigurable level of adaptation 19, 22–3, 25–8
Recursive nonpointwise functions 246–7
Release of redundant resources into additional computations 94
Remote sensor observations 421–77
Replacement algorithm 296
Resource request handler 58
Retirement plan 260
Robotics 550–70
    autonomous navigation 567–9

controlling robot arm in presence of moving obstacles 562–4
HERMIES mobile robots 557–61, 567
hypercube communication 561
message passing in time-critical applications 562
ROSES 551–3
Run-time environment 288–9
Runge–Kutta method 405

SASL 240
Satellite project, TOPEX 391–2
SCALD 138–42, 145–7, 150, 151, 153
    commercial implementation 140–1
    design methodology 138
    original implementation 139–40
Scatter 49
Scheduling problem 551–3
Scheduling program events 285–6
SEASAT spacecraft 437, 446
Seismic waves 498
Semantic analysis and checking 283–5
Semi-Markov process 594
Sensible heat flux 402
Sequent Balance 228, 529
Sequential file 281
Shift permutations 88
Shuttle Imaging Radar instrument (SIR-B) 438
SIMD (single-instruction multiple-data) 356, 399–412, 452, 485
Simulated annealing 553–5
Skewed storage schemes 36
Small-scale integration technology (SSI) 19
Software development 271–91
Soil moisture profile 400

Soil temperature profile 401
Solar system images 437
SOLVE 393, 396, 399
Space overhead 54
Space Shuttle 437, 438
Spatial Lucid operators 248–30
Spatial parallelism 456
Specifications 272
Speed optimization 5–6
STAR-100 5, 6, 9, 11, 18–19, 71–4
STARAN 86–8
STARLETTE satellite 398
STEP MODEL 126
Stereo analysis 438
Stereo matching 438–48
    and ice motion detection 445–6
    major difficulties in 438–40
Stochastic Petri nets 326, 578–613
    definition 585–6
    ergodic 586
    extended (ESPN) 592
    generalized 588–92
    graphical 611
    performance analysis 579–80
    with deterministic and exponential firing times (DSPN) 593–601
    with generally distributed firing times 592–3
    with immediate transitions 588–92
    see also Petri nets 582
Stochastic point process (SPP) 588
Storage management 260–2
Strategic Defense Initiative 569–70
STRETCH computer 70
Structured computer-aided logic design. See SCALD
SUDS graphics editor 139
Supercomputer, use of term 221

Supercomputer architectures 3–105
    evolution 3–6
    gradual and quantitative changes in basic solutions 4
    incomplete utilization of available technological advances 7
    industrial 3
    innovative use of new approaches 6
    performance improvement techniques 7–67
    prototype 3, 6
Switch nodes 29–32
Synchronous operation parallelism 33
Synchronous parallel computing structures 33–49
Synthetic aperture radar (SAR) imaging 437, 446

Tagged versus piped dataflow 236
Task-level adaptations 94
Temporal logic, nonconservation in dynamic multiprocessor systems 564–5
Temporal operators 243
Tentative duration of data exchange (TDE) 56
TESDATA 88 monitor 189
Testing techniques 348–66
Time overhead 54
Time-warp algorithm 501
Timed Petri nets 585
Timed transition Petri nets 585–8
Tomography 499
TOPEX 391–2, 398–9
Toroidal oscillations 536
Tracking algorithms 501
Tree data-dependency structures 131–2

Unisys 1100/90 ISP system 154–220

addressing 166
algorithm to compute logical control expressions 212–14
architectural components organization 158
attributes of 154–5
characteristics 158
code generation for loops with mask expressions 216–17
compiler architecture 167–8
CONTROL dependency, construction 215–16
dependency analysis 195–7
design considerations 187–8
error detection 166–8
flow graph 210–12
FORTRAN compiler 167
FORTRAN vectorization 168–70
hardware 189–90
hardware status registers 161
I/O handling 190–1
IF-to-MASK conversions 207–9
input/output processors (IOPs) 186
instruction processors (IPs) 186
instruction set 162–4
integration 157, 176–8
interactive supercomputing 178–9
interprocessor interaction 191
Livermore Loops 173
loading vectors 166
local storage 162
loop-control registers 159
mailbox 161–2
mask construction 209–12
mathematical libraries 172
memory bandpass 191

Unisys 1100/90 ISP system
(*continued*)
operating system (OS)
code 187
overall structure 156
overlapping instruction
188
overview of 156–76
PEER 171
performance rates 172–3
performance results
176–86
(pi)-graph 197–200,
202–7
pipelines 164–5, 175
processor control 161–2
program debugging 171
quantum timer 161
registers 158
REVERSE dependency
construction 215–16
for expanded scalars
200–7
generation 202
in IF-to-MASK con-
versions 207–5
scalar expansion 200–7
scalar registers 158–9
scheduling algorithm
192–3
scientific processor con-
trol block 162

software 157, 167, 190–1
software debugging
system 160
state registers 160
storage 165–6
storing vectors 166
synergy 173–5
system performance
179–86
results on benchmarks
180–6
results on kernels
179–80
task 187–8
technology 157–8
vector processor 186
vector registers 159
vectorization theory
195–200
vectorizer 170
vectorizing dusty decks
193–219
Unpredictably heedless
operator 236
User-defined functions
244–5

VAL 235
ValidPACKAGER 141
Value packets 259
VAX 11/750 432

VAX 11/780 550, 609
VAX 8650 150–2
VAXELN 274, 289
Vector potential quantum
415
VERTEX 561
Very-large-scale integra-
tion (VLSI) devices
224, 348–66, 550
VIRTEX 566
Virtual-time operating-
system shell 561–6
Vision modules 448–65
Vision tasks 456
von Neumann model 224
Voronoi diagrams 462
Voyager 437

Watershed model 399
Wavefront load array-level
command 354
Wavefront-loading 354
Weak generalized inverse
(WGI) 380
Weather Model 179
Write-back policy 295,
311, 598–600
Write-through policy 295,
600–1
with buffering 601–3
WSI devices 348–66